Changing
Education

We work with leading authors to develop the strongest educational materials in Sociology, bringing cutting edge thinking and best learning practice to a global market.

Under a range of well-known imprints, including Prentice Hall, we craft high quality print and electronic publications which help readers to understand and apply their content, whether studying or at work.

To find out about the complete range of our publishing please visit us on the World Wide Web at: www.pearsoneduc.com

Changing Education

A SOCIOLOGY OF EDUCATION SINCE 1944

Janet McKenzie

An imprint of **Pearson Education**

Harlow, England · London · New York · Reading, Massachusetts · San Francisco · Toronto · Don Mills, Ontario · Sydney
Tokyo · Singapore · Hong Kong · Seoul · Taipei · Cape Town · Madrid · Mexico City · Amsterdam · Munich · Paris · Milan

Pearson Education Limited
Edinburgh Gate
Harlow
Essex CM20 2JE
England

and Associated Companies throughout the World.

Visit us on the World Wide Web at:
www.pearsoneduc.com

First edition 2001

ISBN 0-582-38121-5

British Library Cataloguing-in-Publication Data
A catalogue record for this book can be obtained from the British Library

Library of Congress Cataloging-in-Publication Data
McKenzie, Janet, 1950–
    Changing education : a sociology of education since 1944 / Janet McKenzie.—1st ed.
      p. cm.
    Includes bibliographical references and index.
    ISBN 0-582-38121-5 (alk. paper)
    1. Educational sociology—England—Manchester—Longitudinal studies.   2. Educational
change—England—Manchester—Longitudinal studies.   I. Title.
    LC191.8.M46 M35 2001
    306.43—dc21   00-047912

10 9 8 7 6 5 4 3 2 1
05 04 03 02 01 00

Typeset by 35 in 10/12 pt Sabon
Printed in Malaysia, PJB

Contents

Preface

This book originally emerged from the need to find a resource for my students that would not only provide them with general information about the sociology of education, but also confront the problems involved in studying something that was constantly changing. Although the prime incentive was to provide such a resource, there were two other incentives. I was also experiencing regrets about having carried out an extensive piece of research without thoroughly disseminating and effectively utilizing the findings. How can anyone be justified in receiving research funds if they don't make the most of them? Yet the struggle to cope with the daily pressures of a demanding job constantly took precedence over the need to make people aware of educational experiences in Torytown and Labourville. Even the analysis in this book does not do justice to the mass of data collected. A third incentive was my position as one of a surprisingly large number of academics who have found that their own experiences of educational failure and frustration have actually spurred them on to prove something to themselves, if not to others. So this book has emerged after a long struggle to tackle what seemed to be intellectual inadequacies in a very positive way.

Rapid and continuous changes mean that books about education seem to be out of date as soon as they arrive in the bookshops – and this book is no exception. Yet we still need to reflect on the ways that knowledge is passed on from generation to generation, to be aware of changing assumptions and processes and to critically evaluate the actions of people who are in positions of power within education systems. So the regular output of books about education is vital in order to keep people on

their toes. In adding yet another book to many others I aimed to provide a useful resource for readers who may be interested in education for many wide-ranging reasons. Although it is called 'a sociology of education', sociology is a discipline without clear boundaries and the book takes a multidisciplinary and interdisciplinary approach in its review of the mass of research findings and theories provided by many well-known writers. In general, the aims of the book are to provide a refreshing and stimulating source of information and to help readers to understand and challenge assumptions about what education *has been*, *is* and *should be* like. As you read this book you should try to be active and reflective. Try not to think of what you read as just information that has to be learned; but challenge it, consider who, when and where it comes from and how it relates to your own experiences. Remember too that sociologists are looking for patterns, types, trends, generalities and so on, and that contradictions based on the experiences of *one* individual may not be enough to demolish findings about *common* experiences.

The research findings from Torytown and Labourville provide illustrations of how many of the debates and theories about education can be linked with the experiences of real people in certain settings, but the analysis of those findings is only partly developed. You are expected to carry out some of the analysis yourself and may even develop your own theories. This is why I have taken the unusual step of including biographies in Appendix 1. Although the need for anonymity means that the biographies are brief, and in some cases even vague, they do at least provide some background to the many quotes in the main text and have the potential to be used in a variety of projects.

In Part One you will find chapters about general themes (changing research methods, perspectives, systems and issues) whilst Part Two focuses more on changing contexts, with individual chapters for each of the last six decades of the twentieth century, together with a concluding chapter looking forward to educational futures. The book is designed to allow you to follow through interests in various pathways via common headings in each of the decades in Part Two and links with the general themes in Part One. The main text is also supplemented in various ways in order to help you to understand jargon (Appendix 2, Glossary of terms), get further details (boxed sections include original sources), reflect on what you have read (occasional questions) and follow up ideas (Appendix 1, Family biographies; Appendix 3, Useful websites).

In offering my own theories about the immiseration of education I am aware of putting myself into a high-risk situation. Progress in the development of knowledge is based on critiques of existing theories and mine will be as much subject to critique as any others. There may also be criticisms of the shift from convention, as writers of textbooks usually concentrate on the presentation of other people's findings and therefore manage to minimize claims of personal bias. Yet this book would have had little to offer if it had just reviewed changes in education without the addition of new primary research findings and the attempt to make sense of change at a wider theoretical level. If it is good practice for the writers of more conventional textbooks to acknowledge their own perspectives, it is even more important that someone presenting her own primary research should reflect on the findings and how their presentation could have been affected by personal bias. You will therefore see some of this sort of reflection in Chapter 2 and Appendix 1.

Please take from this book what you can, read it from cover to cover or dip into it occasionally as part of your wider readings. Whatever your interests and successes or failures in education, I hope that you will feel encouraged by my favourite citation (or misquote, as I have lost the full source) from the philosopher Francis Bacon, who said that

> There is no comparison between that which is lost by not succeeding and that which is lost by not trying.

Acknowledgements

This book has emerged from so many years of immersion in 'education' that it would be impossible to thank everyone who has helped me during that time. I am particularly indebted to the people in Labourville and Torytown whose experiences and views have been represented and quoted in this book. Most of the interviews took place in the summer months and on hot summer days they provided cooling drinks and cold flannels for a fevered and flustered interviewer. Meeting and getting to know them, even over long intervals, has been one of the most enjoyable experiences of my academic life. In 1992 the interviewing was shared with Christine Benney. Access to all of these people was made possible by Stephen Edgell and Vic Duke (of Salford University) who started the Greater Manchester Study, selected and labelled the areas 'Torytown' and 'Labourville', carried out the first two phases of the research in 1980/1 (SSRC grant HR 7315) and 1983/4 (ESRC grant GOO23107) and accepted me as their research student. I could not have had more supportive supervisors for my Ph.D. The provision of a competition award by the Economic and Social Research Council (grant A00428624318) and further funding from Salford University, Liverpool Hope University College and Anglia Polytechnic University made my three phases of the research possible. I would also like to thank Julian Thomas and Liz Bradbury (both Anglia Polytechnic University) for each commenting on sections of this book. Heather Warwick supplied some much needed moral support when the book was in its early stages. Former Pearson editor Sara Caro helped to tailor this project into something feasible and her replacement, Matthew Smith, along with Magda Robson, have been a constant source of reassurance and support.

On a personal level I would like to thank the tutor who, in 1976, offered me a place on a degree course at Hatfield Polytechnic (now the University of Hertfordshire), despite my lack of A levels. Hertfordshire Education Department also paid my fees and provided me with a student grant, without which I would not have been able to take a degree. Thanks also to the late Patrick McGeeney (Manchester University) who was an inspiration to his students over many years and who understood the value of education to a single parent experiencing a difficult time. Similarly, the late Michael Wilson (the Open University) is remembered with gratitude for his resounding faith and encouragement. Deep-felt thanks and love to Nicole and Marie for not only tolerating their mother's obsession from an early age, but also learning to love her for it. Particular appreciation and love go to Roddie for enduring my moods and ensuring that this book did not totally control my life. Thanks also to my sister Susan, who designed the book cover and provided the illustrations. Also thanks to John Walsh for providing the maps.

This book is dedicated to my parents Doris and Clifford Nicholls, who have supported and taken pride in not only their children's successes, but also their efforts and many failures. Lacking qualifications themselves they nevertheless demonstrated by example that intellect is about interest, curiosity and creativity, rather than about official recognition. Moreover, whilst some parents punish their children for their failures, mine once spent money they didn't have on a reward for my futile efforts.

We are grateful to the following for permission to reproduce copyright material:

Figure 2.2 from *Research Methods in Education 4th edition* published by Routledge/ITPS Ltd. (Cohen, L. and Manion, L. 1994); Figures 4.3, 4.4 from *Convergence and Divergence in European Education and Training Systems* published by Bedford Way Papers, The Institute of Education, University of London (Green, A., Wolf, A. and Leney, T. 1999); Figures 2.7, 2.8, 5.1, 5.2, 5.8. 5.9 from *Education as a Political Issue* published by Avebury Press/Ashgate Publishing Limited (McKenzie, J. 1993); Figure 5.6 from *Social Trends 1994* published by National Statistics © Crown Copyright 2000; Lists 'Strategies for equal gender opportunities – Equal opportunities and Anti-sexist' adapted from *Just a Bunch of Girls* published by Open University Press (Weiner, G. (ed.) 1985); Figure 5.10 from 'The process of excluding "education" from the "public sphere"' (McKenzie, J.) in *Debating the Future of the Public Sphere* published by Avebury Press/Ashgate Publishing Limited (Edgell, S. *et al.*, 1995); Figure 8.1 from *Social Relations in a Secondary School* published by Routledge & Kegan Paul Ltd./ITPS Ltd. (Hargreaves, D.H. 1967); Figure 9.1 adapted from *Explorations in Classroom Observation* published by Wiley Europe Ltd. (Stubbs, M. and Delamont, S. (eds.) 1976); Figure 9.2 from *Social Mobility* published by Fontana/HarperCollins Publishers Ltd. (Heath, A.F. 1981); Figure 9.3 from 'Black British literacy' in *Educational Research* Vol. 23, 2 published by Carfax Publishers/Taylor & Francis Ltd./ITPS Ltd. (Mabey, C. 1981); Figure 10.1 'Number of Candidates at 1987 General Election Who Were Teachers' published by The Times Educational Supplement, 5th June 1987; Figure 11.1 from *Stress in Teaching* published by Routledge/ITPS Ltd. (Dunham, J. 1992).

We are grateful to the following for permission to reproduce the following texts:

Extracts from quotations in *Education as a Political Issue* published by Avebury Press/Ashgate Publishing Limited (McKenzie, J. 1993); extract from *Convergence and Divergence in European Education and Training Systems* published by Bedford Way Papers, The Institute of Education, University of London (Green, A., Wolf, A. and Leney, T. 1999); Headline 'Race-Equality Advisers' from The Guardian published 15th May 1992; Headline 'Questions for the Party Leaders' published by Manchester Evening News on 29th April 1997; Extract from *The Age of Insecurity* published by Verso Publishers (Elliott, L. and Atkinson, D. 1998).

Every effort has been made to trace the copyright material. However, in the event that any have been overlooked, the Publishers will make the necessary amendment at the earliest opportunity.

Part One

Changing Approaches

1

Introduction: The immiseration of education since 1944

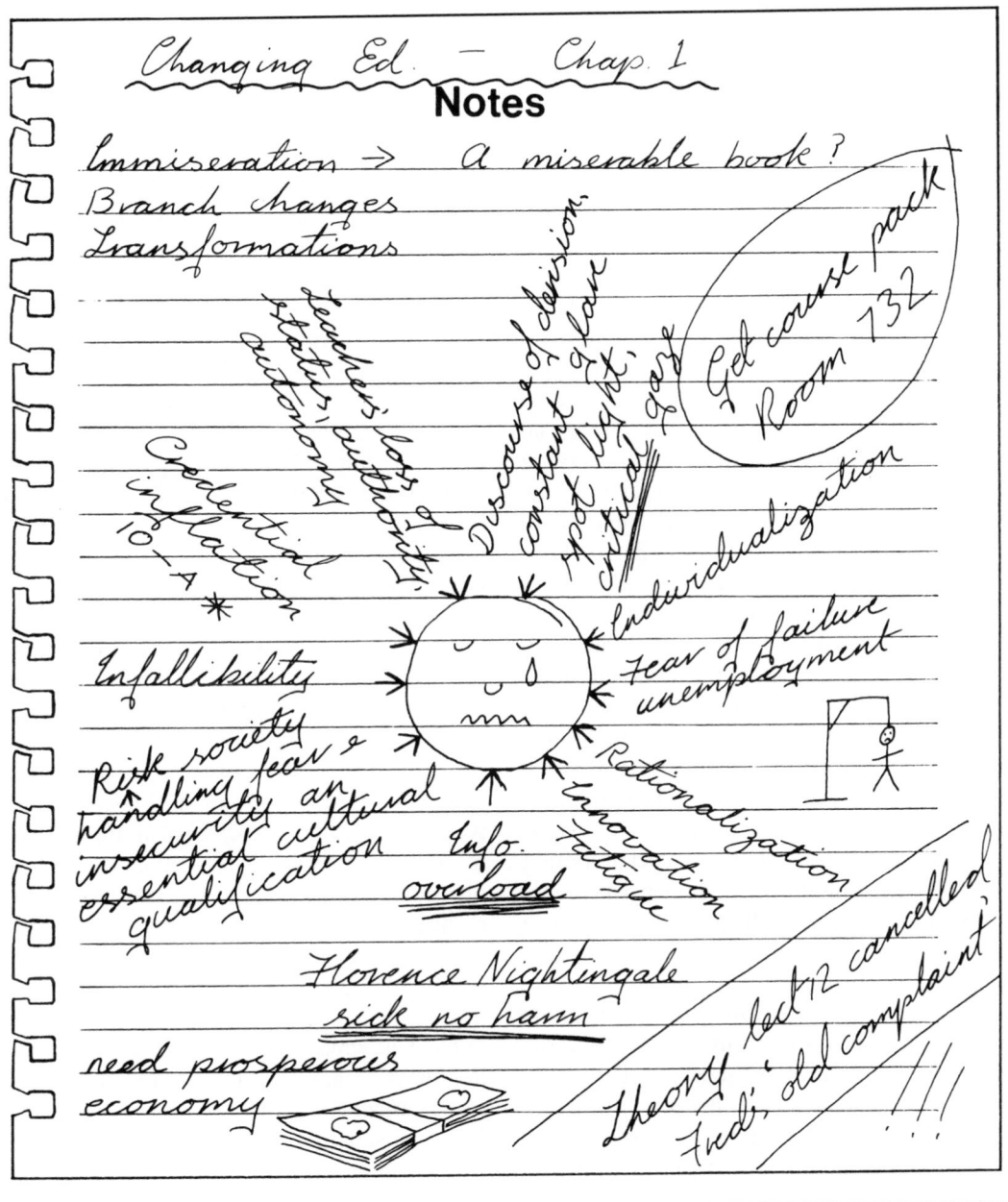

My thesis is that in the risk society we are concerned with a type of immiseration which is comparable to that of the working masses in the nineteenth century, and yet not comparable at all.

Beck, 1992, p 51

Why has British education become so miserable? Although sociological studies of educational change involve many perspectives trying to focus on a constantly moving target, one underlying pattern seems to follow behind recent changes in education: the contemporary history of educational change has been associated with a process of gradual immiseration for many of the people concerned. True, it is always possible to cite heartening illustrations of progress and the sheer pleasure of individual educational achievements, but the one feature that stands out from a sociological study of the often confusing images of educational change is the growth of a new type of misery. This is not the misery of the downtrodden masses of the past, or of the children of the elite, who were expected to follow in their parents' clogs or brogues. Rather it is the misery of constant endeavour to achieve an impossible ideal of perfection, in order to compete against others who are similarly pressed, and to fend off threats of exclusion in an insecure social and economic environment. It is the misery of pupils, students, teachers and workers who know that they will always be regarded as deficient in some way, always have to run in order to keep still and always be aware that unexpected changes may be imposed on them.

This long-term view of changes in education since 1944 shows that social and economic influences have led to new perceptions of what education, and a lack of education, actually signifies for the individual, and genuine fears about personal prospects for the twenty-first century. With its interest in the wider picture, sociology can study the place of education in its changing social context and appreciate how context can influence personal educational experiences. It helps us to appreciate how our personal educational histories belong to a setting in time, place and station.

Despite the many, severe and challenging faults within British education during the 1940s, the spotlight of public debate (discourse) at the time seemed to emit a relatively balmy warmth, based on plans for a new and exciting postwar future in which all children would have greater educational opportunities than ever before. Any changes were likely to be for the better. Yet, by the 1990s, education was wilting after years in the glare of the concentrated and unyielding spotlight of critical discourse, and educationalists faced prospects for the future with a sense of resignation, or even foreboding, based on innovation fatigue. What sociologists called a 'discourse of derision' (e.g. Ball, 1990) meant that, no matter what changes took place in education, more changes would follow, demands would never be wholly satisfied and the critical gaze would continue. Yet the role of sociology in this discourse of derision may be seen as ambiguous because, whilst criticizing the critics, sociologists are themselves critics. It is the job of sociologists to make visible problems that were previously invisible and therefore generate their own critical discourse.

Many changes are obviously essential, as progress through learning is based on a critical understanding of what is already known. Yet a basic understanding of behavioural psychology indicates that rewards, or praise, are at least as necessary as threats or criticisms (some theorists would claim even more so) in any effective training programme. In the UK such praise often seems rare and is usually directed at individual actors or schools when they are seen as outstanding within a generally derided system. The educational 'system' itself is badly in need of succour and sociology should be able to offer some hope as well as criticism. Because of its analysis of what is common (group behaviour, group cultures and social trends), as well as individual, a sociological approach is able to describe and explain what then becomes all too obvious; in this case that the continual reinforcement of negativity can have adverse consequences.

Surely British education must have improved since 1944! It certainly has, and the many radical improvements will be charted throughout this book. Yet, whilst many major and minor problems in education have been tackled effectively, and in some cases apparently eliminated, there was little room for self-congratulation when lingering problems immediately replaced the ones that had been tackled. If the hopes of the 1940s now seem too optimistic, the realism of more recent decades can be experienced as too depressing. In the 1940s it was widely assumed that the new education system would create opportunities for greater social mobility; the working-class child would be able to use education as a way of 'getting on' in life. Passing the 11+ and/or acquiring any qualifications at school-leaving age were regarded as major achievements. Yet a shortage of workers meant that even school leavers without qualifications could find jobs and sometimes choose from a variety of employment options. Despite occasional pressure from parents and teachers, young people knew that school leavers without qualifications were the norm and that they did not have to succeed in education in order to succeed in life. Once employed, promotion in 'jobs for life' often resulted from practical experience and longevity, rather than academic credentials. Competitiveness could be balanced by the sense of mutual dependence emerging from wartime experiences. The late 1940s was not a 'golden age' in which to experience education, but it was an age of relative optimism about the nature of post-war society. Just as we are currently engaged in exciting debates about the prospects for a new millennium, policy-makers and public alike were then fascinated by the prospects for life in a new society fit for heroes and built upon the experience of wartime comradeship. Public discourse about education was generally positive and optimistic and, given the scarce educational opportunities that existed before 1944, it was quite realistic to assume that anything would be an improvement.

Teachers too experienced a relatively comfortable educational environment, with high status in communities that respected them as autonomous professionals and had faith in their ability to determine the 'secret garden' of the curriculum. High wages, self-regulation, short hours, long holidays (when compared to the long hours and short holidays of other workers at the time) and a confident sense of authority meant that teaching came to be regarded as a relatively easy life. Although this positive image conceals a mass of educational problems, education was under a warm and pleasant spotlight, rather than the heat and glare experienced in recent years.

Many, significant, improvements have taken place during the past 60 years, but there is a sense of something not right, a feeling that British education is failing the country and that we are not developing the skills needed in order to compete with other countries in a global community. We are experiencing a never-ending search for perfection and those involved in educational institutions (as students and staff) are subject to increasing surveillance, without serious attention being paid to their emotional well-being. Along the way we may have lost an appreciation that the subjects of this critical gaze are thinking, feeling and emotional humans. Their inputs, processes and outputs are continually monitored as we would monitor those of any factory, and although some interest is shown in educational welfare (e.g. attendance, discipline and so on), happiness in the educational workplace is not a priority or a major issue for public debate.

Individualization, rationalization, mass unemployment and stiff competition for jobs have created a competitive and highly critical culture in which we are all being constantly evaluated. A competitive environment gives rise to a fear of failure, our experience of continuous criticism creates severe anxieties, and we may sense feelings of alienation from the education system itself. Moreover, whilst monetary inflation is the prime concern of most governments, the toll of credential inflation has been ignored. School leavers must now acquire as many qualifications (credentials) as possible; so much so that the highest aspirations of a child in the 1940s could be seen as failure in the child of today. A suggestion that, like monetary inflation, credential inflation could be tackled by limiting the credentials in circulation, would be met by gasps of horror for its educational barbarism. We must aim for the highest possible standards, but such standards can include unreasonable expectations of infallibility, and result in the failure of many individuals who would have been regarded as socially and economically useful citizens in the 1940s. Perceptions of success or failure change according to the criteria against which they are measured. Thus, at one extreme, the most obvious failures are leaving school with literacy and numeracy problems, no hope of a rewarding job and the prospect of social exclusion. Yet sociologists can show (see 'Frank's problems' in this book) that even a lack of apparently essential skills could be balanced by other personal qualities. At the other extreme, those apparent successes who are acquiring advanced technological and other skills (of the sort that would have been regarded as science fiction in the 1940s) may not have developed the reflexive attitude needed in order to effectively utilize, evaluate and monitor that knowledge. There may be little interest in acquiring knowledge for its own sake when students work hard out of fear of the consequences of failure in an increasingly competitive and insecure society.

Teachers too are withering under the pressure to achieve perfection. Their relative reduction in wages, loss of autonomy (with the introduction of the National Curriculum, auditing, monitoring and league tables), long hours and shorter holidays (the leisure time of the past being filled by paperwork and training programmes), loss of status and authority within a changing local community, and severe discipline problems now make teaching a particularly stressful occupation (see Dunham, 1992).

By the end of the century public discourse about the behaviour of young people (e.g. drugs, alcohol, violence and various other criminal activities) was habitually critical of schools and schooling, whilst the potential for immiseration within education tended to be overlooked. Golman therefore created a best-seller (1996) when he suggested that educationalists should concern themselves just as much with emotional intelligence as with academic credentials. It was an idea many educationalists could immediately identify with. Yet the problem is not simply about how education can be used to treat or prevent existing and/or external social problems, as another, overriding problem may be about the pressure on education of social expectations. Just as Florence Nightingale observed that 'It may seem a strange principle to enunciate as the very first requirement in a hospital that it should do the sick no harm' (1863), it is reasonable to observe that the first requirement of an educational establishment is that it does its students no harm. Perhaps a generous spirit could add that it should also do the staff no harm, since we need to feel confident that the work they do will benefit the students.

How and when did the shift from the optimism of the 1940s to the misery of the 1990s take place? In general, although an effective education system is often seen as essential for a prosperous economy, the reverse is very rarely appreciated: *a prosperous economy is essential for a thriving education system*. There were certainly traces of a growing critical discourse during the 1960s but a turning point can be seen in the economic crises of the 1970s. The global oil crisis affected economies and impacted on social systems in various ways and it was difficult for the governments of Western democracies to explain to the public the apparent failure of their economic policies. It was much easier to shift the blame to education systems for not providing the necessary skilled workforce and to subsequently generate the pressure of credential inflation. Education in general, and schools in particular, could easily be treated as what A.H. Halsey *et al.* (1980) called 'the wastebasket of society' or, as Andy Hargreaves described them (1994, p 3), 'policy receptacles into which society's unsolved and unsolvable problems are unceremoniously deposited'. Education provided a neat and simplistic focus for otherwise disparate and complex discontents. Social trends such as mass unemployment, aging populations and changes to the traditional family meant that governments were also becoming overburdened by their responsibilities for social welfare. This provided a supportive environment for the monetarist policies of the New Right (involving cuts in educational spending) and its associated moral underclass discourse (failure in education being discussed in terms of personal inadequacies rather than unequal life chances; see Levitas, 1998). A focus on the never-ending search for better academic qualifications and infallibility in the workplace could easily ignore other, more fundamental needs.

> In the risk society, therefore, handling fear and insecurity becomes an *essential cultural qualification*, and the cultivation of the abilities demanded for it becomes an essential mission of pedagogical institutions.
>
> Beck, 1992, p 76

At the start of the twenty-first century the problems associated with credential inflation, information overload and infallibility are still largely unacknowledged and education is still immiserated by what has become an ingrained critical discourse. Indeed, in many ways it seems that claims that there has been a shift from old- to new-style politics (involving a shift from concerns about emancipation from oppression to concerns about reflexivity and self-actualization) do not fit comfortably with current educational discourse. The arrival of a Labour government in 1997, with its 'Third Way' agenda (Giddens, 1998) as an alternative to the individualist agenda of the New Right, has so far had little impact on the pressures within the education system.

This book will show that, by the 1990s, educational experiences pre-1979 had become what one informant (in the Labourville and Torytown studies) called '. . . a different culture'. In 1990 Stephen Ball described general changes in educational discourse and what he called a 'discourse of derision'.

> Some aspects of the once unproblematic consensus are now beyond the pale, and policies which might have seemed like economic barbarism twenty years ago now seem right and proper.
> Ball, 1990, p 38

The focus in this book will therefore be on how such changes took place and what can be learned from them as we consider prospects for the future. We are not only looking at relatively minor branch changes (see David Hargreaves and Hopkins, 1991), associated with changes in educational practice which may be adopted, adapted or resisted, but also at more fundamental root changes (Andy Hargreaves, 1994), those deeper transformations affecting how education is socially organized and experienced; such as the increasing emphasis on market values. We are not looking at something that is past and finished, but at an on-going project for personal and social advancement. People who experienced these changes are all around us and their experiences impact on our present and future lives by shaping our own identities, understandings and experiences. A sociological study of educational change can, and should, help us to appreciate the wider social context of our individual educational experiences and how even the language used in educational debates (the discourse) has contextual influences over which we have little control. An

understanding of how education has changed in the past will help us to influence its future.

Chapters 1–5 in Part One, 'Changing Approaches', provide a grounding for subsequent chapters by considering general aspects of educational change. Readers can therefore organize their reading according to their specialist interests. For example, someone who wants to read about 'social class' will find a discussion about how the concept may be operationalized for educational research in Chapter 2, a general overview of relevant theories in Chapter 3, relevant information about educational organization in Chapter 4, a discussion about associated issues in Chapter 5 and more detailed chronological accounts in the headed sections of Chapters 6–11.

Chapter 2, 'Researching change', considers various research styles and some of the problems encountered when carrying out research in the sociology of education. It also introduces and explains the case studies of education in Torytown and Labourville and the interviews with a panel of voters in those areas. Findings from this primary research will be used throughout the book in order to show how some individuals experienced educational change for themselves and how their attitudes relate to the various themes discussed in the book. From Chapter 2 onwards you will find boxed extracts from the Torytown and Labourville studies at various points in other chapters. The sources of the many quotes can be found in Appendix 1.

Chapter 3, 'Changing perspectives', considers wider sociological and political perspectives in order to provide a framework for the more detailed theories to be addressed in Part Two. Sociological and political perspectives are combined in this one chapter, rather than in separate chapters, because they are closely related and interact within educational discourse. This will include debates about what some academics perceive as a move from modernity to postmodernity, or late modernity, and associated claims about diversity and fragmentation.

Chapter 4, 'Changing systems', considers the organization of education in the UK in order to provide a framework for the more detailed analysis of its historical development in Part Two. Although largely descriptive, it identifies some of the key debates in educational policy-making.

Chapter 5, 'Changing issues', introduces some key topics in sociological studies of education in order to provide a framework for the more detailed analysis of historical developments in Part Two. It may be used as a point of reference and a means of identifying long-term changes from amongst the contextualized information provided for each decade. Themes and issues are presented as responding to and interacting with their changing social and political context.

Part Two, 'Decades of Change', provides a chronological account of change since the 1940s. There were obviously several possible ways of allocating time frames to individual chapters; for example, a larger number of chapters would have emerged if they had been allocated according to changes in central government. Ultimately it seemed to make sense to use decades, according to common perceptions of time periods, because people often talk about 'the 1950s', 'the 1960s' and so on as distinct periods conjuring distinct social images of cultural change. Thus images of 'the 1960s' may be of the Beatles, hippies, Woodstock, civil rights movements in Northern Ireland and the USA, the building of the Berlin Wall and so on, whilst images of 'the 1980s' may be of punks, yuppies, Live Aid, Thatcherism, the miners' strike, the fall of the Berlin Wall, the arrival of AIDS and so on. Therefore Chapters 6–11 each cover a period of ten years. You will, no doubt, notice that the earlier decades are covered in less detail than the later ones. This is partly because, whilst findings about attitudes to education during the 1940s–1970s generally emerged from secondary sources, the 1980s and 1990s included the fieldwork stages of the Torytown and Labourville studies, which allowed questions to be asked about current issues. It was, nevertheless, reassuring to discover that others have experienced the same pattern of information growing over time: as the well-known historian A.J.P. Taylor noted, 'History gets thicker as it approaches recent times' (1970).

Chapter 12, 'Changing education in the future', brings the book to a conclusion by considering the ways in which an understanding of educational change and wider social expectations may impact upon education in the future. It considers the place of schools in a post- or late modern society, the fears and anxieties experienced by pupils and students and the value of discourses of possibilities. Four scenarios for educational development are outlined and a case is made for the ecological development of education with a greater emphasis on reflexive knowledge. Finally, the commentary provided by the Torytown and Labourville cohort finishes with their reinforcement of the idea that 'Education is our future'.

A NEW FORM OF MISERY?

The Victorian labourer whatever his poverty and sense of social inferiority always enjoyed a psychological comfort. He knew, or could believe, that his station in life was not due to any failing on his part but to the structure within which he was placed. He lacked access to secondary education and the examinations through which he could have advanced himself. Yet his fellows were all in the same boat; there was no need for jealousy of them or recrimination about himself. The late twentieth century unskilled or unemployed labourer, after all the educational reforms, is in a psychologically much more vulnerable situation. He is at the end of a long sequence of failing every examination and neglecting every opportunity placed before him. He is confronted with the fact that his fault lies in himself. As Young notes: 'For the first time in human history the inferior man has no ready buttress for his self regard.' Some indeed see meritocracy as but a new kind of social democratic right-wing society 'where the people at the bottom will no longer have the consolation of knowing that they are there by accident rather than examination'.[1] The dangerous feelings of lack of self worth if not self-loathing that can result from this cruel confrontation already manifest themselves in too many familiar forms of deviant behaviour, the violence, football and other hooliganism and vandalism which are among the nastier aspects of British life.

Sanderson, 1987, pp 86–7

[1] Dennis Potter, *The Glittering Coffin*, 1960, London, p 13.

Questions

Do you agree with the claim that in the late twentieth century unskilled or unemployed workers were 'in a psychologically much more vulnerable situation' than those in Victorian times?

Do you agree that 'his fault lies in himself'?

Do Sanderson's claims also apply to women?

2

Researching change

Changing Ed. — Chap 2

Notes

Researching change — re-searching!

Operationalizing a cow

Ontology
　epistemology
　　Methodology　　indicators
　　　Methods

Positivism　　stop at　　law?
Anti-positivism　red lights?　rule?

Sampling soup
Generalizability — all soup?

breadth　　　depth
Quantitative ← → Qualitative
Ethnography
　customs, communities　Gatekeeper
Validity?　Triangulation
Reliability?　　Action research
Cohort studies　Critical "
— same people　Feminist "
Not you again!!!　Historical "
Alan Anchor 80th??

'Hygienic research' in which no problems occur, no emotions are involved, is research as it is described and not 'research as it is experienced . . .'

Stanley and Wise, 1983

Research can be immensely satisfying, fascinating and creative, but also frustrating, infuriating and tedious! Yet to say that it is what the researcher makes it, and also very creative, implies that there is no difference between social research and works of fiction, which would certainly be wrong. The bonus for the researcher is that at times the truth really is stranger than fiction, sometimes because there are many 'truths', all seen from different perspectives. The opportunity to gain an insight into other people's lives, cultures and perceptions of reality can even generate feelings of escapism from our own apparently mundane realities. Indeed it is the word 'generate' that is important. The data we find in our research is generated via social processes, rather than simply discovered as we would discover a new facial blemish. We make decisions along the way about what we are looking for, who we should study, where we are to go to next, how to get there, how to deal with problems we encounter, what to make of the weird, wonderful, unexpected, or sometimes disappointing, findings and how to tell people about them.

If most research is creative, then research into changing education may be the stuff of science fiction. It not only involves frustrating efforts to study shifting sands but the need to anticipate the direction in which they are going to shift. So, for example, when carrying out longitudinal research or a panel study the researcher may try to anticipate questions that are not only relevant to the present, but also to the future and include topics that have not yet been 'discovered'! Meteorologists, opinion pollsters and those researching social change are all primarily trying to describe current conditions but will find that they are valued by others according to how successful they are in anticipating the future.

Getting started

Researchers are also evaluated for their originality. At undergraduate level the highest marks are given to essays showing a spark of ingenuity, a willingness to move beyond the usual readings for a particular topic, and for enlivening the depressed tutor who has spent hours reading the same things, phrased differently, in essay, after essay, after essay. At Masters degree level originality becomes even more important and at Ph.D level it becomes the single most important criterion for graduation. At a more fundamental, and less instrumental, level it would simply be reasonable to ask what value research has if it adds nothing to what is already known, and how the researcher can maintain interest in following a path that is not only well trodden but also in pristine condition.

In ideal circumstances the researcher is therefore able to choose a topic that is original and has a clear value. How do we do this? First, it must be acknowledged that many researchers are not in this sort of privileged position because the topic finds them, rather than the other way round. The topic may be chosen for them and constraints imposed by the employer or other research organization commissioning the research. Some topics may also be connected with a problem of practice encountered in the workplace: for example, teachers, administrators and social workers will often carry out research in order to evaluate their work or initiate and monitor change in the workplace via action research.

A first step in identifying an original topic usually involves noting a gap or gaps in our existing knowledge and, for this reason, we need to think twice about working in an area with which we are not familiar. Otherwise how do we know that such gaps exist? Familiarity may be gained from all sorts of experiences, not just academic but also experiences in the workplace, in our social lives, our families and so on. For example, a music teacher may also play an instrument in a jazz band and be intrigued by the culture clash between the music taught in schools and the music people experience and enjoy out of school. At post-graduate level research generally emerges almost naturally from an individual's personal obsession. When topics do not emerge in this way they may appear as a result of brainstorming an area; thinking about all sorts of apparently simple, foolish or quirky questions or problems. Why is eleven the usual age for transfer from primary to secondary schools in the UK but not in other countries? What do eleven-year-olds have in common? How do they differ from each other and from ten- or twelve-year-olds? Should other things such as 'intelligence', gender, height, family, area or religion influence the age of transfer?

Operationalizing concepts

Students often report that learning about research methods seems to mainly involve defining words, and they are probably right. If a researcher is studying ethnicity, the meanings of the word 'ethnicity' are obviously vitally important, at even a basic level, and can lead to an original angle for research. In the physical sciences researchers are now studying the meaning of 'age', as there is growing evidence that the age of individuals when defined by years since birth does not closely correspond with the physical aging of the body. Social scientists will also come across this when they find that first impressions of the age, ethnicity or social class of interviewees are totally misleading, and this again may inspire a piece of social research. Researchers call this process of defining terms the *operationalization of concepts*.

Concepts provide meaningful summaries and images of certain aspects of the world. At a very simple level, if you think of the concept 'cow' you will almost certainly see a picture of the animal in your mind. If that image has four legs, udders and is a certain size, such features will be *indicators* of the concept; and these are observable and measurable entities which define the concept in a practical way. You will find that other people share a similar image, with similar indicators, and that a group of people viewing animals in a field would agree that those animals are indeed cows. Similarly, when considering the concept 'age' there may be general agreement that indicators of age include years since birth and some features of appearance such as grey hair and skin texture. However, it is the disagreements about indicators that may be the most interesting. Scientists' disagreements about the meaning and definition of 'age' may prove to be quite fascinating. Since the 1940s social scientists' disagreements about the meaning of 'ethnicity' and the identification of appropriate indicators of ethnicity have generated intriguing and sophisticated debates about how ethnicity should be studied or whether it can be meaningful to study if at all.

HOW CAN WE OPERATIONALIZE ETHNICITY?

Sociologists may feel that the nature of their subject obliges them to allocate individuals into groups. They are also concerned about inequality in education and make such distinctions in order to identify important inequalities in experiences and opportunities. A key problem is that educational research in the UK has tended to categorize individuals into simplistic, and largely incomprehensible, groups; often based on apparent global origins, such as 'West Indian', 'Asian' and 'other', or based on the labelling of skin colour as either 'black' or 'white' in order to identify racism in education. Indeed sociologists themselves could be accused of racism because of their tendency to use the categorization of 'black' to override any other personal characteristic and to label black children (and 'West Indian' children in particular) negatively as 'underachievers'.

These reservations help to explain why figures relating to various ethnic groups have only been included in official, national statistics on education since 1990/1. In recent years the tendency has been to either ask individuals how they identify themselves or use *multiple indicators* so that this contentious concept can be indicated in several different ways.

HOW CAN WE OPERATIONALIZE SOCIAL CLASS?

When trying to operationalize social class we first have to consider whether we are assessing the individual or the whole household. Class is generally perceived as a relationship to the means of production (i.e. an economic concept). Thus social scientists often see the 'household' as the basic unit of economic exchange because the people in it share a common budget. We could use multiple indicators to accommodate the influence of various members of households, and these could include their occupations, income and perhaps even cultural capital in the form of educational qualifications. For example, Ivan Reid (1992) concluded that educational attainment is often associated with occupation and recommended the use of multiple indicators for assessing the influence of the educational attainment of family members.

It is much easier (but not necessarily more accurate) to assess the social class of individuals by measuring their economic activities in the form of employment. Yet the decisions we make concerning the choice of appropriate scales can have an important impact on our findings. For example, Marxists may operationalize social class according to their social perspective, labelling individuals as either the bourgeoisie or the proletariat, or splitting them into more categories such as employers, controllers, petit bourgeoisie and workers. Weber's perception of many class categories and status groups fits more comfortably with the Hall Jones Scale or the Registrar General's Scale. Indeed, although the Registrar General's Scale was updated during the 1990s (to include an underclass), its following classification was used by the Office of Population Censuses and Surveys for a long time and is most familiar to educational researchers.

	I	Professional (including university teachers)
	II	Intermediate (including school teachers)
Middle class	III(N)	Skilled non-manual
---	---	---
Working class	III(M)	Skilled manual
	IV	Partly skilled manual
	V	Unskilled manual

Notice that there was no 'upper class' and no classification for people who were unemployed. This meant that either the researchers considered an individual's last paid employment or that unemployed people were not recognized as being part of the economic system. It is also clear that, if social class is affected by income, scales such as this are overlooking differences between part-time and full-time workers: for example, part-time clerical workers could be assigned a higher class category than full-time manual workers.

Sociologists also faced problems in operationalizing the social class of children. They have traditionally labelled a child according to the father's occupation when assessing children's social class and measuring social mobility, and in the 1940s and 1950s this may have been appropriate. However, as the century progressed, more mothers took paid employment, some of them took jobs in a lower or higher class category than their partners and many became single-parents. It may be that, with increasing numbers of absent fathers, it is now more appropriate to label children according to their mothers' occupations.

Patrick Dunleavy *et al.* (1985) suggested the use of sectoral cleavages as a possible alternative way of categorizing relationships with the means of production. Households could then be allocated to consumption sectors according to whether they consumed mainly private or public facilities (education, health, housing and transport). Individuals could be allocated to production sectors according to whether they worked for a private company, in the public sector or were unemployed.

Progressive focusing

The operationalization of concepts helps us to make the links between formulating researchable ideas, identifying researchable problems and translating them into practical research. So, we cannot study 'education standards' without considering the problem of definition and how standards may be defined by identifying appropriate indicators. This is all part of the lengthy process of *progressive focusing*, which means gradually narrowing the focus on to a relatively small area of research, a central theme, a central question or a research hypothesis.

Suppose you are vaguely interested in three areas: *education, employment* and *ethnicity*. By focusing in on a theme that includes all three you may decide that you are interested in *comparing the prospects for promotion of teachers from various ethnic groups*. This is still so general that you would not know where to start any *primary* research (i.e. research done by you, rather than the *secondary* research you base on findings generated by other researchers) and you need to focus in further. Secondary research into what others have done and discovered will help at this stage as you need to know what is already known and what problems others have encountered. It may be that 'promotion' can only be operationalized by using salary scales as indicators. Now you have focused in further on *comparing the position of teachers from various ethnic groups on salary scales*. Rather than giving this an indirect title you may prefer to construct an even more focused research question, such as, *Do the proportions of teachers from various ethnic groups on salary scales correspond with their proportions within the whole teaching workforce?* You have now focused in a long way

from the original three areas of interest but the choice of topic has raised even more questions to be tackled in the research:

How will ethnicity be operationalized?
What indicators of ethnicity will be used?
What ethnic groups are going to be studied?
Will the research include teachers in both state and private sectors?
Will the research focus on one local education authority, one region (e.g. England, Wales, Northern Ireland, Scotland), one country, or make international comparisons?
Could something else be confused with ethnicity as an effect on promotion?

At this point you may agree with the first sentence in this chapter, that research can be frustrating, infuriating and tedious. It can take a jolt to remind the researcher that such work is also satisfying, fascinating and creative, and this usually happens when work moves from the desktop to the outside world of fieldwork and the researcher meets the people being studied. Alternatively a researcher who is primarily engaged in secondary analysis of existing survey data may find that intricate patterns seem to be emerging from the computer screen as research questions and hypotheses are tested, retested, rephrased, tested and retested again. It sometimes seems that the researcher is juggling several balls at once as ideas accumulate via computer analysis.

Instead of formulating their focus as a research question, researchers may describe it as a *hypothesis*, which is a statement, a proposition, or set of propositions, to be tested in the research. It is often an untested assertion about the relationship between two or more concepts. So, for example, you could state that *White, British teachers are more likely to be situated at high points on their salary scales than other teachers.* This is not the same as a question and the aim is not to find evidence to support it, but to find evidence to challenge or dispute it. Why? In this case it may be easy to find examples of white, British teachers who are high on their salary scales and it seems likely that most teachers near the top of their salary scales will be white and British. If we were only looking for evidence to support the hypothesis we would give up once evidence of this was found. Looking for evidence to challenge it is more demanding and requires more depth and rigour. We need to think about it more carefully and, in this case, our calculations should accommodate the fact that most British teachers appear to be white and British. In order to challenge the hypothesis we should compare the proportions of white, British teachers at each level on the scale with the proportion of other teachers at each level on the scale. It may be that, although non-white, non-British teachers are in a minority within the teaching workforce, a higher proportion of this minority are at the higher levels of the scale. For example, visiting teachers from other member states of the European Union may arrive at a situation high on the scale or may be paid a high wage by their home country whilst on an exchange package. It is also a possibility that there may be proportionately more 'non-white' teachers at high pay levels but that this may be because of their hard work, resilience, imagination or other qualities that may have helped them to overcome (hidden) institutionalized racism. Operationalization of the concepts 'white' and 'non-white' are obviously important. If one indicator is self-rated identity we may find that, in a complex multi-ethnic society, some teachers who are labelled by others as 'white' or 'non-white' will label themselves otherwise. Therefore, a rigorous researcher will try to consider all possibilities and appreciate that, even if there seems to be strong support for the hypothesis, great care should be taken in interpreting the findings. Thus, the search for evidence to challenge the hypothesis may lead us to rephrase it, reject it or state that there is *strong support* for it. Researchers are usually too hesitant about their findings to use strong words such as 'prove' or 'disprove' because their findings will be open to criticism by other researchers and academics who will also be trying to challenge them.

QUESTIONS

See Chapter 1 in this book.
How are claims about the immiseration of education since 1944 presented?
What efforts are made to anticipate prospective criticisms?
Are the claims too forceful or not forceful enough?

Methodology

Sociologists often confuse their students and others by using the word 'methodology' when they mean 'methods' and vice versa. This is usually because they are not aware of the difference, rather than them playing some sort of cruel sociological game. Basically, researchers *discuss* methodology and *use* methods.

Discussions about *methodology* involve philosophical and theoretical debates about the nature of reality and how to study it and whether it will be influenced by individual ontologies (which we will discuss further in Chapter 3). Basically *ontologies* consist of perceptions of the nature of reality and are generally very wide ranging. For example, someone with a feminist ontology will be particularly aware of gender inequalities whilst someone with a Marxist ontology will be particularly aware of the negative effects of capitalism, and these different perceptions will affect how they choose to study the world about them. Apart from their particular interest in gender inequalities, feminists have also produced highly developed critiques of social research and have a distinctive approach to their own work, which they bring into methodological debates.

Just as an ontology affects methodological debates, so both ontology and methodology affect *epistemology*, by which we mean philosophical theories about knowledge and how we know what we know. So, someone with a feminist ontology will see the nature of reality as a world strongly influenced by gender inequalities (ontology), will bring feminist ideas into debates about how research should be carried out (methodology) and will regard knowledge about gender inequalities as particularly important and significant (epistemology).

In addition to the researcher's own ontology, methodology and epistemology, they may be influenced by a current *paradigm*, which is a consensus or model of 'normal' research, the rules to be followed and what constitutes acceptable knowledge. New researchers familiarize themselves with existing theories and the conventions of academic practice, knowing that if they wander too far away from convention their work may be misunderstood or ridiculed by those immersed in the current paradigm, rather than seen as an original and radical illumination of the topic (see the writings of Thomas Khun, 1962 and Karl Popper, 1961). At first glance this looks incompatible with the assessment of research for its originality, and sometimes it can be. Perhaps George Bernard Shaw was right when he suggested (in *Annajanska*) that 'All great truths begin as blasphemies'. Yet, an understanding of the current paradigm also means that the researcher will benefit from what has been learned by others and be equipped to present findings in an accessible way. A paradigm therefore creates problems and solutions but, in the case of sociology, researchers will be in a quandary concerning the nature of a dominant paradigm. Indeed George Ritzer has suggested that sociology is a 'multiple paradigm science' because a wide range of perspectives are competing for centre stage and sociologists often take the pragmatic approach of dipping into them whenever they seem to have something to offer.

If any one paradigm has dominated sociological practice it is probably that of the idealized model of scientific research. A model is a device sociologists use in order to simplify reality and it usually has *heuristic value*; in other words, it can be used as an analytical tool. In the case of the *idealized* model of scientific research (see Figure 2.1) it is now rarely seen as anything other than a source of debate because most sociologists regard it as too idealized.

The idealized model seems to provide a clear image of research processes as the researcher progresses around the circle, starting either at the top, with a theory, or at the bottom, with an interesting observation. If the researcher starts at the top, s/he is using a process called *deduction* (sometimes called the hypothetico-deductive method), which involves moving from a theory or theories (i.e. the general) to the creation of a hypothesis, the operationalization of concepts and then to observation (i.e. the particular) in order to test the hypothesis. Analysis of the findings may lead to adaptation of the original theory, the development of a new hypothesis and so on, round the circle again. If the researcher starts at the bottom of the circle, s/he is using a process called *induction* (sometimes called *ex post facto* theory or grounded theory), which involves moving from observation or findings (i.e. the particular) through analysis towards the development of a theory. This theory may lead to the development of a hypothesis, which is tested by further observation, analysed and so on, round the circle again (see Glaser and Strauss, 1968, for more about grounded theory). Researchers often speak of *empirical* testing, which means testing by observation.

This model looks very straightforward, and this seems to be its main failing. First, the experience of actually carrying out research is not so straightforward, is often downright untidy and may include all sorts of unexpected happenings. Second, observation and theories often develop concurrently rather than sequentially. For example, a researcher observing classroom behaviour may arrive at the school with some already developed theories but will be developing them further, and even identify new theories, test them and analyse them during the observation. Third, identification of a starting point on the circle may be a chicken and egg situation. Which came first, the theory or the observation? Researchers' ideas may have been developing since childhood and related to life-long experiences. A final problem associated with the idealized model may be related to the researcher rather than faults in the model itself. Some researchers simply do not know when to stop their research and could continue circling the model, testing theories and developing theories in a frustrating search for perfection. Indeed some research students never complete their

Figure 2.1 The idealized model of scientific research

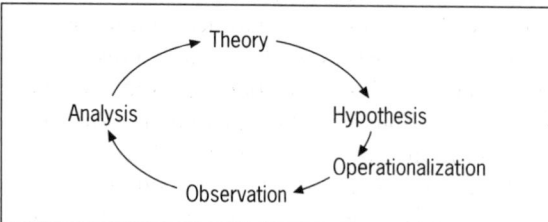

Ph.Ds or take too long because they are continually raising new ideas and some researchers are only forced to complete their work because they run out of time or money.

The main criticism of the idealized model of scientific research is that it simplifies the reality of research in the physical sciences and transfers it directly to the social sciences, where it is less appropriate. This practice of emulating the physical sciences has raised wider methodological debates between those who are either for or against a positivist approach. *Positivism* has a long tradition in sociology, dating back to Comte who coined the term 'sociology' and assumed that this new science could be shown to be scientific by emulating the methods used by the physical scientists of the time (see Chapter 3). As physical scientists aimed to objectively identify laws of nature and generalize their findings, it was assumed that social scientists could objectively identify laws governing human nature and generalize them. This meant that detached observers should monitor and measure behaviour and involved numeric comparisons between clearly operationalized variables in order to identify laws of cause and effect. *Variables* are characteristics that vary and consist of two or more values, such as gender (its two values being 'male' and 'female'), age (with values usually consisting of many individual years or a few age groups) and social class (consisting of six values when the traditional Registrar General's Scale has been used as an indicator of the concept in the past). Operationalization of concepts and the identification of suitable indicators is obviously an important part of this process, as researchers tend to use a variable as both a concept and the operationalization of the concept. For example, the variable 'religion' is also a concept, which may be indicated by many values such as 'Roman Catholic', 'Muslim', 'Jewish', 'Atheist' and so on, and it may be very difficult for a researcher to decide which indicators and values are appropriate.

Many sociologists have argued that the subject matter of the social sciences is different to that of the physical sciences and that a different approach should be taken (see Figure 2.2). These *anti-positivists* emphasize the importance of sensitivity to the subjects (people) being studied and the need to be aware that (unlike much of the subject matter of the physical sciences) people can react to their circumstances in a variety of ways. This is often illustrated by speculation about how Martians could explain the behaviour of this strange species of humans. Suppose they saw motorists and cyclists stopping at a red traffic light and setting off when the light changed to green. Taking a positivist approach they would assume that this was a law of human nature and that people reacted to the changing lights automatically. It would be a simple case of cause and effect, of one variable (the colour of the lights) affecting another variable (stationary or moving traffic). An anti-positivist would point

---

Normative/Positivist	Interpretive/Anti-positivist
Society and the social system	The individual
Medium/large-scale research	Small-scale research
Impersonal, anonymous forces regulating behaviour	Human actions continuously recreating social life
Model of natural sciences	Non-statistical
'Objectivity'	'Subjectivity'
Research conducted 'from the outside'	Personal involvement of the researcher
Generalizing from the specific	Interpreting the specific
Explaining behaviour/seeking causes	Understanding actions/meaning rather than causes
Assuming the taken-for-granted	Investigating the taken-for-granted
Macro-concepts: society, institutions, norms, positions, roles, expectations	Micro-concepts: individual perspective, personal constructs, negotiated meanings, definitions of situations
Structuralists	Phenomenologists, symbolic interactionists, ethnomethodologists

Source: Cohen and Manion, 1994, Box 1.10, p 39

Figure 2.2 Differing approaches to the study of behaviour

out that there was nothing automatic about this aspect of human nature and that motorists were following a rule, which could be broken, rather than a law of nature, which could not be broken. People internalize such rules, attach their own meaning to them and may respond to them in unexpected ways (for example speeding through a red traffic light). Therefore, sociologists who are phenomenologists, symbolic interactionists or ethnomethodologists (see Chapter 3) are particularly interested in *interpreting* behaviour by discovering the meanings behind actions and investigating what is taken for granted. They study not only the subjects being investigated but also the role of the researcher in generating findings, acknowledging that the researcher is involved in the research process rather than assuming that the researcher is a detached observer from the outside. Meanings are seen to be negotiated, constructed and dependent on personal perspectives.

> There is no absolutely 'objective' scientific analysis of culture or [social planning] independent of special and one-sided viewpoints according to which . . . they are selected, analysed and organised.
>
> Weber, 1949, p 72

You will see that what was said earlier in this chapter, about the generation of findings, tended to favour an anti-positivist approach, but that should not suggest a total rejection of every characteristic of positivist research. Notice in Figure 2.2 that normative/positivist and interpretive/anti-positivist approaches tend to focus on different levels of society. A normative/positivist tends to approach society from a macro level, being interested in social structures and social norms and often using large-scale research in order to generalize findings from a sample to the rest of the population. Thus, findings from large-scale surveys (such as opinion polls and other attitude surveys) may be said to represent what would be found in the wider population. An interpretive/anti-positivist tends to approach society at a micro level, being interested in small-scale interactions and how people relate to social life, preferring to achieve a deep understanding of the behaviour of a few people who may not be representative of the rest of the population. Thus, findings from interpretive studies (such as classroom observation

and in-depth interviews) may not represent what would be found in the wider population, but they should provide a clear understanding of the people who were studied. Normative/positivist approaches may therefore be particularly useful for monitoring changes in the social structure and interpretive/anti-positivist approaches may be useful for monitoring changes in social interaction. Indeed, many sociologists take the pragmatic option of using whatever approach seems to be appropriate, using some of the ideas associated with positivism (such as statistical analysis of survey data in order to study cause and effect) and some of the ideas associated with anti-positivism (such as in-depth interviews in order to evaluate the meanings). This was done in the Torytown and Labourville studies which will be described later.

Research methods

Methods are the more practical aspects of social research (such as surveys, interviews and observation) and when we talk about strategies we mean more detailed techniques (such as sampling techniques, questioning techniques and ways of recording data during observation). There are too many research methods to cover in one chapter; here, expediency allows for only a simple acknowledgement of some of the methods that are often found to be particularly appropriate ways of studying education in general, and educational change in particular.

We have already seen that choice of methods can depend on the researcher's ontology, epistemology, methodology and the influential paradigm of the moment. Yet this only partly explains choice of method. The main question to ask when deciding how to study a topic is, *What method(s) is (are) appropriate?* Most researchers have their own favourite and least-favourite methods and an honest appraisal of their own capabilities may show that they are limited in what they are able to do. Sometimes they may even choose topics to fit their favourite methods, rather than the other way round, but even then, the main criteria for selecting methods should be how appropriate they are for the topic. We have already seen the different aspects of society studied via normative and interpretive approaches and have seen that progressive focusing will generate questions and problems which will influence decisions about research methods.

Sampling

Our earlier example of progressive focusing led us to ask how various concepts should be operationalized and what sorts of people should be studied, and it is usual for both questions to be considered at once. Decisions about what teachers to study would depend on how the concept of ethnicity was operationalized, so that we could choose to study teachers from various ethnic groups. They may also depend on any theories we may be testing, so that when sociologists talk about *theoretical sampling* they are referring to the decisions about sampling that will help them to focus on testing an existing theory, or theories. Yet we could not study all teachers from all ethnic groups and need to decide what sort of *sample* should be used. Just as a cook tastes a spoonful of soup in order to discover what the whole soup tastes like, sociologists study a sample of the population they are interested in to learn more about the whole population (for example, a sample of voters in order to study voting behaviour). They may also study a sample of certain types of settings (e.g. classrooms, playgrounds, staff-rooms) in order to learn more about such settings in general.

There are many types of sampling techniques and most books about research methods will provide lists and explanations of a wide range of them. These can seem rather confusing unless it is remembered that the main point is to find an appropriate sample for an individual piece of research and that there are many unique pieces of research. Such lists can be simplified if you are aware that the two main categories into which most sampling techniques fall both relate to *generalizability*, which means the extent to which research findings apply to subjects or settings other than the ones which the researcher used.

Random (or *probability*) *sampling* is most like the spoon-in-the-soup technique and tends to be used by researchers taking a normative approach, who hope to claim that their sample represents the wider population. They can claim *generalizability* if they really do represent the wider population, but how can this be known? First, all members of the chosen population should have a known and equal chance of selection. This means that the researcher must have a *sampling frame*, which is a list of the whole population from which the sample is to be drawn (such as a list of the electorate in a voting district or a list of all of the children in a school). When *simple random sampling* is used, selection is like a lottery and everyone on the list has an equal chance of being chosen. This means that potential bias is eliminated from the selection procedure, as the researcher cannot just choose people who seem to be particularly approachable, easy to contact, helpful, attractive and so on. If this process is faithfully adhered to, the researcher meets the requirements for generalizing from the sample to the total population (e.g. from a random sample of pupils to all of the school's pupils). The researcher can even calculate the sampling error in order to evaluate how much faith should be placed in generalization from the findings. Other types of random sampling also involve the use of a sampling frame (e.g. the selection of every tenth, twentieth or thirtieth person on the list) but may be less genuinely random and we may feel less confident in generalizing from findings to the wider population.

Non-random (*non-probability*, or *purposive*) *sampling* does not allow the researcher to claim that all the members of the relevant population had a known probability of being selected at the outset. As a result, a sampling frame may not be needed and the findings cannot be generalized to the wider population. The sampling techniques falling into this category allow the researcher to choose certain types of people within the whole population (such as voters of a certain age or children from certain school year groups). This is commonly done via *quota sampling*, which involves splitting the population being studied (e.g. children in a school) into sub-groups and taking quotas of the desired numbers of sample cases from each sub-group (e.g. ten children from the first year, ten from the second year and so on). Another common and interesting technique is *snowball sampling*, which is often the only way of getting access to a population that is difficult to trace or contact (such as ethnic minorities, groups operating group closure or deviants and criminals). The researcher makes initial contact with one or more members of the population, who then introduces him/her to others in the population, who then introduce the researcher to others and so on until the sample grows into the required size.

Qualitative and quantitative methods

Tutors have often asked their students to discuss the advantages and disadvantages of qualitative and quantitative methods even though the question is virtually meaningless. We cannot say that either a qualitative or quantitative approach is superior to the other or has advantages over the other without referring to how appropriate they may be for a particular research topic. It is therefore more appropriate to discuss the strengths and weaknesses of qualitative and quantitative methods and how researchers trade off the strengths of one against the weaknesses of the other (see Figure 2.3).

Qualitative and quantitative methods may overlap so much that they are virtually indistinguishable. When students ask what is the minimum sample that can be meaningful for quantitative research I usually cite Dixon, Bouma and Atkinson's advice that 30 would be a reasonable number for a student project (1987). It can be used for simple statistical analysis such as splitting responses into fractions although statistical analysis involving percentages would look ridiculous when based on such a small sample. Yet students do often present findings based on very low figures in the form of bar charts, which are meant to impress but look far too simple. It is just as reasonable to ask what is the maximum size of a sample that can be meaningful for qualitative research. Again there is no straightforward answer because qualitative research has been used to study crowds of football fans and mass demonstrations. A very large number of interviews can also be studied qualitatively using an appropriate computer package (such as NUD*IST or NVIVO) which helps the researcher to analyse huge amounts of data, organizing concepts into categories and sub-categories. Many reports based on qualitative research include some quantitative data and vice versa; for example, a report based on interviews about experiences of gender inequalities in the workplace may include statistics from Social Trends outlining differences between male and female incomes, and a report based on such statistics may include a reference to other findings based on in-depth interviews. The number of people being studied therefore provides little guidance regarding whether the research is primarily quantitative or qualitative, as it is more meaningful to consider how the findings are to be analysed.

Research based on analysis of qualitative data is not usually associated with hypothesis testing because it cannot demonstrate cause and effect via statistics. However, qualitative research can be used as a preparatory stage in which a hypothesis is identified, and this can then be tested later with quantitative research. Thus, the aim of qualitative research is to achieve depth of understanding whilst the aim of quantitative research is to achieve greater breadth in order to evaluate cause and effect and/ or generalize findings to a wider population.

> It [qualitative research] tends to focus on exploring, in as much detail as possible, smaller numbers of instances or examples which are seen as being interesting or illuminating, and aims to achieve 'depth' rather than 'breadth'.
>
> Blaxter, Hughes and Tight, 1996, p 60

Figure 2.3 Trade-offs when using qualitative methods of research

+	−
Depth/understanding	Lacks breadth/generalizability
High in internal validity	Low in external validity
Useful for studying a natural setting	Can't control the setting
Can identify categories, types, concepts, etc.	Can't control variables

Surveys

Surveys are often wrongly associated only with quantitative research because it is assumed that they are fundamentally intended to achieve breadth rather than depth. This is a very limited view of what surveys actually are. Basically they involve the systematic collection of data from more than one person (usually many) which is then studied by identifying variables (such as age, gender, ethnicity, attitudes) for each person. This data is then analysed via a variable-by-case matrix, which allows the researcher to compare responses. By *cases* we mean each of the individuals or other subjects of the research (such as each school if we were comparing schools), and these are usually listed down the left side of the matrix. Variables are listed across the top and the appropriate values of each variable is inserted into the relevant cell (box on the matrix) next to the individual case (see Figure 2.4).

Figure 2.4 Extract from a variable-by-case matrix

id	rsex	partyid1	edspend1	tea
620	2	1	4	4
621	2	3	8	1
622	1	10	1	1
623	2	98	2	1
624	1	2	3	3
625	1	10	3	1
626	1	2	3	1
627	2	6	4	2

rsex
Label: Respondent's sex [interviewer's observation] Q16
Value labels:
 1 Male
 2 Female
 3 Don't know
 9 Not answered

partyid1
Label: Party identification
Value labels:
 1 Conservative
 2 Labour
 3 Liberal Democrats
 6 Scottish Nationalist
 7 Plaid Cymru
 8 Other party
 9 Other answer

10 None
95 Green Party
98 Don't know
99 Not answered

edspend
Label: 1st priority for extra spending on education Q706
Value labels:
 1 Nursery children
 2 Primary children
 3 Secondary children
 4 Special needs children
 5 College students
 6 None of these
 8 Don't know
 9 Not answered

tea
Label: Terminal Education Age Q795
Value labels:
 1 15 or under
 2 16
 3 17
 4 18
 5 19 or over
 6 Still at school
 7 Still at college/university
97 Other answer
98 Don't know
99 Not answered

Source: Adapted from the British Social Attitudes Surveys dataset, 1994. Available to be analysed using the Statistical Package of the Social Sciences (SPSS), Windows version.

Questions

What do the coded responses mean for the person with identification number 627?
What assumptions would it be reasonable, and unreasonable, to make about the implications of terminal education age?
Look at the information provided in Appendix 1. Would there be any value in codifying the responses of a sample of this size and analysing the findings via SPSS?
Would it be appropriate to analyse the findings via NUD*IST?

It is wrong to associate surveys only with quantitative research because it is actually possible to carry out a survey in which qualitative data from as few as four interviews is adapted and compared. Nevertheless, surveys do seem to be most commonly used for quantitative research as the data generated by large-scale surveys is open to sophisticated statistical analysis and (if a random sample is used) may be generalized to the wider population. When there are many cases researchers generally collect the data via *questionnaires*, which are structured lists of questions on which respondents write their own answers. These can be delivered by post and therefore administered more cheaply than *interview schedules*, which may look similar to questionnaires but require an interviewer to note the answers on behalf of the interviewee.

The arrival of the annual British Social Attitudes Surveys in 1983 meant that researchers were provided with a valuable means of monitoring attitudinal change, and the surveys have provided a mass of systematically collected data that can be used to complement research on many topics. Before the 1980s opinion pollsters were already very active, but the most well-known source of attitudinal data was Butler and Stokes's electoral studies (1974). Their questioning on educational topics was, however, very limited, including for example a question in 1969 about respondents' 'warm' or 'cold' feelings towards comprehensive schools. By the 1980s easier access to computers, more sophisticated computer packages (especially the various versions of SPSS, the Statistical Package of the Social Sciences) and accessible databanks (such as the ESRC Data Archive) meant that even the less generously financed researcher with basic statistical skills could analyse data generated by large-scale surveys. Data from the Greater Manchester Panel Studies of 1980/1 and 1983/4 was analysed for the Torytown and Labourville studies and data from national surveys (British Social Attitudes Surveys) was used for comparison with findings in Torytown and Labourville. In this way the study of attitudes to educational issues could be widened beyond Torytown and Labourville and linked to developments at a national level.

Ethnography

The most well-known type of qualitative research is ethnography. This should not be confused with ethnomethodology, which is a theoretical perspective and not the same thing. The term *ethnography* was originally used to describe the study of the institutions and customs in small, well-defined communities in relatively simple societies but is now also used to refer to the detailed study of small groups of people within a complex society. Its emphasis is usually on forms of social interaction, and the meanings which lie behind these, and it may involve a wide range of methods of data collection, including interviews, observation and analysis of documents.

Although its emphasis on small-scale studies seems to suggest an interpretive/anti-positivist approach, ethnography was influenced in its early days by anthropological studies of societies as social systems, such as the work of Malinowski and Radcliffe Brown. These early anthropological studies were heavily influenced by positivism and functionalism and the researchers' 'objective' detachment has sometimes been associated with colonial assumptions of racial superiority. More recently feminists such as Mies (1993) have accused ethnographers of exploiting the people being studied by using 'smash and grab' techniques in which they collect data from their subjects, and use up their time, but leave nothing in return.

Ethnographers have in recent years become more sensitive to the feelings of the people being studied and less likely to take a positivist approach. Their research now tends to focus on interpretation of how people behave in 'natural' settings; they use a range of unobtrusive sources and have become more heavily influenced by theories of social action. They want to reach a deep understanding (Weber, 1949, called it 'Verstehen') of what meanings various social actions have to those in a particular context, making their values explicit and reflecting on their own (the researchers') role in the setting. As the aim is to achieve a valid interpretation of the data, the *informant* (person providing the information) is regarded as the expert and even apparently incongruous behaviour must be seriously explored.

Ethnographers take a holistic approach, which means that, although their commitment is to depth of understanding, they must provide 'thick' description of any aspect of the whole context which may influence the findings. Thick description can include layer upon layer of data as the researcher constantly searches for more and more detail in order to challenge or support findings and interpretations. This is necessary because the only way in which the validity of findings can be assessed is via a test of congruence; in other words, asking whether the detail provided would allow another researcher to fit into the setting. If another researcher does visit the setting later it may be possible to assess the validity of the original findings and monitor change. However, the need to take a holistic approach and provide thick description means that the researcher can easily suffer from data overload, and this problem is tackled by 'winnowing' (Wolcott, 1991) away most of the data by progressive focusing.

The ethnographer progressively focuses on concepts, identifying and codifying patterns as they emerge from the data. This usually involves *theoretical sampling* in the first instance or progressively focusing (when selecting the initial setting(s), types of actors, types of events and so on) so that identification of a sample, data collection and analysis are all interwoven. Ethnographers also look for 'essences' constituting ideal types (such as Willis's ideal type of 'lads' and 'ear 'oles', 1977; see Chapter 9).

> An ideal-type is formed by the one-sided accentuation of one or more points of view and by the synthesis of a great many diffuse, discrete, more or less present and occasionally absent concrete individual phenomena, which are arranged according to those one-sidedly emphasised viewpoints into a unified analytical construct. In its conceptual purity, this mental construct cannot be found empirically anywhere in reality. It is a utopia.
>
> Weber, 1949, p 90

Analytic induction is part of the logic of discovery in ethnography. It involves the systematic search for falsifying evidence by examining cases which differ in known ways, and the modification of theory until no further disconfirming evidence can be found. It should be seen as a continual process rather than a once-and-for-all test of a hypothesis.

Although ethnographic research often involves observation, that observation can be done in many ways. For example, ethnographers may choose *non-participant, covert* observation, which means that they do not participate in the setting and observe via a two-way mirror, video cameras and other secret ways of viewing a scene. This means that the researcher has not influenced the setting by his/her presence or own interaction with the people being studied and the subjects have not changed their natural behaviour because they do not know that they are being watched. However, it raises ethical questions about the rights of a researcher to study people without their permission. Covert observation is usually only carried out when there is no alternative and when the importance of the research may justify it. *Participant observation* may be covert or *overt* (i.e. the subjects know that they are being watched) and this involves the researcher joining a group of people in their natural setting, participating to a greater or lesser extent in what they are doing, observing patterns of social interaction and talking informally with them. Such informal talk may be simply spontaneous conversation or may include more carefully planned interviews. The whole group may (overt) or may not (covert) know the true purpose of the observer's presence and it is possible that some of the group may know whilst others do not. An introduction or other form of access to a group is usually through a contact researchers call a *gatekeeper*, who will help the researcher to fit into the setting. Thus, a participating gatekeeper may know more about the research than others in the group and help the researcher to deal with the various problems that may be encountered.

Interviews are often an essential part of ethnographic research, either in the natural setting being observed or simply as a way in which subjects can provide their own descriptions, explanations and reflections about their lives. Subjects who have been informed about the nature of the research (although sometimes not in great detail) may agree to lengthy interviews in a comfortable setting (usually their own homes) where they can provide a detailed and naturalistic account. These sorts of interviews are usually unstructured or semi-structured. *Unstructured interviews* are generally unplanned and allow the interviewee to identify topics of interest to themselves. They are usually used when the researcher is studying a *life history* and is therefore trying to elicit an autobiography of a single informant, through repeated unstructured interviews.

Semi-structured interviews are planned by the researcher in advance in order to ensure that various topics are covered and, whether this involves the preparation of a detailed *interview schedule* (a list of questions) or a more flexible *aide memoire*

(noting the topics to be covered), semi-structured interviews still allow the interviewee considerable freedom of response.

Ethnographic research is therefore particularly appropriate when a researcher is trying to generate ideas, explore an area that has not yet been studied, or test existing theories with observation. However, it would be very difficult to maintain objectivity (and it has been noted that ethnographers have been criticized for trying to), it is seldom possible

---

LEARNING TO LABOUR: PAUL WILLIS'S ETHNOGRAPHIC APPROACH

Samples

Town: 'Hammertown', an old industrial town in a Midlands conurbation.
School: 'Hammertown Boys' School', a non-selective secondary modern school. Exclusively working-class intake, including many West Indian and Asian minorities. Reputation as a 'good' school.
Main study: Twelve non-academic working class lads selected on basis of friendship links in an oppositional culture within Hammertown Boys' School.

Comparative studies:

1. Group of conformist lads in the same year of Hammertown Boys.
2. Group of working-class conformist lads in a Hammertown mixed secondary modern school, which was known as a 'rougher' school.
3. Working-class conformist lads in single-sex Hammertown Grammar School.
4. Similar group in a comprehensive school near the middle of the conurbation of which Hammertown is a part.
5. A mixed-class male non-conformist group in a high-status grammar school in the most exclusive area of the larger conurbation.

Methods

1. Initial contact with the group at the beginning of the second term of their penultimate year. The research followed them through to the first six months of their working lives.
2. Observation and participant observation in class, around the school and during leisure activities.
3. Regular recorded group discussions, informal interviews and diaries.
4. Taped conversations with parents, teachers and careers officers.
5. Followed all the main group and three boys from each other group into work, worked alongside them, taped interviews with them.
6. Taped interviews with foremen, managers and shop stewards.

From Willis, 1977, pp 11–51

Question

What further information is needed in order to evaluate Willis's methods?
(Note that Paul Willis describes his methods throughout the book, but especially on pages 11–51, 160–170.)

---

to generalize to a wider population, it is difficult to assess validity and it may be regarded as particularly intrusive. Those studying education must also be particularly aware of the ethical issues involved in studying children and of the power structures within the educational setting.

Validity

If sociologists are considering many perspectives and constantly aware of the subjectivity of their interpretations then surely their research is a waste of time and their findings are meaningless! This is the usual criticism from people who do not understand the rigorous nature of good sociological research. The rigorous researcher will constantly evaluate what is being done, how it is being done and the quality of the findings. This *reflexivity* involves a continual monitoring of the whole research process. It requires the researcher to make explicit in the subsequent report the process by which the data and findings were produced. *Validity* is the extent to which the findings can be trusted, the extent to which they accurately represent reality. In quantitative research validity generally means the extent to which a test, questionnaire or other operationalization is really measuring what the researcher intends it to measure. In ethnographic research it refers to the extent to which the actors' expectations, perspectives, meanings and so on are accurately represented and reported in the research report. It also involves the researcher in trying to anticipate all the objections that could be raised against the research process.

This looks like a tall order but some strategies for improving validity can be learned. In particular the researcher must learn to ask all sorts of awkward questions. In checking the *internal validity* of findings, and therefore the accuracy of their own interpretations of the findings, researchers search for alternative explanations (e.g. asking whether it is ethnicity or the poverty arising from racism that is affecting educational outcomes). When checking the *external validity* of findings the researcher considers the extent to which results may be generalized beyond the immediate population (*population validity*) and immediate setting

or sample (*ecological validity*). The researcher will also check for *reactivity*, which is the effect the researcher has on who and what is being studied. The possible effects of the researcher's gender, ethnicity, social class, age and so on must therefore be considered. Although a thorough evaluation of many characteristics may seem too demanding, it is possible to identify the most obvious aspects of reactivity. For example, when asked about their attitudes to gender differences or ethnicity, some interviewees may feel free to express their sexist or racist views when interviewed by someone of their own sex or ethnicity.

Reliability

Many students confuse validity with reliability, but they are quite different. *Reliability* means the extent to which a test would give consistent results if applied more than once to the same people under standard conditions. In the natural sciences we could, for example, consider the reliability of a tape-measure by ensuring that its measurement of a centimetre is exactly the same as the measurement of a centimetre on other tape-measures. In the social sciences we are more likely to be concerned about the reliability (i.e. consistency) of a team of interviewers engaged in an individual research project, and may try to achieve reliability by training them all to ask the same questions in the same way. When evaluating qualitative methods we consider the possibility that a different researcher would have generated different results.

Triangulation of methods

It is also possible to evaluate and improve the validity of the findings by using a triangulation of theories, methods or researchers. If the same conclusions are reached using different methods or sources then it is likely that no peculiarity of method or source has produced the conclusions and confidence in their validity increases.

The heuristic value of competing perspectives is considered in Chapter 3, but it should not be forgotten when considering methods. Indeed *triangulation of theories* becomes a habit as sociologists dip into and compare various perspectives and theories in order to understand their findings. The term *triangulation* has been used for a long time by military strategists (considering attack and crossfire from several positions) and maritime navigators (when locating their ship's position). *Triangulation of methods* tends to become a habit for many researchers as they cross-check the findings generated by using one method with the findings generated by other methods. Do the findings emerging from semi-structured interviews match those from a highly structured survey, those from observation, from reading about other researchers' findings and so on? The researcher will find that it is useful to collect data by different methods which each entail different strengths and weaknesses and threats to validity. Similarly, *data triangulation* involves the collection of varied data on the same phenomena (such as from different participants and different phases of fieldwork). In the Torytown and Labourville research two Likert attitude scales were used in order to create two scales of educational radicalism from different sources and therefore increase validity. The writer most commonly associated with triangulation is Denzin (1970), who described three particular types of data triangulation (time, space and person) and three levels of data triangulation, relating to how groups of people are studied (aggregate, interactive and collectivity). The huge amount of information emerging from this sort of layering of data can often generate what some writers call 'thick ethnography'. In order to tackle problems of reactivity or limited perspectives, research sometimes involves *investigator triangulation*, whereby data is generated by more than one researcher (sometimes through the adoption of different roles in the field).

An illustration of the value of triangulation can be seen in the work of Sanger (1997). Sanger showed that a boy called 'Ashley' was a very convincing liar during his interview. He provided a lot of detail about his use of computers at home and talked about his elder brother. Only when a researcher visited his home was it discovered that he had no computer and no elder brother.

Triangulation therefore seems to be a good idea, but we can still ask whether the researcher should use triangulation or just one method. In an ideal world perhaps triangulation is best. Yet in the real world some researchers favour certain individual methods because they feel comfortable with them or avoid some methods (often quantitative) because they feel particularly uncomfortable with them. They may therefore avoid research topics that necessitate use of a certain method or form a research team with other researchers so that each can contribute the method(s) appropriate to their skills. Also in the real world researchers may not have the time or other resources needed in order to triangulate methods.

Action research

We have already seen that much research is simply aiming to generate a greater understanding of the social world. However, even without intending to do so, some descriptive research of this sort can, by actually increasing knowledge, lead to social change. We are now moving on to consider types of research that actually aim to initiate or implement social change.

Action research is sometimes simply defined as research that aims to change something, but this definition is very wide. It would be more precise to note that *action research* studies changes before, during and after they happen and actually involves the researcher as a participant in the process of change. This means that implementation is not an after-thought, but built into the actual research, and that the research involves a partnership between the researcher and the other participants. Often the research is carried out by researchers who are initiating change in the workplace; for example, teachers trying new teaching practices or social workers trying out new ways of recording case notes. Someone engaged in action research may therefore have a dual role as participant and researcher. As it is their own workplace they are able to identify and specify problems, formulate possible solutions, take action to solve the problem and evaluate the effectiveness of the action.

Although some action research can be rather large scale (e.g. the research associated with the

Plowden Report, 1967, which led to the identification of Educational Priority Areas), most of it involves relatively small-scale projects. Roper and Tosh (1991) studied the role of schools in the construction of masculinity and suggested strategies for working with boys and for in-service work with teachers (including workshops, anti-sexist initiatives and strategies for getting boys to talk more openly and honestly). Doreen Grant (1989) worked with parents in a Glasgow slum, helping them to overcome their own negative experiences of education and teaching them to have pride in their role as educators of their own children.

Action research is generally perceived as being reformist, introducing rather moderate changes, and this seems to be both its strength and weakness. Radicals may claim that it does not initiate the major social changes needed in order to tackle more fundamental social problems, whereas action researchers may argue that piecemeal change is more realistic than revolutionary change.

Critical research

Critical research is associated with critical theory and more radical ideas about how research can initiate social change and the sort of changes that must be initiated. Influenced by Marxist and neo-Marxist critiques of structural conflict, critical researchers tend to assume that social inequalities are maintained by false consciousness and that their research should aim to enlighten people about the nature of their oppression. Once enlightened, the oppressed can be empowered in order to overthrow their oppressors, be emancipated and transform society. It is difficult to clearly identify critical research in education, partly because critical researchers would be wary of declaring the ultimate aim of their research in case their motives seem too extreme or unrealistic.

QUESTION

Look at Freire's (1970, 1972) efforts to promote conscientization via the education of the poorest people in Brazil. Is this critical research?

Feminist research

There are some similarities between feminist research and critical research as both aim to enlighten and empower people in order to achieve social change. We can also see that a Marxist ontology or a feminist ontology will inspire a researcher to focus on certain social inequalities. Here we can clearly see the links between ontology, epistemology and methodology.

Although feminists may use any of the methods used by other researchers their feminist ontologies and epistemologies make them particularly aware of how research can relate to inequalities of power. They are critical of research for having provided knowledge which supports the continuation of male domination, and are particularly critical of positivist approaches for having treated (and exploited) the people studied as objects rather than subjects. For this reason some sociologists wrongly assume that feminists will not use the quantitative methods that have been particularly associated with positivism; an assumption that again simplifies quantitative and qualitative methods. Feminists challenge any claims to objectivity (as, for example, academics cannot be truly gender-blind) and sometimes seem to favour qualitative methods because they see no separation between the subject (person) being studied and the sociologist studying that person. The research process is a shared experience and should empower rather than exploit the person being studied. Positivists and other researchers are also criticized for their idealized image of 'hygienic research', which does not equate with most researchers' experiences of confusion and, sometimes, extreme anxiety.

> The methodological principle of a value-free, neutral, uninvolved approach, of a hierarchical, non-reciprocal relationship between research subject and research object – certainly the decisive methodological postulate of positivist social science research – drives women scholars into a schizophrenic situation. If they try to follow this postulate, they have to constantly repress, negate or ignore their own experience of sexist oppression and have to strive to live up to the so-called 'rational' standards of a highly competitive, male-dominated world.
>
> Mies, 1993, p 67

A feminist approach emphasizes, not only what is known, but also how it has come to be known by analysing the processes producing knowledge and the role of the researcher within those processes. The aim is to create unalienated knowledge; that is, knowledge that is not separated from the process of its production. Feminist research therefore often tries to uncover what has been ignored in the past (literally 're-search'), enlighten and empower women and challenge gender inequalities within the academic/research communities producing knowledge as well as within the wider society. For example, when monitoring change in gendered socialization feminists have scrutinized textbooks and readers to identify gendered language and/or gendered assumptions (e.g. that 'Jane helps mummy' in the kitchen whilst 'Peter helps daddy' to clean the car).

The main problem associated with feminist approaches to research methods concerns how they relate to approaches by men or by women who would not describe themselves as 'feminists'. There are also so many types of feminist perspectives that not everyone who calls themselves a feminist will adhere to the principles associated with feminist methods. Yet, feminist critiques have been very influential and have led 'non-feminist researchers' to evaluate their own approaches, taking on board some, or most, of the principles of feminist research. In particular, it is not only feminists who have criticized researchers for exploiting the people being studied (especially when they are in oppressed or relatively disadvantaged groups). Therefore, the term *non-oppressive methods* is often used as an alternative to 'feminist methods' in order to prevent concerns about the exploitation

---

A TYPOLOGY OF LIFE HISTORIES AND THEIR MODES OF PRESENTATION

Types

Retrospective life history. A reconstruction of past events from the present feelings and interpretations of the individual concerned.

Contemporaneous life history. A depiction of an individual's daily life in progress, here and now.

Modes of presentation

Naturalistic. A first-person life history in which the life story is largely in the words of the individual subject, supported by a brief introduction, commentary and conclusion on the part of the researcher.

Thematically-edited. Subjects' words are retained intact but are presented by the researcher in terms of a series of themes, topics or headings, often in chapter-by-chapter format.

Interpreted and edited. The researcher's influence is most marked in his/her version of a subject's life story which the researcher has sifted, distilled, edited and interpreted.

Adapted by Cohen and Manion (1994, Box 2.7, p 60) from Hitchcock, G. and Hughes, D. (1989), *Research and the Teacher: A Qualitative Introduction to School-based Research*, London: Routledge.

Questions

Does the research in Torytown and Labourville include 'life histories'?
Does the mode of presentation of data from the Torytown and Labourville interviewees fit any of these types?

---

of subjects from being primarily associated with a feminist approach. Non-oppressive methods generally aim to ensure that the people being studied will benefit from the research in some way (e.g. in at least a minor way by providing feedback about the findings).

Historical research

Cohen and Manion (1994, p 45) note that historical research is 'an act of reconstruction' of a previous age and that 'researchers often have to contend with inadequate information so that their reconstructions tend to be sketches rather than portraits'. Ideally it should be holistic, because even specific events can only be understood if the researcher relates them to a broader view of their whole social, economic and political context. Yet a holistic approach (as seen in this book) can never be totally satisfactory because even people who have lived through the relevant period of time will have different experiences and interpretations of their social context. So the researcher tries to ensure that the sketch outlines key features and provides an image as closely aligned to reality as possible. At the very least the aim is not to mislead or misrepresent.

In doing historical research we can trace the origins of the knowledge we have today, the source of current educational processes and, hopefully, learn from previous mistakes. Travers (1969) observed that a better understanding of the history of education would help to tackle the tendency of educational ideas to move in cycles, eventually returning to their starting point and effectively meaning that educationalists had just been engaged in 're-discovering the wheel'.

Historical research obviously includes life histories and, in the case of education, the lives and teachings of well-known educators can help us to understand the history of ideas in education. The educational experiences of less well-known individuals can help to fill the gaps in a historical sketch of more general changes in education. Cohen and Manion listed various types of life histories (see previous page).

Longitudinal research

If historical research in general can be described as a reconstruction or sketch, then longitudinal research describes the changing views from a moving train. Longitudinal research studies not only present relationships, between people or variables, but also the way those relationships change over time. Data is therefore gathered over a long period and the process can last for several years. It is also gathered by several well-known organizations in order to monitor changes in education (e.g. teachers' unions, the National Foundation for Educational Research and OFSTED, the Office of Standards in Education).

There are many types of longitudinal research and one of the most common is the *cross-sectional longitudinal study*, which involves studying different samples at different points in time. *Retrospective longitudinal studies* involve research into what has happened to a sample who have reached a certain point; for example, what led a group of newly qualified teachers to decide on a career in teaching.

Cohort studies

Cohort studies are a type of longitudinal research in which the same sample (called a 'cohort' or 'panel') is studied at different points in time. There are, for example, some well-known studies of samples of children born at the same time (e.g. the National Child Development Study, 1958 onwards, reported by Douglas, 1964, 1976; Douglas, Ross and Simpson, 1968) which allow researchers to monitor the children's personal and social development, identify influences on that development and trace causal relationships. The researcher can also identify social trends that may influence that development.

ADVANTAGES OF COHORT OVER CROSS-SECTIONAL STUDIES

1. Some types of information, for example, on attitudes or assessment of potential ability, are only meaningful if collected contemporaneously. Other types are more complete or more accurate if collected during the course of a longitudinal survey, though they are likely to have some value even if collected retrospectively, for example, length of schooling, job history, geographical movement.
2. In cohort studies, no duplication of information occurs, whereas in cross-sectional studies the same type of background information has to be collected on each occasion. This increases the interviewing costs.
3. The omission of even a single variable, later found to be important, from a cross-sectional study is a disaster, whereas it is usually possible in a cohort study to fill the gap, even if only partially, in a subsequent interview.
4. A cohort study allows the accumulation of a much larger number of variables, extending over a much wider area of knowledge than would be possible in a cross-sectional study. This is of course because the collection may be spread over many interviews. Moreover, information may be obtained at the most appropriate time, for example, information on job entry may be obtained when it occurs even if this varies from one member of the sample to another.
5. Starting with a birth cohort removes later problems of sampling and allows the extensive use of subsamples. It also eases problems of estimating bias and reliability.
6. Longitudinal studies are free of one of the major obstacles to causal analysis, namely, the re-interpretation of remembered information so that it conforms with conventional views on causation. It also provides the means to assess the direction of effect.

Adapted from Douglas, 1976, by Cohen and Manion, 1994, Box 3.2, p 72

Questions

Evaluate the strengths and weaknesses of cohort studies (see Cohen and Manion, 1994, pp 69–72). Examine the strategies used in actual cohort studies and other types of longitudinal studies (see Cohen and Manion, 1994, pp 72–81).

The Greater Manchester Study, 1980–1997: Using a cohort

Themes in this book are occasionally illustrated via the educational experiences and attitudes of a sample of the electorate, who were born between 1910 and 1979. This is a primary source in that most of the data used was collected by the writer herself. The aim is to bring some of the themes in this book alive by reproducing the words of people interviewed in Torytown and Labourville, an approach that does not fit the definition of life histories, but may be described as contemporaneous, with their words thematically interpreted and edited.

QUESTION

Use what you have read about research methods in this chapter in order to evaluate the collection and use of primary data from Torytown and Labourville; for example, considering validity, reliability, generalizability, reflexivity and bias.

At this point I must therefore shift to writing in a more personal style as we are looking at my own work. My involvement in the Torytown and Labourville studies started with a failed job interview for a post as research assistant on the early stages of the research. I retained information about the research and used it when constructing a research proposal as one element of the assessment for my part-time M.Sc. When Salford University advertised full-time postgraduate studentships I submitted the proposal, was interviewed by Edgell and Duke and, starting in 1986, carried out full-time research for a Ph.D (funded by the Social Science Research Council, now the Economic and Social Research Council).

What I will now call the Torytown and Labourville Studies actually started under the title of the 'Greater Manchester Panel Study' (GMS), under the direction of Stephen Edgell and Vic Duke who were based in the Department of Sociology, Salford University. A panel of informants in two areas of Greater Manchester (labelled 'Torytown' and 'Labourville' by Edgell and Duke) were interviewed in 1980/1 and again in 1983/4. The two areas were actually electoral wards within Greater Manchester, chosen by the original researchers because of their equivalent socio-economic structures and contrasting political control. Torytown was represented by Conservatives in the House of Commons and at council level and had a Conservative majority in its council, whereas Labourville was represented by Labour politicians in the House of Commons and at council level and had a Labour majority in its council. *Simple random samples* of voters in the two wards were chosen for Phase 1 and as many as possible of those who were interviewed in Phase 1 were again interviewed in Phase 2 (see Figures 2.5 and 2.6). In the first two phases of the GMS, information was collected about attitudes to public spending cuts and a range of public services. Edgell and Duke have subsequently published their findings in two SSRC/ESRC reports, several academic papers and a book (1991).

I was particularly interested in this research because of the different school systems in the two areas and the questions asked in the interviews about attitudes to educational issues. Torytown retained a system of selection at the age of 11+ for grammar schools and secondary modern schools whilst Labourville provided a comprehensive system of secondary education. (More detail about their different systems are provided in Chapter 4.) It would be interesting to compare the responses of people in the two areas to their different systems and educational issues.

My early work involved statistical analysis of existing data (using the Statistical Package of the Social Sciences) from the first two phases of the

Figure 2.5 Phases in the Labourville and Torytown studies

Phase 1 – interviews during 1980/1, sample size 948, Edgell and Duke.
Phase 2 – interviews during 1983/4, sample size 685, Edgell and Duke.
Phase 3 – interviews during 1988, sample size 52, McKenzie (47 originals, 5 new members of the electoral register; 28 from Torytown, 24 from Labourville; 28 female, 24 male).
Phase 4 – interviews during 1992, sample size 51, McKenzie and Duke (45 originals, 4 who were new in Phase 3, 2 new members of the electoral register; 26 from Torytown, 25 from Labourville; 25 female, 26 male).
Phase 5 – interviews during 1997, sample size 28, McKenzie (19 originals, 2 who were new in Phase 3, 7 adult children of panel members; 15 from Torytown, 13 from Labourville; 15 female, 13 male).

Figure 2.6 Samples in phases 3–5

	1988	1992	1997
From phase 1 and 2 panels	47	45	19
From phase 3 or 4 panels	–	4	2
Replacements	5	2	7
Torytown	28	26	15
Labourville	24	25	13
Male	24	26	13
Female	28	25	15
Total	52	51	28

Total interviewed at some time between 1988 and 1997 = 73

GMS and the British Social Attitudes Surveys of 1983, 1985 and 1987, and the reading of early drafts provided by the researchers carrying out the British Political Participation Study of 1984/5 (Parry, Moyser and Day, 1992). From these sources (and wider general reading) I developed provisional *scales of educational radicalism* (see Chapter 5) and various theories emerged for testing with qualitative data. I therefore designed a *theoretical quota sample*, based on area, consumption of education, experience of further education, employment sector and gender. The aim was to collect qualitative data from a sample selected in order to explore and test theories emerging from analysis of the quantitative data. I tried to get equal numbers from each area in order to identify any different attitudes in the two areas. Theories about consumption sectoral cleavages (e.g. Dunleavy and Husbands, 1985) suggested that public employees might have more left-wing attitudes to those who were employed privately. Therefore, I tried to get equal numbers of private employees, public employees (e.g. working in the NHS, local government, education) and unemployed (including pensioners and students). Quantitative data showed that, at any one time, only approximately one-third of the population are parents with children of school age and that these were the people most likely to be interested in educational issues. Again I tried to balance the sample accordingly. Similarly, efforts were made to balance experience of education after school-leaving age (further education – FE) according the national trends. Claims that women were more interested in educational issues could also be tested by having equal numbers of males and females (M, F).

Figure 2.7 shows the intended sample of 12 people in each of the three employment sectors in each area, resulting in a total of 24 people in each employment sector when the quotas for the two areas were combined. This was obviously an ideal and would have resulted in a total of 72 but the final sample was of 52 people overall (see Figure 2.8).

Figure 2.7 Case study quotas in Torytown and Labourville, each employment sector (public, private and unemployed)

Employment Sector 12							
Parents 4				Non-parents 8			
Had FE 2		No FE 2		Had FE 4		No FE 4	
M	F	M	F	M	F	M	F
1	1	1	1	2	2	2	2

Figure 2.8 Case study final sample in 1988

Labourville
7 public sector, 8 private, 9 not employed
9 parents, 15 non-parents
15 had FE, 9 no FE
14 female, 10 male
Total 24

Torytown
8 public sector, 12 private, 8 not employed
11 parents, 17 non-parents
13 had FE, 15 no FE
16 female, 12 male
Total 28

QUESTION

What possible explanations could there be for differences in the characteristics of the sample originally identified and those of the actual sample (in 1988)?

Interviews in phases 1 and 2 were carried out using *structured interview schedules* and a team of trained interviewers in order to maximize validity. Many of the original questions were also asked in the last three phases, in order to compare responses over time, and some new questions were added in each phase, in order to raise current issues. This provides an illustration of the problem discussed at the very start of this chapter: How do we anticipate topics of future relevance? Nearly all interviews in phases 3–5 were carried out in the informant's own home (except one memorable interview with a police officer in a cell at his station) and lasted between one and three hours (when an informant drank beer throughout, got drunk and talkative, and began to sort out the troubles of the world).

The original plan for phase 3 was to carry out *semi-structured interviews* (using an *interview schedule*) with the sample in 1988 in order to provide qualitative data to supplement existing quantitative data, write-up the findings, acquire a Ph.D and stop there. However, together with Vic Duke, I later applied for funding to finance more fieldwork in 1992, and in 1997 obtained funding to finance my own last phase. This means that a long-term cohort study was not anticipated or planned, making this research a less than ideal model of hygienic research. Ultimately sixteen members of the cohort were interviewed five times during a period of seventeen years (in 1980/1, 1983/4, 1988, 1992 and 1997) and three others from phase 1 were also interviewed in phase 5, a figure that is not particularly low given house moves, deaths, holidays and sickness. As the original cohort were an aging population (the youngest was 35 years old in 1997) and may have been biased towards people who are not geographically mobile, it was decided to add some new additions to the electoral register to their number at each stage. By 1997 some of the panel members' children had reached the age of eighteen and were voting in a general election for the first time. Seven of these adult 'children' were therefore added to the sample, with interesting results. It is now possible to analyse the 'children's' recollections of their own education and attitudes to educational issues and compare them with those of their parents, both in 1997 and in earlier phases of the research.

QUESTIONS

How was cohort depletion and replacement tackled? Could it have been tackled any other way?
What arguments could be made for and against supplementing the original cohort with new members? Could any claims for generalizability be made from the samples in phases 3, 4 and 5?

The data from the five phases of the research now provides an opportunity to explore how subjects' attitudes towards educational issues changed according to life cycles, experiences and political developments. However, this type of analysis has not progressed far enough to be included in this book. It has involved learning how to use NUD*IST (a computer package for analysing qualitative data) and how to manipulate a formidable amount of data from various sources. Efforts were made to test the *validity* of findings by *triangulation of methods*, including observation at political meetings in Torytown and Labourville, interviews with local politicians and analysis of local and national newspapers.

Interviews for this final phase of the GMS took place during the summer following the 1997 general election. This could be seen as a timely end to a longitudinal study covering a lengthy period of

Conservative government. Alternatively, it could be appreciated that contacts with original panel members are unlikely to extend beyond 1997, and that this phase is a natural conclusion.

QUESTION

Discuss arguments for and against interviewing the cohort again.

Reflection on the research now raises many problems and the good researcher should try to identify problems in the research before anyone else does. This can only be done briefly in an already lengthy chapter on research methods. First, the area of study was far too broad and I do not appear to have followed the advice I gave earlier in this chapter about progressive focusing. As Best noted (in 1970, cited by Cohen and Manion, 1994, p 48), an experienced historian will aim for a '... penetrating analysis of a limited problem, rather than the superficial examination of a broad area'. My problem was that, as some theories came more clearly into focus, other ideas emerged unexpectedly and became all the more fascinating because of this. Second, in 1986 I had no plans to write this book and did not design my work accordingly, my main aims being to earn money, support my family, complete the thesis, get a Ph.D and stay sane. All but the last were material objectives and took priority over more highbrow academic motives or more altruistic motives (e.g. providing the feedback to interviewees that most good researchers regard as essential). From what you have seen earlier in this chapter you should now be aware that, although researchers must adopt a meticulous approach and aim for the elusive ideals of rigorous social research, any claims that perfection has been achieved should be treated with suspicion. Feelings of failure often seem to be part of the job, but there are also achievements.

The box describing the advantages of cohort research does not mention the real pleasure and feelings of privilege that may be experienced by someone who does this sort of research. Of course, it is very demanding and can result in frustration and failure, but the opportunity to gain a long-term insight into other people's lives must be appreciated. Often researchers find that the people being studied at a distance via statistical analysis of survey data become depersonalized objects, no matter how determined we may be to avoid a positivist approach. Ethnographers can really get to know the people they interact with in their natural settings, but know that they are only getting a glimpse of current events and may be curious about what happens after they have left the scene. Researchers carrying out cohort studies may also be curious about what happens to their sample after they have ceased their research (in some cases on retirement as other researchers take over) but the longevity of the research can be very satisfying as their relationship with the cohort moves from objectivity to subjectivity to familiarity.

Operationalizing and comparing changing educational standards

Problems arising from efforts to study changing standards of education are being introduced here, rather than with other issues in Chapter 5, because the problem of *operationalizing* standards is central to *research* into educational change. As you meet the samples from Torytown and Labourville for the first time you will see that there is a fundamental problem in operationalizing the concept of 'standards'. Here we can see that common indicators included competence in reading, writing and arithmetic (the three Rs), the number and level of qualifications, the market value of educational achievements, attitudes and behaviour, and equal opportunities. Some informants had problems providing any sort of definition and others mentioned a wide range of indicators. We will also return to the issue of changing standards in Chapter 5, where some of these indicators are mentioned again.

Even if we accept the usual official preference for measuring standards according to examination passes, we face fundamental problems when calculating change and comparing schools for academic 'league tables'.

VIEWS FROM TORYTOWN AND LABOURVILLE: OPERATIONALIZING STANDARDS

What do you mean by standards?

Reading, writing and arithmetic

At least every child should be able to read and write when they leave school.

Frank, 1988

Ordinary everyday things such as the three Rs. There's too much fancy work done in education today – not enough work is done on the three Rs.

Albert, 1992

The basics, that's what one needs. They last you a lifetime. Mine have. Reading, writing and arithmetic, history, geography, English. I can still put things right in library books. Their English grammar is terrible, their spelling and so on. In a shop they'd be lost without computers and them machines. And with my grandchildren. I say, 'Did you not do it the easy way – mental arithmetic?' I should think children's eyesight will be awful in a few years time with these computers. Will they be able to do mental arithmetic? I doubt it.

Annie, 1992

The ability to read, calculate, spell and to write legibly. All of these are worse. There are too many experimenters on education and the teachers have too much to do.

Clifford, 1992

The three Rs and being taught to read so that they enjoy it. I love reading. Children don't read and therefore their spelling will be very difficult.

Caroline, 1992

The basics such as the three Rs. There's not enough emphasis on these. But I'm no longer personally involved in education, so perhaps I shouldn't say.

Elizabeth, 1992

I think they should stick to reading, writing and arithmetic. They should get the basics right and then other things can come after that.

Monica, 1992

Getting qualifications

To get qualifications applicable to your abilities with the help of good, trained teachers.

Henry, 1992

Percentages in an exam rather than percentages in coursework. I know there are some unfortunate characters who, faced with an exam, can be very very clever and just go to pieces and can't answer exams to save their life, and they're probably very good and very competent people. But I think there's a certain amount of fiddling that can go on when you rely too much on coursework, like, 'You do my coursework, Fred, because you're dead good at it and make sure I pass the exam'.

Lawrence, 1997

A higher rate of passing of exams, a greater depth to the understanding of what they have passed exams in and better focus on what the whole point of it is about, as in having a job and being of some use when you leave school.

Richard, 1997

Marketability

Marketability of the end product. Is it of any use to anybody?

Richard, 1992

Qualifications. Getting whatever grades they need to go after a job. Where I work in social services they're advertising for someone to replace a girl who's leaving and asking for three O levels for it – it's just as a simple invoice clerk. They need O levels now.

Georgina, 1992

Attitudes and behaviour

I don't think it's got anything to do with passing examinations (though education's got a lot to do with that) but it's got to do with people's attitudes.

Polly, 1988

Basically respect for their parents, the school and the teachers and the environment.

Graham, 1988

Equality

It depends what stage you're at. Standards is a level of education that gives each child the best of its own ability. That's very difficult to achieve with big classes.

Bernard, 1992

Every child should have the right to show what it can do and be helped to be brought on. They should all have an equal chance.

Emma, 1992

Many things

The whole education. Not only academic but the virtues of developing things in children; the talents and respect for other people, adapting the needs of the child and preparing them for a job, their next school or whatever.

Laura, 1988

Giving a good whole education across the curriculum, providing opportunities, good resources and catering for the individual.

Laura, 1992

Examination passes. What is available for the pupils. The state of the buildings. Are there the right number and type of teachers? A broader choice of subject areas.

Jeremy, 1992

Keeping a good teacher:pupil ratio and keeping up with things like computer studies, a good library, a good set of textbooks. Everything. Keeping up with the times.

Paul, 1992

Questions

These are just some of the themes emerging from responses to this question:
What do standards mean to you?
Can the concept of educational standards be operationalized? (a) If yes, how? (b) If no, does the concept have any value?
Look at the backgrounds of the people quoted (see Appendix 1) and consider how these may have affected their perceptions of standards.
See Chapter 5 for more responses to the question about changing standards.

HOW DO WE COMPARE STANDARDS?

It is a good idea to control for prior attainment of pupils and social-context effects if you are trying to gauge how schools are performing relative to each other or to some average standard, but you have to be aware of the pitfalls.

The first is a basic statistical one, and it concerns the accuracy with which we can estimate averages based on small groups of pupils. For a large secondary school with about 200 pupils in a year group, we may be able to estimate the value added by the school with a moderate degree of accuracy. In a primary, with say 30 pupils in a year group, just one or two high or low-scoring pupils can make a big difference to the overall results.

The second point is about what you use as a baseline measure of pupils' attainment when starting a particular phase of education . . . [We face the] question of how reliable and reproducible the intake measures are, between schools and across time . . . Another issue is how finely-differentiated the results are. National curriculum levels, each roughly equivalent to two years of schooling, are of little use as an intake measure for value-added purposes.

A *third problem* with using the outcomes of one stage as inputs to the next is the danger of 'negative coupling'. If a school, either in reality or through some technique which 'massages' the results, achieves above-average results for its pupils at the end of one stage, then those pupils have to produce even better scores at the next stage for a good value-added result . . . So the moral here might be: if you want to look good at A-Level, make sure your pupils do quite badly at GCSE. This obviously cannot be right statistically, let alone educationally.

[Schagen suggests that measures of prior attainment] . . . should just measure where pupils are without having any further consequences for anyone or any institution. They should be consistent countrywide and from year to year, and should be simple to administer and to mark, while giving the measures of pupils' prior attainment which are as valid and reliable as possible.

At the National Foundation for Educational Research, we have developed systems which allow schools to judge which departments are 'adding significant value'.

There is a case for publicly available data about schools, in the name of accountability. But what that data should be, and how it is used, must be carefully thought out and the consequences weighted. Let us try to measure what is important, rather than letting what we can measure be all that is important.

Ian Schagen, head of statistics at the National Foundation for Educational Research,
'Value added taxes the statisticians', The Times Educational Supplement, 7 March 1997

Question

See the section of this chapter about methodology. How might positivists and anti-positivists differ in their approaches towards the measurement and evaluation of educational standards?

Political attitudes towards educational research

It is worth noting that Margaret Thatcher, perhaps the most influential person in British education since the mid 1970s, trained as a physical scientist with a distinctly positivist approach. This, combined with a firm belief in the supremacy of market forces, a consumer(parent)-led education system and commercial culture in general, set her at odds with many researchers in education and the social sciences. As Mrs Thatcher's government did not perceive the social sciences as science, and regarded sociology as a 'non-subject', it was quite significant that during the 1980s the main source of funding for research in the social sciences changed its name from the Social Science Research Council to the Economic and Social Research Council. This culture clash was described clearly in a speech made by Patricia Broadfoot on becoming the new President of the British Educational Research Association in 1988.

Researchers may also complain of feelings of alienation from the knowledge they are trying to produce. Sometimes this is because the emphasis on objectivity associated with positivist influences can lead them to feeling estranged from their experiences and the people they are studying (see Cohen and Manion, 1994, p 24). Sometimes alienation is experienced because of daunting power structures within the academic mode of production, which have been subject to particular criticism by feminists. In *Feminist Praxis* (1990), Liz Stanley analysed research communities as one would analyse any workplace; by looking at the academic marker, powerful gatekeepers, the technical division of labour, social division of labour and sexual division of labour.

> For at least the last twenty years one of the aims of academic feminism has been to join them; but another has also been to dismantle at least some of the sources and uses of their power over 'peers'.
>
> Stanley, 1990, p 5

EDUCATIONAL RESEARCH: TWO CULTURES

The world of academe is quite literally another world, or, as I want to propose tonight, another culture. It is characterized by values, goals, ways of working and rewards which are fundamentally at odds with those of *laissez-faire* individualism and profit, market-forces and competition. It cannot, as I shall argue in what follows, be squeezed into a conformity with the prevailing political culture.

. . . The . . . history of social and educational research is full of examples of concepts – such as intelligence or cultural deprivation . . . – being used as the basis for policy decisions when subsequent research, conducted in a different cultural climate would challenge not only their significance but their very existence.

. . . an extension of the Rothschild formulation of the customer-research relationship first put forward in the early 1970s represents a considerable strengthening of capitalist principles. Not only does it reflect a considerable tightening in accountability between sponsor and sponsored; it also, more significantly, represents the elevation, and hence imposition, of one set of value criteria – those of the sponsor over those of the researcher with which it may well be at odds. The former is likely to look for maximum pay-off for minimum investment, the resolution of short-term goals and specific problems. Sponsors may look for research to support a particular policy stance or product. By contrast the researcher's criteria of worth will lie in the care with which the study is carried out, the sensitivity of the conclusions drawn and the relevance of the findings produced to the larger body of scholarship in a particular field.

Broadfoot, 1988, adapted from pp 4–7

Questions

Provide an example of educational research or concepts (paragraph two) 'being used as the basis for policy decisions when subsequent research, conducted in a different cultural climate would challenge' its significance or existence.

Identify five sources of sponsorship for educational research.

To what extent should educational research (paragraph one) 'be squeezed into a conformity with' *any* political culture?

Sometimes feelings of alienation are also experienced by researchers who do not recognize their research findings when described by others. An accurate representation of original research findings may be lost as readers are tempted to skim through and simplify lengthy research findings, or simply read what others have to say about them. Indeed, how many sociologists have cited Durkheim's book *Suicide* (1897) without actually reading it?

Politicians of all political parties obviously have a vested interest in distorting some findings, usually via selectivity or exaggeration. The name of the politician mentioned in the following exchange (see box, below) is therefore deleted, as he is seen as representative of what ethnographers may identify as a type. Political bias may be least visible to those who suffer from it the most.

CRITICISM OF *EDUCATION AS A POLITICAL ISSUE* (McKENZIE, 1993)

This is a brave and conscientious attempt by a mature, female, post-graduate working in what her supervisor describes as 'difficult circumstances' to examine the ideological framework of the educational debate, notably the relationship between voters' attitudes and the education policies pursued by central and local government in the 1980s. The work is weakened, however, by the baleful influence of Stephen Edgell and Graham White who seem to have steered the author to adopt a sub-Marxist, culturally determinist approach to her subject, and by the methodological difficulty of resting conclusions about public attitudes upon a statistically unrepresentative sample of only fifty-two.

F MP, 'Book Notes', *Political Studies*, 212(1), March 1994

F goes on to mention 'some useful discoveries' but does not acknowledge the central critique of Conservative policies. I responded with the following letter of complaint to the editor of the journal.

When my book (*Education as a Political Issue*) was published I was prepared for a variety of responses, but did not expect serious misrepresentation in a journal with a reputation for academic excellence. [F's] Book Note is not the sort of critical review one would expect in *Political Studies*. In a few words he goes well beyond normal academic discourse, demonstrating ignorance, selectivity to distort and a patronizing attitude. Given his background he should have known better.

His critique suggests that he has only read (or only chosen to comment on) the Foreword, Acknowledgments and part of the final chapter. He starts by saying that this '. . . is a brave and conscientious attempt by a mature, female, post-graduate working in what her supervisor describes as "difficult circumstances" . . .' This information was gleaned from the Foreword and slanted to provide a negative and patronizing intonation, instead of the flattering tone intended by the writer. He goes on to suggest that the research was weak – but implies that we should not blame the poor woman who carried it out! I would not like my academic credibility to be killed by such kindness. Far from being an 'attempt', the research was at least successful at one level: my academic peers decided that it was worth the award of a Ph.D. They also found that there was no need to comment on my gender, and I wonder why F mentions it within the word limit imposed by such a short review. My full name was given in the heading.

F also regrets the '. . . baleful influence of Stephen Edgell and Graham White who seem to have steered the author to adopt a sub-Marxist, culturally determinist approach to her subject . . .' Do I not have the academic integrity to steer myself in whatever direction I choose? Stephen Edgell was my supervisor, but why does F cite Graham White? I met Graham for the first time when I had a job interview at Liverpool Institute of Higher Education, and this was *three years* after I started my full-time research. He was my head of department at LIHE. Indeed I was still wondering where F had got this impression when I found a 'thankyou' in the Acknowledgments to Graham and other staff at LIHE for their understanding and support during the writing-up period. Does this mean that colleagues in my new department should avoid showing me any kindness or support in order to escape the dubious honour of a mention in future acknowledgments?

What does F mean by a '. . . sub-Marxist, culturally determinist approach . . .'? Is the expression 'sub-Marxist' some new form of insult? I used a variety of perspectives in my research and regard Marxist ideas as useful analytical tools. Indeed new students of the social sciences are usually presented with Marxism as one of a few well established analytical perspectives. I did not limit myself to any one perspective and regard this as one of the strengths of my research. Chapter 5 deals with 'Knowledge bias and the framework of educational debate' and F would do well to read it. On pages 61–2 he would find a clear and honest exposition of my theoretical approach and personal 'bias'.

The criticism that left me feeling most outraged concerned '. . . The methodological difficulty of resting conclusions about public attitudes upon a statistically unrepresentative sample of only fifty-two'. I simply did not generalize from a sample of fifty-two and F would have realized this if he had read the book, or even looked at the content pages and list of tables. My research started with secondary analysis of national and local survey data; including the British Social Attitudes Surveys of 1983, 1985 and 1987, the Greater Manchester Panel Study of 1980/1 and 1983/4, the British Political Participation Study of 1984/5 and various opinion polls. From these I developed provisional scales of educational radicalism and designed a theoretical quota sample of fifty-two (taken from the GMS panel). The voters in this quota sample provided qualitative data to supplement and test the existing quantitative data. I also observed political meetings in my two case study areas ('Torytown' and 'Labourville'), interviewed politicians and studied media reports. Theories were generated by a triangulation of methods and I was very careful and hesitant in any claims I made from the fifty-two interviews.

Finally, I am less concerned about F's selectivity in not referring to those findings that challenge his own government's policies. This is to be expected. I just hope that the publication of such a damning misrepresentation of my work will not put too many people off reading it (and subjecting it to proper, academic rigour). Otherwise it would be too easy for someone who has established his own career to damage the academic credibility of a relatively unknown author.

In October 1994 the editor replied to this letter, noting that it was raised as a matter of policy in a discussion involving the full editorial team. They were concerned to establish whether the review

. . . goes beyond the acceptable range of remarks which we would allow a reviewer to make. I have to tell you that our conclusion is that the review does not. The job of reviewer is obviously to offer a critical judgment. That critical judgment may be right or wrong. Reviewers often are wrong; but, right or wrong, [F's] note does not, in our view, go beyond the limits of critical comment. In these circumstances I am sorry to tell you that the journal cannot publish your response.

Editor of *Political Studies*, letter dated 11 October 1994

Questions

What are the limits of critical comment?
Were those limits exceeded in the case of this small Book Note?
How should a researcher respond if s/he feels that findings have been misrepresented?
What would be the *positive* and *negative* consequences if researchers were more resolute in their efforts to defend their work?

When analysing any piece of research we should consider how bias on the part of the researcher may have affected the findings. Yet, whilst probing deeply into their subjects' backgrounds, researchers rarely provide any information about their own. For this reason the sort of information provided about the members of the cohort has also been provided about the author of this book (see the end of Appendix 1). This must necessarily be a short sketch, but it does indicate that the route towards a good education has not been an easy one. It has generated a natural sympathy for the problems encountered by the many individuals who struggle with education, but may be no more biased in this respect than the bias of those academics who have themselves had a relatively easy route towards a good education. Whilst one may have difficulty in empathizing with confident high-achievers, the other may have difficulty empathizing with anxious strugglers.

Given my background it may be no surprise to find that I feel closest to a socialist feminist ontology (not the same as Marxism; see page 53 in Chapter 3). Eclectic epistemological interests in education come from a personal and professional fascination with learning, labelling and inequalities of opportunity. It is much more difficult to describe a particular methodology as I employ a triangulation of theory and methods, favouring feminist and interpretive approaches, but also feeling that positivist ideas and models have *heuristic value* (i.e. they are useful analytical and discursive tools). Throughout this book you should therefore consider how personal background, ontology, epistemology and methodology could have affected (the inevitable) selectivity of materials and the interpretation of findings, whilst acknowledging that someone with a different social background could be equally, or more, biased (for example, the anonymous F, above, came from an affluent background, was educated at a public school and was a Conservative MP).

Conclusion: The value of hygienic research

You should now be aware that research can be a very messy business and that comparisons between research experiences and an idealized model of educational research can be very dispiriting. Researchers are constantly searching for perfection, constantly being criticized and criticizing each other and are often (see 'Feminist research', above) working in relatively low-paid, insecure jobs. In the real world researchers are often faced with limited resources, including time, money, competencies, contacts and access. Competing demands on the researcher's time sometimes means that research is low on the researcher's list of priorities, after teaching, administration, families and a social life. When studying educational change it may be easier to manage short, intensive, periods of work, rather than the long-term commitment and overall demands of longitudinal research. Identifying and focusing on a topic that is necessary and practical can be a problem, although researchers will often find that the topic is chosen for them as part of their jobs (whether this involves an individual teacher comparing students' results from year to year or a researcher employed to contribute to an existing educational research project).

An idealized model of research is, nevertheless, important as researchers need standards, rules (however loose these may be) and targets to help them to direct their energies. They may therefore see themselves as always the apprentices to some idealized craftworker, continually developing and honing their skills in pursuit of a perfection that may be unattainable. No wonder Mies wrote about the search for perfection driving scholars 'into a schizophrenic situation' (Mies, 1993) and no wonder other feminists have criticized the image of 'hygienic research' (Stanley and Wise, 1983). Yet the rewards for such efforts should not be underestimated as its overall value lies in providing information that otherwise would not exist. Research can provide a public voice for individuals who might otherwise have none and raise issues that might otherwise be overlooked. Whatever its faults, once in circulation it is open to public criticism and provides a clear example of how we can all learn by others' mistakes. As Isaac Newton apparently observed, we all progress on giants' shoulders.

COMMON PROBLEMS IN HISTORICAL RESEARCH REPORTS

1. Defining the problem too broadly.
2. The tendency to use easy-to-find secondary sources of data rather than sufficient primary sources, which are harder to locate but usually more trustworthy.
3. Inadequate historical criticism of data, due to failure to establish authenticity of sources and trustworthiness of data. For example, there is often a tendency to accept a statement as necessarily true when several observers agree. It is possible that one may have influenced the others, or that all were influenced by the same inaccurate source of information.
4. Poor logical analysis resulting from:

   (a) Oversimplification – failure to recognize the fact that causes of events are more often multiple and complex than single and simple.
   (b) Overgeneralization on the basis of insufficient evidence, and false reasoning by analogy, basing conclusions upon superficial similarities of situations.

(c) Failure to interpret words and expression in the light of their accepted meaning in an earlier period.

(d) Failure to distinguish between significant facts in a situation and those that are irrelevant or unimportant.

5. Expression of personal bias, as revealed by statements lifted out of context for purposes of persuasion, assuming too generous or uncritical an attitude towards a person or idea (or being too unfriendly or critical), excessive admiration for the past (sometimes known as the 'old oaken bucket' delusion), or an equally unrealistic admiration for the new or contemporary, assuming that all change represents progress.

6. Poor reporting in a style that is dull and colourless, too flowery or flippant, too persuasive or of the 'soap-box' type, or lacking in proper usage.

Best, 1970, cited by Cohen and Manion, 1994, pp 53–4

Question

To what extent does this book manage to avoid each of these six problems?

3

Changing perspectives

Changing Ed— Chap. 3

Notes

Perspectives

Changing eq. = in 40s 50s / Choice ⋯ in 80s?
discourse

Naturally Bright 💡 →Biological determinism
IQ, 11⁺ + bell curve

Social causes → Cultural determinism

Durkheim   Critical   social action
Functionalism Theory   Bourdieu   Weber
  Marxism Ideology   econ. + cultural Feminism
  Rescuing   cap.   @1900
  Ed.!   @1960s

Poststructuralism → Modernity
Hyperreality   late mod? or Postmod
Man = a terminal of networks

Reflexive modernity → Risk (of poison!!) Trust?
'Managing ontological insecurity

Keynesianism One Nation Cons → New Rt. (monetarism)
  Socialist Labour → New Lab. (stakeholder
                              democracy)

Sarah card
Tues

Biological determinism – Social construction – Functionalism: structure and continuity – Marxism: conflict and change – Bourdieu: cultural capital – Social action: interpreting micro levels – Feminist perspectives – A shift from modern to postmodern or late modern society? – Postmodernism – Poststructuralism and deconstructionism – Reflexive modernity – Political perspectives – One Nation Conservatives and the (Socialist) Labour Party – The New Right – New Labour – Liberal Democrats – Conclusion: The heuristic value of theories

A radical pedagogy and transformative democratic politics must go hand in hand in constructing a vision in which liberalism's emphasis on individual freedom, postmodernism's concern with the particularistic, and feminism's concern with the politics of the everyday are coupled with democratic socialism's holistic concern with solidarity and public life.

Giroux, 1992, in Halsey et al., 1997, p 128

Not many people enjoy reading about theories and, looking at this quote from Giroux, it is easy to understand why. Giroux is explaining his own vision of education and how it could be related to what he regarded as the best features of several theoretical perspectives. Yet who can say that his vision is the best? How can we get to grips with such complex ideas and what value do they have in a study of changing education? It may be difficult enough to understand the wide range of sociological and political perspectives but even more difficult to apply them to developments in education since 1944. Yet by the end of this chapter you should be able to return to this quote, understand what he was getting at and perhaps engage in a discussion about how realistic his ideas were.

Changes in theoretical perspectives about education may be compared with how the media devise new ways of viewing and presenting changing images and messages. During the 1940s advanced technology existed and most people in the UK had access to a radio, but no television or telephone. Today most people have access to a radio, television, phone, perhaps even a video, compact disc player and computer; and who knows what sort of technology will be available in the future! Yet we know that new technology may raise new problems, such as recurrent images of violence, couch potatoes, repetitive strain injuries for computer workers and possibly even brain damage for users of mobile phones. Similarly, changing images of education can be viewed and presented in many ways; building on our previous knowledge and understandings, whilst raising old and new problems and suggesting that not all progress is inevitably positive. A wide and widening range of theoretical perspectives can have *heuristic value*;

in other words, they can be used as tools to aid our understanding, allowing us to create more complex images than those provided by just one medium.

The widest type of perspective is an *ontology*, a term which acknowledges that individuals and groups who share the same views see different worlds around them. Thus, someone with a feminist ontology will see gender inequalities all around them, someone with a Marxist ontology will perceive the majority of people suffering the consequences of an inhumane capitalist system and so on. It is therefore very difficult to argue with an ontology; we might as well try to persuade the people of the Stone Age that the world was not flat, when so much that they saw suggested otherwise. The trick is to try to slip into their shoes and understand how they see the world in general, or in this case how they see education in particular. This also takes us out of the limits of our own experiences for however short a time it may be.

Once we understand the nature of an individual ontology we can start to appreciate the associated *epistemology*; that is, what someone perceives as relevant and useful knowledge. Thus, someone with a feminist ontology will search for a greater knowledge of gender inequalities, someone with a Marxist ontology will search for a greater knowledge about the effects of capitalism and so on. Again it is difficult to argue with an epistemology because it means that alternative forms of knowledge are seen as lacking credibility, just as a radio 'ham' or a computer 'nerd' will each see their own interests as superior to the other's interests.

Ontologies and epistemologies go on to influence *methodologies*; the philosophical and theoretical decisions impacting upon how we carry out research into the area of interest. Thus, this chapter steps back a pace from the discussion about research methods in Chapter 2 in order to explore the origins of the research and findings discussed in other chapters. It also looks at many *theories* about education and society, theories generally being more focused than wide-ranging perspectives and ontologies. For example, although it still makes sense to talk about Marxist theories in general, it is possible to focus in on one of Marx's theories, such as his theory about the alienation of workers from the product of their labour.

There are not only many ontologies, epistemologies, methodologies and theories at play at any one time, but they will shift, adapt, disappear or be replaced over time. One way of trying to trace this fluctuation is by looking at how public debates (*discourse*) about education have changed over time, how the context of those debates has changed, the changing themes, changing assumptions and changing rhetoric involved. A *discourse* is a mixture of beliefs, ideas, concepts and rhetoric which become established as knowledge or as an accepted worldview and create a powerful framework for understandings and actions in social life. Thus, an equal opportunities discourse during the 1940s and 1950s involved debates about social class, meritocracy, intelligence testing (and other themes) but by the 1980s had been replaced by a discourse about choice and individualism, involving debates about social diversification, parentocracy, the National Curriculum (and other themes). This chapter therefore takes a more or less chronological approach in order to study the development of perspectives over time. Yet the arrival of relatively new perspectives does not mean that the old have been superceded. In fact, many perspectives have been around for a very long time and continue to be very influential in educational discourse.

> Perhaps it is time to study discourses not only in terms of their expressive value or formal transformations, but according to their modes of existence.
>
> Foucault, in Rabinow, 1984

This chapter is introducing the bones of various perspectives and more muscle will be added in other chapters; for example, each chapter in Part Two, 'Decades of Change', will present some of the contemporary work carried out by various theorists, but this chapter provides the background to their work. As the aim here is to follow a basically developmental approach, we shall start, as early sociologists tended to start, with a critique of biological determinism.

Biological determinism

Biological determinism tends to have two elements; firstly, a belief in intelligence tests as a means of statistically calculating and comparing individual abilities and, secondly, a more extreme concern about the inheritance of inferior physical and mental qualities. The big debate associated with the two extremes of biological determinism and cultural determinism is often called the nature-nurture controversy. To what extent is intelligence biologically determined (innate) and to what extent is it culturally determined by our social experiences? Indeed the assumptions associated with biological determinism are still very much in evidence in public discourse: 'He is just naturally very bright', 'She went to university because she takes after her mother', 'The family's artistic ability just seems to be in their genes'. We have also seen that many (perhaps most) people regard themselves as naturally 'bright' or 'dim'! This sort of approach often appeals to our common sense assumptions and provides a simple explanation of, and justification for, social inequalities.

It may be that biological determinism appeals to our common sense because it has such a long history and we commonly assume that when we talk about intelligence we know what we mean. Intelligence tests are still highly regarded and may have the status of being 'scientific' when their value is actually very contentious. In 1905, in France, Alfred Binet devised his first intelligence tests and scale by calculating the normal mental capacities for each age from a large sample of Parisian schoolchildren and in 1911 the German William Stern devised his Intelligence Quotient (IQ) on the basis of Binet's work. The promotion of IQ testing in Britain is largely associated with the work of the psychologist Cyril Burt who, in 1909, wrote his first study on experimental tests of general intelligence and went on to become Professor of

Psychology at London University. Burt was the most influential advocate of the notion of intelligence as 'innate, general, cognitive ability'. He believed that intelligence was inborn, a product of genetic, hereditary factors and that, although knowledge increased with age, IQ remained constant throughout life. Therefore, intelligent professional parents could feel assured that their children had a right to places in elite academic schools because they had inherited their parents' abilities. For these reasons it made sense to test children at an early age in order to channel them into schools suiting their 'needs' and, by the 1940s, it seemed clear that selection at 11+ was a good idea. However, the 11+ came in for more and more criticism and, towards the end of his life, Burt used material now known to be fraudulent to 'prove' a decline in educational standards since the introduction of comprehensive schools (e.g. Burt, 1975). He was later discredited in a book by Hearnshaw (1979), although in 1989 Joynson claimed that Hearnshaw was wrong.

In 1919 the local authority in Bradford started using Burt's intelligence tests in local scholarship examinations and, in 1925, Godfrey Thomson at Edinburgh began to develop the Moray House tests which came to be commonly adopted by school boards. Between 1925 and 1944, 38 local education authorities used the Moray House tests and 49 did not, but by 1944 belief in the concept of intelligence had become widespread and entrenched.

Alongside a belief in the quality of intelligence tests as a means of calculating future development there existed various claims about the inheritance of inferior physical and mental qualities. At its most extreme, the eugenics movement in the nineteenth and early twentieth centuries campaigned for the genetic improvement of the human species. In the late nineteenth century Herbert Spencer was applying the findings of Charles Darwin to people in what has often been called social Darwinism; in other words, claiming that people, like animals, evolved via the survival of the fittest. Later, Galton and Pearson promoted the eugenics movement, which claimed that defects in the individual (including mental disability) could be eliminated by selective breeding. Eugenics was discredited to a certain extent by the extremes of fascism and the experiences of the Second World War but ideas associated with biological determinism were still very much in evidence in the 1940s. More recently Jensen (1969) and Eysenck (1971) claimed that educational attainment was heavily influenced by biology. Their findings were hotly disputed for being inherently racist, although supporters claimed that they were misrepresented. However, what many have regarded as a more acceptable analysis of biological determinism has since emerged in the form of sociobiology (in particular via the writings of Dawkins, 1976), with its more contemporary emphasis on genetic structures.

Old ideas about biological determinism are, nevertheless, still being offered in new guises and from the mid 1970s onwards emerged again in the form of the moral underclass discourse promoted by the New Right. The moral underclass discourse emphasizes the moral and behavioural delinquency of the excluded themselves. It demonizes supposedly criminally inclined, unemployable young men and socially irresponsible young mothers and assumes that the only way to challenge their dependency culture is to prevent them from living off the state. This discourse is not new, as the Black Papers of the 1960s and 1970s also suggested that poverty was caused not by social inequalities, but by personal inadequacies.

> No amount of money poured into the 'Educational Priority Areas', enthusiastically espoused in the Plowden Report, is likely to bring any appreciable proportion of slum children up to the standards of university entrance . . .
>
> The suppression of these truths by progressives leads to a whole series of false deductions. One of the most serious is that it is the fault of society that slum dwellers are impoverished and their young do so badly at school. To the young red guards, it follows that society is unjust and must be overthrown. They do not realize that slum dwellers are caused principally by low innate intelligence and poor family upbringing, and that the real social challenge is posed by this.
>
> Lynn, 1970, p 30

In the 1990s this perspective came to be particularly associated with the New Right and the writings of the American Charles Murray. Steven Fraser (1995, *The Bell Curve Wars: Race, Intelligence and the Future of America*) described *The Bell Curve: Intelligence and Class Structure in American Life*, by Richard J. Herrnstein and Charles Murray, as 'clearly the most incendiary piece of social science to appear in the last decade or more'. The writers assumed that intelligence (what some psychometricians call *g*) is quantifiable and can be measured across differences in history, culture and environment. They argued that if we understand the role of statistically measured intelligence, we will also understand the social arithmetic that creates the rich and the poor, the powerful and the powerless. Without this understanding we are likely to tackle the symptoms of social inequalities rather than the causes. Innate low intelligence is a major cause of unemployment and poverty and lies behind all sorts of social problems, including school failure, crime, irresponsible parenting, unmarried mothers, welfare dependency and broken families. If social hierarchies are determined by innate low intelligence then public policy is unable to do anything about such problems. However, combined with this fatalism, the writers conveyed a sense of missionary purpose. They were concerned about 'dysgenesis' or what others characterized as the dumbing down of America due to the higher fertility rates of what they called the 'cognitive underclass'. They tentatively suggested that changes in immigration law and welfare and public health reforms might arrest the genetic degradation of the national stock.

In *The Bell Curve Wars: Race, Intelligence and the Future of America*, Fraser and others note their many criticisms of such claims:

- They ignore the past 100 years of biological and psychological research that challenges the notion of a single, uniform, and innate human intelligence, or *g*. Howard Gardner argued instead for a concept of 'multiple intelligences' – practical, social, musical, spatial, and so on.
- They ignore the important role of training in the attainment of any kind of intelligence.
- The book was published at a time when its explanation justified right-wing politicians' reluctance to commit resources towards the eradication of poverty.
- They did not analyse the criminal behaviour of the white-collar 'cognitive elite'.

There are therefore many criticisms of biological determinism, but the main sociological criticism is

that, however we choose to define 'intelligence', any natural abilities cannot be separated from social and cultural influences.

Social construction

The sharpest contrast to biological determinism is provided by cultural determinism, but sociologists often regard this as also being too extreme. This is because cultural determinism is sometimes defined in terms of attitudes to ethnicity, as the tendency to assume that ethnic groups have a homogeneous culture. Thus extreme cultural determinism does not accept that cultural character is also influenced by the changing economic and social context in which ethnic minorities find themselves. Sociologists today tend to be wary of theories claiming that behaviour is determined by any one, specific element. Instead they prefer to consider the many ways in which society influences educational experiences. In particular, they challenge common sense assumptions and, although accepting that some aspects of educational ability may be biologically determined, it is clear that sociologists would reject the sort of biological determinism illustrated above; for example, the development of children with various levels of autism may depend on how society treats them. Indeed, the following quote (from a left-wing critic of education) can be compared to Richard Lynn's biological determinism.

> This [improving the schooling of working-class children] would undoubtedly be the most effective way of eliminating the social problems of the so-called delinquent areas, a name which masks a much wider social problem – the failure to integrate the unskilled and semi-skilled working class into a society which is becoming predominantly governed by the values and standards of the professional middle class.
>
> Vaizey, as cited in Centre for Contemporary Cultural Studies, 1981, pp 78–9

Theories about social influences are by no means new. The French philosopher August Comte (1798–1857) is usually credited with inventing the term 'sociology' to describe a new science of society. He adopted a positivist approach which assumed that social life can be understood and analysed in the same way that scientists already studied the 'natural world'. Thus social scientists should be able to study the behaviour of people in the same way that physical scientists study nature and animal behaviour. Positivists assume that phenomena exist in causal relationships and these can be empirically observed, tested and measured in a detached and objective fashion. The aim is to identify laws governing human behaviour in the same way that physical scientists identify laws governing the universe. Although this approach was criticized by late twentieth-century sociologists for not being appropriate in the study of human beings, it still has some heuristic value.

Early sociological theories about education in particular are often associated with another French philosopher, J.J. Rousseau, whose book *Social Contract* (1762) begins with the much quoted statement 'Men are born free, yet everywhere they are in chains'. Rousseau believed that people were naturally good but corrupted by the social institutions imposed upon them. In his book *Emile* (1762), he applied this to a study of educational processes in which the emphasis was on the enhancement of self-expression and individual liberty, rather than conformity and following convention. This work still has a great impact on many who are dissatisfied with the rigidities of educational convention and favour radical change and was particularly influential in the movement towards 'progressive' education during the 1960s.

Functionalism: structure and continuity

Emile Durkheim (1858–1917) is often presented as one of the 'founding fathers' of sociology and his work included criticisms of the then orthodox view that educational achievement was entirely based on individual ability, and that this ability was determined at birth. He argued the merits of studying social aspects of education at a time when education was largely seen as a matter for individuals only. This sort of approach emphasizes the role of education in maintaining consensus and reproducing the social structure and is often primarily descriptive. As a socialist, Durkheim was concerned about social inequality but, as a positivist, he also believed that, before change could take place, it was necessary to describe society objectively.

> I regard as the prime postulate of all pedagogical speculation that education is an eminently social thing in its origins as in its functions, and that, therefore, pedagogy depends on sociology more closely than any other science.
>
> Durkheim, 1956, p 114

In sum, education, far from having as its unique or principal object the individual and his interests, is above all the means by which society perpetually recreates the conditions of its very existence. Can society survive only if there exists among its members a sufficient homogeneity? Education perpetuates and reinforces this homogeneity by fixing in advance, in the mind of the child, the essential similarities that collective life presupposes. But, on the other hand, without a certain diversity, would all co-operation be impossible? Education assures the persistence of this necessary diversity by becoming itself diversified and by specializing. It consists, then, in one or another of its aspects, of a systematic socialization of the young generation. In each of us, it may be said, there exist two beings which, while inseparable except by abstraction, remain distinct. One is made up of all the mental states which apply only to ourselves and to the events of our personal lives. This is what might be called the individual being. The other is the system of ideas, sentiments, and practices which express in us, not our personality, but the group or different groups of which we are a part; these are religious beliefs, moral beliefs and practices, national or occupational traditions, collective opinions of every kind. Their totality forms the social being. To constitute this being in each of us is the end of education.

Adapted from Durkheim, 1956, pp 114–116

Durkheim accepted the existence of schools that were not run by the state. In the interests of the public the state must allow other schools to exist, but not be aloof from what happened in them. He said, 'On the contrary the education given in them must remain under its control' (Durkheim, 1956, p 80).

Following the tradition established by Durkheim, other functionalists also emphasize the important function of education in socializing the individual to fit into, and perpetuate, the social system.

Although society has been created by people, individuals are seen as being born into a society which already has an identity of its own, and education is seen as serving the function of passing on the collective consciousness, or culture, of that pre-existing society. Functionalists see specific 'functional imperatives' (needs which must be met if society is to survive and prosper) and are likely to identify three vital functions served by education. Education

- helps to develop the human resources of an industrial nation;
- through its selection processes serves to allocate individuals to the various levels of many occupations;
- contributes to social cohesion by transmitting to new generations the central values of society.

Functionalism was particularly influential in the UK until the 1970s, but then came under criticism from sociologists because it seemed that, first, the skills provided in schools do not clearly fit the requirements of industry, second, selection may not simply be on merit but may be related to ascriptive characteristics (such as social class, gender or ethnicity) or personal contacts and, third, it is not clear what the central values of society are. Furthermore, like other perspectives emphasizing the influence of the social structure, functionalist approaches could be viewed as over-deterministic if they ignore the reactions of individuals to their educational experiences. Some individuals may resist many negative influences on their education.

Marxism: conflict and change

Conflict perspectives emphasize inequalities of educational opportunities and the need for social change. They have emphasized the use of education as a means of perpetuating or shifting structural inequalities within society, focusing their attention on education as a source of not only continuity, but also conflict and change. This approach has varied from the revolutionary writings of Marx and Engels to more moderate appeals for reforms within the existing social system.

MARX ON EDUCATION

The communists have not invented the intervention of society in education; they do but seek to alter the character of that intervention, and to rescue education from the influence of the ruling class.

The bourgeois claptrap about the family and education, about the hallowed co-relation of parent and child, becomes all the more disgusting, the more, by the action of modern industry, all family ties among the proletarians are torn asunder and their children transformed into simple articles of commerce and instruments of labour.

From Marx and Engels, 1888 (1969), pp 66–7

Equal elementary education? What idea behind these words? Is it believed that in present-day society (and it is only with this one has to deal) education can be equal for all classes? Or is it demanded that the upper classes also shall be compulsorily reduced to the modicum of education – the elementary school – that alone is compatible with the economic conditions not only of the wage workers but of the peasants as well? . . .

'Elementary education by the state' is altogether objectionable. Defining by a general law the expenditures on the elementary schools, the qualifications of the teaching staff, the branches of instruction, etc., as is done in the United States, supervising the fulfilment of these legal specifications by state supervisors, is a very different thing from appointing the state as the educator of the people! Government and church should rather be equally excluded from any influence on the school.

From Marx, in Feuer, 1969, pp 170–71

Questions

Do you think that children today are 'simple articles of commerce and instruments of labour'? What do you think Marx meant when he differentiated between the role of the state in ensuring that the system operates effectively and the 'state as the educator of the people'?

The German philosopher Karl Marx (1818–83) was another 'founding father' of sociology, whose emphasis on social influences can be summed up in his own well-known observation that 'The history of all hitherto existing society is the history of class struggles' (*The Communist Manifesto*, 1888, p 1). Marx himself wrote relatively little about education. However, Marxist sociologists and philosophers have said a great deal. A basic feature is the belief that education promotes an ideology that supports capitalism and that, instead, it *should* empower workers by developing in them a critical intelligence.

Classical Marxists have maintained this emphasis on the primary influence of the capitalist economic infrastructure and the secondary role of education in perpetuating the necessary supportive ideology. However, since the 1920s, *critical theory* (another strand of Marxism associated with the Frankfurt School) has focused on the role of the ideological superstructure in perpetuating social inequalities. The Frankfurt School for Social Research was founded in 1923 but its leading figures emigrated to America with the rise of Hitler and some of them remained there after the war. Other prominent sociologists joined the school later. Its most well-known figures include Adorno, Horkheimer, Marcuse and Habermas.

Other well-known European Marxist theorists include Lukács, Gramsci and Althusser, who shared with the critical theorists of the Frankfurt School an interest in what Marx referred to as superstructural phenomena. However, each differed in his focus and interpretation. For example, Lukács developed Marx's theories about *false consciousness*; that is, illusions or deceptions concealing the reality of social inequalities. Gramsci's writings included a strong interest in the notion of *hegemony*; that is, a situation in which the interests of the ruling class are represented as universal interests and therefore used to legitimize the existing social order. Althusser was particularly sceptical about Marx's view of history as consisting of a linear progression towards communist societies and self-realization. Instead he searched for a more 'scientific', less humanist approach to the study of historical developments. This involved an effort to understand science as the social practice in which knowledge is produced and education as playing a vital role within the *ideological state apparatus*. We can see the relevance of each of these three writers to an analysis of the part played by education in generating the sort of knowledge that perpetuates inequalities by conditioning the masses to accept the status quo. Although writing during different periods, their writings had the greatest impact during the 1960s and 1970s (for example, Gramsci's prison notebooks were written during the 1920s and 1930s, whilst he was a political prisoner in Mussolini's gaols, but were translated and published in English in 1971).

QUESTION

Consider changing interests in the sociology of education during the 1970s. What evidence is there that Marxism (and certain types of Marxism) was influential?

Bourdieu: cultural capital

Marxists argue that education transmits the language and behaviour of the ruling class. Therefore, children from middle class families are already advantaged because they come to school already equipped with some of the skills, attitudes and language which correspond with the education system's expectations. Once in school it seems that the system is specifically designed to exclude working-class children so that their failure, and the success of middle-class children, are both legitimized. This is partially conducted through systems of assessment, as standards are set by the dominant class and exams are written and marked by the dominant class. This is legitimized because it is seen to be a rational and meritocratic system in which all have equal chance.

Pierre Bourdieu has referred to this as *symbolic violence*, leading the middle class to achieve more, not as a result of physical force, but by communication, particularly language. To Bourdieu success in education depends fundamentally on the education children acquired in their earliest years. Middle-class children already possess the 'code of the message', whilst working class children are penalized because their style is different from that of the dominant culture and they cannot decode the language used by their teachers. They lack the access to necessary knowledge and the *cultural capital* necessary to succeed in education. By cultural capital Bourdieu means the extent to which individuals have absorbed the dominant culture. Just as financial capital provides economic power, cultural capital forms the basis of a cultural power which transmits values and ideas of the dominant culture, thus protecting and legitimizing dominant class interest. Bourdieu claims that the greater degree of cultural capital individuals possess, the more successful they will be in the educational system. This form of capital emerges from the individual's *habitus*, Bourdieu's term for the everyday habitual practices and assumptions of a particular social environment. To him, people are at once the product of, and the creators of, their *habitus*.

BOURDIEU ON CULTURAL CAPITAL

... capital can present itself in three fundamental guises: as economic capital, which is immediately and directly convertible into money and may be institutionalized in the form of property rights; as cultural capital, which is convertible, on certain conditions, into economic capital and may be institutionalized in the form of educational qualifications; and as social capital, made up of social obligations ('connections'), which is convertible, in certain conditions, into economic capital and may be institutionalized in the form of title of nobility.

Cultural capital can exist in three forms: in the embodied state, i.e. in the form of long-lasting dispositions of mind and body; in the objectified state, in the form of cultural goods (pictures, books, dictionaries, instruments, machines, etc.), which are the trace or realization of theories or critiques of these theories, problematics, etc.; and in the institutionalized state, a form of objectification which must be set apart because, as will be seen in the case of educational qualifications, it confers entirely original properties on the cultural capital which it is presumed to guarantee.

[Criticizes economists because] Their studies of the relationship between academic ability and academic investment show that they are unaware that ability or talent is itself the product of an investment of time and cultural capital (Becker 1964a: 63–6). Not surprisingly, when endeavouring to evaluate the profits of scholastic investment, they can only consider the profitability of educational expenditure for society as a whole, the 'social rate of return,' or the 'social gain of education as measured by its effects on national productivity' (Becker 1964b: 121, 155). This typically functionalist definition of the functions of education ignores the contribution which the educational system makes to the reproduction of the social structure by sanctioning the hereditary transmission of cultural capital ...

It can immediately be seen that the link between economic and cultural capital is established through the mediation of time needed for acquisition. Differences in the cultural capital possessed by the family imply differences first in the age at which the work of transmission and accumulation begins ... and then in the capacity, this defined, to satisfy the specifically cultural demands of a prolonged process of acquisition. Furthermore, and in correlation with this, the length of time for which a given individual can prolong this acquisition process depends on the length of time for which the family can provide him with the free time, i.e. time free from economic necessity, which is the precondition for the initial accumulation (time which can be evaluated as a handicap to be made up) ...

Because the material and symbolic profits which the academic qualification guarantees also depend on its scarcity, the investments made (in time and effort) may turn out to be less profitable than was anticipated when they were made (there having been a *de facto* change in the conversion rate between academic capital and economic capital) ...

The volume of the social capital possessed by a given agent thus depends on the size of the network of connections he can effectively mobilize and on the volume of the capital (economic, cultural and symbolic) possessed in his own right by each of those to whom he is connected.

Bourdieu, in Halsey *et al.*, 1997, pp 47–51

Questions

How can cultural goods (second paragraph) be 'the trace or realization of theories or critiques of these theories, problematics, etc.'?

Can you find any evidence for and against the claim that economists only consider 'the profitability of educational expenditure for society as a whole' (third paragraph)?

The last three paragraphs try to explain how economic, cultural and social capital may be related. Can you support or challenge these claims from your own experiences of education and/or work?

Bourdieu has been criticized for being too deterministic in his assumption that class is passed from generation to generation and his assumption that (all) lower-class pupils will fail in education. Raymond Boudon also claims that Bourdieu overemphasizes the primary effects of stratification at the expense of ignoring the secondary or material and practical effects on older working-class pupils. For example, some young people may have to leave education at 16 or 18, not because they have done badly, but because they are not in a financial position to go on to higher education.

Social action: interpreting micro levels

The perspectives considered so far have tended to emphasize the way that social structure influences social behaviour, particularly emphasizing social class inequalities. This is sometimes called a *macro level* approach (which may also be used when studying gender and ethnicity) and we could compare it to studying the structure of a mountain as a whole. However, there are many ways to study a mountain. If we wanted to study its smaller features, such as particular flora and fauna, we might even need a microscope. For this reason the closer analysis of smaller features of society are sometimes called *micro level* approaches, social action theories or interpretive approaches. They concentrate on the micro level of social life, in order to show how interpretation, arising out of interaction with others, gives rise to social action.

Structural concerns could be viewed as overdeterministic if they ignore the reactions of individuals to their educational experiences. Early functionalism in particular was influenced by positivist ideas and challenged by claims that such an approach was not appropriate to the study of human beings. From the 1970s onwards the influence of Weber and other action theorists was becoming more noticeable in educational research.

Although Max Weber (1864–1920) and Emile Durkheim lived at about the same time, Weber was influenced less by the positivist tradition and instead saw a distinction between social science and the natural sciences. Instead of looking for causal explanations and associated universal laws governing human behaviour, Weber thought that the more appropriate task of sociology was to identify patterns and rules influencing human behaviour.

> We have a perfectly clear understanding of what it means when somebody employs the proposition $2 \times 2 = 4$ or the Pythagorean theorem in reasoning or argument, or when somebody correctly carries out a logical train of reasoning according to our accepted modes of thinking. In the same way we also understand what a person is doing when he tries to achieve certain ends by choosing appropriate means on the basis of the facts of the situation, as experience has accustomed us to interpret them. The interpretation of such rationally purposeful action possesses, for the understanding of the choice of means, the highest degree of verifiable certainty.
>
> Weber, 1922/1968, p 5

Although Weber did not discount the positivist emphasis on the need for objectivity, he argued that, once value judgements had been made about the election of a subject to study, the sociologist should strive for the ideal of value freedom. Notions of value freedom, and much of his work in general, depended upon assumptions that human beings generally act rationally. Thus, educational researchers who are studying social action often observe classroom interaction or carry out interviews in order to seek out the reasoning behind the actions of the people (actors) involved. Weber emphasized the importance of Verstehen, or understanding of the meanings behind various actions, and that to achieve this the sociologist has to interpret the actions seen. From the late 1960s onwards more sociologists started to present findings based on classroom observation and interview data (the best known of these being provided by Hargreaves, 1967; Lacey, 1970; Willis, 1977; Ball, 1981). They were trying to understand the meanings individuals and groups attached to their behaviour, and to develop and test various theories (see Chapter 2 for the idealized model of scientific research). However, it would be a simplification to depict these as just interpretive studies when often they have been motivated by an interest in how structural inequalities are maintained by educational processes. Indeed, Weber's theories span both macro and micro levels of analysis and the recent emphasis on showing how many micro studies of classroom interaction incorporate macro issues could be seen as a natural progression from his work. It also reflects a general move towards the triangulation of methodological and theoretical perspectives. One distinguishing feature is that researchers following a social action (or interpretive, or micro) approach reject determinist explanations of intelligence, stress that identities are not fixed and note that outcomes are created by the interactions of those involved. So, for example, Willis (1977) shows that the working-class 'lads' he studied were involved in rationalizing and creating their own educational failure through their interactions with others. Yet Fuller (1980) found that a group of black girls in comprehensive school created an anti-school subculture but still rationalized their academic achievement as a form of resistance.

Weber also provided an alternative analysis to Marx's analysis of social class by arguing that, rather than being determined by the individual's relationship to the means of production (which Marx claimed), social class could be defined by the sharing of a common market position leading to shared life chances and rewards. Whereas Marx identified two main class categories, the working class (or proletariat) and the middle class (or bourgeoisie), Weber's theories allow for many classes and allow sociologists to identify housing classes (perhaps distinguishing between tenants and owner-occupiers of various sorts). He also influenced the sociology of education through his work on status groups, rationalism, bureaucracies, institutions and ideal types.

Feminist perspectives

If you look back to the extract at the end of Chapter 1, you will see that Sanderson consistently referred to the subjects of interest as male, 'he' 'him' 'his' and so on. Yet this was written in 1987, many years after the start of what has often been called the 'second wave of feminism' in the 1960s. Feminists have regularly attacked the gendered use of language in textbooks and have often been criticized for being too sensitive in doing so. In the 1940s sexist language was so common as to be

virtually invisible to eyes that had not been sensitized by feminist critiques, yet its cumulative effect was to render women invisible in much academic literature.

> Dear Sirs, man to man, manpower, craftsman, working men, the thinking man, the man in the street, fellow countrymen, the history of mankind, one-man show, man in his wisdom, statesman, forefathers, masterful, masterpiece, old masters, the brotherhood of man, Liberty, Equality, Fraternity, sons of free men, faith of our fathers, god the father, god the son, yours fraternally, amen. Words fail me.
>
> Stephanie Dowrick, cited in Exley, 1993, p 41

> In fact he was a bit upset when I went through a book which has a boy and a girl in very traditional roles, and changed all the he's to she's and the she's to he's. When I first started doing that, he was inclined to say 'you don't like boys, you only like girls'. I had to explain that that wasn't true at all, its just that there's not enough written about girls.
>
> Statham, 1986, pp 43, 67

Feminists share a common concern about gender inequalities in society (i.e. a structural emphasis) but the diverse range of (sometimes competing) feminist theories often seem to share little else.

> I myself have never been able to find out precisely what a feminist is: I only know that people call me a feminist whenever I express sentiments that differentiate me from a doormat.
>
> Rebecca West (1892–1983), cited in Exley, 1993, p 39

> [Feminism is] all ideologies, activities, and policies whose goal it is to remove discrimination against women and to break down the male domination of society.
>
> Lovenduski and Randall, 1993, an adaptation of the definition used by Drude Dahlerup, 1986, p 6

Although the term 'feminism' only came into use as perspective on gender equality in the late nineteenth century, there has been a long tradition of theories that are definitely 'feminist'. This tradition has been largely ignored with the result that, whilst relatively minor male philosophers have achieved prominence, feminist theorists, writing from the seventeenth century onward (such as the adventuress, activist and writer Aphra Benn; see Spender, 1982) have remained hidden. Although the 'first wave' of feminism (at the end of the eighteenth century and into the early nineteenth century) coincided with the early days of sociology, we habitually refer to the 'founding fathers' of sociology (as I have done already) and relegate the contributions of major female philosophers (such as Mary Wollstonecraft, 1792) to a second division within the academic league. The founding fathers set the scene for male domination within mainstream sociology, or what many feminists have called *malestream* sociology and *patriarchal knowledge*. Thus, social class inequalities took centre stage as the focus for early studies in the sociology of education and it was only the 'second wave' of feminism that generated greater interest in gender inequalities (including an interest in gendered language in textbooks), along with its emphasis on the need to develop feminist consciousness. Indeed feminists often argue that women in general have been *hidden from history*. Moreover, until black feminists started to state their case, the activities of black women had been virtually *lost* in history. Thus, although the work of Florence Nightingale might be familiar to children in primary school, the achievements of black nurse Mary Seacole (who was also honoured by Queen Victoria) did not enter the curriculum.

> [A]t the core of feminist ideas is the crucial insight that there is no one truth, no one authority, no one objective method which leads to the production of pure knowledge. This insight is as applicable to feminist knowledge as it is to patriarchal knowledge, but there is significant difference between the two: feminist knowledge is based on the premise that the experience of all human beings is valid and must not be excluded from our understandings, whereas patriarchal knowledge is based on the premise that the experience of only half the human population needs to be taken into account and the resulting version can be imposed on the other hand.
>
> Spender, 1985, p 5

There are many types of feminism, and indeed students' essays are often criticized for portraying feminism as just one perspective. Whilst feminists or all sorts share a common interest in reducing inequalities between women and men, they may have different, fundamental interests. A short, and simplified, list of some of the differences illustrates the point.

SOME TYPES OF FEMINISTS

Liberal feminists – emphasize the need for legal and administrative changes in order to incorporate women into existing institutions as equals. They focus on the need for equal access to education for both sexes. This moderate perspective dates back to 'first wave' feminism, has been the most clearly acceptable form of feminism and is associated with the equal opportunities legislation of the 1970s.

Radical (or patriarchal) feminists – emphasize male domination as a universal feature of human societies and use the phrase *the personal is political* to draw attention to issues of sexuality and violence in interpersonal male–female relationships. They have promoted the need for women-focused education and consciousness-raising through education and dominated 'second wave' feminism during the 1960s and 1970s.

Marxist feminists – emphasize the gender inequalities associated with capitalism, such as women's unequal place in the labour market and their provision of unpaid domestic labour. This approach emerged more forcefully in the late 1970s as a critique of liberal and radical feminism.

Black feminists – emphasize women's different experiences of racial inequality, such as the double oppression of women as domestic and slave labour (which was the focus of 'first wave' feminism in the USA). This emerged as a forceful critique of other feminists' assumptions that women share a common experience and in education has focused on institutionalized racism, racial prejudice and self-conscious empowerment.

Socialist feminists – are interested in the effects on women of a combination of structural inequalities (e.g. class, gender and ethnicity).

Ecofeminists – emphasize ecological issues, women's spiritual relationship with nature, their role as life-givers and their interest in maintaining life, providing images of women as 'earth mother'.

Lesbian feminists – provide a political critique of the ideology of heterosexuality (promoted in schools) as a source of male supremacy.

Psychoanalytic feminists – emphasize how the oppression of women affects their emotional life and sexuality. They use Freud's theories about the unconscious in analysing the construction of femininity in order to challenge patriarchal society. In order to free themselves women must learn to challenge the roots of their oppression which are buried deep within their psyche.

Postmodern feminists – are critical of other feminists' claims that it is possible to define an essential female nature, claim that all knowledge is interpretive and open to criticism and are particularly critical of male-centred definitions of knowledge.

Questions

How might various types of feminism approach differently the following topics?

(a) Findings that, although most primary school teachers are female, a disproportionate number of primary school headteachers are male.
(b) Recent concerns that, in general, girls' educational achievements are now better than boys'.
(c) Clause 28 of the Local Government Act 1988 (see Chapter 10).

These are only some of the many feminist perspectives and any attempt to chart them all would be futile because there are so many and they are constantly changing. In her introduction to feminist thought, Tong (1989) distinguished seven categories of feminist thought: liberal, Marxist, radical, psychoanalytic, socialist, existentialist and postmodern. Arnot and Weiner (1987) identified three perspectives which they thought had made the most impact on education: 'Equal rights in education' (i.e. liberal feminism), 'Class, race and gender: structures and ideologies' (Marxist/socialist feminism), and 'Patriarchal relations' (radical feminism). Feminist perspectives, however, are not passive critiques as they aim to enlighten and ultimately empower women and girls in order to help individuals to challenge inequalities. The many variations and combinations of feminist ideas have created forceful critiques of gender inequalities in education, which will be discussed in Chapter 5, where you will see how gender issues engage with personal development. Many feminists (with the possible exception of liberal feminism) also share a critique of positivist approaches, which they see as fitting into a patriarchal malestream sociology, and more of this is seen in Chapter 2.

A shift from modern to postmodern or late modern society?

In Chapter 1 it was claimed that dramatic social changes during the 1970s were associated with dramatic changes in British education. The societies being studied by Durkheim, Marx and Weber were radically different to those we are familiar with today, not simply as a result of scientific discoveries, but because of radical changes in social institutions and the way that people relate to their social context. Philosophical debates were still influenced by the early modern period, known as the Enlightenment, when radicals posited rationalism against the dominance of state controlled religion and progress through science against traditional myths and practices. 'Man' was the subject of most interest. It was believed that science could help people to understand and transform the world and metanarratives could offer all-encompassing explanations of social change; Marxism saw change as relating to the economy and Durkheim could see the transmission of

Modern		Postmodern/Late modern
Industrialization, mass production.	*Economic*	Smaller units, specialization, computers.
Urbanization, social class.	*Social*	Urban decline, fragmentation of classes.
Enlightenment, rationalism, decline of religious domination.	*Philosophical*	Uncertainty, relativism, alternative religions and lifestyles.
Growth of mass education, influenced by social class.	*Educational*	Diversity of schooling, influenced by parental choice.

Figure 3.1 Characteristics of modern and postmodern (or late modern) development

culture via socialization processes. These links between beliefs and economic conditions are seen as fundamental characteristics of *modern* development (see Figure 3.1).

If we look at British society during the 1940s we can see that it still had most of the characteristics of a modern society: it was industrialized, with thriving heavy industries; industries were often nationalized; standardized goods were mass produced; urbanization had developed so far that there were dense urban populations; individuals generally identified themselves as belonging to specific social classes; workers tended to stay in the same job for most of their working life; politics was often class-based and involved strong trade unions; material issues of comparative wealth and poverty tended to dominate the political agenda; women had primary responsibility for unpaid domestic work; men were usually regarded as the family 'breadwinners'; families usually consisted of two parents living with their children (the nuclear family) and close to other relatives (the extended family) and it was assumed that social change would involve positive progress. Educational discourse tended to focus on the nature–nurture debate, intelligence testing and equal opportunities relating to social class in particular. If the production of material goods could be rationalized, standardized and mass produced, so could education, the ultimate aim being to identify each individual's abilities and put them to their best use in the workplace (whether in paid work or in unpaid domestic labour).

By comparison, if we look at British society during the 1990s we can see that most of these characteristics have gone, been transformed or remain as mere remnants of their modern form. Some theorists claim that the modern period is now over and that we are now experiencing a *postmodern* era, whilst (as we have seen) others claim that modernity has not ended but has evolved into a *late modernity* (see Figure 3.1). Social characteristics in keeping with this postmodern or late modern climate include: the decline of heavy industry to be replaced by work carried out in smaller, more specialized units, often high-tech and involving expert systems; urban decline; mass unemployment; an underclass of people with long-term dependency on state benefits; social exclusion; one-parent families; the deconstruction of social categories; fragmentation of inequalities and identities; a crisis of masculinity as many men lost their role as the 'breadwinner'; the reality of a double shift as women manage both paid employment and unpaid domestic labour; lifestyle politics, postmaterialism, alternative religions and lifestyles. If the production of material goods could be diversified and employment could be competitive, with associated risks, then so too could education, the ultimate aim being to provide future workers with generic (transferable) skills to help them to adapt to a flexible and changing job market.

The cumulative effect of these changes meant that by the late twentieth century sociologists were talking about fundamental social change in terms of a shift from modernity to postmodernity, or late modernity, and the ideas of the 'founding fathers' started to look out of date because of their association with modernity. The status of science as a source of human progress was challenged by fears about atomic warfare, nuclear fuel and other environmental hazards. At a socio-political level the downfall of communism in Eastern Europe considerably weakened the status of the traditional Marxist metanarrative. Indeed Francis Fukuyama (1989) claimed that liberalism's global triumph over other ideologies would result in societies in which the loss of the dialectic of ideas associated with a struggle between ideologies would also mean a loss of passion and cultural creativity. Other theorists (e.g. Stuart Hall, writing about New Times) have retained a Marxist influence by arguing that, although Western societies may have entered a post-industrial, post-Fordist era, with an end to the mass production of the past, the economy is still a driving force in their social and political systems. Daniel Bell (1973) was one of the first writers to spot such dramatic social changes and he too claimed that modernity was not entirely over, because theoretical knowledge (and therefore creativity) would be the most important feature of the new 'information society'.

Sociology also changed, from its previous emphasis on the material inequalities associated with social class, gender and ethnicity at a national level to a greater emphasis on individualization, social exclusion, risks and the global society. In Germany an emphasis on the analysis of changing times

is called *Zeitdiagnostische Soziologie* and in the UK and North America it can be seen in writings about education by Andy Hargreaves (1994) and Michael Fullan (1991). Hargreaves argues that in many respects school systems are modernistic (or even premodern) in a largely postmodern world. He suggests that, although modernity is on the wane in other parts of society, it remains in schools (particularly secondary schools) with their large-scale, factory-like, inflexible bureaucracies promoting impersonalized systems and alienation. He associates modern school systems with what Habermas called technical rationality and with 'Narrowness of vision, inflexible decision-making, unwieldy structures, linear planning, unresponsiveness to clients' needs, sacrifice of human emotion for clinical efficiency and loss of meaningful senses of community' (p 11). Yet schools, and educationalists, too often respond to postmodern pressures by either aiming to reinforce modernity, or retreating into romanticized notions of premodernity, with an emphasis on community spirit and a sometimes naive attempt to respond to local needs. Hargreaves (Chapter 4) suggests that teachers need to tackle seven key dimensions of postmodernity: flexible economies; the paradox of globalization; dead certainties; the moving mosaic; the boundless self; safe simulation; and compression of time and space.

HARGREAVES'S SEVEN DIMENSIONS OF POSTMODERNITY

1. *Flexible economies (occupational and technological complexity).* Teachers need to develop skills and flexibility in their students but also need to address and discuss the uses of technology and patterns of unemployment and underemployment which many young people will face.
2. *The paradox of globalization* creates national doubts and insecurities. There is a danger of resurrecting traditional curricula of an ethnocentric and xenophobic nature, and reinforcing subject-based structures that inhibit organizational learning.
3. *Dead certainties (i.e. moral and scientific uncertainties)* have reduced confidence in the factual contents of what is taught. In response, teachers may be involved in developing their own missions and visions, or placed at the moral mercy of the market force of parental choice, or forced to extol the standards, traditions and basic skills of those who nostalgically reconstruct mythical certainties of ill-remembered pasts.
4. *The moving mosaic (organizational fluidity)* challenges the separation of subjects in secondary schools and addresses the need for more collaboration and shared occupational learning in contexts that are larger and more complex than those provided in small schools.
5. *The boundless self (personal anxieties)* involves a continuous psychological quest in a world without secure moral anchors.

6. *Safe simulation (technological sophistication and complexity) of reality* can be more perfect and plausible than the more untidy and uncontrollable realities themselves. In a world of instantaneous images and artificial appearances, contrived co-operation and contrived collegiality are examples of safe simulations that can deny the collaborative process its vitality and spontaneity.

7. *Compression of time and space* brings real benefits, including increased turnover, quicker travel and communication, speedier decision-making, more responsive services, and reduced waiting times. It also brings the following costs:

- Expectations of such rapid responsiveness mean that decision-making is too swift and leads to error, ineffectiveness, etc.
- Innovation, accelerated pace and so on mean that people experience an intolerable overload and feelings of guilt about their inability to meet goals.
- People may concentrate on the aesthetic appearance of change or performance rather than on the quality and substance of change or performance itself.
- Uncertainties can be exacerbated as knowledge is produced, disseminated and overturned at an ever increasing rate.
- The possible erosion of opportunities for personal reflection and relaxation can lead to increased stress and loss of contact with basic goals and purposes.
- We can place such a premium on implementing new techniques and complying with new mandates that more complex, less visible, longer-term and less measurable purposes, which involve care for others and relationships with others, are diminished in importance or sacrificed altogether.

To Hargreaves, the challenge in reconstructing and redesigning teachers' work is to develop more flexible and responsive structures and processes which also deal effectively and reflectively with the pressures of overload, multiple innovation and accelerated change.

Adapted from Hargreaves, 1994, Chapter 4

Question

Consider each of the first six dimensions and

(a) whether you agree that it exists;
(b) what means could be used to tackle it.

Discuss the costs and benefits of the last dimension. Can anything be done to tackle the costs?

Postmodernism

The main characteristic of theories about post-modernity (rather than late modernity) is a rejection of the grand narratives or metanarratives which provide overarching philosophical explanations of history and change. Such metanarratives include Enlightenment claims about the progress of freedom and reason and the Marxist belief in the forward march of progress via class conflict and revolution. Postmodernists question claims that reason can be objective and instead argue that what we may see as knowledge or truth is actually the product of forms of power exerted by particular discourses. This challenges the ideas of human rationality associated with Weber and action theories, as the development of particular discourses is seen as defining knowledge and perceptions of social reality. Thus, postmodernists (e.g. Lyotard and Baudrillard) are sceptical about notions of creative autonomy and have become particularly interested in studying language and tracing discourse as a way of identifying definitions of knowledge.

There have been many forms of resistance to postmodern assumptions about the implications of a diversified society. From a critical theory perspective, Habermas rejected the whole notion of postmodernity for its denial of reason and rejection of the Enlightenment project of increasing self-consciousness and self-determinism (Habermas, 1987a, p 338). Others (such as Bauman, 1992) accept that significant social change has taken place but suggest that a sociology of postmodernity or late modernity is still meaningful. Laclau also claims that postmodernism does not signify an end to human progress because, by dissecting discourses and the power relations behind them, postmodernists can initiate change and humanity can construct its own history (Laclau, 1988, p 80).

Habermas and other critics have claimed that postmodern ideas can be used to justify social inequalities. Postmodernists see identity as fluid and shifting so that, although it may make sense to discuss multicultural and multi-ethnic societies, it does not make sense to talk about national cultures, 'women' in general, 'Africans' in general and so on. It is possible that, rather than acknowledging the uniqueness of individual interests and aptitudes, but still expressing concern about social justice, a postmodern emphasis on diversity and fragmentation can present inequalities as natural; for example, justifying educational decisions based on parent power.

QUESTIONS

Do you accept the claim that societies have become more fragmented?
Is educational research into social class, gender and ethnicity still useful?

Poststructuralism and deconstructionism

There often seems to be some confusion about distinctions between postmodernism, poststructuralism and deconstructionism. Basically, they are similar in that all acknowledge fragmentation and reject metanarratives or grand narratives. The differences are that poststructuralism involves an emphasis on the deconstruction of literature, language and philosophy and leaves politics and society to others. As human identities are perceived as constructed by linguistic practices, those linguistic practices should be the focus of study. Moreover, approaches emphasizing linguistic practices are primarily associated with the work of various French writers, including Foucault, Lyotard, Baudrillard, Derrida, Kristeva, Lacan and Barthes.

According to poststructuralism, the media do more than just communicate ideas, as they construct them, along with a new 'electronic reality' of symbols and images. Baudrillard claims that the media have helped the world to become unreal, based on simulations, symbols and images which replace reality with a hyperreality in which it is not possible to distinguish one from the other. For example, Disneyland consists of more than just fictional images as it has an identity of its own and represents the hyperreality of American life. Los Angeles includes areas and communities called Hawaiian Gardens, Ontario, Venice, Naples and so on, which do more than just simulate other countries and cultures because their cultural mosaic represents Los Angeles itself. Instead of 'man' being the centre of this cultural analysis 'he' becomes just a terminal for multiple networks, like an astronaut in a capsule through which electronic messages flow. Baudrillard sees this as creating a new form of schizophrenia in which there is a feeling that there is no defence or way of retreating from the experience of being 'a switching centre for all the networks of influence' (1983, p 133). Whereas Bell has associated the information society with human progress, Baudrillard has a more resigned attitude towards what he perceives as images of despair.

Lyotard (1984) suggested that, although the universal claims of the grand narratives should be abandoned, it would still be possible to provide an analysis based on little narratives. These are based on local or customary knowledge and therefore provisional and grounded in context. They determine their own criteria and (like the popular stories of traditional societies) may include what seem to be illogical arguments and false reasoning. This leaves open a way of studying education via little narratives about individual schools or the communities they serve. To replace the permanence of social institutions and organization described within metanarratives, these little narratives could involve studies of flexible and loosely connected networks of communities.

Obviously poststructuralism may provide some insight into educational issues because of its focus on the deconstruction of knowledge and the possibility of little narratives. Yet poststructuralists are often criticized for their difficult writing style, together with the apolitical detachment and lack of direction associated with postmodernism.

QUESTIONS

What impact could the growth of hyperreality have on education?
In what ways can grand narratives and little narratives contribute to a greater understanding of education?

Reflexive modernity

In Chapter 1 it was claimed that education has undergone a process of immiseration and that this is influenced by the experience of living in a risk society. One problem is that education is primarily evaluated by politicians according to its vocational utility (the market value of the skills produced) and the risks to those involved in education are relatively neglected. What Beck says in *Risk Society* (1992) could equally be said of education. Beck notes that 'The first priority of techno-scientific curiosity is *utility for productivity*, and the hazards connected with it are considered only later and often not at all' (1992, p 60). Thus, when a German government decree outlined the acceptable levels of toxicity in the pesticides used on foodstuffs, its principle was that people could be poisoned up to a certain level. To claim that people should not be poisoned at all was dismissed as unrealistic and utopian and, instead, consumers could be provided with a regular ration of standardized poison (Beck, 1992, pp 64–5). Among sociologists, therefore, the term *risk* is now being used to refer to people's experiences of danger in late modernity. Increasingly, the threats we face are side-effects of social development and reflection on such risks can

undermine our confidence in systems of knowledge, expertise and social organization. We are nevertheless expected to *trust* large-scale, abstract systems of knowledge, expertise and social organization beyond our full understanding or control.

Beck and others argue that it is important to recognize the significance of risk and trust. They claim that, in the more advanced industrialized liberal democracies, the Enlightenment project of self-actualization is still unfinished business, and that we are experiencing a later stage of modernity in which there are greater possibilities for self-actualization through reflection on social experiences. Lash (in Beck, Giddens and Lash, 1994, p 115) also promotes the idea of reflexive modernization and suggests that there are two relevant types of reflexivity: first, *structural reflexivity*, when the agent (individual) reflects on the 'rules' and 'resources' of the social structure and his or her conditions of existence and, second, *self-reflexivity*, when the agent reflects on her/himself and is therefore self-monitoring. Thus, when stating his case against the rationed poisoning of consumers, Beck is suggesting that the consumer should engage in structural reflexivity and the producer (of the poison) and administration should engage in self-reflexivity. Beck's work has become most well known for its theme of the risk society and concerns with ecology and the management of scientific and technical risks. Giddens, however, is also concerned with insecurity, but in his case with the problem of how the agent manages *ontological insecurity* (also see R.D. Laing, 1960); how we cope with doubts and worries about social hazards whilst maintaining stable societies and personalities. Whereas Beck sees expert systems as associated with scientific risks and therefore obstacles to feelings of security, Giddens tends to see in them the potential to enhance security by helping us to interpret, reflect on and cope with such feelings (Beck, Giddens and Lash, 1994, p 117).

Unlike the rather pessimistic message offered by many postmodernists as an end to the subject ('man') of sociological analysis, these appeals for a reflexive modernization have become quite popular because they seem to offer some purpose or meaning to social progress. Indeed, in Germany they are associated with a Zeitdiagnostische Soziologie and are seen as offering a more exciting insight into studies of social change via such concepts as risk, trust, and expert systems. In the UK, Giddens has linked his work on reflexive modernity with a wider range of influential political theories.

QUESTIONS

What elements of risk and trust are involved in education?
In Chapter 1, I asked, 'How did education become so miserable?' Do postmodernism, poststructuralism and theories about reflexive modernity provide any answers?

Political perspectives

We have now seen conflicting views concerning the extent to which radical social change can take place as a result of individual actions. Biological determinism, functionalism and postmodernism have often been described as apolitical, but for different reasons: biological determinism because it accepts extreme social inequalities as natural and therefore unalterable; functionalism because it tends to focus on describing elements of consensus and continuity, rather than the conflict and change associated with political power struggles; and postmodernism because it rejects any metanarrative favouring radical social change.

QUESTIONS

Do you accept such brief summaries of potential reasons why biological determinism, functionalism and postmodernism may be regarded as apolitical? Can a perspective only be regarded as political if it presents an agenda for social change?
These three perspectives are often presented as being non-political and inherently conservative at the same time. Is that possible?

A contrast can be seen with the more radical and socially active perspectives associated with feminism, Marxism, critical theory and reflexive modernity. These approaches are generally regarded as inherently left-wing in that they present agendas for social change involving an emphasis on certain types of equality. This link between social theory and political perspectives is most clearly seen in Marxist influences on communist societies. More recently, in the UK we have seen how the work of Anthony Giddens has had a direct influence on the policies of the British Labour Party and a link with what Giddens (1998) and others have called a *Third Way* in the politics of various liberal democracies.

Although relationships between sociological and biological perspectives and political perspectives may be influenced by an emphasis on passivity or activity it is important to note that this is not what politics is primarily about. Politics is primarily about *power* relationships and, at an even more basic level, about assumptions concerning human nature. This obviously relates to education policies, and we can see here how Lawton saw educational ideologies as relating to a polarity ranging from extremes of pessimism and optimism about human nature.

> At one extreme we have the seventeenth-century philosopher Hobbes (1588–1679) who was pessimistic about human nature, seeing human beings as essentially selfish and therefore needing 'society' to ensure order by means of social control. Without strong control from society, life would be 'nasty, brutish and short'. This view, I suggested above, also represents one important strand of traditional Conservatism.
>
> Lawton, 1992, p 12

Thus, right-wing (Conservative) views about education include not only what are often claimed to be apolitical and passive perspectives, but also approaches favouring a very active stance in controlling children who are inherently selfish and nasty. This could be seen when we looked at biological determinism and Lynn's comments about the social challenge posed by 'slum dwellers' (see page 45). In contrast, more left-wing approaches tend to have more optimistic views about human nature, assuming that children are born good and it is society that makes them bad. This could be seen when we looked at social construction and Vaizey's comments about the failure to integrate working-class children into a society governed by the values of the middle class (see page 46).

In Chapter 5 you will see how Lawton differentiated between three overlapping levels of thinking about ideology and education, ranging from the very general (Level 1) to the specific (Level 3). In this chapter we are looking at Level 1 and the basic ontologies giving rise to more specific views about society and education. Yet it is by no means certain that most people distinguish between the ontologies and education policies of different political parties at even a basic level. Many individuals in the Torytown and Labourville cohort did not distinguish between the education policies of the main parties. Although several members of the cohort favoured the Liberal Democrats' plans to spend more on education by raising taxes, few had sufficient interest in education for it to influence their vote (see Chapter 5) and many felt that the Liberal Democrats were not a credible future government.

> All of them have good bits, but none of them have
> a whole national education policy. All of them
> are too far removed from what actually goes on
> in schools, or how close the system is to collapse.
>
> Mark, 1992

> I like the Lib Dems idea of having a targeted
> amount of tax (I think a penny) attached to
> education. I think now there's not much difference
> between Labour and the Conservatives as regards
> their attitudes to education and things like
> inspections and the National Curriculum and so
> on. So I'm not very happy with either of them as
> regards the pressure they're putting on schools. I
> don't know enough about the Liberal Democrats
> policy in that respect to be honest.
>
> Jeremy, 1997

Similarly, since 1944 various writers have criticized both the Labour Party and the Conservative Party for not having a clear and cohesive education policy.

More recently, Lawton considered the emergence of what have since been described as New Labour policies in order to look for remaining distinctions between the Labour and Conservative parties.

> What is lacking is a principle or set of principles
> which would clearly differentiate Labour Party
> policy from that of the Conservatives. Crosland,

LEFT-WING CRITICISMS OF THE LABOUR PARTY

In 1981 the Centre for Contemporary Cultural Studies criticized the Labour Party for not being radical enough, claiming that it:

1. Was committed to educational progress through state policy and neglected a more direct, popular educational connection. Its commitment to the existing political system meant that it organized education from the top down. Instead of 'popular' education (promoted by, for example, workers' organizations) it had organized an 'unpopular' form of schooling.
2. Was mainly concerned about equal access to education and neglected matters of 'control' and 'content'.
3. Left teachers and other educationalists to fill the gap by raising the issues of content and control.
4. Concerned itself with a weak version of equal opportunities rather than real egalitarianism.
5. Had, with the onset of the Great Debate, moved from seeing schools as a solution (to working-class failure) to presenting schools as problem (failing the country's economy).
6. Had too often seen equality as a means to an end (such as social cohesion) rather than as an end in itself. To the CCCS the Labour Party 'has always served two masters' by accepting the capitalist system whilst claiming to support the interests of the working class.

Questions

Compare the criticisms above with the Marxist and critical theory approaches described in this chapter. See Chapter 5 for further information about equal access, equal opportunities and egalitarianism (items 2 and 4 above).

Paul Willis was a research fellow at the Centre when his book *Learning to Labour: Why working class kids get working class jobs* was published in 1977. Can you see any relationship between the theories he explores in the book and the CCCS criticisms?

and before him, Tawney, focused on the ideal of 'equality' – a word which was so ambiguous that it became misleading. (There were endless disputes about whether it meant equality of opportunity, equality of outcome or equality of regard.) Equality will no longer serve, but if we examine clearly what has developed as one of the remaining guiding principles of Labour Party policy it is social justice or fairness. This too has problems of definition, but it is an ideal difficult to oppose in principle, although theorists of both wings of the New Right have tried.

Lawton, 1992, p 30

Notice that Lawton identified 'both wings' of the New Right, which is often regarded as a 'wing' itself. In fact there are many right-wing perspectives but, as we are considering changing education, it makes sense to explore the long-term movement from the old style of Conservatism associated with the 1940s to the New Right emerging in the 1970s. We should also look further at the movement from the 'old' Labour of the 1940s to the New Labour of the 1990s.

One Nation Conservatives and the (Socialist) Labour Party

By the 1940s British politics already had an established *liberal democracy*, with the necessary political institutions, free elections of Members of Parliament and processes in place for the peaceful election and removal of governments. This was also commonly seen as a *pluralist* system, in which central and local government responded to changing public opinions and aimed to reach compromises between a plurality of influences. In a pluralist system power is spread across a wide range of social locations and organizations representing various interests, and no one interest group is allowed to dominate. As sociologists we can see how this relates to Durkheim's argument that social solidarity is based on an acceptance of diversity. Yet it is clear that there were flaws in this image of the perfect pluralist, liberal democracy.

During the 1940s Conservatives tended to accept the concern expressed over a hundred years earlier by Disraeli (1835, pp 22–5) that the UK

was dangerously split between the 'two nations' of rich and poor, between whom there was very little understanding. Indeed this split had become more noticeable as the 'two nations' came into closer contact, and their interdependence became more apparent, during two world wars. 'One Nation' Conservatives therefore advocated social reform, which would generate a more equal, but not totally egalitarian, society. Although these more moderate Conservatives saw society as a hierarchy, they had a benevolent, paternalistic attitude and a sense of *noblesse oblige*, combined with a fear of unrest. They saw their own wealth as held in trust for the common good, and this helps to explain why many Conservatives supported the development of a welfare state. The provision of at least a good basic education for all was regarded as essential in order to promote social continuity and cohesion and provide an educated electorate.

By the 1940s the Labour Party was clearly associated with a reforming style of socialism, distinct from the revolutionary socialism favoured by the (more Marxist) Communist Party. Emerging from a strong labour movement, the party promoted a community ethic, social emancipation and an end to the exploitation of the many by the few. During the 1930s and 1940s Hugh Dalton and Herbert Morrison were particularly influential in developing ideas of corporate socialism, centralized planning of a mixed economy using Keynesian economics, nationalization (social ownership of public services) and a strong welfare state. The provision of a strong system of state education was regarded as essential in order to provide opportunities for the children of working-class families and break down class barriers.

Conservatives and Labour politicians had very little in common during the 1940s, but the forced unity they experienced during the wartime coalition government and their concerns about the sort of country that would emerge from the destruction of war meant that there was a relatively common sense of purpose when compared with their situation at the end of the twentieth century. They were also linked by the common influence of various political and economic theories. A new form of political liberalism (associated with John Maynard Keynes and William Beveridge) advocated systems for the redistribution of wealth from the rich in order to help the poor and to promote positive freedoms, including the capacity to make real choices regarding education, employment and leisure. However, this type of liberalism was more paternalistic than egalitarian, arguing that the state should intervene in the capitalist system in order to promote economic growth and social ends such as full employment. Keynes's (1936) economic theories suggested that government spending on social investment (such as education, the health service, housing and welfare benefits) was productive because it increased purchasing power; therefore, it increased demand for the goods produced by industry, minimized unemployment and led to greater affluence for all. This economic impetus was supported by the socio-political theories of T.H. Marshall. In his essay 'Citizenship and social class' (1947), Marshall suggested that it was possible to trace the historical development of three types of citizenship in the UK: civil citizenship (representing equality before the law), which grew as civil rights increased during the nineteenth century; political citizenship (representing the right to vote and express political views), which grew with the expansion of the franchise during the early twentieth century; and social citizenship (representing welfare rights and liberation from insecurity), which he expected to grow with the expansion of social rights during the middle and late twentieth century. Thus the expansion of education was supported by an economic emphasis on the beneficial effects of government spending and beliefs in the desirable spread of social citizenship.

Nevertheless, Conservatives influenced by this type of liberalism still had in common with other Conservatives a rejection of egalitarianism, the image of a chain of command, deference to authority, respect for the law, allegiance and patriotism. Their common zeal about social control and law and order issues was still based on concern about the inherent depravation of the individual and its destructive potential. The Labour Party too had radical and moderate factions, some favouring more radical means for the redistribution of wealth and some favouring slow, incremental reform.

Yet changing discourses and contexts mean that what may have been regarded as moderate in the past is regarded as radical today, and vice versa. The early 1940s to the mid 1960s is often regarded as a time when the UK was close to achieving consensus politics. However, after the election of a Labour government in 1966, the two parties started to move further apart. The Conservative Party gradually moved further to the right, away from One Nation Conservatism and towards the more extreme policies favoured by the New Right. The Labour Party seemed to move further left in the late 1960s, and during the 1970s, as its policies became more radical and egalitarian (see Chapter 5 for an explanation of egalitarianism). Although Labour's 1997 election manifesto indicated a radical move to the right, the Conservative Party had shifted so far to the right by then that the two parties were still far apart on many issues. Meanwhile the Liberal Party (and its most recent incarnation, the Liberal Democratic Party) has maintained a consistent position slightly left of centre since the mid 1960s.

The New Right

Having looked at the new form of liberalism associated with Keynes and Beveridge and how this influenced the politics of the 1940–60s, we can now see how a resurgence of an older form of liberalism led to changes within the Conservative Party during the 1970s. 'Liberalism' includes a wide range of sometimes competing theories and early classical liberalism emphasized a negative form of freedom, involving freedom from oppression, but without the support from society advocated by theorists in the mid twentieth century. In Britain its origins are associated with the work of John Locke (1690), who saw human nature as capable of being educated into responsible citizenship, with an emphasis on toleration, natural rights, individual liberty, the consent of the governed, representation, constitutional checks and balances and limited government powers. This included the economic freedoms promoted by Adam Smith (1776), who criticized the protection of trade involved in the eighteenth-century mercantilist system and promoted *laissez-faire* (free trade), and the ideas of radical philosophers such as Jeremy Bentham, James Mill and his son John Stuart Mill. Herbert Spencer argued further, that the poor should not be protected from the consequences of their behaviour by welfare provision.

By the late 1970s Keynesian economics were in doubt as the state had taken on more responsibilities and was facing chronic monetary inflation. This was worsened by a global economic crisis. Appeals to the ideals of early classical liberalism, with an emphasis on self-sufficiency and a reduced role for the state, were therefore starting to look quite attractive to politicians. Such policies were supported by the contemporary political and economic theories of Friedrich Hayek and Milton Friedman. Both writers rejected welfare rights, arguing that a welfare state is monopolistic and state bureaucracies were not to be trusted as they can act in their own interests and become too expansive. Consequently, bureaucracies and their activities should be kept to a minimum. Friedman also promoted a monetarist policy in which the government would control and minimize the circulation of money by reducing its own spending in order to reduce both inflation and taxation. Indeed, the last Labour government of the 1970s started to cut public spending and consequentially ended its term of office with a high rate of unemployment. In 1979 the Conservative Party won the general election with the slogan 'Labour isn't working', but then went on to cut government spending even further and increase unemployment even further.

Since the mid 1970s the Conservative New Right have emphasized the idea of letting market forces operate naturally, without government interference (using the phrase 'rolling back the state'). This means that they have favoured a market system in education where parental choice has been emphasized, competition between institutions has been promoted and some schools have been allowed to decline and eventually close. The New Right have also tended to reject pluralist ideas, claiming that a search for consensus within a diverse population is a waste of time. All of the people cannot be satisfied for even part of the time. This means that Conservative governments have not felt the need to satisfy the disparate views of educationalists and helps to explain various conflicts between governments and teachers, lecturers and managers. Furthermore, Prime Minister Margaret Thatcher claimed that there was no such thing as society, only individuals and their families. This individualization meant that educationalists' concerns about various types of inequalities (including social class, gender and ethnicity) could be rejected on the grounds that such groupings were not meaningful and that governments could not tackle natural differences between individuals and their families.

QUESTION

It was noted earlier that functionalism has been regarded as inherently conservative. Look again at Durkheim's views and compare them with One Nation Conservatism and a New Right perspective.

Before moving on it should be noted that a trawl through the origins of the New Right in the UK would be misleading if it suggested that this perspective is only a British phenomenon. Indeed, it has been very influential in many other (particularly English-speaking) countries, where the ideas of classical liberalism have also been regenerated (see Kenway, 1997). It has been rather less influential in countries with different philosophical traditions.

> I live in the Australian state of Victoria, a state governed by radical conservatives who, since coming to power less than two years ago, have vandalized the school system, removed 8,200 teaching positions, closed or amalgamated over 230 schools, wound back the provision of educational support services, pushed schools into a market mode, instituted a model of management which has turned educational leadership into a form of institutional management devoid of educational concerns, undermined the morale of teachers, almost totally destroyed the teachers' unions, officially removed the concept of social justice from the educational agenda, shaved $300 million off the state education budget and increased aid to private schools by 15 per cent in real terms. I agree that there is an urgent and pressing need for educators to speak out strongly and courageously against those types of educational manoeuvres, to deconstruct the truth claims which have been mobilized to justify and legitimate such moves and to name them for what they are.
>
> Kenway, 1997, p 131

New Labour

Despite some claims that the Conservative Party and Labour Party moved further apart from the 1960s onwards, left-wing critics of the Labour Party have recently claimed that the lines between them have become more blurred and that, in particular, the Labour Party has adopted some Conservative education policies. Certainly the fact that a Labour government introduced student fees came as a surprise to many Labour voters. Yet it may be more appropriate to argue that, whereas the New Right has been criticized for being a strong version of Conservatism, New Labour has been criticized for being a weak version of socialism.

Since 1944 the fundamental problem within the Labour Party has been the clash between the two major influences of pluralism and Marxism and how to accommodate both. Labour Party supporters have ranged from the extreme left (for example, the Militant Tendency) to the more moderate who have sought to maximize the appeal of Labour policies to as many voters as possible. The lengthy period of Conservative governments from 1979 to 1997 meant that Labour leaders faced an important question – Should Labour's 'left-wing' policies be moderated in order to ensure that Labour could win the next election?

'The reason we have been out of power for fifteen years is simple – society changed and we refused to change with it' (Tony Blair, July 1994). 'New Labour' is the name Tony Blair started to use in 1994–5 to signal the changes that had taken place in the Labour Party. Although his predecessors Neil Kinnock and John Smith had tried to make Labour less dependent upon its traditional industrial working-class base, Tony Blair went further by abandoning Clause 4 of Labour's Constitution which, in theory, had bound the party to a policy of nationalization of industry. New Labour now embraces the concepts of enterprise, individual responsibility and the market economy, and tries to address the concerns of what political commentators have labelled 'Middle England'. This distinguishes New Labour not only from the extreme left within the party, but also from those moderates who still favour the policies espoused by earlier Labour governments (including Keynesian economics and a strong welfare state supported by relatively high taxes). Yet, unlike Conservative governments, New Labour has apparently tried to retain an image of responding to a plurality of views. For example, it has apparently been aiming to balance the interests of business and workers by involving representatives from business in its policy-making, and accepting much of the Conservatives' regulation of the trade unions (including teachers' unions), yet trying to maintain some of its traditionally good relations with the unions.

The two main theoretical influences on New Labour have been Will Hutton and Anthony Giddens. Hutton (1995) has been particularly influential in his writings about the political economy of the state, emphasizing the notion of a 'stakeholder democracy', in which all would feel that they had an economic stake in society and trade unions would become partners in the management of a less degenerate form of capitalism. Democracy would also be enhanced by the devolution of power and an emphasis on obligations as well as rights. This helps to explain why New Labour has continued the Conservatives' emphasis on parental choice (i.e. rights) in education, although it has added a stronger emphasis on parental responsibility (i.e. obligations). In this respect it has also been influenced by communitarian theories about moral values and social responsibilities associated with the writings of Amatai Etzioni (1993). Hutton also argued that the middle-class exodus from public services should be discouraged and this meant that although private schools could be retained, their public subsidies and associated tax incentives should be withdrawn. Private schools should be compelled to form partnerships with the state sector and their charitable status should be dependent on educating a high proportion of non-fee-paying children. Hutton also favoured the revival of grammar schools and 'grammar school streams' in comprehensives in order to encourage more middle-class parents to send their children to state schools.

The second major influence on New Labour has been the work of the sociologist Anthony Giddens (e.g. 1991, 1994, 1998). Giddens's work on reflexive modernity (with Beck and Lash, 1994) has already been discussed and you will see many references to his work in this book; for example, in Chapter 5 we will look at his explanation of how, by the end of the twentieth century, a new style of politics was starting to define equality in terms of social inclusion and exclusion. He has also written extensively on democracy and citizenship, stating the case for the 'democratization of democracy', involving a dialogic democracy, reflexive citizenship, life politics and the devolution of power.

When interviewed in August 1997, even sympathetic members of the Torytown and Labourville cohort were still sceptical about change under the new Labour government.

I think the government should listen more to what the grass-roots are saying. There's always a danger

GIDDENS ON THE THIRD WAY

The overall aim of Third Way politics should be to help citizens pilot their way through the major revolutions of our time: globalization, transformations in personal life and our relationship to nature.

1. Third Way politics should preserve a core concern with social justice, while accepting that the range of questions which escape the left/right divide is greater than before.
2. Freedom to social democrats should mean autonomy of action, which in turn demands the involvement of the wider social community.
3. Third Way politics looks for a new relationship between the individual and the community, a redefinition of rights and obligations.
4. One might suggest as a prime motto for the new politics, *no rights without responsibilities*. The government has a cluster of responsibilities for its citizens and others, including protection of the vulnerable. With expanding individualism should come an extension of individual obligations. It is up to the government to ensure that welfare systems do not discourage the active search for work. This value applies to all; the affluent as well as the less affluent.
5. Democratizing democracy. The Third Way argues that what is necessary is to reconstruct it – to go beyond those on the right who say government is the enemy, and those on the left who say government is the answer.
6. No authority without democracy. Reform of the state and government should be a basic orienting principle of Third Way politics; a process of the deepening and widening of democracy. Government can act in partnership with agencies in civil society to foster community renewal and development.
7. The economic basis of such partnership is what Giddens calls the *new mixed economy*.
8. Free trade can be an engine of economic development, but given the socially and culturally destructive power of markets, its wider consequences need always to be scrutinized.
9. Economy can be effective only if existing welfare institutions are thoroughly modernized.
10. Third Way politics is one-nation politics. The cosmopolitan nation helps promote social inclusion but also has a key role in fostering transnational systems of governance.
11. Philosophic conservatism – a pragmatic attitude towards coping with change; a nuanced view of science and technology, in recognition of their ambiguous consequences for us; a respect for the past and for history; and in the environmental arena, an adoption of the precautionary principle where feasible. In an era of ecological risk, modernization cannot be purely linear and certainly cannot be simply equated with economic growth.

Adapted from Giddens, 1998, pp 64–70

Questions

Consider how each of the eleven points may affect education.
Since 1997 what has the Labour government done to address each of these points?

that when they get into power they loose touch. You just have to look at what happened with the Conservatives. There's a lesson there for everyone to learn.

Henry, 1997

As far as I'm aware of what the policies are, most pupils have got a better chance of getting a better education. I do have doubts about whether it'll work, but my impression is that they're going to try and give a better chance. Which is all you can do is give them the chance of getting a better education for into the next century.

Karl, 1997

Liberal Democrats

The former Liberal Party and its successor the Liberal Democratic Party have often been perceived as forming the moderate centre ground between the Conservative and Labour parties. Indeed some voters may support them because of this public perception. Most Liberal Democrats would, nevertheless, argue that this is not the case, as their policies are radical and seeking major social changes. Their most distinctive aims are to defend and enhance civil rights, freedom of belief and speech, the protection of minorities, tolerance and equal opportunities. Rather than being a centrist party, they seek recognition that some of their radical policies have been 'stolen' by other parties.

Liberals first espoused the idea of a welfare state and, in 1942, the Liberal William Beveridge produced his Report on Social Insurance and Allied Services, which laid the foundations of a welfare state. However, the Labour Party won the 1945 general election and received most of the credit for implementing the report's recommendations.

Liberal Democrats have also aimed for radical political change via the decentralization of power and the reform of an electoral system that has regularly produced a disproportionately small number of Liberal Democrat MPs when compared with their actual votes. During the 1990s the Labour Party developed a greater acceptance of both these aims, and it is reasonable to ask how much difference there is between the Liberal Democratic Party and New Labour. One distinction between the education policies of the two parties is that not only do Liberal Democrats favour a larger increase in government spending on education, but they also advocate increased taxation in order to pay for it. In the 1997 general election campaign they recommended an increase of one penny in the pound on income tax, specifically destined for educational spending. Cynics responded that, at a time when voters favoured low taxes, this policy would be a vote-looser but, as they had no chance of winning the election, it did not matter! Liberal Democrats have also been opposed to the introduction of student fees, they favour reduced class sizes and they want further devolution of powers to local schools and communities.

QUESTION

Find out more about the Liberal Democrats' education policies. How close are they to the 'new' style of liberalism that was so influential during the 1940s?

Conclusion: The heuristic value of theories

At the start of this chapter it was claimed that the wide, and continually widening, range of theoretical perspectives can have heuristic value in allowing us to generate complex images and understandings of educational realities. No one perspective has been presented as *the* perfect tool for the analysis of changing education; rather it has been argued that different tools may be needed for different crafts. For example, feminism has reflected on various types of inequality; functionalism has considered the role of education in promoting social cohesion and continuity; postmodernism has raised questions about significant social change.

> . . . postmodernism does more than wage war on totality, it also calls into question the use of reason in the service of power, the role of intellectuals who speak through authority invested in a science of trust and history, and forms of leadership that demand unification and consensus within centrally administered chains of command.
>
> Giroux, 1992, in Halsey *et al.*, 1997, pp 118–9

QUESTION

Look again at the quote from Giroux at the start of this chapter. How much has the chapter helped you to understand what he was saying?

The theories described tend to be useful because of the questions they raise, rather than any answers that they may tentatively offer and, as we tackle these questions, we identify even more. Any answers provided are generally bound to their context in time and place and superceded by social change. So, whilst arguing that modernism, postmodernism and feminism offered valuable opportunities for rethinking learning processes and relationships between schooling and democracy, Giroux acknowledged that theories were also unfinished business.

> To invoke the importance of pedagogy is to raise questions not simply about how students learn but also how educators (in the broad sense of the term) construct the ideological and political positions from which they speak. At issue here is the discourse that both situates human beings within history and makes visible the limits of their ideologies and values. Such a position acknowledges the partiality of all discourses so that the relationship between knowledge and power will always be open to dialogue and critical self-engagement.
>
> Giroux, 1992, in Halsey *et al.*, 1997, p 128

However, according to Giroux, the partiality of discourse does not exclude an agenda for using education in a transformative and political way. In the quote at the start of this chapter you can see his explanation of how, to him, sociological theories about education are (and should be) inextricably linked to education policies. Yet, as Kenway argues, it sometimes seems that theorists become so concerned with their own internal logic that they ignore the real world of education.

HAS FEMINISM LOST ITS EDUCATIONAL GROUND?

I believe that in recent times feminism in and for education has become so preoccupied with its own 'internal' theoretical and political difficulties and differences that it has not paid due and proper attention to what is going on in the rest of the 'restructured' educational world. I also believe that it has become so infatuated with various versions of poststructuralism and/or postmodernism, so influenced by the concerns and interests and intrigued by the debates and challenges of these fields that it has, in many senses, let the educational policy world go by. Certainly exploring the implications of these theories for education policy has not been high on the agenda. This is not to say that any of its postmodernist concerns are unimportant, rather it is to say that a great deal of other really important educational ground is being lost and that feminism seems to be sacrificing much of its critical edge in those Political (the big P is intentional) circles where education policy is made. It seems to be off in a space by itself somewhere, meanwhile something is burning, and it's not Rome . . .

Indeed, it hasn't been my feminist work that has led me to be as concerned as I am. It has been my work examining the market forms in education in association with other major policy shifts and in the context of the commodification and technologization of western culture. This complex world of practice, commentary and analysis in and beyond but connected to education is barely touched by the ideas of feminists in education and yet it is this world which is largely shaping education's future.

Kenway, in Halsey *et al.*, 1997, p 132

Question

Do you agree that some theory seems to be off in a space by itself somewhere whilst education burns?

4

Changing systems

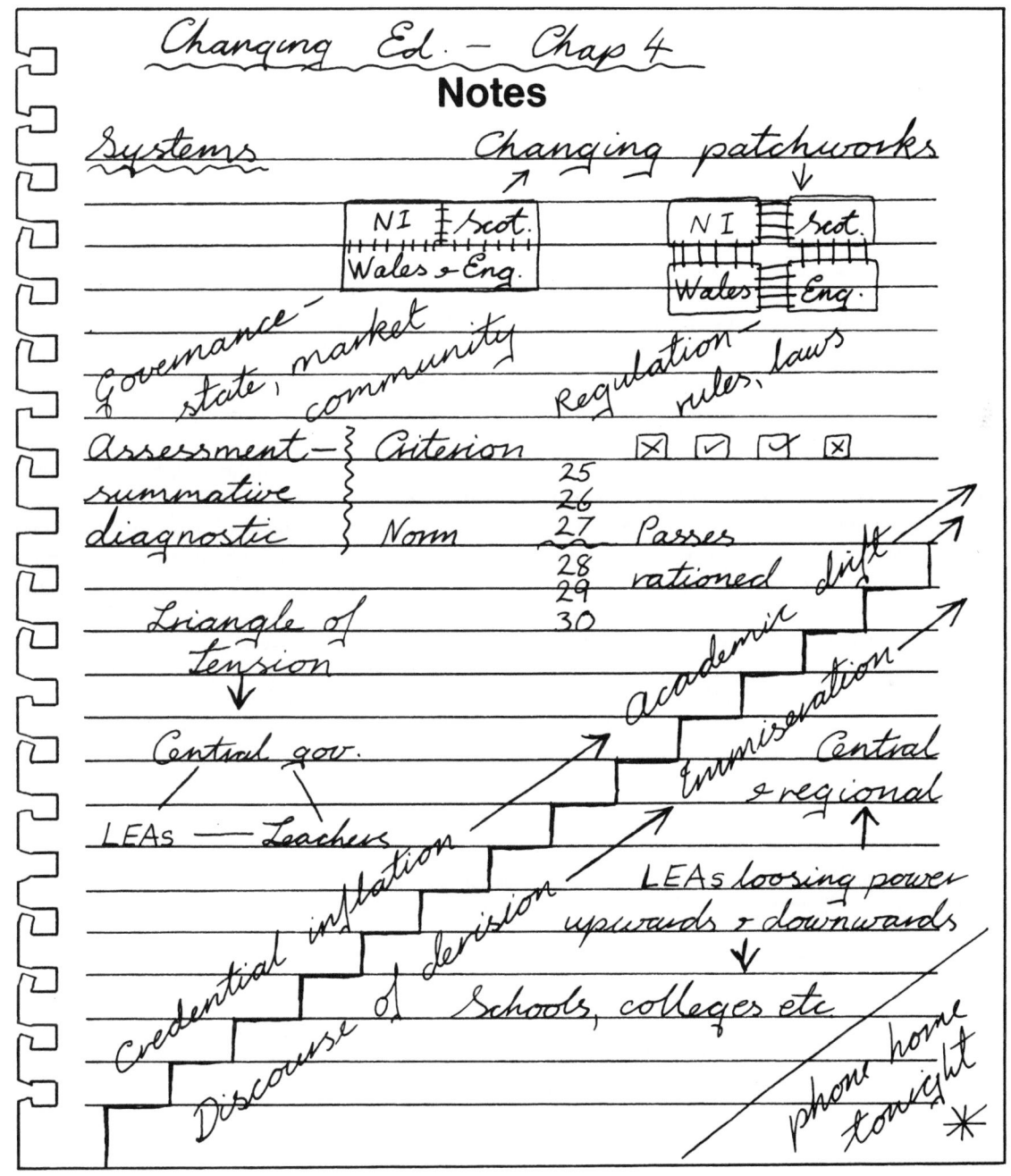

Socio-economic change – Systems theories – Bureaucracy – Governance and regulation – Assessment and academic groupings – Special educational needs – The curriculum – Types of schools – Control of individual schools – Further and higher education – National systems – Education in Wales – Education in Scotland – Education in Northern Ireland – Local education authorities – Torytown and Labourville – Teachers and lecturers – Conclusion: Economic influences on education systems

How a society selects, classifies, distributes, transmits and evaluates the educational knowledge it considers to be public, reflects both the distribution of power and the principles of social control.

Bernstein, 1971, p 47

How can sociologists make any sense of the constantly changing systems of education within the UK? We may labour long and hard to understand them and then find that, whilst we were reading, they changed behind our backs. To confuse matters even more, we will find that not only do systems of education change over time but the language used in the study of systems also changes. So, in order to make some sense out of the chaos, my own way of understanding the UK's education systems involves seeing it as a patchwork quilt! In the mid twentieth century the quilt seemed to consist of the three main sections of education, in England and Wales (generally classed as sharing the same system), Scotland and Northern Ireland. Researchers were interested in the three sections, as well as in how the different sorts of education provided by the many local education authorities within each section were starting to cohere as a result of the 1944 Education Act. Educational rhetoric (perhaps the plain or fancy stitching in the quilt) tended to be about bureaucracy, rationalism, equal opportunities and the ideas of universal provision. Yet, by the end of the twentieth century, devolution to the regions meant that the quilt was starting to look like four more distinct sections, as education in Wales started

to distinguish itself more from English education and the four sections developed their own patterns. Differences in the sort of education provided by local authorities (and other providers) within the four sections had also become more pronounced. Interest in systems of education had also widened as a result of British membership of the European Union and the process of globalization. This means that British education systems can no longer be studied in isolation from international influences, and that my image of the quilt as a separate item is now looking decidedly weak.

A more useful model of changes in British education systems was provided by Dale (1989) and Trowler (1998) when they considered the way that roles and responsibilities shifted between the various groups who could influence education policies (see Figure 4.1). Between 1944 and 1974 many decisions were negotiated between the government ministry, local education authorities and teachers' unions. Parents had very little say in matters of education policy However, during the 1970s and 1980s the political party in power gradually started to play a more dominant role, asserting its policies through the government ministry to effectively enfeeble LEAs and teachers and replace them with

	1944–74	1974–88	1988–97
National ministry	Overseers	Limited assertiveness	Minister's instrument
Political party in power	Reserve power	Electorally opportunist	Dominant
LEA	Active partners (managing director)	Squeezed	Eunuchs
Teachers	Active partners (executive director)	Problems	Proletarianized
Parents	Who?	Constructed as 'natural' experts/moral guardians	Consumers
Industry	Indifferent (full employment)	Concerned (increasing unemployment)	Consultants

Source: Adapted by Trowler, P., 1998, p 15, from Dale, 1989, p 115

Figure 4.1 Changing roles in the structure of education 1944–97

a market system where the roles of parents and employers apparently took priority.

QUESTIONS

As you read this chapter you should consider the following:

(a) How have these shifts taken place and do they amount to radical changes or more gradual, incremental reforms?
(b) Who has been included or excluded from decision-making and why?
(c) How much uniformity and diversity is there within the education system(s) in the UK as a whole?

Socio-economic change

Soon after the Second World War the UK, like other European countries, experienced a 'baby boom', class sizes were growing and many politicians were committed to a rapid expansion of educational opportunities and facilities. Supported by a belief in Keynesian economics, public spending on education grew quickly, along with spending on other public services. For many years to come spending on education was seen as a good investment, not only as a way of supplying a workforce with the necessary skills, but also as a way of equipping individuals with the valuable social skills and promoting healthy personal development.

By the late 1970s declining birth rates (throughout Europe) meant that young people became a smaller proportion of the total population and educationalists were faced with a surplus of school places. If this had been the only problem faced by policy-makers then a simple response may have been to reduce class sizes and thus create a more favourable teacher–pupil ratio. However, at the same time unemployment was starting to rise, bringing with it a wide range of socio-economic problems and increasing pressures on public services. The new Conservative government of 1979 was also committed to a reduction in public spending, and this included the rationalization of the education system and schools in particular. Spending per student is largely determined by three things: the

ratio of teachers to students, how much teachers are paid and the level of non-teaching costs. Savings could therefore be made by allowing classes to get larger, restricting teachers' pay rises and cutting non-teaching costs such as capital expenditure on buildings and books.

Cuts could not, however, be made across the board, as declining birth rates and the reducing proportion of young people in the population was not matched by a reduced demand for further and higher education. Indeed, demand for continuing education actually increased, largely because of the growth in unemployment and the credential inflation arising from employers' ability to select from increasing numbers of job applicants. Young people knew that they had to get more qualifications in order to compete within a highly competitive job market.

Together with changes in the demand for education, the dominant political attitudes also changed. During the 1940s the socializing and integrating function of education was seen by all political parties as vitally important. It was seen as maintaining some national stability at a time of international disorder. By the 1970s worldwide economic crises had become the main focus and were inclining politicians towards a greater emphasis on the economic function of education in providing the necessary vocational skills. From 1979 onwards New Right, Conservative governments promoted individualization within a competitive market economy, together with Margaret Thatcher's claim that there was no such thing as society. The fragmentation of social classes, existence of many ethnic groups and divisions and changing family structures meant that it was, indeed, becoming increasingly difficult to perceive such a thing as society. Yet by the end of the twentieth century, a relatively new 'Third Way' Labour government was committed to an end to individualization and the re-introduction of community ideals, with an emphasis on not only rights but also responsibilities. Green, Wolf and Leney (1999, p 23) claim that, by the end of the twentieth century, after years of emphasizing the importance of education for economic competitiveness, there was again a growing awareness of the importance of its civic role. The European Commission was already taking a lead in promoting European citizenship ('Accomplishing Europe', Study Group, 1997, and other reports). Perhaps the traditional function of education in promoting social cohesion may have become more important as the fragmentation of postmodern, or late modern, societies was becoming increasingly apparent.

Systems theories

Some of the cohort in Torytown and Labourville had their own views about systems of education. Unlike various theorists, they perceived them as actually lacking system; in other words, being disorganized and incoherent.

> There's a problem with education that they follow, if you like, fad management. Whatever seems to be the flavour of the month they chase this, wasting money right, left and centre, and change for the sake of change, which I think isn't necessarily in anyone's interest.
>
> John, 1997

> In education, which I know more about, they [Conservative governments] did too many things without thinking them through and had to change them and created a lot of extra work and hassle and torment for people and then changes were made, which made more work whereas if they'd thought them through properly then it would have been more successful. Unfortunately I think the present government are following the same path, diving into things. For example, the student fees, which they obviously hadn't thought through and found that it was going to create problems and now they're having to back-track.
>
> Jeremy, 1997

It is therefore possible that systems theorists live in an idealized world of imagined coherence unrelated to the lived experience of teachers such as John and Jeremy. Alternatively it is possible that the 'system' actually has more coherence than can be appreciated in a hectic working environment. Perhaps it is a bit of both, as the criticisms above relate to changing education policies and it is possible that, underlying frequent policy changes, there may be some sort of fairly stable foundation for the day-to-day management of education. What follows is a review of how sociologists have tried to make sense of what may often seem to be confusing social structures, procedures and relationships.

Systems may be defined as structured relationships between various entities which together form a sense of a unity. Obviously that sense of unity in the systems we are looking at is provided by their common interest in the provision of education and, of the various sociological perspectives, functionalism (see Chapter 3) has had the most to say about how education systems operate by looking at the way that parts of the system interrelate. Parsons described a systems approach as referring

> . . . both to a complex of interdependencies between parts, components and processes that involves discernible regularities of relationships, and to a similar type of interdependency between such a complex and its surrounding environment.
>
> Parsons, 1968, p 458

Parsons's most well-known analysis of social systems involved the identification of four subsystems that respond to internal and external 'functional prerequisites of a system of action' (1937), which sociologists tend to memorize as the AGIL model:

- Adaptation (how the system adapts to and utilizes available economic resources).
- Goal-attainment (the system's polity, aims, decisions).
- Integration (how the system fits into the social community).
- Latency (the system's latent function of socialization).

Even when focusing on classes within the school, Parsons noted that functionalists were primarily concerned with the problems of, first,

> . . . how the school class functions to internalize in its pupils both the commitments and capacities for successful performance of their future adult roles and, second, of how it functions to allocate these human resources within the role structure of the adult society.
>
> Parsons, 1959, p 297

To a certain extent functionalists see schools as taking raw products (the students) and processing them with the result that an 'educational product' emerges when a young person leaves school. Func-

tionalists probe further by raising questions about the 'processing' that takes place in schools and the influence of the organizational structure of schools. Their approaches to the study of systems therefore help us to identify and dissect what we are looking at, but they have been criticized for stopping at description and not being concerned with the problems of social inequalities, social conflict and social change (as they tend to assume a gradual movement towards equilibrium). For example, when Richardson used this approach in the study of a comprehensive school in Bristol (1973, 1975) she found that the open systems model was defective because schools could not be detached from the influence of the wider society.

Since the 1970s the effects of radical educational reforms has meant that sociologists have tended to shift their interest away from the study of education structures towards the analysis of policy-making and the effects of policy-implementation. This does not mean that functionalist ideas and systems theories are without their uses, as a complex understanding of both can contribute more to our understanding of social systems. The systems analysis associated with the political scientist David Easton (1966) has often been included in the study of education policy. For example, Brown and Howell (1983) used Eastonian systems theory to shed light on two pieces of British education policy: the Inner London Education Authority's review of its Vocational Further Education service, and London University's introduction of a B.Ed degree. This involved identifying inputs, processes, outcomes and the effects that outcomes may have on new inputs (the feedback loop). Thus, the flow of effects from the wider social environment, including subsystems (also called 'parapolitical' systems, such as universities, LEAs, churches and companies) and the parent system (the national system), could influence inputs into the system which are converted into demands, support and then outputs. Brown and Howell explain the difference between *wants* and *demands* as follows.

> The main disturbance to which the political system is subject consists of those wants of members whose fulfilment appears to require an authoritative allocation. Wants do not automatically become allocations, since they are filtered both at the point of entry into the system, and in their path through it, by gatekeepers such as interest groups, political parties and administrators. Those wants which succeed in entering a system become 'demands'. Wants are reduced through collection and combination into a common demand; they are both broadened in scope and pruned to a more restricted number on which attention can be focused. A demand therefore is a want which has reached the political agenda as a basis for a political decision. Clearly the number of wants expressed at any time is far greater than the number of demands.
>
> Brown and Howell, 1983, pp 18–21

Brown and Howell show how the input and processing of demands can be combined with various types of support (again from the wider social environment) in order to determine outputs (which again stimulate inputs). This analytical approach helps to explain how some kinds of wants are not identified as demands and some demands take higher priority than others. It also explains the interrelationship between demands, support and policy-making.

Bureaucracy

One common perception of education systems is of structures in which individual identities can be lost among the procedures, tasks and huge assortment of officials involved in its administration; in other words, these structures are perceived as bureaucracies. Studies of bureaucracies often start with what Max Weber identified as their five characteristics:

1. An administrative hierarchy with a structure of command.
2. Specialized training and a clear career structure.
3. Areas of expertise with a division of labour among experts.
4. Specific rules and procedures according to which the bureaucracy completes tasks.
5. Formalized and impartial methods of dealing with clients.

Weber was particularly concerned about bureaucracy as a source of power.

Once it is fully established, bureaucracy is among those social structures which are among the hardest to destroy . . . and where the bureaucratization of administration has been completely carried through, a from of power relation is established that is practically unshatterable. . . . After all, bureaucracy strives merely to level those powers that stand in its way and in those areas that, in the individual case, it seeks to occupy. We must remember this fact – which we have encountered several times and which we shall have to discuss repeatedly: that 'democracy' as such is opposed to the 'rule' of bureaucracy.

> Weber, 1968 (original 1922), p 987ff., cited in Lee and Newby, 1983, p 193

QUESTIONS

Do you agree with Weber's claim that democracy is opposed to the 'rule' of bureaucracy? Consider your own educational institution.

(a) Does it fit Weber's five characteristics of a bureaucracy?
(b) Could your institution be described as a democracy?

Weber's interest in bureaucracies was linked to his concern about the negative impact of processes of rationalization and we can see more up-to-date expressions of this concern amongst educationalists. For example, Broadfoot (and others) saw the rhetoric used, and its emphasis on administration and efficiency, as a means of legitimating Conservative ideology during the 1980s.

> So powerful is the appeal of scientism at the present time that in curriculum, management and finance there is a growing tendency for issues to be defined as simply technical problems, to which an optimum solution exists. The effect of this trend is not only to preclude explicit discussion of the different educational values that might be involved in any particular issue, but also to conceal a growing lack of consensus over educational priorities in general by defining them off the agenda of debate. Arguments couched in terms of efficiency and rationality thus provide a spurious but extremely effective legitimation for the pursuit of particular educational priorities.
>
> Broadfoot, 1985, p 273

Governance and regulation

An analysis of education systems also relates to broad issues of governance and regulation and by the end of the twentieth century these terms were assuming greater importance in debates about education systems. The term *governance* can be widely defined beyond the image of a 'government', in a traditional sense, to include various processes of co-ordination and collective decision-making from micro (e.g. family) through to macro (e.g. government agency) levels. It includes an interest in how institutions are changing the way in which they are 'governed', in ways that might be perceived to be legitimate or illegitimate. The term *regulation* relates to a more distinct process. In political science this is concerned with particular aspects of public policy-making (such as public choice theory) and includes specific areas such as environmental regulation, the regulatory state, international regulatory regimes, debates about the future regulation of the welfare state, deregulationism and so on.

Roger Dale showed how we may study the governance and regulation of education via a simple analytical model in which he considered regulation as one area of governance activities (see Figure 4.2). This table allows us to identify and analyse influences on the governance of education by splitting governance activities into funding, regulation and provision/delivery, and splitting coordinating institutions into the state, market and community. It

Figure 4.2 A simple representation of the governance of education

Governance Activities	Co-ordinating Institutions		
	State	Market	Community
Funding by	Taxation	Private	Organizations, e.g. churches
Regulation	Rules, laws, state control	Deregulation, removing barriers	Organizational rules
Provision/ Delivery to	Citizens	Consumers	Members

allows us to see how each may differ from system to system.

Funding may take many forms and Dale lists some common features. It may be

- directed to organizations, individuals or both;
- available to members of, and/or organizations within a given population or targeted at particular groups or individuals;
- subject to conditions;
- available only on a competitive basis;
- in the form of grants, loans, investment or subsidy.

The only method of *state funding* is through taxation and the state may try to reduce public expenditure on education in order to reduce taxation. *Market funding* can involve the provision of private (non-maintained) schools, supported by fees paid by parents, but also including some state subsidies and community funds (for example, from religious or voluntary organizations). *Community funding* involves funding from, and to, identifiable groups (such as religious or voluntary organizations) which decide how to allocate them. In the UK all three types of funding have been influenced by the state-induced proliferation of 'non-state' funding of education, whereby user fees have grown as a proportion of educational funding in 'state' schools as well as in private schools.

Regulation can also take more than one form. Dale notes that it is shaped by the ultimate ability of the state to determine policy and sanctions through the law. This means that there are some *rule-governed* forms of regulation, providing constraints within a legal framework, controlling inputs, channelling demands and generally influencing behaviour 'before the fact'. *Goal-governed* forms of regulation, however, come 'after the fact' (*ex post*), involving a focus on outputs and operational procedures and an evaluation of how these have conformed to performance targets.

Dale described three of the most common characteristics of *state regulation*. First, it may actually involve *deregulation* and, indeed, this does seem to have happened in many countries, where the pattern has shifted from a European model (of state intervention as a response to the failure of the market to provide) to the traditional American model of non-interference in the educational market.

The aim is to encourage new providers of education to enter the market in order to remove some of the pressure on the state. Second, it may involve *juridification*; in other words, the use of the law in structuring social, political, cultural and economic life. This involves constraining political actors by constitutional means. Third, it may involve *new public management*, which emphasizes the importance of public accountability and is the policy expression of public choice theory.

Market regulation obviously relates to what has already been said about state deregulation as it involves the removal of barriers to encourage greater consumer choice of schools. The assumptions behind this have led to many criticisms, including those of Polanyi (1975) who noted that markets are not natural institutions because they are still shaped by patterns of state regulation.

According to Dale, *provision and delivery* can focus on citizens of the state, consumers in the market or members of communities. When provision is for *citizens*, the state tries to ensure that everyone has access to good-quality education. As it is provided by universal entitlement this is likely to involve highly centralized bureaucratic controls. If the image is of provision for *consumers*, the central focus is on efficiency and issues regarding equal opportunities tend to be played down or excluded. As the basic principle is one of ability to pay, the possession of material and cultural capital leads to high-quality education, whilst those without it receive low-quality education. When provision and delivery is by the community the important principle is one of *eligibility of membership* to the community. Educational benefits will only be given to recognized members. This involves a shift from a welfare state (involving universal provision for citizens) to what Santos (1991) has called a 'welfare society', involving a new form of particularism based on social or class privileges or membership of an identifiable group.

Green, Wolf and Leney (1999) state that governance and regulation have become the most contested areas of educational reform in countries within the European Union (EU). By the end of the twentieth century education systems in the EU seemed to have become too complex to be administered centrally and decentralization was one way of relieving financial pressures on central government, achieving more efficient use of resources and spreading responsibility for unpopular austerity measures. There has been a widespread tendency in EU countries to devolve some decision-making and operational powers (see Figure 4.3). Decentralization also tackles the problem of social fragmentation and pressures from various social groups (religions, ethnic minorities, the changing middle classes) for more choice and autonomy in education. In this way it can be presented as a way of enhancing democracy and appeals to various political parties. New Right governments have favoured decentralization through a (quasi-)market system, and the New Labour government since 1997 has retained some aspects of the market system whilst favouring decentralization through a community-orientated approach, involving partnerships and 'stakeholder democracy'. In both cases we can see an extension of partnerships in educational decision-making beyond the traditional 'triangle of tension', between central government, teachers' unions and local authorities (influential from the 1940s to the 1970s),

to include the social interests of 'consumers', in the form of parents, and 'stakeholders', in the form of employers and local interest groups.

Assessment and academic groupings

Systems of education are obviously influenced at a very fundamental level by assumptions about the nature of 'intelligence', 'knowledge' and 'ability' and how such attributes can be measured. This is also considered elsewhere in this book (e.g. Chapter 2 about researching educational standards and Chapter 3 about biological determinism and social construction), but here we will look at how various ideas about the purpose of assessment can influence education systems. Assessment is rarely as objective as it is generally perceived to be, as it is, after all, a social process.

First, is the purpose of the assessment seen as 'summative' or 'diagnostic'? *Summative* assessment aims to describe an individual's current intelligence, knowledge or ability. This may lead to a grading, or some other type of summary or label (for example, cumulative grades at GCSE or SCE will show up in a 'league table' of schools). Yet, even a descriptive assessment of this kind can lead to a variety of results. Objectivity is very difficult to achieve, and examiners may disagree about what questions should be asked, what skills should be tested, and how results should be interpreted. *Diagnostic* assessment is likely to include a summative assessment but will go further by providing an indication of what the next stage of the learning process should be (for example, by identifying special educational needs). Positive action can be taken, but again we can reasonably ask how objective the assessor's recommendations can be.

Decisions also have to be made in the selection of a standard, or standards, against which individuals are to be judged. When *criterion-referencing* is used, there is some sort of list of criteria available to provide guidance concerning the standard that has been reached. An individual is assessed according to how the criteria have been satisfied, and the assessment can be made by a tutor or by

Figure 4.3 Models of regulation and governance

	1975	1995
Centralized (with some devolution)	Luxembourg Portugal Greece France Italy Austria Spain Sweden Finland Belgium	Luxembourg Portugal Greece France Italy Austria
Regional devolution (by language, community and region)	Switzerland (non-EU) Germany	Switzerland Germany Belgium Spain
Local control (ecclesiastical)	Denmark UK Ireland	Denmark Finland Sweden Ireland
Institutional autonomy in quasi-market	Netherlands	Netherlands UK

Source: Green, Wolf and Leney, 1999, Figure 2.2, p 80

the student (e.g. self-assessment using a tutorial on computer). When *norm-referencing* is used, the performance of one individual is ranked in comparison with that of others. Usually the aim of this approach is to ration the number of 'passes' or qualifications (for example, in the use of an 11+ examination to allocate children to a limited number of grammar school places).

Once students have been graded, decisions still have to be made about how the results from tests in a range of subjects should be used to determine the way they are grouped within an educational institution. Should they be grouped according to aggregate scores from a range of subjects (*streaming*), should different competencies in different subjects be taken into account (*setting*) or should students of diverse abilities be grouped together (*mixed ability grouping*)? Norm-referencing and streaming gradually became less common during the second half of the twentieth century as the National Curriculum set targets for criterion-referencing and made different abilities in different subjects more noticeable.

Where *streaming* did (and sometimes still does) exist the whole year group was divided into different classes according to overall ability, such as classes A, B and C, with the A stream having the highest aggregate grades and the C stream having the lowest aggregate grades. Sometimes schools gave streams alternative names in order to conceal positive or negative labelling but staff and students still tended to be aware of the differentiation and respond accordingly. Hargreaves described this in his study of Lumley Secondary Modern School (1967) when he developed an ideal type model to explain the different cultures in different streams. Lacey also identified some of the social processes associated with streaming in his study of Hightown Grammar School in Greater Manchester (1966 and 1970). In the mixed ability first year all boys displayed a high commitment to the norms of the school but, once they were streamed in the second year, they became more polarized into pro- and anti-school cultures. Such studies discovered that teaching staff also become 'streamed' into high- and low-status groups, the 'best' teachers teaching the 'best' pupils with no allowance made for extra skills needed for teaching children with a low aggregate ability.

Setting was already popular in many schools before the introduction of a National Curriculum in which targets were set for different subjects. This involves allocation to a particular group according to ability in a particular subject; for example, a pupil may be in the 'top set' for maths and the 'bottom set' for English. This does not necessarily mean an end to the anti-school subcultures associated with lower streams because some students will consistently appear in most of the top sets or most of the bottom sets. Moreover, Lambart's (1976) study of Mereside Grammar School in Greater Manchester identified a group of third-year (year 9) girls called the 'Sisterhood', who formed an anti-school culture although they were labelled as above average ability and put in the same sets.

A combination of streaming and setting can be seen in what is generally called *banding*. In this system pupils are subdivided into broad ability groups, such as above average, average and below average, and within these groups parallel classes are established which contain pupils of similar ability. This could be seen in Ball's (1981) study of Beachside Comprehensive where, of ten classes in each year group, four constituted Band One for the most able students, four were in Band Two and two were in Band Three for the least able. His findings were similar to those of Lacey in that Band Two pupils were regarded by teachers as a discipline problem and Band One as the ideal type of pupils. Ball also found that pupils made friendships mainly with others in their band and were to some extent hostile to those in other bands. Beachside changed to mixed ability grouping while he was there.

Mixed ability grouping means that pupils may be distributed randomly (or purposely) into classes containing an assortment of different abilities. However, Barker-Lunn (1970) and Nash (1971) both found that streaming occurred in non-streamed schools in a covert way; for example, when teachers allocated pupils to different tables according to how 'bright' they thought they were. Ball (1981) found that when Beachside Comprehensive School changed to mixed ability grouping it helped to prevent the development of an anti-school culture but did not prevent sharp divisions in friendship according to ability and social class. Moreover, the aspirations of working-class pupils were reduced as they could no longer aim to be top of the class.

Another type of grouping not generally found in UK schools is that of *grading*. This involves allocation to a class according to attainment and irrespective of age group. Pupils of different ages may therefore study together, as some who are struggling repeat a year and some who are doing particularly well work with others who are older than themselves. This system is widely used in some other countries (including the USA, Australia, Belgium, Austria, Italy, Luxembourg and the Netherlands).

Special educational needs

The changing position of children and adults with special educational needs has possibly been more radical than any other aspect of the UK's education systems. Indeed, until the changes initiated during the 1970s, children with physical or mental disabilities were usually categorized by certain medical terms and regarded as being primarily the responsibility of the medical professions, rather than having a place within the schooling system. Since then the whole discourse and rhetoric associated with special needs has changed dramatically. Until the 1940s children with severe learning difficulties were generally described as 'idiots' or 'imbeciles' and between 1945 and 1981 they were called 'subnormal', all terms which, by the end of the twentieth century, had become not only politically incorrect but also abhorrent.

In 1978 the report of the committee chaired by Baroness Mary Warnock recommended that medical categories should be replaced by a more general concept of 'special educational need'. Such needs include temporary as well as permanent requirements, in recognition of the finding that, although the usual medical categories only covered about 2 per cent of the school population, it is likely that about 20 per cent of children may have some sort of special educational needs at some time during their school careers. The committee also recommended new diagnostic assessment of needs via the completion of a detailed statement (since then often called 'statementing'), more care-

ful consultation with parents and the integration of children with SEN into mainstream schools where possible (an approach that had already been partially initiated in the 1976 Education Act). It distinguished three types of integration:

- Locational, involving the provision of special units or classes on the site of an ordinary school.
- Social, meaning that children with SEN share time and space with other children outside the classroom.
- Functional, meaning that children with SEN share lessons with others on a full-time or part-time basis.

It also noted that positive discrimination of this kind required extra resources (material, human and in terms of expertise).

The 1981 Education Act implemented many of these recommendations and, since the 1980s, the proportion of children with SEN who are educated in 'special' schools has declined. However, the Act was criticized for its lack of commitment to the extra resources Warnock deemed essential for successful integration (see Chapter 10) and for concentrating on the 2 per cent who were expected to have statements.

> The whole concept of 'statementing' for only a few children, with the rest supposedly having their needs met according to what individual schools can provide, must be radically rethought. And this is more urgent as schools become increasingly competitive over examination results and have to manage their own finances . . .
> With hindsight, what is happening now should have been expected. Parents are pressing in increasing numbers for statements for their children since only then, it seems, can they be assured of special provision. Local authorities are increasingly drawing up statements, not in accordance with the child's assessed needs, but with what they think they can afford.
>
> Warnock, 1992

Since 1981, new measures have gradually been introduced to improve educational provision for children with SEN, including the introduction of 'whole school' involvement in the development of relevant policies and the requirement (since 1994) that local education authorities follow a Code of Practice on SEN and report on its management to parents. Colleges and universities are also required to provide access and facilities for students with SEN. However, it is clear that structural changes alone are not enough and in Chapter 5 we will consider some of the wider issues associated with special educational needs.

The curriculum

Just as assessment is not a natural process, decisions about the content of the curriculum are influenced by cultures, norms and competing perspectives (see the quote at the start of this chapter). Also see the section about the curriculum in Chapter 5 where the cultural relativism of curriculum contents will be discussed. Here we will just consider how control of the curriculum has changed.

Until the 1980s the school curriculum was generally determined by the school and its teachers and the expression 'the secret garden of the curriculum' was commonly found in educational discourse as outsiders were often unaware of what information was transmitted within the classroom. As far back as 1976 the Labour Prime Minister James Callaghan voiced his support for a national core curriculum in his Ruskin speech and (despite some opposition when it was introduced in 1988) some form of National Curriculum now has considerable cross-party support. Indeed it now seems that opposition to the principle of a National Curriculum mainly comes from some Liberal Democrats and nationalist parties, whose policies

have traditionally maintained a strong emphasis on decentralization. Sociologists too have started to accept the benefits of a National Curriculum (for example, as a way of reducing gendered subject choice and creating a greater understanding of normative standards), although they are still concerned about the content of the curriculum, its potential or actual overloading, its modes of assessment and the reporting of comparative standards.

The potential overloading of the curriculum has become a particular problem as demands for new subjects and types of skills have increased over time. Children now need to understand more sophisticated developments in the mass media and information technology. The European Commission's White Paper, *Teaching and Learning: Towards the Learning Society* (1995) identified the development of effective education-industry links as a priority and noted that there was a pressing need for more information technology skills within the workforce, and therefore to equip every school with up-to-date computer technology. In 1995 the European Commission also showed how the influence of new technology and work organization could be seen in changing ideas about the meaning of responsibility, expertise, interdependence and learning (see Figure 4.4). Globalizing processes such as membership of the European Union helped to shift languages from being an option for those in grammar schools who were regarded as academically able to being compulsory in nearly all schools (although the requirement to learn a language has existed longer in Scottish schools than in other schools in the UK). Decentralization and increasing awareness of national identities has also increased the use of the Welsh language in Welsh schools. Increasingly

Factors of competence	Old content	New content
Responsibility	Based on behaviour – such as effort and discipline	Based on taking initiatives
Expertise	Related to experience	Cognitive – identify and solve problems
Interdependence	Sequential; hierarchic	Systemic; group working
Training	Acquired once and for all	Continuous
Learning	Passive learning – being trained	Responsible for own learning – self-learning, lifelong

Source: European Commission (1995b) adapted by Green, Wolf and Leney, 1999, Figure 3.3, p 128

Figure 4.4 Shifts in competencies deriving from new technologies and new work organization

multi-cultural and diverse societies have also led to an emphasis on civil, social and individual behaviour and attitudes. The loss of job security has led to a greater awareness of the need for flexible or transferable skills and competencies such as learning to learn and think, solve problems, show initiative, work in a group and work independently. There have been attempts to introduce work experience into secondary education (such as the Technical and Vocational Education Initiative, TVEI) and students in many schools now expect a short period of work experience. Yet as the curriculum has become increasingly diverse, and students have been stretched, there have been concerns about the potential loss of more basic skills and renewed pressure to improve literacy and numeracy skills.

QUESTIONS

The National Curriculum has changed since its introduction in 1988 and was amended again in the year 2000. Consider the following questions in order to study its current constitution. (See Longman's annual *Education Yearbook*.)

What core and foundation subjects are included in the National Curriculum?

What are key stages, attainment targets, programmes of study and strands?

How does the National Curriculum differ in England and Wales, Scotland and Northern Ireland?

How is the National Curriculum managed in the school timetable and classroom?

How does the National Curriculum apply to children with special educational needs?

What sort of assessment is used in the National Curriculum; descriptive or prescriptive, criterion-referencing or norm-referencing?

Can a National Curriculum be politically neutral?

Types of schools

There are so many types of schools provided in the UK that they cannot all be considered in this chapter (although many more are described in the Glossary). Here we will simply consider some common types of schools (see Figure 4.5) accord-

Figure 4.5 Stages in UK education

School	Age	Year	National Curriculum Key Stages 1–4 and other qualifications
Infant	5–6	1	
	6–7	2	1
Junior	7–8	3	
	8–9	4	
	9–10	5	
	10–11	6	2
Secondary	11–12	7	
	12–13	8	
	13–14	9	3
	14–15	10	
	15–16	11	4
School leaving age	16		GCSE or SCE (Scottish Standard Grade)
6th Form or college	16–17	12	SCE (Scottish Higher Grade) or A levels/BTEC/GNVQ
	17–18	13	
	17		Start of a Scottish degree
	18		Start of a degree in the rest of the UK

ing to their modes of selection, the age of their intake and the form of funding.

Primary school provision could consist of one school covering the whole age range of children aged five to ten or eleven or may be split into two schools; an *infant* school for children aged five to seven (ending at Key Stage 1), and a *junior* school for children aged seven to eleven (ending at Key Stage 2). In some areas children leave primary school early (e.g. aged eight) and move to secondary school late (e.g. aged thirteen). The intervening years are then spent at a *middle* school. *Secondary* schools consist of any type of schools for children aged eleven to sixteen (ending at Key Stage 4 with General Certificate in Secondary Education, GCSE, or Scottish Certificate of Education, SCE, examinations) and sometimes include a sixth form (years 12–13) for young people aged sixteen to eighteen who take A level GCSE examinations, Scottish Highers or BTEC courses. As secondary schools are designated just according to age range, the wide range of school types can seem rather confusing (including high schools, comprehensives, grammar schools, secondary modern schools, technical schools and city technology colleges; see the Glossary).

Such a diverse range of schools (especially secondary schools) exists in the UK that the term 'school system' no longer seems as appropriate as it was in the 1950s (when most children were educated in a bipartite system) or 1960s (when comprehensive schools were more common). Indeed it is modes of selection that helps to distinguish between the many types of secondary schools. When studying the convergence and divergence of education systems in the European Union, Green, Wolf and Leney grouped the various ways in which children are allocated to secondary schools into three types or models.

A TYPOLOGY OF ADMISSION POLICIES

Model 1: Zoned comprehensive. In principle a mixed ability and mixed social intake, delayed specialization into vocational, academic or other tracks, a broad curriculum. There may be four ways of trying to achieve a mixed ability intake:

1. Children are obliged to attend their nearest secondary school and/or one linked to their feeder primary school. This works when local areas have a relatively mixed social composition.
2. Children are 'bussed' into zones in order to achieve a social balance. This has been an unpopular practice in some parts of the USA and has not been government policy in the UK (although there has been some bussing of students to integrated schools in Northern Ireland).
3. School catchment areas may be drawn up in ways that include a mixture of social and economic community types.
4. Parents may choose from a range of schools but their applications are judged by schools according to various selection criteria, in order to achieve a socio-economic balance.

Model 2: Open enrolment in comprehensive and partially comprehensive systems. This gives parents more freedom of choice and allows schools to compete with each other for students and, therefore, resources. However, an element of choice suggests diversification in the type of schools provided and this may contradict the principles of comprehensivization, which is based on the notion of equal entitlement to common learning experiences. In the UK diversification has been encouraged without an emphasis on equality. Since 1997 the Labour government has allowed comprehensive schools to select up to 15 per cent of their pupils on the basis of ability and has retained grant maintained (now called 'foundation') schools and city technology colleges. This obviously promotes status differentiation between schools.

Model 3: Selection by ability. Children are selected according to an assessment of their abilities. This selection may be by examination, by teachers' recommendations or by a mixture of both. Germany has traditionally maintained a selective system for admission to its *Gymnasien, Realschulen, Hauptschulen* and *Gesamtschulen*. In the UK this is common in Northern Ireland, less common in England and Wales and quite rare in Scotland. Selection by ability does not allow for real parental choice, although some parents will make a great effort to ensure that their children go to a high-status academic school.

Adapted from Green, Wolf, and Leney, 1999

Question

Consider arguments for and against the bussing of students from one area to a school in another area. Green, Wolf and Leney claim that, within the European Union, there has been growing pressure to move towards Model 2. Why might that be the case?
Do you favour one of the models? If so, why?

The *bipartite system* of selection (see Green, Wolf and Leney's Model 3) was the most common form of secondary provision between 1944 and the 1960s and still exists in Northern Ireland and some other areas of the UK. In this system children are assessed during their final year of primary education and allocated to (usually) a *grammar school* or a *secondary modern school* on the basis of their results. Criticisms of what was largely a bipartite system gradually gained strength during the 1950s and 1960s. These were mainly concerned with the assumptions, firstly, that intelligence could be assessed accurately at the age of 11 and, secondly, that the abilities identified at that age would be fixed for life. It was also found that relatively few children from working-class backgrounds were 'passing' the 11+ to find a place on the 'ladder' of educational opportunity and that girls were often discriminated against in the allocation of grammar school places. There were also regional disparities in the provision of grammar school places, making it more difficult to 'pass' the 11+ examination in some areas than in others. Although a bipartite system still exists in some LEA areas, and grammar schools still have widespread public support (McKenzie, 1993, pp 161–5), the case for this sort of selection was lost in mainstream British sociology a long time ago.

Since the 1940s the majority of current EU countries have gradually moved towards the comprehensive model. However, there are still essentially selective systems in Austria, Belgium, Germany, Ireland (in part), Luxembourg and the Netherlands and it is interesting to see that most of these countries have been influenced by German language and culture, which includes strong traditions of social partnership, craft traditions and high levels

SELECTION AT 11+ IN TORYTOWN

Until the 1990s the Torytown LEA remained committed to a policy of selection at 11+. Pupils in the Torytown area were assessed during their last year at primary school by a mixture of written tests (one in the autumn term and one in the spring term) and continuous assessment by their teachers. Teachers placed pupils in a numerical rank order for their class or school. If a child was ranked tenth by the teacher and came fifth in the test, his/her actual examination mark would be added to the test mark of the child who actually came tenth. The final mark was a combination of the two and therefore depended not only on the child's own examination result but also the result of the child coming tenth. At the time of the second test in the spring teachers again placed pupils in a rank order. The averages from the autumn and spring examinations and rankings were used to find the final average for the child. Parents were informed of the results of the practice tests but not the actual tests and assessments used for selection at 11+. As they would not know how the system worked, they could not appeal on the grounds that a teacher had underestimated their child or that the result of the child who got the mark that teachers predicted for their child was particularly low.

In 1989 this numerical ranking was replaced by a system of ranking into three groups by the headteacher, the groups being secondary modern school, grammar school and borderline cases. There were no standard activities and the assessment was based on observation in class together with activities and testing during the last two years at primary school. If the test result contradicted the headteacher's assessment, the pupil's case was referred to a Review Panel. However, in 1989 over 450 cases were considered by the Review Panel and this had to be done in a short time, raising doubts about how much attention could be devoted to each child.

The pass rates for individual primary schools in Torytown tended to differ according to the socio-economic composition of their catchment areas. In the most affluent, rural areas of Torytown it was usual for nearly half the candidates to reach pass standards, whilst in the less affluent, urban areas it was often the case that less than 25 per cent reached that standard. Some schools in one particularly deprived area rarely obtained any passes. Before 1975 assessment results were therefore adapted by applying different pass rates in different areas, in order to improve the opportunities of children in deprived areas. Thus, a child attending one school could get a grammar school place with a lower grade than a pupil attending another school. Since 1975 no notice has been taken of the child's school or area and the grade needed for a pass is the same for all.

Results of 11+ assessments could also be influenced by the gender of the child. It was originally decided that equal percentages of boys and girls should go to grammar schools. As more girls tended to do well in the examination, some of them had to get a higher grade than boys in order to pass. In 1989 the Equal Opportunities Commission insisted that a new method of selection should be used and that the pupils' sex should not be considered. As a result, in that year, 34 per cent of boys were selected for grammar schools compared to 41 per cent of girls. When a Torytown Education Officer was interviewed for this research he argued that the previous system was fairer because it helped under-achieving boys to get a grammar school place.

Some of these problems have been tackled by many LEAs via the existence of what has sometimes been called a 13+ selective process. This means that, when teachers and/or parents feel that a child was wrongly allocated at 11+, or had since shown signs that s/he would benefit from a grammar school place, it might be possible to move from a secondary modern school to a grammar school. (Cases of movement in the opposite direction, from grammar school to secondary modern school, are virtually unknown.) Some students have also moved from secondary modern schools to grammar school sixth forms to take A levels. When two of the Torytown cohort expressed satisfaction with their children's secondary modern school education it was found that their children had later moved to grammar schools.

> [Torytown] have a good arrangement that if you fail the 11+ you can be reviewed at twelve to go to the grammar school. You can move at any age. It was easy for my daughter to move to a grammar school from a secondary modern to do A levels.
>
> Caroline, 1988

SELECTION AT 11+ IN LABOURVILLE

In 1988 one of the Labourville cohort (Hugh) noted that, years earlier, whilst his son was at a grammar school, he had attended a public meeting about proposals to change Labourville to a comprehensive system, which lead him to question the bipartite system. A grammar school headteacher spoke at the meeting about the different 11+ pass rates applied to various schools in the area in order to give children in socially disadvantaged areas a better chance of passing. Hugh had thought that the same pass rate applied to all and, although he was concerned about socially disadvantaged children, he decided that whether or not allowances were made for differences between schools, the whole problem meant that the 11+ system was unfair. His son's school, in Labourville, became part of a comprehensive school whilst his son was still a pupil there and the family had no complaints.

Jeremy was a primary school headteacher who, as a child, went to a Labourville grammar school before comprehensive schools were introduced in that area. He believed that 'real' comprehensive schools offered the best all-round education and provided a distinction between 'real' or 'true' comprehensives and those that are comprehensive in name only.

> A lot of the schools in [Labourville] are really secondary moderns called comprehensives, but that's the nature of the area. The grammar school I went to in [Labourville] – lads came to it from all over the place, not just [Labourville], as there were not enough Catholic boys from [Labourville] of that ability. In [Labourville] now most comprehensives accommodate people who probably would have gone to a secondary modern. A true comprehensive would have the facilities, staff and width of the curriculum to offer a wide choice.
>
> Jeremy, 1988

Questions

Should there be different pass rates for different schools?
Should schools aim to include equal numbers of boys and girls?
Can the existence of a 13+ resolve the problems associated with selection at 11+?
Is it possible to ensure that comprehensive schools are 'true' comprehensives, rather than comprehensive in name only?

of unionization. These characteristics have legitimized a system which differentiates young people into different tracks, each with its own identity, status and social value and usually leading to different occupational destinations. This sort of legitimacy for selection has not been sustained in the UK because of the declining influence of craft traditions and the trade unions.

Types of schools can also be distinguished according to their source of funding, of which there are four main types. *Maintained* schools are all types of 'state' schools, financed (i.e. maintained) by public taxation. This may be taxation paid to central government, which funds *foundation* (previously grant maintained) schools or taxation paid to local councils, which funds *community* schools (previously local education authority – LEA – schools). Most *maintained* or *community* (since 1997) schools are supported by funds from their local education authority. *Foundation* schools have generally continued the sort of funding arrangements made in the past for grant maintained schools and direct grant schools, which were supported by a grant from central government.

Before the 1980s schools funded by central government grants were called *direct grant* schools and were situated on the boundary between the state and the private sector. Although partly financed by fees, they also received a government grant on condition that they supplied some free places for children who had been to state primary schools. The local authorities could therefore use high-status, direct grant schools as an additional source of grammar school places. The 1979–97 Conservative governments introduced *grant maintained* schools by encouraging schools maintained by LEAs to apply for grant maintained status (i.e. 'opt-out' of LEA control). When a Labour government was elected in 1997 most of the existing grant maintained schools took up the new option of changing their name to foundation schools. In theory a grant maintained or foundation secondary school can still have the characteristics of a comprehensive, grammar or secondary modern school.

Voluntary aided or *aided* (since 1997) schools are supported by a mixture of local education authority funds and church funds. Since the 1944 Education Act three types of schools established by a church body became voluntary aided schools, differing mainly in the extent to which the LEA finances and controls them; *aided*, *controlled* and *special agreement*. In 1997 the new Labour government effectively renamed voluntary aided schools as *aided schools*. Although some maintained schools (including grant maintained and aided) may be partly funded by private sources, parents are not officially required to pay fees for their children to attend.

HOW INDEPENDENT ARE INDEPENDENT (i.e. NON-MAINTAINED) SCHOOLS?

Non-maintained schools are often supported by the state in various direct or indirect ways. Since 1944 costs to the state may have included the following:

1. Tax concessions for fee-paying parents and for schools classed as charities. In 1983 indirect tax concessions amounted to nearly £500 million a year.
2. Fees paid by the state for children of VIPs serving abroad.
3. State services – training teachers, facilities for special educational needs, travel costs, etc.
4. Assisted Places were introduced by the 1980 Education Act. These involved means tested grants from central government to parents of 'academic' children towards the cost of fees at recognized schools. However, in 1988 a DES survey found that 10 per cent of these places were not used and in the same year an ISIS survey found that 60 per cent of parents had not heard of Assisted Places.
5. Some fees have been paid by LEAs. In 1985/6 a total of 1,576 Torytown children attended non-maintained schools. Most of these were funded by the LEA to attend non-maintained Roman Catholic grammar schools because the authority could not provide state grammar schools for its Catholic students. In the same year only 11 Labourville children attended non-maintained schools. (More information about this is provided later when we consider local education authorities.)

Non-maintained (*independent, private* or *public*) schools may be supported from various sources, including fees paid by parents, businesses and some state concessions. During the 1980s and 1990s some 'academically able' children from less affluent backgrounds were granted an 'Assisted Place' at a suitable non-maintained school, which meant that central government at least partly financed their education. The most elite non-maintained schools are called *public schools*.

Control of individual schools

As you can see above (Figure 4.3), the UK is one of only two European Union countries to move towards the creation of autonomous school management within a quasi-market system but this change has not been consistent throughout the four British regions. In England and Wales increasing proportions of school and college budgets have been delegated to individual institutions since 1988 (a modified policy being used in Scotland) through the introduction of local management powers, and since then financial delegation has risen to 90 per cent of the whole budget. Local management of schools and colleges has been advocated as a form of deregulation, providing an incentive for innovation, allowing teachers, lecturers and governors to respond to local needs and work effectively. It also complements any long-term movement towards decentralization either via a quasi-market or via an emphasis on community. Researchers have tended to find that local management of schools has positive effects on efficiency but their findings about improvements in teaching and learning have been mixed (Arnot, Bullock and Thomas, 1992; Levacic, 1995). Local management of schools can also have negative effects on teacher morale, as increasing workloads distances heads from classroom teachers (Fitz, Halpin and Power, 1993) and workloads for all teachers can affect health and morale (Dunham, 1992; Maychell, 1994).

As a result of the 1986 Education Act local education authorities lost their majority on school governing bodies, some of their places being taken by local employers and parents. The powers of school governors were also increased by the 1988 Education Reform Act, which also gave parents the right to send their children to any school, irrespective of its catchment area or local authority. Local authorities were obliged to pay for the education of children living in their areas but going to schools outside the area.

When studying individual schools, one fundamental question raised by sociologists and others is, *How much difference does the type of school attended have on educational outcomes?*

Answers to this question obviously depend on how we measure the effectiveness of a school and this is a major problem. 'Open enrolment' (Green, Wolf and Leney's Model 2) means that schools compete for pupils in the market place but, in order to allow parents free choice from a range of schools, the effectiveness of individual schools would obviously need to be monitored by measuring the performance of students. The publication of 'league tables' has been criticized for not measuring performance in absolute terms (i.e. by not taking into account the nature and abilities of the student intake; see Chapter 2). There are, nevertheless, many advocates of the need to measure 'school effectiveness' who challenge what they see as an earlier emphasis by sociologists on the external social influences on school achievement. Advocates of an approach that focuses more on individual schools have emphasized the importance of clear goals, high expectations, parental support, teacher participation in decision-making, strong leadership, rigorous academic standards and order and discipline (Chubb and Moe, 1990; Sexton, 1987). Sexton, Chubb and Moe are also concerned about the constraints imposed by bureaucratic control and the professional self-interest of teachers and suggest that schools should be able to compete with each other for students and resources in a type of market system.

As school choice was introduced in Scotland before other parts of the UK, researchers were able to study its effects in Scotland at quite an early stage. Adler, Petch and Tweedie (1989) found that the number of parents actively choosing their children's schools rose from 10,456 in 1982 to 23,075 in 1987, although nine out of ten Scottish children still attended their local school. The researchers found that, although some children from areas of multiple deprivation were able to move to better schools in nearby areas, the changes were leading to a 'two-tier' system of wider educational inequalities, as many children remained in schools in deprived urban areas. Since then other researchers (e.g. Gewitz, Ball and Bowe, 1995) have found that unpopular schools have entered a 'spiral of decline' as a result of limited resources and low teacher morale. Gewitz, Ball and Bowe (1995) and others (such as Bush, Coleman and Glover, 1993) also found that schools were using covert methods of selection in order to 'cream off' the best students and thus improve the school's performance and status. This 'creaming' included giving preference to children from middle-class homes and limiting the number of children with special educational needs (Vincent *et al.*, 1995).

The main problem associated with a quasi-market system in education is that the supply of schools is not elastic. They have fixed costs, cannot expand easily without it affecting the quality of their services, new schools cannot be established quickly and unpopular ('sink') schools may face a long period of gradual decline before closing; and this decline is likely to have negative effects on the remaining students. The introduction of market forces into state schools (together with support for private education) has involved increasing the

PARENTAL CHOICE IN TORYTOWN AND LABOURVILLE

That's a sore point that [choice of schools]. The choice was denied for the secondary school. We were given a place at one, so we asked for a place at another one; they told us we couldn't have it, so we ended up going to a third one. We went to appeal with the other two [children], they started off at one school and they moved the school to [. . .], we did get a choice with that. We got a choice with the primary schools.

Ryan, 1997

I know they can do [opt out] and I don't think it's a good idea. It's with the schools, whereas parents are supposed to have a choice. The choice is down to the headmaster, who selects which kids they want. Our daughter-in-law visited a school and the headmaster asked her about her child, because they wanted to assess him before accepting him, rather than her choosing the school.

Hugh, 1992

[Choice of school] I didn't. I went to [. . .] Junior which is over here and [. . .] Grammar which is just next door, all my friends went there and they said I had to go to [. . .] Grammar, which I didn't even know existed. There was five of us from our school. My mum and dad went to a tribunal and everything. I was really upset about it, but that didn't do any good, so we had to go to [. . .]. We were just on the borderline. They didn't have enough pupils. Presumably it was because we were near the bus-stop. Basically, that's what it boiled down to. [It was about a 10-minute walk to school she wanted, but instead she had to catch the bus.] We were about a metre outside the thing. They had a man out with a trundlemetre at the tribunal. It was barmy.

Sharon, 1997

All I know is from the people that I work with that they have awful trouble getting their children into the schools that they want them to go to. It's a real headache. It must be very stressful for young children to have to go through not only the 11+, but also the entrance exams to schools as well. To enter certain schools they need to take another exam.

Katherine, 1997

It was a bit difficult to get what we wanted, but in the long run we did get what we wanted. [Was this your first choice?] No. [How far down the list was it?] Second. But, having said that, I'm quite happy that its turned out this way now.

Kirsten, 1997

[Kirsten's son could have gone with most of his friends to the high school for which his primary school was a 'feeder' but the family visited other schools and chose another.] It's a very old school but I was quite impressed going into it. I know it may sound silly but it's kept nice. It's old but it's kept nice. You see we did go to look at [. . .] High and I got the shock of my life. It was horrible. And I do believe that it does matter, your surroundings. It does matter. It matters if you work in a horrible place. I mean the windows were broken. It was dirty. It's a shame because it just seemed to me like it was falling down and I thought, 'I don't want him to go there. I want him to go where he can learn then . . .' I was very shocked. It was horrible to see how it had been let go inside.

Kirsten, 1997

In 1993 Hackney Council distributed a circular setting out the options for increasing the number of co-educational places at borough schools. Angela Phillips highlighted some of the problems:

> There are four girls' schools, four mixed schools and two boys' schools in Hackney. People do not like boys' schools so they are under-subscribed; people do like girls' schools so they cannot be touched; but most of all people want co-ed schools which, given the above, they cannot have . . .
>
> If Hackney Council introduced co-education at one of the girls' schools . . . there would almost certainly be a campaign to protect it and then a vote to opt out of local authority control . . .
>
> Instead of facing this battle they will attempt to integrate girls into the first year of the roughest and least popular boys' school. If they succeed . . . they will have created the new co-ed school that parents have asked for and the numbers of girls in the other co-ed schools will drop still further . . .
>
> If people refuse to send their daughters to this school the council will be able to satisfy themselves that people don't want co-ed schools. Problem solved, subject closed.

Quotes and adaptation from Phillips, Angela, 1993

Questions

To what extent was genuine integration of the sexes possible in Hackney's co-educational schools?
Explain why more parents favoured girls' schools and co-educational schools than boys' schools.
Should efforts to provide parental choice (in Hackney and elsewhere) be abandoned?
See government websites for more up-to-date information about schools in Hackney.

---

many types of schools available, promoting parental choice, providing information about school performance and making funding dependent on school enrolments and outcomes. Yet many studies have found that, rather than diversifying educational experiences in many directions, educational markets are more likely to polarize intakes (Ambler, 1994, pp 454–476; Hughes *et al.*, 1996).

QUESTION

In economics, the concept of consumer sovereignty means that consumers decide what is produced. The mechanism of supply and demand suggests that if prices are too high, demand will be too low and, if prices are too low, demand will be too high. Can these assumptions about supply and demand be applied to education?

Further and higher education

The main change in further and higher education since 1944 is that it is continually moving further

and higher! It was noted in Chapter 1 that what seemed to be a good level of educational attainment in the 1940s was regarded as relatively inferior by the end of the twentieth century. The social, demographic and economic changes described earlier in this chapter help to explain why we are now faced with an apparently continuous process of *credential inflation*. This started during the 1960s when grammar schools lost their monopoly over the provision of examinations at school-leaving age, continued with the raising of the school-leaving age to sixteen in 1972 and gained speed as mass unemployment since the 1970s (especially among young people) made the competition for jobs particularly fierce. In 1984, 47 per cent of sixteen-year-olds were in full-time education but by 1994 it was 72 per cent, with the remainder mainly involved in part-time education or apprenticeships (EUROSTAT, 1997; European Commission, 1996). Indeed, although the school-leaving age has not officially been raised since 1972, the age at which young people leave education is continually being raised in practice, as most young people delay the start of work because they need to get more qualifications in order to improve their job prospects.

In some cases, when young people have left school with few, if any, qualifications, this delay is involuntary as the only alternative is unemployment. Young people, and their parents, are not only aware of the competitive labour market but also of the job insecurity associated with changing economic trends.

The lack of a 'job for life' also means that the availability of apprenticeships (so commonly found by even unqualified school leavers in the UK during the 1940s) has declined since the 1970s. The more markets have fluctuated, the less inclined employers are to invest in, and commit themselves to providing, lengthy training programmes which may also involve training staff who move on elsewhere. In the UK apprenticeships remain for very few skilled occupations, and they are associated with a few, often gender-specific, jobs such as hairdressing, construction and engineering (unlike in Germany, Austria, Denmark, the Netherlands and Switzerland where apprenticeships are still common). In the early 1990s some 'Modern Apprenticeships' were introduced in the UK, involving some government regulation and funding and it is possible that this may expand further. It is, however, difficult to find a recent, accurate figure of apprenticeships that are primarily based in the workplace (which most were during the 1940s) as some figures include young people who are primarily being trained in colleges. Writers such as Green, Wolf and Leney (1999) claim that thriving systems of apprenticeships are most likely to exist in countries with strong traditions of professional identities, social partnerships and intervention by the state in order to co-ordinate the roles of the various partners and regulate the labour market to maintain a link between qualifications and employment. In the UK there is a relatively loose linkage between qualifications and employment (Wolf, 1997), unlike some other countries, such as Germany and France, where national collective agreements and statutory regulations have linked qualifications with a wide variety of jobs.

Although employers have become less unwilling to meet the expenses involved in providing apprenticeships, many (particularly large-scale) employers are willing to promote work-based or work-related continuing vocational education for existing employees. This often involves short-term courses introduced to help employees to adapt to changes in the workplace by developing new skills. Indeed, Green, Wolf and Leney claim that, in the UK, participation in job-related training rose by 70 per cent between 1984 and 1990, although they also note that opportunities for further education often go to those who are already highly skilled and better educated. This means that a distinction has appeared between further education for existing employees and lower-status vocational training for the unemployed. In general, Bransma, Kessle and Munch (1995, p 24) suggest that vocational education in EU countries tends to serve the common functions of adaptation, innovation, promotion, second chance, curative and preventative, the last two relating to unemployment in particular. They also note that such diverse functions mean that it is only possible to speak of a 'system' of vocational education with great reservations.

It is, however, possible to identify a clear pattern of *academic drift* throughout the EU, by which educationalists mean the tendency of the public to perceive academic qualifications as superior to non-academic or vocational courses and therefore to favour academic routes. This status differentiation has been criticized by sociologists for the past 50 years, dating back to earlier concerns about the way that young people were labelled as 'sheep' and 'goats', according to whether or not they were academically inclined. The term *academic drift* also suggests that by the 1990s young people were moving into academic courses from a range of directions, with vocational/non-academic courses often taken as an alternative form of access. Indeed, the British government expressed its intention that, in addition to their vocational function, GNVQ (in Scotland GSVQ) qualifications should also provide a route into higher education. Students may therefore see the vocational benefits of such courses as less important than their role in providing entitlement to enter university. Vocational qualifications are also becoming more general in content in recognition that they may be treated as preparations for higher courses as well as to serve employers' demands for transferable skills. More young people are now working towards more than one qualification in order to improve their labour market position. This may involve failing one course and moving on to another or topping-up one qualification with another. For example, it was found that in England and Wales over a third of those who dropped out of Advanced GNVQs moved straight into another course of study (Further Education Development Agency *et al.*, 1997).

Green, Wolf and Leney's image of the previous structure of recruitment is of a pyramid, with the elite at the summit and the masses below. This meant that the masses could find reassurance by comparing themselves with others in a similar position. However, their new image (and one that is commonly used by other educationalists) is of those who fail in education constituting a long, thin tail to a relatively bulky animal (Green, Wolf and Leney, 1999, p 164). This group may conclude that, as they have not done well in education in the past, they will not do well in the future and become marginalized. For others, as more people get more

---

CREDENTIAL INFLATION AND ACADEMIC DRIFT

In 1950s Europe, only 3 per cent, not 33 per cent, of the age cohort attended university. In that situation, any employer knew that the vast majority of able and desirable employees were to be found in the non-graduate pool. It might be very enjoyable to go to university, and, indeed, be the route to the *élite*, to the top of the occupational pyramid. But for most people, in most working and social environments, it was simply irrelevant. Young people's decisions about what to do in life, and the vast majority of lifetime careers, were made without any reference to university at all.

Growth in participation triggers yet more growth because people – notably gatekeepers in employment and education – perceive skills and intelligence to be unequally distributed. (The *actual* way in which intelligence, or ability, or achievement are distributed in the population is quite irrelevant here. The important issue is how people *perceive* it to be distributed.) The normal distribution is a very useful encapsulation of this: of how people generally tend to see the world, and also of the way in which young people very definitely experience it. As a rule, people find it easy to distinguish the very good and the very bad. However, the bulk of examples tend to be perceived as in the middle and much less easy to rank and separate.

An employer, in a world where 3 per cent went to university, and when only 5 or 6 per cent took the upper secondary leaving certificates, perceived that tiny academic *élite* as concentrated at one extreme of the distribution, representing members of the upper rank of ability. However, that same employer also knew that such people were hard to get hold of, because so few, and that the vast bulk of the distribution, which had not got university degrees or higher certificates, included some very able people; this was the area from which he had to recruit.

But what happens when participation rates start to move up fast? Suppose one moves to a situation where three-quarters of the young population have baccalaureates and the like, and a quarter have degrees? At this point one is well into the large middle 'ability' group; and perceptions, and actions, will change. It is, theoretically, perfectly possible that many or most of the new graduates do not actually come from the top end of the distribution in terms of 'real' ability at all, but are scattered all over it. However, this is not a very obvious or indeed plausible conclusion for an employer or anyone else to reach. It is much simpler to conclude that the increase in the academically qualified population has all come from the upper end of the distribution. In practice this is exactly the simplifying assumption that employers do make. They hire the academically qualified.

Green, Wolf and Leney, 1999, pp 162–3

Questions

Do you agree with the writers' understanding of how gatekeepers (in employment and education) perceive the distribution of ability?

Do you think there is such a thing as 'real' ability?

---

qualifications, more people feel that they also have to have them. Even young people who are a moderate success in education will be aware that they will become more disadvantaged as their qualifications become more common. Students and their tutors have therefore become more concerned about the acquisition of transferable skills and during the 1990s they started to discuss 'graduateness'; that is, the various qualities (such as initiative, confidence, citizenship and communication skills) associated with being a graduate. Thus, graduates face a job market so competitive that it is not enough 'merely' to have a good degree; it is also necessary to display further credentials of excellence. They must aim for infallibility.

The constitution and types of students found in institutions of education have undergone radical change since the 1940s. A first stage was seen in the mass expansion of entry into higher education initiated by the introduction of polytechnics and the Open University during the 1960s. Such developments brought with them a growth in the number of mature undergraduates, more part-time undergraduates and more students who were working class, female, from ethnic minorities or had special educational needs. Universities have gradually introduced and improved their equal opportunities policies, starting with the most obvious issues associated with gender, ethnicity and social class and moving on to consider special educational needs and differentiation according to sexuality and age. Yet social class inequalities in access to higher education remain, as people from higher socio-economic groups are still more likely to attend university and the main beneficiaries of expansion have been the middle-classes (although it must be acknowledged that middle-class occupations have grown since 1944). The effects of unemployment and international economic competition led to a second stage of rapid growth during the 1980s and 1990s. As central governments found that support for higher education created a severe financial burden, they gradually withdrew student grants during the 1990s before introducing means-tested fees in 1998. This means that most students now have part-time (or even full-time) jobs whilst taking a full-time degree and/or face heavy debts after graduation as they pay back their student loans. Yet the pressures of credential inflation mean that they are almost forced into a never-ending search for academic perfection.

The tradition (or even rite of passage) of leaving home to study in a university has gradually started to decline with the growth in the numbers of mature students and as a result of financial pressures on younger students. More undergraduates now study at a local college of further education which may have effectively become a *college of further and higher education* as it provides all or part (typically the first year) of degree courses, using pathways franchised from their partner universities. Thus, although the binary divide between polytechnics and universities was ended in 1992, when polytechnics were given university status, new status divisions have opened up between universities and other colleges offering degree courses. New systems of competitive funding mean that money has been primarily channelled to universities according to their research, with teaching quality being a secondary criteria. This has helped to reinforce or extend existing institutional hierarchies. There has been a dramatic increase in marketing activities by colleges as a result of their greater autonomy and need to improve their funding by getting more students within a competitive market.

New funding mechanisms and reductions in unit costs have led to tough efficiency targets and in some cases colleges and universities have run into financial difficulties and there have been redundancies. Efficiency gains have also been made by reducing staff–student contact hours which, for some full-time courses, have fallen from an average 28 hours per week to about 15 (Further Education Development Agency *et al.*, 1997). Some institutions have responded by increasing resource-based learning to supplement the time spent with teachers, but doing so assumes that more students have an autonomous attitude towards their learning than may be the case (e.g. it may negatively affect the middle-ability students arriving in higher education because of academic drift). Success must be measured not only by the output of qualifications, but also by drop-out rates. Green, Wolf and Leney show (pp 49–50) that although the proportion of young people participating in further and higher education has increased, this is not necessarily matched by increases in satisfactory completion. In 1984, 24 per cent of the UK population aged 25–34 had completed tertiary education but by 1994 this figure had dropped to 23 per cent. They note that such figures must be treated with caution because of changes in the courses offered but they suggest possible concerns about policy. Until the 1990s British universities had very high completion rates, and high drop-out rates may be associated with widening access and increasing financial pressures on students.

Alongside the localizing features of higher education there is also a process of internationalization, as students who can travel long-distance for their studies have become even more geographically mobile. More British students are now taking all or part of their courses in other countries (especially in the European Union) and more students are coming to the UK from other countries. The European Union has introduced its own programmes such as ERASMUS and SOCRATES as well as facilitating international exchange programmes in general as a result of its policies of co-operation and co-ordination between member states. Researchers are also far more likely to work with researchers in other countries. Universities have created their own international offices, or administrative equivalents, in order to tackle issues such as international marketing and the comparability of credentials.

Britain has moved further than any other EU country towards the development of quasi-markets in education. Colleges and universities have faced rising student:staff ratios whilst still facing financial stringency in what is becoming a highly competitive market system. Since the 1970s management has been devolved to institutional levels whilst increasing central control has been exercised over curricula, qualifications and funding. Standards have therefore been monitored and new, more visible quality control procedures have emerged. Along with the development of new management evaluation, universities lost control over much of their quality assessment practices as they were brought within a national system of government-dominated assessment. Since the 1970s governments have encouraged universities to seek more private funding and a private university has been established (the University of Buckingham). As management has become engrossed in the problem of meeting the targets associated with student numbers and efficiency, it is possible that it will loose sight of the creativity of its students and lecturers.

QUESTION

Assess the positive and negative effects of the expansion of further and higher education.

National systems

If the organization and administration of education in the United Kingdom is rather confusing, it is largely because the UK itself is very confusing. The words 'Britain' and 'Great Britain' refer to England, Scotland and Wales and do not include Northern Ireland, whereas the 'UK' does include Northern Ireland, and the 'British Isles' includes the whole of the UK and the Republic of Ireland. Most importantly, the UK is united in that it constitutes a *state*, which has clearly defined geographical boundaries and some sort of central government (in Westminster). In the UK there are also separate national assemblies in Scotland, Wales and Northern Ireland and laws can vary between the nations. The word *nation* refers to a sense of identity or belonging which can exist among people who may be dispersed across the globe. It therefore makes sense to talk about the national pride and identity felt by Scots living in England, Wales, Northern Ireland or Australia! It also makes sense to talk about the *system* of education in the UK and the *systems* of education in England, Wales, Scotland and Northern Ireland.

Some sense can be made of the many variations in education systems if we note the claim made by Kellecher and Scott (1996) that systems of education in the EU have been responding to a common set of pressures and problems to which they have diverse solutions, depending on their national histories and institutions. Green, Wolf, and Leney (1999) split these national differences into four areas.

Education in Wales

Much of this book will refer to education in England and Wales as one regional system because that is how it has been perceived historically. England and Wales share the same qualifications, basic structure of institutions, and legal and financial framework for education, although Welsh schools have long had a different curriculum, giving a special place to the Welsh language (see Chapter 5 on ethnicity). However, like the Scots, the Welsh have their own political culture and less emphasis on competition between institutions.

In 1997 a referendum in Wales resulted in a vote in favour of the creation of a devolved Welsh parliament with various powers over its education system (although not including tax-raising powers). Indeed, in the lead-up to the actual vote for members of the assembly, the education minister for Wales (Peter Haine) experimented with the notion of diversity as an advertisement for the benefits of devolution and in April 1999 a plan was published

for the integration of all post-16 education in Wales. In 1998 the government at Westminster also decided to slim down the primary curriculum in England to make more time available for English, mathematics and science. However, Haine introduced a less vague and more interventionist approach for Wales, which involved making specific cuts in each of the non-core subjects to make sure that teachers dropped none of them.

In their campaigns leading up to the election of a Welsh assembly in May 1999 the main political parties provided a much clearer indication of how the Welsh and English systems may split in the future. The Labour Party promised to provide a nursery place for all three-year-olds in Wales. It was not committed to reforming A levels but seemed likely to revive plans for a broader baccalaureate qualification in view of a proposal by the Institute for Welsh Affairs for a WelshBac, based on the experience of providing the International Baccalaureate in Wales. The Liberal Democrats promised maximum class sizes of 30 for all primary schoolchildren (an extension of the government's pledge for five- to seven-year-olds) and a longer-term goal of no more than 25 to a class. They proposed a relaxation of the national curriculum to allow teachers more freedom for professional judgement and called for an emergency programme to provide financial incentives for councils to make school buildings fit for the twenty-first century. The Welsh nationalist party Plaid Cymru also proposed moving towards a Welsh baccalaureate and promised to abolish league tables, reform the school inspectorate and introduce new funding arrangements to eliminate competition between schools. Priority would be given to 'childcare' for children in their early years and to lifelong learning for later years. The absence of any major Conservative presence in Wales may mean that the Conservative Party has even less influence in the immediate future than it does as the main opposition party in Westminster.

Even before the election it was clear that the new assembly planned to set up a single agency to take control of education and training in school sixth-form colleges, employer-led workplace schemes and local authority-led adult education. It planned to oversee local consortia of education and training providers who would be encouraged to co-operate to find the best opportunity for each student, instead of competing as if they were rival businesses. There were also plans to cut the funding premium that has given school sixth forms an advantage over further education colleges.

QUESTION

Update these findings about education in Wales. In what ways has education in Wales become more distinct from, or similar to, education elsewhere in the UK?

Education in Scotland

Scotland can be distinguished from other parts of the UK by its different laws, churches and education system. Its educational provision has a better international reputation than that in other parts of the UK and seems to have avoided the sense of crisis that has existed in English education since the 1980s. This may be because the New Right had less influence in Scotland, where education policy is more consensual, change has been more incremental and more consultation has taken place. Teachers are also generally regarded as being more influential than elsewhere in the UK. The Scottish Joint Negotiating Committee (the staffroom union power base) continued to fix pay and conditions during annual talks and all deals between unions and councils have been legally binding throughout Scotland.

During most of the period covered by this book, education in Scotland (including higher education) has been funded and influenced by its own government department, the Scottish Office Education Department (SOED). At a local level education was administered by 12 education authorities until they were replaced in 1996 by 32 unitary education authorities (EAs).

Scotland has a long tradition of community education, which has often been church-centred; most church schools are Roman Catholic. There is a larger proportion of small (i.e. less than 50 pupils), rural schools than elsewhere in the UK and a smaller pupil : teacher ratio in primary schools than elsewhere. Opinion polls also suggest that there is far more public support for comprehensive education in Scotland than in other parts of the UK, the only major division in secondary education being that between Roman Catholic and non-denominational schools. In 1994 nearly all Scottish secondary schools were comprehensive (compared to 99 per cent in Wales, 85 per cent in England and a much lower percentage in Northern Ireland). State schools are generally described as 'public' schools in Scotland (see Glossary), unlike in the rest of the UK where 'public' schools are elite private schools. The Scottish equivalent of the grant maintained (or foundation) school is the self-governing school but in 1994 there was only one, Dornoch Academy.

By the end of the twentieth century it was clear that the move towards a quasi-market in education had been less successful in Scotland than elsewhere in the UK. Class sizes were being minimized as a result of a statutory agreement between teacher unions, and local authorities keep them under control. Only about 3 per cent of children in Scotland attended non-maintained schools, which was about half the proportion of English children attending non-maintained schools.

The rigid National Curriculum imposed on other UK schools has not been implemented in Scotland, although it has been influential. There are, however, curriculum guidelines for children up to fourteen, as they pass through six levels of attainment, from A to F. Teachers generally have more flexibility in their choice of what to teach and Scotland has a history of mass disobedience against unpopular change (as with the Scottish rejection of the Poll Tax). In 1991, whereas less than 100 schools in England and Wales avoided the compulsory testing of their seven- and eleven-year-olds, in Scotland two-thirds of pupils aged seven and eleven were not tested. Scottish Minister Michael Forsythe could not effectively impose sanctions on rebellious schools or teachers because the Conservative Party had relatively few Scottish MPs and local councillors and therefore relatively little influence north of the border. Local authorities may not have orchestrated disobedience but they could facilitate it and their responses to disobedience varied from withholding teachers' pay (in Strathclyde) to inviting individual parents to declare whether or not they wanted their children to be tested (in Tayside).

Examinations taken at school-leaving age also differ from those elsewhere in the UK. Since 1986 students have taken the Scottish Certificate of Education (SCE) Standard Grade examination at the age of sixteen (comparable to the GCSE elsewhere). Although it is taken by all students there are three levels of study and award (Foundation, General and Credit). Students receive a certificate at the end of their fourth year, giving a 'profile' of their attainments.

Highers (SCE Higher Grade) are, unlike the A levels taken elsewhere in the UK, taken at the age of seventeen, one year after the Standard Grade SCE and are taken over four or five subjects (rather than the two or three usually taken at A level). Three passes are minimum for university entrance. More advanced pupils can take up to five at one sitting, a year earlier than A levels, although they also allow a slower pace over two years. Students can also take the Certificate of Sixth Year Studies (CSYS) after a year of study following Highers. In 1996 the Conservative government was con-

sidering the introduction of Advanced Highers to replace CSYS, requiring study over two years after SCE (with 320 hours of study over two years).

In 1994 the government document (Scottish Office) *Higher Still: Opportunity for All* announced the introduction of a unified system for post-16 education in 1997 (although the implementation was subsequently postponed until 1999). This keeps Highers but adds three less demanding levels and one more demanding one, the Advanced Higher, which is intended to be at least as tough as an A level examination. The system includes all subjects, including vocational subjects, with the first courses starting in May 1999. However, continuation until the age of eighteen in order to gain Advanced Highers can overlap with the first year at university and, even when it was introduced, it was uncertain whether, or how, universities would give credit for Advanced Highers. Since 1984 the SCOTVEC (Scottish Vocational Education Council) has offered a National Certificate, which is modular in form, with students receiving credits for units of up to 40 hours of study. This is regarded as equivalent to the RSA and CGLI in the rest of the UK.

Until 1992 Scotland had sixteen Central Institutions, which were similar in function to polytechnics in England and Wales (though always controlled by the Scottish Education Department rather than local authorities). This binary divide in Scotland was dissolved in 1992. Degrees at Scottish universities last for four years (usually from the age of seventeen) and it is the norm to start a degree by taking a broad range of subjects before going on to specialize. This means that when central government gradually withdrew student grants and then introduced means-tested student fees, the changes had to be adjusted for Scotland. In October 1997 the new Labour government announced exemption from the £1,000 annual tuition fee in the fourth year of a Scottish course, but only for students from Scottish homes and those from EU countries other than the UK. Students from other areas of the UK would have to pay for each of the four years. Yet students from other parts of the UK make up nearly half the students at universities of Edinburgh, St Andrews and Dundee and about 20 per cent at other Scottish universities. The government claimed that there would be no unfairness to such students studying in Scotland, as in other parts of the UK students spend a year longer in the sixth form and could opt to enter the second year of a four-year Scottish course, thus gaining a Scottish degree after paying for three years of tuition. However, the National Union of Students claimed that relatively few students from other parts of the UK started in the second year of a Scottish degree course.

In September 1997 a Scottish referendum resulted in votes in favour of the creation of a devolved parliament with tax-raising powers. The issue of student fees was most prominent during the campaign before the election of a Scottish Parliament in May 1999. The Conservative, Liberal Democrat and Scottish Nationalist parties all promised to abolish student fees, leaving Labour as the only main party wanting to retain them. It was, nevertheless, clear to all that the removal of fees in Scotland would have serious repercussions for universities in other parts of the UK and that this would severely challenge movement towards the further decentralization of educational decision-making powers.

During the campaign the Conservative Party retained its pledge to further devolve the control of schools by increasing the number of grant maintained (now foundation) schools, although such an attempt while in government only led to 2 out of about 2,500 Scottish schools opting out. The Liberal Democrats promised to increase spending on education, providing 2,000 more teachers, £100m for buildings and doubling the books and equipment budget in year one. The Scottish National Party also planned to provide more books and equipment and a one-third cut in teacher paperwork. The Labour Party too promised more for education, with 5,000 classroom assistants, more computers, private finance for school buildings and a tougher attitude to deficient teachers. There were also signs that the Labour government might be planning to take on the very powerful main teachers union, the Educational Institute of Scotland, abolishing negotiating rights, 'modernizing' contracts and making school management more flexible. Scottish teachers were complaining that what had been a relatively better rate of pay than teachers in other parts of the UK had now moved into deficit and that morale was very low.

QUESTION

Update these findings about education in Scotland. In what ways has education in Scotland become more distinct from, or similar to, education elsewhere in the UK?

Education in Northern Ireland

Schools in Northern Ireland are mostly organized on sectarian lines, with Protestant and Catholic voluntary aided schools, and a mainly bipartite system. This involves selection, not only according to measured ability at the age of 11+ (for places in grammar schools and secondary modern schools), but also selection according to religion and gender. Most schools in Northern Ireland reflect (and possibly promote) the sectarian divide by being either Roman Catholic or Protestant and there are many single-sex secondary schools. There are also some comprehensive schools and a few integrated schools, which aim to break down sectarian differences by educating children of different faiths together.

The Department for Education in Northern Ireland (DENI) has a statutory duty to encourage the creation of more integrated schools, but in 1992 the fifteen integrated schools educated only about 1 per cent of children in Northern Ireland. The Northern Ireland Council for Integrated Education (NICIE) works as an umbrella body, bringing together integrated schools, and within Northern Ireland there is a strong campaigning movement towards religious integration via the introduction of more non-denominational schools. Within the integration movement it is claimed that any religious ratio worse than 40:60 undermines successful coexistence. However, although a balance can be maintained in mixed areas, there are problems elsewhere and some children travel to and from an integrated school from politically polarized areas.

Local education authorities in Northern Ireland are called Education and Library Boards (ELBs) and there are five of them. Thus, governance and regulation of schools has generally been influenced by central government through DENI and by local government through ELBs. The types of schools to be found in Northern Ireland are listed below.

1. *Controlled schools* are managed and funded by ELBs through boards of governors. These include primary, secondary intermediate, grammar and special schools.

   Controlled integrated schools were introduced by the 1978 Education (Northern Ireland) Act. Four such schools existed in 1996.
2. *Voluntary (maintained) schools* are managed by boards of governors, consisting of representatives of the trustees, parents, teachers and ELBs. Capital expenditure comes partly from the DENI (about 85 per cent) and running costs from the ELBs. There are several integrated primary schools and one integrated secondary school.
3. *Voluntary (non-maintained) schools* are managed by boards of governors, which may include representatives of DENI or an ELB. They are mainly grammar schools and most are separate Protestant and Roman Catholic schools. Capital expenditure is partly met by DENI (about 85 per cent) and running costs come partly from DENI and partly from fees.
4. *Grant maintained schools*. In the Education Reform (Northern Ireland) Order 1989, integrated schools were given grant maintained status, and the enrolment rules forbid selection on the grounds of religion. In 1994 there were nineteen such schools.

Three interconnected bodies of government for Northern Ireland were introduced (by the Good Friday Agreement 1998): a Northern Ireland Assembly, a North/South Ministerial Council and a Council of the Isles. Yet so severe have been the problems in this region that their description in this book must still be tentative. For example, it was agreed that the Assembly would be suspended if it did not set up the Ministerial Council within a year. *The Northern Ireland Assembly* has an executive committee of twelve ministers (including a head of the new education department), has legislative powers and its first duty was to set up the North/South Ministerial Council. *The North/South Ministerial Council* provides a forum for ministers from Dublin and Belfast to promote joint policies. *The Council of the Isles* includes representatives from the Assembly, the Dublin government, the Westminster government, the Scottish Parliament and the Welsh Assembly. It meets twice each year but has no administrative of legislative powers.

QUESTION

Update these findings about education in Northern Ireland. In what ways has education in Northern Ireland become more distinct from, or similar to, education elsewhere in the UK?

Local education authorities

The role and powers of local education authorities (LEAs) have undergone radical change since the 1940s, when they shared the 'triangle of tension' for educational policy-making with central government and representatives of the teachers' unions. Until the 1970s, often uneasy and difficult negotiations took place between the three but negotiations *did* take place and LEAs were generally regarded as a force to be reckoned with. For example, when governments issued circulars instructing LEAs to introduce selective or comprehensive education in their areas some LEAs chose to ignore or circumvent instructions. By the end of the 1990s the balance of power had shifted away from LEAs and teachers' unions, although they were still able to circumvent some instructions from central government. LEAs have seen many of their powers (and in particular much of their control of spending) move upwards, to central government and regional assemblies, and downwards, towards individual schools, colleges and other agencies. Indeed, it may be that the relative power of LEAs has been exaggerated in the past because of the variation in how much power and influence has been exerted by Secretaries and Ministers of State for Education since 1944. Furthermore, although central government could try to keep LEAs under control or even abolish them (as it did with the Inner London Education Authority in 1988), LEAs have not been able to mount an effective challenge when they have been critical of central government.

Much of LEAs power over education in the past came from their control of most of the public spending on education. Indeed, in the 1980s local authorities still controlled about 84 per cent of public spending on education (Statham *et al.*, 1989). Although no particular proportion of local authority finance has been earmarked for education, it has usually accounted for about half of each authority's whole budget and thus constituted the largest spending commitment for any local authority. However, the proportion spent on education started to decline in the late 1970s, from over 54 per cent of all English authorities' total expenditure in 1978/9 to 49 per cent in 1986/7 (CIPFA, 1988). This was partly explained by the falling birth rate during the 1970s and the corresponding reduction in the number of pupils being educated. Yet expenditure in real terms per pupil per annum on books and equipment also declined. In secondary schools this was from £50 in 1975/6 to £45 in 1985/6, although it dropped as low as £39.80 in 1980/1 and 1981/2 (Statham *et al.*, 1989, p 131). In the mid 1970s the rate support grant from central government was 66.5 per cent of local authority income but this fell to 61.0 per cent in 1979 and 46.3 per cent in 1987 (Statham *et al.*, 1989, p 116).

Whilst the proportion provided by government grants fell, local authorities found that their ability to levy rates to compensate had also been severely constrained. In this respect the effects of central government policies were similar to those on other welfare state services. However, in the case of education, the degree of change was particularly great as it moved from being the most rapidly expanding service within the welfare state (Dennison, 1985, p 34). As a percentage of total government expenditure on public services, education fell from 14.4 per cent in 1978/9 to 13.3 per cent in 1986/7 (White Paper, 1988, Chart 1.10). Education spending also declined as a percentage of the UK gross domestic product, from 5.5 per cent in 1981/2 to 4.8 per cent in 1985/6 (DES, 1987, Table 1).

The shift of power to central government can also be clearly seen in the introduction of a National Curriculum and new centralized directives regarding management and quality assessment, implemented in schools by inspectors from the Office of Standards in Education (OFSTED) and by other offices responsible for further and higher education. This shift of power was sustained by the 'discourse of derision' (Ball, 1990) and its allocation of blame for educational 'failures' to LEAs

and teachers. Conservative governments (1979–97) gradually reduced the amount of influence LEAs had on the types of schools provided in their areas (for example, by promoting grant maintained schools and city technology colleges) and acquired a tighter control of LEA spending. To a certain extent Conservative governments regarded the influence of Labour-controlled LEAs as incompatible with, and challenging, their own policies, and acted accordingly. For example, the largest Labour-run LEA, the Inner London Education Authority (ILEA), was seen as a major challenge to Mrs Thatcher's government, which abolished it in 1988/9. LEAs have, nevertheless, managed to maintain some flexibility in their implementation of government directives. For example, it has already been noted (see Education in Scotland) that the National Curriculum and associated testing may be taken up differently by different LEAs and schools, leading to different outcomes that may work against the notion of a *National* Curriculum (Bowe and Ball, 1992). Furthermore, LEAs still have some influence on the types of schools found in their areas.

Local politicians will favour certain types of schools according to their own political perspectives, together with local educational cultures and traditions, and their decisions about local schooling have been influential throughout the twentieth century. Decisions have not always followed party lines, as we can see with the introduction of some of the first comprehensive schools by Conservative LEAs (and see Chapter 5). The variety of approaches to education at LEA level therefore makes it very difficult to generalize about local policies and decisions. Indeed, the findings in Torytown and Labourville studies are used in this book to illustrate the changing nature and influence of political perspectives on the local provision of education, but they cannot be generalized to other areas.

Torytown and Labourville

The two LEAs in Greater Manchester, initially called Torytown and Labourville by Edgell and Duke, were introduced in Chapter 2, where you were guided through the background to the research. There are remarkable variations between the sorts

	Torytown	Labourville
Nursery education	Part-time and attached to primary schools.	Full-time and in separate nursery schools.
Pupil:teacher ratios in LEA schools	Higher proportion of pupils than national average for England and Wales.	Lower proportion of pupils than national average for England and Wales.
Selection at 11+	Yes. 'Passes' went to state or private grammar school. 'Fails' went to state 'high' or 'comprehensive' school.	No. All went to state comprehensive school.
Private education	LEA paid some fees. Over 1,500 children in Torytown privately educated.	LEA did not pay any fees. Less than 20 children in Labourvillle privately educated.
Spending per pupil (unit costs) in state schools, compared to all schools in Metropolitan LEAs	−£84 in primary schools. −£42 in secondary schools.	−£26 in primary schools. +£15 in secondary schools.
Number of local children educated by another LEA – number coming from another LEA	100+ more primary children leaving. 200+ more secondary children leaving.	300+ more primary children arriving. 50+ more secondary children arriving.

Adapted from: *Education Statistics 1985–86 Actuals*, CIPFA, Statistical Information Service, SIS Ref. 52.87

Figure 4.6 Educational provision in Torytown and Labourville, 1985/6

of schools provided by LEAs throughout the UK, and these two areas cannot be seen as representing particular types, yet they do provide illustrations of the changing links between political perspectives and systems of education. (For more detailed information about the two areas see McKenzie, 1993.)

Since 1944 there have been many changes in the administration of Torytown and Labourville. Before the mid 1970s one was part of a county and one was part of a metropolitan borough. Although changes since 1944 are considered in this book, fieldwork for the case studies began in 1980, when the Labourville ward had a Labour MP, Labour council and comprehensive schools, and the Torytown ward had a Conservative MP, Conservative council and selection at 11+. By the end of the fieldwork, in 1997, the political identity of Labourville and its influence on schooling still fitted its old Labour heritage, whilst Torytown could more appropriately be called 'New Labour-town'. Control of the Torytown council and local representation in Parliament had now changed from Conservative to Labour and its New Labour identity could be seen in its retention of some Conservative education policies (retaining selection at 11+, subject to the approval of local parents).

A brief summary of the major differences in educational provision, in the mid 1980s, in Torytown and Labourville is provided in Figure 4.6.

In 1985 the wider borough including the Labourville ward had an estimated population of 22,000 more than that in Torytown (both had populations of between 210,000 and 240,000) and these differences must be considered in any comparisons between educational statistics for the two boroughs. However, this has little effect on the type of statistics used for comparison in Figure 4.6.

In 1985/6 Labourville had more than twice as many under-fives in full-time education as Torytown, whilst Torytown had nearly twice as many under-fives in part-time education as Labourville. Nursery provision in Labourville was very generous, its nurseries providing health and community care as well as education, and thus serving the needs of families in particularly deprived areas within the wider Labourville borough. Both areas had 'comprehensive' schools, but in Torytown this was as a result of its policy of not calling secondary modern schools by their correct name. Instead they were called 'high' schools or (in one case) a 'comprehensive' school.

The number of Torytown children being privately educated can be explained by its policy of paying the fees for Roman Catholic children to attend independent Roman Catholic grammar schools if they passed both the local 11+ assessment and the individual school's entrance examination. This meant that Torytown had more children in this category than any other LEA in England and Wales. However, this figure not only represents those children financed by the Torytown LEA, but also some children who were either financed entirely by their parents or partly funded by an Assisted Place financed by central government. An insight into the proportion of each type of funding was provided in figures supplied by the Torytown Education Department in 1989, when half of all Torytown first-year pupils entering independent secondary schools were not supported financially by the Torytown council (about 20 per cent of these having failed the 11+).

Independent schools, with their (usually) low pupil : teacher ratio are not included in the CIPFA figures describing the pupil : teacher ratios in Torytown and Labourville. In 1985 the average pupil: teacher ratio in independent schools (primary and secondary combined) was 11.7 to one (Statham, Mackinnon and Cathcart, 1989, p 72). The average pupil : teacher ratios for all of England and Wales in 1985/6 were: primary 22.2 to one; secondary 16.1 to one; overall average 17.8 to one. In comparison, the Labourville ratios were better than average at each level and the Torytown ratios worse than average at each level (Figure 4.6). This tendency for Labourville to provide more generous state education provision was confirmed when the expenditure of the two areas was compared (McKenzie, 1993, Tables 6.1 and 6.2). When interviewed in 1989 a senior Torytown Education Officer thus presented a misleading impression when he claimed that the selective system generated better than average pupil : teacher ratios in Torytown. Such healthy ratios were more likely to be experienced by the many Torytown children attending independent schools than those attending state schools in the Torytown area.

Torytown's spending on state schools (unit costs mean spending per pupil) was lower than Labourville's and considerably lower than the average for all Metropolitan LEAs in 1985/6. It was also found that Torytown was loosing more of its local children to schools in other areas. In

August 1985 fewer children were arriving in Torytown than were leaving to go to school elsewhere, whilst the corresponding figures for Labourville showed larger numbers arriving than leaving.

Torytown was, however, in a state of political flux for most of the 1980s and 1990s. For a long time the future of education in Torytown had been uncertain, as arguments about the respective merits and defects of the existing bipartite system were used by politicians at successive elections. When the qualitative research started in 1986 (relating to phases 3–5 of the fieldwork) Labour had minority control of the Torytown council, the balance of power being maintained by seven Liberal councillors. A scheme for the reorganization of education along comprehensive and coeducational lines was proposed by the Labour and Liberal groups. This would have involved a radical change from single-sex grammar and secondary modern schools to coeducational comprehensive schools. As a result of a compromise between Labour and the Liberals, school leavers would be offered a choice of further education including tertiary colleges (favoured by Labour), colleges of further education and sixth-form colleges (a combination of the last two being favoured by Liberals). During the mid 1980s a lengthy period of consultation was taking place and meetings between parents, teachers and LEA representatives were called at various schools. However, the local elections in May 1988 returned an overall Conservative majority of one, and the proposals for reorganization were abandoned.

During the 1990s falling rolls affected both Torytown and Labourville. In Torytown two single-sex grammar schools were merged to become a coeducation grammar school. Controversy about assessment at 11+ continued as administrative blunders meant that some children had to resit it. More radical change occurred in 1997 when the new Labour council refused to pay fees for Torytown children to be privately educated. One of the Torytown cohort explained the situation.

> Well at St [Roman Catholic independent school], some of the children from [Torytown] had places there paid for by [Torytown], and now [Torytown] Council have said that because there are two Catholic schools already in the borough they now won't pay the places at St [. . .]. So there's been quite a fuss about it, because the

people who've got children at St [...] have staged a protest at the Town Hall, because they think that [Torytown] should pay for the children, but [Torytown's] Labour leader has said that he wants to put the money somewhere else where it can be, where it's needed for something else, as there are two Catholic schools already in the borough. I think they stop paying next year.

Georgina, 1997

Meanwhile, political control in Labourville changed very little during the 1980s and 1990s. Labour still has an overall majority within the council and has maintained its commitment to the existing comprehensive system. Local debates about education have tended to focus on cuts in education spending and the closure of schools as a result of falling rolls. During the 1990s Labourville cuts included redundancies among central support staff, cutting the number of places at nursery schools, closing some nursery schools and creating nursery units attached to primary schools. The problem of falling rolls particularly affected Labourville's Roman Catholic schools, which led to amalgamations and even the threat of closure.

> One of our local Catholic schools [X] (just down the road) is not viable because of student numbers. Another Roman Catholic school [Y] had a similar problem, so the idea was to amalgamate them. Then the feeling was that enough parents wouldn't be prepared to travel from this area to where the other place is, or from there to down here to make the new amalgamated school viable, so there was a suggestion that they would close them both and not replace them. There was an outcry, public meetings, protests and eventually it's been decided that they are going to amalgamate the schools and it is going to be on the [X] site and they feel that enough people have committed themselves to sending their children to make it a viable proposition. They're also going to try to make it a centre of excellence for technology.
>
> Jeremy, 1997

Changes have taken place in both areas, and have been met with some resistance, yet over the years members of the cohort have often explained that voters have become used to the policies of one party.

> [Which party has the best education policies?]
> It's difficult to say because the Conservatives have been in so long. You know what you've got [the

system] and you're told that if Labour got in you'd have something different, but we've nothing to compare it with. We've got a Conservative local authority and unless I lived in [Labourville] or [...] I wouldn't know what others are like.

Megan, 1992

> [Why did you vote Labour in the local election?]
> ... In this particular area, if three-quarters of the population didn't bother to turn out to vote, Labour would still get in because it's such a Labour area.
>
> John, 1997

Teachers and lecturers

This book started with the question, Why has education become so miserable? Nowhere is this process of immiseration more noticeable than in the changes to the teaching 'profession' since the 1940s. Changes have been so profound that even the appropriateness of the word 'profession' is now debatable, as teachers have lost much of the relative status, affluence and job security that they could take for granted fifty years ago. There are still, of course, many teachers who gain a great amount of personal satisfaction from their work, but positive individual experiences often seem to be lost amid the shadow of negativity covering many staffrooms. Students' experiences of the pressures associated with education at the end of the twentieth century have been temporary, but teachers may feel the pressures constantly over a lengthy career.

At the end of the Second World War it was possible to train as a teacher over a period of two years and, without a degree, obtain a teaching post which brought with it a well-paid job and a position of high status and authority within the local community. Emergency measures for the training of new teachers after the war continued in order to meet the baby boom of the 1950s. Yet, as the emergency abated and teachers' qualifications increased to the level of an obligatory degree, the status of teachers started to decline. To work in maintained schools, teachers now need at least four years in higher education, acquiring either a B.Ed, which includes teacher training and lasts for four years, or a three-year degree (or part-time equivalent) followed by one year of postgraduate training to attain qualified teacher status. Teachers in many non-maintained (private or independent) schools do not need qualified teacher status.

During the 1960s the public started to criticize those teachers they perceived as using 'trendy' new (progressive) teaching methods and there were a few, well-publicized, scandals when teachers at some schools were accused of failing their students. Sociologists could see how the problems of a few schools could escalate into a moral panic about education in general. This was reinforced by student demonstrations during the late 1960s and the ease with which it was possible to label *all* university and polytechnic students and *all* teachers as dissolute and profligate. A negative image was supported further by the Black Paper critiques published during the 1960s and 1970s. Nevertheless, whilst teachers were suffering a negative public image at that time, their workloads, autonomy in the workplace and relative income still meant that they had comparable working conditions to those of other professionals. This began to change during the 1970s as governments started to blame education for the country's economic problems. In 1970 Margaret Thatcher was made Secretary of State for Education in a Conservative government and set about withdrawing some spending on education. In 1976 the Labour Prime Minister James Callaghan made a speech at Ruskin College, Oxford, in which he was very critical of education for not preparing young people effectively for the workplace. This initiated what some sociologists (e.g. Ball, 1990) have called a 'discourse of derision' in which education has been blamed for many social and economic ills. During the lengthy period of Conservative government, from 1979 to 1997, a major shift of influence took place as the previous 'triangle of tension' was gradually replaced by the allocation of more power to central government, at the expense of LEAs and the teachers' unions. Cuts in public spending on education resulted in poorer resources (e.g. less capital spending on the upkeep of schools, fewer books, the sale of playing fields) and a radical downward spiral in teachers' working conditions in general.

Since the early 1980s newly qualified teachers and lecturers have found it more difficult to obtain a post and many posts are on part-time and/or temporary contracts. Local management of schools and colleges also means that LEAs are no longer obliged to find new jobs for teachers and lecturers who have lost their posts due to institutional restructuring. During the mid 1980s teachers' unions took industrial action, in protest not only about their pay, but also about conditions of work and changes in the education system. The government responded by withdrawing their negotiating rights. Together with the radical increase in students taking courses in further and higher education there has also been a relative reduction in lecturers' salaries. Green, Wolf and Leney (1999, p 45) note that it is not just a UK tendency, as spending on teachers' salaries grew more slowly than per capita GDP in most OECD countries between 1985 and 1993, despite the aging of teaching personnel. By the end of the twentieth century 40 per cent of teachers in OECD countries as a whole were between 40 and 50 years of age (CERI, 1996, p 56). The higher salaries given to more experienced teachers have therefore been offset by the tendency of teachers' and lecturers' salaries in general to decline in relative value over time. The aging of teaching personnel also means that many teachers are now retiring and will have to be replaced through new expansionary recruitment programmes. It is difficult to see how this can be done without improving the pay of teachers to bring it in line with that of other graduates.

There have also been deleterious effects on teachers' working environments. Greater autonomy for individual institutions means that senior staff take on demanding managerial roles which can separate them from other teaching staff. Lower-grade teachers and lecturers have faced increasing amounts of administrative work on top of the normal workload associated with classroom teaching. The introduction of a National Curriculum means that teachers must constantly update their knowledge of its amendments and assessment requirements. Teachers also need professional updating to keep them abreast of the continual changes in educational technology and teaching and assessment methods. Continual monitoring and visits by OFSTED (the Office of Standards in Education) inspectors involves far more paperwork than did the visits by Her Majesty's Inspectors in the past.

In colleges and universities new funding mechanisms and efficiency targets resulted in revisions to lecturers' conditions of service, demands for greater flexibility and much higher workloads. Some colleges and universities having financial difficulties even took the unusual step of introducing redundancies at a time of rapid expansion in further and higher education. Higher student : teacher ratios meant less contact time. These new pressures led to a five-year dispute between the lecturers' unions and employer organizations and widespread evidence of stress and low morale.

As you will see in Chapter 5, sociologists studying changes in teaching have used terms like *proletarianization* in order to describe the declining socio-economic status of teachers. The continuing feminization of teaching, with men still tending to take a disproportionate share of senior teaching and managerial posts, also sustains relatively poor financial rewards for lower-grade staff. Yet one of the most notable changes has been the move from a relatively autonomous working environment to one in which surveillance by a highly controlling management system generates and promotes self-control by self-surveillance. Indeed, some aspects of Foucault's theories, emerging from his study of punishment and control (1975) and surveillance via the panoptican (a type of prison building that allows for the continuous surveillance of prisoners), could be applied to the experiences of teachers at the end of the twentieth century. Continuous processes of external assessment and evaluation can be experienced as a sort of disciplinary gaze, which workers are aware of and respond to. This may result in what some sociologists have called *panoptic management*, or self-surveillance, as workers internalize the idea that they are being watched by others and manage themselves accordingly. Teachers may experience this sort of management through deficiency as they become constantly concerned about what they have been persuaded are personal inadequacies and control themselves accordingly. As they try to comply with an idealized image of how teachers should present themselves and/or see themselves as playing an increasingly competitive role, they may experience ever increasing levels of stress.

In July 1997 the new Labour government published a White Paper, *Excellence in Schools*, in which it suggested ways in which some of this demoralization could be tackled. A General Teaching Council was introduced to raise the status of the profession and integrate teachers (as general members and with seats on the council for union representatives) in more key education policy decisions. Similarly, plans were made to create an Institute of Learning and Teaching for lecturers. The appointment of Lord David Putnam to chair the General Teaching Council means that teachers now have a new advocate with a remit to raise their status in society. Putnam initiated the new, annual national teaching awards and seems to have a genuine commitment to teachers' best interests. However, concerns have been expressed about a move towards selecting some teachers for particular praise and it may be that the Council's powers are not as meaningful as hoped. Many of its powers are negative, such as creating quicker procedures for disciplining incompetent teachers. At the end of the century it therefore seemed that teachers' prospects were improving in some ways, but the study of changing education systems can lead to cynicism as we see that intentions are rarely mirrored by outcomes.

Conclusion: Economic influences on education systems

Much of what has been said in this chapter relates to the impact of economic crises and insecurities on education systems. Although responses to economic pressures have varied according to region, locality and even individual school, it is still possible to see the influence of several trends. First, there has been a gradual shift in power structures away from the influence of LEAs, with decisions about allocation to schools being made by authorities, towards a quasi-market system in which the principle of parental choice has been emphasized. Yet this raises problems, as education should not only benefit the individual but also the community as a whole. The drift towards privatization under the Conservatives (1979–1997) has been at least partly halted by a Labour government committed to community benefits but the century still ended with a strong emphasis on education serving the needs of the economy, rather than vice versa. Second, the threat of unemployment has lead to credential inflation and academic drift. Yet this leads to a type of immiseration for both the loosers, who feel excluded, and the winners, who may suffer constant pressure to achieve an unnatural level of personal perfection. Limits to growth in education mean that when one person gains a high level of education, the relative position of other people will be lowered. As some writers have noted (Green, Wolf and Leney, 1999), when a whole crowd stands on tiptoe, no one sees any better. Perhaps it could be added that standing on tiptoe for any length of time is very tiring.

5

Changing issues

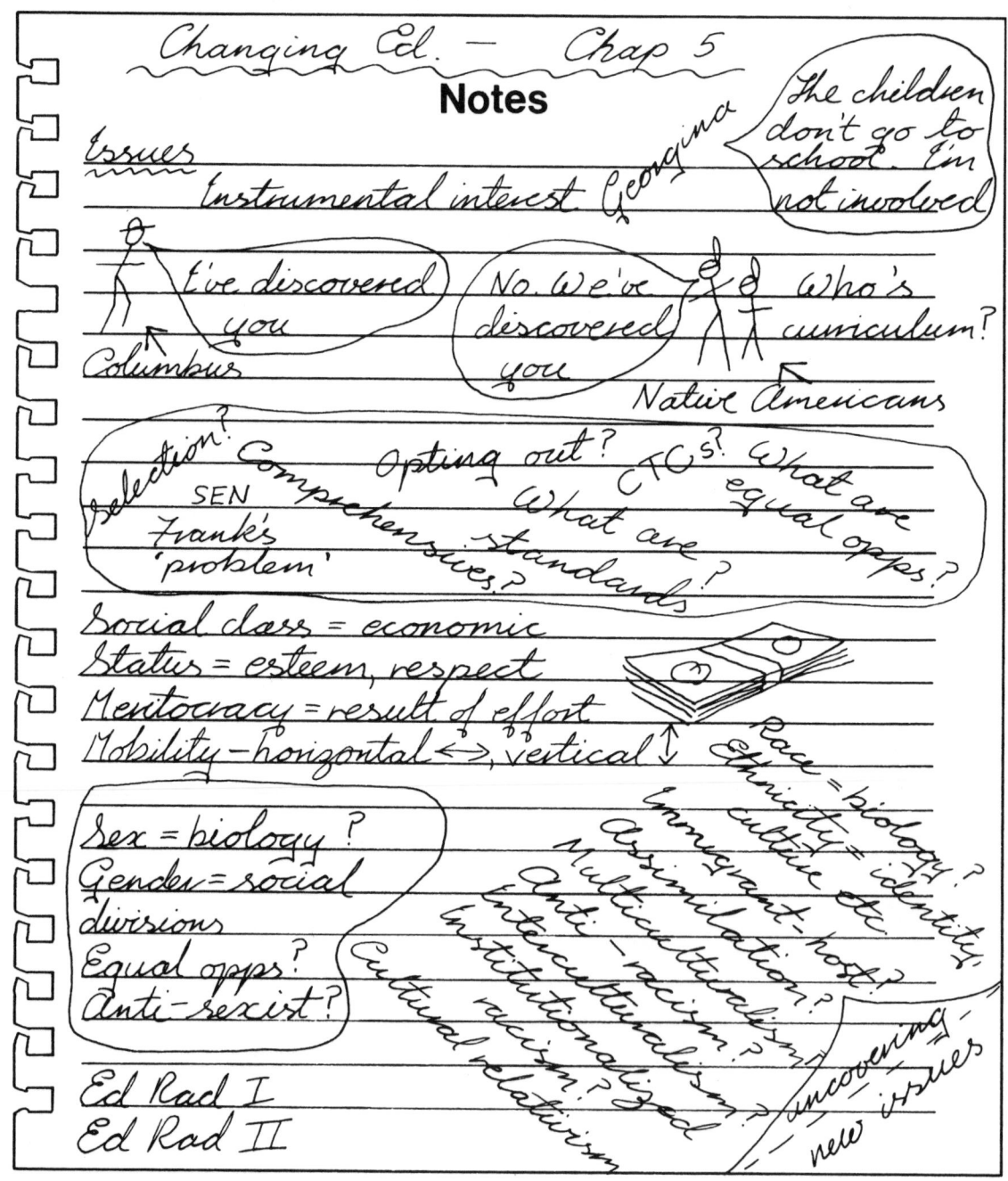

What is an issue? – Instrumental interest – Attitudes – The curriculum – Testing – Special educational needs – Private schools – Grammar schools and secondary modern schools or comprehensive schools? – Opting out of LEA control – City technology colleges – Further and higher education – Teachers and lecturers – Changing standards of education – Political and socio-economic change – Equal opportunities – Class and status – Gender – Tackling sexism – Sexuality – Race and ethnicity – Tackling racism – Are educational outcomes most influenced by social class, gender or race? – Religion and cultural relativism – Behaviour – Apparent contradictions in attitudes to issues – Conclusion: Issues in flux

Education has also been seen as a means to social emancipation. It is through education that socialists and feminists, for instance, have come to know their everyday unhappinesses aren't the fault of personal inadequacies but are common experiences, shared by others, and produced by particular social arrangements.

Johnson, 1983, p 20

In this chapter you will see how perceptions of what issues are will vary in a very personal way. Yet, the experiences of different generations at different times can be used as a means of interrogating education policies and exploring the importance of wider sociological concerns. Many personal and political issues are in a constant state of flux, whilst some will provide a consistent background, and may even be taken for granted. For example, a woman from an ethnic *majority* may take her ethnicity for granted, but pursue interests in gender inequalities in the workplace because she is a worker who feels herself to be disadvantaged by her gender. Once she retires, gender inequalities in the workplace may be replaced by a new interest in ageism and pensions. Contrast this with a woman from an ethnic *minority* whose minority status is constantly in the background (or in the foreground) to whatever changing issues arise in her life. Our interest, or lack of interest, in educational issues is often personalized and selective. Thus, my own interest in a wide range of educational issues arises because I have chips on both shoulders, rather than just one!

The section headings in this chapter provide indications of how some themes have provided a consistent background to educational debates for many years, although not necessarily for the whole sixty years covered by this book. For example, 'special educational needs' were barely acknowledged during the 1940s because such needs were generally seen as medical rather than educational problems. Similarly, we now tend to discuss 'ethnicity' rather than 'race' because we have uncovered some of the many problems involved in using 'race'

as a concept. Indeed, the real value of the sociology of education is in revealing what was previously hidden. Sociologists are constantly identifying and probing new, as well as existing, areas of interest, asking awkward, even apparently ridiculous questions and identifying problems where there previously seemed to be none. No wonder they are unpopular with many politicians! Not content with being unpopular, sociologists have stubbornly expanded their interests into education policy-making in order to understand why many of their research findings seem to have been ignored or misrepresented. This reflects a gradual politicization of the sociology of education as sociologists have moved from an emphasis on identifying and describing educational problems towards a more active interest in education policies and their impact on educational experiences.

What is an issue?

At a very basic level an issue could be compared with a television programme or a movie. Suppose the latest *Star Wars* film was showing at your local cinema. It would be available for viewing whether you decided to watch it or not, and your decision to see it would be based on your own personal interests, income, free time, perhaps age and so on. Some *Star Wars* fans can display an almost (or actual) obsessive interest in the genre, some people will view the film simply because they expect to enjoy it, and others will choose not to view it for a variety of reasons. Educational issues and attitudes towards them are similar. Once established, educational issues can exist whether or not many individuals take an interest in them; some people may become almost obsessively involved, some may display a more restrained interest and some may ignore them entirely. Such responses may also be manipulated by influential individuals (such as politicians or film critics) who are in a position to label the issue/film as not worthy of interest. Indeed, in a previous paper (McKenzie in Edgell *et al.*, 1995) I argued that after 1979 Conservative governments tended to define changes in the education system as technical, rational and non-political; that is, not issues at all. This could result in potential issues being unavailable for 'viewing' or being regarded as not worthy of our individual interest.

Even if we have our own educational problems, it is easy to personalize them so that we do not perceive links between our individual experiences and relevant social influences. Indeed this is perhaps more easily done in the case of educational issues than in the case of other policy issues, such as health and employment. We may be more likely to attribute our educational failures to personal inadequacies ('I'm just thick') than to attribute our health problems to personal lifestyles. Thus, although C. Wright Mills has helped to clarify the difference between a personal 'trouble' and a public 'issue', the overlap between the two is remarkably complex.

> Troubles occur within the character of the individual and within the range of his immediate relations with others: they have to do with his self and with those limited areas of social life of which he is directly and personally aware . . .
>
> A trouble is a private matter: values cherished by an individual are felt by him to be threatened. Issues have to do with matters that transcend these local environments of the individual and the range of his inner life. They have to do with the organization of many such milieux into the institutions of a historical society as a whole, with the ways in which various milieux overlap and interpenetrate to form the larger structure of social and historical life. An issue is a public matter: some value cherished by publics is felt to be threatened. Often there is a debate about what that value really is and about what it is that really threatens it. This debate is often without focus if

only because it is the very nature of an issue, unlike even widespread trouble, that it cannot very well be defined in terms of immediate and everyday environments of ordinary men. An issue, in fact, often involves a crisis in institutional arrangements, and often too it involves what Marxists call 'contradictions' or 'antagonisms'.
> Wright Mills, 1970, pp 8–9 (original 1959)

Instrumental interest

The metaphor of a cinema film was used to reflect how individual tastes and interests vary and how an educational issue can be important to some people and not to others. This is rather an obvious point, but it becomes more interesting when we consider not only who is interested and who is not, but also how many people manage to ignore even blanket coverage of certain issues by the media.

My first interviews were carried out when what was to become the 1988 Education Reform Act was passing through its final stages in Parliament. It seemed logical to assume that the high profile given by the media to educational issues at that time would have been reflected in a relatively healthy public awareness of, and even interest in, these radical changes. However, the majority of my informants in 1988 expressed little, if any, interest and questioning in 1992 and 1997 drew similar responses. Media coverage and high-profile political debates about educational issues seemed to be just as likely to generate or degenerate any potential interest.

In 1988, 1992 and 1997 I asked informants whether they had heard of seven subjects emerging from current local and national events. Those who had heard of a subject were asked if they had any interest in it and what they knew about it. The number giving any accurate details in 1988 are listed in Figure 5.1. Although based on a small, non-random sample, and not therefore generalizable (see Chapter 2), it was interesting to see similar patterns emerging in 1992 and 1997.

The seven subjects mentioned in 1988 were:

1. Changes or proposed changes in the local provision of education.
2. The Assisted Places scheme.

Figure 5.1 Knowledge and interest frequencies (interviews in 1988)

Number of debates	Heard of	Interest	Detail
0	3	32	8
1	5	9	14
2	6	3	13
3	10	1	5
4	11	2	5
5	7	3	4
6	4	0	0
7	6	2	3
Total	52	52	52

3. City technology colleges.
4. The Education Reform Bill (currently passing through Parliament).
5. Proposals to let schools opt out of LEA control.
6. The proposed abolition of the Inner London Education Authority.
7. Recent events at Burnage High School in Manchester (the MacDonald Report into the murder of a pupil in the playground had received extensive press coverage in recent months).

From this sample of 52, only 28 had heard of four or more topics, 7 expressed some interest in four or more and 12 were able to provide some accurate information about four or more. Item 7 drew more *apparent* knowledge than other items; because it related to somewhere fairly local, it was reported in local newspapers and some interviewees had personal knowledge of the area and people involved. However, this was not necessarily *accurate* knowledge, as you will see later when we consider ethnicity and racism. In the framework of educational debate the 'truth' is a very illusive concept indeed, as knowledge of educational issues is acquired after a process of communication in which some facts are omitted, some distorted and many are reinterpreted several times. Some interviewees got their information from other people, who got their information from other sources and so on, like a game of Chinese Whispers in which the final message bears little resemblance to the original 'true' message. It is even possible that some of the 'facts' about local events may become even more distorted than the 'facts' about more distant events as local gossip involves many voices in a process of exaggeration. Indeed, strong opinions often emerged from a very weak knowledge base and were often apparently unrelated to personal experience.

In 1987 I interviewed Labourville's Chief Education Officer, who clearly explained what he saw as the nature of interest or lack of interest in education as a political issue.

> I happen to think that education's the most important thing in the world . . . It's easy for education to be vitally important if you're living in a nice house, you've got a good job and you want to see your children in the same situation; education's vitally important, isn't it? If you sit in the inner city where you see a certain amount of hopelessness about your own position and the fact that no matter how well your children might do at school – is that going to get them a job? – education may not seem as relevant as it does to the middle-class areas. I can understand that. I think that there are issues that are considered important. Housing is obviously important. Employment, or rather lack of employment, is extremely important to many. I think that support for one-parent families – the sort of support they need to sustain themselves in the city – is important. I think that those issues to those people are clearly more important.
>
> Chief Education Officer, Labourville, 1988

The point is that, as issues relating to personal survival (for example, unemployment, social security, housing) have assumed a more obvious and immediate importance to many people, education has been viewed as a luxury item on a personal issue agenda. Even at a personal level, education is often associated with long-term planning and short-term interests are, of necessity, regarded as most important. A low level of interest in education as a political issue has also been indicated by many other sources. For example, in their British Participation Study of 1984–5, Parry, Moyser and Day found that only 8.9 per cent of their sample had education on their (free response) personal agendas of 'issues, needs or problems' which had been most important to them 'over the past five years or so' and which they 'might consider taking action on' (Parry, Moyser and Day, 1992, p 243). Just 6.4 per cent of all of the issues mentioned were about education, which compared with 15.3 per cent about the environment and planning, 15 per cent about economic issues (excluding unemployment) and 9.6 per cent about unemployment.

People who are working in education, consuming education (including parents with children in education), public employees and those who have been in education the longest are generally more aware of, interested in, and knowledgeable about educational issues. You will therefore find many lengthy quotes from teachers, public employees and parents of children currently in education in this book simply because they had more to say on the subject than others who were less involved. Parry, Moyser and Day (1992) also supported this conclusion in their findings that the significance of education within the public sphere was mainly recognized by the relatively small proportion of the electorate who had an instrumental interest in the subject. They found that those respondents with college or degree qualifications were twice as likely as other members of the public to refer to the topic. Whilst constituting only 20.9 per cent of all their respondents, those who had received higher education offered 42.3 per cent of the education issues. A British Social Attitudes Report (Jowell, L. *et al.*, 1985) on personal action scores offered further verification of these findings; those who had been longest in education were most willing to become actively involved in education and politics.

In families it is often the mother, rather than the father, who is assigned the role of prime educational carer, having more contact with the schools and frequently demonstrating greater knowledge of educational issues. This was particularly noticeable when the members of the cohort were approached for the first time for qualitative research, and education was mentioned in the introduction to the interview. Men frequently suggested that I interview their wives or tried to enlist the help of their wives or children in answering questions about schooling. The reverse was not the case, and women were generally prepared to deal with questions unaided. (In subsequent interviews the existing cohort understood the need to interview the same person again.) Such findings reinforced those from the first Greater Manchester Survey (1980–1) when Edgell and Duke reported a greater cuts consciousness among parents in general and among mothers in particular. They found that the perceived impact of education spending cuts among women with dependants in all age groups was greater than that of men in the same situation. Yet it was noticeable that women without young dependants did not report a greater impact of spending cuts. Gender inequalities have also been noted in the annual British Social Attitudes Reports; for example, in the 1986 Report (Jowell *et al.*, 1986, Table 7.2) the writers found that women were becoming less likely to choose 'smaller classes' as the main priority for improving primary schools and they claimed that the gradual drop in the proportion of large primary classes was a factor that was probably more apparent to women because of their more direct contact with their children's schools.

INSTRUMENTAL INTEREST: VIEWS FROM TORYTOWN AND LABOURVILLE

Megan said of proposed changes to the education system in Torytown:

> I'm very interested with having children in school and working in school.

Her children were at primary school and, when asked about the Assisted Places scheme, she showed little interest.

> I've not really thought about it. I suppose I'm thinking about my children's immediate needs. It's one of those things I might think about if and when it arises.
>
> Megan, 1988

> My daughter is a teacher – therefore education's important. I found it difficult to position the last three [on a list of issues, i.e. benefits, transport and housing] as they don't apply directly to me.
>
> Freda, 1992, gave education highest priority for government spending

---

I suppose I'll have to say 'Yes' because of my children. If I didn't have children I'd say 'No', probably, not because I didn't care, but because I would never have thought about it much. But, having said that, I don't know whether it's the same in all boroughs, but in Torytown nearly every single primary, if not every primary, has got a really good nursery facility anyway. My eldest has just come out of it, and it'll be a year before [. . .] goes into it. So I can see that it's important but it seems fine as it is.

Sharon, 1997, prepared to pay more tax to increase spending on nurseries

Education on a selfish level, because obviously my employment depends on that.

John, 1997, noted education as one of his main interests

Trouble is I don't listen much to arguments about education. As the children don't go to school I'm not that involved nowadays.

Georgina, 1992

With the family grown up we don't take a lot of notice. We've had about twenty years of that, and that's enough.

Eamon, 1992, when asked about schools opting out of LEA control

It's not relevant to me now as I'm forty. It depends where you place it in your life. You can be in education at any time in your life.

Nicholas, 1992

Now I'm a bit stuck for education because I've no children at school anymore, mine are all grown up now, but I think it's very important for the future that it's kept on top of, you know. I mean I've no grandchildren yet, but I mean I would expect, I would be very keen again, and I'm in a period now where mine are grown up and I've no grandchildren to think about with education, but when I do then I'll be thinking about it properly then, you know.

Georgina, 1997, priority for government spending

Once your own children finish you don't tend to pay as much attention as I would have done. I have briefly caught sight of headings in the local paper, just recently about some of the schools, but I can't remember for the life of me what the detailing was. Are they stopping sort of like grant status, local funding or something? I read something, I just read a headline. I'm not sure if one of the schools was in [local area], was it [. . .]? I can't remember any details.

Nicholas, 1997, aware of changes in local education

I was looking at the list from a socially responsible point of view, but I'm looking at this from a personal point of view. I don't want my answers to appear to contradict each other.

Richard, 1992, comparing priorities for spending on education with interest in subjects

Questions

Should we be concerned about

(a) the lack of public interest in education and
(b) the lack of public knowledge about education?

Explain your answers.

Attitudes

Attitudes towards educational problems and issues are important because they help us to understand how educational change may facilitate, reflect or contradict changes in the climate of opinion. There may be a gulf between the attitudes of one individual, the force of public attitudes in general and the government (including LEA) education policies, and the direction of influence between one and another may be uncertain. Has government policy influenced voters' attitudes or vice versa?

A fascination with this chicken and egg situation meant that, in the early stages of my involvement in the Greater Manchester Study, I chose to study the relationship between consumption of education (in this case operationalized as having a member of the household attending school or college) and party identification. Figure 5.2 shows the findings from Phase 2 of the Greater Manchester Study, at a time when the Conservatives were still dominating the polls in Torytown and at national level. The finding that consumers were more likely to vote Labour than non-consumers is particularly noticeable, although it is important to remember that this is still a weak association. It was possible that this was just a local trend (perhaps associated with the nature of local educational provision) and so had to be tested against national data. You will see in Figure 5.2 that, when similar variables in a British Social Attitudes Survey (BSA, Jowell *et al.*, 1984) were cross-tabulated, the Conservative Party received more support from both consumers and non-consumers, although consumption still seemed to have a slight influence.

QUESTIONS

How could the different operationalization of variables in the GMS and BSA affect the findings (see Chapter 2)?
What other factors could influence the relationship between consumption of education and party identification?
How would you test these findings with more recent data?

Figure 5.2 Education consumption and party identification: Torytown, Labourville and national data compared, GMS 1983/4 and BSA 1983/4

		Conservative	Labour	Alliance
	n=	%	%	%
Torytown				
Consumers	84	33	40	26
Non-consumers	204	45	30	25
Labourville				
Consumers	103	29	55	16
Non-consumers	200	38	47	15
BSA				
Consumers	682	44	39	17
Non-consumers	835	45	38	17

Source: Edgell and Duke, GMS2, computer analysis; BSA, 1984

My own theories about the relationship between attitudes towards education and political identity tend to centre around three conflicting or mutually supportive elements: the *priority of basic needs* (which means that other interests often take priority over interest in education); the *pressure of experience* (our personal educational experiences affecting us in many important, but often inconsistent, ways); and the *pull of tradition* (which involves a common respect for educational 'traditions'). In later sections you will see that many interviewees in the Torytown and Labourville cohort supported the long-established types of educational institutions with which they were familiar. This was often expressed as a sense of reverence for the traditional image of the grammar school (whilst its usual partner, the secondary modern school, was often ignored), private education and Oxford and Cambridge. Indeed the pull of tradition could even be seen when some interviewees expressed their dislike of the elitism associated with such institutions (see Jane's comments on social class later in this chapter).

One potentially useful way of examining attitudes is offered by Denis Lawton (1992, pp 10–19) who suggested that it may be helpful to think of ideology and education as a set of three (overlapping) levels, ranging from the very general, at Level 1, to the specific, at Level 3. *Level 1 (General/Political)* is where general ontologies (see the start of Chapter 3) give rise to more specific social and moral views, for example, about the purpose of education, functions of schooling, appropriateness of teaching methods. This may loosely accommodate those members of the cohort who expressed no interest in, or particular knowledge about, education but still tried to express views based on their more general ontologies. *Level 2 (Interest Group Level)* involves those ideologies associated with groups particularly concerned with education. For example, Raymond Williams (1961) talked about the influence on the curriculum of three 'groups': old humanists, industrial trainers and public educators. The *old humanists* perceive the education of their own children in terms of character-building and the development of good tastes and manners and are therefore associated with upper-class elitism. This group includes some parents in the Torytown and Labourville cohort.

The *industrial trainers* emphasize the practical, utilitarian aim of producing economically useful education, and a well-trained and obedient work-force. Although it may be imagined that members of the cohort who were employers would fit this category, it was not always the case. The *public educators* aim to educate the whole population for a democratic society, with political or civic aims. *Level 3 (Education/Teaching or Pedagogic Level)* is a more specific level where we can find educational or teacher ideologies; for example, how teachers and administrators envisage their own role, the aims of education and so on. Here we can see the teachers in the cohort, who may not share a common perspective, but who often provided very detailed comments about education systems and experiences.

The curriculum

Many competing perspectives and attitudes to education can be seen in the issues we encounter when considering what sort of knowledge should be taught in schools and how it should be taught. Decisions about the content of the curriculum are heavily influenced by changing cultures, norms and competing perspectives and what is valid knowledge today may be invalid tomorrow. This means that those who convey this disputed knowledge may easily stray from convention and be regarded as subversive. As you can see in the cases of Galileo and Darwin, it is possible that George Bernard Shaw was right when he wrote that 'All great truths begin as blasphemies (*Annajanska*, 1972)'.

During the twentieth century Check Anta Diop encountered similar problems when his Ph.D thesis was initially rejected for its findings that not only did the ancient Egyptians have black skin, but the whole human race was descended from black-skinned people. During the 1940s and 1950s common assumptions about the inherent superiority of fair-skinned Europeans and the (therefore) relatively light skin of ancient Egyptian academics meant that such ideas could not be accepted. It was only the subsequent reinforcement of Diop's findings by other researchers that allowed them

---

TEACHING AS A SUBVERSIVE ACTIVITY

When Galileo, using scientific method, suggested that Western man would have to unlearn the concept that he was the centre of the universe, the institutions devoted to the conservation and transmission of this concept responded with something less than enthusiasm. Galileo had the choice of shutting up about this 'subversive' new concept or being shut up. He was scientific enough to figure out that he wouldn't be able to say anything if he were dead . . .

Along similar lines . . . when Charles Darwin, again employing the method of science, made certain observations with his naked eye (Galileo had used an 'unholy' instrument consisting of a tube with lenses in it) that led him to suggest that the concept of the origin of man depicted in Genesis might require unlearning, the institutions committed to the conservation and transmission of this concept were, again, less than delighted. The response to Darwin, however, was quantitatively different . . . from that to Galileo. A number of cracks in 'concept monopoly' had developed between Galileo and Darwin . . . so Darwin did find some support (mostly among scientists), whereas Galileo did not. One of the hazards of being first is that you leave everyone else behind.

Postman and Weingartner, 1971, pp 197–8

---

to be given credence (see Van Sertima, 1987, for Check Anta Diop's life story).

Furthermore, the biased nature of the curriculum throughout the twentieth century may not have been missed by the students on the receiving end. For example, Mac an Ghaill found considerable resentment among the Black Sisters, a group of girls of Asian and Afro-Caribbean origins in a sixth-form college in the Midlands.

With me like I go into school and I listen to the teacher and I put down just what they want. Christopher Columbus discovered America, I'll put it down, right. Cecil Rhodes, you know that great imperialist, he was a great man, I'll put it down. We did about the Elizabethans, how great they were. More European stuff; France, equality, liberty and fraternity, we'll put it all down. At that time they had colonies, were enslaving people. I'll put it down that it was the mark of a new age, the Age of Enlightenment. It wasn't, but I'll put it

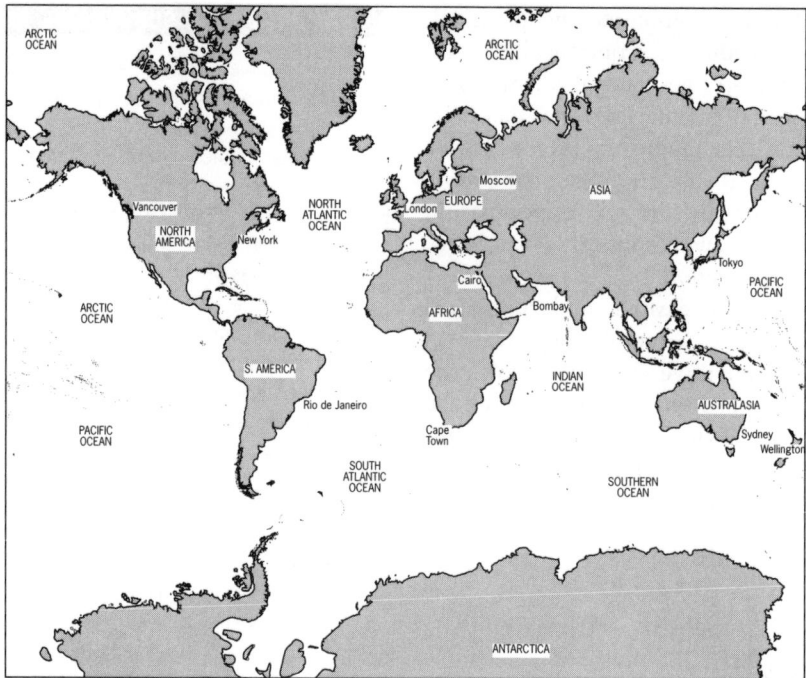

Figure 5.3 Mercator's projection map

down for them, so that we can tell them that black people are not stupid . . . I'm just saying to them, 'I can do it right, and shove your stereotypes up your anus'.

> Mac an Ghaill, 1988, p 28

These sorts of examples of the relative nature of the curriculum can be found in any academic subject and affect the way we perceive the world we live in. One of the most well-known developments has meant that children in schools today are likely to use a different map of the world to the one that was familiar to many of the cohort (see Figures 5.3 and 5.4).

The Mercator map was used in British schools throughout most of the twentieth century but was eventually criticized for distorting the size of the continents in favour of the continents in the north, its lines of latitude having been moved further apart the nearer they were to the poles. This also meant that the size of the British Isles was grossly exaggerated. Geographers claim that the Peter's projection map represents the size of the continents more accurately, according to their surface areas.

QUESTIONS

Compare the maps.
What impact could the different proportions have on students?
Identify and discuss other relevant examples of changes in the 'knowledge' provided in educational institutions.

The changing and relative nature of school knowledge creates major problems for curriculum planners and is one reason why the introduction of a National Curriculum in British schools met with some fierce opposition. Whether the curriculum is determined by politicians or teachers, it is socially constructed and therefore biased in various ways. If it is influenced by politicians, it is also influenced by their perspectives and could result in overt or covert political indoctrination; if it is decided entirely by teachers, it may not only be influenced by their individual biases, but also result in a lack of coherence for the system as a whole. Maclure (1988, 1989, 1992) and Ball (1990) have provided detailed analyses of the debates surrounding the

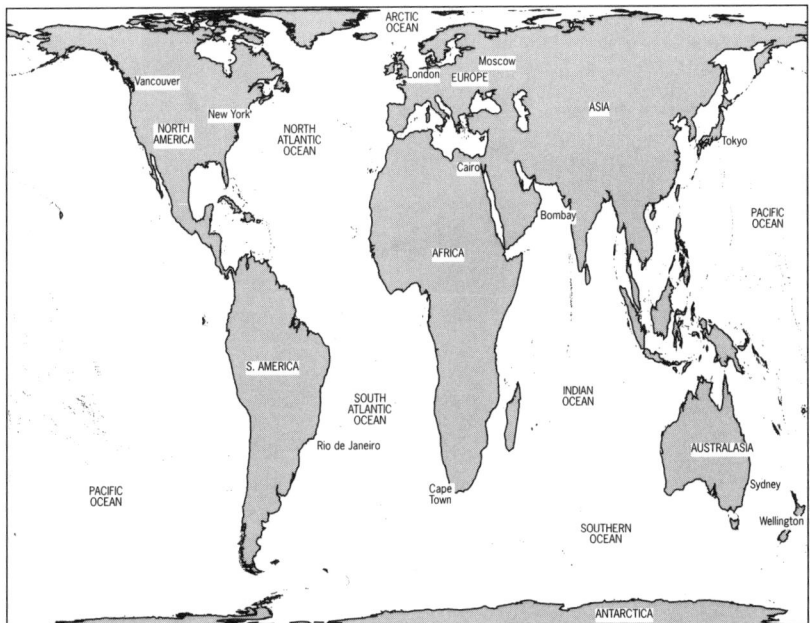

Figure 5.4 Peter's projection map

introduction of the National Curriculum. The main concerns were about who influenced the contents of the curriculum and how they influenced it. For example, when discussing the 'rivals at court', who were trying to influence the government, Ball (1990) concluded that representatives of the LEAs and teachers' unions were noticeably absent. He therefore noted his particular interest in the matter: 'In terms of curriculum policy the key question that is addressed here is not which curriculum prevailed but rather whose curriculum prevailed' (Ball, 1990, p 160). This is also the key question when considering more recent and future developments in the curriculum.

THE CURRICULUM: VIEWS FROM LABOURVILLE AND TORYTOWN

When the Torytown and Labourville cohort expressed their views on the National Curriculum they tended to focus on more practical issues. It was also interesting to discover different responses when they were asked if they favoured a National Curriculum and when they were asked, 'How much of what is taught in schools should be up to individual schools, the local education authority and central government?' Although most favoured a National Curriculum, very few gave central government the main responsibility for deciding what is taught in schools.

Teachers should have some input, but there should be national standards and therefore some government input. I don't know how much should be up to schools or local authorities but schools need to have some individuality in order to meet local needs, for local industries and local interests.

Iris, 1992

They're pushing the same thing into children at the moment. Every child of seven to eight is learning about Egypt at the moment but different schools might want to have their own topics.

Monica, 1992, thought that schools, LEAs and central government should have an equal influence on what is taught in schools

---

As long as they are willing to revise it, as we've got so many problems. We need more contact time for assessment.

Laura, 1992, in favour of a National Curriculum

I agree with what the Conservatives have done in introducing the National Curriculum . . . but in the National Curriculum too much is expected in too short a time.

Jeremy, 1992

In 1997 Jeremy said a lot about the need for wide consultation and negotiation (including schools, universities, colleges, industry) before planning a National Curriculum and

I believe in a National Curriculum and I believe it should be centrally agreed, but I don't believe it should be imposed without everybody having the opportunity to contribute.

Jeremy, 1997

At the end of the day central government. You realize later on in life that central government are far more aware of what's happening in the world than local government and local people.

Nicholas, 1997, central government should have 50 per cent responsibility for deciding what is taught in schools

I think it should be changed more to suit the children. Every child's an individual and I think it should be more suitable for individual children rather than they've all got to do certain things. They still need something, but it needs to be changed, I think, to show that even children that aren't as able as maybe the ones who can do things are showing what improvements they've made. Maybe they're not meeting their targets, but they are improving. You get used to it, don't you, you get used to working to a certain way, I suppose, so it would be hard if it was changed again to something different.

Valerie, 1997, did not know whether we should retain a National Curriculum

Questions

What possible reasons could there be for the different responses to the question about the National Curriculum and the question about who should decide what is taught in schools?
Who do you think should determine the content of the curriculum?

Testing

With the introduction of the National Curriculum came plans for the testing of children at the ages of seven, eleven and fourteen. In Chapter 4 you were shown how responses to these plans varied across the UK, with some local authorities in Scotland accommodating local objections. Although there was some variation in responses at a local level and in individual schools, the Torytown and Labourville LEAs tended to follow the guidelines provided by central government. Yet Chapter 4 also introduced the ideas of norm-referencing and criterion referencing, explained some of the problems associated with assessment at 11+ in Torytown and indicated that decisions about testing are often subjective. Cohort members often found it difficult to say whether they were or were not in favour of testing at seven, eleven and fourteen and showed in their responses that the issue is not at all straightforward.

TESTING: VIEWS FROM TORYTOWN AND LABOURVILLE

Concerns about testing in general

It should go on the full twelve months' work because some children have the knowledge needed but when it comes to exams they can't do it. A few children, they know. Their year's work is very good, but when it comes to exams . . . !

Audrey, 1997

But it depends what they do to them after the testing. They shouldn't be put on the scrapheap.

Leonard, 1992

But it should be a proper system, not one that they can't cope with. That's just a farce.

Monica, 1992

I'm not against testing per se, but it's going to limit what's being taught. In the National Curriculum you will be taught to do the test.

Natalie, 1992

I quite enjoyed school, it's just I was never very good at exams. It was 'Oh, you're doing well', but when it come to exams I just froze up. It comes down to what is intelligence and what do you need for an exam, intelligence or a good memory. The way I look at intelligence – intelligence is the ability to use what you've got rather than remember what you've been taught.

Karl, 1997

I'm not in the school sector and don't know much about it. I've heard that they [teachers] are bitterly opposed to it. [Read about it in the newspapers] I agree in principle that there has to be some testing but whether it should be as much as that . . . ?

John, 1997

Testing is a good idea

For the sake of the bright ones in particular. I'm dead against levelling down. I myself wouldn't have worked at school if we hadn't had exams to face.

Caroline, 1992

When we were at [. . . primary] we used to always do spelling tests every week. You were tested all the time, and now they just don't seem to be doing as much as we did when we were at infants and junior school, and at the high school I think the standards have gone down a lot.

Teresa, 1997

Concerns about the testing of seven-year-olds

They've got to be tested, but I don't see anything wrong with inspectors coming round. One hears awful tales about the quality of teachers nowadays. There has to be some sort of inspection – but seven is a wee bit young. I'm against government intervention provided the system is already working well, and it seems to be.

Bernard, 1992

It depends how pressurised it is. There's no harm if they're just to give a general idea but there shouldn't be pressure – especially at seven.

Nicholas, 1992

I think it's too young. I know it's an awful thing to say but [. . .] is extremely bright and she'll undergo tests at those ages as it stands now, and I know that she'll always do well, I think it's too young for a lot of children because, some children, it takes them a while to get going. I suppose it depends how the information's used, I mean if it's just to say at seven, it's like turning round and saying 'Your child isn't good enough, or whatever'.

Sharon, 1997

The testing of seven-year-olds is a good idea

They're bringing some sense into this testing so that they must now have a fair idea about what they can do. If they find that they're not doing well at seven they can get them to pull their fingers out. It's terrible the numbers that can't read or write.

Brenda, 1992

Questions

Why is testing necessary?
Look again at Chapter 4 (Assessment and academic groupings) and discuss forms of assessment and testing of children at various ages. Is it possible for your group to reach an agreement about desirable forms of assessment?

Special educational needs

Just as decisions about the content of the curriculum and forms of assessment are heavily influenced by changing norms and perspectives, so too are assumptions about other educational needs. In 1944 a child who was left-handed was often regarded as being physically incapacitated and in need of treatment! Indeed, my one interview with Frank (who died before I returned in 1992) seemed to generate more information about changing education than any other single interview, because Frank was an intelligent man who also happened to be illiterate.

> I was left handed and they tried to make me write with my right. I didn't stand a chance. I couldn't read when I left school so it would have been waste going anywhere else. I was clever in different ways. I had a photographic memory. I could picture something before I made it. If I'd been able to read and write I could have gone right to the top.
>
> Frank, 1988

Problems at school were not compensated by help at home because Frank's parents took no interest in helping him to read and write. Yet, when I met him, Frank was well 'read' and very well informed about current events because he was an avid listener to Radio Four. He explained that he had been able to keep his illiteracy secret for many years because his wife or daughter read his mail and did his paperwork. Jobs were plentiful when he left school and he obtained work by calling at businesses and offering to work free of charge for a week in the hope that a satisfied employer would keep him on. This worked quite well; Frank eventually became skilled at understanding instructions for craftwork by looking at pictures and diagrams and when I called he showed me work he had done on his own house in order to justify his claims.

Frank's problem seemed to be that his education suffered, not as a result of his own 'disability', but because of a system that was disabled in that it was not able to meet his needs. It is possible that, even if he had not been left-handed, he might still have had literacy problems; but it is certain that many children today are suffering, not because of their own personal problems, but because of disabilities in the education system and in society in general. Although there have been some structural improvements in education, much more needs to be done before education can play a significant part in generating a genuine form of social integration for people with special educational needs.

> All disabled people experience disability as a social restriction whether these restrictions occur as a consequence of inaccessible built environments, questionable notions of intelligence and social competence, the inability of the general public to use sign language, the lack of reading material in Braille or hostile public attitudes to people with non-visible disabilities.
>
> Oliver, 1990, p xiv

The 1981 Education Act defined children who had special educational needs as having '... significantly greater difficulty in learning than the majority of children of his [sic] age' or '... a disability which either prevents or hinders him [sic] from making use of educational facilities of a kind generally provided in schools, within the area of the local authority concerned for children of his [sic] age'. This meant that children could only be labelled as having special needs as a result of comparisons with other children and reference to the sort of educational facilities 'generally provided'. Implicit in this was the assumption that other children were 'normal' and facilities were generally adequate and it is this normalization that seems to be most pronounced in some of the comments made by cohort members in Torytown and Labourville. For example, although Frank complained about his treatment at school, he also spoke of his problems as natural and resulting from his own inadequacies, rather than seeing them as being socially constructed.

Ian assumed that some abilities were natural but also understood the benefits of extra help.

> They've [his daughters] done very well considering, they're only ordinary, I think they took after me you see. My wife's side are clever, but they took after my side, but they've applied theirselves, so they've done well really. They're not brilliant, but they're above average sort of thing, so they've done well. My other girl was dyslexic so she's really had to work hard, my oldest girl, but she's really worked hard at it, she's really stuck at it, she's done well. The school recognized her dyslexia, but it was towards her last year when she was leaving really. We sent her to a chap round here with his lessons and he put her right. They didn't really know, did they, at [the school]. She was struggling, it was spelling. It's usually spelling isn't it, I think. Anyway, I mean her spelling isn't 100 per cent, well obviously she's tons better.
>
> Ian, 1997

Henry explained the affects of his long-term illness.

> From eleven to thirteen I was hospitalized, so I didn't get to a technical high school until I was thirteen. I passed me 11+ to go to [school] but I couldn't go because I was hospitalized, that's why I eventually went to [. . .] Tech. That was the highest level they could get me to.
>
> Henry, 1997

Whilst trying to show concern about children with disabilities, Henry still seemed to assume that a disabled child was not 'clever'.

> You don't want the disabled child to feel any different than a normal child. But if it's put in too clever a class it's putting unnecessary pressure on it so its got to be very carefully monitored how you do that. You need skill to point them in the right direction.
>
> Henry, 1997

One of Sharon's daughters attended a nursery school with children with special needs.

> At [. . .]'s nursery they had a little boy that was autistic and one that wasn't hyperactive, but he had hyperactive tendencies (I'm not sure what the proper term for it is), which I was quite surprised at. It didn't bother me, obviously, but I remember reading something about how they want to try and keep as many as possible in mainstream education, you know like with hearing difficulties and eyesight difficulties and stuff like that. That's fair enough, for the children themselves, but if they have special needs, like if they have mental difficulties, then I think they should have their own schools, for their own sakes really as much as anything. I know it sounds really awful, but kids are cruel, aren't they? I don't think being made fun of and stuff is going to help them in any way. There's quite a few special schools in this area anyway, so I think people are quite aware of it.

Was having children in the nursery with special needs OK? Sharon could not help out in the nursery because she had a younger child, but she knew other mothers who helped out on a regular basis. They told her that

> Quite a lot of them they have trouble with. They're very naughty. They've got a few little naughty boys. One little boy, he only actually managed to go something like one morning a week and sometimes they had to phone his mum to get her to bring him home because they couldn't cope. Well presumably they're not trained to cope, which can't be good for the child. But at nursery level I don't know that it makes that much difference, but I suppose it puts an extra strain on primary teachers in having to deal with children that they're not trained to deal with. Which is why they're better off in their own – you know what I mean – that sounds really awful, but . . . [answer ends]
>
> Sharon, 1997

Kirsten worked for an organization dealing with children with special educational needs.

> Most of the children do go to special needs schools but some are in mainstream, those that are able, and the schools that are willing to take them really – if they're not too badly – with support, because there's support teachers in with them as well. Most of [. . .] children go to special needs schools, but there are one or two that are in mainstream. I suppose it depends how badly they're disabled.

[What do you think of that system?]

Personally, I think if we could have the facilities, yes, but the children, like the Downs Syndrome children, perhaps that aren't too physically (sometimes they have the hearing defects, don't they). But if they could go. I think it's good for people. It's good for my child to . . . I think people have different attitudes today anyway. I mean I grew up with a next door neighbour who had a Downs Syndrome boy and we just grew up with him and accepted him, but they did move away and my mum used to keep in touch and they said they had quite a few problems because the people didn't know him where they'd moved to, you know while he was still quite young. And I think it's an acceptance of people. I mean even now, I see some children, really very, very badly disabled (because we have the facilities there for them, you know playrooms and that) and I know the people who care for them, the support workers, I don't know whether I could do that, because some of them have gastrostomies, you know have to be fed through a tube right directly into the stomach, and I don't know whether I could do that, although I love children, and I love seeing them. I think we need to – because they're still children aren't they? And those that are able to go to mainstream schools I think should. Even ramps for wheelchairs – and I think that's sad, if that stops them, if it's just the physical aspect and if the school can't take them because they haven't got ramps, or they, you know – and they could join in, they could join in academically.

[Do you think the local schools are well equipped for them?]

I don't really. Some probably are better than others. I think that [names a school] is OK.

Kirsten, 1997

Jeremy was a headteacher and had many children with special educational needs in his school. He outlined some variations in the implementation of policies.

Certainly in the authority where I work they've found that they've got too many statemented children in maintream schools. When I say too many, they've got a higher percentage of statemented children in mainstream schools compared to other authorities. Now (whether they've been told to get this down, or whether it's a decision within the authority) its getting more difficult within our authority to get a statement written about a child than it was, say, two years ago. There now seems to be a move back towards some children going back into special schools who would have been catered for in the mainstream, but given additional support. We've just had a child who has been in mainstream all through from reception, and got as far as the end of year four, and now it's been decided (and we've been saying every year that she's not been making sufficient progress and would be better in a special school), and now they've decided to do it. And the last few children we've referred (thinking that they would be formally assessed and maybe have a statement made) have been put on hold and told that it would be monitored and looked at again in twelve months' time. Whereas two years ago practically everybody who we referred as needing a statement, they were being written.

[Is it better to educate children with SEN in mainstream schools?]

Basically, providing they've got the right kind of support, then I think they are probably better in mainstream education, but it sometimes becomes too expensive and it's difficult sometimes to target the way that you offer this support because you could have one child in a class with thirty children who has a statement of SEN. With that child comes a parcel of money, and it's not a vast amount of money (I think it's currently about £1,700–£1,800). If they've got particular needs then there may be extra funding available, but for the average child with special needs (say learning difficulties) that would be what would happen. What we've done is to add up the number we've got and we've employed a teacher part-time who withdraws children to give them intensive work on certain things like reading and spelling, and then they're back in the class for the rest of the curriculum. With other children (for example we've got three hearing impaired children at our school at the moment) they've got a non-teaching assistant who helps them. There's also all kinds of technical equipment to enable them to hear better, such as phonic ears and so on, so the teacher wears a device and they wear a device and they can pick out the teacher's voice from the sounds going on around them. And also we have a teacher who's been trained for the hearing impaired who comes in and does so many sessions a week working with them. So, if you've got that level of support then we feel, and the authority feels, that those children are better off going to a mainstream school than going to a specialist school, say for the deaf. However, depending on the particular need. I know of a child who is visually impaired and the authority wanted to teach her in mainstream and her parents fought against it because they thought she would be better placed – there's a school in Liverpool apparently that is superb. The authority resisted that because it costs a lot more to send a child outside the authority. But the parents have won. The child isn't at our school but the parent is a teacher at our school, so that's why I know that. She feels that their child benefits more from the specialist teaching she gets, and obviously the rest of the pupils are also visually impaired. So, that was an argument that went against the normal run of things. I would say that normally most children, if they've got the right kind of support, are better in the mainstream because it gets them used to coping with society generally and certainly people who are in the hearing impaired service feel that children in mainstream who are hearing impaired come on better than children who go to specialist schools because the expectations are higher and the things that the children are asked to do and they learn to socialize better. I don't know enough about what happens in the special schools to really argue about that but, my experience of the children we've had is that they have come on in leaps and bounds, socially as well as academically. The problem is even if you've got the money, getting the right kind of people, and sometimes the money just doesn't go far enough.

Jeremy, 1997

Questions

What particular special needs mentioned by the cohort would have been unknown or given an alternative label fifty years ago?
What other changes in the treatment of children with special educational needs are identified by the cohort?
Discuss your personal experiences of special educational needs (your own or those of someone you know).
How would you evaluate responses from teachers and others involved in educational institutions?

Private schools

When considering attitudes it was claimed that many people are attracted by the 'pull of tradition', a sort of respect for historical longevity that legitimizes types of educational institutions despite occasional criticisms. It was, for example, interesting to discover that the majority of informants were against the abolition of private schools, without any personal experience of them and although many thought of them as out of reach for families like their own. During the 1980s and early 1990s few had heard about Assisted Places, either by their correct name or, by definition, as an opportunity for children from less affluent families to go to independent schools. In general, it seemed that the importance of private education as an issue was reduced by its lack of visibility to those whose only experiences were of state schools.

PRIVATE SCHOOLS: VIEWS FROM TORYTOWN AND LABOURVILLE

When Nicholas was interviewed in 1988 and 1992 one of his sons had an Assisted Place at a single-sex private grammar school. Nicholas and his wife had to contribute towards the fees, and sometimes found this difficult, but he was generally pleased with the schooling his son received.

It was brought to our attention that he was very bright and suited to it. He had a couple of years when whatever school he was at would have got him down but now he's got over it. He felt pressurized and took it personally. But now he's in the sixth form and has grown up.

Nicholas, 1992

When Nicholas's son Timothy was interviewed in 1997 he provided a less positive account of his experiences.

> I personally wouldn't have chosen the private education that I got. I think it probably did me a lot of good educationally, I got taught well, but I think it puts you off too much from the real world and people perhaps in your own area, because being a private school I had to travel to get there. The friends I met there generally lived a long distance away, so I didn't see them as often. These teachers there, I'd say that half of them were very good and were really into what they were doing, whereas the other half had a mercenary attitude and were there just for the money and couldn't really care less whether you passed your exams or not. So I've got mixed feelings. I told my parents that I wasn't satisfied, and they told me to stick it out until the sixth form and to then make my own decision whether I wanted to stay or to perhaps move to a local grammar school. The teachers there, they thought I should stay, because I was doing well there. In my own mind I didn't really have a very happy time there, so I've got mixed feelings about it really. I think the reason I didn't move in the end was because when it came to the last two years to take my A levels it would have been such a big change again that it seemed a waste of time at the time.
>
> Timothy, 1997

Many interviewees thought that private schools were entirely funded by the fees paid by parents (see Chapter 4 about their funding) and felt that families should be able to spend their money as they please.

> They [the government] don't pay for them. We've got to have brains at the top otherwise we couldn't have brains in the middle. If I had the money, I'd have sent mine. You've got to have highly educated people.
>
> Frank, 1988

> Let them that's got the money pay and let them that's not got the money go to others. If people don't have to rely on the state, let them. Then there's more for them that do.
>
> Jennifer, 1988

In 1992 Richard was asked whether the government should abolish private schools which are outside the state system. He was unsure of his answer and asked whether they received a government subsidy. After I explained charitable status and tax relief (information I did not provide to other interviewees) he said 'Yes', but noted that he would have said 'No' if I had not answered his question.

When interviewees objected to private schools it was often because of unfavourable comparisons with state schools.

> The state system should be good enough. The more people opt out of it, the more of a dumping ground it would become.
>
> John, 1992

> Because it's elitist. A good education should be available for all. If all state schools were good then I wouldn't object so much.
>
> Natalie, 1992

> I don't see the value of it. They can get that level of education at a standard school. It's too elitist for me.
>
> Rodney, 1992

Some interviewees objected to private schools for other reasons.

> I don't think that education should be paid for. It should be every child's right.
>
> Michelle, 1992

> His teacher wanted him entered for [named two public schools] but I refused on ideological grounds. He also wanted to go where his friends had gone the year before.
>
> Natalie, 1992

> [Assisted Places.] They're available for the so-called poorer children to go to private or direct grant schools. But actually the money comes off other children. The middle class benefit because the working class don't know about it, generally speaking.
>
> Natalie, 1992

Some interviewees had more mixed views.

[Abolish private schools?] I'm a moderate and some of these schools are good. If I had to lean in one direction, I'd say 'Yes'. None of my children had a private education and they've all done well, but I could imagine the feelings of some parents whose children have not got a place at a grammar school and can't afford a private school. Still, if children are educated privately at primary level, they shouldn't bring them back into the state system.

Jean, 1992

I couldn't afford it. At one time I didn't agree with them but I'm changing my views a bit because I don't feel they're [her children] getting a proper education. The seven-year-old can't read or write properly.

Olivia, 1992

There's a few very, very special situations, like say Oxford or Cambridge, where they have the sort of tuition where they talk one to one, and things like this, really supersonic education, but basically I think that if a person's got it inside them, he's going to come out anywhere. I don't think sending him to anywhere super special is going to make that much difference in the long run. Other than if you're going to somewhere really swanky like Oxford, where you're going to get one to one tuition or something, then I suppose that has got to be something really good, hasn't it. I think that if you've got the talent and you're going to show that you've got the capabilities of doing things and passing exams, I think it's going to come out anywhere; I don't think it makes that much difference.

Lawrence, 1997

[How likely was she to send her children to a private school?] Definitely not. Well, (a) we couldn't afford it and (b) the school that she's actually going to – if it was at [names local private school] I might have said 'Maybe not'. I know it sounds really silly but if we did win the Lottery – because we do actually say this – if we won the Lottery, what would we do? Would we send her to private school? But there's only one in this area, and they've changed it all recently, and I don't like it, and I'd rather she stayed where she was. It depends how much we won though, I suppose.

Sharon, 1997

Questions

Do you agree with the claim that there is a 'pull of tradition' legitimizing private schools?
Can private schools be abolished realistically?
Would you send your child to a private school if you could afford to? Why?

Grammar schools and secondary modern schools or comprehensive schools?

Most Torytown voters were aware of the continuing debate about the selective system in their area but few had any detailed knowledge about how the selection process worked. This is not peculiar to Torytown, or to this period of time, as most of us who were selected for a particular type of education at 11+ have little knowledge about how the process in which we were involved worked. Interviewees also tended to have little knowledge of a secondary school system that they had not experienced personally and often favoured the system with which they were most familiar.

The most interesting finding from each interview phase was that many people believed that, irrespective of any complaints they might have had, they and their children had the right sort of education. Again it was a view of education as a natural process, combined with particular respect for some long-established institutions. Yet this pull of tradition meant that, when asked which system of schooling they preferred, grammar schools were compared with comprehensive schools and secondary modern schools were rarely mentioned. When interviewees talked at greater length about their experiences of schooling, their views of secondary modern schools were sometimes more positive (see Lawrence and Georgina).

In many direct or indirect ways, the grammar school took priority when interviewees favoured a bipartite system.

> I agree that there should be grammar schools, but that means making secondary modern schools second class. I suppose in comprehensives they still get segregated but I think that grammar schools should still exist.
>
> Monica, 1992

> They've been arguing so long about going comprehensive, but I support grammar schools. Each of my children went to the right school. We paid fees for one to go to a direct grant school because she was accepted there and we didn't qualify for assistance.
>
> Caroline, 1992

Some interviewees praised grammar schools for the opportunities they provided for working-class children.

> I'm changing my views about that. At one time I was in favour of the comprehensive idea but now I feel that scrapping the grammar schools (as they have done in most areas) was a mistake. It was an avenue for ordinary lads like myself from working-class families, who perhaps were able to cope academically. And I know that if I'd gone to a comprehensive, I probably wouldn't have done as well as I did going to the grammar school because I would have gone off with the wrong gangs and things like that. In the grammar school it was more geared towards achieving success and, although I wasn't a brilliant pupil, I probably did better than I would going to a comprehensive. And I think that's happening to a lot of people today.
>
> Jeremy, 1997

Some interviewees disapproved of comprehensive schools because of the mistaken assumption that all classes included children of mixed abilities.

> . . . because I don't think that mixed abilities can be taught in one class. I know they are to a certain extent but I think that grammar and secondary schools are much better.
>
> Freda, 1988

> In comprehensives it seems to be that everybody gets thrown into a big melting pot and when you cook that way you don't get the same standard of food.
>
> Bernard, 1988

Megan favoured comprehensive schools but was still not aware that children were placed in academic groups within comprehensive schools.

> I'm quite happy with the children's schools, but not the system. I'm not a great one for the 11+, but I still favour streaming once they get past eleven. My daughter's doing quite well in a high stream [in a secondary modern school].
>
> Megan, 1992

Some of those favouring a comprehensive system were aware of differences between comprehensive schools.

> I fully believe in the comprehensive system, provided the infrastructure's there, because there can be a vast difference between a comprehensive school in the inner city and a comprehensive school in a middle-class area . . .
>
> I think it depends on where the school is, where it's situated, the internal structure. There's so many variables on that but I think that a good comprehensive school is as good, if not better than many of the grammar schools.
>
> John, 1997

> But it depends on the catchment area of the schools. In [Torytown] it wouldn't make any difference because the parents of secondary modern school children are still anxious for them to do well.
>
> Mark, 1992

Lawrence and Georgina noted the different demands placed on their children by grammar schools and secondary modern schools and each saw some advantages in a secondary modern school education for their children.

I have a son of fifteen who failed the 11+, but knowing him as a person and the way he approaches work, he's gone to exactly the right school. If he'd have gone to a grammar school, he'd have been the unhappiest person in the world, because to be quite honest they don't seem to get very much homework and don't seem to do a great deal. It seems very relaxed and laid back. I'm not saying they're not interested but he consistently comes home with ten minutes' homework, whereas my daughter, at the stage that he's at, was coming home with hours and hours of it, and supposedly they're doing the same course. If he had more homework he wouldn't do it anyway, he's gone to the right school, the school that suits him, and all be it he's not going to come out Professor [. . .], Head of Chemistry at So and So University; he might come out as labourer at the local brick factory or something. As for if it suits him, yes it does. The system's worked for him. He is at a boys' school, and he doesn't seem bothered, and I'm not bothered either because at his age I wasn't bothered either. My daughter is seventeen and is doing A levels; she got in her O levels, eight A-stars and one A, which is a bit on the high side apparently. She is now doing her A levels in Biology, French, Economics and General Studies, which is compulsory. She wants to go to university and she wants to study Law, specifically Company Law. Her education opportunities are perfect for her, just perfect. She would have been like a fish out of water at a secondary modern school and my lad would have been like a fish out of water at the grammar school; it worked for them, because they're different people and they behave and do different things . . . The quality of teachers, even at my lad's school where he comes home with virtually no homework and nothing else, the teachers seem very keen and, you know. Obviously my daughter's in with a sort of more elite crowd and the teachers seem great there, they're no problem with either of them. I think they all do their best, you know.

Lawrence, 1997

The one who passed for grammar school would have been better if she'd not passed and she'd gone to the secondary school, because the one who went to secondary school was a lot happier, and coped with it a lot better, because the one who went to grammar school, she was a borderline case. So she struggled a lot at the grammar school, and we found at [. . .] Grammar School, if you were very bright, really bright, you came on, you were encouraged; if you were in the lower down, you struggled. So she would have been better, and she wasted a lot of time and when it came to exams she was messing about, and so I took her down to [college of further education] and got her on a catering course then and said, 'This is your last chance'. The tutor said to her, 'We don't mess about here. If you don't do the course you're out', because, he said, 'It's not school; we don't have to have you here'. So that pulled her round. She did brilliantly, she got every exam she went in for with distinction, but she'd wasted her years at grammar school.

Georgina, 1997

Questions

Consider the type of school you attended. In what ways did it suit you or not suit you?
Compare comprehensive schools with a bipartite system. Can your group agree on which is best? Explain your conclusions.

Opting out of LEA control

Chapter 4 explained that for many years some schools have been funded by grants from central government, rather than by funds from LEAs. These have included direct grant schools, grant maintained schools and foundation schools (since 1997). This type of funding became a significant issue when the Conservative governments between 1979 and 1997 tried to encourage individual schools to leave the control of LEAs (opt out) in order to be maintained by a grant from central government. Often members of the cohort regarded such schools as superior is some way, without actually appreciating that they were still state-funded. Yet this may have been a realistic impression of elitism, as schools funded by central government have often been better resourced than other state schools.

There was some confusion about what opting out actually meant.

I can't see that it's going to help them. An overall pattern (whether comprehensive or like us with the 11+, which I favour because it stops brighter children from being held back) is needed. Where do they go after they leave opted-out schools? Can they get into higher education? Private school children used to be able to get in. I don't agree with opting out. So often the wrong people are making the decisions.

Caroline, 1992

Some people saw freedom from LEA control as a good thing and some saw it as a source of problems.

They're given their own money and are not at the mercy of the people in the council. They [the council] couldn't run a barbecue!

Annie, 1992

It's usually the ones threatened with closure, but it means that the LEAs can't plan their numbers properly. They get more money at present than those who have not opted out, but this will change. It's been used as a political ploy.

Natalie, 1992

Two nurses compared the system to the introduction of hospital trusts.

I can't think of any in [Labourville]. I know that they can manage themselves and hold their own budget and are responsible for the hiring and firing of staff. They're similar to hospital trusts because they're both financed by central government.

Margaret, 1992

I don't know of any in [Torytown] planning to do this. I know they have their own budgets now and presume that they're like hospital trusts in that they get their money from central government.

Megan, 1992.

Question

How have debates about whether schools should be funded by central government or LEAs changed since the 1940s?

City technology colleges

During the 1980s Conservative governments promoted the creation of city technology colleges as a way of encouraging the private funding of state schools whilst helping to improve the quality of education in, sometimes troubled, inner-city areas. Although called 'colleges' they are secondary schools providing particular specialism (usually, but not always, in technology) and extra, appropriate resources. Some were created and have been very successful, but the scheme was not established as intended because businesses were reluctant to fund schemes that

they could not see as a profitable investment. Ultimately, central government was forced to contribute more to the funding of such schools than it had intended.

Public debates about city technology colleges had tended to subside by 1997, when the last interviews were conducted in Torytown and Labourville. However, while they lasted, these debates had been confused, mainly because some people could not clearly distinguish between city technology colleges and the old technical schools that were meant to be part of the tripartite system introduced in the 1940s. In general, therefore, very few interviewees had anything to say about city technology colleges.

Further and higher education

In Chapter 4 we considered a wide range of problems encountered in further and higher education. Critics argue that their rapid expansion since the 1940s was not matched with a rapid expansion of the necessary funds and that staff and students have suffered the consequences of financial constraints mixed with increased surveillance and unreasonable pressures to succeed. Credential inflation means that ever-increasing numbers of students are drifting into further and higher education in order to acquire extra qualifications, which are devalued as more people acquire them (see Chapter 4 for more on credential inflation and academic drift). Problems such as these raise questions about whether the expansion of further and higher education has led to a more highly educated population or to a fall in standards as more people pass through the systems (also see debates about standards, below). These debates were reflected by the interviewees in Torytown and Labourville, who often had strong but oppositional views about the standards, benefits and problems associated with further and higher education.

John, however, worked as a lecturer in further education and was grateful that he had experienced the benefits of further education himself, but was feeling totally demoralized and wanted to stand on a 'bandbox' to talk about his complaints at length.

> I was going to leave [his job], because I'd just had it up to here with the way that we'd changed from education as a means to an end in itself, that if you educate somebody, that person blossoms or improves. Under the Tories (and I think this was deliberate, and I could stand on a bandbox with this for hours), it's as though they wanted people with a very narrowly defined skill so that you've got the laws of supply and demand working at their maximum, where you can't bargain with that skill because there's so many people with the same qualification. And I was bitterly opposed to NVQ, because in my opinion all it is is simply a very narrowly defined training where you can do a particular task. It's task orientated so that you can do a task – but then so can hundreds and hundreds of other people. And so you de-skill jobs and compartmentalize them so that those people can never use that as a bargaining chip to increase their standard of living, because hundreds of other people can all do it. It's just simply a training. The means to the end is just simply to turn somebody out who can do a particular skill.
>
> Now I benefited from the old FE. They taught me more than I learnt all the time I was at school and they caused me to learn as well. I went on and studied myself. I could teach myself then. I became somebody who could just simply go off and research stuff and take external examinations. I didn't need teachers as such anymore. I became a self-reliant person who could go out there, study and come up with a qualification if I needed it, and absorb information from all various sources. And I feel that this has stopped in FE. Not completely because, the area that I'm moving into now, the old order still exists. This is why I wanted to get out into this other area, because I'm deadly opposed to the NVQ as it stands. It could be modified, it could be knocked into shape, it could be improved, but I think that they threw out a lot of what has been built up over many, many years, that the City & Guilds had done. The City & Guilds was superb. They didn't need taking under this NVQ umbrella because all they've become now is a rubber stamp. So I'm very sad about the way it's gone because they've allowed the private sector to move in (and that again was another death knell) to just simply churn people out as fast as possible with a very, very low level of understanding. They're just simply operators, functionaries. They don't really understand what they're doing and I think, right the way through, since the Tories came to power it's been a case of teach them so that they know as little as possible. Don't teach them anything about history, or they might find us out. I think all the way through it's been designed so that people just become robots to work for (if you like) the ruling class. It's not what I came into education for – to push people on so that they could reach their ultimate potential.
>
> John, 1997

Some of John's criticisms were supported by Sharon.

> [Did two year BTEC in business and finance, then] I went to university doing law but I didn't last very long [two terms] because I didn't realize how blooming difficult it was going to be. That's about as honest as it gets. It was a nightmare. I just made a bad choice. I didn't think about it. I just picked something out of the air and thought, 'Right, I'll go for that'. I was amazed that I got on the course in the first place. BTECs don't prepare you very well for it, I don't think. When you're at school you do your GCSEs and it's all essays and everything, you do your A levels and everything, you continue in that same sort of discipline. But with BTEC it's all continuous assessment and you don't have the same sort of pressure on you and it was just a big shock to the system.
>
> [Getting a place at university.] It's the only place that accepted me, but I had to get, I think it was five out of six distinctions. I got a distinction in every subject. I did so well! But that was the only place. Nowhere else would consider me because I did a BTEC.
>
> Sharon, 1997

In 1997 Sharon was considering starting another degree but hesitating because she and her husband were getting a mortgage and, although her husband was supportive, she did not want him to end up resenting it.

Despite her problems, Sharon was the sort of student Richard envied because he was studying part-time.

> . . . you weren't a student as most students remember being a student, as in the social aspect of it. That's when I talk to most full-time students or people who were full-time students, what they remember mostly was the piss ups and the

good times, and, incidentally, they had to go to a few lectures and then they'd cram for a couple of months and take their exams. But a part-time degree in engineering or a part-time MBA, it's not like that. There's no going out getting 'aled up' and if you go out and have a skinful at the weekend, you pay for it, because that was a loss of your spare time you could have done your studying in; it's just a different culture, it's a different experience. You experience it as a chore rather than a social event, which most people at university see it as, you know. Even Oxbridge students you see on telly seem to have a bit of a laugh, you know what I mean, they've got all day, haven't they, they've got all day and all night; you're at work from nine to five.

Richard, 1997

Timothy's experience of being a full-time student did not seem to match Richard's description.

[At university] it was very much like still being at school; you had homework and it was all very rigid, there was no real freedom. That's what I was hoping, that at university it would change, but I think due to the nature of the course being a very sort of new thing it had to prove itself to probably the heads there. It was very long hours as well. I think being so far from home probably did me no favours because I was in with new people. I made friends quite quickly, but it was such a big step after being in a single-sex school, generally, and being locally with all my friends; I think the combination just pushed me away. I think a lot of it was the fact that while I was at school the teaching methods weren't good, I didn't agree with a lot of it, especially at the boys' school; there was a strict punishment if you perhaps failed in a test. I thought that perhaps it might be unjust, you'd done the work but you just couldn't, you didn't understand perhaps what they were teaching you, and you'd be punished for it and made to do lines or whatever it may be. I didn't think that helped at all; I'd rather have had a teacher help me out to try to sort whatever problems I had. I got quite a chip on my shoulder with the whole system, I think, and then for it to reoccur when I went to university, it all being very rigid. I thought it should perhaps be bit more relaxed, the atmosphere, and because you'd actually chosen to do this course. I didn't think they should be treating you like kids, which they definitely did. National events in education definitely affected me at university because within the first month or so I was there, the teachers, the lecturers, were on strike practically every few days, two or three days. It didn't really help us settle down at all.

Timothy, 1997

Katherine did badly at school and valued her further education as a second chance that should be available to others.

I was lucky to get my education because I could pay for it. I did get some help from work, but mostly I paid for it myself. My nephew who was unemployed for a number of years – I felt that it was difficult for him to get higher education – financially really. I felt that he could have had more opportunities. I think its a shame that higher education is getting so expensive. Going back to the people who are in a lower social class, I think that if it was made available for people who, like me, left school without an education (of any academic qualifications) then it would be available for them to lift themselves up as they got more mature and more sighted on what they wanted to do, because I think that children as a whole, from just my own experience of seeing children, they have to make decisions at such an early age of what they want to do when they leave school, and I wasn't ready to decide at that age.

Katherine, 1997

Question

Do the interviewees provide any evidence of middle-ability students arriving in higher education because of academic drift (see Chapter 4)?

In Chapter 4 we also saw how the rapid expansion of further and higher education since the 1980s was made possible by the gradual reduction and phasing out of student grants and LEA contributions to fees. Again the Labourville and Torytown cohort had very mixed views about the changes and such views tended to be based on personal experience or (sometimes) lack of experience of further or higher education.

Although there tended to be less opposition to the loss of grants than to the introduction of fees, interviewees who had some personal contacts with higher education were most likely to be opposed to either or both.

[Should not replace grants with loans.] But when a student drops out through laziness or is kicked out, then they should be forced to pay some back. My daughter wasn't earning proper money for four years after she graduated. There should be grants but there should be a tightening up on attendance to make sure that grants are justified.

Caroline, 1992

. . . pupils are going to have to pay for education, their fees. That's going to hit one of my grandchildren, I think. Plus the fact that his argument was that it's related to the parents' income, but he is responsible for paying it back. So because his parents earn quite a lot of money, he will be paying more back than somebody else whose parents are earning less. When it comes that he's got to pay back, he's got to be earning over a certain figure. This is what they've got in mind anyway, so surely what the parents are earning doesn't matter; they pay back on what they're earning, so they should all be paying the same. I just don't understand the way that works. You know, if I'm a pupil and my parents are poor, she's a pupil and her parents have got plenty of money; because she comes off parents that have plenty of money then she starts earning a certain figure, even though I'm earning the same figure. She'd be paying twice as much back that I do, and I just don't think that's fair. I think that's very wrong.

Donald, 1997

At the moment I can't quite see how it's fair. Now whether it hasn't been explained properly or whether they haven't sorted out the nitty gritty. I don't think that if you've got working parents that you should pay because one of the things they actually said (I've forgot his name – the man who studied it or brought it out) was that it was the accepted feeling that if you had a degree that you would go into a job that was better paid than someone without a degree, which makes me think, 'Why does it matter what the parents earn?' It should be that you pay it back if you get a degree and that the onus should be on the student, not the parents. And that I would agree to, because I think that then is fair, because it's not the parents who get the degree. And that's the only thing I've felt particularly strong about – because it involves me.

Margaret, 1997

When [. . .] was at university we had to pay a lot really because we're reasonably well off in education terms. But since [. . .] was at university things have got much worse, which I don't think is a good thing. How can students start off with a debt? It doesn't seem right. It should really come out of taxation.

Henry, 1997

In both cases she [his daughter Sharon] chose the wrong subject and she was out of her depth. The fact that she got to university and didn't give it a go was very disappointing. From a parent's point of view, apart from the disappointment, it put the finances under quite a strain because we had to pay for it over several years.

Henry, 1997

. . . they are now likely to pay about £1,000 or be in debt to the tune of £1,000 tuition fees, which is the one thing Labour have done since they got in power that I wasn't happy with because I don't remember them broadcasting this very loudly before the election and it's a bit hypocritical because most people in the past didn't pay. And that's the one thing that they've done that surprised me. OK, they can blame it on advisers, but I was still surprised.

John, 1997

I know my niece [who was at university] says she's busy trying to pay off her overdraft, and I think most students are not prepared for how much they're going to end up owing in a very short time. She certainly wasn't.

Karl, 1997

Clifford voiced the common views of other interviewees who had no contact with higher education.

I know banks have schemes for students and the government's been pushing that they should pay towards their education, which I do believe in. I mean, it's a big gain to get a degree and it gives you a hell of a step forward against people that can't get that high, and I think you should contribute to it. I don't think it should be a free gift. I don't know how they're going to contribute, I don't see how they can contribute when they're at university. I assume they can give so much of their salaries afterwards, but I don't know how it's going to be done really.

Clifford, 1997

Negative attitudes towards students were very common and affected views about student finance.

It's only what I read last weekend about it, that they've got to pay towards the university fees. They were giving a 'for instance' of one young man who gets a grant, I think it's £2,000 and his outgoings are about £4,000 a year, because he spends £50 a week on beer. That was all, it was just general reading in the paper, you know, I didn't take an awful lot of notice of it.

Georgina, 1997

I did my degree one day a week and paid, while I worked four days a week. There's no need for thirty hours of lectures each week. These full-time students have lots of parties and so on. Why should I pay for it?

Richard, 1992

I've spent eleven, twelve years at university and colleges since leaving school and I met loads of people who were just doing pointless courses, who don't want to work, don't want a job, and they just put it off, put it off, put it off, and they have no intentions of doing anything. They've no idea what they want to do, and that's OK, but somebody's paying for all that, there's somebody out there doing a job they don't want to do, to pay taxes so they can carry on just being indifferent, you know.

Richard, 1997

Both my degrees I got part-time, so I did a forty-hour working week as a project engineer at the same time as doing my degrees. So, I've got a degree in Mechanical Engineering and an MBA, and I see them whingeing on telly about how they've got to get a job in McDonald's or a bookstore or whatever to help pay, and I also see statistics like the biggest consumer of beer in Scotland is the students' union buildings on one of the big universities, and I watch them all on Oxford Road, pissed out of their head in the morning, staggering about, still drunk from the night before. You go in any of the pubs along Oxford Road, in the back of Manchester, at night and it's full of students. They all seem to have dough to spend on ale, and it's very hard for me to have much sympathy for them, you know. I know I was on a full engineer's pay at the same time, but, you know, you've got to go to work, and I had to do the same exams as them. It was at the University of Manchester and the Manchester University's degrees; well, it wasn't the OU, so I couldn't spread it out indefinitely and take your time, I still had to meet the deadlines, particularly with the MBA. I struggle to have a lot of sympathy for them. I don't think it would do them any harm, I think it would make them think long and hard about whether they really wanted to.

Richard, 1997

Questions

Why do you think there was less opposition to the loss of grants than to the introduction of fees?
Does the relative lack of financial support for many students in further education justify the loss of grants and introduction of fees for students in higher education?
Is there a solution to the problem of student finance?

Teachers and lecturers

We have already considered various issues relating to teachers and lecturers in Chapter 4 and will now focus on associated public debates. Indeed, the most noticeable changes have involved the growing visibility of teachers and lecturers since 1944, as they have gradually been scrutinized more and more in the public arena. From a common acceptance that teachers knew best, public discourse has shifted through concerns about trendy teachers with dangerous progressive methods (especially since the 1960s) to a common belief that, unless they are closely monitored, teachers would fail to serve the best interests of the children in their care. Teachers themselves experienced what many saw as a process of proletarianization, as their status, relative income, job security and autonomy were seen to decline whilst the pressure of work increased dramatically. Moreover, in the 1990s, central governments made strenuous efforts to identify and sack poor teachers, whilst grading other teachers according to their levels of competence. Similar patterns can be seen in the changing public discourse about lecturers. Since 1944 (and especially since the 1980s) lecturers in colleges and universities have also seen their status, relative income, job security and autonomy decline, again whilst experiencing growing pressures at work as they have had to deal with the ever increasing numbers of students.

Interviewees in Torytown and Labourville were often most scathing in their comments about teachers when their opinions were based on very little knowledge about contemporary schooling. As few people had insider knowledge, opinions were often speculative, even when they were sympathetic. Sometimes opinions were based on the fear, resentment or respect they had for their own teachers. Hargeaves explained his theory about this.

When members of the public judge teachers, and do so on the basis of the many teachers they themselves have known over the years, they judge them through children's eyes – eyes that have seen the teacher teaching, but not preparing, marking or meeting. This is why, to the public, teachers' work often seems less difficult and demanding than it really is.

Hargreaves, 1994, p 12

TEACHERS AND TEACHING: VIEWS FROM TORYTOWN AND LABOURVILLE

I remember my school days and the teachers were crap and they deserved a lot of the kicking they've had in the last ten to fifteen years . . .

I'm heavily influenced by my own school days. I remember how bad they were. Teachers didn't give a toss, you know. I presume they've all retired or been sacked by now, because I can't imagine they carried on like that for another twenty years. If I met them again, to a man or woman, I'd tell them what I thought of them, you know. They just were lousy at their job, and they didn't give a toss. It was the 70s, you know, Leyland strikes, coal miners going on strike, it was a different culture, a different sort of attitude to work, but they're dealing with children, you know, and they didn't give a monkeys. I do hold a grudge about teachers.

Richard, 1997

Good teachers were often seen as those who could maintain control.

We had very good teachers. [Why do you think that?] They had control of the classes. They taught everything and you could understand what they were saying. And if you wasn't paying attention – well you had to pay attention, so you was made to.

Audrey, 1997

[Quality of teaching] When I was there it was a very, very good school but we had a very strict headmistress and I think things have gone down since the headmistress left. Everyone was frightened to death of her. She was very frightening. We daren't put a foot wrong.

[Would you prefer to have a headteacher like that?] Looking back at the time now – yes – but at the time it was horrible, but looking back now, definitely.

Teresa, 1997

Henry commented on the changing problems faced by teachers and associated them with control in the classroom.

[Thought that standards had fallen.] I think that over the years governments have meddled too much with education policy. They've tried to update it and in many ways they've made it go backwards. I think they've been too obsessed with results and not going back to basics. I know Mr Major tried to go back to the three Rs policy and I know in many ways you've got to update it, but what many people don't recognize is that society's changed so much since the 1950s and 1960s and that's not been reflected enough in the training that teachers have been given. Children these days, because of television and other factors, are a completely different group than they were in my day, so a teacher's got to be armed with the necessary tools to understand that and how to handle those sorts of children. If you took a teacher from the 50s who had to handle the modern-day class, it wouldn't necessarily be the right person to do it, because he wasn't used to the modern society. A lot of them don't seem to have any respect for anything, so the poor old teacher's got no chance. And I don't think governments take that into account. All they're obsessed with is good teachers and bad teachers. But it's like any profession, if you don't arm that person with the necessary training to cope with the input they've got, unless you're particularly talented or lucky . . . Governments are too detached to get that far into education.

Henry, 1997

Variation in teaching quality was often noted.

I feel at the moment, the way the education system works, it seems to push out the good teachers, they seem to be the ones who lose out and get fed up with it all, whereas the bad teachers seem to be getting (bad teacher is probably not a way to express it, but the teachers who don't seem to care as much for the children as our future), they seem to do fairly well.

Timothy, 1997

I know some of the teachers who are going to school now and two especially are exceptionally good. But then I know someone else who, if I had a child, I wouldn't like to put them under them, you see. It comes down to if they can control the children, and it's not their fault because they're not allowed to. Our teachers used to get their ruler out and you got a little whack if you . . . And it didn't hurt, it never hurt.

Audrey, 1997

Labour, they're too new to say, but they're trying to put money into education, which I agree with, and they seem to be trying to wheedle out what they describe as bad teachers, but I'll go back to the point I made earlier on, that I don't think they're going into enough fine detail and look at it from a teacher's point of view.

Henry, 1997

Positive and negative attitudes towards teachers could affect their status.

They used to be on strike a lot when I was at school. We were forever having supply teachers, but you don't hear so much about it now. But maybe they're not respected, not looked upon as – you know, like a doctor – you think, 'Oh, a doctor', and lawyers and stuff, but teachers – you don't really think of them that much as how it's a teacher. But primary school teachers, I think they're ridiculously important, because that's where it starts. It's the interest. If you've got a good teacher, you gain the child's interest and with a bit of luck you hang on to it. A lot of the ones at secondary school are a waste of time.

Sharon, 1997

They're not underpaid from what I know of them. Some of them are overpaid. They want paying in washers. You can't put a blanket over all of them. Some of them are good but some of them aren't. We used to have a smashing headmaster up here [points], but he's retired. You've got to have a good head to start with.

Annie, 1992

When trying to gauge teachers' pay, some interviewees considered how it suited their personal needs.

I don't know what they're paid. I've got some friends who are teachers and they seem to have an acceptable standard of living, but they're women and not a family living on a single wage.

Margaret, 1992

Teachers we know don't do bad – but they're all two-parent working families.

Nicholas, 1992

I'm better off, but it's not because I'm paid any more money, but because my children are grown up.

John, 1997

Some evaluated teachers' pay by comparing it with the pay of other workers.

I don't know what their wages are. They're like nurses in that they're absolutely vital in the social structure and should be paid accordingly. They say they're underpaid. When I worked at the university I was astonished that the pay of the lecturers was not great at all.

Bernard, 1992

I know what they're paid and it's not the same as people in industry. I think they're overworked more than underpaid. Some are very underpaid but some don't earn the money.

Megan, 1992

Probably varies enormously. From what I know of them, they're on about the same as a copper. So I suppose compared to a copper they're underpaid, but they only work two thirds of the year, they get that many holidays off; but if you translate that into an hourly rate it probably puts 25–30 per cent on their pay anyway, you know, compared to the rest of us. Probably about right.

Richard, 1997

I think, generally, if I look at what I was earning as a building inspector one time, and look at their pay scales now, although we have been treated outrageously recently, I think they have as well. I think in the public services they have across the board. So I tend to look at what other people are earning in the public services. I think it's not so bad, but when I look at the private sector I get annoyed. But I've not felt it as much personally because other colleagues in the public sector aren't doing any better or any worse than I am.

John, 1997

[Do you think teachers are better paid than you?]

At one time we [in FE] were slightly better paid than the schoolteachers but that's turned right round. A lot of the schoolteachers at the top of the scale are better paid than we are. And I think the universities have done reasonably well. FE has been pilloried really. In fact it got to the point where it was just site bargaining and you'd look up the road to another college, and you've got this dog-eat-dog – well, they're paid only £10 an hour now. And then you get this college from hell where these part-timers are so desperate for work. The lowest I've heard is £6.75 an hour, which is outrageous. They were paying cleaners and labourers in our workshop £5 an hour, yet they wanted to pay a lecturer – But of course they were changing the definition and the name 'lecturer' was disappearing with a whole area of Newspeak, which were 'facilitators', 'tutors', 'instructor grades', 'trainer grades'. And I thought, 'This is time to get out. This is time to go'. And then I thought, 'I might as well stick it out and see'. Because if Labour hadn't got in at this last election I would have gone. Even though it would have meant a drop in money, I would have definitely gone, because I could see that it was only a matter of time before they would replace us with the type of man or woman at the factory gate. 'I'll work for less than her, or him. Let me have his job.' And then you don't see what happens to them twelve months down the road, and that they're sacked and somebody's brought in to work cheaper than they were prepared to work.

John, 1997

Other interviewees reinforced John's views.

The people at the top are getting more powerful, materially and in every way. I work in education and the morale is very low. A friend of mine works in the health service and morale is very low there too.

[In her job] There have been a lot of cutbacks and they offered early retirement and redundancy to some. Some are retiring and not being replaced because of cuts in the budget. In education it's not really about the individual anymore as it's how much you cost. They avoid employing people who are on the top of the scale. It's become more money orientated through local management of schools . . .

We've got little power now. The teachers' unions are nearly dead . . .

There are things in teaching that are not right and morale is very low, which is not best for the children, but the unions don't have any influence at all. Mrs Thatcher killed the power of the unions . . .

Laura, 1992

The teachers interviewed tended to have problems when asked what social class they belonged to.

I'm technically middle class but see myself as working class.

Mark, 1992

Changing standards of education

Just as ideas about teachers and knowledge in general are heavily influenced by society, perceptions of educational standards are not based on an objective definition of what standards are (see Chapter 2) or how they may have changed. Indeed, some may seem to cancel each other out. Thus, we find that the introduction of computers into the classroom can be seen as both an indication of declining standards and of improving standards.

Arguments about a supposed fall in educational standards are contradicted by statistics concerning the proportion and level of examination passes but supported by subjective views about discipline and literacy. Before a debate on that subject could be reasonably attempted, agreement would have to be reached about how to measure 'standards' and elements of bias identified. Yet the identification of bias again assumes some recognition of

the truth, some firm ground or framework within which the debate can take place, and this poses problems of its own. It is common for favourable/unfavourable measures (the firm ground) of 'standards' to be chosen according to the perspectives of the combatants; examination passes and school league tables may, for example, be considered sufficient evidence from one perspective but not from another. From Melanie Phillips's perspective, standards had fallen because pupils were not taught the basic structures of their subjects; for example, language students were expected to 'pick up the codes of language by a kind of osmosis' instead of being taught correct grammatical structures.

When interviewees in Torytown and Labourville were asked whether they thought that standards had improved since they were at school, what emerged was a wide range of perspectives, including an emphasis on the range of subjects, depth of understanding, qualifications achieved, facilities, discipline, numeracy and literacy, tuition and capacity for independent thought.

Here in a nutshell is one of the driving impulses behind the thinking that has caused educational standards across the board to implode. At some point in the last few decades, the educational world came to agree that its overriding priority was to make children feel good about themselves: none of them should feel inferior to anyone else or a failure. At the same time, such people came to believe that children from relatively impoverished backgrounds, who unarguably started at a clear disadvantage, were somehow incapable of learning what other, more forward, children could learn. There was of course not a shred of evidence for such a belief. What disadvantaged children needed above all was more structured teaching, greater attention paid to those elementary rules of language or of arithmetic and a heavier emphasis on order. These were all the features which were second nature to those children from more favoured homes but which tended to be lacking in their own.

But the educational world, heavily influenced by other profound currents of thinking which all conspired to undermine every form of external authority . . . decided in its wisdom that disadvantaged children simply couldn't learn those 'difficult' things. Moreover, since it now held that no child should be allowed to do any better than any other, it decided that no child would learn them. Thus was created an examination system – the GCSE – which was structured so that many more children would be able to pass it . . .

At a meeting of the Conservative backbench education committee in 1995, Peter Saunders, professor of maths at King's College, London said: 'I don't see how you can teach skills and operations without facts and techniques. How can you operate with nothing to operate on? How do you teach any mathematics when the students lack the fluency in technique and the knowledge of the previous levels to follow what you are saying? It's hard to learn fractions if you aren't confident with arithmetic, it's hard to learn algebra if you aren't good at fractions and it's hard to learn calculus if you are still uncomfortable with algebra. It's also hard to navigate your car through a strange town if you haven't yet learned to change gears without thinking about it' . . .

The educationalists' absolute horror of 'rote learning', repetition and memory work meant that they were fundamentally opposed to the very techniques which were essential for children to achieve mathematical fluency.

Melanie Phillips, 1996, pp 12 and 15

Question

Compare Phillips's argument with those of other writers (e.g. Edwards on Creole interference and Bernstein on language codes) who claim that the importance of standard English has been exaggerated. What are their implications for students' progress?

Have standards improved since you were at school?

Yes – there are more subjects

It was just a matter of reading, writing and arithmetic when I went to school. There's a lot more goes on now.

Frederick, 1988

There are more opportunities than we ever had. For example, we never took languages.

Hugh, 1992

Teachers are not as good as they used to be but there is a greater variety of subjects. There's less emphasis on the three Rs.

Audrey, 1992

Yes – there's more depth

They're higher now because I don't know half the things that they're doing now. They leave me standing. When our [eldest] was doing maths I hadn't a clue what she was going on about. They're definitely higher . . . [About teaching standards.] Higher. They seem to go into depth more with everything. They don't seem to just give them set work to do. They stretch their minds more. They're not just satisfied with an answer. They ask why or how they reached that answer.

Naomi, 1988

They study in more depth now and make it more interesting. There's more project-based interdisciplinary study and more school trips.

Naomi, 1992

Yes – more qualifications

It's so different to when I was at school. Standards are higher now because they need to have more qualifications for the jobs they go after. There are so many other kids to compete with.

Georgina, 1992

More children are given a good education because more go on to university. So education must have improved.

Jane, 1992

Yes – there are better facilities

They must be higher because there's far less children in classes than when I was at school. I'm talking about forty-three children in a class when I was at school, so they must be better.

Jane, 1988

It's a totally different environment. There's so much that I'd call electronic schooling, computers and so on. Whether it's better – that remains to be seen. I suppose if we go off numbers entering university nowadays then it's higher.

Edward, 1992

We only used to do our ABC and 1, 2, 3. We didn't even know what computers were.

Emma, 1992

Well, computer-wise – and when I was going to school you were left to your own devices, like reading and writing and spelling. You had the slides and things like that to show to pupils. Today they have television.

Eamon, 1997

. . . the fact that when I was at school you never had any computers and stuff like that. I mean every classroom has a computer in it, so all the kids are coming out computer literate, whereas when I was at school nobody knew how to work a computer, so that's one of the main achievements that we've had in schools.

Ryan, 1997

Yes – they are better in other ways

They're far better. They've got it at their feet. In them days there was nothing. There was just the three Rs and that was your lot . . . [About teaching standards.] Fabulous today, but not then. I've been in schools and I've seen it. The teachers put it over to the kids better. In them days it was all the cane and God knows what. I think we learned more about religion but I think, with the teaching standards, they've got everything today.

Emma, 1988

Seven-year-olds in 1955 would probably not know as much as they do in 1992. For most kids, general standards are better. Children are also treated better in that they're not just sitting in rows and not having a say. Kids are more confident than they were. But there are some areas where standards are lower, such as spelling.

Natalie, 1992

Probably my seven-year-old is tackling work that we covered one or two years later. Probably my memory is playing tricks. They go to a particularly good school and I'm very happy with the standard of their education.

Rodney, 1992

No – the discipline is worse

Discipline [asked for it to be underlined] is appalling now. The three Rs. They're both worse.

Freda, 1992

Well, I mean, when I was at school, I mean you had respect for the teachers. They were good teachers, I mean I wasn't really academic, but that was my fault, but I think the teachers were good if you were prepared to buckle down. You respected them, and if you was out of line you got the cane and that was it. The discipline was there, but it all seems to have gone now, it's all slid away.

Ian, 1997

When you first said standards, I thought about the behaviour and the attitude of children. I think children are more unruly now in schools.

Michelle, 1997

No – literacy and numeracy are worse

There's more technology today (more computers) but most can't add up unless they've got a computer in their hand. This is progress, isn't it?

Philip, 1992

I don't think children today know the three Rs thoroughly enough. I mean, computers and calculators, they're rubbish. Even my wife today can reckon up as fast as any calculator. You go in a shop, you know what the change is, you get these girls using a calculator for 30p. Certainly they don't seem to be able to do basic mathematics. I think education's worse. I'm not saying the range is worse, the range is probably infinitely better, but on the basics it's not good.

Clifford, 1997

They should be able to read and write proficiently and do most other things capably, such as arithmetic. I've not come across it but I hear of them leaving school barely able to read.

Hugh, 1992

No – there is a lack of tuition

Children are not given enough direct tuition and they're left to get on with things themselves. Therefore, a non-motivated child can get away without working. It's the fault of the system rather than the teachers.

Katherine, 1992

They don't get taught properly. Some of the teachers can't spell. It's the teachers' fault.

Luke, 1992

In [son's] case, when he was at school . . . there seems to be a tendency these days to them teaching themselves. He was given books and then, 'Off you go'. At my school we were taught together as a class and given more attention.

Neil, 1992

No – they are worse in other ways

Because of government policies on education (towards teachers in particular), standards have not been given the priority that, say, the police service has been given.

Henry, 1992

Standards are the same

The standards are probably about the same, all be it the schools like to crack on that they're higher, but I don't think they are; I think they've done that just by fiddling the books and relying more on coursework.

Lawrence, 1997

I went to a parents' evening with the lads and the school seems to have kept up. Like they've got a computer room. There's no difference between teaching me to leave school and teaching the lads. They've just kept up with the times.

Paul, 1992

Standards vary

Any education would be better than what I had. But I think standards vary across the country. Southern schools seem to be generally better equipped.

Leonard, 1992

They're not lower. In some ways they're higher because some of the things they do are in more depth than I ever did. There seems to be a wider range of subjects as well. It's the level of knowledge. They seem to go into more depth.

Margaret, 1992

I left school at fourteen. Already they've got a longer school life nowadays. Nowadays they teach more subjects. Perhaps the range of education is wider. But they seem to be having trouble with the three Rs, the simpler things.

Edward, 1992

But it's hard to say because I was in a selective system. There's greater pressure on children now than when I started teaching seventeen years ago. The only standard you can use is examination results. The standard of literacy may have fallen but the opportunities are greater nowadays.

Mark, 1992

In the schools I come into contact with, it's higher – but I don't work in a deprived area, and my children don't go to school in a deprived area, and local schools have a lot of parental support, whereas when I went to school your parents didn't get involved. The thing that most concerns me is the class size and I don't think that's changed since I was at school, and the classes are still too large – especially in primary schools.

Megan, 1992

I'm not really talking about high schools, because I don't think they're improving, but I think primary schools are improving, because it's starting from lower down in the school, you know. A lot of the education starts lower in schools now, which is really good, but at high school I don't think enough's done. The type of education that starts in primary school is everything really, maths and English. I don't think they're strict enough with children and if something happened in the classroom it would disrupt the whole class, so it's the ones who wanted to work that lost out, instead of the ones who were being silly or whatever. I think children are just getting out of hand in high schools.

Valerie, 1997

Students are not learning how to think

I sometimes wonder. The more you spend and the less they're getting educated. Well, the less they're learning to use their brains. They have no imagination. Everything has got to be technical or else they do not comprehend it. They have no forward thinking. Everything's got to be today. If it's not happening today then it can't be worth bothering about . . .

Standards is overall living, ways of thinking, whereas children today need everything spelt out. They've got to have it in living images. Television is partly, but not necessarily it. They cannot visualize things, I find, and it all stems from that. If they can't visualize the possibilities, they won't even work towards the possibilities or use their imagination in any way. The standards they're looking for is what's on an advertisement, whereas we didn't have that advertisement, so if we had had advertisements we'd probably be just exactly the same.

Karl, 1997

But – we can't make comparisons

Schools here probably have similar standards to when I was at school, but it's difficult to compare them as the world is such a different place now.

Iris, 1992

I was at school in the postwar boom period when there was a population explosion, but we got a good education. We concentrated on the three Rs, although there was not much choice of subjects. There are more going on now into higher education, but as for the general standard of education as far as reading and the essentials . . .? Now children are more worldly and get a broader aspect of education. When I was at school there was a narrower sphere but less illiteracy.

Jean, 1992

If you're talking about standards at primary school level (you know, can children read, write, add up and do arithmetic) I don't think they're much further on than when I was at school. But I don't think they're dramatically worse. So overall I'd say that they're about the same. From the age of eight I went to a prep school to prepare for grammar school and everybody but two or three in my class passed the 11+, so I don't have much to compare with. Everybody could read. I don't remember anyone in the class who struggled with things like that. Now, regards the other ways of measuring, we can't really compare the results at seven and eleven because we didn't have the tests at seven and eleven then. We had the 11+ but that was a different kind of test. But, when we look at GCSE and A level results, every year it seems to get better and better. I know the suggestion is that the exams are getting easier, but the exam boards say they're not so I don't know any different, and so I would guess from that that standards are rising – if you measure them by exam results.

[How do you measure them?] I don't measure them in that way, because I don't measure them. I see them in terms of individuals. What was this child like when he came to me and what was he like after he's had the contact with me.

Jeremy, 1997

Question

How might individuals' perceptions of changing standards vary according to their personal experiences? (See Appendix 1.)

Political and socio-economic change

The UK experienced a severe economic depression during the 1930s and, when the Education Act was passed in 1944, it was still at war. Feelings of insecurity were obviously very common. This was followed by the lengthy period of the Cold War in which there was real concern about the prospects of atomic warfare. Yet the thirty years after the Second World War involved a growing sense of economic security for many people. Although extremes of poverty and wealth remained, public discourse tended to assume economic progress and increasing prosperity, and this reflected on positive public attitudes towards education.

It is possible that the real turning point in educational change occurred during the 1970s, when economic recession led to increasing pressures on public services. The welfare state was no longer seen as providing a safety net against the effects of unemployment, illness or old age and those in work often felt that they were experiencing longer hours and more stress. Whilst schools were having to cope with the impact of recession on individual families, politicians were 'rolling back' state support for education and simultaneously blaming education for failing the economy. The attitudes of interviewees in Torytown and Labourville to such wide-ranging socio-economic changes were interesting. Not only did they often blame politicians (and Conservative governments in particular) for job insecurity, cuts in spending on education and personal economic difficulties, but they also occasionally attributed their increasing personal affluence to government policies.

Bernard and Freda offered opposing views about the effects of Conservative governments, providing contrasting impressions of poverty and affluence.

That period will take another fifty years to come into perspective. Mrs Thatcher (whether you like her or don't) has had a phenomenal influence. She virtually broke the trade unions and changed the country economically. The country's not as strong as it was. The industrial changes might have taken place with or without her. Many young people now will never be in jobs. Isn't that awful? In many ways I'm quite glad that I don't have very long to go. It's the likes of you that will reap the rewards of the Thatcher era.

Bernard, 1992

There just seems to be more and more people losing jobs and no signs of jobs being created for them. Each year they seem to be cutting back more on what councils can spend. Even [Torytown], which is a Conservative council and very good on its economics, has got capped.

Neil, 1992

They have done a lot of good in some areas. The world recession was responsible for unemployment. They've made things affordable for people, such as cars (most people have one or two) and television – everyone has that now. Everyone has holidays abroad, whereas prior to the 1980s people stayed here for their holidays.

Freda, 1992

Many interviewees *said* that they were prepared to pay more in taxes in order to support education, although political scientists (e.g. Crewe, 1992) have suggested that lower taxation was a prime motivation for voting Conservative in the general elections between 1979 and 1992.

I'd rather give money to make society a better place (on health and education etc.) than have money in my pocket. That's why I vote Labour.

Laura, 1992

I've got education pretty high [on his spending priorities]. I think it's important, it's important for the future of the country, isn't it. I think it's been sort of run down by the Conservatives, or they've frozen spending on it, when in actual fact it should have at least gone up with inflation or something . . .

I'd rather see the odd extra pennies here and there. It would only take a penny or tuppence or something, a penny towards education and a penny towards health and I think it would be, for millions and millions of people paying these pennies, it would make a fantastic difference to the services that are available.

Lawrence, 1997

Many of the global economic changes affecting educational issues have been discussed in earlier chapters. Yet they were rarely mentioned by interviewees because they were not perceived as relating to personal experience. We have also considered how the fragmentation of inequalities and identities led to theories about postmodernity or late modernity. Later in this chapter we will consider equal opportunities and the complex and diverse ways in which divisions of class, ethnicity, gender and sexuality shape life chances, identities and educational experiences.

Perhaps the most obvious sign of socio-economic change since the 1960s has been the dramatic rise in unemployment and, in this respect, Conservative economic policies simply exacerbated trends that already existed. Heavy industry, other types of manufacturing and the manual work they provided had started to decline by the 1970s, and this was a pattern that was occurring in most industrially developed countries. This led to the loss of both skilled and unskilled jobs and an end to the notion of a linear career involving a steady progression through phases of education, training and up the employment ladder. Instead there has been a shift towards frequent transitions between various states and combinations of employment, family responsibilities, studies, voluntary work and so on, involving the constant acquisition of new skills. Schools (as Green, Wolf and Leney suggest, 1999) will need to prepare young people with new attitudes and expectations in order to be adaptable, live with uncertainty and be more creative in inventing their career paths. The role of education is seen as no longer feeding students with information but teaching them how to learn.

> This means they need to have acquired the attitudes and dispositions which allow them to embrace change positively and proactively. Young people need to have developed the foundations for learning before entering the labour market so that they can adjust to the changing demands of their employment and so that employers may feel they are trainable without excessive costs. They need to have developed the basic skills and tools for learning, the motivation to learn, and the ability to learn both from others and by themselves.
>
> Green, Wolf and Leney, 1999, p 10

Social inequalities have changed shape as new factors emerge, such as the problem of the *information poor*, who lack an adequate preparation for new, demanding working environments. Although workers may need to acquire new physical skills, a higher premium is placed on the need for higher levels of abstract and conceptual thinking, involving analysis, problem solving and effective communication skills. Some enterprises have become *learning organizations* (Green, Wolf and Leney, 1999, p 9), managing continuous adaptation and change by ensuring that their employees frequently acquire new and multiple skills at different levels of complexity. Not only are employees constantly learning and adapting but one of the functions of the enterprise is seen as engendering and sustaining a stock of collective *organizational intelligence*.

Whilst employers have shifted towards an emphasis on organizational intelligence, government schemes for work-based training have been met with growing cynicism amongst the Torytown and Labourville cohort. It was clear that many did not believe that the government was dealing effectively with the effects of economic change.

ECONOMIC INSECURITIES: VIEWS FROM TORYTOWN AND LABOURVILLE.

Getting a job

When I left school you could choose from hundreds of jobs (in 1954) but now you've got to be well educated to stand a chance of a job. There used to be that much industry in [area near Torytown] that anyone could get a job.

Neil, 1988

There's not the jobs for them [the working class]. They don't get the opportunities that other people do, or the education, and there always seems to be more unemployment where there's a lot of hardship.

Paul, 1992

I've had a lot of short-term jobs really, no proper long-term job. There's no job safety anymore.

Ryan, 1997

Most interviewees had cynical attitudes towards youth employment and youth training schemes

One of my sons is being made redundant in September. The other is on a youth training scheme and the wages he has are bobbins and I've lost my single parent's allowance for him, but he only gets £29.50 per week, yet he does the same work as others that get real money.

Paul, 1992

My daughter has had bad experiences on a youth training scheme. It's just a cop-out for the government.

Naomi, 1992

I'm not against the schemes as such. I don't think they're run properly. Mind you, I'm not up to date on that. I got most of my information from my daughter. When she graduated she was a year trying to get a job and went on some courses, which was a waste. That's one reason why she has emigrated.

Bernard, 1992

At the moment it's impossible for youngsters to get jobs. There should be apprenticeships as there used to be. We've got some youngsters on job training at my place but they're only temporary and would be better off on the dole. Most wouldn't do it for that money.

Philip, 1992

They're just a con. It's like slave labour now and there are no proper apprenticeships.

Leonard, 1992

They need proper youth training, not just six months of cheap labour and then they can't get a job.

Monica, 1992

Personally, I understand them to be a bit of a sham, no more than a way of massaging the unemployment figures. I don't know of anyone who's said they're any good. It would be just as useful for a plasterer to go on an evening course at night school. I don't know if there's a market for people with that sort of training.

Richard, 1992

We had to manage ourselves. The more they get, the more they want.

Freda, 1992

Opportunities for graduates

Bernard's daughter was unemployed for twelve months after graduating.

> She got various little jobs, but not a proper job. She got one job for £40 per week and stuck it for a day. She could have got a suitable job if she had been prepared to move but she wouldn't leave her boyfriend. They're married now and have emigrated.
>
> Bernard, 1992

Edward's son graduated in 1991.

> There's a Social Security-run sort of job club that he's a member of. He says it mainly consists of reading newspapers for vacancies.
>
> Edward, 1992

> [Thinks that good qualifications don't necessarily lead to a good job.] Because people go to university, don't they, and then they come out of it and they still don't get a good job.
>
> Valerie, 1997

Equal opportunities

The notion of equal opportunities has changed dramatically since 1944, although it must be acknowledged that it has always been defined in many ways. There seems to be an almost universal assumption that 'equal opportunities' are a 'good thing' yet if we try to clarify the concept it is likely that individual meanings will differ. In educational studies we acknowledge and consider the many weak and strong definitions of 'equal opportunities', although the weakest definitions could be more appropriately associated with definitions of inequality. The various approaches we are about to describe tend to make different assumptions about human nature (e.g. that we are basically competitive or basically co-operative) and the purpose of formal education (e.g. to emphasize the needs of the child and/or of the economy). They also tend to fit the discourse (or more than one discourse) of the moment and can be seen to change as their contexts change.

Many writers have noted that equality is not the same as equal opportunity; for example, we can be equal before the law but unequal in aptitudes and capabilities. Recognition of equality in one area may even be compatible with recognition of inequality in another.

> To have the opportunity of doing something is not the same as being able to do it. Yet just as surely

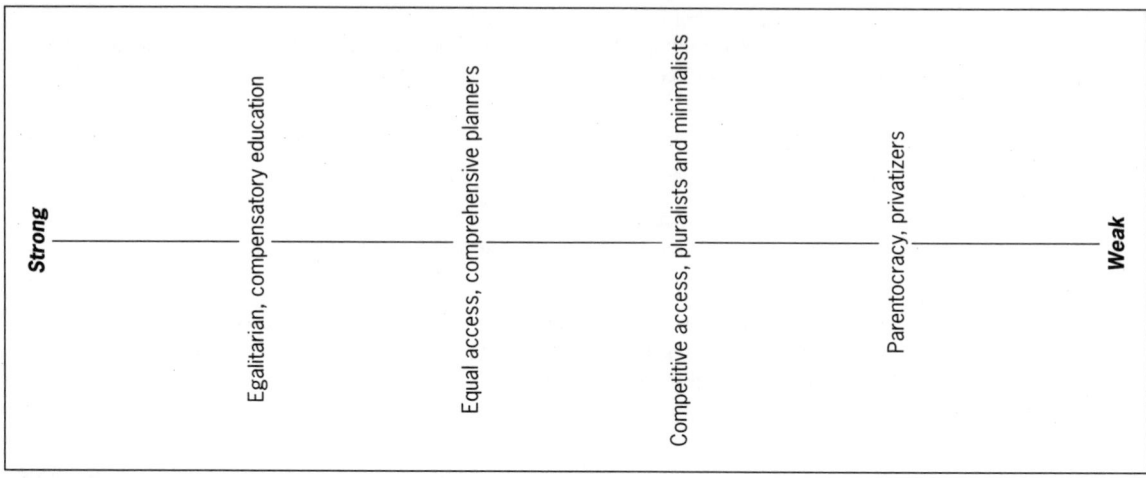

Figure 5.5 A polarity of views on equal opportunities

not to have the opportunity of doing something is the same as not being able to do it. Some would argue that to offer a superior education to those with already superior natural abilities is to compound the unfair inequality of nature with that of human institutions. Others would hold that to offer the same equal education to children of unequal levels of ability is to treat the able unfairly and unequally. This could be seen as the 'unfair' counterpart of counteracting the disadvantages of the dull child by buying him a superior private education.

Sanderson, 1987, p 89

It may be possible to describe notions of equal educational opportunities as a polarity, moving from one extreme (biological determinism) to another (egalitarianism) but here we are considering changing education and will consider how perspectives have changed since 1944. See Figure 5.5 for a model of the polarity of views on equal opportunities.

QUESTION

Before reading further, consider what 'equal opportunities' mean to you.

It has already been noted (Chapter 2) that during the 1940s and 1950s Conservative and Labour politicians managed to ameliorate their different education policies to a certain extent and find some common ground. The principles of Keynesian economics and pluralist ideas tended to dominate.

During the 1940s and 1950s the Labour Party seemed to be what Lawton (1992, p 17) called *pluralists* in their perception of equal educational opportunities. Although they regarded independent schools as elitist, belief in freedom of choice prevented them from legislating them out of existence. Pluralists therefore wanted to provide a state system so good that there would be little or no incentive to use independent schools. Yet, whilst allowing independent schools to remain, pluralists also promoted the expression 'parity of esteem'.

There are serious contradictions in this position: pluralism and 'parity' are difficult to reconcile, as are freedom and equality of opportunity, privilege and meritocracy. These contradictions . . . partly account for the past weakness of Labour Party education policies.

Lawton, 1992, p 19

This type of attitude was expressed by two influential Labour Party theorists, R.A. Tawney and Anthony Crosland. Tawney went to public school himself and was very critical of them, but did not suggest that they should be suppressed. Instead, he hoped that the state system would become so good that state schools would become equally attractive as independent schools and independent schools would become a 'minor category' within the system. He was not therefore prepared to let his views on equality override his support for liberty. Later, Anthony Crosland was also critical of public schools, but would not support their abolition even when he became Minister of Education in the 1960s and was under increasing pressure from others in the Labour Party.

This relatively weak view of equal opportunities emphasizes *competitive access*. Its vision is of a competitive system in which only a few children can find a place on the narrow ladder to success. In the 1870s T.H. Huxley, addressing the London School Board, called for 'a great educational ladder, the bottom of which should be in the gutter and the top in the university and by which every child who had the strength to climb might, by using his strength, reach the place intended for him' (Philpott, 1904, pp 153–4, cited by Sanderson, 1987, p 76). This metaphor became very common in the early twentieth century, enabling critics of the education system to even refer to 'missing rungs' or the 'lack of a firm footing'. Superior educational provision was seen as being rationed according to ability, the less able being provided with the sort of education that would equip them for relatively undemanding working lives. This sort of definition has supported the provision of scholarships, or the 11+ examination for entry into grammar schools and rests on two assumptions: first, intelligence can be identified at an early age and, second, basic aptitudes do not change considerably over the years.

Whilst the Labour Party of the 1940s and 1950s seem to fit Lawton's description of 'pluralists', the Conservative Party at that time tended to fit his image of the 'minimalists'. *Minimalists* believe in a mixed economy in education, accepting that the state should provide basic schooling but that parents must have the right to buy extras or of opting out of the state system altogether. Here we can see that a significant distinction between One Nation Conservatives (see Chapter 2) and the Labour Party of the time rested on their attitudes towards independent schools. Although the Labour Party has consistently held ambivalent attitudes towards private education, Conservatives have consistently supported it *and* held it in high esteem.

QUESTION

Compare New Labour policies with regard to equal opportunities with those of the 'pluralists' and the 'minimalists'.

During the 1960s and 1970s the views of the Labour Party and Conservative Party began to diverge as the Labour Party started to adopt stronger definitions of equal opportunities and the Conservative Party started to adopt weaker definitions (and this helps to explain why Crosland was put under increasing pressure to abolish private schools). Many Labour ideologists tended to fit the image of what Lawton (1992, p 17) described as *comprehensive planners*, a generic title for those who wanted high-quality education for all and believed that this was best achieved by a unified, planned system in which equal access to a high-quality education, with equal resources, was to be provided for all. The image is of a broad staircase to which all should have access; and it is this sort of definition that supported the provision of comprehensive schools attended by children of all abilities and (in theory) all social backgrounds.

Some comprehensive planners (e.g. Raymond Williams, 1961) advocated a common curriculum for English schools and Lawton explained the reasoning behind such views.

> In practice, comprehensive schools have found it very difficult to escape completely from the 'dead hand' of the grammar school. The curricula of most comprehensive schools has tended to be a watered-down version of the grammar school curriculum for the more able pupils and a sad neglect of the needs of the least academic. There has also been a tendency to equate less academic with less intelligent, less worthy and less important. Comprehensive planners have therefore tended to place great emphasis on curriculum reform as a means of achieving a better and fairer education service.
>
> Lawton, 1992, p 20

In the past this emphasis on *equal access* was seen as quite radical because of its insistence on equal treatment for all, irrespective of social origins. It is still popular today, but is limited in its application to social inequalities by the existence of a diverse range of schools, and its success is more noticeable in policies relating to gender and racial issues. For example, efforts to ensure that individuals are not discriminated against on the grounds of gender or race include the Sex Discrimination Act of 1975 and Race Relations Act of 1976. Proposals such as these, couched in terms of equal access, were able to gain more popular and political support than some of the more radical, egalitarian action promoted by the Equal Opportunities Commission and Commission for Racial Equality. The discourse of derision helped to generate a climate that was generally disparaging of anti-sexist and anti-racist ideas, but could tolerate 'weaker' versions espousing equal access.

Legislation has therefore been more successful in generating less discriminatory practices than in changing public attitudes. There have been many other initiatives since the 1970s in which the aim of changing attitudes had to take a back seat to the achievement of equal access. For example, the Girls Into Science and Technology initiative aimed to encourage more girls to take science and technology courses, and it had some success, but it was less successful in challenging the high status often associated with 'male jobs' or the low status associated with 'female jobs' (Kelly, 1981).

The strongest definitions of equal opportunities are often described as *egalitarian* and emphasize equality of outcomes, in which identifiable social groups are not over- or under-represented among high or low achievers. This means that the proportion of a social group represented among university graduates (and also among those without qualifications) should correspond with the proportion of that group in the whole population; for example, if 50 per cent of the population is female, about 50 per cent of all graduates should be female. When we go on to look in more detail at social class, gender and race we will see how far we are from such equal outcomes.

Egalitarian arguments have supported the need for compensatory education, such as the Educational Priority Areas promoted by the Plowden Report in 1967. In other words, some children are seen as needing extra resources and extra help in an effort to compensate for wider social inequalities. However, according to egalitarian approaches, social inequalities cannot be tackled by education alone. A new educational power base and other changes in education (such as anti-racism, anti-sexism and anti-heterosexism) are promoted, but egalitarians present these as just part of the necessary shift towards a more equitable and caring society in general.

The ideals espoused by egalitarians are, however, seen in a much different light by others. Critics, such as the writers of the Black Papers, argue that egalitarians see education as a handicap race in which some children have to be held back in order to let others progress. Far from arguing that some children should be held back, some of these critics (such as Sir Keith Joseph) have cited John Rawls's theory of justice and the view that inequalities of outcome result in benefits to the most advantaged, which also benefit the least advantaged. Although it is not possible to eliminate distinctions of natural ability and privileged education, these can work to the benefit of all. Thus, a better education for a prince, a surgeon and an army general will mean that they have qualities that will benefit the prince's subjects, the surgeon's patients and the soldiers in the general's command. Such views are commonly found among what Lawton (1992, p 17) called the *privatizers* (the New Right in the 1970s–1990s), who take an uncritical approach to inequalities in education and advocate generating educational opportunities via a market-led system. From this perspective stronger definitions of equal opportunities are unrealistic and impractical. They are unrealistic because they do not accommodate our competitive natures, and they are impractical because they demand too much action from the state via the education system. Margaret Thatcher's criticisms of the 'nanny' state were supported by her conviction that the state, and therefore education, can and should do very little that interferes with individuals' private lives.

Although similar to an emphasis on competitive access, this approach no longer sees competition as being only among children, but also among parents, who are expected to act in their children's best interests by sending them to the best possible schools. The ultimate aim is to provide a free market education system in which only those high-quality schools that attract parents will survive. As schools and families become more self-sufficient, the pressures of education on the state should decrease and consumer-led education should lead to optimum consumer satisfaction.

Brown (1990) called this perspective the *ideology of parentocracy*. However, an emphasis on this sort of competitive access does not allow parents complete freedom of choice, or eliminate selectivity on the part of the school. Some popular schools have had to adopt stringent criteria for the selection of pupils, and 'parental choice' raises uncertainties about who is really being selected in this sort of competitive system. Is it parents and/or their children?

QUESTION

Can you see traces of some of these definitions of equal opportunities in New Labour policies at the turn of the century?

Where New Labour differs is in its emphasis on parental duties as well as rights, and in its concern about equal opportunities in terms of social inclusion, social exclusion and social justice. In the next section you will see how the rhetoric associated with social inequalities has changed.

Class and status

Debates about social class and social status have always been problematic, but they have become increasingly complicated since 1944. In 1944 class and status seemed to be meaningful concepts. Yet we have seen (Chapter 3) that theories about modernity and postmodernity suggest that they are at least problematic and at worst no longer meaningful concepts. Indeed, the rhetoric used in debates about social inequalities has shifted from an emphasis on social class inequalities, equal opportunities and meritocracy (e.g. Tawney, 1922; Jackson and Marsden, 1963; Willis, 1977) to social inclusion, social exclusion and parentocracy.

Social class relates to an individual or group position within the economy or, as Marxists state more precisely, relationship to the means of production. It is therefore generally influenced by the sort of paid work done by an individual, or by that individual's family members, and in Chapter 2 we considered the practical problems involved in defining (operationalizing) an individual's social class. Such problems have been confounded by gradual shifts in the nature of the economy as a whole and jobs in particular.

It may be that status is a more meaningful concept than class, yet status also shifts according to changing social contexts. *Status* relates to the respect or esteem attributed to an individual or group by others. It may be achieved through one's own

effort or ascribed by others with no effort on your part (which obviously includes inherited status).

QUESTIONS

To what extent do social class and social status operate together?
Can you think of any examples of people with low status and high social class or vice versa?

Between 1944 and the mid 1970s meritocratic ideas tended to dominate in educational discourse. The image was of an idealized *meritocracy* in which status, class position and their associated rewards would be achieved as a result of individual efforts. Those who did best in the educational system would be given the most powerful, well-paid and high-status occupations. Even during the 1990s it was possible for some politicians (e.g. Prime Minister John Major) to claim that the UK had a meritocracy. However, claims that a meritocracy really does exist can be criticized for various reasons.

One way of assessing the influence of social class and status is to look at changes in the social class or status of family members over time. This involves monitoring *social mobility*, but there are

---

CRITICISMS OF THE CONCEPT OF A MERITOCRACY

It idealizes education and is wrong to assume that

- there is 'perfect' educational opportunity;
- there is perfect entry into occupations via educational qualifications alone;
- promotion in the workplace is via educational qualifications alone.

It ignores influences other than education, overlooking

- the significance of elites;
- the importance of personal contacts;
- the many types of selection criteria used by employers.

Questions

Can you think of any other criticisms?
Can you answer these criticisms?

several types of mobility, including *horizontal or lateral mobility* (change from employment in one place to employment in another, with little or no change in the job done), *vertical mobility* (movement up or down the social scale), *intragenerational mobility* (how far a person has moved up or down the social scale during his/her lifetime) and *intergenerational mobility* (how much difference there is between a parent and a child's occupation). Most research has looked at vertical and intergenerational mobility but in Chapter 3 we have seen that, as the twentieth century progressed, the difficulties involved in monitoring social mobility have become more apparent.

QUESTIONS

What problems are involved in monitoring social mobility?
Look at the family chronologies in Appendix 1. How much evidence of social mobility can you find and what sort(s) of social mobility?

By the end of the century sociologists were finding it easier to talk about social inequalities in terms of extremes rather than as social class categories.

> The gap between the highest-paid and lowest-paid workers is greater than it has been for at least fifty years. While the large majority of the working population are better off in real terms than twenty years ago, the poorest 10 per cent have seen their real incomes decline.
>
> Giddens, 1998, p 105

Put simply, social scientists and politicians started to use the terms *inclusion* and *exclusion* to refer to such extremes, although they acknowledged that the privileged as well as the underprivileged could be excluded. According to Giddens, privileged groups had started to exclude themselves voluntarily within 'fortress communities' as they sheltered from the discontent of those who were excluded at the other extreme and therefore 'cut off from the mainstream of opportunities' (1998, p 103). Ultimately, 'Exclusion is not about gradations of inequality, but about mechanisms that act to detach groups of people from the social mainstream' (Giddens, 1988, p 104).

> The new politics defines equality as inclusion and inequality as exclusion, although these terms need some spelling out. Inclusion refers in its broadest

sense to citizenship, to the civil and political rights and obligations that all members of a society should have, not just formally, but as a reality of their lives. It also refers to opportunities and to involvement in public space. In a society where work remains central to self-esteem and standard of living, access to work is one main context of opportunity. Education is another, and would be so even if it weren't so important for the employment possibilities to which it is relevant.
>
> Giddens, 1998, pp 102–3

QUESTIONS

How could the privileged and underprivileged be detached from the 'social mainstream' because of their relationships to education? Do you think that they are?

UNEQUAL CONSEQUENCES OF RESISTANCE TO SCHOOLING

> The crucial point though – and one that brings questions of class and structure back into the debate – is that the rejection of the offers and advantages of schooling has differential class consequences. Aggleton (1987) found that middle class students who resist schooling are advantaged in the labour market in general terms. The labour market defines class and advantage in the clearest sense (Weiss, 1990). At a time of high youth unemployment, all of Aggleton's middle class resisters were in employment six years after his study. They were involved either in service industries or in industries related to symbolic production and the arts. The available evidence suggests that resistance has differential racial, ethnic and gender consequences as well.

Whilst middle-class resisters may still be advantaged, working-class students who comply may still be disadvantaged.

> Willis' counter image to that of the voluntary walk onto the shopfloor, i.e. of 'Armies of kids' who have absorbed 'the rubric of self-development, satisfaction and interest in work', 'equipped with their "self-concepts"' . . . fighting to enter the few meaningful jobs available, and masses of employers . . . struggling to press them into meaningless work' (Willis, 1977), is as powerful and applicable an image now as it was then.
>
> McFadden, 1996, pp 297–306

Even if we agree that children from some privileged families are detached from the social mainstream, it is still clear that they arrive and leave school with many advantages (also see Bourdieu on cultural capital in Chapter 3). McFadden (1996) explained the different consequences of resistance to education for socially advantaged and disadvantaged students.

Many other sociologists have argued that social class is still a meaningful concept, even though it may be hard to pin down! Indeed, the cohort in Torytown and Labourville seemed to reach the same conclusion. In each of the five fieldwork phases, a large majority in both areas answered that they were aware of the existence of social class, and a majority also felt that social class affected opportunities. Yet it was also found that most were opposed to the abolition of private schools (which was partially explained earlier).

SOCIAL CLASS: VIEWS FROM TORYTOWN AND LABOURVILLE

How private education affects class

Well, social class is connected to people that can afford to give their children private educations. That's an advantage, isn't it, to them? Obviously the poor can't send their children to private schools, I suppose. It affects opportunities a lot.

Clifford, 1997

The old boy system still exists. Classes tend to stick together.

Clifford, 1992

If you've got the right connections and the old school tie it helps a lot. It may not be a guarantee, but it helps.

Karl, 1992

The old school tie comes into it. Perhaps not as much as before. It has altered in the last thirty years or so, but it's still there.

Ian, 1992

It affects every opportunity we have. If you're part of the old boy network you can get away with murder. Royals have been done for speeding and so on but they get off lightly.

Mark, 1992

There are distinct classes. Three: the working class, middle class and upper class. Education's important. Your type of business, employment and subsequent earnings determine your class. But now even coalminers earn a lot of money. Whichever class you're born into gives you a basis for life. My daughters went to a private school, which they feel gave them a grounding in what they would do.

Freda, 1992

If you've got money you can go to a private school. You can have private tuition. There's more guarantee of higher education than the normal working-class child. And I think to a certain extent there's still an old boys' brigade mentality within the country, particularly within, say, the London area and it's the old adage, it's not what you know, it's who you know. I still think that still applies, even in 1997.

[Reminded him that he said earlier that private schools should not be abolished.] Even though I've pointed out the privileges of being well off, I don't think the government's the right body to say you cannot have a private school. If they started doing that, you're becoming a dictatorship instead of a democratic country.

Henry, 1997

I know I've already said that higher education doesn't necessarily lead to a job but people with more money can afford to do it. You're expected to do it. You know, public school, you go to university, you get a good job, whereas if you were lower class, a lot of the time, if you want to go into higher education and you want to go for that better job, you've got to push yourself to do it. So it does affect it a lot. You're just expected in a way, and obviously they can afford it, but its not just that; it's like their social attitudes or whatever.

Sharon, 1997

In law [i.e. the legal profession], in certain areas, people are still recruited from the public schools. In the civil service in particular (central government civil service) there is still almost, you know, the bowler hat image. It's still there, very deeply ingrained. The army, the Church of England. I think that class order is still very much alive and thriving. I think it regressed very dramatically in the 60s, but under Thatcherism it flourished.

John, 1997

Powerful groups

I think there's a definite case – if you're employed anywhere – that it's a case of them and us all the time, and that's a form of social class.

Edward, 1992

The old aristocracy has now virtually ceased to exist but the new rich tend to defend their territory, and that may be worse than anything we have encountered before. A lot of them are extreme right-wing Thatcherites.

John, 1992

You've got to have the leaders and the followers, and the private schools produce the leaders. That sounds awful because I hate them, but they're there and I think they're necessary. We're a very class-conscious country and, even though I don't like it, it'll always be that way. You've got the upper class, the middle class and the working class, and the upper class become the leaders and the working class become the workers. And I think that's why this country is falling apart – because we're forgetting what class we're in.

Jane, 1988

It's difficult to put into words. It's very difficult for people who are not empowered by their position to actually influence decisions and get out of the state that they're in. It's easier for middle-class people to improve their condition than it is for the unemployed – or unclassified now. We've got a tremendous unclassified group.

Iris, 1992

It's who you know and where you know them from. It's partly being in the right place at the right time but if your face don't fit, it's not going to fit.

Karl, 1997

Accent

Accents have a lot to do with it. The higher class can get jobs because it's who you know and they help each other, whereas the working class have to help themselves.

Kirsten, 1992

Well, I think if you can speak better than me and you come from a better address than me, I think you stand a much better chance of getting a better job. And if that's not class I'll eat my hat.

Donald, 1997

If a [Labourville] child with a [Labourville] accent is going for a job together with another with a southern accent, then the southerner would get it.

Olivia, 1992

All workers are working class

I think we're all working class, because we all go to work, don't we. I suppose if you don't go to work, you're either ill or you're a very privileged person, or you've just won the Lottery or something, but I think we all work. I wouldn't see it as different classes, no.

Lawrence, 1997

General comments

It's not as bad as it used to be. There is and always will be. In my day, if you were born in the working class, you stayed in the working class. You hadn't a cat in hell's chance of getting out. You can today. It certainly does help to come from a good home and a well-to-do family but the underprivileged have a better chance today.

Albert, 1988

[About social class affecting opportunities.] It does. There's the rich, the middle class and the poor – so it does seem to have some effect. Naturally, the poor can't be like the middle class and the middle class can't live up to the rich – so you've all got your own grades.

Emma, 1988

I think it's very good for the people in Britain, how they get together like and mix, whereas they're on different paths like in Northern Ireland. There's sort of two lots at each other's throats all the time like, you know. Britain's very good in that sense.

Eamon, 1997

There's still a north and south thing, isn't there, I think. Well, it can affect opportunities like. It's not as bad as it was, but I think it does the old school type, but it's certainly not as bad as it was. It's still and it will probably always be there, but it's not as bad as it was.

Ian, 1997

There are fewer chances for those from the lower classes as they may get less encouragement from their parents than in the higher classes, and it's education which leads to jobs.

Katherine, 1992

You will always get a certain class because of the different standards that people have. Some of the wealthiest men I've met have been the most charming, ordinary people and you never think of them as a higher class. Conversley, some people have been snobs with nothing to be snobbish about. My husband had a public school education but he could get on with anybody. On holiday we got on famously with people he would not normally have met through school. The people at the bottom of the scale are the ones trying to impress.

Caroline, 1992

I should hope it doesn't but it probably does – but Mr Major's going to make us classless [sarcastic tone] so it should be less of a problem! I'm aware of class attitudes. Some people I work with have strong class attitudes, which annoys me because I'm also working class. It annoys me when some parents say, 'If it was good enough for me, it's good enough for them', as though they shouldn't get on.

Megan, 1992

I once thought I was going to achieve middle class, but I realize now that middle class (what I thought as a child was middle class) now is – I think middle class now is closer to upper class. I think middle class doesn't exist in a way, if you know what I mean. I used to think of middle class as like middle management positions and what have you. Well there aren't so many of those around anymore, so you've got like lower class, upper low, lower middle, and I think what I thought as a child was like they're middle class; I don't think there's many of those around.

Nicholas, 1997

[Sons would have had periods of unemployment but worked for the family business. Son . . .] similarly had to wait a year before he started this course that he's just completed. Now in that year he would have been in one respect unemployed, but he didn't claim unemployment benefit and I kept him busy anyway. So, you know, because of the family situation, what you class as being unemployed or not, I don't know, it's not normal.

Nicholas, 1997

It tends to be involved in recruitment and selection at all levels and is a distorting factor. Value is put on perceived class that isn't related to ability.

Richard, 1992

Gender

Sociologists distinguish between sex and gender because their focus is on the study of society and social groups rather than individuals. *Sex* is related to biological differences between males and females, is relatively stable and is therefore of greater interest to other types of academics. *Gender*, however, relates to social divisions associated with notions of masculinity and femininity and such divisions vary according to changing contexts. Indeed, it is interesting to find that in some societies the norms of masculine and feminine behaviour are reversed: for example, UK educationalists have for many years tried to tackle the image of mathematics as a 'male' subject, whilst it

has been seen as a 'female' subject in some Eastern European countries.

Until the 1960s discussions about equal opportunities generally focused on social class differences (usually between men and boys) and gender and ethnicity were not really on the agenda. Gender inequalities in schools were seen as so natural that it was assumed that boys would study woodwork, metalwork and technical drawing whilst girls would study cookery, needlework and other domestic subjects. Even today, sports lessons may be effectively segregated (particularly among older students) as it is assumed that boys and girls will be interested in different activities.

As gendered experiences changed from the 1960s onwards, education started to play a dual role (Pascall and Cox, 1993), with girls experiencing

	1975/6		1990/1		1991/2		1995/6	
	Boys	Girls	Boys	Girls	Boys	Girls	Boys	Girls
5 or more GCSEs grades A–C	7	10	12	16	13	17	41	51
A level*	18	16	25	29	28	31	20*	23*

Sources: *Social Trends* 1994, Chart 3.18; Statham *et al.*, 1996, Fig. 11.5; *Social Trends* 28, 1998, Table 3.16.
* Note that A level figures represent one or more A level passes between 1975 and 1992 and two or more A level passes in 1995/6.

Figure 5.6 Highest qualification attained by school leavers: by sex

the reinforcement of domesticity in their schools *but* mature women starting to use further and higher education as a source of liberation from domesticity. Indeed, similar mixed messages with regard to gender issues have been a feature of changes in education since the 1960s. Although educational institutions have responded to concerns about equal (gender) opportunities it has not been possible to separate women's experiences of apparently equal opportunities within education systems from their experiences of unequal opportunities outside of education; for example, Edwards (1993) studied the processes by which women tried to manage conflict between their education and family 'commitments'. Moreover, it is still possible to identify inequalities within educational communities (see Chapter 2 about feminist research) because they cannot operate in isolation from wider social influences. Parents, for example, have been more likely in the past to pay for their sons, rather than their daughters, to attend private preparatory schools and top public schools (Statham *et al.*, 1991, p 71).

QUESTION

The most prestigious public schools in the UK include Eton, Harrow, Charterhouse and Marlborough. Has the gender of their intake had anything to do with their prestige?

Macfadden's comments about how social class can affect the results of resistance or conformity to schooling could equally be applied to gender. The crucial point is that, although female educational achievements have improved dramatically since

1944, men with the same or fewer qualifications are still advantaged in the labour market.

In previous chapters we considered feminist critiques of gender inequalities and examples of how girls were discriminated against in the past, most obviously seen when girls had to achieve higher scores in the 11+ examination in order to pass. Discrimination of this sort was tackled by equal (gender) opportunities legislation during the 1970s, which had long-term effects on girls' educational experiences, ultimately leading to what Wilkinson (1994) called a 'Genderquake', as women achieved more qualifications (see Figure 5.6) and started to raise their personal aspirations. Although it still made sense to write about girls 'Learning to Lose' in the 1980s (Spender and Sarah, 1989), it was more realistic to write about boys learning to lose in education during the 1990s.

As boys started to fall behind in education, more concerns were raised about the femininization of the educational workplace. The growing gender imbalance among teachers (especially at primary school level) was influenced partly by men choosing not to have a teaching career and partly by assumptions that, as women were still primarily responsible for the domestic, 'private' arena, they (women) would be particularly suited to *emotion work* (see Hochschild, 1983). This concept has two elements, referring to the work involved in dealing with other people's emotions and the work people do on their own emotions in order to conform with social rules about how it is appropriate to feel in various situations. The concept labels as 'work' the efforts which are usually not noticed and which are often gendered, as it is assumed that women have a greater capacity to recognize, label and disclose feelings (Cohen, 1990). Many feminists argue that doing emotion work is another form of exploitation of women as it means that they subordinate their own needs to those of others and collude with male power. This can be seen in the efforts made by women students and teachers to work effectively in both their domestic and educational roles. It also matches my finding in Torytown and Labourville that many interviewees assumed that mothers knew more about educational issues than fathers because of their caring role within the family.

> ... to state that women learn political lessons in their 'private' world, even to argue that those lessons are crucial correctives to a 'masculine' political ethos is problematic. It implies that women have a unique responsibility for bringing the humanistic principles derived from the experience of nurturing and caring in the private world of personal relationships and family to bear on the public sphere. This skirts perilously close to recommending that women shoulder responsibility for humanizing a public arena brutalized by men's neglect. It ignores the potential for transformation of men's consciousness, and, far from exploding artificial divisions between public (male) and private (female), it threatens to institutionalize those divisions within the heart of the public sphere itself.
>
> Siltanen and Stanworth, 1984, p 199

By the end of the twentieth century it was clear that many previously invisible gender inequalities had been made visible and many had been tackled effectively. However, it also seems that in education and the workplace (including the educational workplace) expectations according to gender have in some ways been reversed. Whereas in the 1940s it was assumed that boys and men would achieve better educational qualifications and go on to support their families as responsible 'breadwinners', by the end of the twentieth century it seems that the reverse is expected, and it is commonly assumed that girls and women will achieve better educational qualifications than boys and men (at least at school-leaving age) and go on to support their children as responsible (often single) parents. More seems to be expected of women as social expectations have shifted from assigning women

to domestic roles to expecting the attitudes and application of a superwoman, without expectation of commensurate rewards. They may suffer from role strain once they become mothers as they strive for perfection in their dual roles as carers and employees, balancing a double shift that is rarely expected of men. Moreover, single women who are not mothers may still suffer the consequences of employers' assumptions that they will change that status at some time in the future. Meanwhile, men (whether fathers or not) may still be advantaged in the job market and be promoted beyond the 'glass ceiling' that many women perceive as holding them back.

Although few interviewees in Torytown and Labourville were well informed about recent educational issues, many were aware of changes in the educational achievements of boys and girls and they often assumed that girls were more 'responsible' than boys. They also provided illustrations of their own experiences of gender inequalities. Some male interviewees expressed real concerns about the way that education was used to reinforce masculine stereotypes and that this was particularly noticeable in boys' schools, where a traditional image of masculinity was reinforced by an authoritarian ethos.

It is also possible to trace changes since 1944 from an early tendency to ignore females (and make generalizations based on all-male samples) to a growing awareness of female disadvantages (associated with the second wave of feminism and the growth of courses in Women's Studies) and, more recently, to the opening up of new avenues of research into the construction of masculinity (for example, Roper and Tosh, 1991). Indeed many sociologists and educationalists are concerned about the role of education in promoting or tackling negative masculine stereotypes.

Experiences of gender inequalities

Albert said about his wife's lack of qualifications at school-leaving age:

> Her father was one of the old-fashioned sort. Girls didn't need them, so she never sat them.
>
> Albert, 1988

> [Mother's education.] For a while she was at a girls' private boarding school. Her father died. Therefore she left and I don't know where she went. She got some further education and a Pitman's shorthand typing qualification.
>
> Jean, 1988

Olivia said of her mother, who left school at fourteen:

> She didn't go to grammar school because, although she passed the exams, her father wouldn't pay for her. He could afford to but didn't. She went to an ordinary school.
>
> Olivia, 1988

Girls achieving better results than boys

> I only know fully what goes on in primary schools and I would say that, on the whole, girls do better up to eleven but the system expects less of girls at secondary age. At primary school it's easier to teach girls than boys because they're more eager to please.
>
> Jeremy, 1988

> I think girls mature sooner than boys do. My daughter, when it got to her GCSEs, was super keen, and she did dead well. My lad, on the other hand, he takes his in twelve months' time, and he couldn't care less whether he passes one or one hundred, he's just not interested. He likes playing his guitar, listening to pop music, going out with his mates, and he's not interested at all in school, not interested at all. I think it's a bit of male in him, but I think it's just his make-up. I can remember my education at the sort of age group that my kids are at, or certainly the age my lad's at. I did basically nothing at the secondary school for four years, and then it suddenly dawned on me in the fifth year that, my God, this time next year, I won't be here, I could be anywhere, and I'm going to have no qualifications whatsoever because I messed about. I really got stuck in and worked very hard in the last year, but it was too late. I came out of it all with what the headmaster said is the absolute bare minimum, and he said, 'If you come out with any less than this then you've completely wasted your time'. I got five O levels but there were certain subjects I suddenly realized I had to put a lot of work in, but there wasn't enough time to catch up with all the subjects, and I had to start axing subjects and saying, I'll have to cross that one off my list and forget it, and I'll have to cross that one off. I'm going to have a similar chat with my lad very shortly, and say, 'Look, you've left it all desperately too late; let's look at a rescue policy for some subjects, and the only way to rescue a few is to abandon some of the others and just say, "I will take no interest whatsoever in these, and I'll just concentrate on a few"'. I've got a horrible feeling that he's still going to come out with nothing at the end of it anyway. He's just not interested, but I'm going to try. I feel I've got to try and do something.
>
> Lawrence, 1997

> Well, I'll just go off my children, and my daughter is doing what she wanted to do and she was given every encouragement at school, so I'm very satisfied with her education. My son's a bit of a disappointment, but that was nothing to do with the school, it was his own, he didn't work, so, but he was given every opportunity.
>
> Michelle, 1997

> He was grammar school material anyway, so in [son's] case everything was there. More than enough. It's just that, like me, he doesn't particularly take to education in general, as a whole. He takes out certain things and enjoys doing that, but [of his sons] they don't take to or like the sort of regime and if they think a teacher is, putting it mildly, a fool then they immediately turn off to that person, like that guy's a fool. They're both very intelligent lads and they know what they want, and if it's not there, or they don't particularly take to things, then there's not a lot you can do really. I walked out of school, I didn't even take my O levels. I just walked out of school. It's not something I'm proud of. It was [. . .] Grammar. I was bright enough. This is where I can't fault my lads, because they inherited something.
>
> Nicholas, 1997

> Girls seem to buckle down better than boys. They seem to get less distracted.
>
> Henry, 1997

Sharon, 1997, knew that girls were achieving better results than boys. During the interview her four-year-old daughter told me, 'I'm clever. I'm going to go to college'.

> I know a lot of the girls in [son's] class are brighter than the boys but, generally – it's certain subjects as well, isn't it. I think it's how they're taught because boys are more in the sciences, aren't they. They're supposed to do well, aren't they, better than girls. But I don't know how true that is.
>
> Kirsten, 1997

> [Not surprised when he read in newspaper that girls were doing better than boys.] Overall, I've worked with more women than men and my opinion of most men is distinctly not over-confident in their abilities to think. Women may appear to be a bit silly at times but, when it comes to thinking things through, I've always found that they work it out a lot better.
>
> Karl, 1997

Single-sex or coeducational schools?

Although most interviewees had no strong feelings for or against single-sex education, those who did comment were mostly in favour of coeducational schools. Ryan was typical in being quite satisfied with his own education but 'I would have preferred to have gone to a mixed school, because probably I'd have learnt more social skills' (1997).

> I just heard that when boys and girls are together that generally boys do worse. They tend to do less well compared to when they're on their own in a boys-only school, although I have my own feelings about that. I went to a boys' school, and it changed when I entered the sixth form; it started bringing girls as well, and I thought it was a bit of a – I don't know – I don't think it did me any favours by it being boys only, socially anyway.
>
> Timothy, 1997

> It was a single-sex school up until the last two years I was there, and then the girls were brought in in stages. They brought them into the sixth form and started from the first year; it would have taken a few years for it to be mixed properly. The girls were just in the sixth form when I was there, and it was a ratio of about ten to one, so even then it wasn't really mixed. The fact that it was a boys-only school was one of my biggest complaints about the school. I don't think it helped at all, because it just cut you off too much socially with girls, you didn't know what to do or how to talk to them and, you know, social environment and so I don't think it did me any favours. It affected the ethos of the school, things like the games; everything had a very – you had to be a real man in every sport you did. If for any reason you couldn't keep up, you'd be knocked down for that. I thought that perhaps they'd be more lenient if there were girls there. You could tell that by the sort of sports they were doing there as well – and they had their own swimming pool, and things like that. There were no female-type subjects on offer, nothing at all. I don't think I would have taken them anyway, but it would have been nice to have the opportunity.
>
> Timothy, 1997

Sharon attended a single-sex grammar and met her husband there after it changed to a coeducational school in 1986.

> [Single sex school.] I don't believe in it. For a lot of the kids it's a big shock to the system [means her school changing to coed] because at that age, you're like fourteen or fifteen, hormones are running amock, you're trying to concentrate on your exams, you've had boys up until the age of eleven (and I know they're a pain, they really drive you mad when they're that age, they really do) but I don't see the point in separating them because all it does is increase the interest even more. I know the point of keeping them apart was to concentrate on their studies, but I don't think it works.
>
> Sharon, 1997

> [Attended a single-sex secondary school.] It didn't bother me at the time but, looking back, I think it would have probably been better for our own personal development if it had been coeducational because we had a strange attitude to girls. They were like other beings. Because you didn't mix with them in school we were very chauvinistic.
>
> Jeremy, 1997

> I didn't mind it being an all-boys school. I think at eleven – I don't think you recognize girls for what they are, you know. They're a nuisance I suppose when you're eleven, so it was better at a boys' school, I suppose.
>
> Clifford, 1997

Tackling sexism

No one can make you feel inferior without your own consent.

Eleanor Roosevelt, 1884–1962,
cited in Exley, 1993

Many sociologists and feminists are likely to argue that sexism in education *has* made many people feel inferior without their consent *but* that we must consider what we mean by 'consent'. The point is that sexism may have been legitimized, normalized and internalized by its victims, who can then go on to collude in their own oppression. Sociologists studying classroom interaction have, for example, had to deal with their encounters with schoolgirls who feigned ignorance because they believed that boys would find it more attractive than intelligence.

Thus, feminists have not only challenged the more obvious forms of sexism associated with a biased curriculum, sexist language in textbooks and negative stereotyping by teachers, but have also tried to empower girls and women; for example, in Women's Studies by providing a discursive space where women can write, read and think as women and about women.

The revolt of women, unlike the explosion of the French Revolution, is a creeping revolution, a sub-revolution proceeding like a cat: on cat's paws but always with claws. Wherever it touches it changes industrial society's sensitive underside, the private sphere, and reaches from there (and back?) into the peaks of male domination and certainty. The sub-revolution of women, which directly cuts up the nervous system of the everyday order of society, despite setback, can certainly give society

---

STRATEGIES FOR EQUAL GENDER OPPORTUNITIES

Equal opportunities	*Anti-sexist*
Persuading girls into science and technology	Recognizing the importance of girl-centred study; for example, 'herstory' as well as 'history', or girl- and woman-centred science and technology
Providing a compulsory common core of subjects to include 'hard' sciences for girls and humanities for boys	Providing girls with skills and knowledge to challenge the male system in the workplace and the home
Analysing sexism in textbooks, readers and resources	Widening girls' horizons while not denigrating the work of their mothers, female friends and women in the community
Reviewing school organization – for example, registers, assemblies, uniform, discipline	Changing the nature of schooling: replacing hierarchy, competitiveness, authoritarianism and selection with co-operation, democracy, egalitarianism and community
Producing in-service courses and policy guidelines	Exploring the relationship between sexuality, women's oppression and sexual harassment in school and the workplace
Establishing mixed-sex working parties to develop and monitor school policy	Establishing schoolgirls' and women's support groups
Creating posts for equal opportunities	Decision-making through wide consultation and collective working

Adapted from Weiner (1985), quoted in Arnot (1986)

Questions

What do the two approaches have in common?
Which approach do you think has been most successfully followed and why?

a different face. One need only venture this thought experiment: a society in which men and women were really equal (whatever that might imply in detail) would without doubt be a new modernity. The fact that walls to prevent this are built from nature, anthropology and ideas of family and maternal happiness with the deliberate co-operation of women is another matter. It is not the least of all the shock precipitated by the failure, in the view of many women, of the permanent feminist revolution which serve as a measure of the changes that will face us from its success. As social science studies show, the broad variety of fundamentalisms are patriarchal reactions, attempts to reordain the masculine 'laws of gravity'.

Beck, in Beck, Giddens and Lash, 1994, pp 26–7

QUESTION

Consider Beck's 'thought experiment'. What would an education system be like in which males and females were really equal? What are the 'walls to prevent this'?

Gaby Weiner's (1985) summary of gender-related policies and strategies may provide a useful over-all view of changes since the 1970s. The 'equal opportunities' approach is similar to what has already been described as an equal access approach to equal opportunities. It reflects a fairly moderate interpretation of equal opportunities, compared to the stronger, egalitarian 'anti-sexist' approach.

There are many problems involved in study-ing sexism in education but one of the most sig-nificant is that of trying to isolate sexism from other sources of oppression affecting education: as Spelman (1990) observed, all women are women but no woman is only a woman. Some feminists have argued that debates have been dominated by certain types of women, thus ignoring the needs of girls and women who are black, disabled, gay or experience other forms of oppression.

Sexuality

In 1944 any sex education provided in schools was primarily about biology and reproduction, the assumption being that sexual relationships were between married heterosexual couples. Male homo-sexuality was illegal at any age, lesbianism was generally ignored, abortions were illegal, birth control clinics were not open to young, unmarried people and the pill was not yet available. What has often been described as a sexual revolution in the 1960s had long-term effects on sex education in schools, as more emphasis started to be placed on debates about morality, relationships and new family structures. This reflected ideas about the fragmentation and diversification of society and included acknowledgement of various types of sexuality.

Jones and Mahony (1989) studied the historical background to debates about homosexuality and education and criticized the sociology of education for the way it had ignored the promotion of hetero-sexuality and homophobia in the past. Schooling has been a major influence on the development of attitudes towards sexuality, whether that influence may come from the curriculum or from playground banter. The inclusion or exclusion of any references to homosexuality in the curriculum has implications for the social construction of knowledge. Inter-pretive sociologists have also generated accounts of the, often negative, experiences of homosexuals in academic environments.

Tackling debates about homosexuality is as much a problem for teachers today as tackling debates about pre-marital sex was in the past (and in the present in some, especially religious, schools). Indeed, during the early 1980s, when teaching in a Roman Catholic sixth-form college, I found that, in essays on population changes, my students ig-nored what we had discussed in class about the effects of developments in birth control. In their educational environment it was a sensitive issue and best not put down on paper. Similarly, in 1988 there was much public debate about Clause 28 of the Local Government Act, which aimed to pre-vent the teaching of homosexuality as a normal family relationship and I asked the Torytown and Labourville cohort whether they had heard about it. Although many had heard about it, they did not tend to supplement very brief answers with their usual lengthy comments and some looked decidedly uncomfortable. Perhaps Margaret was an exception because she was a nurse.

This is Clause 28. I'd never heard of them as a kiddy. I've learned about homosexuality as an adult and therefore accept it. I wouldn't want children to accept it as a norm. Learning about them when you're older, you just accept them for what they are – full stop. I don't think they should be emphasized.

Margaret, 1988

Sociologists have acknowledged uncertainties about whether, or how, teachers should tackle debates about sexuality, noting that they may have a considerable influence on social attitudes.

While pre-marital sex is now accepted as 'normal' behaviour, there is no such acceptance of sexual relations among same sex adults. Indeed, there is considerable dispute about whether homosexuality is a biological aberration (an essentialist view) or one particular manifestation among the range of sexual categories and behaviours that display historical and cultural variability over time (the social constructionist view). If such conceptual differences are influential in determining attitudes towards homosexuality, then education is likely to be an important force in encouraging attitudes that are more supportive of different sexual orientations.

Scott, 1998, p 821

Several researchers, including Scott (1998) have discovered that higher education has a liberalizing influence on attitudes towards homosexuality. This can be seen in data collected for the annual British Social Attitudes Survey (e.g. Wellings and Wadsworth, in Jowell, Witherspoon and Brook, 1990) which repeatedly shows that graduates tend to be more tolerant of homosexuality than non-graduates.

Historically, ideas about gender and sexuality have been inseparable from racist beliefs and practices. Racial stereotypes often include assumptions about gender and sexuality as well as race, and these can sometimes be revealed in educational research (e.g. as shown by Willis, 1977).

Race and ethnicity

Race and ethnicity may have a major impact on life chances and identity even though (like social class) they are difficult to define and may even appear trivial (Donald and Rattansi, 1992). A growing aware-

ness of this paradox means that terminology has changed over time and that, whereas sociologists in the middle of the century tended to write about 'race', today they often prefer to write about ethnicity.

The word *race* emphasizes biological differences often based on skin colour, whereas *ethnicity* relates to a sense of identity, of belonging to a community with common cultural traditions. If we use the word 'race', we are in danger of *reifying* biological categories (i.e. treating them as something real and independent, with their own qualities) and therefore exaggerating their significance in education. Yet if we use the word 'ethnicity', we are also in danger of reifying ethnic categories and promoting a sort of ethnic absolutism (a conceptual and political view of ethnic groups which sees them as possessing distinct cultures, which are fixed and absolute), thereby providing simplistic educational responses.

By the 1990s many sociologists preferred to use the term 'ethnicity' because of their interests in how identity and culture may affect education. Yet ignoring 'race' means that we may discount experiences of educational inequalities arising from prejudiced responses to skin colour or other physical features. In Chapter 2 we looked at the problems associated with operationalizing ethnicity in view of the many and varied ethnic identities. Here we saw that sociologists, like many other people, have tended to use skin colour to group students in very simple ways in order to study their educational experiences. Yet there appears to be no solution to the problem of classification. Some sort of classification is necessary in order to monitor educational experiences, but classifications are constantly changing. During the 1940s people were often described as 'negroes', which is now regarded as unacceptable. Before the 1970s people with dark skin were often called 'coloured', but this term was also criticized for many reasons (e.g. implying that white people had no colour). Although the word 'black' was previously seen as pejorative, since the 1960s the term has been claimed as a source of pride by radicals and has been commonly used in academic discourse. Yet, during the 1990s, Asian academics and activists in particular argued over its validity as a blanket term for all people who are not white.

This growing sophistication in the analysis of ethnicity and education ran parallel to changes in the educational achievements of various ethnic minority groups. Indeed it is likely that we have only been able to appreciate these achievements because of improved research methods. Research during the 1980s (e.g. Rampton, 1981 and Swann, 1985) supported previous findings about the under-achievement of 'West Indian' or 'Afro-Caribbean' children when compared with 'white' or 'Asian' children. Yet there was growing evidence of the relationship between the different socioeconomic backgrounds of 'West Indian', 'Asian' and 'other' children and their educational achievement. Throughout the 1980s relatively small-scale studies, taking an interpretive approach, generated further information about racism in the classroom, and how black and Asian pupils sometimes responded by forming anti-school subcultures (which were not necessarily the same as anti-learning sub-cultures). Researchers also started to move away from simplistic categorizations and, by the 1990s, negative images of the educational problems associated with ethnicity were continually being countered by growing evidence of the different educational achievements of pupils and students from a wide range of ethnic groups. Once colleges and universities started to monitor the ethnicity of applicants and entrants it even became clear that some ethnic minority groups were over-represented in further and higher education and that representation could vary according to the subject being studied. Globalization also impacted on findings about ethnicity and education as increasing numbers of students started to take at least part of their degree in a foreign country. Improved communications between education systems throughout the world mean that there are fewer boundaries between British education, British students and their counterparts elsewhere. Simple descriptions of ethnic groupings become meaningless when personal contacts impress us with the many variables that could affect educational achievement.

Tackling racism

The term 'racism' only entered common usage after the Second World War as a response to the holocaust but, because of its association with the war, it tended to be associated with fascism and anti-semitism and it was easy to overlook other forms of racism in the UK. During the 1940s and 1950s blatant racial discrimination was common in areas such as housing and employment and many immigrants who had achieved good qualifications in their home countries found that the UK certainly did not offer them a meritocracy. In such cases the cultural capital they provided for their own children meant that subsequent generations were advantaged in at least some ways.

As with perspectives about equal opportunities in general (see Figure 5.5), there are wide-ranging views about how racial or ethnic inequalities should be tackled in the education system (see Figure 5.7). Notions of *biological determinism* suggest that nothing can be done to effectively redress natural inequalities. However, most education policy-makers have acknowledged social influences and tended to favour policies between the centre and left of the model. In the twenty years after the Second World War there was a mass influx of migrants from Europe, the Caribbean and Asia and the approach to racial or ethnic inequalities in British education was primarily influenced by the *immigrant-host model*. This model presented *assimilation* as the solution to educational disadvantage, based on the view that the problems experienced by the children of immigrants arose from their situation as new arrivals. The role of education was to assimilate these children into mainstream culture so that the normal consensus and stability of British society would be restored. This assimilation was embedded with ideas about the superiority of British culture and traditions, simplistic assumptions about alternative cultures and a tendency to ignore racism. Indeed, although efforts have been made to tackle this sort of racism in education, the immigrant-host model is still influential.

Children were presented with a world view in which blackness represented everything that was ugly, uncivilized and underdeveloped, and our teachers made little effort to present us or our white classmates with an alternative view. Having been raised on the same basic diet of colonial bigotry themselves, they simply helped to make such negative stereotypes and misconceptions

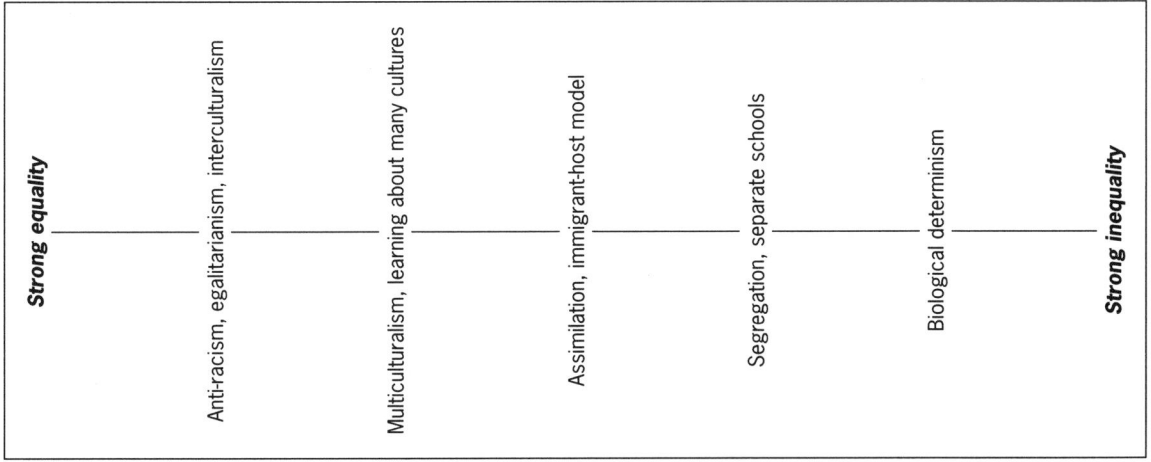

Figure 5.7 A polarity of perspectives and policies on ethnicity and education

about us more credible . . . According to them, we 'could not speak English' and needed 'special' classes where our 'broken' version of the language could be drilled out of us. We were quiet *and* volatile. Best of all, we were good at sports – physical, non-thinking activities – an ability which was to be encouraged so that our increasing 'aggression' could be channelled into more productive areas.

Bryan, Dadzie and Scarfe, 1987, p 93

Legislation in the 1960s and 1970s outlawed discrimination on the grounds of race but has meant that, as it is illegal, racism in education today is usually disguised. It can consist of violence and bullying but may also consist of attitudes and practices which are rarely made explicit. In education this may include institutionalized racism in schools, colleges, universities and other educational processes generating or reproducing disadvantage. Some sociologists have moved from looking at motives to looking at outcomes because policies not directly constructed in relation to race may have a side effect of disadvantaging minorities; for example, schools whose entry requirements include evidence of regular church attendance will exclude the children of non-Christian minorities.

Since the 1960s various types of multiculturalism have been promoted in education as a way of tackling intolerance. *Mutliculturalism* acknowledges and accommodates a variety of different cultural practices and means that schools are now likely to teach about and celebrate a wide variety of lifestyles and traditions. The assumption is that if children can learn about cultures other than their own, a greater degree of tolerance will be cultivated, in the individual and in society as a whole. However, this approach has been caricatured as just being about 'saris and samosas' and criticized for both dividing up societies neatly into homogeneous traditions or communities and being naive in its understanding of the true nature of racism. By emphasizing ethnicity it ignores the racism endured by the many children with black or brown skin who are born into indigenous 'British' families and in a British culture.

QUESTION

Is there such a thing as a British culture?

Remnants of the immigrant-host model can be seen most clearly in Conservative Party policies. As Conservatives emphasize individual liberty, state intervention is regarded as only making problems worse, and a 'colour-blind' approach is taken, assuming that children from a wide range of backgrounds will be incorporated into the existing British culture, submerging their own cultural heritage in the process. A New Right approach, with its emphasis on individualism, tends to be more accepting of cultural diversity but assumes that social cohesion can be maintained and promoted by market forces. On the most extreme right there are more traditional, authoritarian perspectives, favouring 'repatriation', enforced *segregation* or forced integration of some sort. Yet these are not exclusively the views of white extremists. Some black fundamentalist religious groups also favour segregation in education in order to maintain their traditions and cultures.

Centre ground and left-wing perspectives tend to involve stronger concerns about racism and the negative effects of racial inequalities, but also vary in their proposed solutions. *Anti-racists* therefore argue that it is racism, rather than just cultural diversity, that must be confronted. From this point of view the role of education is to challenge racism in society as a whole by, for example, providing children with positive images of 'blackness'. This approach challenges what is described above in the extract from Bryan, Dadzie and Scarfe. However, a third approach (and there are probably more) tries to assimilate multicultural and anti-racist approaches. *Interculturalism* promotes a recognition and acceptance of the uniqueness of the individual and the superficiality of labelling anyone simply by their skin colour, 'culture', social class, gender, disability etc.

Studies of racism in schools have been beset with difficulties, due to its often covert nature. There are, however, many 'victim reports' of the sort furnished by Bryan *et al.* (1987) and other studies into the nature of racist bullying and name-calling (for example, Cohn, 1988). Some of these were inspired, or commissioned, by the Macdonald Report (1989), which investigated the murder of an Asian boy in his school playground. Similarly, concerns about the inadequate response of police officers to the murder of Stephen Lawrence (a black teenager) led to renewed efforts in the 1990s to tackle 'institutionalized' racism in all public services. Although sociologists are aware of the problems involved in studying ethnicity and education, it is still clear that racism must be acknowledged as a fundamental problem and the role of education in the transmission or amelioration of racism must be considered.

The common problem of accessing ethnic minorities emerged in phases 3–5 of the Greater Manchester Study, as these involved small samples taken from sampling frames containing no record of ethnicity (see Chapter 2). It was not possible, therefore, to elicit information about interviewees' personal experiences of racial disadvantage, although informants sometimes offered their general views. The most relevant question asked in interviews in 1988 was about the interviewee's knowledge of the murder of an Asian boy at Burnage High School (which led to the Macdonald Report, 1989) and responses to this question are considered elsewhere.

In 1988 one white interviewee (not included in the quotes above) led me into a researcher's nightmare when he persisted in trying to gain my agreement to his views in favour of repatriation. Despite the relative lack of questions about race and ethnicity, he wanted to express his strong views that many national and educational problems resulted from the mixing of various colours and cultures. Past research training had led me to believe that the interviewer's response should be impartial, which meant that I resisted for as long as possible. At the end of the interview I calmly explained that I did not support his views and we parted

> ## ETHNICITY AND RACISM: VIEWS FROM TORYTOWN AND LABOURVILLE
>
> In junior schools, sometimes there's a lot more in the class than there should be. Sometimes there's about thirty and you can't give them individual attention. They've got Asian and English children together and learning Purdah and different languages. English children are going to be confused with it all.
>
> Emma, 1992
>
> Some of the lads at work are not happy with Labour, because of Jack Straw, the education guy for Labour. They felt he was compromising his position because he's in a Blackburn constituency. He's got a very Muslim electorate and were going to allow them various things, and a lad at work lives in an area where the Muslim population is very active in the school. Jack Straw's going to offer them Muslim schools and my colleague feels that he's sold them out.
>
> Hugh, 1992
>
> [About social class affecting opportunities.] It's mainly the colour of your skin. I feel that a lot of coloured people are being prejudiced against.
>
> Neil, 1992

In 1986 the London borough of Brent's Labour council launched a multi-million-pound programme of race-equality advisers in its schools. The intention was to provide in each school a teacher responsible for monitoring and advising on racial issues. Advisers were appointed by the LEA and reported back to the LEA. Only 56 advisers of the planned 181 were recruited – possibly because of bad publicity. Staffing costs for the four years were over £3.2 million and about 75 per cent of the costs were financed by the Home Office, which monitored the scheme.

The scheme was criticized by the national press and by some local teachers and governing bodies. Some teachers regarded advisers as 'race spies' and criticisms reached their peak when the LEA produced unsubstantiated allegations that primary head teacher Maureen McGoldrick had made racist remarks.

A Home Office advisory committee chaired by Baroness Caroline Cox (who contributed to the Black Papers and was a member of the Hillgate Group) produced its report on the scheme in 1992. Its findings were that:

- Many advisers did useful work that was appreciated by schools.
- The policy was based on assumptions rather than on research into what minority pupils needed.
- The LEA did not know the ethnic origins of its school population. There was 'an almost total lack of systematic information, collection and analysis'.
- There were no systematic attempts to identify areas of under-achievement.
- The scheme was so badly organized that it was not possible to assess its value.

Adapted from the *Guardian*, 15 May 1992

Questions

What can be learned from this case about relations between the LEA and central government?
Are race-equality advisers still necessary?
What other ways are there of tackling racism in schools?

---

amicably. Yet I was appalled by the experience. On the one hand it was necessary to be polite and friendly in the hope that he would agree to be interviewed again in the future (and when a colleague interviewed him in 1992 she reported that he was a very nice man who expressed no racist views whatsoever), but on the other hand my instinct was to aim for the jugular vein! Even an impartial response could suggest covert support for his views, yet an amicable disagreement meant that I had both failed to be impartial and failed myself at a personal level.

QUESTION

How should a researcher react when faced with views that s/he finds totally repugnant?

Are educational outcomes most influenced by social class, gender or race?

Race, social class and gender must be recognized as sources of educational inequalities, but their effects and interrelationships must not be distorted by over-simplification. Sociologists are faced by a particular problem in matching their primary interest in social groups with an acknowledgement that individual experiences of the affects of such groups on educational experiences will vary. Even the improved educational performance of girls and women does not provide a regular pattern of educational achievement and more equal opportunities.

For example, the Policy Studies Institute found that in 1992, holding all other variables constant, women were still significantly less likely to be admitted to universities than men.

Interrelationships between gender, ethnicity and social class are particularly interesting. Many sociologists have asked whether research that intends to study 'race' or 'ethnicity' is actually studying social class. Rex and Tomlinson (1979) argued that the position of many black people in the UK could be understood in terms of an underclass occupying a systematically disadvantaged position in comparison with the bulk of the white working class in relation to employment, housing, education and political influence. Although Rex and Tomlinson started from a neo-Weberian perspective, a similar argument has been used by some neo-Marxists, who have maintained that black people constitute a 'sub-proletariat' (Sivanandan, 1982; Castles and Kosak, 1985). Some neo-Marxists claim that racism and the use of migrant labour plays an important part in determining positions within a capitalist social structure and that education plays an important role in that process of allocation. Others (e.g. Stuart Hall, John Solomos and Paul Gilroy) claim that analysis of race (and gender) in the contemporary world points to new issues of inequality and power not adequately addressed by classical Marxism.

We have now seen how social class, gender and ethnicity work together to produce quite diverse patterns of inequality because many pupils and students suffer double or multiple oppressions. Yet the impact of these oppressions varies between groups and according to contexts. Individuals and groups may respond differently, perhaps allowing their lives to be governed by social disadvantage and the negative messages they may receive in education, or using education itself as a form of resistance to social disadvantages.

Religion and cultural relativism

Religious education in schools has become more pluralistic, moving from an emphasis on Bible reading to a greater emphasis on the study of spiri-tuality, morality and comparative religions. Yet education in the UK has been both assimilative and divisive. Just as the immigrant-host model (most common in the 1940s and 1950s) for the treatment of ethnic minority groups gradually gave way to a greater acceptance of cultural diversity, so has an earlier emphasis on the study of Christian scriptures shifted towards a greater acceptance of religious diversity and different moral codes. This is not a simple progression because in many schools it is still not an unconditional acceptance. Churches can no longer be relied on to teach religion and morality because attendance has declined and, as the trend towards secularization has been particularly noticeable among the young, there have been recurring debates about the importance of teaching Christian religion in schools. National governments have tried to reinforce Christianity as a norm, whilst allowing some deviation; for example, promoting the maintenance of Christian school assemblies but allowing some children to be withdrawn from attendance. At the same time some religions have been able to establish their own private schools and have campaigned for state support. In particular there has been a growing appeal of religious orthodoxy among some of the UK's many Muslims. Thus we can see two separate developments: a shift towards greater acceptance of diversity and a fundamentalist response, asserting the validity of individual religions in the face of secularization.

During the 1940s–1960s religious and cultural identities were relatively fixed and absolute but, as society has become more diverse, individuals have often been faced with uncertainties about hybrid identities emerging from a variety of influences. One response is to forcefully assert an identity (such as Englishness, Scottishness or other, minority identities) and there been various campaigns about issues such as the right of Muslim girls to wear headdresses to school and the state funding of Islamic schools.

Sociologists tackle such debates about comparative identities by discussing cultural relativism. *Cultural relativism* acknowledges the social and cultural forces affecting the conditions under which knowledge is produced. It notes that it is impossible to distinguish between 'real' knowledge and culturally produced knowledge and denies that any one way of living is superior to others (see Michael Young, 1971). Yet people in powerful positions can ensure that certain cultural practices are regarded as superior or inferior. In education this has meant that children from some ethnic minorities have experienced problems as they have tried to balance the dictates of their religious/cultural background with their school rules.

QUESTION

Can you think of any examples of clashes between school rules and the traditions of ethnic minorities?

Behaviour

Not only have attitudes towards religion become more pluralistic but so have ideas about morality and codes of behaviour. It is normal for each generation to express concern about standards of behaviour among the younger generation. This means that parents today who were the mods and rockers, hippies or punks of the past are concerned about the degenerative moral climate experienced by their own children! Yet the reality of social change can best be appreciated at a distance. Thus, we can see that during the late 1940s the UK experienced a period in which community spirit and mutual support was emphasized within a strict moral climate. During the 1950s more concerns were expressed about the younger generation and the 1960s has been seen with hindsight as a period in which many social norms and expectations started to be challenged. The 1960s are associated

with the development of a permissive society, although change of this sort was very slow. For example, only 24 per cent of couples had cohabited before marriages contracted between 1965 and 1974, but this rose to 63 per cent for marriages contracted between 1985 and 1992 (Buck and Scott, 1994). The economic individualism of the 1980s matched a greater sense of individual freedom to choose an individual lifestyle. Indeed, Weeks noted the irony of President Reagan and Margaret Thatcher both being proponents of traditional families whilst presiding over 'probably the greatest revolution in sexual mores in the twentieth century' (Weeks, 1995, p 29).

The relaxation of moral restraints in society in general has obviously had repercussions for education. Not only was education commonly blamed for economic depression from (at least) the 1970s onwards but it was already being blamed for not fulfilling its function as a source of social control, for the degenerating behaviour of the younger generation, sexual immorality, crime and a general decay in day-to-day civility and security. The abolition of corporal punishment in state schools in 1987 has often been cited as having a negative influence on the behaviour of children in schools, but debates about this are confused by counter-claims that adults' use of corporal punishment sets a bad example. Nevertheless, many of the interviewees in Torytown and Labourville expressed real concerns about their personal security and older cohort members were particularly fearful. This often complemented what they had to say about a perceived lack of control within schools, whether it related to the abolition of corporal punishment or simply pupils' lack of respect for their teachers.

BEHAVIOUR: VIEWS FROM LABOURVILLE AND TORYTOWN

Memories of school

When I was at school we had the same teacher and she stayed with you all day and we had respect for her. There were fifty or more in the class but they were all under control. It was a little village school with a bobby to keep an eye on you. It was great.

Annie, 1992

School culture

My son's seventeen and a half now and he left school at sixteen being classified an under-achiever, and he hated school. A lot of this was caused by the indiscipline in the school. The school went from being a very disciplined society to a very indisciplined one. There were a lot of reasons for this, not just the fault of the headteacher who seemed to be doing the best he could under the circumstances. But there was a definite change of emphasis in the school and a definite swing away from a very disciplined society to one that was drug-ridden and so on. There's disaffection in a great many of the schools in [Labourville]. My son, much to my great respect, avoided it. If you can survive when a school is going down the road to where a lot are taking drugs, it takes a strong kid to keep saying 'No', and at the end he hadn't got any friends because all the rest of them were drug freaks. He was an outsider. So he hated school. This is why I don't like sixth-form colleges being attached to schools. When he left there and went to [. . .] Sixth-Form College he almost overnight blossomed. He came back to the child I once knew, where he was happy, outgoing, mixing with different people; he left all those other people behind and he started to progress. [He did some resits and another music course.] The school that he attended in [Labourville] can take no praise for this at all. The only person that can take any praise for that in the school was his music teacher, who was a wonderful woman, Mrs [. . .], who asked him to join [a brass] band, which again kept him clear of some of these idiots who were on the slippery road to ruin. Most of his friends, or what were his friends, were into drugs and petty crime, some of them. It was so heartbreaking for their parents. He steered clear of this due to the influence of music, which had been denied him at school. We'd given him the opportunity here, but he hadn't any inclination to take up music until it came via this band.

John, 1997

[Wife's job.] She's a midday assistant, that's like a dinner lady-type job at an infant school. She's making sure that the kids don't kill each other at dinner time. She pulls them apart when they get really violent.

Lawrence, 1997

Crime

Well I think education is vital, isn't it really, for the children, and certainly the crime rate. If you can get that down they would probably benefit financially on the money that must be wasted; it would probably help towards – go off other things, you know. I mean crime, it's terrible, isn't it, and they don't seem to do much. Well certainly education is vital, isn't it, for the future.

Ian, 1997

I'm in construction and I do maintenance on petrol stations and places. Regularly, once every couple of weeks, I get called out to burglaries. So I see, almost at first hand really, what is going on, and obviously education is the long-term answer, but if in the short term the only answer is to increase policing, then something's got to be done.

Nicholas, 1997

Teachers and parents

From what I hear around, some of the teachers don't know what they're talking about, so how can they teach the children? There's good teachers and there's some who just don't know what they're doing.
[In what way?] In some cases they can't control the children and this is mainly because they're not allowed to and this is wrong, I think, because when we were at school your teacher, you had to take notice of them and a lot of children don't these days, mainly because when they go home and say the teacher said something, parents go to the school and remonstrate with them. Where if we went home and said something about the teacher, mother would say straight away, 'Well what have you been doing?' So the parents are in some ways to blame because they don't get to the bottom of things.

Audrey, 1997

Apparent contradictions in attitudes to issues

Although at the start of my involvement in the Greater Manchester Study I did not expect to find that voters would fit into neat attitudinal types, I was nevertheless surprised to discover how their views seemed to lack internal or external coherence. It was, for example, possible to find that an interviewee could resent private schools but still feel that they should not be abolished, could believe that the LEA and individual schools should have the main influence on what is taught in schools but favour a National Curriculum, and could enjoy being at school but not enjoy having to learn. Yet some of these apparent inconsistencies were explained by the interviewee's own internal logic when the background to the response was probed more deeply.

Similarly, interviewees might vote one way in a general election and another way in a local election and might vote for a political party with which they had very little sympathy. Again this was not simply a case of being inconsistent. Many individual voters did not seem to have consistently left-wing or right-wing attitudes to the large range of individual sub-issues within the field of education.

In order to assess the cohesion of attitudes to a variety of sub-issues, I created two exploratory scales of educational radicalism for the analysis of the survey data that was available before I carried out my first interviews in 1988. My interest was in discovering the extent to which voters expressed consistently left-wing (most radical) or consistently right-wing views (least radical) attitudes. The first scale (Ed Rad I) used three questions asked in the second phase of the Greater Manchester Study. These were:

1. Should the government establish comprehensive schools in place of grammar and secondary modern schools throughout the country?
2. Should the government abolish the private schools which are outside the state education system?

SOME APPARENTLY INCONSISTENT ATTITUDES IN TORYTOWN AND LABOURVILLE

When attitudes seemed to be inconsistent, the wording of the question and the place of the statement within the flow of the interview must be considered. Emma agreed with a statement that 'The welfare state makes people nowadays less willing to look after themselves' and said,

> That goes for these hangers-on that have no intention of getting a job and all those people that abuse it. That's why it's gone to pot, because it's been so badly abused.
>
> Emma, 1988

Yet, when asked for any other comments at the end of the interview, she expressed concern about inadequate welfare provision, and was particularly concerned about how young people on the dole managed.

> It must be disheartening having no future and wanting what other people have, constantly struggling to make ends meet. It's no wonder that some steal things.

She said that she and her husband had enough money to manage at the moment but she did not know how they would manage once he retired. After listing their regular payments (rates, electricity, gas, etc.) she said they would not be able to afford them once he retired.

At one point Audrey said that she enjoyed school but she later said that she did not enjoy it. I asked her to explain.

> Well I enjoyed being in the classes with all the children and we were all good pals together. It was a village so we were really all happy together. There wasn't any bullying or anything like that. And the teachers were excellent. I didn't enjoy having to study. It wasn't me at all. I wanted to go to work. I enjoyed the teachers, although I didn't enjoy the teaching. I could have gone on to grammar school but didn't want to. Some friends were talking about it in the last twelve months and they said that the one thing was that when my school moved on to the secondary school there was more children in the top levels than there were from the other schools.
>
> Audrey, 1997

3. The government collects taxes and rates for a variety of services. Would you like to see more spent on education?

An answer of 'Yes' to any of these questions was labelled as 'radical'. When responses were scored and analysed (McKenzie, 1993, Table 8.11, p 214) it was found that, although consumers expressed the most left-wing views, the most common response from consumers and non-consumers was politically slightly right of centre. This came as no surprise after many years of Conservative government in which the favoured public discourse was generally right wing.

A second scale of educational radicalism was created by using three questions asked in the British Social Attitudes Survey of 1983 (Jowell *et al.*, 1984):

1. Should opportunities to go into higher education be increased, reduced or stay the same?
2. Choose between three options: reduce taxes and spend less on health, education and social benefits; keep taxes and spending on these services the same; increase taxes and spend more on health, education and social benefits.
3. Should there be more private schools, about the same number as now, fewer, or no private schools at all?

The most radical score would require an answer to question 1 of 'increased', to question 2 an answer favouring increased taxes and spending, and to question 3 an answer favouring no private schools. Again (McKenzie, 1993, Table 8.12, p 215) consumers were found to be slightly more left-wing than non-consumers but the most common response was again politically just right of centre.

Further analysis showed that there was also a weak association between educational radicalism and political partisanship (McKenzie, 1993, Tables 8.13 and 8.14, pp 216–7). When the scales of educational radicalism were cross-tabulated (compared) with political partisanship (i.e. whether a strong or weak supporter) the most common response was also politically right of centre, although there was also a weak association between educational radicalism and political partisanship (see Figures 5.8 and 5.9).

QUESTIONS

Carry out a similar statistical analysis of data from a more recent British Social Attitudes Survey.

(a) What problems do you encounter?
(b) How do you tackle them?
(c) What criticisms do you now have of the way that data was analysed for Figure 5.9?

Although voters cited education as one of the most important issues at the time of the 1987 and 1992 general elections (see Figure 5.10), its actual influence on the election results was very limited.

		Least		Educ. radicalism				Most
		−3	−2	−1	0	+1	+2	+3
	n=	%	%	%	%	%	%	%
Conservative:								
strong	127	7.9	30.7	48.8	6.3	4.7	0	1.6
weak	99	4.0	25.2	45.4	12.1	9.1	1.0	3.0
Alliance:								
strong	47	4.2	10.6	46.8	17.0	12.8	4.2	4.2
weak	76	3.9	9.2	48.7	11.8	15.8	5.3	5.3
Labour:								
strong	161	0	1.2	22.4	16.2	23.6	9.9	32.9
weak	86	0	4.6	38.4	12.8	27.9	5.8	10.5
Source: Edgell and Duke, 1985, adapted by computer								

Figure 5.8 Political partisanship and educational radicalism, Ed Rad I, GMS (1983/4 interviews)

	n=	Least −3 %	−2 %	Educ. radicalism −1 %	0 %	+1 %	+2 %	Most +3 %
Conservative:								
strong	421	46.3	4.5	36.6	1.2	10.4	0.2	0.7
weak	255	36.9	1.5	39.2	2.0	16.9	0.8	2.7
Alliance:								
strong	81	23.5	1.2	45.7	1.2	24.7	0	3.7
weak	177	28.8	2.3	42.4	1.1	22.6	1.1	1.7
Labour:								
strong	306	15.7	2.0	36.6	3.3	26.8	0.6	15.0
weak	278	18.7	2.5	38.8	2.9	29.1	1.8	6.1

Source: BSA, 1983/4, adapted by computer

Figure 5.9 Political partisanship and educational radicalism, Ed Rad II BSA (1983/4)

Figure 5.10 Proportion of the sample mentioning an issue as one of the two most important in influencing their vote

	1987 %	1992 %
Unemployment	49	36
NHS/hospitals	33	41
Education	19	23
Taxation	7	10
Defence	35	3

Source: Gallup post-election survey, 10–11 June 1987; Gallup post election survey, 10–11 April 1992

Crewe argued that, on the basis of declared attitudes to such issues, Labour would have won the 1987 general election. However, his well-known conclusion was that the influence of individual issues was outweighed by an association between the Conservative Party and private prosperity.

> When answering a survey on the important issues respondents think of public problems; when entering the polling booth they think of the family fortunes.
>
> Crewe, 1987

Comments made during interviews in Torytown and Labourville tended to support Crewe's claim.

> Education only lasts a short time but you pay tax all your life.
>
> Ian, 1988

Among those who mentioned the top three issues listed in Figure 5.10, Labour was considered to be the most capable party and Crewe believed that education lost the Conservatives votes. The majority (including the majority of Conservative voters) felt that conditions had deteriorated regarding the top three issues. Crewe concluded that it was an association of personal prosperity with the Conservative Party that led many to vote Conservative. By a 55 per cent to 27 per cent majority, respondents believed that a Conservative government was most likely to bring 'prosperity'.

Conclusion: Issues in flux

We have seen that educational issues are part of a very wide and changing public discourse but that they often only seem to assume any reality when they are experienced personally as part of an individual's unique and real world. These varied realities often seem to be very confusing but it is still possible to identify some patterns among diverse impressions. First, sociology shows us that educational experiences are not as unique as we might imagine. People who share some particular characteristics often share their misfortunes or their good fortunes. Second, some large issue areas have been an important part of public debate since 1944 but their features have changed and continue to change. So, for example, interests in social class and meritocracy have regenerated to focus on social exclusion and parentocracy. The issues of gender and ethnicity have emerged from previous assumptions about biological determinism and been refined to accommodate an incredibly diverse range of experiences. Third, apparently new issues are regularly uncovered and will continue to be uncovered so that this book, as with other books about education, will soon start to look out of date.

Even the language used to analyse issues changes into a new discourse in order to accommodate new issues. Yet, a fourth and final point is that we should recognize the way that unequal power structures can often manage, hide or reveal new issues, present them from certain biased perspectives and try to control the way they are perceived. Although issues seem to be in a constant state of flux, they do not change in a totally uninhibited way.

Part Two

Decades of Change

6

The 1940s

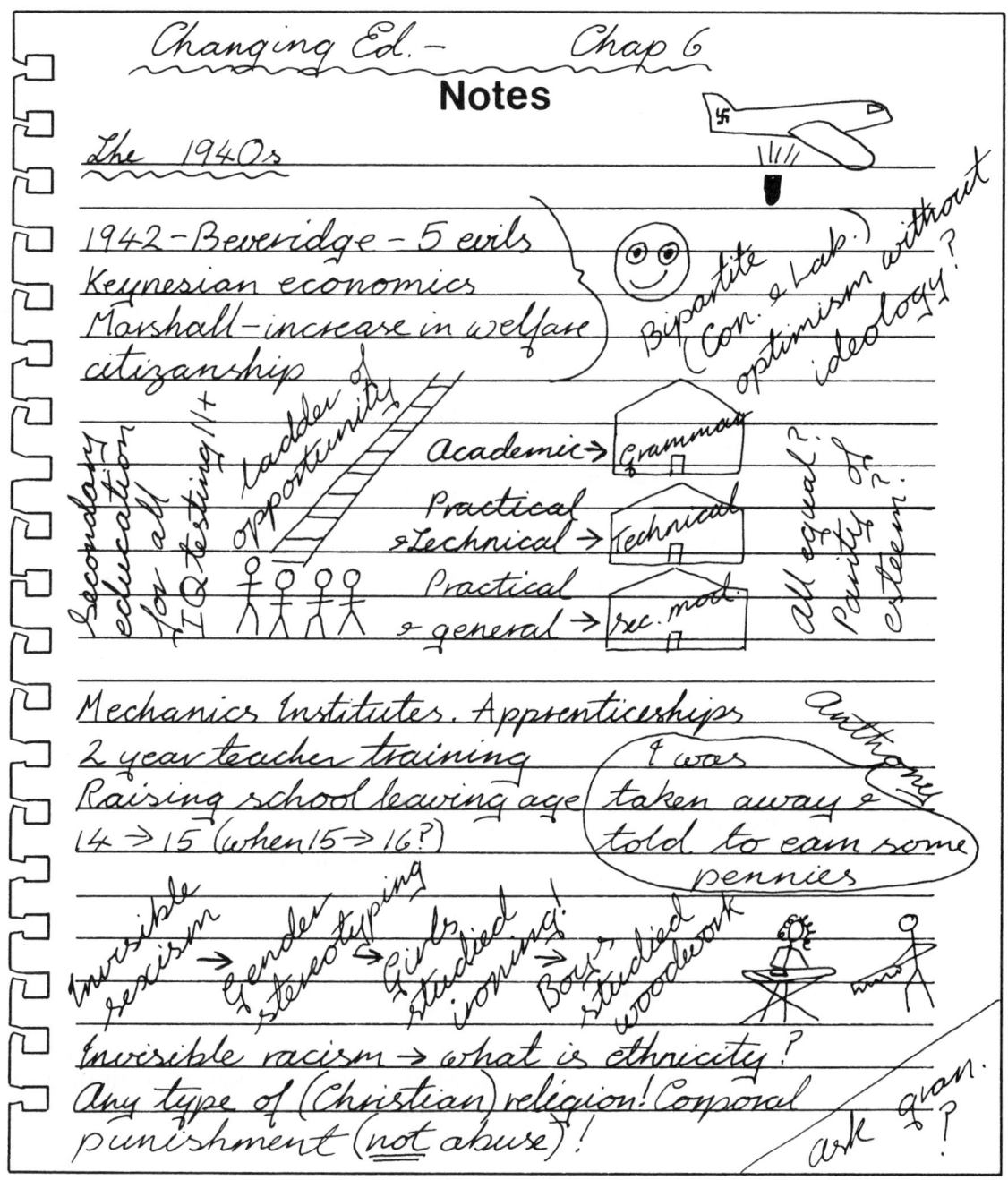

Changing Ed. — Chap 6
Notes

The 1940s

1942 – Beveridge – 5 evils
Keynesian economics
Marshall – increase in welfare
citizanship

Bipartite
(Con. & Lab.)
optimism without
ideology?

Secondary education for all
IQ testing 11+
Ladder of opportunity

Academic → Grammar
Practical & Technical → Technical
Practical & general → sec. mod.

All equal? Parity of esteem?

Mechanics Institutes. Apprenticeships
2 year teacher training
Raising school leaving age
14 → 15 (when 15 → 16?)

Anthony?
I was taken away & told to earn some pennies

Invisible sexism → Gender stereotyping → Girls studied ironing! → Boys studied woodwork

Invisible racism → what is ethnicity?
Any type of (Christian) religion! Corporal
punishment (not abuse)!

ask gran.?

Socio-economic change – Changing perspectives – Changing school systems – Further and higher education – Teachers – Class and status – Gender – Race and ethnicity – Religion – Special needs – Behaviour – Unfinished business

Hammered on the anvil of war, our nation has been shaped to a new unity of pride and purpose. We must preserve this after victory is won if the fruits of victory are to be fully [given] and that unity will, by this Bill, be founded where it should be founded, in the education of youth.

R.A. Butler, introducing the Bill for the 1944
Education Act to the House of Commons, January 1944

Socio-economic change

When R.A. Butler introduced the Education Bill in 1944 he was speaking not on behalf of his own governing party, but on behalf of a broad coalition government with widespread public support. The UK was still at war and experiencing a rare moment of national consensus which favoured the expansion of welfare provision.

Although its origins were much earlier, the 'welfare state' is a term that came into general use during the Second World War, largely as a result of the Beveridge Report, *Social Insurance and Allied Services*, in 1942. Initially the coalition government set up the committee to simplify the social security system but Beveridge believed that the time was right for a massive shake up in welfare. He was supported by a groundswell of public opinion in favour of democracy and equality because the war was being experienced by all social classes and all had suffered its consequences. In his report, Beveridge argued that 'The object of government in peace and in war is not the glory of rulers or of races, but the happiness of the common man'. Thus, he cited the five 'giant evils' in society to be tackled by the new welfare state.

1. Disease: meaning that medical care was needed.
2. Ignorance: to be combated by the Education Act of 1944.
3. Squalor: to be tackled by adequate housing.
4. Idleness: to be discouraged by full employment.
5. Want: to be tackled by social insurance, services and benefits for children, the elderly and the unemployed.

The one point on which most politicians and educationalists were agreed was that social origins could have a profound, and often negative, affect on educational achievement and that something should be done about it. British people had memories of hardships endured before the war, when it was often assumed that children would leave school at a very early age in order to work to support their families. Members of the Torytown and Labourville cohort could still remember this.

My father had an accident and he wasn't expected to live and there was my mother and my brother and I wanted to go out to work to bring some money in, so much so that I left school when it was my birthday and went to work in an office, and the school board came and told mother (and I've got the letter now) that I hadn't to leave school, I had to stay until the end of term, and I said, 'But I'll loose my job. I won't be able to go to my job if I leave it now'. And he said, 'Don't worry about that. I'll send a letter'. So he sent a letter to the firm and told them that I hadn't to leave school until the end of term. And I've got the letter now. They sent a letter back saying that they would keep my job open for me until the end of term. So I went back to work.

Audrey, 1997

[Father] went to a type of 'ragged school' and at fourteen won a scholarship for a free place at [a private school] but his father died and he had lots of younger sisters, so he had to go and get a job to support them.

Richard, 1992

For the first time, the 1944 Education Act provided free secondary education for all and therefore created a 'ladder' of educational opportunity for working-class children.

The effects as I see it will be as much social as educational. I think it will have the result of welding us all into one nation . . . instead of the two nations that Disraeli talked about.

R.A. Butler, newsreel footage,
From Butler to Baker, BBC2.

In a period of postwar excitement, the aim was to act quickly and resolutely, building on close partnerships between central government, local education authorities (school boards) and teachers. However, it was not until the mid 1950s that the changes introduced in 1944 really took shape. Thousands of schools had been bombed during the war and others had fallen into disrepair. A massive building and repair programme was needed. Many teachers and prospective teachers had been drafted into other war work or had even lost their lives during the war. It was therefore necessary to implement an emergency training programme in order to supply the teachers needed for an expanded education system.

In 1945 a Labour government was elected and remained in office until 1951. Richard Law replaced R.A. Butler as Minister of Education but Law was soon replaced by Ellen Wilkinson, who was replaced in 1947 by George Tomlinson.

Changing perspectives

During the 1940s Keynesian economics dominated in all of the main political parties. This meant that the payment of taxes in order to support thriving public services was assumed to be a good thing. Indeed, criticism of alternative views could be summarized in one phrase often attributed to Keynes: 'The avoidance of taxes is the only pursuit that still carries any reward.' The 1944 Education Act, as with other legislation expanding the welfare state, was a product of wartime bipartisan optimism about a better postwar world. Furthermore, T.H. Marshall's belief that the twentieth century would see an increase in welfare citizenship fitted in with the cross-party consensus of all the British political parties. This view lasted throughout the 1940s, 1950s and 1960s, due largely to the wartime spirit and a growing sense of community.

However, a consensus about the need to expand educational opportunities seems to have concealed more practical divisions of opinion about what those opportunities should look like.

For many the function of the Labour Party was to represent working-class views on social issues but there were divisions of opinion within the party regarding what working-class interests were. Some Labour supporters were concerned about raising the school-leaving age, because this would reduce family incomes, whilst others supported it because it would reduce unemployment. Although ideas about comprehensive education were already being mooted, Ellen Wilkinson and George Tomlinson both favoured grammar schools as a working-class child's alternative to elite public schools. Various critics (including Tawney before the war and Lawton in 1992) have also claimed that the greatest weakness in the Labour Party was its lack of an ideology. Lawton observed that the 1945 Labour Party election manifesto, *Let Us Face the Future*, contained no educational thinking but simply gave support to the 1944 Education Act. As a result, the new Labour administration of 1945 was faced with the task of implementing an Act about which it had no clear policy. Moreover, according to Lawton, Labour exaggerated the importance of purely administrative changes in education and almost completely ignored the importance of the curriculum.

The Conservative Party of the 1940s has also been criticized for its lack of a clear ideology. Robert Dunn (Lawton, 1992, p 32) argued that for nearly 40 years after the 1944 Act the Conservative Party had no real education policy or central philosophy. Although the paternalism of One Nation Conservatives tended to dominate during the 1940s, some Conservatives regretted the need for direct state participation in education.

. . . the 1944 Act was profoundly alien to Conservative philosophy. The idea that state officials should allocate children to different kinds of school, on the basis of the decisions of experts about what kind of occupation they are best fitted for, is part of the philosophy of socialism and the planned society. The Conservative tradition is surely one of individual families making decisions for themselves.

Lynn, 1970, p 32

Nevertheless, whilst the Labour Party was divided on the subject of comprehensive schools (often called multilateral schools during the 1940s), most Conservatives favoured selection for different types of secondary schools.

Ideas about selection at the age of eleven were underpinned by a firm belief in the value of intelligence tests. The assumption was that a child's innate abilities and capacity for learning were so well established at the age of eleven that they would be unlikely to change in later life. Research into intelligence by Cyril Burt and others seemed to provide conclusive evidence of the value of the intelligence test as a legitimate, scientific process for measuring innate intelligence. This also had an impact on sociology during the 1940s, which was mainly concerned with behaviour in class, social control, knowledge and IQ. When Mannheim lectured in London between 1940 and 1945, he was interested in the sociology of knowledge and behaviour in class. Taking a relatively conservative approach, he was concerned with restoration of order and not with structural inequalities or a search for social justice. More critical approaches were taken by those influenced by the work done by Tawney between the wars (e.g. 1922, 1931). Tawney argued that 'The hereditary curse upon English education is its organization upon lines of social class' (1931, p 142). Such arguments won some support within the Labour Party but the effects were rather muted.

> . . . the Labour Party has usually merely taken the existing education system and suggested minor adjustments to it in order to try to make it serve the interests of working class children more fairly. Tawney's Secondary Education for All (1922) came close to being an expression of desirable policy, but even that was essentially a criticism of the status quo and lacked the wholehearted support of the Party.
>
> Lawton, 1992, p 23

Although equal opportunities was a key concept during the 1940s, they were defined rather weakly, the prevailing view being that the separation of children by test at the age of eleven was acceptable provided that *parity of esteem* was maintained. No child was meant to be regarded as inferior or superior as a result of IQ tests, merely different. In a climate of public optimism and good intentions, it seemed to many that this ideal would actually work.

Changing school systems

Before 1944 over 80 per cent of children left school at fourteen, after elementary school. Some took an exam at eleven to compete for scholarships to secondary schools but places were only given to those with exceptional ability. Even when children from working-class families did pass scholarships they were often prevented from attending secondary school because the family could not afford uniforms or other expenses. Only about 2–3 per cent of working-class children actually attended a grammar school before 1944, about 1 in 7 moved from elementary school to secondary school and about 12 in 100 had the opportunity to continue education until the age of sixteen. In general, it was expected that working-class children would become 'factory fodder'; that is, follow their parents into low-grade manual work. Clifford explained how he became one of the fortunate few who progressed to a secondary school.

> In my day I don't think they called them state schools, they were council schools. I was educated down south for part of my education. I went to Wimbledon Tech for a start, which might sound a bit daft, but it was actually in Kingston. In the war no one was educated in the south of London area and Wimbledon's just inside, so they moved us just half a mile outside. Big difference from the bombs that half mile, I think! I sat an exam after about eleven, whether it was called the 11+ I don't know, but you had to pass it and, if you didn't, a free place was the first half-dozen, I think. There's only twenty-four allowed in the school and you paid after that, but we're talking about (I don't know how my dad paid it), we're talking about £3 a quarter, in those days. You had to go into this exam and there was about six hundred went in for it and the fortunate twenty-four passed it. I remember the first essay we ever did when I went there was how lucky you were to be in these twenty-four – which you were, you know. It was a very competitive education, so it was like a scholarship. Yes, scholarship was the word I wanted. I went to Wimbledon Tech with the

scholarship, which was an all-boys school. Well, they had all-girls schools as well, you know, in those days. Commercial colleges were girls' schools, although boys did go to commercial colleges.

Clifford, 1997

The 1944 Education Act followed the publication of several discussion and policy documents. These included *The Green Book* in 1941, which explained what the government meant by *equal opportunities* and *parity of esteem*.

Equal opportunity means . . . Acceptance of the principle that the accidents of parental circumstances or place of residence shall not preclude any child from receiving the education from which he is best capable of profiting . . .

It will be clear from what has been said that by 'secondary education for all' is meant not the provision of the same type of education for all at the secondary stage, but that all types of full-time education at this stage should be regarded as on a parity and should receive equal treatment in such matters as accommodation, staffing, size of classes etc.

The Green Book, cited by Halsey, Heath and Ridge, 1980

In 1943 more official papers reinforced the need for a fairer system of secondary education. The *Report of the Consultative Committee on the Secondary School Examinations Council* (Norwood) reinforced views expressed in earlier reports (e.g. Spens, 1938) in favour of a tripartite system of secondary education. A White Paper, *Educational Reconstruction* (Board of Education, 1943), was also critical of the existing arrangements allowing preferential access for children whose parents could pay fees.

It has been noted that the children who are most successful in the examination taken at 11 secure places in secondary schools, but this is not to say that all the places in secondary schools are filled by the ablest candidates for admission. The Board's Regulations do not do more than require that 25 per cent of the yearly admissions should be confined to pupils whose admission is independent of their ability to pay the prescribed fee, and although this percentage is very often greatly exceeded, it remains true that many children get the benefit of secondary education owing to the ability of their parents to pay fees.

Seeing that these fees represent only a proportion (on the average about one-third) of the cost of the education given in the secondary schools, it follows that a parent by paying only one-third of the cost of education can buy a place in a secondary school for his child, possibly to the exclusion of an abler child whose parent is not in that position. A system under which fees are charged in one type of post-primary school and prohibited in the other offends against the canon that the nature of a child's education should be determined by his capacity and promise and not by the financial circumstances of his parents.

White Paper on *Educational Reconstruction*, 1943, Cmd. 6458, paras 17 and 20, cited by Halsey, Heath and Ridge, 1980, p 27

In the same White Paper the government noted that it did not intend to introduce competitive examinations for access to secondary schools and said that

There is nothing to be said in favour of a system which subjects children at the age of eleven to the strain of a competitive examination on which, not only their future schooling, but their future careers may depend.

Cited in Douglas, 1964, p 14

According to the White Paper, the 1944 Act would replace the Special Place examination with a system whereby children would be classified

not on the results of a competitive test, but on an assessment of their individual aptitudes largely by such means as school records, supplemented, if necessary, by intelligence tests, due regard being had to their parents' wishes and the careers they have in mind.

White Paper, 1943, para 27, cited by Halsey, Heath and Ridge, 1980, p 27

The White Paper argued that, in order to promote parity of esteem, the grammar school should not be presented as a superior institution, educating superior minds, but as simply providing an appropriate education for some children.

An academic training is ill-suited for many of the pupils who find themselves moving along a narrow educational path bounded by the School Certificate and leading into a limited field of opportunity. Further, too many of the nation's abler children are attracted into a type of education which prepares primarily for the University and for the administrative and clerical professions; too few find their way into schools from which the design and craftsmanship sides of the industry are recruited. If education is to serve the interests both of the child and of the nation, some means must be found of correcting this bias

and of directing ability into the field where it will find its best realization.

White Paper, 1943, para 28, cited in Halsey, Heath and Ridge, 1980, p 28

Some technical schools already existed but, according to the White Paper, not enough.

THE 1944 EDUCATION ACT

(This Act is often called the Butler Act, after the then Minister of Education.)

- Replaced almost all of the previous legislation.
- Replaced the Board of Education with a Ministry of Education.
- Gave the Minister of Education more powers and responsibilities. The Minister was to be arbiter of disputes between local authorities, school governors and the public. S/he had to be consulted by local authorities over their general development plans and any proposals to establish, close or alter schools.
- Abolished the distinction between elementary and higher education. It created a unified system of free, compulsory schooling from the age of five to fifteen. Pupils could receive this education in local authority schools, schools maintained by other organizations, or, in certain circumstances, 'otherwise' (usually at home).
- Formulated a relationship between the county and voluntary sectors. Voluntary schools were given the choice of becoming 'aided' or 'controlled' schools and provision was made for a few 'special agreement' schools. Standards were set to which all school premises had to perform.
- Made it possible for all children to receive secondary education. The Act itself did not specify a particular structure of secondary education but directed education authorities to provide pupils with 'such variety of instruction and training as may be desirable in view of their ages, their abilities and aptitudes, and of different periods which they may be expected to remain at school including practical instruction and training appropriate to their respective needs' (Section 8, para 1b). However, official policy supported the introduction of a *tripartite* system and the aim was that all children were to be assessed at the age of 11+ and categorized as having specific abilities that made them suitable for one of three types of secondary education.
- The types of secondary education were: grammar schools (academic ability), technical schools (practical/ technical ability), secondary modern schools (practical/general ability). Children were to be regarded with 'parity of esteem', that is, no type of school was supposed to be superior to the others.
- The school leaving age was to be raised to fifteen from 1945 (it was actually raised in 1947).
- Created a variety of services to support the basic structure of primary and secondary education; for example, transport, free milk, medical and dental treatment. School meals were to be provided for all children who wanted them.
- Extended the concept of education to cover the needs of those above and below school age, and to include the community's needs for culture and recreation. Local authorities could provide nursery schools and classes and they could provide or finance holiday classes, camps, play schemes, swimming baths, community centres and recreation facilities.
- Set up two Central Advisory Councils for Education (CACE), one for England and one for Wales, to advise the Minister of Education. Until 1967 a number of major reports were produced in this way.
- Required every LEA to appoint a Chief Education Officer.

Adapted from Mackinnon and Statham, 1999, pp 54–55

Planned to give a general education associated with preparation for entry to one or other of the main branches of industry or commerce they have grown up in close relation to the local needs and opportunities of employment. But their progress in numbers has been comparatively slow and their chances of attracting the most able children *vis-à-vis* the Grammar Schools have been adversely affected by the fact that they normally recruit at the age of 13. With altered conditions, and with a more rapid development in the future, they hold out great opportunities for pupils with a practical bent.

> White Paper, 1943, para 30, cited in
> Halsey, Heath and Ridge, 1980, p 28

Of secondary modern schools, the White Paper said:

Lacking the traditions and privileged position of the older grammar school they have less temptation to be 'at ease in Zion'. Their future is their own to make, and it is a future full of promise. They offer a general education for life, closely related to the interests and environment of the pupils and of a wide range embracing the literary as well as the practical, e.g. agricultural sides.

> White Paper, 1943, para 29, cited in Halsey,
> Heath and Ridge, 1980, p 28

Acts are often seen as the implementation of plans already drawn up in White Papers but, as it passes through the Houses of Parliament, legislation is generally amended. As a result, not all the ideals of the 1943 White Paper were advanced by the 1944 Act.

As with many pieces of educational legislation, some of the changes favoured by many critics of the existing system were not included in the Act and some measures that were included in the Act were not implemented. The Act did not tackle the private schools and did nothing to deal with potential conflicts between parents' wishes and children's aptitudes. Few technical schools were ever introduced and, in effect, most local authorities provided a bipartite system. Places at grammar schools also had to be rationed because the demand for places far exceeded supply. As a result, the 11+ examination system was introduced, which looked remarkably similar to the Special Place examination. Despite efforts to retain the ideal of parity of esteem, the reality was that children were seen as 'passing' the 11+ examination and going to a grammar school or 'failing' and going to a secondary modern school. Mary Warnock (1977) observed that the equal opportunity offered by the Act was an equal opportunity *to compete* for the best education for which they could be selected. The assumption was that if a child did not win a grammar school place, s/he at least won what was best for them, since the prize would not have been suitable for them. Estimates from various sources (e.g. Halsey, Heath and Ridge, 1980) suggest that about one in four children were mis-allocated to a school after taking the 11+. From the start there was a wide variation in the number of places available at grammar schools in different areas; for example, in parts of Wales as many as 40 per cent were given places at grammar schools, compared to rates as low as 10 per cent elsewhere. There were also structural defects in a bipartite or tripartite system because separation into different schools meant that there were few opportunities to meet children from another social class.

In 1946 another Education Act specified some of the responsibilities of LEAs and governors and in 1947 the Education Act (Northern Ireland) initiated dramatic changes in Northern Ireland. The existing system of public elementary education in Northern Ireland was replaced by a unified system of primary, secondary and further education; education was to be compulsory from five to fifteen, collective worship and religious education were to be compulsory in all county schools and various directives were made regarding the duties of local authorities. Rules were laid down for the management of schools and provisions were made for the setting up of voluntary schools.

In 1949 the Evans/Aaron Report, *The Future of Secondary Education in Wales* (CACE Wales), detailed recommendations for the organization and curriculum of secondary education in Wales under the 1944 Education Act. Unlike the previous directions applying to England, it suggested that secondary education should take the form of either 'multi-lateral' schools or a dual system of grammar/technical schools and modern/technical schools (rather than the tripartite system), although it must take into account variation in ability and aptitude between children. It also suggested that education should be 'child-centred', recommending that the curriculum should emphasize free creation and co-operative inventiveness rather than passive assimilation. The study of history, geography and literature should give a central place to Wales.

The 1948 Clarke Report, *Out of School* (CACE England), extended government guidance to 'the natural interests and pursuits of schoolchildren out of school hours'. It urged LEAs to increase and improve facilities for children's play and recreation outside school hours, and suggested that the government should give financial support to voluntary bodies serving the out-of-school interests of schoolchildren. Not only did it recommend that LEAs provide training courses for those who worked with children, but that they should also provide courses for parents (an idea that has subsequently been raised many times).

We can therefore see that, although many changes in education took place during the 1940s, and some of these were heavily criticized, the most radical change was the introduction of secondary education for all children. It is the expansion of secondary education that is most often associated with the 1940s and this is what often leads people to think most positively about the period as one of optimism and opportunity. Yet, during the long time it took to implement the changes, it gradually became clear that idealism was not going to be matched by reality.

Further and higher education

Many of the people who would normally have progressed to higher education during the 1940s were drafted into the forces or other war work. As this would affect any figures representing the number of students in higher education it may be more useful to note that during the last recorded period of stability, in the academic year 1938/9, there were 50,000 university students and 13,000 student teachers (Halsey, Heath and Ridge, 1980, p 310). If we compare these figures with the approximate 400,000 university students in 1992, we can immediately see that access to higher education during the 1940s was for a relatively small, privileged minority.

It would be more difficult to estimate the number of people taking some sort of further education, as definitions have changed. For example, the many apprenticeship schemes available during the 1940s often brought with them high status as they involved the transmission of high-level, and respected, craft skills. These may include day release at local colleges or be entirely provided in the workplace. Yet when I asked older interviewees in Torytown and Labourville what qualifications they had, few of those trained in one of these apprenticeships cited them as a valid qualification.

QUESTION

Can the devaluing of apprenticeships just be attributed to credential inflation?

Similarly, during the 1940s and 1950s many areas still had mechanics' institutes, where working men (initially they were seen as male-only institutes) could advance their education without necessarily getting formal qualifications. They provided opportunities for the working class to expand their reading and general knowledge as well as skills associated with hobbies (such as woodwork and art), but this was often seen as primarily for self-development, rather than for the advancement of a career. It was generally assumed that, although being born into a working-class family meant that individuals would stay working class, it was still possible to value education for its intrinsic value rather than for entirely instrumental reasons.

According to the 1944 Education Act it was

> the duty of every local authority to secure the provision for their area of adequate facilities for further education, that is to say, (i) Full-time and part-time education for persons over compulsory school age; and (ii) Leisure time occupation in such organized cultural training and recreative activities as are suited to their requirements, for any persons over compulsory school age who are able and willing to profit by the facilities provided for that purpose.
> Section 41 of the 1944 Education Act, cited by Trowler, 1998, pp 26–7

The Act also set up adult education centres and required LEAs to co-operate with other voluntary agencies to ensure that adequate facilities were provided for recreation and social and physical training. As a result, the number of adult students attending evening classes rose from 300,000 in 1947 to more than a million in 1967 (Trowler, 1998, p 27).

During the 1940s most of the government initiatives relating to post-school education were about transition from school to employment, rather than from school to formal further or higher education. In 1945 the *Report of the Special Committee on Higher Technological Education* (Percy) recommended upgrading some technical colleges to colleges of advanced technology. The 1947 Clarke Report, *School and Life* (CACE England), examined 'the transition from school to independent life' and called for a dramatic increase in spending in order to reduce pupil : teacher ratios and improve unhealthy and unsuitable school buildings. It made recommendations about a wide range of topics, including relationships between school, home and neighbourhood, youth clubs and voluntary organizations, the health of children at school and young people at work, and 'compensatory' further education for workers in routine jobs. The main conclusion about education and employment was that schools should not prepare pupils for particular types of employment because industry itself benefited from the teaching and learning of basic educational skills.

Teachers

It is possible that during the 1940s teachers had a higher social status than at any time since, primarily because of their scarcity value. In 1938/9 there were 13,000 student teachers (Halsey, Heath and Ridge, 1980, p 310), but many teachers who later enlisted in the services, or were engaged in other war work, did not return to teaching in peacetime. As very few had been trained between 1939 and 1945, there would have been problems running existing schools after the war, but the problem was compounded by the 1944 Act's introduction of secondary education for all. Furthermore, the raising of the school-leaving age to fifteen in 1947 brought about 400,000 extra children into schools.

In 1944 *The Report of the Committee on Supply, Recruitment and Training of Teachers and Youth Leaders* (McNair) recommended that efforts to raise the status of teachers should include a three-year training course and the increasing of their salaries. However, the severity of the shortage meant that teachers had to be trained as quickly as possible, and most teachers followed a two-year training scheme to teach in state schools. Those who had degrees but were not qualified teachers often chose to teach in private schools. (Since the 1940s this situation has been reversed as a degree and qualified teacher status is necessary to teach in state schools but not in private schools.) The status of teachers was further enhanced by a relatively close working relationship between central government, local authorities and teachers' unions. Teachers were regularly consulted on policy issues even though their views were not always followed.

With hindsight, the late 1940s looks like a relatively cheerful period in which to teach, with its plentiful supply of high-status jobs, good career prospects, relative autonomy and the ear of the government. Even the sociology of education, with its emphasis at the time on the sociology of teaching (see Waller, 1932, reprinted in 1965), tended to have a less critical approach than in later years, as it was most concerned about practical issues such as behaviour in the classroom. However, a taste of things to come could already be seen in the availability of one quote that was to be used to insult teachers for many years to come: 'He who can, does. He who cannot, teaches' (George Bernard Shaw, 1946).

QUESTION

Consider what might be the advantages and disadvantages for pupils and students in having teachers with a high degree of autonomy.

Class and status

Some concerns about social inequalities have already been explained because they are related to socio-economic context, perspectives and school systems. At a more practical level, social inequalities were often identified most clearly when the school-leaving age was considered, and many educationalists commented on the waste of the many who were selected for grammar schools but left before taking their School Certificate at sixteen. In 1945, 23.1 per cent of boys and 25.5 per cent of girls left grammar school early, compared with 14.5 per cent of boys and 17.6 per cent of girls in 1949 (CACE, 1954, p 5), and it was children from lower social groups who tended to leave early. Whereas children with semi- or unskilled parents made up 20.9 per cent of grammar school pupils, they made up only 7.3 per cent of those in sixth forms. It seems that only 11 per cent of early-leaving boys and 18 per cent of early-leaving girls left early because their parents could not afford to keep them on and that other reasons included social assumptions and parental attitudes.

When interviewees in Torytown and Labourville were asked why they left school at school-leaving age, their responses often took an incredulous tone at the apparent stupidity of the question. They left because that was the age to leave! When they were asked further about the school-leaving age of their parents, it often emerged that school-leaving age was determined by family

---

VIEWS FROM TORYTOWN AND LABOURVILLE: SCHOOL-LEAVING AGE

Audrey (born in 1918) said that her mother left school at fourteen to look after her mother, who had had a stroke. Her father ran away from home at fourteen because his parents wanted him to work down the local mine.

Donald was born in 1929 and said that his mother left school at eleven,

> ... which was allowed in those days if you had a one-parent family.
>
> Donald, 1988

Anthony left school at fifteen because of the financial needs of the family.

> My father came out of work, so I was taken away and told to earn some pennies.
>
> Anthony, 1988

Cecil said that his mother left school at twelve and that he had to leave his elementary school at fourteen, although he would have liked to have had a better education.

> They [his parents] were both from big families. They had to leave school to help keep the family.
> [Why informant left at fourteen.] Because I had to. Because I had to go and get a job and start work to help keep me brothers and sisters. [His preferred education.] I would rather have gone to an all-boys' school. In them days there was no such thing because your parents couldn't afford it. Mine couldn't anyway.
>
> Cecil, 1988

Other families tried to pay for their children to be privately educated but had problems in keeping up the payments. Jean was born in 1944 and compared her education with that of her mother.

> [Mother's education.] For a while she was at a girls' private boarding school. Her father died. Therefore she left and I don't know where she went. She got some further education and a Pitman's shorthand typing qualification.
>
> Jean, 1988

> [Elizabeth left her private school at fifteen.] It was just at the end of the war and I was off school a lot. Mother was ill and I wasn't doing well in my exams, so dad said I'd better get out and go to work.
>
> Elizabeth, 1988

> [Father] went to a boys' secondary modern school because they couldn't afford to let him go to the grammar school because they had to buy their own books and were so poor that they couldn't afford them at that time.
> [Mother's education.] She went to grammar school but left at fourteen. They pulled her out before the end because they couldn't afford to keep her there.
>
> Justin, 1988

income or other family pressures. From this small sample there emerged many examples of the effects of relative deprivation on educational opportunities. To many of the interviewees and their parents, education beyond the usual school-leaving age was totally out of the question because of the family's need for an extra wage.

Efforts to create a more meritocratic system also included proposals for improving access to private education. In 1944 the Fleming Report, *Public Schools and the General Education System*, recommended that public schools should gradually be integrated into the state system by taking pupils who would be given state grants and that eventually all places should be open to pupils with state grants. However, this scheme never came into effect.

Gender

It is easy to imagine that gender did not exist during the 1940s! Despite great strides towards the emancipation of women, gross inequalities between the sexes still existed and in education they largely existed unseen. Following the introduction of votes for women in 1918, the University of Oxford finally allowed women to take degrees in 1920, yet it was only in 1947 that the University of Cambridge followed suit; until then women had been allowed to take courses but were not awarded with degrees.

In the 1930s mass unemployment meant that men often had priority for jobs and women were encouraged to stay in the home. Yet, during the 1939–45 war women again (as in the First World War) showed themselves capable of doing heavy manual work as well as other 'men's' jobs. Again, some women were replaced by men returning from the war, but a shortage of workers in the 1940s and 1950s still meant that there was a demand for women workers. Women could be particularly useful as teachers, a profession that was seen as well suited to their natural 'caring' instincts. Indeed, women were encouraged to enter teaching by the 1944 Education Act, which removed restrictions on married women working as teachers.

After 1944 improved access to a grammar school education helped more girls to get academic qualifications, although they often had to perform better than boys in order to pass the 11+ examination. In secondary modern schools training for manual work was still generally sexist; girls studying domestic subjects (cookery, needlework and housework, often in mock houses or flats, where they could practice the full range of domestic duties such as ironing, washing up, etc.) and boys studying technical subjects (metalwork and woodwork in workshops). Here we can see how a woman writer explained that girls took domestic science seriously because it related to their futures.

> Domestic science is another popular lesson. The girls regard it as a serious business and are prepared to work hard at it. This attitude appears to be fairly general. An older girl who said that she did as little work as possible when she was at school . . . still thinks of 'cooking and laundry' as lessons which did not turn out to be a waste of time. Senior girls, who perhaps spend one whole day a week, for six months, in the school kitchen, set about their work in a business-like manner, are not afraid to handle ovens, and have a confidence in their own abilities that is in marked contrast to their hesitating approach to such subjects as letter-writing or history . . . A good many girls indicate that they do not really think school work has any bearing on their future . . .
>
> Pearl Jephcott, 1942

Gender stereotyping was generally accepted as the norm because it was largely unseen. Yet there were some signs of rebellion, even in conventional publications such as the *Ladies Home Journal*, which famously noted in 1947 that 'The average girl would rather have beauty than brains because she knows that the average man can see much better than he can think' (cited in Exley, 1993). Any rebellion was, nevertheless, muted and feminism was at such a low point during the 1940s that, even when Simone de Beauvoir published *The Second Sex* (1949), she declared that she was not a feminist. Still she argued that cultural (rather than biological) factors were important in women's oppression and that women's oppression came from their positions as the 'Other', not only separate from men, but inferior to them. However, she also believed that the class struggle was more important than gender inequalities and that women's rights would come with the achievement of socialism.

Race and ethnicity

In 1944 the UK was already a multi-ethnic state, including the descendants of slaves, Vikings, Romans and Moors and more recent immigrants from the Commonwealth and many European states. Some ethnic minorities were particularly visible because they lived close together for mutual support, such as the Jewish community in the East End of London and the Chinese in Chinatown, but many were unobtrusively integrated. The experience of war had increased this existing amalgam as Allied forces and refugees established themselves and mixed with the local population. Thus the war babies, who experienced education in future years, came from many and varied backgrounds. Yet common perceptions were of a mainly white population, tolerant of ethnic differences because such differences were inconsequential. It was only when intolerance surfaced at a personal level that ethnicity, or rather *race*, seemed to become significant. *Ethnicity* was a word that was rarely used at that time.

The UK had fought a war against the assumption that some races were inferior to others, but attitudes towards race were not at all straightforward. The United States of America was one of the Allies during the war, whilst maintaining a system of racial segregation in many of its own states. In the UK it was common, and legal, for blatant racial discrimination to exist in housing and employment, but discrimination was likely to be more covert in education. Elite ruling-class families in various Commonwealth states could already send their children to the top British public schools in order to ensure their social as well as educational advantage. Yet theories about the inheritance of intelligence and the value of IQ testing could still be claimed to support ideas about the inferior intelligence of various races.

Within the UK the long-standing sectarianism in Northern Ireland continued but was to explode into relatively large-scale violence much later, in the 1960s. Scottish nationalism existed but much of it had been contained by loyalty to the British state during a time of war. Similarly Welsh nationalism had been contained, although in education there was the continuing problem of how to manage two languages. The 1949 Evans/Aaron Report, *The Future of Secondary Education in Wales* (CACE Wales), paid particular attention to problems caused by the prevalence of two languages and the rural and sparsely populated character of much of Wales. It recommended the concentration on the pupil's first language (whether it was English or Welsh) but argued that English must be taught well in predominantly Welsh-speaking areas, and that Welsh should be available as an option for all children in predominantly English-speaking areas.

Religion

Before the introduction of state education in 1870 most formal religious instruction took place in Sunday schools, and this was often the only formal education children had. However, with the development of state education, the key argument in favour of including some form of religious instruction was for its civilizing influence, in creating compliant citizens. Although it was not seen as essentially vocational, it did serve a purpose in preparing children for work by teaching them to obey rules and adopt high moral standards. Religious education was therefore already an integral part of state schools before secondary education was expanded in 1944.

The 1944 Education Act included guidelines for religious instruction. All state schools, whether county (i.e. controlled by a local authority) or voluntary (controlled by a church) must start the day with a corporate act of worship, although parents had the right of withdrawal and local authorities could rule that it was impracticable to assemble all pupils at one time. All schools must also provide religious instruction (the only part of the curriculum prescribed by law, until the 1988 Education Reform Act), and this must be non-denominational except in voluntary schools. In practice 'non-denominational' still generally meant that, although it included different denominations within the Christian church, it did not include other types of religions. When exceptions were made in voluntary schools this meant that the school could teach the religion of the particular Christian church to which the school was attached (usually Church of England or Roman Catholic).

Special needs

Frank's problem, as described in Chapter 5, helps to explain how perceptions have changed dramatically since the 1940s. Problems we may consider to be relatively minor today were regarded as quite severe at that time and, if being left-handed was a problem then, it is easy to imagine how children with more severe conditions, such as cerebral palsy or Down's syndrome, were categorized.

Until the 1940s children with severe learning difficulties were described as 'idiots' or 'imbeciles' and between 1945 and 1981 they were called 'subnormal'. Indeed, until the changes initiated during the 1970s, children with what we would now call special educational needs were usually categorized by certain medical terms and regarded as being the responsibilities of the medical profession, rather than having a place within the schooling system. The 1944 Education Act tried to do something about this by requiring local authorities to ascertain the needs of children in their areas for special educational treatment, and recommending that they be educated in ordinary schools wherever possible. It also established ten categories of handicap, including the new one of 'maladjusted' (these categories were abolished in the 1981 Education Act). Nevertheless, many children with what we would now regard as physical disabilities were wrongly assumed to have mental disabilities, to be uneducable and were institutionalized in psychiatric hospitals. Others attended special schools, where they were supposed to receive more specialized attention according to their individual needs, although some adults who attended such schools as children have since complained of the inhumane treatment they received (see Humphries and Gordon, 1992, for a historical account).

Behaviour

It is tempting to develop an idealized image of behaviour in the classroom during the 1940s. Interviewees in Torytown and Labourville reinforced this image by comparing discipline in the classroom in the 1990s unfavourably with discipline in the past. Yet they mixed rosy images of pupils' civilized behaviour with harsh memories of corporal punishment and fear of the teacher. Indeed, when one interviewee insisted that corporal punishment did not hurt, the claim was probably based on memories dulled and romanticized over time. Many types of corporal punishment were legal during the 1940s and they were not altered by the 1944 Education Act. As a result, children could be left with deep cuts or bruises from what today would be regarded as physical assaults or with the effects of humiliation that today would be regarded as mental torture.

QUESTION

Do the rigours of corporal punishment in the past challenge this book's central claim that education has undergone a process of immiseration since 1944?

During the 1940s sociologists were already interested in studying control of children in the classroom, primarily as a way of helping teachers to function effectively. Theorists were also influenced by the experience of the Second World War and debates about how education could be used to create a new and better society (see Mannheim, 1943). It was only later that sociologists really started to tackle the problems of behaviour in the classroom when viewed from a pupil's perspective.

Unfinished business

One interesting feature of changing education will be noted in each of these chapters on decades of change: it is that each decade ends with a lot of unfinished business. Sometimes:

- apparently important initiatives and directives that seemed to be certain of implementation simply seem to get lost along the way;
- hindsight allows us to see them as being too unrealistic in the first place;
- it simply takes a long time for ideas to actually bear fruit.

An example of the last of these was the raising of the school-leaving age, which was unfinished business left over from a recommendation by the Spens Committee in 1938, initiated by the 1944 Education Act but only implemented in 1947. Yet the Spens Committee actually recommended the raising of the school-leaving age to sixteen and in 1947 it was only raised from fourteen to fifteen. The 1944 Act suggested that it should be raised further to sixteen when practicable – and this is the important point. Educational policy-makers have to make long-term plans, setting themselves targets which they may or may not reach. As a result, there is an almost inevitable sense of failure when an ideal is not attained, even though the identification and targeting of an ideal has led to more progress than would have been achieved otherwise.

The study of unfinished business is also useful for identifying impossible ideals or particularly intransigent targets and, by reflecting on the 1940s, we can already see that it was difficult for the government to influence private education or implement compulsory further education. The 1944 Act introduced a scheme for the registration of private schools but it was not enforced until 1957. In 1944 the Fleming Report, *Public Schools and the General Education System*, went further, recommending that public schools should gradually be integrated into the state system by taking pupils who would be given state grants. Eventually all places should be open to pupils with state grants. However, the scheme never came into effect. The 1944 Education Act also gave LEAs the responsibility to ensure that all young people up to the age of eighteen, and not otherwise in education, received part-time further education by attending a 'county college' for the equivalent of one day a week. This too was never implemented.

QUESTION

Why do you think these targets were so intransigent?

7

The 1950s

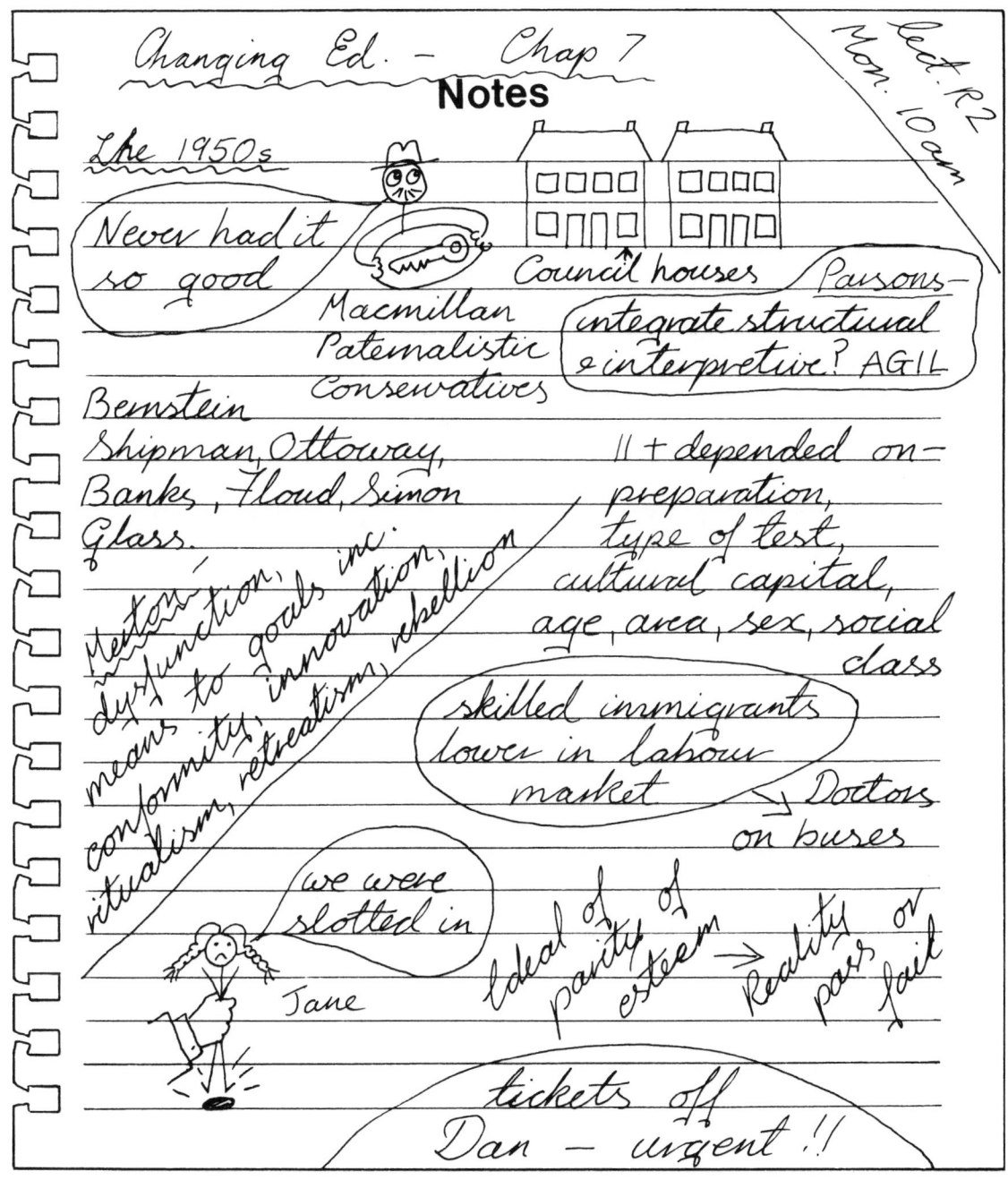

Socio-economic change – Changing perspectives – Changing school systems – Further and higher education – Teachers – Class and status – Gender – Ethnicity – Special needs – Behaviour – Unfinished business

Most of our people have never had it so good.

Harold Macmillan, speech at Bedford football ground, 20 July 1957

Socio-economic change

In the 1950s it was easy to claim that most people had never had it so good when comparisons were made with the economic depression of the 1930s and wartime experiences during the 1940s. At a personal level, a still relatively new welfare state brought with it some sense of relief from habitual fears of sickness, unemployment, old age and poverty. Although there were still major social inequalities, it seemed that progress was being made to tackle them. At both a national and international level the 1950s was a period of consolidation and expansion, but also a period of disappointment. European states were starting to experience economic regeneration after the Second World War, but the Cold War between the liberal democracies of the West and the communist states of the (mainly) East helped to support a climate of suspicion towards some of the socialist ideals promoted during the 1940s.

In education the changes introduced in 1944 were still being implemented but faults were becoming more noticeable. Most clearly it was possible to see that, despite the expansion of secondary education, and although many jobs were available, most children still had predetermined life chances.

LEARNING TO BE MINERS

Ninety-three Ashton persons selected at random were asked about their attitude towards encouraging a son to work in the mining industry. The vast majority, 66, said that they would not or did not encourage their sons to take this step, many of them expressing themselves most emphatically. Many added, however, that they would allow the boy to choose for himself. This latter statement, however, is obviously significant, since despite the fact that parents apparently do not encourage their sons to be miners, the great majority of them do in fact become miners. Indeed, this question was only asked in order to confirm the statement heard many hundreds of times in the Yorkshire coalfields since 1945 – 'I hope no son of mine ever works in the pit'. When the same persons were asked if they thought it advantageous to have a grammar school education for both boys and girls 79 answered in the affirmative but a few added their opinion that a good education for girls was likely to be wasted since they 'only get married'. It is unlikely that this preference for grammar school education has any effect on reality . . . Only very few Ashton children actually get a grammar school education and very few develop interests broader than those of their parents whose interests can be satisfied by life in Ashton . . .

We have given two examples of the failure to coincide of parents' expressed wishes and the actual fate of their children. In each case an important consideration is the fact that the position of the parent in the social structure unfits him or her for the task of (a) holding his ideas very strongly or practically and (b) carrying them out. These two disadvantages, not by any means directly perceived or understood by all parents, reinforce that characteristic we have already described as 'basic' – the approach to life on only a day-to-day footing. Miners, like many other industrial workers, are often very cynical about 'book-learning' in anything to do directly with their own work and life. They recognize the value of book-learning for 'getting on' in school and as a training for professions out of their experience, but for their own lives, and in contact with their own people, they are sceptical about 'theory', so that any child not showing exceptional talent with 'books' at school is given little encouragement to study. The vocational training available in mining institutes after leaving school is seen as much more valuable.

Dennis, Henriques and Slaughter, 1956, *Coal Is Our Life*, 235–6

It was a different life in them days. We lived in the same street as Councillor [a current Labour councillor] and his was the only house to have a bath. The local Conservative councillor's family ran the local laundry and even they had no bath.

Philip, 1992

I went to a state school, it was just an all-girls secondary modern. I took my 11+, but I didn't pass it. They were all single-sex schools in the 50s, it was quite normal then. I left school in 1954, when I was fifteen, with no qualifications. I wanted to stop on another year, but my mother wouldn't let me, because she thought that I would be wasting my time. There was four of us, four children, and she thought it would be better getting a job. Actually when I got a job I was better off because I learnt to type. I did better when I left school than I did in school. I always had a good job. I could always move from one job to another because I picked things up at work; I got women who already worked there to show me how to work different things in the office and the typing and everything, so I picked things up and then, you know, went from there. I started as just a clerk in a place in [. . .] in an office in [. . .] and then I started learning to type. I went to, there was a college in [. . .] called [. . .] College, and I learnt shorthand and typing there.

Georgina, 1997

I think there's more competition now, I think they've got to get more results to get better jobs nowadays. There seems to be fewer jobs and you need more qualifications, because when I left school at fifteen you could go to the Labour Exchange and you could take your pick, any job you wanted. That was the way it was in the 50s, so. Now people have to get more and more qualifications because firms want higher qualifications, higher standards.

Georgina, 1997

Question

How were life chances predetermined in the 1950s?

Changing perspectives

In 1951 a Conservative government was elected under the leadership of Harold Macmillan, who was later succeeded by Douglas-Home. Both came from aristocratic families, with a paternalistic attitude towards the poor which fitted the mould of One Nation Conservatism. Indeed, Harold Macmillan was particularly proud that he looked after the poor and claimed that his government had handed over more keys to new council house owners than had any Labour government. Yet there were some traces of the political perspective we more closely associate with the New Right of the 1980s. For example, the new Minister of Education, Florence Horsborough, was described by Ronald Gould (representative of teachers' unions) as 'The girl who can't say yes', because she introduced cuts in educational spending. Horsborough was replaced in 1954 by Sir David Eccles, who was popular with teachers and local authorities and got on well with Gould and William Alexander (representative of LEAs). In January 1957 Lord

Hailsham replaced Sir David Eccles and in September 1957 Geoffrey Lloyd replaced Lord Hailsham. However, by the end of the 1950s (from October 1959) the most popular of these, Sir David Eccles, was again Minister of Education.

Despite years of division, the 1950 Labour Party Conference passed a resolution calling upon the Labour government to implement the party's policy on comprehensive schools.

> The tripartite system, it was claimed, rested upon, and indeed perpetuated, those class distinctions which the Labour movement was pledged to destroy. The aim of the common school has accordingly been envisaged as the promotion of social unity and the destruction of class barriers – it is hoped that the creation of the common school will promote equality within the social as well as the educational system, and so prevent the new aristocracy of brains which . . . threatens to supersede the aristocracies of wealth and birth.
>
> Banks, 1968, p 283

By 1951 the Labour Party had fully adopted a policy favouring the comprehensive school for secondary education and the Labour pamphlet *A Policy for Secondary Education* (1951) was essentially a brief for the comprehensive school. It suggested that the first two years at a comprehensive school should be mainly diagnostic, and that the remainder of the children's school career should seek to provide them with courses adapted to their specific abilities and aptitudes. Yet, despite Labour's adoption of a policy favouring comprehensive schools, few plans were made for comprehensive education until the new Labour government of 1964. There were still concerns that comprehensive schools would dilute educational opportunities and prevent particularly able pupils from achieving their full potential. Some people in the Labour Party, such as Crosland (1956, cited by Sanderson, 1987), thought a degree of eliteness was inevitable and desirable in any society as the aim was not to create a mediocre society in which everyone was levelled down to the same denominator.

During the 1950s and 1960s two themes in the sociology of education were emerging. The first was more practical in its applications, with an emphasis on home-school relations and compensatory education, and this suited the majority of courses about education, which were mainly for the training of teachers. The second had a more theoretical emphasis on structural functionalist approaches to equal opportunities and the school as a social system (including the work of such writers as Bernstein and Shipman). Sociologists were particularly concerned with educational opportunities since the 1944 Education Act as the changes since then provided a focus for their critiques. In 1953 the first British sociology of education book was published by Ottoway and the same year saw the publication of Brian Simon's book, *Intelligence Testing and the Comprehensive School*. Simon provided a sociological and psychological critique of intelligence tests explaining (his and others') doubts about the relationship between intelligence and environment.

During the 1950s Talcott Parsons was writing in the United States about his own version of functionalism and his theories gradually had an impact on the sociologists in the UK (1937; 1949; 1951; 1959). Although he did not focus just on education, he did note his interest in the problem of, first,

... how the school class functions to internalize in its pupils both the commitments and capacities for successful performance of their future adult roles, and second of how it functions to allocate these human resources within the role structure of the adult society.

Parsons, 1959, p 297

In this way Parsons was aiming to integrate structural and interpretive approaches by emphasizing how the social structure influences the roles of individuals within the education system. His work is relevant in both sociology and psychology and is an example of how unrealistic it would be to make sharp distinctions between structural and interpretive approaches. It is, nevertheless, more often cited in the sociology of education as a 'structural functionalist' approach simply because he did not emphasize the routine small-scale classroom interactions that provide a focus for interpretive approaches. He was interested in the 'patterned expectations' (rules and regulations) that have developed, governing how individuals should behave in order to maintain social order and continuity. More specifically, education was seen as serving the four functional requirements that all societies have in order to survive.

Adaptation: education adapts itself and individuals to changes in the cultural, technological and physical environment. It helps to emancipate the child from dependence on the family.
Goal attainment: education helps individuals to identify and realize their personal and collective needs. Differentiated achievements can contribute to an effective division of labour.
Integration: education provides some coherence between the relative influences of, for example, family, legal system, church, employment and the wider economic system. It helps individuals to identify themselves within a wider social system.
Latency or pattern maintenance: educational processes lead to the reproduction of common values and social norms. It teaches us not only how to conform, but also how to think.

Here we can see a continuation of Durkheim's positivist approach (see Chapter 3), with its emphasis on description, rather than criticism. Its implication that education contributes towards a meritocratic system (in which pupils' educational achievements are only based on ability and effort) has, however, been challenged as research has repeatedly highlighted the profound effects of social inequalities on educational outcomes. Critics have also argued that education can contribute to both social cohesion and social conflict, and that education does not necessarily serve the needs of either the economy or the individual. There are, moreover, no clear and agreed sets of 'needs' that can be functionally fulfilled.

It would, however, be wrong to assume that functionalist approaches to education are no longer influential. Some aspects have indeed been adapted or developed more fully to incorporate criticisms. For example, theories about social dysfunction (Merton, 1957; see his work later in this chapter when we look at behaviour) help to explain how education can not only fail to serve the needs of society, but actually work against the interests of society. It can also reasonably be claimed that it is just as important to observe the role of education in maintaining society as to observe the manifestation of conflict within education.

Changing school systems

Criticisms of what was largely a bipartite school system gradually gained strength during the 1950s. These were mainly concerned with the assumptions, first, that intelligence could be assessed accurately by testing at the age of eleven, second, that this involved pure tests of mental ability, untouched by bias and, third, that abilities would be fixed for life.

In addition to the many problems involved in making an assessment at 11+ it became clear that few technical schools were provided and that selection at 11+ had become synonymous with a great divide between a grammar school and a secondary modern school education. The aim of 'parity of esteem' was being lost to the actual experience of 'passing or failing' a grammar school entrance examination and, in her book on the issue, the sociologist Olive Banks (1955) showed the impossibility of the policy of 'parity of esteem' ever succeeding. Yet the Labour Party's new official policy in favour of comprehensive schools had very little impact and by 1954 there were only sixteen comprehensive schools in England and Wales (Halsey, Heath and Ridge, 1980, p 32).

It was the introduction (in 1951) of the General Certificate of Education in England and Wales that was to be largely responsible for the gradual end of nationwide testing at 11+. The GCE could only be taken by pupils who stayed on at school past the school-leaving age of fifteen and was at first only taken by grammar school pupils. Whilst all grammar schools provided education until the age of sixteen and aimed to prepare their pupils for the GCE, it was generally assumed that pupils would leave secondary modern schools at the age of fifteen with no academic qualifications (and usually no qualifications at all). Yet many children left grammar schools at fifteen, without taking examinations, and gradually secondary modern schools started to allow some of their pupils to stay at school until sixteen in order to take GCEs. It was therefore possible for some children to leave a secondary modern school with more qualifications than others leaving grammar school, which clearly challenged assumptions that life-long intellectual ability could be tested at 11+. Although such contradictions were not particularly apparent for most of the 1950s, it was apparent that decisions about school-leaving age were crucial.

Some of the reasons for early leaving may appear to be individual; for example, a study of early leaving from Southampton grammar schools in the early 1950s found that the chief reasons for this were: low ability, 31.7 per cent; home conditions, 30.2 per cent; no will to work, 10.1 per cent; and wanting an early career, 17.8 per cent (Dempster, 1954, pp 107–8). Yet, if we look at these reasons, it is quite easy to see that all may be affected by a pupil's socio-economic status and that this could explain why many grammar school children left school at fifteen.

In 1954 the Gurney-Dixon Report, *Early Leaving* (CACE, England), also considered the

1. Selection was not just taking place at 11+. Much was decided before then as pupils in primary schools were usually streamed and often the children in the higher streams were given more intensive preparation for the exam.
2. There was no single type of national test at 11+. Each separate LEA used its own combination of any of nineteen or more criteria (including intelligence tests, use of English, a general paper, interviews and school records).
3. When English tests were used their demands for a wide vocabulary and flexible use of language advantaged children from cultured middle-class homes. They were not so much testing capacity for thought as the possession of cultural capital.
4. Children supposedly being tested at 11+ actually ranged in age from ten years and six months to eleven years and five months. The older children were advantaged by maturity and the fact that they may have been in school for six years, compared to others who had been in school for five or five and a half years.
5. There were regional disparities in the provision of grammar school places, making it more difficult to 'pass' the 11+ examination in some areas than in others. Access to grammar school often depended more on the number of places available at local grammar schools than on measured IQ. Douglas showed that there were wide regional variations in the opportunities to attend grammar school in 1959. This varied from a 35 per cent chance in the South West and a 33.5 per cent chance in Wales to an 18 per cent chance in the South and a 22.4 per cent chance in the North East (Douglas, 1964, p 24).
6. Girls were often discriminated against in the allocation of grammar school places in order to compensate boys for their supposed late maturation.
7. It was not really about allocating children to the education most appropriate to their needs (academic, technical, general) as there was no fixed standard of what each constituted. In effect it was more about competition for a limited number of grammar school places. For example, technical skills were not usually assessed. Where a tripartite system existed, candidates who only just failed the 11+ went to technical schools, thus assuming that children who were not quite academic enough for grammar school had technical or mechanical abilities.
8. There was growing evidence of a major misallocation of talent with many trapped in an inappropriate environment. Stephen Wiseman found that in 1951, 14 per cent of the brightest children in his sample of fourteen- and fifteen-year-olds were in secondary modern schools and in 1957 the figure was still 11.2 per cent (1964, pp 21, 132). Yates and Pidgeon (1957) claimed that approximately 70,000 children were being allocated each year to the wrong type of school.
9. Although one aim was to improve the access of working-class children to a grammar school education, it was found that relatively few children from working-class backgrounds were 'passing' the 11+.

factors influencing school-leaving age and found that it was closely linked to the occupational status of the pupil's father. The report recommended that not only should more grammar school places be provided, but there should also be more financial provision for pupils who remained at school after school-leaving age. In general, it cast grave doubts over the effectiveness of the 1944 Act in reducing social class-based inequalities in education.

The 1959 Crowther Report, *Fifteen to Eighteen* (CACE), confirmed the Gurney-Dixon Report's findings about the effect of social class on school-leaving age. It also supported a tripartite system but noted that such a system had never really been established. Whilst accepting that some comprehensive schools should be set up, it suggested further divisions within secondary and further education. The report argued that in secondary modern schools the top third of pupils were capable of taking and benefiting from external exams below GCE level but the majority of pupils there should be excused them.

As you progress through the various decades in this book you will note that far more is said about state schools than about private schools. This is because governments have paid relatively little attention to private schools and, when they have, any changes in them tend to be either delayed or implemented very slowly. In 1957, for example, one piece of unfinished business left over from the 1940s was completed when the registration of private schools, introduced in the 1944 Act, was finally enforced. Since then, private schools have been inspected by HM Inspectors before being registered and private schools have been expected to apply to be recognized as efficient.

During the 1950s relationships between central governments and their partners (including links with private education) were sometimes strained but relatively amicable when compared with later years. What some educationalists have called the 'triangle of tension' (e.g. McNay and Ozga, 1985) between central government, LEAs and teachers' unions was still relatively healthy, although at the time this sometimes seemed otherwise. For example, in 1957 the percentage grant system for funding LEAs was abolished and it seemed that the partnership between central and local government was starting to deteriorate. However, relationships seemed to depend more on the character of the Minister of Education than on central government policy. Personalities and the local context often seemed to influence educational experiences more than central government directives.

Further and higher education

The numbers of students in higher education increased dramatically during the 1940s and 1950s and by 1954/5 there were 82,000 university students and 28,000 student teachers (Halsey, Heath and Ridge, 1980, p 31). However, there were growing concerns about the influence of social class on access to further and higher education.

In 1959 the Crowther Report, *Fifteen to Eighteen* (CACE), considered the education of fifteen- to eighteen-year-olds and was the first report to really look for sociological answers. Its extensive research confirmed the findings of Gurney-Dixon about the relationship between father's occupational status and pupil's educational attainment. The report argued that there was considerable 'wastage' of talent, and focused on the 'neglected educational territory' of pupils who left school at fifteen to follow a craft or a technical rather than an academic career. It recommended the implementation of the section of the 1944 Act initiating compulsory part-time further education and that, of sixteen- to eighteen-year-olds, half should be in full-time further education by 1979, compared with 12 per cent at the time of the report.

Despite the recommendations of the 1944 Education Act and various reports, compulsory part-time further education was not introduced during the 1950s. The experiences of the few members of the Torytown and Labourville cohort who left school during the 1950s were therefore varied.

I became an apprentice in the building industry. My saving grace, if you like, was because we then had a very, very well-structured apprentice system. I remember leaving school and being so glad to leave and then being told I had to go to a further education college, and I dreaded this because I thought it was going to be like school and found that it wasn't. It was completely different because we were treated like adults and were actually taught. For the first time since I'd been at primary school I actually started to learn. And I became very receptive to the subjects that were being taught there. We had a formal grounding there in maths, English, science. It was wonderful.

John, 1997

At the time, yes, I was quite happy with the educational opportunities. I just wish I'd have had the opportunities that they've got now. Maybe as I get older I realize what I didn't do but I don't think that the opportunities were there. I don't think we had the same chances. You were slotted into things when we were at that age, but now they've got the opportunity to say, 'I don't want to do that. I want to do that'. And they let them do it. But I think when I was at that age, you weren't given that opportunity. You were slotted into this little space and they said, 'That's what we think you are capable of doing and that's what we'll teach you to do'. And you were never given the chance to say, 'Do you really want to do this?' I think nowadays they're given the chance to say, 'No that's not what I want to do. I want to do this'. And the further education wasn't offered to you in the same way that is now. I think they only offered it to the children that they thought were bright enough to accept it but now they'll say that further education is there if you want it. And it doesn't matter whether you're bright or not, the opportunity's there. But they never gave you that opportunity when I was young. Only if you were really bright and then they'd say you could do something better, and then they'd say to you, 'Yes, I think we should put you into something else'. But they never gave it to other children. They only offered it to certain children.

Jane, 1997

I left school at sixteen (that must have been in 58) with five O levels and worked for the post office. Then I got into computers because I answered an advert wanting people with post office experience and experience of handling money. You didn't need computer skills as they trained you on the job. In hindsight, I should have taken my A levels because as an individual I feel under-qualified education-wise. [What prevented you?] The need for an extra wage to come into the household.

Henry, 1997

Teachers

Efforts to tackle the shortage of teachers after the war worked gradually and by 1954–5 there were 28,000 student teachers (Halsey, Heath and Ridge, 1980, p 31). During the 1950s the status of teachers was still relatively high and it was clear that they played an important role in making decisions about their pupils' futures. In many areas the teachers' report constituted an important part of assessment at 11+, whether this was as in the assessment of all pupils or just in cases where the results were on the borderline. However, this responsibility meant that any errors left them open to criticism. Respect for teachers meant that most families seemed to accept their judgement without question, but sociologists had less belief in their infallibility. For example, when Floud and Halsey (1957) compared the proportion of children that teachers would have selected for grammar school with the proportion that actually was selected on the basis of the 11+ examination, they found that teachers were more likely to make decisions influenced by social class. Growing evidence of the biased nature of IQ testing was therefore supplemented by growing concerns about the influence of the teacher.

Class and status

During the 1950s sociologists gradually focused more on the impact of social class on educational opportunities; for example, Glass considered social mobility (1954), Banks criticized theories about parity of esteem (1955) and Floud showed disparities in access to grammar schools. Floud, Halsey and Martin (1956, p 33) found that in the years 1931–1941 just under 10 per cent of working-class boys reaching the age of eleven entered selective secondary schools (mostly grammar schools). In 1953 in south-west Hertfordshire the proportion was 15.5 per cent of working class boys (compared to 22 per cent of all children in the area) and in Middlesbrough it was 12 per cent (compared to 17 per cent of all children in the area).

For the 1954 Gurney-Dixon Report (*Early Leaving*, CACE, England) data were collected from a 10 per cent sample of all grammar schools, whose headteachers supplied details of the 'background, school record and potentialities' of the 1946 intake. It was found that his or her father's occupational status strongly affected a pupil's academic record, what the headteacher judged to be the pupil's 'promise' and the tendency to leave school early. The higher that occupational status, the more likely the child was to succeed and stay at school after school-leaving age. Differences also increased during secondary school as the achievements of children from lower-status occupational groups declined from their 11+ position relative to higher groups. These findings were confirmed by research for the Crowther Report (1959, *Fifteen to Eighteen*, CACE), although the occupational group 'skilled manual workers' was so large that their children were still the largest single group in all types of schools.

Gender

Although social class inequalities were receiving an increasingly high profile during the 1950s, questions about gender inequalities were still not being raised. Indeed, we are often faced with an idealized image of family life during the 1950s.

> Nostalgia for the traditional idealizes the past. Broken families were almost as common in the UK in the nineteenth century as now, although the main reason was death of a spouse rather than separation or divorce. Historical research is revealing more and more about the dark side of the traditional family, where violence against and sexual abuse of children were much more frequent than most historians used to believe.
>   . . . when rightist critics speak of the traditional family, they don't in fact mean the traditional family at all, but a transitional state of the family in the immediate post-war period – the (idealized) family of the 1950s. The traditional family by this point had all but disappeared, but women hadn't yet entered the labour force in large numbers and sexual inequalities remained pronounced.
>
> Giddens, 1998, pp 91–2

Indeed, idealized images of family life during the 1950s ignore the many families who had lost fathers, husbands and other family members during the war. Nevertheless, the existence of an extended family and the introduction of an expanded welfare state helped to ameliorate the increasing strains associated with lost parents and the increasing birth rate ('baby boom').

Idealized images of schooling during the 1950s also ignore the rationalization of sex discrimination in selection at 11+.

> If the pass marks are made equivalent for the two sexes the number of girls admitted to grammar schools will in most areas substantially exceed the number of boys. In view of the fact that these differences exist at the age of eleven and that there is considerable uncertainty as to when and to what extent they eventually disappear the most satisfactory course ... to adopt would seem to be to treat boys and girls separately for the purpose of allocation to secondary school.
>
> Yates and Pidgeon, 1957, pp 168–9

Once selected for the 'appropriate' school, gender divisions continued according to the occupations boys and girls were expected to take after leaving school. In secondary modern schools girls were still trained for a domestic role and boys for a job-for-life in low-grade manual work (as seen near the start of this chapter when they were 'Learning to be miners'). Gender divisions within technical schools were possibly even more pronounced, as boys were trained in technical drawing and craft skills whilst girls would be more likely to learn shorthand, typing and other office skills. In some areas technical schools admitted only boys, whilst girls were expected to gain any office skills in a secondary modern school.

Ethnicity

Race became an increasingly high-profile issue during the 1950s due to the threat to postwar prosperity posed by labour shortages in key sectors of the economy. It has been estimated (Skellington with Morris, 1992, using OPCS and Labour Force Surveys) that in 1951 approximately 0.4 per cent of the British population was drawn from ethnic minorities and that by 1961 this had increased to approximately 1 per cent. More women were entering the workforce but gender inequalities meant that they were not encouraged to do so in large enough numbers to compensate for labour shortages. Many of the shortages were for 'men's' jobs and the government and businesses initiated recruitment campaigns in foreign countries in an attempt to solve the problem. Workers were also encouraged to move because of the underdevelopment they experienced in their own countries. Many of these colonies suffered from over-population, political instability and economic crises and citizenship of the New Commonwealth countries gave migrants the right to settle in the UK permanently.

People arriving from the West Indies in the 1950s and 1960s saw the UK as the 'mother country' and fully expected to participate in British life. When immigrants arrived from India and Pakistan, they too found that open discrimination was lawful. This meant that, whatever qualifications and skills they brought with them, they tended to be fitted into the lower levels of the labour market. Although plenty of low-grade work was available, there was a housing shortage and they often ended up living in areas and accommodation where others did not want to live. Their children would suffer the consequences in education as they faced not only many of the social inequalities experienced by other working-class children, but also prejudices based on their colour and the struggle to learn a new language (in the case of many Asian children) or patois (in the case of many West Indian children). Unlike many other countries (for example, the USA where federal troops were used to protect the first black children attending some schools) the UK already had a history of racial integration and did not face wide-scale political unrest. However, the children of immigrants had to endure many problems associated with prejudice and it was only in the 1960s that many of these started to be identified.

Special needs

Although the effects of the changes initiated by 1944 Education Act could gradually be seen in most areas of education during the 1950s, relatively little was done to help children with special needs. Special educational needs were still labelled as primarily medical problems and the vagaries of the Act meant that many children who could have been educated in ordinary schools were educated in special schools or received little education at all. As such excluded children included those who had physical or mental disabilities, more action was taken with regard to the education of children who were 'maladjusted', a term that entered common usage after the 1944 Act. In 1955 the Underwood Report, *Maladjusted Children*, recommended the use of day, rather than boarding, schools wherever possible, the setting up of a Child Guidance Service in every LEA, with a strengthened role for educational psychologists, and the introduction of preventative measures such as increased nursery provision.

Behaviour

During the 1950s more sociologists started to study behaviour in classrooms from the pupil's perspective. Many still took a functionalist approach, but this approach was changing and heavily influenced by the ideas of Parsons and Merton. Like Parsons, Merton (1957) was writing about social systems such as education but he considered how they could exert pressure on individuals not to conform as well as to conform. He claimed that social systems provided both goals and the means of attaining those goals but that groups of people would have different means of attaining the goals. People may,

for example, want to seek the goal of wealth but will have different ways of attaining it, such as conformity, innovation, ritualism, retreatism or rebellion. Ivan Reid later (1978) adapted this pattern and applied it to education (see Figure 7.1). Here we can see that the formal culture of the school involves hard work as a means to the goal of academic success but that not every pupil will accept both the means and the goals.

John's memories of his schooling during the 1950s did not, however, fit even comfortable images of how the school could promote conformity.

I failed my 11+ and was then sent to this school from hell, where I can't remember learning anything. It was [. . .] School. The school was – it defies belief. I've still met people of my generation who remember the teachers at that school and they can't think about them without being traumatized. It was that bad. Every teacher had a cane. Every teacher used that cane. All day long we were caned for the most trivial of things. They were sadists really. Many people who attended that school have very, very bitter memories. This is why I get so upset when I remember – we weren't taught anything. We were just beaten all day long. And this is no exaggeration, it's the absolute fact.

[What year did you leave?] I wasn't at that school very long (thankfully) because I went to [. . .] High when it first opened. This would be about 1957. My last year or two were spent at [. . .] High, and at that time it was like dying and going to heaven. It was completely different to this school from hell.

Adaptation	Goals*	Means*	Description
Conformity	+	+	Successful pupil, well liked by teachers
Innovation	+	−	Orientated towards success but normative background, lack of stability/personality inhibits adoption of means
Ritualism	−	+	Well-behaved non-achiever
Retreatism	−	−	School is meaningless since pupil identifies with neither goals nor means
Rebellion	±	±	Uses school for purposes and in ways which are different to those of the formal culture

*Key + = acceptance
     − = rejection
     ± = rejection and substitution

Devised by Reid (1978, p 53) from Merton (1957, Chapter 5)

Figure 7.1 Types of individual adaptations to the formal culture of schools

[He left with no qualifications] because, quite honestly, we weren't taught anything. The only thing I can remember being taught – in fact I learned more at the primary school than I learned in the whole of the secondary modern input. I left the moment I was fifteen.

John, 1997

Unfinished business

Some of the unfinished business left over from the 1940s was still unfinished in the 1950s. As in the 1940s, one of the unattained targets was the raising of the school leaving age to sixteen. The Crowther Report (1959) recommended that this should be done, together with the other unattained target of compulsory further education. Perhaps demonstrating an appreciation of how long-term this aim actually was, the report recommended that, of sixteen- to eighteen-year-olds, half should be in full-time further education by 1979, compared with 12 per cent at the time of the report. Actually major expansion of further education finally came in the 1980s as a result of high levels of unemployment among school leavers.

8

The 1960s

Changing Ed. — Chap 8

Notes

Dan Lickets Now!!

The 1960s
Labour 1964 – 7 inc.
→ Integrating public schools?
→ Plowden EPAs Compensatory ed.
→ Circular 10/65 – comprehensives
Conservative inc.
→ Mandatory stu. grants   Progressive Ed?
→ ILEA   vv Black Papers

race & IQ
Jensen, Eysenck
D
MENSA

Bio. determinism Newson 1963 –
home craft for – some girls who
are far from enthusiastic

Enoch Powell – River Liber   Expansion of HE
foaming with blood   Douglas – efficiency
                                    of pump
Robbins – principal of access, polytechnics
Open University
Class Douglas, Jackson & Marsden, Turner
manifest & latent values,
sponsored & contest   Marcuse, civil rights,
mobility, Hargreaves &   Vietnam, Northern
Lacey streaming – class   Ireland etc. etc.

Socio-economic change – Changing perspectives – Changing school systems – Further and higher education – Teachers – Class and status – Gender – Ethnicity – Religion – Special needs – Behaviour – Torytown and Labourville – Unfinished business

The young always have the same problem – how to rebel and conform at the same time. They have now solved this by defying their parents and copying one another.

Quentin Crisp, 1968

Socio-economic change

Those of us who were teenagers during the 1960s often bore those who were not with tales of a golden era in which opportunities seemed boundless and the UK seemed to be the centre of the world. So many share such impressions that it does seem certain that a wave of idealism swept through the UK in the 1960s. Young people started to be identified as a separate group with its own cultural identities during the late 1950s, under the influence of American icons such as Elvis Presley and James Dean (copied by British imitations such as Cliff Richard). However, more of the icons of the 1960s were home-made (including the Beatles and the Rolling Stones) and products of an apparently new, progressive and optimistic youth culture. With continually expanding opportunities for employment and a rapidly advancing standard of living for many people, it seemed that education could also make a significant contribution to a rising meritocracy.

There were, nevertheless, many less optimistic trends during the 1960s. Not only did the Cold War between East and West continue but it reached menacing new heights in the early 1960s with the Bay of Pigs incident and the Cuban Missile Crisis, when it seemed that the world was very close to a nuclear war. Before the end of the 1960s the Vietnam War was having an effect much wider than its national boundaries as it served as a major focus for discontented youth. Civil rights marches in the USA were helping to generate new social movements and ideas about alternatives to formal political action, thus inspiring anti-racists elsewhere, women's liberationists and student radicalism throughout Western Europe. In Northern Ireland civil rights marches helped to publicize the unequal treatment of Roman Catholics and generate more extreme activities by those republicans who felt

that peaceful protest was not enough. It seemed that the optimism and confidence of youth during the 1960s had combined with their critical awakening and led to a determination to tackle newly exposed social wounds.

In education it was apparent that not only had the high expectations raised by the 1944 Education Act not been fulfilled, but also that some of these expectations may have been too low. It seemed unreasonable to predetermine future progress at the age of eleven because many 11+ 'failures' were achieving more than expected and many 11+ 'successes' were achieving less. The comprehensive school was therefore promoted as not only a way of creating a broad highway of educational opportunity, but also a way of addressing wider social class inequalities. Perhaps, just as the idealism of the 1940s led to unreasonable expectations of selection at eleven for a tripartite system, the idealism of the 1960s led to unreasonable expectations of what comprehensive schools could achieve.

The idealism of the time can also be seen in *progressive education*, which gained favour in some schools during the 1960s, although it was perhaps not as common or radical as was assumed at the time. Indeed, the concept of progressive education can have many meanings, including support for comprehensive education, the reaction of some schools against traditions such as corporal punishment and rote learning, the use of a child-centred approach in primary schools (often with an integrated curriculum of the sort described by Bernstein as weak classification and framing) and, at the most extreme, the creation of independent progressive schools promoting the maximum freedom of the individual (see A.S. Neill's book about Summerhill School, 1962). Yet, despite the vagueness of the term and doubts about how widespread it became, progressive education was heavily criticized by writers such as the contributors to the Black Papers (Cox and Dyson, 1969, 1970, 1971; Cox and Boyson, 1975, 1977) for reducing educational standards in general and discipline in the classroom in particular.

Certainly it seems that, in the 1960s, many young people felt that (like their favourite pop stars) they could achieve great things without good educational qualifications and that this may have impacted on their motivation. We can see this in the recollections of some of the few members of the Labourville and Torytown cohort who left school during the 1960s.

TORYTOWN AND LABOURVILLE: COHORT EXPERIENCES

Nicholas and Mark had casual attitudes towards their education during the 1960s.

I suppose I must have been about fifteen when I walked out, and I left before I took any exams. I just refused to take them, because I knew what I was going to succeed in, I knew what I would achieve, and I would do very well in them. I was top in art, top in woodwork, top in English and that was it, but I was bottom in maths, bottom in French, all the, in those days, subjects that really mattered. The best any of the teachers would ever say to me was, 'Have you considered being a woodwork teacher? Have you considered being an art teacher?' and all these sort of things. Well, I, for a couple of years prior to that had been playing semi-professionally in groups and I was earning more money than all my mates that actually had left school and got jobs, and I was just doing it in the evenings. So, it got very close to the mock O levels and I suppose, to put it bluntly, my bottle went and I just walked out of school. I only found out for certain that's what happened when I was at the dentist a year ago and I bumped into an old schoolmate of mine that I hadn't seen for like twenty years; he was sat there reading, you know, the National Geographic or whatever it was. 'Bloody hell,' he says, 'I remember you,' he says, 'do you remember the day you walked out of school?' I says, 'No, I don't know, why?' He says, 'You were sat next to me in English,' he says, 'and all of a sudden you said to me, "Stuff this, I've had enough, I'm going," ' he said, 'and you just got up and walked out, and nobody ever saw you again.' I said, 'No, I'm not proud of this, man,' you know, it's all been history now. My parents had been split up for a few years, right, and I lived with my mum. That's why I could get away with it I suppose, I didn't have a father figure, but my old fella used to still call round on a fairly regular basis. He actually went to see the head, the headmaster tried to get me back and then he went to see the headmaster and said, 'He's coming to work for me and I'll put him through a further education, you know, get him some sort of constructional qualifications in civil engineering or something, you know'. Basically, I just ended up digging holes for my dad after that. Playing in bands at night and digging holes in the daytime, but then there was some sort of a recession. He found it very hard to keep everybody employed, and [Nicholas's son] was on his way, and we'd just committed ourselves to buying a house and I thought, 'Sod this, I'll have a go on my own, I've got nothing to lose'. That was how it all sort of started really, so my father sort of helped me out through the hardest times and then I decided to go it alone.

Nicholas, 1997

Mark also had an affluent, self-employed father and stayed at his grammar school until he was nineteen, later graduating and becoming a teacher.

I left school at nineteen because I failed my O levels the first time and had to take an extra year. I was sport mad and spent more time on that than in the classroom.

Mark, 1988

[Failing the 11+ was no big deal.] You did a bit of revision. I remember my parents buying a couple of books that you did things in but I'm glad to say you were never made to feel it was the be all and end all. A few passed, and everyone was very glad for them, but I've never been pressured about education. I left at fifteen (that's the only pressure) because my dad wouldn't let me stay on to do the O levels. [Why was that?] Money. Needed money. Because I should have stayed on, but I didn't. I suppose I resented it at the time but it's never stopped me doing anything. [Did you manage to get jobs in 1965 without qualifications?] Oh there was loads then. Three jobs lined up. It wasn't a problem, was it?

Margaret, 1997

Changing perspectives

The 1960s started with a Conservative government but was dominated by the Labour governments of 1964–70 under Prime Minister Harold Wilson. In 1962 (July) Sir Edward Boyle replaced Sir David Eccles as Minister of Education and in 1963 Boyle (a Conservative) expressed his own concerns about the 11+ leading to a waste of talent. Quintin Hogg (Viscount Hailsham) replaced Sir Edward Boyle in April 1964 with the new title of Secretary of State for Education and Science. However, Hogg was not in place for very long before the election of a Labour government and his replacement in October was Michael Steward. In 1965 Steward was replaced by Anthony Crosland who (despite his reservations) was more forceful in trying to introduce comprehensive schools. Crosland was replaced by Patrick Gordon-Walker in 1967, who was replaced by Edward Short in 1968.

During the 1960s the tone of political debate and sociological research seemed to become more radical and egalitarian as educationalists grew more persistent in their claims that changes in the school system were not enough to improve working-class opportunities. Among others, work by Halsey, Floud and Anderson (1961), Jackson and Marsden

---

INTELLIGENCE *IS* INNATE

No amount of money poured into the 'Educational Priority Areas', enthusiastically espoused in the Plowden Report, is likely to bring any appreciable proportion of slum children up to the standards of university entrance.

The suppression of these truths by progressives leads to a whole series of false deductions. One of the most serious is that it is the fault of society that slum dwellers are impoverished and their young do so badly at school. To the young red guards, it follows that society is unjust and must be overthrown. They do not realize that slum dwellers are caused principally by low innate intelligence and poor family upbringing, and that the real social challenge is posed by this.

Lynn, 1970, p 30

INTELLIGENCE *IS NOT* INNATE

To take intelligence as a fixed quantity, from the ordinary thinking of mechanical materialism, is a denial of the realities of growth and intelligence itself, in the final interest of a particular model of the social system. How else can we explain the very odd principle that has been built into modern English education: that those who are slowest to learn should have the shortest time in which to learn, while those who learn quickly will be able to extend the process for as much as seven years beyond them? This is the reality of 'equality of opportunity', which is a very different thing from real social equality. The truth is that while for children of a particular social class we have a conception, however imperfect, of a required minimum of general education whatever their measured intelligence might be, we have no such conception, or a much lower conception, for the majority of those outside this class. This fact in itself, together with other social processes, magnifies natural inequalities, in a persistent way. For of course there is no absolute correlation between intelligence and membership of a particular occupational group. The mean IQ of children of such groups varies, but the differences within groups are greater than those between the groups. And then, if longer education can be bought by a few, and if more favourable learning environments are perpetuated by the social inequality resulting from previous inequalities of real opportunity, natural inequalities are again magnified and take on a direct social relevance. While we shall always be faced with substantial differences in learning ability among all children, we have to face the really hard fact that we are now meeting the problem in a particular way which serves in the end to magnify the differences and then pass them off as a natural order.

Williams, 1992 edition (first published in 1961), pp 146–7

Question

Discuss Lynn's claim that less money should be spent on the education of children with 'low innate intelligence' and Williams's claim that more money should be spent on those who are 'slowest to learn'.

(1963), and Douglas (1964) emphasized the need to make schools more accessible to working-class parents and to involve parents more fully in their children's education. This coincided with political initiatives by the Labour government aimed at generating greater equality: for example, Circular 10/65 instructed LEAs to replace a bipartite system with comprehensive schools and the Plowden Report recommended the introduction of Educational Priority Areas (to provide compensatory education for children living in poor areas). Thus the growing interest in home–school relations and compensatory education that was noticeable during the 1950s had precipitated change in the 1960s.

Functionalist approaches remained important in the sociology of education but sociologists themselves were gradually looking more left-wing as they drew on and adapted Marxist critiques of education as a source of social control by the dominant middle class. Debates about IQ testing and the influence of biology on intelligence continued, although supporters of biological determinism gradually started to look like an extremist minority. Raymond Williams summed up many of the criticisms of biological determinism in *The Long Revolution* (1961). However, by the end of the 1960s, Black Paper critiques were building on Jensen (1969) and Eysenck's (1971) claims that educational attainment was heavily influenced by biology in order to argue against many of the reforms introduced by the Labour government. The Black Papers were published in the *Salisbury Review* between 1969 and 1977 as a series of critiques of current trends towards the introduction of comprehensive schools, progressive education and Labour Party education policies in general (Cox and Dyson, 1969, 1970, 1971; Cox and Boyson, 1975, 1977). They were edited by Brian Cox and contributors included Rhodes Boyson (who became a Conservative government education spokesman during the Thatcher government), Caroline (now Baroness) Cox and Richard Lynn.

Changing school systems

During the early 1960s the Conservative government remained on many of the paths outlined during the 1950s, consolidating the effects of the 1944 Education Act and addressing some of the associated criticisms. In particular they started to tackle the criticism that there were no opportunities for children in secondary modern schools to obtain school-leaving qualifications (The Crowther Report, 1959). In 1960 *The Report of the Committee on Secondary School Examinations* (Beloe) recommended the introduction of a Certificate of Secondary Education and its suggestion was partly endorsed by the Newsom Report (1963, *Half our Future*, CACE), which advised that all sixteen-year-old school leavers should be provided with some form of 'internal leaving certificate' containing a 'general school record'. The first examinations for the CSE eventually took place in 1965.

The Newsom Report (1963) was concerned with children aged thirteen to sixteen of average and below average ability. It still favoured a tripartite system but was concerned that schools for the less able were sometimes poorer in the standard of buildings, quality of teaching and other ways. The Report recommended the maintenance of existing structures, but with redistribution of spending to the benefit of the less able. It also recommended the provision of a more stimulating and demanding curriculum so that pupils had a wider choice of courses, including some 'broadly related to occupational interests', and others concerned with personal and social development, and 'imaginative experience through the arts'. Another recommendation was the establishment of an experimental building programme 'to try out different forms of school organization and teaching methods in buildings designed for the purpose' but this was met with criticisms from those (for example, writers of the Black Papers) who felt that experiments with less formal education in open-plan settings would undermine educational standards.

A further revision of the 1944 Education Act came in the 1964 Education Act, which allowed the break between primary and secondary school to come between the ages of ten and twelve, to cover the development of middle schools. Such schools were to be classified as either primary middle schools (normally 8–12) or secondary middle schools (normally 9–13).

In private education more schools continued to be registered after inspection by Her Majesty's

Inspectors and many also applied to be recognized as efficient. Yet politicians (particularly Labour) were still disturbed by their inability to monitor standards of education in private schools to ensure that they at least met the standards expected of state schools. In 1965 over half of all English private schools were still not recognized as efficient. According to Halsey, Heath and Ridge (1980, p 30), out of 2,762 independent primary and secondary schools in England, 1,188 held this status.

During the early 1960s the Conservative government also introduced various changes in local government and administration. In 1962 Eccles announced the creation of a Curriculum Study Group within the Ministry of Education. This was met with some resistance because it suggested that the balance of power between central government, LEAs and teachers was not being maintained and consultations eventually lead to the replacement of the CSG by the Schools Council, which was jointly run by LEAs, teachers and central government. Although relationships were often tense, the Conservative government was still anxious to demonstrate its adherence to a pluralist system of government in which consultation ranged as widely as possible. It now seems ironic that in 1963 the London Government Act (passed by a Conservative government) created the Inner London Education Authority, which was abolished in 1990 by a Conservative government (via the 1988 Education Reform Act), despite public resistance. The new ILEA was responsible for twelve inner-London boroughs and the City, whilst twenty outer-London boroughs each constituted a separate LEA. Indeed the ILEA was unique in that it dealt only with education, whereas all other local authorities were responsible for education alongside their other local government responsibilities. In support of an ILEA it was argued that co-operation between boroughs would help to tackle the unique demands placed on education in central London.

QUESTIONS

What particular demands could be placed on education in central London?
Are these demands different to those placed on education in other cities?

From 1964 onwards a period of Labour government was characterized by political initiatives aimed at generating more equal educational opportunities. This involved tackling the problems experienced as a result of selection at 11+ and moving towards a system of comprehensive secondary education.

More problems with bipartite or tripartite systems were identified as the 1960s progressed. Soon after the 1944 Act it was realized that some children would be wrongly allocated and measures were introduced to transfer some children from secondary modern to grammar school at thirteen. However, very few transfers were made (only about 2 per cent of secondary school children, according to Douglas, Ross and Simpson, 1968, p 43), many parents were not aware that transfers were possible and it was often the case that, once in secondary modern schools, children would conform to low expectations. Moreover, other types of transfers (such as from grammar school to secondary modern school) were not generally considered. Yet the most severe criticisms were raised with the introduction into secondary modern schools of assessment at school-leaving age. During the 1960s increasing numbers of secondary modern school pupils passed CSE examinations and GCE O level examinations and some 11+ 'failures' left school better qualified than some grammar school pupils.

QUESTION

How can the ability of children in secondary modern schools to gain good results at school-leaving age be used as an argument in favour, as well as against, selective education?

By the 1960s Labour Party policy was committed to the introduction of comprehensive schools and in 1965 the government's Circular 10/65 (*The Organization of Secondary Education*) asked LEAs who had not already done so to introduce a system of comprehensive secondary schools. The circular requested LEAs to prepare and submit to the Secretary of State plans for reorganizing secondary education on comprehensive lines, and offered guidance as to methods of achieving this. By the end of the 1960s, out of 163 LEAs in England and Wales, 129 had schemes for comprehensive systems either implemented or approved. Of these, 108 authorities had schemes implemented or approved covering the whole or greater part of their areas, and a further 21 authorities had schemes implemented or approved for part of their areas (DES, 1970, pp 34–5). However, having read about the development of education since the 1940s, you will now be aware that plans may be very different to action. The 1944 Education Act gave LEAs the power to decide the pace of any changes and many (particularly Conservative) authorities were either opposed to comprehensive schools or internally divided on the subject. Some LEAs resisted by citing particular constraints or using delaying tactics, such as submitting patently unsuitable plans.

With a growing and fluctuating population, other pressures on both central government and LEAs were also increasing and the government acknowledged this in 1966 (Local Government Act) and 1967 (Rate Support Grant, Pooling Arrangements, Regulations) when it made changes to LEA spending by introducing the Rate Support Grant. This made LEAs (rather than central government) responsible for paying for school meals and milk, and allocated funds to LEAs for the payment of staff employed specifically for the education and welfare of immigrants. The changes also provided for the pooling of expenses incurred by LEAs on teacher training, advanced further education, the education of pupils not belonging to the area of any authority and the training of educational psychologists.

Differences between LEAs were identified again in the Plowden Report (CACE, 1967, *Children and their Primary Schools*), one of the most memorable initiatives during the 1960s. This was the result of extensive research by teams of sociologists studying all aspects of primary education and transition to secondary schools. The Report highlighted the inequalities of educational opportunity associated with the geographical location of primary schools and suggested that there should be positive discrimination to help schools in deprived or 'educational priority areas' (EPAs). Other suggestions (some mentioned elsewhere in this chapter) included a broader curriculum, expansion of nursery provision and the reorganization of primary education into first and middle schools.

In keeping with its policies in favour of equal opportunities, the Labour government also established a commission to advise on the future of public schools. The commission's first report (1968, Newson Report, Public Schools Commission) concluded that public schools should be abolished, integrated into the mainstream system, or allowed to remain but without their traditional tax privileges. As a step towards integration, it recommended that a number of public schools should accept some of their pupils (eventually at least half) from maintained schools, using the criteria of comprehensive selection and social needs (rather than selection according to ability). Fees would still be paid but such pupils would receive financial assistance. It was suggested that these arrangements should be voluntary if possible, but statutory if necessary.

> A special system of schools, reserved for children whose parents have larger bank accounts than their neighbours, exists in no other country on the same scale as in England. It is at once an educational monstrosity and a grave national misfortune. It is educationally vicious, since to mix with companions from homes of different types is an important part of the education of the young. It is actually disastrous, for it does more than any other single cause, except capitalism itself, to perpetuate the division of the nation into classes of which one is almost unintelligible to the other.
> Tawney, 1964 (fourth edition), p 145

QUESTIONS

What do you think were the strengths and weaknesses of positive discrimination to help educational priority areas?

What is the difference between a public school and a private school?

Why do you think the Newson Report (1968) did not make similar recommendations for the integration of all private schools?

Further and higher education

It appeared to many that during the 1960s 'youth' and 'youth cultures' were becoming more meaningful concepts than they had been in the past. During the 1950s young people were starting to congregate in coffee bars and to create their own group identities; for example, as Teddy Boys. The Albemarle Report (1960, *The Youth Service in England and Wales*) reviewed the youth service, which was thought to be demoralized and unprepared to deal with the increasing demand from the 'baby boom' children who were reaching adolescence. It supported the continuation of a mixture of statutory and voluntary provision but recommended better training and improved status for youth leaders, a building programme of new premises and facilities, and the setting up of a Youth Service Development Council. Unlike many reports, most of its recommendations were actually implemented and by 1966 a special college had opened in Leicester and the number of trained youth workers had doubled.

Although politicians were concerned about how to deal with youth cultures and wanted to expand opportunities for further education, their initiatives for opening up access to higher education were more memorable than their initiatives within further education. Nevertheless, recommendations of the Haslegrave Report (1969, *Technical Courses and Examinations*) had an impact because they lead to the creation of a Technical Education Council and a Business Education Council to oversee courses and exams. These were later amalgamated to form what became the Business and Technology Education Council (BTEC).

Higher education had continued to expand throughout the 1950s but by 1963 there were still only twenty-four universities, with 15 per cent of all students attending either Oxford or Cambridge (Trowler, 1998, p 27). In 1963/4 there were 118,000 university students and 55,000 teacher trainees (Halsey, Heath and Ridge, 1980, p 31) and critics argued that this was not enough, adding to previous concerns about the loss of talent as young people left school early, without acquiring any qualifications.

> In recent discussions there has been a tendency to assume that there is only a limited number of persons who can benefit from higher education and that there is a clearly defined 'pool of talent' on which to draw for university places. It has been said, however, that what is extracted from the pool depends much less on its content than on the effectiveness of the pump; it is clear from the present study that the pump is leaking badly

at the points of secondary selection and early leaving. The pool of talent found at the end of the secondary school period is likely to be only a portion of that which would be found if it were possible to draw fully on potential rather than realized ability.

> Douglas, 1964, pp 127–8

One effort to improve the effectiveness of the 'pump' was the 1962 Education Act. This required all LEAs in England and Wales to provide grants for all first degree courses in accordance with income scales ('mandatory awards') and allowed them to provide grants for further and postgraduate education ('discretionary awards'). It also authorized the Secretary of State to award grants for postgraduate courses and for older students.

THE 1963 ROBBINS REPORT, *HIGHER EDUCATION*

Perhaps the most well-known effort to improve access came with the Robbins Report (1963, *Higher Education*). Research for this report found that the proportions of children from each social class entering higher education remained much as in the 1920s, although the absolute numbers had increased steadily. Concluding that there was a huge, untapped 'pool of ability' in the population, it recommended a massive expansion of higher education (from the 216,000 places available in 1962/3 to 390,000 in 1972/3 and 560,000 by 1980). It stated what became known as 'the Robbins principle', that 'Courses of higher education should be available for all of those who are qualified by ability and attainment to pursue them and who wish to do so'. In order to ensure expansion it recommended the granting of university status to the ten colleges of advanced technology (this was accepted), the establishment of special institutions for scientific and technological education and research (which was not implemented) and the creation of the Council for National Academic Awards (CNAA) to grant degrees to students in non-university establishments (which happened the following year). This led to the creation of new universities and thirty polytechnics.

Along with creation of new universities and polytechnics for full-time students, the Open University was established in Milton Keynes in 1969. This indicated a move even beyond the Robbins principle, as students were not required to have the usual formal qualifications on admission, just a determination to work hard and pay their fees for part-time studies.

The Robbins initiatives were least successful in the case of science and technology and research for the Dainton Report (1968, *The Flow of Candidates in Science and Technology into Higher Education*) studied the shift away from science in sixth forms of secondary schools, which ran counter to the proposed expansion of science and technology in the universities. The Report called for changes in the sixth form, with less specialization and some mathematics for all pupils. However, these recommendations were not well received. There was a shortage of appropriately qualified teachers and many grammar and public schools were determined to defend the notion of sixth-form study in depth. Indeed, debates about the value of depth or breadth continue today.

The 1960s are therefore remembered as a time of massive expansion in higher education. Yet they are also associated with the radical student activism that will be considered when we look at behaviour.

QUESTION

Do you think there was some sort of connection between the expansion of higher education and student unrest?

Teachers

The expansion of teacher training continued into the 1960s and in 1963/4 there were about 55,000 teacher trainees (Halsey, Heath and Ridge, 1980, p 31). In 1962 the length of teacher training courses increased from two to three years and in 1963 the Robbins Report recommended raising the status of teacher training colleges to colleges of education offering B.Ed degrees. It also recommended the integration of colleges of education into universities, although this only happened in part. Expansion

of teacher training courses, both with regard to length and availability, brought with it increased opportunities to study sociology of education. We can therefore see a dramatic expansion in educational research and sociological publications both as a stimulus and response to growing interests.

Not only were the numbers of fully qualified teachers growing but efforts were being made to increase the number of classroom helpers. The Plowden Report (1967, *Children and Their Primary Schools*) called for a new group of staff called 'teachers' aids' to be recruited with a similar status to nursery assistants. These assistants would be particularly useful in schools where many children had multiple problems associated with deprived backgrounds. The Report also cited a problem that was to remain in education for many years: the relatively low status of primary school teachers meant that there was a shortage of males, graduates and specialists in mathematics and science and the Report argued that more of these types of people should be encouraged to become primary school teachers.

QUESTION

How could the feminization of primary school teaching staff be tackled?

Until the 1960s relationships between teachers' unions and the government had remained amicable, despite occasional strains. This was largely because the (widely respected) Burnham Committee negotiated teachers' pay rises and any recommendations it made were generally accepted by the government. However, in 1961 the Conservative government had a 'pay pause' policy and Eccles refused to implement Burnham's recommended pay rise. This was repeated in 1963 when the new Minister of Education, Boyle, did not accept Burnham's recommendations. This more serious impasse only ended when the government legislated that it could decide teachers' pay and the 1965 Remuneration of Teachers Act set up committees for negotiations on teachers' pay. At this point the 1965 Teaching Council (Scotland) Act helped Scottish teachers to establish their independence of the rest of the UK by setting up a General Teaching Council for Scotland to deal with the training, registration and professional conduct of Scottish teachers.

Class and status

During the 1960s there seemed to be a deluge of findings about the effects of social class on educational experiences. Some of these were based on research that had been going on for a long time (e.g. Douglas, 1964), some came from recent research (e.g. Hargreaves, 1967) and a lot of research was carried out for government-sponsored reports (e.g. Plowden, CACE 1967). Research focused on many different angles, including the effects of schooling, value orientations, social mobility and social interaction. Indeed, 1963 alone saw publications from three sources that were to have a major impact in future years: *Education and the Working Class* (Jackson and Marsden, 1963), the Newsom Report (CACE 1963) and the Robbins Report

(1963). All three found that social factors deprived poor children of educational opportunities.

The Newsom Report (*Half our Future*) did not accept that secondary modern schools should be poorer than others in the quality of the teaching, buildings or any other respect and recommended not only the maintenance of existing structures, but also the redistribution of spending to the benefit of the less able (including the rebuilding of inadequate secondary modern schools in slum areas).

The Robbins Report (1963, *Higher Education*) found a high correlation between social class and educational achievement and, even with controls for measured intelligence, the correlation remained high. At extremes, a child of professional parents was about twenty times more likely than a child of semi-skilled as unskilled workers to enter full-time higher education. However, social class

---

THE HOME AND THE SCHOOL

In 1964 Douglas *et al.* produced their findings from a cohort study of all children born in the first week of March 1946 in England and Wales. The cohort consisted of over 5,000.
The study found that:

1. The educational disadvantages of working-class children compared with middle-class pupils persisted even when their measured intelligence was identical.
2. Streaming was a self-fulfilling prophesy. Between the ages of eight and eleven children in upper streams improved their test scores (the less able improving the most) but the scores of children in lower streams deteriorated (the most able deteriorating the most).
3. While middle-class and working-class pupils in the upper stream both improved, the middle class improved the most. In the lower stream middle-class pupils were more likely to improve than working-class pupils.
4. Between seven and eleven, middle-class children's test scores increased whereas working-class children's declined.
5. 79 per cent of high-ability boys from the upper middle class were expected by their parents to enter the professions compared to 39 per cent of lower-class boys of the same ability.
6. Of children in the above-average ability band, 51 per cent from the upper middle class, 34 per cent from the lower middle class, and only 22 per cent from the lower working class were allowed entry into grammar school.
7. In an earlier study Douglas *et al.* used a measure of parental interest, including teachers' comments on parents' attitudes and records of the number of times the parents visited the school. They found that higher levels of interest from middle-class parents (and especially fathers) were a key factor governing their children's chances of entry to grammar school.

Questions

How could the affects of streaming on test scores be explained?
What factors could explain the different number of school visits by working-class and middle-class parents?

---

influence on attainment seemed to cease with university entry and, once admitted, working-class students performed as well as middle-class students. The Report concluded there was a huge, untapped and unsuspected 'pool of ability' in the population, especially in lower socio-economic groups.

Like Douglas, the Plowden Report (1967, *Children and Their Primary Schools*) concluded that parents' attitudes to education were of supreme importance in influencing their children's educational success. However, Plowden researchers found that parents' attitudes were more influential than their own education, occupational status, material circumstances at home, and schools themselves. The report therefore recommended that schools should do more to encourage parental involvement and that schools should become more involved in their communities. It also suggested that there should be positive discrimination to help schools in deprived or 'educational priority areas' (EPAs) and that nursery provision should be expanded.

Not only Douglas and Plowden were finding that parents' attitudes had a major influence on educational achievement. Other researchers were also finding that parents of children who were successful in school provided more encouragement, had more contact with the school, valued education more highly and had higher occupational aspirations. Sociologists labelled such values relating most directly to education as *manifest values*, but they were also interested in the *latent values* with only a tenuous or indirect relationship to education.

Sugarman (1966) reinforced some of Kluckhohn and Strodbeck's findings about the influence of latent values in a survey of London secondary school boys. It was found that high scores on the three value orientations associated with the middle class did relate to school achievement, but that these values were middle class only in the sense that they separated the high achievers (destined for middle-class jobs) from the low achievers (destined for working-class jobs). Within each social class, high-achieving boys were those with the sort of value orientations associated with the middle class but, interestingly, there was no significant relationship between the boys' values and their fathers' social class.

VALUE ORIENTATIONS AND ATTITUDES TOWARDS EDUCATION

Kluckhohn and Strodbeck (1961) suggested five important value orientations and used three of these to investigate parents' and children's latent values and relate them to educational performance. Value orientations were measured by questionnaires in which respondents were given statements and a five- or six-point scale for responses, ranging from 'strongly agree' to 'strongly disagree'. Questions included the following:

Activity: 'You must accept life as it is for there is nothing much you can do to alter things.' (Disagreement labelled as active orientation.)

Time: 'You have to give up having a good time now to do well later on.' (Agreement labelled as future orientation.)

Relations with others: 'Keeping in contact with friends and relations is more important than moving up in the world.' (Disagreement labelled as individualistic orientation.)

Analysis of the responses found that some value orientations were particularly common among working-class respondents and others particularly common among middle-class respondents.

	Working class	Middle class
Activity	Passive	Active
Time	Present	Future
Relations with others	Familialistic	Individualistic

Question

Would these, or other, value orientations be useful in the study of parental influence today?

Swift (1967) went on to observe that a variable related to success could be shown to operate in each social class and operationalized 'mobility ideology' in three ways:

1. Parental social horizons. Parents of successful children had high aspirations for them.
2. Parental social class identification. Those with successful children were more likely to see themselves as middle class or upper working class.
3. Fathers' mobility pessimism. In the working class the most pessimistic fathers tended to have successful children whilst in the middle class this was reversed and a lack of pessimism was linked to their children's failure. Swift argued that these differences resulted from intervening variables which confused the picture.

QUESTION

Can you think of any possible explanations for Swift's third finding?

Sociologists found, however, that the values of parents were not the only values affecting their children's long-term prospects. Turner (1961) examined the education systems in England and the USA and argued that, although both provided mass education, there was a contrast between the system of sponsored mobility in England and the system of contest mobility in the USA. In the USA, 'Elite status is the prize in an open contest and is taken by the aspirants' own efforts' (p 122), whereas in England 'elite recruits are chosen by the established elite or their agents, and elite status is given on the basis of some criteria of supposed merit and cannot be taken by any amount of effort or strategy' (p 122). Although Turner claimed that both modes could occur in all societies, in England early segregation for different schools meant the early socialization for elite roles and early allocation of elite credentials. Turner also noted that the most obvious control problem in such a system was ensuring the loyalty of the disadvantaged to a system which gave them very little. Whereas in a contest system everyone felt that they could compete for a position, a sponsored system involved the training of the masses to

regard themselves as incompetent. Some sociologists argued that Turner's two ideal types were too basic and in the 1970s Hopper (1971) substituted his own categories.

Findings about the impact of value orientations still left sociologists with questions about how they actually manifested themselves in educational settings and the 1960s saw the completion of some classic observational studies. During the 1960s Colin Lacey carried out his ethnographic research at 'Hightown Grammar School' in Greater Manchester and published some of his findings (1966, 1970). His research identified the social processes associated with streaming. For example, in the mixed ability first year all boys displayed a high commitment to the norms of the school but in the second year they were streamed and became more polarized into pro- and anti-school cultures. Hargreaves too (1967) found that streaming lead to different cultures when he studied 'Lumley Secondary Modern School'. Both Lacey and Hargreaves developed models to describe the differentiation and polarization of pupils in streams and Hargreaves reported the subcultural divide between fourth year streams, ranging from the highest stream (4A) to the next to lowest stream (4D, excluding 4E because they had specialist teachers and special friendship groups), as shown in Figure 8.1. The dominant values of the highest stream were academic and the dominant values of the lowest stream were delinquescent (although Hargreaves noted that this was not synonymous with delinquency).

Figure 8.1 Subcultural differentiation in Lumley Secondary Modern School

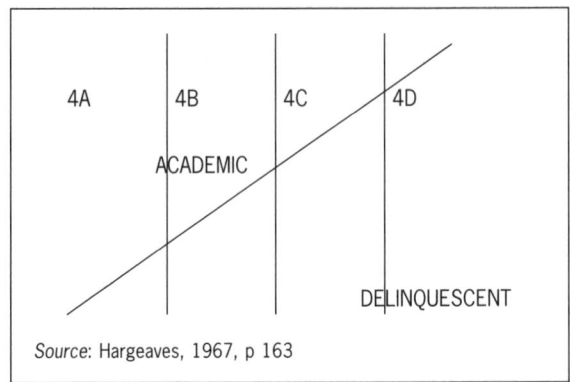

Source: Hargeaves, 1967, p 163

How do findings that anti-school subcultures existed in both grammar schools and secondary modern schools relate to Turner's claims that grammar school children experienced privileged access to sponsored mobility?

Gender

In 1961 Kathleen Ollerenshaw claimed that women 'have largely won the battle for equal educational opportunity with men', yet, with hindsight, it seems that the battle had barely started. In theory, females and males had equal educational opportunities but in practice girls were still discriminated against (for example, in assessment at 11+) and sexist assumptions were made about the curriculum and job prospects. The publication of Betty Friedan's book *The Feminine Mistique* (1963) is commonly seen as signalling the beginning of the women's movement in the USA, but it took some time to establish itself there and cross the Atlantic. In the USA this second wave of feminism (the first wave being associated with liberal feminism and the right to vote) was stimulated by the influences of other social movements, such as the civil rights movement and the anti-Vietnam peace movement, but political protest in the UK was more often related to inequalities of social class or religion (for example, sectarianism in Northern Ireland). Until the 1970s it seemed that social class inequalities were more visible than inequalities of gender or ethnicity. Most sociologists, educational researchers and politicians were male and many were able to adopt the blinkered privileges of power.

In 1974 Wolpe criticized reports published by the Norwood Committee in 1943, the Crowther Committee in 1959 and the Newsom Committee in 1963. She illustrated how they reproduced assumptions about women and marriage and helped to perpetuate an education system that did not open up new opportunities for most girls. In the following extract from the Newsom Report we can see that, although boys were rarely expected to take lessons in housecraft, even girls who resented the domestic work they had to do at home were expected to take an interest.

The domestic crafts start with an inbuilt advantage. They are recognizably part of adult living. Girls know that, whether they marry early or not, they are likely to find themselves making and running a home; moreover some quite young schoolgirls, with mothers out at work are already shouldering considerable responsibility, a fact which needs to be taken into account in school house-craft programmes. There may also be some girls who are far from enthusiastic, because they have had their fill of scrubbing and washing-up and getting meals for the family at home; and yet they may need all the more the education a good school can give in the wider aspects of homemaking and in the skills which will reduce the element of domestic drudgery.

Newsom Report, 1963,
cited by Sharpe, 1976, p 121

It seems that although, by the 1960s, educational opportunities had improved in general, the different opportunities of boys and girls had barely been acknowledged. During the 1960s women were far more likely to go to college or university than in the past. The expansion of higher education meant that more women, as well as men, took degrees, but access was still a problem. In 1962, 26,192 women were at university but Oxford and Cambridge still clung to their all-male colleges, and there were only 680 women at Cambridge among 7,318 men, which was similar to the position in 1922 (Holdsworth, 1988). The 1960s also saw the creation of more coeducational schools, although this may have resulted from the shift towards comprehensive schools rather than a planned policy of mixing the sexes.

Although relatively little research into gender and education was completed during the 1960s, there was some evidence that girls were achieving more than boys at an early age, and this raised questions about discrimination against girls in 11+ assessments. Douglas (1964) provided evidence that girls obtained superior academic results in all areas of the primary school curriculum, apart from mathematics, and also ranked girls more highly than boys for behaviour. However, the only tests that Douglas considered valid for comparing changes in the achievement of boys and girls in the primary school were those for reading and vocabulary, with girls obtaining higher scores than boys at the ages of eight and eleven. The picture for mathematical ability was more confusing and Douglas showed that, whilst girls surpassed the performance of boys at the age of eleven, middle-class boys produced better results than middle-class girls, but manual working class boys did not perform as well as manual-working-class girls.

Ethnicity

In Chapter 2 we considered the difficulties involved in researching race and ethnicity, which mainly revolved around the operationalization of concepts. Bearing these limitations in mind, various estimates (Skellington with Morris, 1992, using OPCS and Labour Force Surveys) have suggested that, in 1961, 1 per cent of the population were drawn from ethnic minorities and, by 1971, the figure had increased to 2.3 per cent. Such figures help to get the extent of these changes into perspective. Indeed, if we consider the many British people who were emigrating during the 1960s (when Assisted Passages to Australia were available at a cost of only £10) the effects of migration on population figures as a whole seem minimal. Yet immigrants were obviously more visible than emigrants and some people were concerned about the mixing of races and cultures and the potential for racial violence. The music of Tamla Motown (from the USA), reggae (from the West Indies) and the Indian sitar (popularized by the Beatles) impacted upon black and white youth cultures and helped to generate new hybrid cultural forms. Mixed marriages generated images of 'coffee-coloured people' (in the words of one pop record) living in harmony but, to some, raised fears of a change in general or the dilution of the 'superior' white 'race' in particular. Changes were welcomed by those who felt a sense of optimism about the decline of racism and resented by others who saw them as a prelude to social conflict.

> As I look ahead, I am filled with foreboding. Like the Roman, I seem to see the River Tiber foaming with much blood.
>
> Enoch Powell, speech about immigration, Birmingham, 20 April 1968

Enoch Powell's views not only reflected those of many others but actually contributed to a climate of prejudice and fear that was bound to affect education.

Prejudices were soon compounded by the writings of Jensen (1969), who sparked a controversy when he claimed that the higher average IQ score of white Americans over black Americans was due largely to genetic difference and that it justified different approaches for educating black pupils and white pupils. Jensen was writing in the USA but the controversy emerged (or re-emerged) in the UK during the late 1960s and escalated with the work of Eysenck in the 1970s.

Governments responded to immigration during the 1950s and 1960s with some limited efforts to cater for the educational welfare of immigrant children. In 1966 the Local Government Act allocated funds to local authorities for the payment of staff employed specifically for the education and welfare of immigrants. The Plowden Report (1967) also recommended greater attention to the needs of the children of immigrants. Yet concerted action was largely left until the 1970s, when detailed research findings about the experiences of ethnic minorities started to emerge. Meanwhile, the creation of the Inner London Education Authority provided a supportive grounding for current and future research.

The relatively large numbers of children from ethnic minorities attending many London schools, and the links the ILEA provided between areas, helped to alleviate some of the practical problems associated with research into ethnicity. As a result, Little and his associates carried out research in the ILEA during the 1960s that was reported in the 1970s (Little, 1975, 1978; Little and Mabey, 1972). This research included comparisons between children from three wide ethnic groups, who had been fully educated in the United Kingdom, to see what proportion from each group were placed in the upper bands for English, Mathematics and verbal reasoning on transfer to ILEA secondary schools. Of the three groups, children of Asian origin did nearly as well as children of UK origin, but children of West Indian origin were far behind and also had a reading age one year below the national norm for their age group.

Research into the particular experiences of Welsh children continued during the 1960s for the Gittins Report (1967, *Primary Education in Wales*, CACE, Wales). This committee was set up at the same time as the Plowden Committee, with the same aims and some overlap in membership. The group shared Plowden's educational philosophy and reached similar conclusions. However (like the 1949 Evans/Aaron Report), it also considered the prevalence of two languages, the existence of large rural areas with a sparse population, and the high respect widely felt for education and teachers. It recommended the fostering of both Welsh and English (especially Welsh as a second language) in predominantly English-speaking areas.

Religion

Religious education changed very little during the 1950s and 1960s and, in 1963, the Newsom Report (*Half our Future*) reiterated earlier recommendations that schools should provide adequate religious instruction and positive guidance on sexual behaviour. Yet the world outside the established curriculum was changing in many ways. Immigration by peoples of different religions was putting pressure of schools to accommodate wider knowledge of many cultures and, although changes were not universal, some individual schools were responding. However, whilst throughout the rest of the country there was pressure to expand religious instruction beyond Christianity, in Northern Ireland radical Catholics and Protestants, emerging from the generally moderate civil rights movement, were increasing sectarian divides between people who regarded themselves as Christians. The beginning of the 'Troubles' in Northern Ireland meant that the sort of changes introduced elsewhere in the UK did not gain momentum and education in Northern Ireland remained divided by religion (mostly Protestant and Roman Catholic schools), gender (many church schools were single-sex) and class lines (a bipartite system).

Special needs

The 1960s were generally a period of consolidation with regard to special educational needs, accommodating more psychological as well as physical needs. Within its wide remit, the Plowden Report

(1967) recommended that greater attention should be paid to the needs of slow learners, and handicapped children. In 1968 the Summerfield Report (*Psychologists in The Education Service*) recommended that the educational psychologist's brief should be extended beyond the traditional testing and assessing of children, and some remedial teaching, to include 'an extended range of treatment', which had previously been the responsibility of the psychiatrist within the Child Guidance Service. The report also recommended an increase in the numbers of educational psychologists, aiming at a proportion of 1 per 10,000 children. Finally, the 1969 Children and Young Persons Act gave local authorities powers and responsibilities for children not receiving proper education or in need of care and control.

Behaviour

The experiences described by John in his 'school from hell' (see Chapter 7) at last started to be tackled during the 1960s when informal advice was given to at least limit forms of corporal punishment in schools. The Plowden Report (1967) recommended the ending of corporal punishment in primary schools but, rather than being a formal directive, this was simply an appeal to schools and their teachers to change their habits. Even when individuals accepted that corporal punishment should not be meted out to young children, they may still argue that it was necessary for older children. Yet some researchers were now starting to question the value of physical punishment as a form of social control.

Other assumptions were also being questioned, including the idealized image of the family and of parents as people who had their children's best interests at heart. A growing realization that parents' value orientations could have a negative impact on their children's educational achievements (see the earlier section on 'Social class and status') also tended to fit findings by other researchers who were studying the family. Indeed, one of the most memorable quotes to emerge from the 1960s was Leach's claim that 'Far from being the basis of the good society, the family, with its narrow privacy and tawdry secrets, is the source of all our discontents' (Sir Edmund Leach, in the BBC's *Reith Lectures* for 1967; lecture reprinted in the *Listener*).

During the 1960s academics (and sociologists in particular) not only described society but also influenced it. Many of their critiques of capitalism, materialism, racism and imperialism added substance to the activities of civil rights movements and the peace movement and were seized on enthusiastically by the newly expanding number of students in higher education. Students could cite the work of critical theorists (especially Marcuse's attack on capitalist materialism in *One Dimensional Man*, 1964) in support of their protests against the failures of capitalism and associated injustices. They not only demonstrated against social inequalities in the wider society but also against what they perceived as suppression within their own institutions, arguing that they should have more democratic and less elitist constitutions.

The wave of unrest among students in many countries seems to have started in 1964 in the University of Berkley, California, as part of the American civil rights movement and spread throughout the USA and Europe. Various sources (e.g. Bell and Kristol, 1969) have claimed that, until then, students tended to be politically apathetic. Researchers also found that the number of radical activists in individual universities may have been very small, but influential through their mobilization of other students (Peterson, 1968). Unrest seemed to be more likely in large institutions, partly as a reaction against the anonymity of a large bureaucracy as well as the increased mathematical probability that some student(s) would want to take some sort of action.

Studies of activists in the United States indicated that they were mainly the left-wing children of left-wing parents, from permissive (rather than authoritarian) families and often particularly able students taking courses in the humanities or social sciences (Lipset, 1969). Meanwhile, a study by Blackstone *et al.* (1969) of students at the London School of Economics (which was a focus for much student activism in the UK) found that there was little difference between activists and other students in terms of academic ability or social class background. What students from diverse backgrounds had in common was an interest in a wide range of issues relating to human rights, including racial discrimination in general, apartheid in South Africa, opposition to the Vietnam War and a loss of faith in the authority of the older generation. Indeed, the year of 1968 saw wide-scale protests by students in many Western countries (including the UK, France and the USA; see Habermas, 1987b; Degroot, 1998), which led to growing concerns by many (e.g. the writers of the Black Papers) that not only were young people out of control, but also that the education system and sociologists in particular were to blame.

QUESTION

What do you think have been the long-term effects of the student demonstrations of 1968?

Torytown and Labourville

Although not necessarily typical in their responses to government directives, we can see in Torytown and Labourville how the political identity of local government could have an impact on educational change during the 1960s. Labourville's traditionally Labour council responded quite eagerly to Circular 10/65, established comprehensive schools and did little to challenge their character in future years. Meanwhile, Torytown's Conservative council began a process of avoiding such central government directives, which lasted until the election of a Conservative government in 1979.

Although the Torytown council eventually made plans for over half the schools in wider Torytown to change to a comprehensive system, its reluctance helped to delay essential progress. Working parties deliberated very slowly and identified many problems, and the result was that plans for the whole area were not completed. Nevertheless, most LEAs in what is now Greater Manchester changed to a comprehensive system and Roman Catholic direct grant schools in the two nearest diocese were asked to decide whether to become independent or move to the state system as comprehensive schools. The interests of the Roman Catholic direct grant schools were also the interests of the Torytown council because Torytown sent Roman Catholic pupils who had passed the 11+ to such schools. When the schools to which Torytown sent its Roman Catholic pupils decided to become independent there began a long-standing agreement that Torytown would pay the fees for Roman Catholic children who were being privately educated. Not only did Torytown retain its grammar schools but it also retained its single-sex schools, splitting a coeducational grammar school into two single-sex grammar schools despite the national trend to move towards coeducational schools. Torytown still retained some of these single-sex schools in the 1990s.

In a period of educational expansion and optimism, new schools were built by many LEAs during the 1960s, including Labourville and Torytown. However, one Torytown interviewee noted that the splitting of the coeducational grammar school into two single-sex schools was done in what he regarded as typically 1960s fashion.

> [School he and his daughter attended.] It was only built in the sixties and was declared unsafe not so many years ago and it had to be demolished, so they had to quickly shove all the boys in with the girls and they stayed there. That's where they came from in the first place, they were all together until 1961, then they built a brand new boys' school using super-cheap building techniques of reinforced concrete and the cheapest and fastest way of building things, the way that they did in the sixties. I can remember when I went there they had great big props propping the roof up, from day one when it first opened, and apparently it had to be demolished about five years ago and it was only about twenty-five years old, the building. It had to be razed to the ground, because it was unsafe. I don't think they did it purely on moral grounds, I think they were kind of forced into it.
>
> Lawrence, 1997

Unfinished business

Once again the many recommendations to raise the school-leaving age to sixteen had no effect. The Newsom Report (1963, *Half our Future*) recommended raising the school leaving age to sixteen and the establishment of an experimental building programme 'to try out different forms of school organization and teaching methods in buildings designed for the purpose'. Yet new, open-plan buildings tended to materialize for primary schools, rather than secondary schools. Similarly Newsom's recommendations regarding the assessment of 'less able or average' pupils were not entirely followed. In practice the curriculum for many pupils became geared towards the new external CSE exam, contrary to Newsom's explicit recommendation. Only in the late 1970s did many schools begin to use pupil profiles and records of achievement similar to those recommended by Newsom.

One of the most noticeable development in education during the 1960s was the expansion of comprehensive education. However, resistance by many Conservative councils (such as Torytown) meant that the Labour government did not fully achieve its aim and Circular 10/65 was only partially successful before it was withdrawn by a Conservative government in 1970.

Although the Plowden Report had a profound effect on the way both professionals and parents viewed primary education, few of its practical recommendations were immediately acted upon. Teachers in 'difficult' schools received an extra £75 annually (although £120 was recommended by the Report) but the expansion of nursery provision did not begin until 1973 (and was cut back not long afterwards). Money was found for school building projects, especially in educational priority areas (EPAs), but ten years later 20 per cent of all primary pupils were still being educated in pre-1903 buildings, many with outside toilets. The recommendation that a new group of staff called 'teachers' aids' should be recruited with a similar status to nursery assistants was never widely implemented. Corporal punishment was eventually forbidden in all state schools from 1987.

The Dainton Report's (1968) recommendations to increase the flow of science and technology students into higher education were not well received and came up against a shortage of appropriately qualified teachers and the determination on the part of the grammar and public schools to defend the notion of sixth-form study in depth.

Finally, the Central Advisory Council for Education (CACE) was gradually wound down as no council was constituted between 1967 and 1986 (when the provision was repealed), and later government reports have been issued by committees set up to consider particular issues.

9

The 1970s

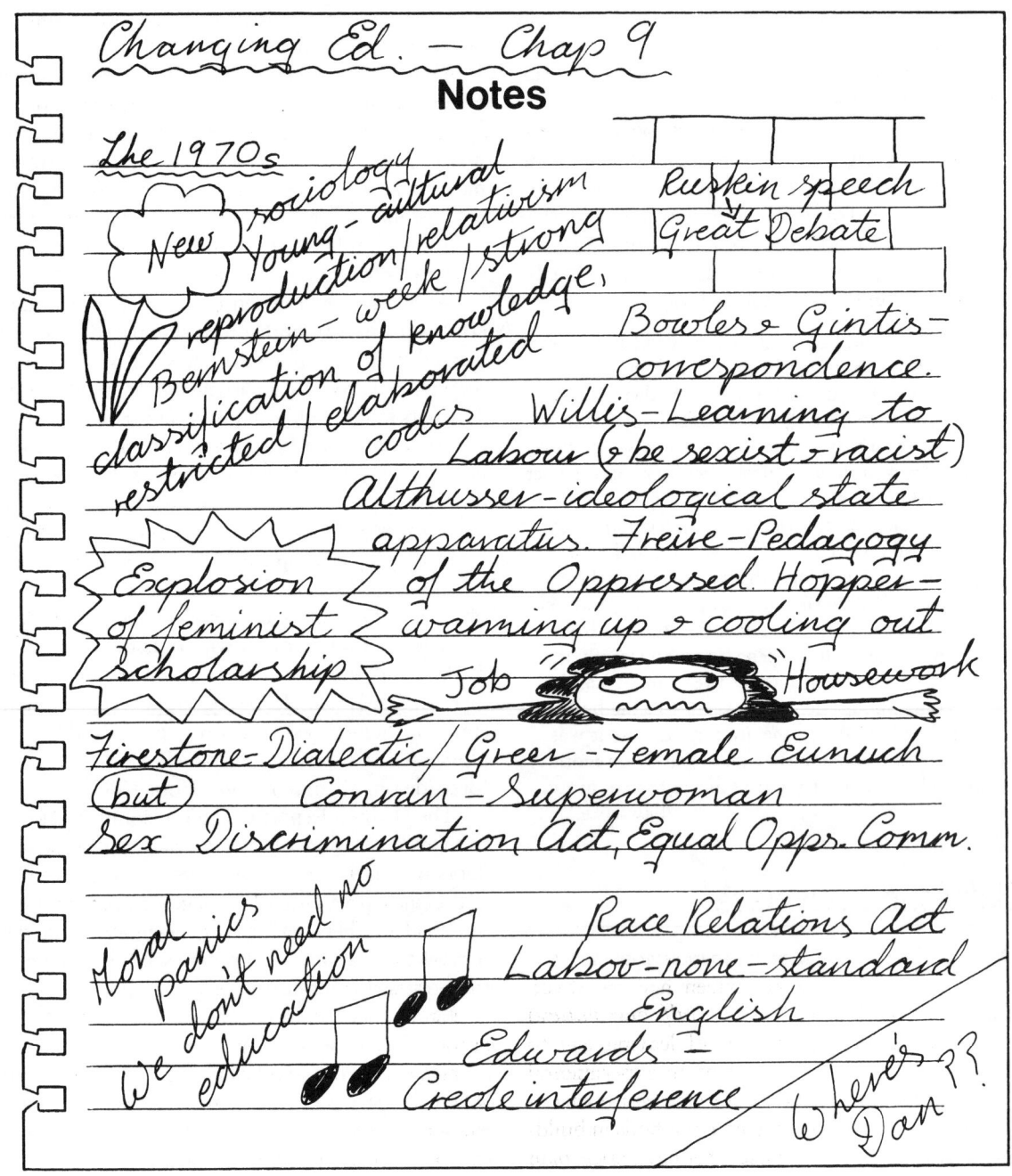

Changing Ed. — Chap 9

Notes

The 1970s

New sociology

Young — cultural reproduction/relativism

Bernstein — week/strong classification of knowledge.

restricted/elaborated codes

Ruskin speech

Great Debate

Bowles & Gintis — correspondence.

Willis — Learning to Labour (& be sexist + racist)

Althusser — ideological state apparatus. Freire — Pedagogy of the Oppressed. Hopper — warming up & cooling out

Explosion of feminist Scholarship

Job "   " Housework

Firestone — Dialectic / Greer — Female Eunuch

(but) Conran — Superwoman

Sex Discrimination Act, Equal Opps. Comm.

Moral panics
We don't need no education

Race Relations Act

Labov — none-standard English

Edwards — Creole interference

Where's Dan ??

I am concerned on my journeys to find complaints from industry that new recruits from schools sometimes do not have the basic tools to do the job that is required.

Prime Minister James Callaghan, Speech at Ruskin College, Oxford, 1976

Socio-economic change

The 1970s was a turning point for the immiseration of education as the optimism of the 1960s slowly turned into an awareness of painful realities. Research and social critiques were making inequalities more visible and this seemed to generate a sense of despair rather than progress. Progress was being made via equal opportunities legislation, race relations legislation and a greater understanding of children with special educational needs but, as some problems were tackled, more seemed to materialize. Even a falling birth rate seemed to bring little relief because, as primary school rolls began to fall from the mid 1970s onwards, headteachers were finding that they still could not create smaller classes. From the mid 1970s onwards some sociologists were identifying the development of *moral panics*; that is, escalating public fears about the behaviour of certain groups of people, including teachers, young people and black youth in particular (e.g. Hall *et al.*, 1978; Cohen, 1973). Indeed the 'punk' scene of the mid 1970s could be seen as just another of the increasingly reprobate youth subcultures.

The gradually worsening national and global economic crisis had a profound affect on attitudes during the 1970s. In 1973 and 1974 there were dramatic international rises in oil prices, which have often been associated with the start of a 'recession' in the UK. By the mid 1970s economic issues had become uppermost in political debates, as economic crisis followed economic crisis, and by the end of the 1970s, the crisis was dominating all aspects of government. Unemployment increased to over one million and governments seemed to be facing a legitimation crisis (Habermas, 1975).

The economic crisis was reflected in a new emphasis on the role of education in serving the needs of the economy, an emphasis that was associated with the start of the 'Great Debate', which lasted for at least twenty years. Its trigger is generally cited as a speech by the Labour Prime Minister James Callaghan at Ruskin College, Oxford, in October 1976. To say that one speech was solely responsible for the Great Debate would be a gross simplification, but it was followed by a period of intense political activity around a theme of 'vocationalism' that accelerated throughout the 1980s and until the end of the century. Some educationalists noted in particular the way that politicians criticized education for in some way 'failing' the nation (Ball, 1990, called it a 'discourse of derision') and we can see signs of this discourse emerging in James Callaghan's speech.

> I am concerned on my journeys to find complaints from industry that new recruits from schools sometimes do not have the basic tools to do the job that is required.
>
> I have been concerned to find that many of our best-trained students who have completed the higher levels of education at university or polytechnic have no desire to enter industry.
>
> There is no virtue in producing socially well-adjusted members of society who are unemployed because they do not have the skills. Nor at the other extreme must they be technically efficient robots. Both of the basic purposes of education require the same essential tools. These are basic literacy, basic numeracy, the understanding of how to live and work together, respect for others, respect for the individual. This means acquiring certain basic knowledge, and skills and reasoning ability. It means developing lively inquiring minds and an appetite for further knowledge that will last a lifetime. It means mitigating as far as possible the disadvantages that may be suffered through poor home conditions or physical or mental handicap.

Callaghan himself was concerned that the tone of his speech was exaggerated and noted that 'A lie can be halfway round the world before the truth has got its boots on' (speech, 1 November 1976) but, whatever his intentions, the Ruskin speech established a discourse that led education and educationalists away from their earlier optimism.

Changing perspectives

During the 1970s ideas about equal opportunities tended to polarize into the extremes of egalitarianism and parentocracy (see Chapter 5) as the Labour Party promoted stronger definitions and the Conservative Party promoted weaker definitions. Indeed, the decade started and ended with the Conservative Party's growing emphasis on individualism, whilst the middle years saw the Labour Party's socialist agenda being riven with internal disputes.

In 1970 a Conservative government was elected under Prime Minister Edward Heath and in June 1970 Margaret Thatcher became Secretary of State for Education. Unlike many of her predecessors she was not afraid of being unpopular with local authorities, teachers and parents and her strident image soon started to manifest itself via the slogan 'Margaret Thatcher, the milk snatcher' (because of her withdrawal of milk from secondary schools in 1971) and the story that, after receiving a school prize at the age of nine, she observed that 'I wasn't lucky. I deserved it'. In a speech during a tour of the USA (in 1975) she noted her acceptance of natural inequalities by saying, 'Let our children grow tall, and some taller than others if they have it in them to do so'. Indeed, her beliefs in the ideas of early liberal thinkers were supported by the work of Hayek, who published three volumes of his work on Law, Legislation and Liberty between 1973 and 1979. His work was to be a major influence in the development of neo-liberalism/the New Right.

Whilst the Conservative Party seemed to be moving further to the right during the 1970s, the Labour Party seemed to be moving further to the left. It was having problems accommodating the many varieties of socialism within its ranks and some, particularly radical, local authorities (influenced by a group called the Militant Tendency) were pushing the party to move further left. Labour leaders responded by moving further left, although not as far as their internal critics wished them to. Egalitarian definitions of equal educational opportunities were therefore being promoted by many Labour activists in both central and local government. In the early 1970s the sociologist A.H. Halsey explained his own definition of egalitarianism in education, which matched Labour policies. However, his words provide an interesting reflection of how anti-racism affected social discourse during the 1970s. The word 'negro' was commonly regarded as inoffensive in the early 1970s but started to look offensive by the end of the decade.

> . . . the goal should not be the liberal one of equality of access but of equality of outcome for the median member of each identifiable non-educationally defined group, i.e. the average woman or negro or proletarian or rural dweller should have the same level of educational attainment as the average male, white, white-collar, suburbanite. If not there has been injustice.
>
> Halsey, 1972, p 8

Within sociology at least, the decade seemed to start at a high point with the 1970 British Sociological Association conference on education, which came to be associated with the start of a 'new sociology of education'. Michael Young presented a paper on which his book *Knowledge and Control* was based and that book of readings (1971) became very influential within the field. As the title suggests, this new style of sociology paid more attention to the part played by schools in the creation and validation of knowledge (including consciousness, understanding, world views, etc.), asking questions about who defined knowledge and determined the hierarchy of knowledge and relationships between power and access to knowledge. Cultural reproduction and cultural relativism were therefore regarded as particularly important. The 'new' approach also utilized interpretive accounts, raising questions about what was taken for granted in everyday interactions in schools.

QUESTION

Was the new sociology of education really new? Compare the new sociology of education with descriptions of the sociology of education during the 1940s–60s.

One of the contributors to *Knowledge and Control* was Basil Bernstein, who observed that decisions about the selection and transmission of knowledge reflected power relationships (Bernstein, 1971). Bernstein's theories sometimes seem rather complex but, in order to explain how knowledge may be strongly or weakly classified and framed (usually into subject areas), he compared the organization of knowledge with the spatial arrangements in different types of lavatories!

Thus, the 1970s started with a sociology of education that was critical of authoritarian norms, whilst the government of the time was starting to move further towards authoritarianism. These conflicting stances changed in 1974 when a Labour government was elected under the leadership of

BERNSTEIN ON CLASSIFICATION AND FRAMING

Imagine four lavatories. The first is stark, bare, pristine, the walls are painted a sharp white; the washbowl is like the apparatus, a gleaming white. A square block of soap sits cleanly in an indentation in the sink. A white towel (or perhaps pink) is folded neatly on a chrome rail or hangs from a chrome ring. The lavatory paper is hidden in a cover and peeps through its slit. In the second lavatory there are books on a shelf and some relaxing of the rigours of the first. In the third there are books on the shelf, pictures on the wall and perhaps a scattering of tiny objects. In the fourth lavatory the rigour is *totally relaxed*. The walls are covered with a motley array of postcards, there is a various assortment of reading matter and curios. The lavatory roll is likely to be uncovered and the holder may well fall apart in use.

We can say that as we move from the first to the fourth lavatory we are moving from a strongly classified to a weakly classified space: from a space regulated by strong rules of exclusion to a space regulated by weak rules of exclusion. Now if the rules of exclusion are strong then the space is strongly marked off from other spaces in the house or flat. The *boundary* between spaces or rooms is sharp . . .

Whereas classification tells us about the structure of relationships in *space*, framing tells us about the structure of relationships in *time*. Framing refers us to interaction, to the power relationships of interaction; that is framing refers us to communication. Now in the case of our lavatories, framing *here* would refer to the communication between the occupants of the space and those outside of the space. Such communication is normally strongly framed by a door usually equipped with a lock. We suggest that as we move from the strongly classified to the weakly classified lavatory, despite the potential insulation between inside and outside, there will occur a reduction in frame strength . . .

Lavatory one is predicated on the rule 'things must be kept apart' be they persons, acts, objects, communication, and the stronger the classification and frames the greater the insulation, the stronger the boundaries between classes of persons, acts, objects, communications. Lavatory four is predicated on the rule that approximates to 'things must be put together'. As a consequence, we would find objects in the space that could be found in other spaces. Further, there is a more relaxed marking off of the space and communication is possible between inside and outside . . .

When the rule is 'things must be put together' we have an *interruption* of a previous order, and what is of issue is the authority (power relationships) which underpin it. Therefore, the rule 'things must be put together' celebrates the present over the past, the subjective over the objective, the personal over the positional. Indeed when everything is put together we have a total organic principle which covers all aspects of life *but* which admits of a vast range of combinations and re-combinations . . .

What is taken for granted when the rule is 'things must be kept apart' is *relationships* which themselves are made explicit when the rule is 'things must be put together'. They are made explicit by the weak classification and frames. But the latter create a form of implicit but potentially continuous surveillance and at the same time promote the making public of the self in a variety of ways.

Bernstein, 1975, pp 116–56, in Halsey *et al.*, 1997, pp 76–78

Questions

Is the organization in your educational institution or department strongly or weakly classified and/or framed? Explain your answer with some details about how it is organized.

Can you find any evidence that your institute or department uses either of the two rules described in the last two paragraphs (i.e. 'things must be put together' or 'things must be kept apart')? If so, what is the significance of such a rule?

Prime Minister James Callaghan. The new Secretary of State for Education and Science was Reginald Prentice, who was followed by Frederick Mulley in 1975 and Shirley Williams in 1976. As the sense of economic crisis grew, the government joined sociology in criticizing education, although each had a different agenda. Sociology was critical of political influences on the generation of knowledge and inequalities, whilst the government was faced with claims that it was using education as a scapegoat for its problems in managing the economy.

During the late 1970s sociology continued to change as a result of the increasing influence of feminism, anti-sexism and anti-racism. In the USA Bowles and Gintis (1976) were writing about the correspondence between educational experiences and work experiences, claiming that the social inequalities experienced in the classroom provided a grounding for inequalities in the workplace. Such theories were explored in the UK by Paul Willis when he produced a classic piece of sociology (1977) in which he mixed neo-Marxist and interpretive approaches, drew on the current themes of knowledge and vocationalism and included issues such as sexism and racism. Also in 1977 the Open University course E202 started with strong emphasis on interpretive/micro perspectives, reflecting the new sociology of education's interest in the curriculum and classroom interaction. Furthermore, the sociology of education was demonstrating its rebellious streak via such controversial books as *Deschooling Society* (Illich, 1971) and *Teaching as a Subversive Activity* (Postman and Weingartner, 1971). What seemed to be emerging was a synthesis of structuralist and interpretive perspectives in a sociology with a strong social critique. Indeed, Ronald Inglehart saw this critique as extending beyond sociology to the highly educated masses in Western societies, who were, he claimed, becoming much more reflexive (1977). Yet the growing interest in vocationalism (e.g. Schultz, 1963) was also preparing the ground for the economic liberalism of the 1980s.

Although new social movements (e.g. the women's movement, the peace movement and environmentalism) suggested a relatively new style of politics, largely occupied by the highly educated and most reflexive individuals, individualism and authoritarianism appealed to those of the increasingly affluent working class and middle class who had primarily instrumental interests. In 1979 a Conservative government was elected under Prime Minister Margaret Thatcher and Mark Carlisle replaced Shirley Williams as Secretary of State for Education.

Changing school systems

At the start of the 1970s the traditional 'triangle of tension' between central government, LEAs and teachers' unions was starting to look rather more tense because of varied responses to the Labour government's directive to introduce comprehensive schools. The Conservative government was obviously more sympathetic to those Conservative authorities who had exerted their independence and resisted instructions, and in 1970 issued Circular 10/70 (*Organization of Secondary Education*), which withdrew Circular 10/65. Nevertheless, the movement of LEAs towards comprehensivization continued and such inconsistent responses to government policy strained the already fragile process by which education policy was generated via negotiations between the three groups in the triangle. Major changes to local government were also introduced by the 1972 Local Government Act (implemented in 1974) which reduced the number of LEAs in England and Wales from 163 to 104 by creating some new and larger authorities, although the ILEA remained unchanged. Although the Secretary of State need no longer be consulted about the appointment of Chief Education Officers, reorganization also led to the demise of the Association of Education Committees (of LEAs), which had been a considerable source of power for LEAs within the triangle of tension.

Whilst some changes took place in control of education at a local level there were also some regional changes. In 1970 the government partly acknowledged the particular character of education in Wales by transferring most of the responsibility for primary and secondary education in Wales from the Secretary of State for Education and Science to the Secretary of State for Wales (Circular 18/70, DES; 108/70, Welsh Office).

Changes in the early 1970s also seemed to be signifying the expansion of education. Nearly thirty years after it had been recommended by the 1944 Education Act, the school-leaving age was finally raised from fifteen to sixteen by the 1972 Raising of the School-Leaving Age Order. With an extra year available, the 1973 Education (Work Experience) Act enabled all LEAs to arrange for children under school-leaving age to have work experience during the last year of their compulsory schooling. The Education White Paper of 1972 also assumed a 53 per cent increase in recurrent school expenditure over the next ten years. Yet this was actually the last government move towards an increase in spending on education for a very long time. The predicted expansion in educational spending did not happen and the movement was, instead, from growth to contraction.

When a Labour government was elected in 1974 it, predictably, set about overturning some of the actions of its predecessor. Just as the Conservative government had replaced Labour's circular of 1965, the Labour government replaced the Conservative's circular of 1970 with Circular 4/74 (1974, DES; Circular 112/74, Welsh Office, *Organization of Secondary Education*). The new circular reaffirmed the Labour government's objectives of ending selection at 11+ and introducing comprehensive schools. It required those LEAs who had not already done so to submit to the Secretaries of State, by the end of the year, information about their plans for making their schools comprehensive. Yet again some LEAs still hesitated and in 1976 an Education Act attempted to abolish selection by ability for secondary schools. It laid down a general principle of comprehensive education which should have ended selection over a period (but this principle was repealed in the 1979 Act).

Similarly, plans for changes in Northern Ireland did not come about. In 1976 the Cowan Report (*Reorganization of Secondary Education in Northern Ireland*) investigated ways of changing the bipartite system (of grammar and secondary intermediate schools) in Northern Ireland. It recommended a dual system of 11–16 (two-form entry) and 11–18 (six-form entry) comprehensive schools. Pupils would also be able to transfer from 11–16 to 11–18 schools for sixth-form courses. In 1979 the Benn Report (*Report of the Working party on Voluntary Schools*) investigated ways of allowing voluntary schools in Northern Ireland to continue (as direct grant schools) in the new system recommended in the Cowan Report, 1976. Finally, the Dickson Report (1979, *Report on Preparatory and Boarding Departments*) investigated the legal and admininstrative aspects of the new system recommended in the Cowan Report. However, the period of three years between the publication of the Cowan Report and the election of a Conservative government was not long enough for the changes to take shape and Northern Ireland retained a largely bipartite system.

Although the introduction of comprehensive schools was met with much resistance in Northern Ireland and some resistance in England and Wales, its successful introduction in Scotland was causing some problems. The Munn Report (1977, *The Structure of the Curriculum*) and the Dunning Report (1977, *Assessment for All*) were both set up by the Secretary of State for Scotland to study the curriculum and assessment in the third and fourth years of Scottish secondary schools. Both reports presented complementary recommendations at the same time.

Munn (1977) found some problems arising from the raising of the school-leaving age and rapid expansion of comprehensive schools in Scotland. Too often pupils of average or below average ability were either struggling with work beyond their abilities or following 'improvized' courses. Yet for pupils of high ability, too much of the curriculum was often taken up with preparation for examinations and too little done to stretch them in their earlier years. The report recommended that:

- The first year of secondary schooling (at 12+ in Scotland) should involve mixed ability grouping, but differentiation into ability groups should begin in the second year and be established by the third.
- The curriculum for third and fourth year pupils should consist of a core and an elective area.
- The core should consist of seven subjects: English, mathematics, PE and religion to be taken by all pupils, and a social studies subject, a science and a creative arts subject to be chosen from a list.

- The elective area would be wide ranging, and a further two or three options would be chosen from it.
- Each course would have three syllabuses of different levels of difficulty for pupils of different ability, with some opportunities for transfer between them.

The Dunning Report (1977, *Assessment for All*) considered assessment of third and fourth year pupils of all levels of academic ability in Scottish secondary schools. It recommended that:

- The O grades, taken only by abler pupils, should be replaced by an exam that matched comprehensive education, and that all pupils should take a single national certificate in each subject.
- (As Munn proposed) there should be three syllabuses of different levels of difficulty, with certificates awarded at three corresponding levels, covering the entire ability range. These were termed Credit (the highest), General and Foundation, the last of these to be divided into Pass and CC (Course Completed).
- Awards should be based on continuous assessment of course work as well as on the final external exam.

The major recommendations of the Dunning Committee were eventually accepted and embodied in the Standard grade exam system, which replaced O grades in Scotland. Thus, the Labour government's policy of comprehensivization had varying degrees of success in different parts of the UK, with Scotland not only establishing the largest proportion of comprehensive schools by the end of the decade, but also starting to tackle any problems arising.

Whilst the Munn and Dunning proposals started to take shape in Scotland, other parts of the UK were moving in different directions. The Waddell Report (1978, *School Examinations*) favoured the replacement of assessment for GCE and CSE with a single system at 16+. It recommended three modes, as in CSE, and a single grading system (although with special papers in some subjects for pupils of low or high ability) and that unified courses should be offered from 1983, with first exams in 1985. The first GCSE courses were actually offered in 1986, with the first exams in 1988.

Another key issue of contention between Labour and the Conservative Party was that of private education and, again, changes tended to reflect their different perspectives. In 1970 the Donnison Report (Public Schools Commission, Second Report) included recommendations about both independent day schools and direct grant schools. It recommended that such schools should either admit pupils without charging fees and selecting by ability, or forgo state aid. However, as the report was published during a Conservative government, action had not been taken before there was another change of government. In 1975, the Labour government issued its *Direct Grant Grammar Schools (Cessation of Grant) Regulations* which specified how and when direct grants were to be phased out. Direct grant schools were required to choose either comprehensivization or withdrawal of state aid. Furthermore, the 1976 Education Act limited the powers of LEAs to pay for places in independent schools.

In response to criticisms of schools for their lack of accountability, the Taylor Report (1977, *A New Partnership for Our Schools*) investigated maintained schools in England and Wales and recommended that every school should have its own governing body, consisting of equal numbers of representatives of the LEA, school staff, parents and the local community. Although all powers relevant to school government were formally vested in the LEA, it should delegate these as far as possible to the governing body of each school, who would give the headteacher as much discretion as possible. Governors should define the broad aims of the school, invite the head and staff to devise means of pursuing them and should themselves monitor the school's progress towards them. To increase their effectiveness all governors were expected to attend initial and in-service training courses to be provided by the LEA. In 1979 the Astin Report (*Report of the Working Party on the Management of Schools in Northern Ireland*) made similar recommendations for schools in Northern Ireland. Unlike the proposals made in many other reports, Taylor and Astin's proposals ultimately became very influential. The main recommendations made in these reports were implemented in the 1980 Education Act and extended in the 1986 Education Act, when a Conservative government interpreted them differently and gradually used school governing bodies to promote its ideas of a parentocracy.

When a Conservative government was elected in 1979 it was possible again to see what seemed to be a revolving stage of education policies as it set out once more to undo the work of its predecessor. The 1979 Education Act repealed the 1976 Education Act, which had required local authorities to submit comprehensive schemes and had obliged direct grant schools to join the maintained system or become independent. Thus, at the end of the decade educationalists braced themselves for another period of radical changes to school systems, some of which could be predicted by reading the last Black Paper (1977). Some Black Paper writers assumed a new role, shifting from their standing as radical extremists to being part of the Conservative administration that was to implement some of their views.

Further and higher education

During the 1970s there was a gradual shift away from further education's traditional role of providing leisure activities towards its other, more vocational functions. Growing concerns about the state of the British economy meant that more pressure was starting to be put on to further and higher education to serve the needs of the economy, rather than individual hobbies and interests. At the start of the 1970s about half of adult education was for 'leisure' activities such as cookery, arts and crafts, yoga and other assorted hobbies (Trowler, 1998, p 28).

In 1973 the Russell Report (*Adult Education: A Plan for Development*) examined the already thriving non-vocational adult education sector in England and Wales and suggested little change to the existing division of responsibility for this between LEAs, university extramural departments and voluntary organizations, such as the Workers' Education Association. However, it recommended tighter controls over the sector with the creation of a national development council, regional advisory councils, and local organizations in every LEA, and a stronger role for central government in terms

of financial support and guidance to LEAs. It suggested that employees should have the right to paid educational leave, and that adult education courses should charge fees, but that these should be small. In fact it was only in 1977 that an Advisory Council for Adult and Continuing Education was set up, which was a central body like the proposed national development council but lacking the strong government support called for by the Report. By comparison, the Russell Report's successor in Scotland was much more successful. In 1975 The Alexander Report (*Adult Education: The Challenge of Change*) investigated voluntary, non-vocational adult education in Scotland and recommended that adult education should be combined with the youth and community service into a community education service. Most Scottish education authorities adopted this arrangement.

An increased emphasis on vocationalism during the mid 1970s could be seen in new concerns about the employability of school leavers without qualifications. Until the 1970s it had been relatively easy for anyone to get a job but economic crises were bringing with them a rise in unemployment. In 1973 the Employment and Training Act required LEAs to set up a careers service. This was quite significant, but perhaps even more intriguing in the long term was its creation of the Manpower Services Commission under the Department of Employment. The MSC was to become increasingly influential (until it was disbanded as a separate organization in 1988) and often resented by staff employed in further education as a symbol of increasing government control.

In 1979 two more reports considered the further education of young people who were not following an academic route. The Keohane Report (*Proposals for a Certificate of Extended Education*, Cmnd. 7755) recommended a single-subject qualification at 17+ (the Certificate of Extended Education, CEE), for pupils staying on after the compulsory school-leaving age but not taking A levels. Instead of linking CSE and CEE courses it favoured seeing CEE courses more closely linked to courses in further education (themselves in need of a simpler structure) and with more being vocational in emphasis. Also in 1979, the Mansell Report (*A Basis for Choice*) considered full-time courses (mainly one year) for young people of average ability and attainment who had left school and wanted neither GCE studies nor preparation for specific jobs. It recommended unifying and rationalizing curriculum structures. Courses should consist of three main elements; with the common core occupying 50–60 per cent of the course and the rest of the course spread equally between vocational studies, related to a general idea of employment, and studies specific to a particular job. The report emphasized three principles:

1. courses should encourage development of 'a realistic vocational focus' as students progressed;
2. attainment in vocational courses should receive equal recognition with academic attainment and not restrict future prospects;
3. experience of learning is important itself, as well as the attainment of certain levels of performance.

The massive expansion of higher education experienced in the 1960s was starting to slow down during the 1970s. Although the 1972 Education White Paper envisaged a 63 per cent increase in expenditure on higher education over the next ten years, this did not happen. Spending on student grants was revised in favour of students taking courses below degree level, as the 1972 Education Act excluded postgraduate students from eligibility for LEA discretionary grants (introduced under the 1962 Education Act) and the 1975 Education Act extended grants to include students taking DipHE, HND and initial teacher training courses. Postgraduate students were also considered by the 1974 Swann Report (*The Flow into Employment of Scientists, Engineers and Technologists*), which found that the best graduates in science and technology tended to stay working in higher education rather than go into industry or teaching. The report recommended that in postgraduate training there should be more emphasis on the links between the academic world and industry, and that scientists should be encouraged to contribute to the work of schools.

Teachers

At the start of the 1970s teachers had already started to face growing criticisms but by the end of the decade that criticism seems to have gathered an unstoppable momentum. Teachers still had considerable freedom to decide what should be taught in class (the 'secret garden') but that freedom was being viewed with suspicion by those who had doubts about teaching standards and the supposed political motivations of some teachers (for example, the writers of the Black Papers, Cox and Dyson, 1969, 1970, 1971; Cox and Boyson, 1975, 1977). Some sociologists (for example, Postman and Weingartner, 1971 and Illich, 1971) were contributing to an image of teachers as left-wing radicals, who were also being criticized for their authoritarianism. Teachers were at once dangerous subversives and dangerous authoritarians! In either case they had to be controlled and this could be tackled by reviewing teacher training procedures and key parts of the curriculum.

Teacher training was, in any case, due for review after the rapid expansion since 1944. In 1972 the James Report (*Teacher Education and Training*) examined arrangements for the training and probation of teachers in England and Wales. It proposed the radical reorganization of teacher training to involve three stages: general higher education, professional training and in-service training. The first could take the form of a degree or a new qualification, a two-year Diploma in Higher Education, the second would consist of a year's professional studies followed by a year as a 'licensed' teacher (after which students would be awarded a BA(Ed)) and the third cycle should amount to at least a term of in-service training every seven years for all teachers in post. In response to this report many colleges of education merged with other establishments, such as technical and art colleges to form colleges and institutes of higher education. However, little action was taken to try to implement the 'licensed teacher' scheme.

Attempting to enter into the 'secret garden' of the classroom, the 1975 Bullock Report (*A Language for Life*) looked at all aspects of teaching the use of English. It was mainly concerned with England but took evidence from other English-speaking countries (including Scotland). Research for the report involved a survey of language teaching in 2,000 schools and found a widespread commitment to basic skills, with an emphasis on formal practice. Although evidence was also found that standards of reading were inadequate for present-day society, there was no evidence of an actual decline. The report made many recommendations, some of which involved increased spending on staffing, accommodation and other resources. It recommended that language in education should form a part of initial training for every teacher and that in-service education in reading and language should be expanded.

From the mid 1970s onwards some sociologists were identifying the development of moral panics (e.g. Hall *et al.*, 1978; Cohen, 1973) which were often associated with the behaviour of young people and black youth in particular. At the same time, criticisms of teachers seemed to be escalating into some sort of panic, supported by snap-shot views of localized problems. Parents with children at William Tyndale Junior School in London accused teachers there of being politically motivated in making no attempt to teach traditional basic skills and failing to discipline children. It seemed that resistance to authoritarianism could shift too far towards an excessively permissive culture. In 1977 a BBC *Panorama* programme ('The Best Days', about Faraday Comprehensive School in a deprived area of West London) focused on lax discipline, but it was criticized as biased by staff, parents and pupils. It was easy to exaggerate problems until they escalated into a sense of moral crisis and were generalized to all schools.

Moral panics, combined with criticisms of education for failing the economic needs of the country and critiques from the 'new' sociology of education meant that the spotlight on teachers grew more intense. In 1978 the BBC news from teachers' conferences was reporting signs of declining morale among teachers.

Whilst teachers were facing criticism in the wider society, sociologists studying classroom interaction were showing how their pupils tested them in the classroom. Their findings have, for many years, been useful to student teachers and teacher trainers in identifying and developing 'survival' strategies. One particularly useful model was produced by Gannaway (1976) to examine the dynamic interaction between pupils and teachers in the classroom, as pupils tended to ask three crucial questions: Can the teacher keep order? Can the teacher 'have a laugh'? Does the teacher under-stand pupils? Here we can see some of the hurdles teachers have to jump in order to develop a successful working relationship with their pupils (see Figure 9.1).

In his study of a secondary modern school, Woods (1979) also listed eight 'survival strategies' used by teachers:

- socialization (trying to use school's routines and rules to train pupils for the ideal pupil role);
- domination (verbal or physical discipline);
- negotiation (involving exchange principles such as bribes, flattery, appeals, etc.);
- fraternization (including identification with youth culture and tolerating some behaviours in order to establish friendship, interest and co-operation);
- absence or removal from the classroom (including physical or mental absence from the classroom);
- ritual and routine (which can be addictive for teachers and pupils);
- occupational therapy (engaging pupils in practical activities to occupy the mind);
- morale boosting (teachers' groups solidarity, humour in the staffroom).

Like Paul Willis (1977, who noted the importance to the 'lads' of 'having a laff'), Woods emphasized the importance of laughter in the school. Woods (1976) distinguished between various types of laughter: in particular natural laughter (with teachers and friends), institutionalized laughter (what teachers described as silly and childish behaviour) or subversive laughter (to undermine the authority of the teacher).

Class and status

During the 1970s five particular areas tended to dominate sociological research into social class and equal (or rather unequal) opportunities. First, there were continuing doubts about systems and, in particular, how the organization of secondary schools (into bipartite, tripartite or comprehensive schools and segregation into maintained and non-maintained systems) could reflect and affect opportunities. Second, sociologists were interested in how patterns

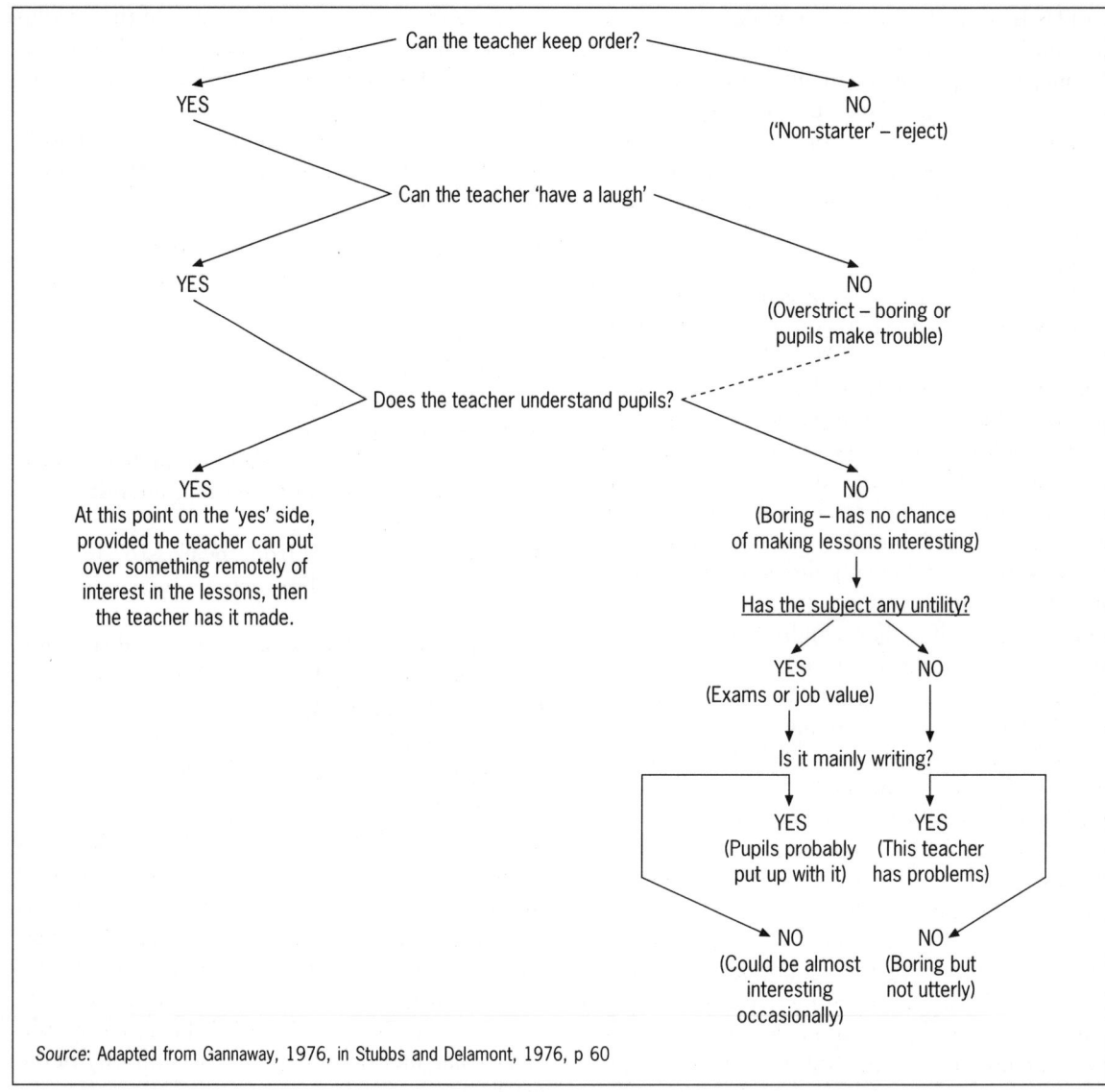

Can the teacher keep order?

YES / NO ('Non-starter' – reject)

Can the teacher 'have a laugh'

YES / NO (Overstrict – boring or pupils make trouble)

Does the teacher understand pupils?

YES
At this point on the 'yes' side, provided the teacher can put over something remotely of interest in the lessons, then the teacher has it made.

NO (Boring – has no chance of making lessons interesting)

Has the subject any untility?

YES (Exams or job value)   NO

Is it mainly writing?

YES (Pupils probably put up with it)   YES (This teacher has problems)

NO (Could be almost interesting occasionally)   NO (Boring but not utterly)

Source: Adapted from Gannaway, 1976, in Stubbs and Delamont, 1976, p 60

Figure 9.1 Pupils' evaluation schema for teachers

of social inequalities and social mobility were changing and could impact on education. Third, there were concerns about interaction in the classroom, including teachers' differential expectations of the capacities of children from different classes and the self-fulfilling prophesy (i.e. outcomes in accord with the expectations of teachers). For example, Barker-Lunn (1970) and Nash (1971, 1973) both found that streaming occurred in non-streamed schools in a covert way, with teachers allocating pupils to different tables according to how 'bright' they thought they were. Fourth, sociologists were interested in the impact of the family and home environment on educational achievement, including differences in encouragement, values, language patterns and peer groups. Finally, sociologists were concerned about how education prepared young people for their future working lives.

Although many people had experienced a noticeable rise in their standard of living during

	Respondent's class (% by row)								
Father's Class	I	II	III	IV	V	VI	VII	Total	N
I	48.4	18.9	9.3	8.2	4.5	4.5	6.2	100.0	582
II	31.9	22.6	10.7	8.0	9.2	9.6	8.0	100.0	477
III	19.2	15.7	10.8	8.6	13.0	15.0	17.8	100.1	594
IV	12.8	11.1	7.8	24.9	8.7	14.7	19.9	99.9	1223
V	15.4	13.2	9.4	8.0	16.6	20.1	17.2	99.9	939
VI	8.4	8.9	8.4	7.1	12.2	29.6	25.4	100.0	2312
VII	6.9	7.8	7.9	6.8	12.5	23.5	34.8	100.2	2216
%	14.3	11.4	8.6	9.9	11.6	20.8	23.3	99.9	(8343)

Source: Heath, 1981, p 54; based on the Oxford Mobility Study
*'Outflow' means destinations of men from different social classes.
Sample: Men aged 25–64 in 1972.
The classes were defined as follows:
I   Higher-grade professionals, administrators, managers in large establishments, larger proprietors.
II Lower-grade professionals, higher-grade technicians, lower-grade administrators, managers in small establishments, supervisors of non-manual employees.
III Routine non-manual (clerical) employees, sales personnel, other rank-and-file service workers.
IV Small proprietors, self-employed artisans, non-professional 'own account' workers.
V   Lower-grade technicians, supervisors over manual workers.
VI Skilled manual wage-workers.
VII Semi- and unskilled manual wage-workers.

Figure 9.2 Intergenerational mobility in England and Wales 1972: outflow*

the 1960s, sociologists found that there were still extreme inequalities. Wedge and Prosser (1973) found that 6 per cent of British children fulfilled all of the following indicators of deprivation:

1. their family income was so low that they received supplementary benefit and/or school meals;
2. they lived in overcrowded homes and/or lacked a hot water system;
3. they lived in a one-parent family or a family with five or more children.

That 6 per cent of children shared many common features. They were less likely to have pre-school education, likely be older when starting school, to experience larger classes, to have parents who visited school less often, to have a poor level of health, to frequently be absent from school, to have low behaviour ratings from teachers and to have low maths and reading scores at the age of eleven.

Turner had already looked at social mobility during the 1960s but far more was published on

the subject during the 1970s. Findings from the extensive research for the Oxford Mobility Study were gradually emerging (Goldthorpe and Llewellyn, 1977a, 1977b) although they were not published in book form until 1980 (Goldthorpe, Llewellyn and Payne). As well as its wider interests in socio-economic change, the study examined the impact of postwar education policy and the degree of movement between generations in the same family. It used a large sample of men aged 20–64 and the researchers compared men born between 1908 and 1927 with those born between 1928 and 1947. The sample was split into seven class categories (see Figure 9.2) and mobility was recognized as movement into or out of one of these categories. If classes were perfectly self-recruiting, every son would be in the same class as his father, and this was obviously not the case, although it was interesting to find that there were still clear patterns in the relationship between son's class and father's class.

QUESTIONS

Analyse the findings presented in Figure 9.2.
From which class was there the most change?
From which class was there the least change?
Was mobility mainly short-range (i.e. to the nearest class) or long-range?
Was there an increase in upward mobility?
To what extent did the class into which a man was born influence his class in 1972?
Comment on the type of sample and the validity and generalizability of the findings.
How relevant would the same sort of study be if carried out today?

These figures are useful but say little about the process of social mobility. Hopper (1971) followed Turner's (1961) categories (of sponsored and contest mobility) with two categories of his own: ideologies of implementation, which were concerned with how and when mobility occurred, and ideologies of legitimation, which were concerned with to whom and why it occurs. Hopper argued that what Turner saw as sponsored mobility could be seen as a process involving the 'warming up' of students who receive further specialized training and the 'cooling out' of others who are sent into the labour market.

QUESTION

Do you think that your expectations were 'warmed up' or 'cooled out'?

Research into the influence of parental values on educational opportunities continued to develop during the 1970s, building on and challenging earlier theories. It challenged assumptions that groups inhabiting the same social position shared a common culture or subculture and criticized research into parental values for several reasons.

1. It fails to see that the holding of values is a dynamic process. Barker-Lunn (1970) found that streaming affected parental aspirations in both directions; upwards for working-class parents with children in higher streams and lower for middle-class parents with children in lower streams.
2. Working-class parents were socially ill at ease in school and with teachers (Halsey, 1972)

and may avoid them for that reason rather than lack of interest.
3. Acland (1980) found the measures used often combined attitudes with circumstance (for example, family outings involve both) and failed to consider differences in schools' efforts to involve parents.
4. In imputing the effects of parental values on children's behaviour we are ignoring intervening variables.

Nevertheless, some research into the effects of parents' values has been simplified and distorted. When we consider how Bernstein (1970) looked further at the impact of the language spoken in the home, we will see findings that have been habitually misrepresented.

Although sociologists were implicitly critical of society in general and education in particular, a strand of educational research was particularly influenced by neo-Marxism and critical theory, with an interest in hegemony and the role of the ideological superstructure in perpetuating social inequalities. For example, Althusser (1971) saw education as playing a vital role within the ideological state apparatus, perpetuating inequalities by conditioning the masses to accept the status quo. Sociologists were also influenced by the educational writings of Paulo Freire, who worked among poor farmers in northern Brazil during the 1960s. In *The Pedagogy of the Oppressed* (1972) Freire said that the poor were trapped in a 'culture of silence' by being in an economic and social situation in which critical awareness and responses were virtually impossible. What was needed was teaching as a partnership and dialogue through which people could 'achieve significance as people' (1972, p 61).

> Conscientization is a permanent critical approach to reality in order to discover it and discover the myths that deceive us and help to maintain the oppressing dehumanizing structures.
>
> Freire, 1970

Freire's approach was very active in trying to challenge the forces of oppression and some British researchers followed his example (e.g. Grant, 1989). However, others had a more detached approach as they probed more deeply into the processes by which inequality was perpetuated through educa-

Basil Bernstein has been writing about education since the 1960s but his publications were particularly significant during the 1970s when he made important contributions towards what was seen as the 'new' sociology of education. He related social structure to educational achievement via language and is most well known for his concept of two language codes: the restricted and elaborated codes. As concepts these codes were valuable for analysis and tendencies rather than absolutes. It was, nevertheless, easy for students with a basic impression to wrongly interpret the restricted code as only referring to the working class and the elaborated code as only referring to the middle class.

According to Bernstein, use of a *restricted* code meant that speech could be predicted by the observer; it was simple, had limited range, was descriptive and narrative rather than analytical and abstract, relied on common understandings between the speaker and listener, some meanings were implicit, and the manner and circumstances of speech were important as well as the content. Bernstein associated this code with a *positional family role system* in which individuals' differences, intentions and motives were prescribed by the family. This resulted in 'closed' communication which was less likely to encourage verbalization. In such groups the culture emphasized *we* rather than I to reinforce social relationships and create social solidarity. The world would also be viewed as something to be responded to in which the person was relatively passive.

Use of an *elaborated* code meant that speech was often difficult to predict; it was more complex, with a wide range of alternatives, analytical and abstract, not reliant on a common understanding of meanings, and therefore producing explicit meanings in which extra-verbal factors were of little importance. Bernstein associated this code with a *person-oriented family role system* in which decisions were made on the grounds of the psychological and individual differences of members, rather than on their formal status. This resulted in 'open' communication which encouraged discussion and expression of individual differences. In such groups the culture emphasized *I* rather than we and a common identity and understanding could not be anticipated. The world would also be viewed as something capable of being manipulated, where the subject was relatively active.

Bernstein was not saying that people spoke the codes any more than they spoke grammar (because both were underlying principles rather than actual speech). Although associating them with social class in some ways, he did not see them as mutually exclusive or the exclusive property of one class. Everyone had access to a restricted code but some people (in particular some of the working class) did not have access to the elaborated code. The relationship between social class and linguistic codes was imprecise and Bernstein argued that, in order to achieve a proper understanding of them, we would need to consider family role systems.

Questions

As a group, discuss how Bernstein's theories about language codes may relate to the experiences of people in your families.

Can you find any evidence to challenge Bernstein's theories about restricted and elaborated codes?

tion. They were reaching similar conclusions to those of Bowles and Gintis (1976), who analysed the correspondence between children's experiences in school and the inequalities they encountered as adults in the workplace. In this way the school was seen as introducing and reproducing the inequalities of social class that were perpetuated in a capitalist system, normalising them in the process so that the working class were hardly aware of them (and therefore in a state of false conscious-

ness). Bowles and Gintis called this link between education and the workplace the *correspondence principle*.

Alienated labor is reflected in the student's lack of control over his or her education, the alienation of the student from the curriculum content, and the motivation of school work through a system of grades and other external rewards rather than the student's integration with either the process (learning) or the outcome (knowledge) of the educational 'production process'. Fragmentation in work is reflected in the institutionalized and often destructive competition among students through continual and ostensibly meritocratic ranking and evaluation. By attuning young people to a set of social relationships similar to those of the workplace, schooling attempts to gear the development of personal needs to its requirements.

Bowles and Gintis, 1976, p 131

Although this may seem to be a structural approach, we can see that it also rests on findings about how small groups and individuals related to each other in schools and in the workplace. This makes it difficult to see where a structural approach may end and an interpretive approach may start, and divisions between these approaches become even more spurious when we consider the work of a British sociologist, Paul Willis (1977). Willis analysed the attitudes of a group of working-class 'lads' during their last year at secondary modern school and their first year in the workplace and, in the process, greatly enhanced our understanding of how the 'correspondence principle' identified by Bowles and Gintis could work in practice. We considered Willis's research methods earlier (Chapter 2) and you are advised to look at them before reading on. More can also be found in this chapter about how Willis's findings relate to gender and ethnicity.

WILLIS ON *LEARNING TO LABOUR*

At the very beginning of his book (published a year after Bowles and Gintis's book) Willis acknowledged the use of both structuralist and interpretive approaches.

> The difficult thing to explain about how middle class kids get middle class jobs is why others let them. The difficult thing to explain about how working class kids get working class jobs is why they let themselves.
>
> Willis, 1977, p 1

Willis's interests reflect common sociological interests in pro- and anti-school subcultures, the self-fulfilling prophesy and the 'hidden curriculum'. Put simply, teachers' expectations about how well or how badly individuals will behave are likely to influence that behaviour. Pupils are likely to internalize their teachers' expectations and make them their own, eventually matching their behaviour to the predictions made. Expectations may not simply be derived from teachers, but also from familes, friends and society in general and, in this way, social inequalities can be perpetuated by low self-esteem. Willis, however, adds depth to this sort of scenario by illustrating the lads' creative interaction with social constraints as well as the processes by which they reach a predictable structural location. (Other well-known studies of the self-fulfilling prophesy include Holt, 1964, 1990; Rosenthal and Jacobson, 1968; Spender and Sarah, 1980.)

In the following extract, you can see the essential features of interpretive sociology, as he used the lads' own words and tried to communicate their own sense of reality.

> It is essentially what appears to be their enthusiasm for, and complicity with, immediate authority which makes the school conformists – or 'ear 'oles' or 'lobes' – the second great target for 'the lads' [the first target is the teachers]. The term 'ear 'ole' itself connotes the passivity and absurdity of the school conformists for 'the lads'. It seems that they are always listening, never doing: never animated with their own internal life, but formless in rigid reception. The ear is one of the least expressive organs of the human body: it responds to the expressivity of others. It is pasty and easy to render obscene. That is how 'the lads' liked to picture those who conformed to the official idea of schooling.
>
> Crucially, 'the lads' not only reject but feel superior to the 'ear 'oles'. The obvious medium for the enactment of this superiority is that which the 'ear 'oles' apparently yield – fun, independence and excitement: having a 'laff'.
>
> Quotes from Willis, 1977, p 15

Question

Most of the 'lads' found it easy to get jobs when they left school in the early 1970s.
Consider the implications of Willis's findings in view of the level of unemployment today.

Gender

Having started to break out during the 1960s, women at last seemed to become visible during the 1970s. Even Simone de Beauvoir, despite her earlier reluctance, started to call herself a feminist and joined the Women's Liberation Movement, now convinced of the need for women to unite to fight against sexual inequality. The 1970s began with the publication of Shulamith Firestone's book *Dialectic of Sex* (1970) in which she defined society in terms of a sex/class system and stated the case for a feminist revolution. The ideas she developed came to be known as radical feminism, an approach that grew more dominant within the women's movement as the decade progressed. In the UK, Germaine Greer's book *The Female Eunuch* (1971) probably had more impact outside of academia than had any previous piece of feminist writing and feminist publishing houses (such as Virago) started to reflect the raising of women's consciousness together with an explosion in feminist scholarship. Small feminist groups emerged in most large towns, loosely connected via conferences, and by the end of the 1970s some other feminist perspectives had emerged to challenge the dominance of radical feminism, such as Marxist, socialist, lesbian and psychoanalytic feminism.

Although feminist ideas were starting to take hold, they were operating alongside a still dominant ideology that reinforced traditional images of femininity and domesticity. This ambiguous position could be seen in another best-selling book by Shirley Conran (*Superwoman*, 1975), which was described on the cover as a 'guide to household management for today's woman'. Although women were now entering the workforce in large numbers, more and more of them were facing the reality of the 'double shift', as they tried to succeed in both their paid work and unpaid domestic work. Conran wrote that the purpose of her book was 'to help you do the work you don't like as fast as possible, leaving time for the work you enjoy' (p 1).

QUESTION

Was Shirley Conran being realistic in acknowledging social realities or simply pandering to gender inequalities?

The concept of the superwoman says a lot about changing relationships between gender and education as, rather than girls and women having won equality, it seemed that more was expected of them than of boys and men. They were expected to be better! The increasing number of divorces and births out of wedlock obviously meant an increase in the number of one-parent families, but it was easily assumed that such families would be the responsibility of the mother rather than the father. Research for the Finer Report (1974, *One-Parent Families*) found that by 1971 one in ten families with children had one parent and that the vast majority of these parents were female. Its recommendations were therefore aimed at helping women to support their children independently of state help or help from absent fathers. The Finer Report recommended the encouragement of pregnant schoolgirls to continue their education, radical changes in the secondary school curriculum and improvements in the careers guidance offered to girls to enable them to compete equally for better-paid, traditionally male jobs. In fact few of the changes recommended by the Finer Report were implemented and support for one-parent families continued to be minimal long after the 1970s.

Despite continuing problems, a major step towards equal opportunities was made with the passing in 1975 of the Sex Discrimination Act. This prohibited sex discrimination in admission to schools, the appointment of teachers (with exceptions for single-sex schools) and careers advice, and stipulated that neither girls nor boys should be refused access to 'any courses, facilities of other benefits provided' solely on the grounds of their sex. The Act was clearly important for its acknowledgement that such inequalities existed and for initiating a means of monitoring gender inequalities via the Equal Opportunities Commission. Liberal feminists in particular could see how legislation such as this could help to promote equal access to education, although more radical feminists noted that it could do little to change attitudes associated

Like the researchers for the Oxford Mobility Study, Paul Willis (1977) choose an all-male sample for his research. Feminist critics noted that this was a pattern for much of the educational research carried out before the 1980s. It meant that either women were ignored or it was wrongly assumed (not necessarily by the researchers themselves) that findings could be generalized to females. Nevertheless, Willis's research provides a fascinating picture of how the working-class 'lads' learned to internalize and reproduce male stereotypes, celebrating their own sexism and the characteristics that would not only reduce their horizons in the workplace, but also impair their relationships with women.

Willis noted that the main divisions repressing the counter-school culture were those of mental and manual labour and those of gender and that, in its sexism, the counter-school culture reflected the wider working-class culture. The lads rejected mental activity, not only because it was associated with school and unjustified authority, but also because it was regarded as effeminate. Their need to satisfy the masculine stereotype partly explained why that which was conventionally described as the least desirable and satisfying type of work should be taken voluntarily.

> Manual labour is associated with the social superiority of masculinity, and mental labour with the social inferiority of femininity. In particular manual labour is imbued with a masculine tone and nature which renders it positively expressive of more than its intrinsic focus on work . . .
>
> The secret of the continuation of both sets of divisions in labour and gender lies, at least partly, in their lived profane conjunction under the class system of capitalism, and not in their own pure logics . . .
>
> If the currency of femininity were revalued then that of mental work would have to be too. A member of the counter-culture can only believe in the effeminacy of white collar and office work so long as wives, girlfriends and mothers are regarded as restricted, inferior and incapable of certain things . . .
>
> . . . what they take as mental work becomes for 'the lads' mere 'pen-pushing', 'not really doing things' and, most importantly, 'cissy': it is not basically man's work or within the manly scope of action. We see at least why the 'ear 'oles' are likely to be regarded as effeminate and passive 'cissies' by 'the lads', and why other names for conformists include 'pouf' or 'poufter', or 'wanker' . . .
>
> The toughness and awkwardness of physical work and effort – for itself in the division of labour and for its strictly capitalist logic quite without intrinsic heroism or grandeur – takes on masculine lights and depths and assumes a significance beyond itself.

The will to work and to finish a job 'is posited as a masculine logic and not as the logic of exploitation'. Housework is never finished and not regarded as productive, as masculine work is held to be.

> Female domestic work is simply subsumed under being 'mum' or 'housewife' . . . Far from patriarchy and its associated values being an unexplained relic of previous societies, it is one of the very pivots of capitalism in its complex, unintended preparation of labour power and reproduction of the social order.

The male stereotype was imbued in every aspect of their lives, including claims of sexual experience, their clothes, smoking, drinking, sexist and sexual jokes, fighting, fiddling and pilfering and generally being street-wise. Girls were sex objects but must not be sexually experienced and distinctions were made between the 'easy lay' and the steady girlfriend ('the missus'). When girls responded to boys with giggles, crushes or romantic ideas, the lads could see this as a weakness and yet another indication of male superiority.

Quotes from Paul Willis, 1977, pp 148–151

Questions

What role could the school have played in supporting the reinforcement of male stereotypes?
Do you think their teachers could have successfully challenged the boys' attitudes?

Girls and women have been forced and accustomed to embrace a fundamentally ambivalent position. Many have drawn a lot of satisfaction and enjoyment out of activities specific to their 'domestic' role as women, while these are generally assumed by society to be inferior to the activities of men. They are attracted by a role that stands in second place. It is a double-bind situation: if girls go after what society deems most important, succeeding financially and academically in a career, then they may lose in 'femininity'; while if they concentrate on their 'proper' role, it is inherently of lower economic and ideological status . . .

Girls are in an ambivalent and contradictory position. On one level, there is pressure to succeed academically, which is rewarded by school, parents, and the self-satisfaction of doing this. At this level, boys and girls alike may be hindered by the fear of failing, which involves lack of confidence and a reluctance even to try for success. In all the vast literature that has accumulated about 'achievement motivation' in our competitive society, it is the effects of 'fear of failure' that have frequently been emphasized.

For girls the situation is more complex, and girls are often omitted from achievement motivation studies because they do not yield consistent and meaningful results and therefore 'mess up the model'! The increased awareness of feminine role stereotypes particularly those promoted by the media fosters the belief that it is not desirable that girls should be as clever as boys. This implies that 'over-achievement' involves losing an important ingredient of 'femininity'. The majority of the Ealing girls agreed that boys do not like girls to do better than them in school-work. The implication is therefore – if you want to attract boys, don't start by showing how clever you are.

Sharpe, 1976, pp 135–6

with a dominant sexist ideology or ensure strongly defined equal educational opportunities.

Willis's evidence of sexist stereotypes supported an earlier piece of research by Sue Sharpe (1976), who studied 249 girls in the fourth forms of four schools in the London borough of Ealing (they completed a questionnaire and some were interviewed in depth). Most of them were working class, three-fifths were 'white', one-fifth were 'West Indian' and one-fifth were 'Asian'.

One of Willis's colleagues (Griffin, 1985) followed with her own study of 'Typical Girls' which should, perhaps, be read in conjunction with his work. Lambart (1976) also studied female anti-school culture, but in a grammar school (Mereside Grammar School in Greater Manchester) where she found a group of third year girls called 'the Sisterhood', who formed an anti-school subgroup when put into the same sets.

Ethnicity

It has been estimated that, in 1971, 2.3 per cent of the UK's population was drawn from ethnic minorities and that the figure in 1981 was about 3.9 per cent (Skellington with Morris, 1992, using OPCS and Labour Force Surveys). However, new regulations during the 1970s made immigration from some countries (including the West Indies) more difficult and increases in the proportion of ethnic minorities were largely because of the arrival of dependants or the birth of children. The lower than average age of migrants generated higher than average birth rates and public images abounded of black immigration as a threat to national identity. In 1978, prior to her election as Prime Minister, Margaret Thatcher talked of 'the British people's fear' of 'being swamped' by 'alien cultures'. This created a vicious circle as such hostility meant that many of the younger generation from immigrant families sought solace and strength in subcultures (such as Rastafarianism) which then became the targets of further racism.

Although governments started to clamp down on immigration, they finally acknowledged the horrors of racism and started to address it. The assumptions of the immigrant-host model were being questioned as the predicted assimilation and decline in disadvantage did not happen. Writing about racism in 1970s Britain, the Centre for Contemporary Cultural Studies (1981) also argued that the immigrant-host model reinforced racist assumptions by defining immigrants and their cultures as social problems and largely ignoring the influence of structural inequalities. Eventually, in 1976, the Race Relations Act prohibited discrimination on the grounds of race in admission to schools, the appointment of teachers, careers advice, access to facilities and the award of discretionary grants. 'Positive discrimination' in favour of disadvantaged racial groups (e.g. in recruitment or promotion) was not to be allowed, although in some closely defined circumstances, where it could be shown that a particular racial group has a special need with regard to education or training, access to facilities could be restricted or allocated first to its members.

As far as research was concerned, the 1970s started with a continuation of debates by psychologists about genetic influences on the learning potential of different groups and versions of Jensen's theories (1969, 1973) were published in the UK by Hans Eysenck (1971, 1973). Jensen and Eysenck both believed in the validity of IQ testing and for Jensen, 'The problem of Negro-White inequality in reducibility is thus essentially the problem of Negro-White differences in intelligence' (1973, p 355). During the 1970s such claims were criticized by other researchers (e.g. Kamin, 1977) and not simply because of their racist overtones. For example:

- Most of the evidence advanced by Jensen and his supporters came from studies with severe methodological faults. For example, no test of intelligence can separate natural ability from cultural influences and cultural factors can influence children's attitudes to testing.
- Theories about heredity and IQ scores could distract us from more fundamental issues. The objective of education is not the equalizing of IQ scores as the knowledge and skills of a group of pupils can be raised without any alteration to IQ. In any case, Douglas, Ross and Simpson (1968) found that the educational disadvantages of working-class children persisted even when their IQ matched that of middle-class children.
- The policy implications of the concern with the inheritance of IQ could be challenged. Suggestions that inheritance of intelligence entails a reduction of educational support for 'low IQ' groups would be seen as contentious political judgements.

Sociologists such as Little continued their research into inequalities in educational achievements but, unlike Jensen and Eysenck, emphasized the impact of culture rather than heredity. During the 1970s one of Little's colleagues, Christine Mabey (1981), reported on a cohort survey within the ILEA focusing on literacy. The cohort began with over 30,000 children (although some were lost over time) born between September 1959 and September 1960, who were monitored at various stages between the ages of eight (in 1968) and 15 (in 1976). It was found that the reading attainment of some ethnic groups was much lower than others (see Figure 9.3). However, social deprivation, restricted education and attendance at an Educational Priority Area school accounted for about half of the differences between the scores.

QUESTION

Analyse and discuss the findings presented in Figure 9.3.
What are the limitations of such statistics?

Some researchers were particularly interested in the impact of the child's indigenous language on educational achievement, arguing in particular that it was wrong to assume that problems in the use of standard English (often called the Queen's English) indicated lack of intelligence. Although Labov's work emerged at the end of the 1960s, it started to have an impact during the 1970s, at a time when the new sociology of education was emphasizing cultural relativism. Labov (1969) rejected the superiority of standard over non-standard English, arguing that differences from the norm should not be interpreted as deficiencies. Moreover, non-standard English could have its own logical structure and could be very effective as a means of communicating complicated arguments. This can be seen in comparisons between the responses of Larry and Charles, two black Americans. Larry was a rough gang member who was asked what colour he imagined God to be and used non-standard English in his response.

Larry: He'd be white, man.
Interviewer: Why?
Larry: Why? I'll tell you why. Cause the average whitey out here got everything, you dig? And

Age in Years	UK	Eire	WI	IND	PAK	GC	TC	O
8	98.1	94.8	88.1	89.6	91.1	87.3	85.4	93.2
10	98.3	97.9	87.4	89.6	93.1	87.8	85.0	93.9
15	97.8	96.6	85.9	91.4	94.9	87.6	84.9	95.4
N	12,530	229	1,465	137	74	194	139	502

*The word 'mean' signifies average.

Note: UK = United Kingdom; WI = West Indies; IND = India; PAK = Pakistan; GC = Cyprus, Greek speaking; TC = Cyprus, Turkish speaking; O = all other immigrants

Source: Mabey, 1981, p 85

Figure 9.3 Mean* reading scores at eight, ten and fifteen years by ethnic group

WILLIS ON LEARNING TO BE RACIST

'Hammertown Boys' School' had an exclusively working-class intake, including many West Indian and Asian minorities, and within the school there were distinct groups of whites, West Indians and Asians. The headteacher let pupils use form rooms for friendship groups but boys then segregated themselves into one room for whites, one for West Indians and one for Asians. Some forms of discrimination could also be seen among the staff, with the headteacher talking about whites making cups of tea in their room, West Indians 'stamping around' to music and Asians 'jabbering' to each other. In the racist hierarchy it was the Asians who fared worst. West Indians shared some of the lads' counter-culture, including cultural interests, such as 'going out', R & B and reggae music and a lack of conformist achievement. They were, nevertheless regarded as stupid and 'thick' and there was some tension regarding sexual rivalries over girls. Asian boys were seen as 'alien', 'smelly', 'unclean' and associated with the 'ear 'oles'.

To Willis, racism 'marks the bottom limit of the scope of masculinity' (p 153). As immigrants were likely to have the worst, roughest jobs, they were (according to the lads' stereotype) potentially more masculine, and so such jobs were reclassified to fall off the scale of masculinity into 'dirty', 'messy' and 'unsocial' categories. West Indians were accredited with more masculinity than Asians, and some hostility towards them related to sexual jealousy, but their supposed sexual prowess was also downgraded as disgusting. Asians could be associated with 'ear 'oles' because their parents were stereotyped as successful shopkeepers and businessmen, making their sons 'cissy', passive and lacking aggression.

Willis drew from his analysis of racism in the school an interesting insight into future developments. He noted that some second-generation West Indian boys had inherited a culture of wagelessness which they could see as a positive challenge, so that they were learning to take pride in surviving without wages. This attitude could be emulated by white youth in the future.

> As structural unemployment becomes a permanent feature of this society and some sections of white youth are forced into long term unemployment there may well develop a white ethnic culture of wagelessness (borrowing very likely from the West Indian one, though compare the currently emerging phenomenon of punk rock culture). A necessity might be turned into an invention and, through the cultural mediation, the option of not working become a more widespread 'freely' chosen response. The question of the cultural reproduction of an under class is as full of significance as that of the reproduction of the manual working class.
>
> Willis, 1977, see pp 152–4

Question

How useful are these findings and ideas today?

the nigger ain't got shit, y'know? Y'understan'? So – um – in order for that to happen, you know it ain't no black God that's doin' that bullshit.

Charles was college educated and upper middle class, who was asked whether dreams come true and answered in standard English.

Charles: Well. I even heard my parents say that there is such a thing as something in dreams. Some things like that, and sometimes dreams do come true. I've never dreamt that somebody was dying and they actually dies (mhm) or that I was going to have ten dollars the next day and somehow I got ten dollars in my pocket. (Mhm) I don't particularly believe in that, I don't think it's true.

Cited by Reid, 1986, pp 209–210

QUESTION

Compare the responses by Larry and Charles. Which contains the most orderly and effective ideas?

Labov's research was done in the USA, but similar theories emerged from the work of Edwards (1976 and 1979) in the UK. Edwards argued that *Creole interference* in particular played an important role in the underperformance of West Indian children. Although the Creole spoken by many West Indian children (and children of West Indian parents) includes English vocabulary, it has different grammatical constructions and sound systems. Children who are influenced by Creole are not only at a disadvantage because their Creole 'interferes' with their use of standard English, but they also have to endure the commonly held view that they are inarticulate. Unlike children who 'officially' learn to speak English as a second language, children who speak Creole are assumed to be speaking 'poor' English. By comparison, children who learn to speak English as a second language are formally taught in school to speak standard English, with the 'correct' grammatical constructions. Edwards's theories not only complemented those of Labov, but also those of Bernstein (1970) who said that the teacher should accept the language the child brought to school and start from there.

Towards the end of the 1970s some particularly wide-ranging and significant work was also carried out for the Rampton Report (1981) but its findings will be considered in the next chapter because they were published, and had a significant impact, during the 1980s. Meanwhile, we can look again at Willis (1977) in order to recognize findings about the origins of racism that have often been neglected.

Special needs

Just as gender and ethnicity were becoming more visible during the 1970s, so too were special educational needs. This may have happened anyway, as the period of consolidation during the 1960s was followed by new ideas, but special needs also became more dominant in public discourse with the birth of many disabled babies to mothers who had taken the drug Thalidomide. These 'babies' were growing up and starting school, and there was a growing realization that physical disabilities could not be associated with educational inadequacies (although that attitude still remains). Campaigning groups of parents were becoming increasingly vocal and assertive in their demands for a good education for their children.

During the early 1970s legislation continued to make relatively minor changes to provision for children with special needs. The 1970 Education (Handicapped Children) Act transferred responsibility for the education of severely 'subnormal' children in England and Wales from health authorities to the LEAs (which was applied to Scotland by an Education Act in 1974). Also in 1970, the Chronically Sick and Disabled Persons Act required new educational buildings to be made accessible to disabled people, unless this was incompatible with the efficient use of resources. In 1976 another Education Act added further weight to previous recommendations that 'handicapped' children should be educated in ordinary schools whenever possible. However, recommendations and changes had, until the 1970s, often been piecemeal and it was the Warnock Report of 1978 that set in motion more concerted efforts to recognize and respond to some children's special needs.

The Report of the Committee of Inquiry into the Education of Handicapped Children and Young People is often called the Warnock Report after its chairperson, Baroness Mary Warnock. Its remit was to review the educational provision in the UK for children and young people 'handicapped by disabilities of body or mind' and five of its many recommendations are noted below.

1. The ten existing medical categories of handicap should be replaced by a more general concept of 'special educational need' (SEN). This was more wide-ranging than the old medical categories and included temporary as well as permanent requirements. Whilst the medical categories covered about 2 per cent of the school population, the committee expected that about 20 per cent of children would exhibit SEN at some time during their school careers.
2. There should be new forms of assessment of needs, to create a clear and detailed statement. Children whose needs could not be met within the resources of the ordinary school should have a record (which came to be called a 'statement') of their SEN drawn up by a multi-professional team. A detailed procedure was proposed for assessing and 'statementing' children with SEN.
3. Parents should have more rights to be involved in assessment and make known their views.
4. Wherever possible, children with SEN should be educated in ordinary, mainstream schools alongside their peers (the principle of integration). Three main types of integration were identified: *Locational* integration provided special units/classes on the site of an ordinary school; *Social* integration involved sharing time and space with ordinary children outside the classroom; *Functional* integration involved sharing lessons full- or part-time with others.
5. Positive discrimination of this kind required extra resources (material, human and in terms of expertise).

Behaviour

During the 1970s there was growing evidence that young people were rebelling against education whilst still conforming in some ways, either by accepting some aspects of the status quo or conforming to the dictates of their peer group. Evidence of disenchantment could be seen in the many pieces of observational research in schools which revealed the dynamics of classroom interaction and anti-school subcultures. Thus Pink Floyd's record 'Another Brick in the Wall' (1979) could become an anthem for disenchanted youth and a reflection of the spirit of the time. 'Dark sarcasm in the classroom' was not only noted in pop lyrics but also in research findings about the hidden curriculum and the role of the teacher in sometimes reinforcing negative identities. Yet, if there was a new dimension to studies of classroom interaction, it was in revelations about pupils' creative roles in reinforcing their own inequalities (Willis, 1977). By effectively saying that 'We don't need no education' (Pink Floyd) anti-school subcultures were reinforcing their own subordination and supporting the status

quo. Punk rockers could go even further by literally spitting at society and the older generation who seemed to have given them a dismal future! Expectations were not only derived from teachers but also from a society facing a decline into economic crisis, with fewer jobs available and a growing sense of insecurity.

Yet many of the disenchanted youth of the 1970s became Conservative voters in the 1980s, and there may be many explanations for this. Certainly by 1979 there was a groundswell of public opinion in favour of some sort of radical political change. Not only was change desired by social rebels but also by traditionalists concerned about the declining moral character of young people. From the mid 1970s onwards some sociologists were identifying the development of moral panics in response to the (imagined!) behaviour of teachers, young people and black youth in particular (e.g. Hall *et al.*, 1978; Cohen, 1973). Yet those same sociologists were also noting that public reaction and blame was often directed away from government management of the economy and towards the victims of economic crises.

Torytown and Labourville

Although Labourville retained and consolidated its comprehensive school system during the 1970s, changing governments were met with almost predictable responses in Torytown. In 1974 a Labour government (Circular 4/74 and Circular 112/74) once again told LEAs to make plans to form a comprehensive secondary system and Torytown maintained its delaying tactics until the election of the next Conservative government. Indeed, locals claimed that some of the headteachers appointed in the 1970s as heads of the forthcoming comprehensive schools were still heads of secondary modern schools at the end of the 1980s.

The Torytown council managed to resist change from a selective system but could not resist the effects on education of a major reorganization of local authority boundaries in 1974. Although the new authority maintained its support for selective education, it did address one of the anomalies in the process of selection. Until the 1970s the grade necessary for a pass varied from school to school in order to ensure that at least some of the children attending schools in particularly deprived areas moved to a grammar school. As relatively few families appealed against results, it could be assumed that they knew nothing about the system, trusted the decisions of experts, felt incapable of taking action or simply regarded educational successes or failures as personal and private. However, the new LEA introduced a standard pass rate throughout the borough, all children having to achieve the same standard in tests and assessment in order to get a grammar school place. As a result, the proportion of 11+ passes in some particularly deprived areas of the borough became very low and some primary schools sent no children to grammar school.

Unfinished business

As usual, many of the recommendations made in official reports were not applied because of opposition from some educationalists or politicians. Torytown was not the only LEA to resist government directives concerning comprehensivization. As in the 1960s, a Labour government's efforts to introduce comprehensive schools throughout the UK met with different responses from LEAs. Circulars 4/74 and 112/74, the 1976 Cowan and Dickson reports and the 1979 Benn Report were all met with some opposition and their directives and recommendations were largely abandoned when a new Conservative government was elected in 1979.

A core curriculum (proposed in the 1977 Green Paper, *Education in Schools*) was finally implemented in most of the UK as a result of the 1988 Education Act. However, unlike in England and Wales, a Scottish 'national curriculum' was not established by law, and it is difficult to gauge how much influence the Munn Report (1977) actually had on schools. Proposals for a 'licensed teacher' scheme were to be raised in future, but the scheme envisaged in the 1972 James Report met with strong opposition from the teachers' unions and little action was taken to try to implement it.

The 1974 Finer Report on single-parent families was not debated in Parliament until over a year after it was published and few of its recommendations were implemented. Indeed, by the end of the 1970s, action to support the increasing numbers of (usually female) single parents and their children even seemed to be out of place alongside cuts in public spending and a growing moral underclass discourse. Although the 1975 Sex Discrimination Act provided the legal basis for equal opportunities for girls, the 'radical changes' envisaged in girls' curriculum choices were not introduced. Nursery and day care provision was expanded but still did not meet the demand. Care for school-age children outside school hours and in the holidays received little attention. Even in the 1990s little information was available on the extent to which schools were aware of, and providing for, the special needs of children from one-parent families, which by then formed about one-fifth of all families with children.

10

The 1980s

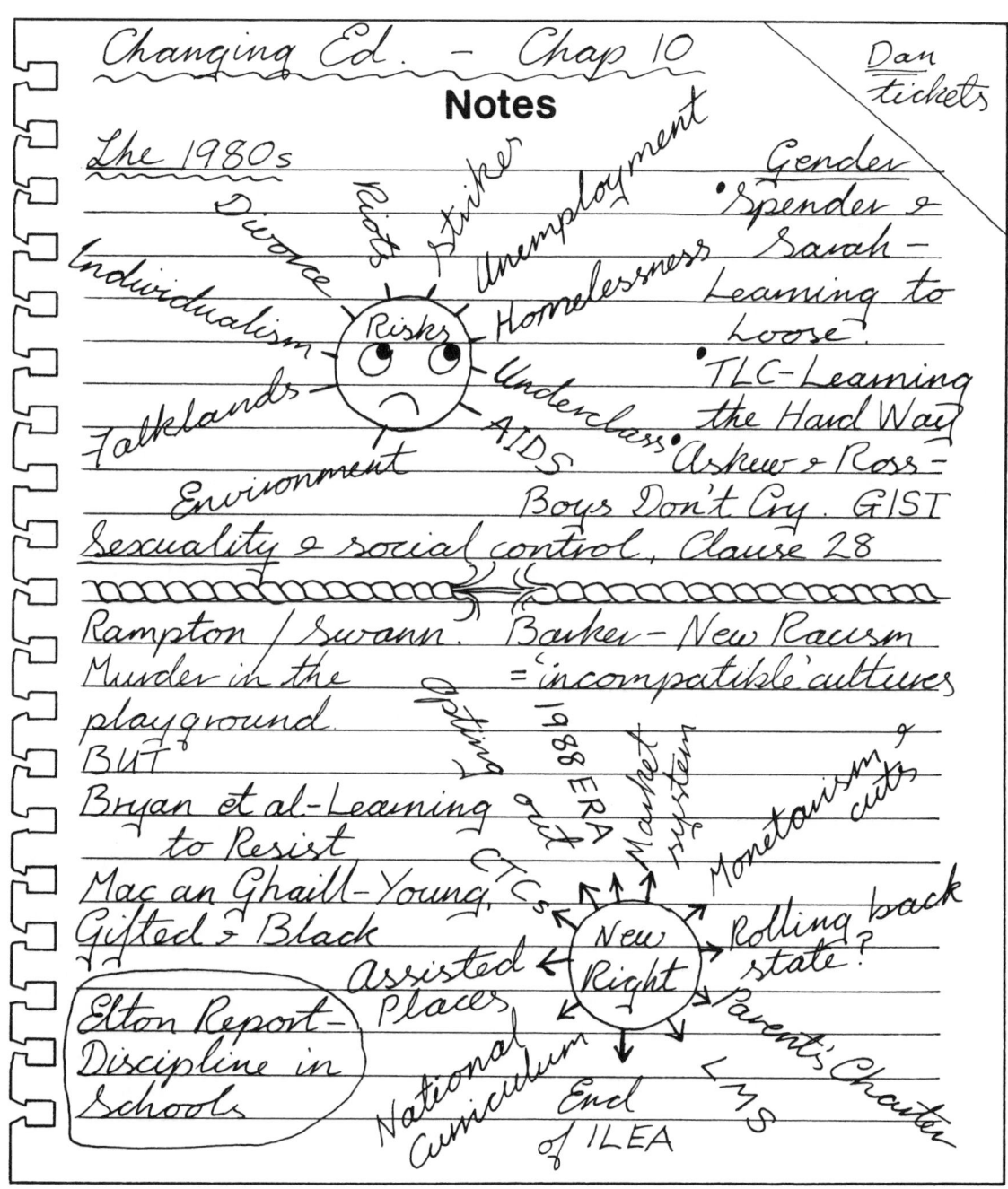

Changing Ed. — Chap 10

Notes

Dan tickets

The 1980s

Risks:
- Divorce
- Riots
- Strikes
- Unemployment
- Homelessness
- Individualism
- Falklands
- Environment
- AIDS
- Underclass

Gender
- Spender & Sarah — Learning to Loose.
- TLC — Learning the Hard Way
- Askew & Ross — Boys Don't Cry. GIST

Sexuality & social control. Clause 28

Rampton / Swann.
Murder in the playground.
BUT

Barker — New Racism = 'incompatible' cultures

Bryan et al — Learning to Resist

Mac an Ghaill — Young, Gifted & Black

New Right:
- opting out
- CTCs
- 1988 ERA
- Market system
- Monetarism & cuts
- Rolling back state?
- Assisted Places
- National Curriculum
- End of ILEA
- LMS
- Parents' Charter

Elton Report — Discipline in Schools

Socio-economic change – Changing perspectives – Changing school systems – Further and higher education – Teachers and lecturers – Class and status – Gender – Ethnicity – Religion and morality – Special needs – Behaviour – Torytown and Labourville – Unfinished business

The Labour left – hard, soft and in-between – hate the idea that people should be able to choose. In particular, they hate the idea that parents should be able to choose their children's education. The Conservative party believes in parental choice.
  Prime Minister Margaret Thatcher, quoted in The Times Educational Supplement, *16 October 1987*

Socio-economic change

With hindsight, socio-economic change during the 1980s seems to be so firmly linked to political perspectives that is hard to distinguish between the two. The economic crises of the 1970s had led both Conservative and Labour parties away from Keynesian economics and towards monetarist policies. Even before the election in 1979 of a Conservative government committed to expenditure cuts, the Labour government of 1974–9 had gradually started to tighten its budgets. The hope was that a reduction in public spending would help to reduce monetary inflation but, for a long time, inflation remained high whilst unemployment also increased. As unemployment reached 1 million, the Conservatives' 1979 general election slogan of 'Labour isn't working' was pasted over a picture of a long queue of unemployed people. Yet the willingness of Conservative governments to introduce more radical spending cuts resulted in even more dramatic rises in unemployment throughout the 1980s.

Responses to the growing climate of individualism and competition (for jobs and material goods) varied. To many it was an almost indiscernible change, as old social norms drifted into new norms but, throughout the 1980s, there was also social unrest as many challenged the government's policies and its authoritarian style. The decade started with urban street riots, which were followed in the mid 1980s by protests about the introduction of a poll tax and a lengthy period of strikes. The miners' strike (1984–5) may have attracted the most public attention but there were also strikes by many other workers, including teachers. Extremes of wealth and poverty were becoming more noticeable as it became easier to identify an underclass of the long-term unemployed.

The nature of family life continued to change as the number of divorces and single-parent families continued to rise, many unmarried couples were living together (including openly gay couples) and more people experienced complex family networks consisting of step-parents, step-children and siblings with different parents. From the early 1980s onwards new fears about AIDS seemed to check a gradual movement towards sexual freedom and contributed towards a moral climate in which those who favoured economic liberalism still felt able to oppose sexual liberalism.

New fears were also emerging about the environment, along with debates about risks and uncertainties. Indeed, as relationships between capitalist and communist states started to improve and fears about nuclear war started to wane, they were replaced by other worries about the viability of the planet. A series of environmental disasters (e.g. at Chernobyl and Bhopal) and concerns about the greenhouse effect and loss of the ozone layer meant that environmental issues entered mainstream public debate and became a more noticeable part of the school curriculum. Such fears were compounded by more immediate feelings of increased vulnerability to unemployment, marriage breakups, sickness and crime. Yet at the same time the 1980s was the decade of the yuppie (young urban professional) and material wealth for many people, particularly for the successful entrepreneurs, those who were engaged in business and finance and many private employees. Unfortunately some sociologists (e.g. Maguire and Ashton, 1981) still found that there is no perfect link between educational achievement and advancement in employment. At a time when the emphasis was on individualism, enterprise and competition, it was easy for even some highly educated individuals to fall behind.

Changing perspectives

By the 1980s it was possible to identify extreme differences between the One Nation Conservatives of the past (now called 'wets' to reflect their softness) and the New Right government under Prime Minister Margaret Thatcher. Mrs Thatcher summed this up in a speech to the Conservative Conference of 1980 when she countered suggestions that she might change her policies (take a U-turn) by saying, 'U-turn if you want to. The lady's not for turning'. The pluralist tendencies of previous Conservative governments were replaced by a firm self-belief that would not falter in the pursuit of even apparently unpopular policies. Paternalist attitudes of the past were abandoned in favour of enforced self-sufficiency and a belief in self-regulation via the introduction of a market system to most public services. Indeed, even the former Conservative Prime Ministers Edward Heath and Harold Macmillan (now the Earl of Stockton) criticized the new style of Conservatism for going too far. In 1986 (speech to the House of Lords) the Earl of Stockton famously accused the government of 'selling the family silver' by privatizing profitable nationalized industries. Even the Black Paper critics of previous Labour governments were not entirely supportive of New Right policies. The 1986 booklet *Whose Schools?* (written and published by the Hillgate Group) maintained the perspective offered by the Black Papers and seemed to be promoting New Right policies. Yet Brian Cox, who edited the Black Papers, resisted the notion that schools could be run as part of a market system.

Throughout the 1980s Mrs Thatcher ensured that each Secretary of State for Education shared her own brand of Conservativism. Indeed, Sir Keith Joseph, who replaced Mark Carlisle in 1981, was one of Thatcher's mentors and was assiduous in developing and promoting the ideas of the New Right. In 1986 Joseph was replaced as Secretary of State for Education by Kenneth Baker, who managed the passing and implementation of the 1988 Education Reform Act, and in 1989 Baker was replaced by John MacGregor.

The Great Debate emerging from the 1970s grew even more intense during the 1980s as New Right governments increased their criticisms of education for not effectively preparing children for work in a competitive economy and not applying enough attention to parents' wishes. At a political level, debates continued to shift from concerns about equal opportunities to the concept of employability and questions about whether schools, colleges and universities produced school leavers and graduates with the sort of skills needed in the market place. Efforts to increase equal opportunities were regarded as a failed social experiment and the supposed move towards progressive teaching methods was seen as having damaged educational standards.

> The false prophets of the 1960s gravely damaged British education. Instead of concerning themselves with standards and skills, they preached the virtues of 'progressive' education and 'spontaneous self-expression'. They tried to use schools as an instrument of social engineering.
>
> Conservative Research Department, 1985, p 282

Here we can see the assumption of being in the right ('false prophets') that was to characterize Conservative rhetoric throughout the 1980s and 1990s. This set the tone for conflicts between governments and social scientists throughout the 1980s, as social scientists habitually identified and examined common assumptions, norms and discourse in general. In his critique of what he called the 'economic utility challenge' to education, Bailey argued that, by virtue of its implicit assumption of consensus about society, the economic utility model of education favoured by recent governments was essentially indoctrinary (Bailey, 1984). Whilst president of the British Educational Research Association, Patricia Broadfoot saw the rhetoric used and its emphasis on administration and efficiency as a means of legitimating Conservative ideology.

> The effect of this trend is not only to preclude explicit discussion of the different educational values that might be involved in any particular issue, but also to conceal a growing lack of consensus over educational priorities in general by defining them off the agenda of debate.
>
> Broadfoot, 1985, p 273

Margaret Thatcher regularly claimed a monopoly of traditional virtues for the Conservative Party and interchanged expressions of truth and value to suggest that they had the same meaning.

Most of us were brought up to respect these values. I respect them today, for they are the traditional values of British life. And as the false values of Socialism fade, so those true and traditional values are returning to our country.

Thatcher, at the Conservative Women's Conference, 1988, quoted in the *Guardian*, 26 July 1988

Even after years of Conservative government, it was still being claimed that too many educationalists were being influenced by 'false values'. In 1987 the *Salisbury Review* (source of the earlier Black Papers) described the Department of Education as being 'rotten with leftist ideology, and well-stocked with conspirators anxious to impose that ideology throughout the world of education'. Baroness Cox, a former contributor to the Black Papers who had been made Conservative education spokeswoman in the House of Lords, claimed that

Education has been turning into indoctrination. There are a growing number of education authorities and teacher groups who are committed to politics in the classroom.

Cox, addressing the Freedom Association in 1987

This image of left-wing teachers was not entirely accurate because, even in the 1983 general election, the Conservative Party was the most popular party among teachers, receiving 44 per cent of their votes. It is possible that they reduced their support for the party in subsequent elections, not because they had become more left wing, but because the party had become more right wing. At the Conservative Party Conference in 1987, Margaret Thatcher provided a long list of criticisms of an education system that her government had already been responsible for for eight years.

And in the inner cities – where youngsters must have a decent education if they are to have a better future – that opportunity is all too often snatched from them by hard-left education authorities and extremist teachers.

Thatcher, quoted in *The Times Educational Supplement*, 16 October 1987

Implicit in such arguments was the assumption that only a Conservative government could be trusted to manage the UK's system of education and to defend it against the threat of dangerous political

(i.e. left-wing) elements. It could even be claimed that politics should be taken out of education, as though education were purely a private and technical problem and solutions could be arrived at objectively (see McKenzie, 1995). After eight years in power, the government had achieved some success in its efforts to disassociate itself from faults in the system by laying the blame elsewhere. Thatcher continued to attack 'anti-racist mathematics', teachers who defended the individual right to be gay and the Labour Party's approach to parental choice. Yet, when making such criticisms she could ignore or sanction possible right-wing indoctrination: for example, during the 1987 general election campaign, she visited Waldersdale Secondary Modern School, where Conservative hats, stickers and flags were handed out to pupils.

Although sociological perspectives during the 1980s tended to be critical of New Right education policies, their criticisms were not uniform because they came from the many perspectives within sociology. The Centre for Contemporary Cultural Studies, for example, was influenced by Marxist critiques and in *Unpopular Education* (CCCS, 1981) argued that the models of equal opportunities favoured by past governments had also been deficient. Such models had involved less interest in the education of children than in their selection and the identification of hierarchies (whether via the 11+ or streaming within schools), which led to the educational failure of many children. From this point of view the education policies of the New Right, with an emphasis on standards and selection in the 1988 Education Reform Act, were not such a departure from the policies behind the 1944 Education Act (Griggs, 1989).

The influence and development of traditional sociological interests could also be seen as feminists studied anti-sexism and sexuality, specialists in race and ethnicity studied anti-racism and work specialists studied vocationalism and the Great Debate. It was, however, possible to see that sociologists and educationalists responded to the government-sponsored discourse by politicizing their studies. Quality, control and accountability had always been considered as part of systems analysis but they took on a new guise at a time when they signified ways that government could monitor the educationalists and administrators they regarded as inept. Similarly, the phrase 'parental choice' symbolized a particular political perspective and sociologists started to make comparisons between meritocracy and 'parentocracy'. University courses and book titles also started to reflect the influence of the New Right; for example, the Open University provided a course called Policy-making in Education, with a set book that summed up the new educational climate, *Policy-making in Education: The Breakdown of Consensus* (McNay and Ozga, 1985).

Changing school systems

The proportion of comprehensive secondary schools continued to grow during the 1980s, although less quickly than in the 1970s. In 1971 approximately 36 per cent of secondary schools in the United Kingdom were comprehensive but by 1988 this was 87 per cent (Educational Statistics for the United Kingdom 1989, London, HMSO). However, proportions varied in different parts of the UK: in 1987/8 the figure in Scotland was 99 per cent, in Wales 98 per cent and in England 86 per cent (Government Statistical Service, 1989, Table 18), but the much smaller proportion in Northern Ireland reduced the percentage in the UK as a whole. The growing numbers of comprehensive schools could still be misleading, as some were situated in an area where partial selection remained.

QUESTION

What sort of partial selection could prevent a school from being genuinely comprehensive?

Throughout the 1980s major changes to school systems undermined the comprehensive ideal and some of them were so dramatic that it is fair to ask whether it was appropriate for the governments of the time to describe them (as they did) as 'reforms'. Indeed, far more official documents (including reports and legislation) were produced during that time than in any previous decade. The 'breakdown of consensus' described by McNay and Ozga (1985) could be seen as a major shift of influence as the previous 'triangle of tension' was replaced by the allocation of more power to

central government, at the expense of LEAs and teachers. This shift was sustained by the 'discourse of derision' and its allocation of blame for educational 'failures' to LEAs and teachers. Conservative governments gradually reduced the amount of influence LEAs had on the types of schools provided in their areas (largely by promoting grant maintained schools and city technology colleges) and acquired a tighter control of LEA spending. Although there had always been conflict between central governments and those LEAs controlled by an opposing party, the Conservative governments of the 1980s were not prepared to tolerate the incompatible influence of Labour-controlled LEAs. For example, the Inner London Education Authority was abolished, despite opposition by most local parents, because its Labour policies were seen as a major challenge to the Conservative government. In theory, the New Right were opposed to centralization and wanted to reduce the responsibilities of central government (by 'rolling back the state') but, in practice, its hostility to local government and teachers was used to justify more government intervention. In effect, many responsibilities were taken away from LEAs and shifted upwards, to central government, and downwards, to schools and parents.

In the 1980 Education Act the shift of responsibilities from LEAs to central government could be seen in various ways:

- Assisted Places were created. Central government would pay all or part (depending on a means test) of the tuition fees for academically able children to move from maintained (usually LEA) schools to selected independent day schools.
- LEAs were no longer obliged to provide free school milk or provide school meals, although LEAs could provide them if they wished.
- It limited the rights of LEAs to refuse to provide primary, secondary or further education for pupils or students not belonging to their areas.
- It restricted the rights of LEAs in other ways.

The 1980 Act was also known as a 'parents' charter' because parents were given extra rights:

- to choose the school they wanted their child to go to, although the LEA could refuse on the grounds of inefficient use of resources (and the parents could appeal);

- to be represented on school governing bodies.
- LEAs and school governors were also required to provide information to parents on such matters as criteria for admission, exam results, curriculum, discipline and organization.

The Act also:

- required all independent schools to be registered but abolished the previous category of 'recognized as efficient';
- noted that the provision by LEAs of education for the under fives was discretionary.

Also in 1980 the Education (Scotland) Act consolidated various measures enacted separately during the 1960s and 1970s. It covered public (i.e. the name for maintained schools in Scotland), grant aided and independent schools. Shifting control upwards, it empowered the Secretary of State for Scotland to issue regulations governing the conduct and responsibilities of LEAs. Shifting downwards, it defined the responsibilities and rights of parents. It also established the Scottish Examination Board to conduct Scottish Certificate of Education (SCE) exams and set up committees for negotiating teachers' pay settlements, laying down arbitration procedures where agreement could not be reached. In 1981 the Education (Scotland) Act also gave parents in Scotland the right to choose which school their children should attend.

In 1980 central government also increased its control of LEAs via the Local Government and Land Planning Act, which introduced a new system for allocating grants to local authorities (block grants and grant-related entitlement). Instead of being based on local authorities' previous expenditure patterns, the levels of grants were to be calculated in future according to the authority's score on a range of factors which the government decided were likely to affect its expenditure. Penalties were imposed for spending above the recommended level.

As the 1980s progressed more and more reports and regulations were produced relating to what was offered by schools, whether this was in terms

of the formal curriculum or regarding the physical resources offered. In 1982 the Cockcroft Report (*Mathematics Counts*) studied mathematics teaching in primary and secondary schools in England and Wales in light of the needs of pupils when they moved to further and higher education, employment and adult life in general. This was in keeping with the growing discourse about employability. It tried to identify needs and addressed detailed recommendations for meeting them in central government, LEAs, examination boards, teacher training and funding bodies for research and curriculum development. More general recommendations included recognition of the diversity of pupils' abilities, and a 'differentiated curriculum', with a range of exam papers provided. In general it advocated a 'new progressive', 'new mathematics' approach which was not consistently well received by traditionalists. Also in 1982 the Schools Council was replaced by the School Curriculum and Development Committee (SCDC) and a Secondary Examinations Council (SEC) and in 1983 the Secondary Examinations Council and School Curriculum Development Committee were formed.

Although changes to the curriculum were being mooted, public debates in the early 1980s were starting to focus on what parents could see more clearly – the effects of spending cuts on the physical resources available in schools. In 1982 Her Majesty's Inspectorate found that an increasing reliance by state schools upon contributions from parents was leading to 'marked disparities' in the standard of schooling between affluent areas and areas serving the poor. Spending on school books in state schools fell in 1984/5 in real terms by £5.1 million, whilst in the same year in the independent sector, spending on school books doubled (Bosely, 1986). The 1984 Education (Grants and Awards) Act reduced LEAs' control over how the block grant was spent by allowing central government to allocate sums of money to LEAs for particular educational purposes. Hopes that LEAs could raise extra funding elsewhere were largely dashed by the 1984 Rates Act, which gave central government the power to set an upper limit to rate increases. The 1984 Education (Grants and Awards) Act enabled central government to allocate directly a small proportion (up to 1 per cent) of the block grant for specific educational projects which the

Secretary of State judged to be important and thus reduced further the local authorities' control over how the block grant was spent.

These changes in funding were noticed by some of the interviewees in Torytown and Labourville.

[Eldest child attended a comprehensive school during the 1980s.] It was a very, very good school at the time. As comprehensives went, it was excellent. That was mainly due to the excellence of the headmistress at the time, Mrs [. . .], who was absolutely first rate, and she created an atmosphere in that school that was conducive to learning. Most of the children there did very, very well. The money was coming into the schools at that time in the early part [of the 1980s], which then trickled, or eventually almost dried up. Certain things that particularly annoy me were subjects like CDT. I remember visiting the school and seeing children making things like skis, actually things that were of value, that the child could stand back and say, 'Yeh, I created that'. The satisfaction the child got must have been difficult to put a price on. And then by the time my son was leaving that school, I was giving them wood; I was getting wood out of the skip at my college and taking it to them and they were making things out of paper, dancing dollies and all sorts. Well, I thought, 'This is pathetic'. So we'd seen a complete turn-round to where CDT was more 'design a kitchen', but they never really made anything, because they hadn't got any materials to make anything with anyway, and the tools had dwindled away. I thought that was outrageous. So that was one area where my son was adversely affected.

John, 1997

The 1985 White Paper *Better Schools* made it clear (e.g. section 286, p 85) that extra government expenditure on education could not be expected and that improvements would have to be financed by improvements in efficiency and effectiveness. Despite what seemed to be a firmly entrenched discourse of derision, the language used in the paper lacked the strident critical rhetoric of other Conservative pronouncements at the time. Yet its reflection on the expansion in education since 1944 could be used to justify its claims that improvements could be made within existing financial constraints.

. . . the school system of England and Wales can take credit for much progress since the war.

Through the addition of two years to the compulsory period, the system now offers to all, not just a fraction of pupils, a secondary phase long and broad enough to lay the foundations for adult life and work in the world of today and encourages 47 per cent (compared with 13 per cent in 1947) to continue in full-time education until at least age 17. So far as the maintained sector is concerned, in 1954 three primary school classes in every five had more than 30 pupils, and half of these had more than 40; in 1984 only one in every five had more than 30, and less than one in a hundred more than 40, pupils. Between 1954 and 1984 the proportion of secondary school classes with more than 30 pupils fell from nearly one-third to less than one in ten. These improvements enable teachers to pay more regard to the needs and progress of the individual pupil. School provision for the under fives now extends to 43 per cent of 3 and 4 year olds compared with 21 per cent in 1972 and 15 per cent in the 1950s and 1960s.

Better Schools, 1985, London, HMSO,
Cmnd. 9469, section 4, p 2

Better Schools set out the action the government intended to take in four areas of policy:

1. to secure greater clarity about the objectives and content of the curriculum;
2. to reform the examinations system and improve assessment so that they promote more effectively the objectives of the curriculum, the achievements of the pupils, and the recording of those achievements;
3. to improve the professional effectiveness of teachers and the management of the teaching force;
4. to reform school government and to harness more fully the contribution which can be made to good school education by parents, employers and others outside the education service.

The fourth of these policy areas was addressed in 1986 in two Education Acts. All maintained schools were required to have a governing body with increased parental representation and a formula was set for the numbers of parents, representatives of voluntary organizations and LEA representatives. Governors were required to present an annual report and to arrange a meeting with parents to discuss it. Governors could determine the school's policy on sex education, prevent 'political indoctrination', and ensure that children with special needs were identified and suitable provision made. Corporal punishment in maintained schools was to be prohibited from 1987 and independent schools could not use it on pupils whose fees were paid by the state.

The first two of the policy areas listed in *Better Schools* were discussed throughout the mid 1980s, as plans were prepared for the introduction of a National Curriculum. The government set up a Task Group on Assessment and Testing (TGAT) to devise assessment arrangements, which reported its findings in the 1987 Black Report, *National Curriculum Task Group on Assessment and Testing*. The TGAT recommended that pupils should be assessed at four key stages, at the ages of seven, eleven, fourteen and sixteen. Assessment would involve teachers' evaluations of their pupils' attainment and pupils' performance in standard assessment tasks (SATs), which would be set nationally (although teachers could select from a wide range of tests). Aggregated tests results would be published in a report about the school's work as a whole. Most of the recommendations of the Black Report were initially accepted by the government, although the aggregated results for schools were ultimately published in the form of 'league tables', and not as intended in the report. The TGAT model was used as a framework by the national curriculum subject working groups when drawing up programmes of study and attainment targets. However, the assessment arrangements were gradually simplified and teachers' assessments were reduced in importance.

Whilst plans were being made for a National Curriculum the government was also planning to increase the number of schools financed directly by government grant, rather than by the LEA. At the Conservative Party Conference in 1987, the Secretary of State for Education, Kenneth Baker, said that the broad scale and intention of the educational reforms to be introduced by the 1988 Act could be summarized as 'choice, freedom, standards and quality control'. These would be improved by an increase in the number of grant maintained schools, which would provide a 'half-way house

in education' between the 93 per cent in the LEA sector and the 7 per cent in the independent sector. The government hoped that a large proportion of maintained schools (as many as 24,000) would in the future 'opt out' of LEA control to be maintained by a government grant. Such plans were met with suspicion, not only from opposition parties but also from education experts. Sir Toby Weaver (ex-Deputy Secretary at the Department of Education and Science) said the idea that so many schools could have a one-to-one relationship with the Funding Council was 'Alice in Wonderland'.

The 1988 Education Reform Act introduced so many changes to schools in England and Wales that we could ask whether the word 'reform' was appropriate. Its directives and requirements included the following:

- It introduced a National Curriculum for pupils aged five to sixteen in all maintained schools (i.e. not in independent schools). Attainment targets were being set for each of its constituent subjects at the ages of seven, eleven, fourteen and sixteen. Although the implementation of these plans suggested increased expenditure, central government did not propose to significantly increase its grants to local authorities.
- The SEC and SCDC were being replaced by a School Examinations and Assessment Council (SEAC) and a National Curriculum Council (NCC).
- LEAs were required to delegate certain responsibilities for financial management to the governing bodies of schools. This has been called local management of schools (LMS).
- Established mechanisms to ensure that limits set to the number of pupils being admitted to a maintained school were not lower than the school was physically capable of accommodating. Parents may send their children to any school that had room for them, provided that it catered for their age and aptitude.
- Allowed a maintained secondary school, or a primary school with over 300 pupils

(extended in 1990 to all primary schools), to opt out of LEA finance and control and be given 'grant maintained' status. This would require a resolution by the governing body, the consent of a majority of those parents who voted in a secret ballot, and the approval of the Secretary of State. If fewer than half the parents voted, a second ballot must be held within fourteen days and its results would be binding, regardless of how many parents voted. The school would then own its own premises, employ its own staff, and receive an annual grant directly from central government. The character and size of the school could not be altered without the consent of the Secretary of State.

- Introduced city technology colleges, which were originally meant to be financed by business.
- Abolished the Inner London Education Authority, transferring its responsibilities from April 1990 to the inner-London boroughs and the City of London.

The 1989 Education Reform (Northern Ireland) Order introduced into Northern Ireland most of the reforms initiated by the 1988 Education Reform Act. There was to be a similar common curriculum and pattern of assessment, and a comparable scheme for delegation of financial management to the governing bodies of schools. However, opting out would only be permitted where a school sought 'grant-maintained integrated status' and moved towards the full integration of Protestant and Roman Catholic pupils.

The 1988 School Boards (Scotland) Act established school boards for Scottish schools, with strong parental and community representation. These had rights to be informed and consulted about their schools' education, disciplinary and financial policies and achievements, and the appointment of senior staff. In 1989 the Self-Governing Schools etc. (Scotland) Act established procedures whereby Scottish schools could 'opt out' of finance and control by education authorities and receive funding directly from the Scottish central government. However, by 1994, only one school had done so.

QUESTIONS

Notice that the 1988 Education Reform Act did not apply to Scotland and Scotland has no statutory national curriculum. What reasons could there be for this?

Discuss the possible reasons why a school may choose to opt out of LEA control.

How rigidly has the National Curriculum been followed in different schools and LEAs? (See Bowe and Ball, with Gold, 1992, for claims that it has been taken up differently, leading to different outcomes.)

Further changes during the late 1980s focused again on the curriculum. In 1988 the Kingman Report (*The Committee of Inquiry into the Teaching of English Language*) recommended a model of how the English language (spoken or written) worked, which would form a basis for teacher training and professional discussion of English teaching. It also recommended how this model should be made explicit to pupils and what pupils should be taught and be expected to understand by the ages of seven, eleven and sixteen. This had considerable impact. However, the 1988 Higginson Report (*Advancing A Levels*) was immediately rejected by the government. It recommended more co-ordination of the work of examination boards, a reduction in the number of separate syllabuses in each subject and a compulsory core common to the remaining syllabuses. A fifth of A level assessment should be based on coursework and full-time students should study a wider range of subjects (five A levels plus one AS level).

Although there was resistance to changes to A levels, in 1988 the General Certificate of Secondary Education was introduced in England, Wales and Northern Ireland. In Torytown Sharon experienced not only a new form of assessment, but also other dramatic changes.

> I think for years and years under the old O levels they just churned out the same old texts, year after year, and I think someone one day just turned round and said, 'Hang on a minute. This is all so completely out of date'. Hence GCSEs. We were the first year to do the new GCSEs, and we were an all-girls school and they amalgamated us with the boys, and it was like all these things all in one go.
> Sharon, 1997

Further and higher education

Changes to further and higher education during the 1980s were largely inspired by changes in the job market and responses to this from a government with a firm belief in market forces. As the job market collapsed, more young people were forced into unemployment or became reluctant stayers-on, thus postponing acquisition of the adult status associated with a job (Brown, 1989). It was clear that the problems normally associated with youth were taking on a new dimension. Donald explained how it affected his son.

> Well, the thing is, his education was all right until he left school and he'd got no job to go to. So he went to these job creation schemes, which is the biggest con there ever was. All it was was cheap labour. I mean, I saw all this because the firm I worked for actually got kids in and the way they were treated was terrible. I had damn big rows at my work about it, because they were working as hard, if not harder than the men that earned the money, but they never got paid for it, and that's just what happened to [son 'Ryan']. The wrong part about his education was the advice that the careers officer gave to [Ryan], that he should go on these job creation schemes instead of going to college, and that was ridiculous. Now all our other children had gone from school to college, and I believed what they were saying [about Ryan], and it's proved wrong. He was nearly twenty-four before he got a permanent job. You know, he had worked all the time but it was only temporary. He did work with the [. . .], he did work for [. . .], and they all said how good he was, and he worked in sports, in a sports complex. They all said how good he was. He was a damn good worker, keen to learn, all this paraphernalia, but as soon as the time came, they got rid of him and started a new one, because it was cheap labour. I think it's all wrong. I shouldn't have listened to the careers officer. That's my only complaint about his education. Now since then, he's started part-time at college and he's doing bloody marvelous at college . . . I think he left school about 79 or 80.
>
> Donald, 1997

In 1982 the Thompson Report (*Experience and Participation*) reviewed the Youth Service and re-commended that a government minister should be appointed to co-ordinate the work of all departments concerned with youth affairs. There should be more funding and clearer national objectives. It also suggested that the Youth Service should be attempting to meet the 'crucial social needs' of the 11–20 age group, especially the unemployed, the handicapped, girls and young women, and ethnic minorities. Most of these recommendations were rejected in a formal government response two years later. Instead, the government focused on new initiatives for the training of school leavers, the assumption being that young people were unemployed because they lacked the skills valued in a competitive job market.

In 1981 a government White Paper (*A New Training Initiative – A Programme for Action*, Department of Employment) introduced one year of training for all school leavers aged 16–7. As part of that initiative, the Manpower Services Commission (in 1983) introduced a Youth Training Scheme (YTS), consisting of employer-based schemes for young people aged 16–17, and the Technical and Vocational Education Initiative (TVEI) for young people aged 14–18. In 1985 the Certificate of Pre-Vocational Education (CPVE) was introduced in the form of college-based schemes for young people aged 16–17. The form of funding for most of these schemes again reflected the gradual loss of local authority control. In 1985/6 the government took 25 per cent of the funding for non-advanced further education from the local authorities' budgets and gave it to the Manpower Services Commission, which was attached to the Department of Employment.

Once such schemes were in place, the government was able to claim that no young person should be unemployed and not in receipt of some sort of training allowance. As (in theory) training places were available for all who needed them, the government withdrew Income Support for 16–18-year-olds in 1988. Problems soon emerged when it became clear that there were not enough training places available and that some young people did not have any means of financial support. Some of those who had no practical support from their families even became homeless and resorted to begging on the streets. Yet Income Support was not restored and begging gradually became a familiar sight on British streets. Homeless people found it difficult to acquire a job or training without an address of their own and so a spiral of social deprivation remained even at the end of the century.

Expenditure cuts during the 1980s also meant that some financial support for students in higher education was withdrawn. Reductions in spending on student welfare not only matched the government's policy of cutting public spending but also matched its plans to expand higher education without increasing costs. Local authorities were still expected to pay students' fees and mandatory student grants but central government was able to reduce its own contribution. In 1984 the reimbursement of student travel costs was abolished (except in Scotland) and in 1985 the minimum maintenance grant for students was also abolished. Special equipment grants for specified courses were abolished in 1986, students' entitlement to Supplementary and Unemployment Benefits during Christmas and Easter vacations was abolished and Housing Benefit for students in halls of residence was abolished.

During the 1980s various reports were produced about higher education before more radical changes were introduced by the 1988 Education Reform Act. In 1982 the Chilver Report (*the Future of Higher Education in Northern Ireland*) recommended changes to the New University of Ulster, Ulster Polytechnic and Queen's University, Belfast, although some of these changes were overthrown in 1985 when the New University of Ulster and Ulster Polytechnic amalgamated to form the University of Ulster. In 1982 the Swinnerton-Dyer Report studied 'The Support of University Scientific Research' and in 1985 the Lindop Report investigated 'Academic Validation in Public Sector Higher Education'. However, as with the school system, it was the 1988 Education Reform Act that dominated change in higher education during the 1980s.

The 1988 Education Reform Act not only reduced LEA control of schools but also its influence on higher education. It also initiated changes to the contracts of staff who had been criticized for having too much power. Changes included the following:

- Polytechnics and some other colleges of higher education were removed from LEA control, making them 'free-standing statutory corporations'.
- LEAs were required to delegate certain responsibilities for financial management to the governing bodies of those larger colleges remaining under LEA control.
- Responsibility for administering the funding provided by central government was given to the Universities Funding Council (UFC) and the Polytechnics and Colleges Funding Council (PCFC). Although officially independent from the government, members of these bodies were to be appointed by the Secretary of State.
- New university teaching staff would no longer be given academic 'tenure' (which had meant that they could only loose their jobs because of professional misconduct) and tenure would be removed from staff in posts who moved to a different university or accepted promotion within the same university.

Teachers and lecturers

Right-wing perceptions of teachers as left-wing subversives pursuing trendy ideas have always been at odds with left-wing claims that teachers are authoritarian conformists, reinforcing the dominant capitalist ideology. Research seems to suggest that it is more accurate to see teachers as being somewhere between both extremes, but with heterogeneous political identities. In the 1983 general election the Conservative Party was still the most popular party among teachers, securing approximately 44 per cent of their votes in England and Wales compared with 26 per cent for Labour and 28 per cent for the Alliance (MORI and TES polls, 1987). They could hardly be described as radical left-wingers. However, it is possible that most right-wing sympathies were with the old style of Conservatism, associated with paternalism and a strong welfare state, rather than with the New Right and its policy of withdrawing support for state education. As the 1980s progressed, the government's policies irritated teachers more and more until, by the 1987 general election, the Conservative Party was the third most popular party among teachers, behind the Alliance and Labour. Even so, as 46 per cent of teachers in England and Wales intended to vote Alliance, 28 per cent Labour and 24 per cent Conservative, the swing was to the middle rather than to the left (MORI and TES polls, 1987). In Scotland and Northern Ireland this swing was less clear-cut due to the impact of nationalist parties. The voting intentions of teachers were, however, noticeably different to those of voters in general, as 43 per cent of the UK's electorate intended to vote Conservative in the 1987 general election (TES, 5 June 1987).

The status of teachers was challenged throughout the 1980s, as their pay fell behind that of other 'professionals', they lost some of the independence they had previously had in the classroom and their representatives were gradually excluded from policy-making processes (McNay and Ozga, 1985). Yet responses to changes in their status, and in education in general, were divided, as some felt that they were barred by professional ethics from taking the radical political action proposed by others. Many teachers experienced a period of slow radicalization, with their complaints directed at a right-wing government, whilst others were more inclined to localize or individualize their problems.

The decade started with the 1980 Chilver Report (*The Future Structure of Teacher Education in Northern Ireland*), but its suggestions for changes were opposed by both Catholic and Protestant churches and not adopted. In 1982 the Cockcroft Report (*Mathematics Counts*) studied mathematics teaching in primary and secondary schools in England and Wales in light of the needs of pupils when they proceeded to further and higher education, employment and adult life in general. It made recommendations about how those needs could be addressed by teacher training institutions, the recruitment and retention of more well-qualified mathematicians through financial incentives, flexible salary structures and guarantees of employment, and increases in in-service training and support. With regard to content, it advocated a 'new progressive', 'new mathematics' approach that was not popular with some traditionalists. Furthermore, in 1984 a government White Paper, *Teacher Quality*, was more critical of teachers and helped to generate more resentment.

By the mid 1980s teachers were not only annoyed at their own treatment by the government, but also resentful about the effects of the government's expenditure cuts on state education. Between 1984 and 1986 there was a particularly intense period of confrontations between teachers' unions and their employers, whether seen as central government or the LEAs. Interpretations of the reasons for strike action were heavily dependent on political perspectives; for example, Phillip Merridale, the Chair of Hampshire Education Committee and Conservative Leader of the Employers' Panel within the Burnham Negotiating Arrangements up to 1987, saw the issue as being about control over teachers and their work (Ball, 1990, p 171). Ultimately the dispute did lead to a shift from teachers being autonomous decision-makers to people who implement policies made elsewhere. Yet, to many teachers, the conflict was about even more than that, as it was about the future of the education system in general.

At a local level, most strike action did not involve a total withdrawal of labour and sending children home from school. It was more likely to involve the withdrawal of some (rather than all) labour, and especially affected extra-hours activities. Teresa and Sharon remembered how it affected them in Labourville and Torytown.

There were not many [teachers' strikes] at [. . .] High. I was only out for maybe a couple of days. What I think they used to do was, sometimes other people who were not on strike would cover their classes, so we didn't get to go home anyway. I may have been out for a couple of days.

Teresa, 1997

When they merged us [single-sex boys' and girls' schools] we were the first year to do the GCSEs. Half of them were off doing teacher training because none of them knew what they were doing, because this new GCSE had just come in, and the rest of them were blooming supply teachers because they were all on strike. It was barmy. English was the worst one, because we used to have a really, really good English teacher, and we used to have supply teachers in and out. Geography was another one. And it does influence you a lot, because if you've got a good teacher you want to stick with it. Because supply teachers are a waste of time.

Sharon, 1997

. . . not one of our major international competitors treats education and training with the contempt we currently do in this country . . .

At a fundamental level we believe it is important to recognize that the education system has been 'hijacked' by a narrow market-determined view of what 'education' should provide. In doing so, schools and teachers have been scapegoats for the broader failings of governmental policy. Education has thus become easy prey for expenditure cutbacks and has laid itself open to the introduction of specious tests of effectiveness and performance. We disagree with this way of looking at the role of education in society. In our view, the so called 'great debate' of the mid-1970s which was supposed to have provided pointers for a more responsive education system, in fact began the process by which schools and the teaching profession officially got a disproportionate share of the blame for Britain's deteriorating economic performance. In effect the 'great debate' has provided a false prospectus upon which the government has launched its attacks on state educational provision . . . In the last few years it would not have mattered how much schools had turned out youngsters according to the model supposedly laid down for them by industry in the 'great debate'. The jobs for these youngsters had simply disappeared. Yet schools and teachers have somehow continued to be singled out for the failures of an economic system that is wholly outside their control.

NUT, 1985, pp 4–5, 9 and 21–23

Question

Discuss arguments for and against the NUT's point of view.

As political conflict over education escalated during the 1980s, teachers responded by dividing further, rather than forming a united force. Teachers could be in one of several trade unions, some of which (for example, the Professional Association of Teachers) refused to take strike action. Others became particularly active in their opposition to government policies, and the National Union of Teachers often provided a vehicle for their discontent. In 1985 The National Union of Teachers published a pamphlet in which it attacked government policies in vehement tones.

Ken Jones (1983 and 1985) argued that professional ideals prevented teachers from being more politically active. Writing of the NUT, he observed that even this supposedly radical union was restrained from taking political action by its concern about the image of professionalism.

A too-consistent pattern of militancy, political alignment and educational controversy seems from the perspective of professional unity to jeopardize the union's highest ambitions, since the conferral of self-government upon an unruly teaching force would be impossible.

Jones, 1985, p 241

The argument rested, he said, on the

. . . belief that the nurture of children is a task which is politically and ideologically unproblematic and must therefore be kept free from political controversy and 'interference'.

Jones, 1985, p 242

Nevertheless, teachers were more active in this particular arena than most other social groups and their action was met with further constraints by central government. In 1986 the right to decide how sex education was taught in schools was taken out of the hands of teachers and LEAs and given to school governors, and corporal punishment in maintained schools was to be prohibited. This was followed by the most contentious of the government's actions when, in the 1987 Teachers' Pay and Conditions Act, it imposed on teachers a formal contract of service with fixed hours of work and abolished the negotiation procedures set up in the 1965 Remuneration of Teachers Act (negotiation via the Burnham Committee). Instead of negotiating pay changes with the teachers' unions, the Secretary of State was authorized to appoint an interim advisory committee to impose teachers' pay and conditions. Later, in 1988, the International Labour Organization ruled that the removal of teachers' negotiating rights did not conform to international standards of freedom and fairness.

It was no surprise that few teachers voted Conservative in the 1987 general election and 77 per cent of teachers regarded education as the most important political issue in the election. Even the occupations of candidates reflected major differences in the relationship between the parties and the education systems, as far more teachers stood as candidates for the Labour and Alliance parties than for the Conservative Party (See Figure 10.1).

Many lecturers were just as critical of government policies as were teachers and in 1988 the NATFHE annual conference passed a motion (in tones that made the NUT pamphlet look moderate by comparison) that England was

> ... a squalid, ugly, uncomfortable place, an intolerant, racist, homophobic, narrow-minded, authoritarian rat-hole, run by vicious, suburban-minded materialist philistines.
>
> Based on a quote from the
> film-writer Hanif Kureishi

Yet, despite such political rhetoric, research by Denver and Hands (1992) actually suggested that teachers' political preferences were not likely to rub off on their pupils. They also found that the teaching of A level politics was relatively safe and innocuous because sixth-formers taking such courses in England and Wales had significantly higher levels of political knowledge and sophistication than those who did not study politics and were more likely to support a party because of its politics than to take a lead from their parents or teachers.

Despite indications that this was already starting to happen, Ball claimed that it was the 1988 Education Act that predicated on an entirely new relationship between the state and teachers (Ball, 1990, p 172). The Act ensured that teachers would in future be treated as employees rather than as professionals. Local management of schools meant that they would be employed by individual schools, rather than LEAs, and no longer bound by LEA equal opportunities policies or by arrangements for the protection of their jobs from redundancy (LEAs could previously move a surplus teacher from one school to another). Falling rolls could also lead to the loss of some jobs. School staff would be split into those with primarily teaching roles and those with managerial roles, as headteachers and their deputies became more involved in budgeting and marketing. The new set of formal expectations and conditions also included a new contract, revised pay structure and appraisal in the workplace.

Class and status

During the 1980s sociologists' interests in socio-economic equalities were starting to change to fit in with changing discourses about the effects of economic crises and the shift towards what many saw as a postmodern or late modern society. Thus, when Halsey, Heath and Ridge analysed data collected during the 1970s for the Oxford Mobility Study (1980) they were interested in the usual concepts of social class, social mobility and meritocracy. In particular they studied the effect of type of school and qualification on the occupational attainments of men in pre- and postwar Britain. They found that before the war middle-class boys had a greater chance of going to grammar school or public school, but that the expected increase in the social mobility of working-class boys after the war had not happened. The occupational gap between service (middle) class and the working class was even greater than the pre-war one and changes in the labour force had mainly benefited marginal members of the dominant class. Following this important but relatively restrained analysis came more radical critiques from the CCCS (1981) and W.J. Wilson (1987). Wilson argued that a new 'underclass' of the dispossessed was emerging in apparently affluent late capitalist societies, and his critique became influential in new sociological analyses of long-term unemployment, homelessness and associated subcultures.

Figure 10.1 Number of candidates at the 1987 general election who were teachers

	Lecturers	Teachers
Labour	102	86
Alliance	89	57
Conservative	24	26

Source: The Times Educational Supplement, 5 June 1987.

Throughout the 1980s an increasing amount of evidence was emerging about the consequences of relative deprivation. For example, in 1987 a BMA report produced a mass of evidence showing how deprivation generated by unemployment and low pay caused sickness and premature death. Wives of unemployed men had higher death rates than those married to wage earners, their babies suffered higher death rates, their children were shorter and young unemployed people were more likely to use drugs. Its findings were, moreover, directly related to education as it noted that

> Young people are held back from achieving their full physical and mental potential by the debilitating effects of unhealthy environment, lack of emotional support or intellectual stimulation.
>
> BMA, 1987

When Income Support for 16–18-year-olds was withdrawn in 1988 it was clear to the government's critics that medical and social problems would be exacerbated.

Evidence of the relationship between socio-economic status and educational achievement continued to emerge throughout the 1980s although, as it was becoming more difficult to operationalize 'social class', researchers were focusing more on clearly identifiable groups such as one-parent families, those who were low paid, the unemployed and the homeless. Records were still, however, showing some relationships between occupation and educational. The DES Statistical Bulletin 13/84 (1984) listed the proportion of homes in an area with a manual or non-manual head of household, which could be related to A level results (Reid, 1986). An average of 28 per cent of homes in England had a non-manual worker as head of household, but in Surrey this was 50 per cent and in Knowsley (Merseyside) 11 per cent. In the same year 15 per cent of pupils in England gained one or more A level passes, compared with 22 per cent in Surrey and 8 per cent in Knowsley. The same bulletin also revealed significant differences in the O level results in different areas.

QUESTION

What other factors could have affected these findings about differences between areas?

Researchers found that children from low-income families were likely to have less time for schoolwork because they were more likely to take paid work in order to meet their basic needs (Finn, 1984). Also housework and unpaid family labour tended to fall more heavily on working-class than middle-class pupils and far more heavily on girls than boys (Griffin, 1985).

By the 1980s some researchers were considering the impact of comprehensivization on social class inequalities but it was difficult to do this at a national level because so many school systems remained. Even where comprehensive schools existed in one area, some of the local children may have been 'creamed off' to attend a selective school elsewhere. Research in Scotland could be more useful because Scotland had a larger proportion of comprehensive schools than other areas of the UK, and there was less 'creaming off'. McPherson and Willms (1987) studied the effects of comprehensive reorganization in Scotland and found that differences in the attainment of middle-class and working-class pupils remained but were smaller in comprehensive schools. The trend towards equality of attainment was especially marked in schools that had been comprehensive for a long time. They found that the result was a raising of working-class attainment rather than a lowering of middle-class attainment and that the feared levelling down had not happened. This suggested that comprehensivization had been successful in undermining class differentials, but it was still difficult to make comparisons as little research had been done into the effects of a tripartite system and many factors other than school type had to be considered. Moves towards new forms of selective education (e.g. parental choice) during the 1980s and 1990s also undermined the potential for further research in other parts of the country.

Research into classroom interaction continued to provide evidence of processes by which socio-economic inequalities were compounded in schools. By the end of the 1980s Brown (1989) was able to identify two general approaches used by sociologists when studying social class and pupil orientations. First, an educational differentiation approach (e.g. Bourdieu and Passeron, 1977; Bowles and Gintis, 1976) emphasized how schools discriminate between pupils in order to cool unrealistic aspirations. This cooling out process persuades pupils to 'voluntarily' abandon ambitions, convincing them that it is not the system that is at fault but themselves. The problem with this approach is that it assumes that pupils are passive and that their educational careers are 'determined' by educational processes or social circumstances, yet pupils can actively create their own identities. The second approach is one of cultural differentiation, which implies that working-class pupils voluntarily 'fail' themselves (e.g. Willis, 1977). Brown criticized both approaches, suggesting that both underestimated the range of responses of working-class boys and girls. A more widespread strategy was that of 'alienated instrumental orientation', a limited form of compliance. Pupils would seek modest successes, including decent jobs with good rates of pay, and many were willing to exchange some effort at school for modest levels of attainment.

In a study of middle-class youth that provided a useful comparison with that of Willis (1977), Aggleton (1987) argued that, whether compliant or rebellious, middle-class pupils who resisted schooling were advantaged in the labour market in general terms. Even at a time of high youth unemployment, all of Aggleton's middle-class 'resisters' were in employment six years after his study. Their jobs also tended to be in service industries or in industries related to symbolic production and the arts, rather than in the manual work (or unemployment) experienced by working-class resisters.

So, what were government reactions to socioeconomic inequalities during the 1980s? In 1987 Walker and Walker (for the Child Poverty Action Group) complained that 'The government views inequality as being helpful to incentives at both ends of the income distribution and does not regard gross inequalities in income and wealth as a problem'. From a New Right perspective inequalities stimulate competition in a healthy market system and efforts by a government to tackle such inequalities would just lead to an overburdened state. Whereas earlier governments had provided free milk and food in schools in order to ensure that poor children received at least some nourishment during their school day, the Conservative government believed that increasing affluence made such provisions out of date and that their withdrawal would help to reduce public spending.

Therefore, the 1980 Education Act removed the obligation for LEAs to provide free school milk or school meals. In 1986 the Social Security Act moved further, stating that (from 1988) LEAs no longer had the power to supply free school meals or milk to any children other than those from families receiving Income Support. Moreover, they would no longer be obliged to supply free school meals or milk to *any* children, even those from families receiving Income Support.

Whilst efforts were being made to reduce spending on state schools, the government was supporting the private provision of education as a way of encouraging self-sufficiency by families who could pay for their children's education and therefore relieving the pressure on the state. The government contributed towards the fees for some children to be privately educated (Assisted Places) and encouraged private businesses to contribute towards the state system via the funding of city technology colleges and sponsorship of various items and activities in other schools. As a result of this new ethos, the independent school population rose from 5.9 per cent of the total of UK schoolchildren in 1980 to 7.3 per cent in 1989. If these figures included the sixth-form school population, the proportions would be even higher. In view of this expansion in private education, in 1989 Oxford University offered an increased proportion of its places (48 per cent) to those from independent schools. By the end of the 1980s one of the authors of *Origins and Destinations* (1980) was noting that the writers' earlier concerns about the level of social inequalities remained.

> So we have a striking contrast. There has been constantly rising educational attainment . . . during the course of the twentieth century. But class inequalities first in access to selective secondary schools then at O and next perhaps A-level, have shown no overall tendency to decline . . . In the face of this remarkable resilience of class inequalities, educational reforms seem powerless.
>
> Heath, 1989, pp 186–7

Gender

The diffusion of feminist perspectives continued throughout the 1980s. Second-wave feminism had been based around notions of a common experience and the common interests of all women but this fundamental tenet of 'sisterhood' was challenged by black women within the women's movement (e.g. Davis, 1981). White feminists were accused of being naive in their judgements about minority lifestyles and of failing to address racism both outside and within the movement. In the UK black radicals argued that the experiences of Afro-Caribbean, African and Asian women challenged feminist orthodoxy (Carby, 1982; Amos and Parmar, 1984) as women from different ethnic groups had distinct traditions and concerns which were not reflected in the women's movement. Similarly, other feminists argued that they were marginalized by the domination of the women's movement by white middle-class radicals. During the 1980s ever-increasing numbers of factions emerged, such as postmodernists, poststructuralists, humanists, Muslims, Christians and ecofeminists, who were particularly inspired by recent threats to the environment.

Although the women's movement showed some signs of fragmentation, there was still a sense of unity against many common problems. Indeed, a United Nations Report summed up the global nature of gender inequalities by saying that 'Women constitute half the world's population, perform nearly two-thirds of its work hours, receive one-tenth of the world's income and own less than one-hundredth of the world's property' (1980).

Along with the rise in unemployment during the 1980s there was also a rise in the proportion of workers who were in part-time and/or temporary employment. The proportion of male workers in part-time work almost doubled from 3.3 per cent in 1983 to 6.3 per cent in 1992 (Green, Wolf and Leney, 1999, Table C.1, p 266), whilst the proportion of female workers in part-time work increased from 42.4 per cent in 1983 to 45 per cent in 1992. School leavers could therefore see that their job prospects were not only affected by rising unemployment, but also by a reduction in the availability of full-time work. Girls were more likely to assume that, even if they married and/or had children, they would be working for many years to come and education had to be responsive to these and other trends. Further and higher education had to accommodate changing life-cycle patterns by providing nurseries, flexible courses and various ways of staging opportunities. Yet girls and women were still stuck with the image of the 'superwoman' that had both inspired and restrained them.

> A modern woman is expected to tag professional success on to domestic bliss. Ever anxious to please, she is determined to give equal weight to both. The sort of single-mindedness that makes for excellence remains largely a male prerogative . . .
> Holdsworth, 1988, p 59

In the well-known book *Learning to Lose* (Spender and Sarah, 1980) researchers showed how girls were socialized to expect and demand less than boys from their education. Other studies (e.g. Stanworth, 1981) also found that boys tended to demand, and get, more of the teacher's attention in class and that girls had unrealistic ideas about their own capabilities. Again the self-fulfilling prophesy could be seen, as boys tended to over-estimate their own capabilities whilst girls under-estimated theirs. Educational achievements could therefore be influenced by self-belief, or lack of it, whether this was because of feelings of inferiority relating to gender, social class or something else. This relationship was, nevertheless, rather complex. More and more women were continuing to enter further and higher education and find there the sort of opportunities that they either lacked, or did not seize, during their school years. In the book *Learning the Hard Way* (The Taking Liberties Collective, 1989) the educational experiences of over 50 women were published, recording how they had encountered, and sometimes challenged, 'oppression in men's education'.

QUESTION

Look at the section in this chapter about social class. Could any of the theories about social class and education shed light on the affects of gender on education and employment?

In 1986 Lees helped to explain how some girls rationalized their lack of achievement in school. She studied the attitudes of 15–16-year-old girls, from various social class and ethnic backgrounds, in three London schools to discover how they

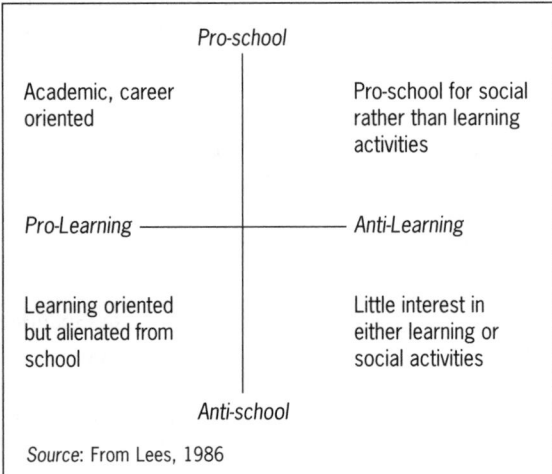

Figure 10.2 Categories of girls' attitudes towards school and learning

```
                        Pro-school

Academic, career                    Pro-school for social
oriented                            rather than learning
                                    activities


Pro-Learning ─────────────┼───────────── Anti-Learning


Learning oriented                   Little interest in
but alienated from                  either learning or
school                              social activities

                        Anti-school
```

Source: From Lees, 1986

described their sexuality and managed their social world. The main attitudes of the girls she studied were categorized into four main groups, as shown in Figure 10.2.

QUESTION

Is this model still useful for analysing girls' (and boys') attitudes and achievements today?

During the 1980s more studies were also starting to emerge about images of masculinity and how these affected education. In *Boys don't cry*, Askew and Ross (1988) studied the role of schools in the construction of masculinity, sexism in school structures and organization, classroom dynamics and women teachers' experiences. They argued that boys were victims of their own socialization, which involved learning to be aggressive and attaching little importance to academic work. Problems were identified in some boys' schools, where it was claimed that a traditional image of masculinity was reinforced by an authoritarian ethos. Askew and Ross also suggested strategies for working with boys and for in-service work with teachers, including workshop sessions, the adoption of anti-sexist initiatives and ways of persuading boys to talk more openly and honestly. Practical advice of this sort was to become even more important in

the 1990s when it was noted that boys' educational achievements had started to fall behind those of girls.

The effects of equal opportunities legislation were becoming more apparent during the 1980s but its effects were limited by attitudes that were still not helpful to equal opportunities. Some LEAs could not understand how their policies could be construed as sexist. For example, in 1984 Bromley Council tried to balance the number of each sex in junior school fourth form classes by keeping eight girls in the third year class for two years. The council acknowledged that the girls had not been kept down due to lack of ability, but nevertheless the girls suffered ridicule from schoolmates and disadvantages in the 11+ examination. In 1988 the Court of Appeal found Birmingham City Council guilty of sex discrimination because in Birmingham there were a total of 520 grammar school places available for boys and only 360 grammar school places available for girls. Girls therefore had to obtain higher marks at 11+ to get a grammar school place.

During the 1980s boys were still more likely than girls to choose science subjects and, in an environment in which science and technology skills were at a premium, this helped men to acquire better-paid jobs. From 1970 to 1985 the most common A levels taken by boys were maths, physics and chemistry, whilst girls' A level preferences during that period changed from English, history and French to English, biology and maths (Statham *et al.*, 1989, p 151). Although more girls were taking a science, biology was still a subject that fitted gender stereotypes (e.g. of female nurses). Such stereotypes were often important to students who even associated them with their personal sexual identity. Measor and Woods (1988) described how a group of girls made a fuss about school regulations requiring them to wear safety glasses for work in physical sciences. It seemed that a distance from the physical sciences was as important to them for demonstrating their femininity as scorn for office jobs was for Willis's lads in order to demonstrate their masculinity. Various schemes, such as the Girls Into Science and Technology initiative, were introduced to encourage more girls to take mathematics, science and technology courses (Kelly, 1981). These had some success, although gendered subject choice was more forcefully tackled by the introduction of a National Curriculum that 'forced' girls and boys into subjects they would not otherwise have chosen. Since then all girls have been required to take a science and all boys to take a language (previously more popular with girls). The monitoring of resources by sociologists and educationalists has also helped to promote more positive images of girls and women in school textbooks.

QUESTION

Did the changes initiated during the 1980s fit the equal opportunities and/or the anti-sexist approach described in Chapter 5?

Not only was the profile of gender inequalities raised by feminist critiques and the women's movement but, during the 1980s, there were also signs that the legalisation of male homosexuality and the development of critiques from the gay movement

---

CLAUSE 28: VIEWS FROM TORYTOWN AND LABOURVILLE

As the debate about Clause 28 of the 1988 Local Government Act was in the air at the time of my first qualitative interviews with the Torytown and Labourville cohort, I asked them, 'Should the government allow teachers to present a favourable view of homosexuality?'

> I think schools need to prepare children for life outside and life as it is, and I think the line should be that there's nothing wrong with homosexuality, but I'm against a strong pro-homosexuality stance. My teaching would be that there are certain people who are like this and, provided they don't harm anyone, let them get on with their lives. I doubt whether a gay teacher could inspire a pupil to be gay unless the pupil was inclined that way.
>
> Jeremy, 1988

Another teacher emphasized the importance of this normative framework.

> I think from a personal point of view that sex education in schools should refer to what the majority of society regard as normal behaviour.
>
> Mark, 1988

Some informants had problems interpreting the supposedly simplified version of Clause 28 in the question.

> Because I don't understand the question. I interpret it as they would be happy to allow them to teach about homosexuality as part of teaching about general life. I wouldn't say, 'No, you can't talk about it or have it in discussion'. It could be just part of their normal teaching about awareness.
>
> Polly, 1988

> I don't understand the question. What's a favourable view? If you said that the government should allow teachers to teach children to tolerate homosexuality I'd say 'Yes'. That's a different thing than teaching them a favourable view. I don't think it's got anything to do with the government.
>
> Jane, 1988

> I don't know the answer to that one. I think that any responsible teacher would not present a favourable view of homosexuality but I think it would be dangerous to ban the subject because, in any discussion you have with pupils about a responsible attitude to growing up, I think it's the teacher's job to answer those questions without bias or prejudice. I think it's an educational matter. If it was found that a member of staff was actually selling homosexuality as a favourable thing then there ought to be some disciplinary action taken by the education authorities rather than the government.
>
> Iris, 1988

Questions

Could the question have been asked differently? If so, how?
Should sex education 'refer to what the majority of society regard as normal behaviour?'
Who should be responsible for deciding on the contents of sex education lessons in schools and why?

---

were also starting to raise awareness of how education represented and treated gay people. This has implications for the social construction of knowledge and interpretive sociologists have also generated accounts of the experiences of homosexuals in academic environments. For example, Trenchard and Warren (1984) found individuals who had been expelled or referred to a psychiatrist when they 'came out'! Jones and Mahony (1989) also criticized the sociology of education for the way it had ignored the promotion of heterosexuality in the past.

Although some sociologists were concerned that teachers were promoting homophobia, some politicians were concerned that teachers were providing a positive image of homosexuality. The government's distrust of teachers was once again shown when in 1986 it shifted responsibility for determining sex education from teachers to school governors and gave governors responsibility for preventing 'political indoctrination'. Section 28 of the 1988 Local Government Act forbade LEAs from promoting 'teaching in any maintained school of the acceptability of homosexuality as a pretended family relationship'. However, many educationalists construed the wording of this amendment as rather vague and questioned the legal right of the government to make such a ruling. It is not certain how much impact this ruling had on schools, although it generated a heated public debate about related issues (see Macnair, 1989, pp 35–9).

Ethnicity

Just as the equal opportunities legislation of the 1970s did not eradicate gender inequalities, so the race relations legislation of the 1970s had a limited impact on racism in education. Once sexism and racism were outlawed at a formal, institutional level, attention was drawn more closely to their more subtle influences on educational experiences. In 1981 Martin Barker claimed that racism had not disappeared but had changed to a stronger emphasis on cultural differences rather than claims to biological superiority. Thus, some minority ethnic groups living in the UK could be regarded

as aliens whilst Mrs Thatcher argued that it was necessary to fight over the sovereignty of the Falkland Islands (about 8,000 miles away from the UK) because 'Their way of life is British; their allegiance is to the Crown' (quoted in Miles, 1993). Barker (1981) described the emergence of a *new racism*, which based its arguments on difference rather than superiority. New racism defined groups not as biological types, but as cultural communities, and claimed that the significance of racism in contemporary societies was exaggerated. Rather than hostility towards other groups being racist, 'new racists' saw it as resulting from the incompatibility of various cultures and the 'natural' wish to be with one's 'own' people.

The implication of Barker's work is that, rather than operating with a single definition of racism, we should talk of many racisms based on different cultural groups. In the early 1980s efforts were made to tackle this by making British education less *ethnocentric* (which means unable to understand the validity or integrity of cultures other than one's own) and aiming to reduce hostilities by providing more *multicultural* schooling (i.e. aimed at teaching pupils about a wide range of cultures). Instead of trying to assimilate children into some sort of British culture, the aim should be to generate an appreciation of cultural pluralism. However, by the 1980s educationalists were observing that a multicultural approach still could not address forms of racism based on appearance rather than cultural differences.

In Chapter 9 we considered why West Indian children, who spoke English as their first language, were falling behind Asian children, who were more likely to speak English as their second language. Research during the 1980s continued to support previous findings about the underachievement of West Indian children (or children with a West Indian background), although the analysis probed further. In a review of 33 studies of the performance of ethnic groups in schools, Tomlinson (1980) noted that 26 of them showed that West Indian children were scoring lower than 'whites' on individual or group tests and that they were over-represented in the category of 'Educationally Sub-Normal' (ESN) children and under-represented in the higher streams of schools. Mabey (1981) continued to study the literacy of children attending Inner London Education Authority schools and found that 'black British' pupils achieved very low scores compared with other groups. Their attainment was only marginally affected by the length of education they had received in the UK, yet those 'Asian' children, who had been fully educated in the United Kingdom, scored as well as indigenous 'white' children. However, many variables must be considered when studying attainment; for example, Mabey also noted that social deprivation accounted for about half of the difference in the scores of black and white children.

The most well-known official reports published during the 1980s were the 1981 Rampton Report and the 1985 Swann Report. In fact both were reports from the same committee, which was set up in 1979 by a Labour government but had its membership finalized by a Conservative government. The committee was to investigate the education of children from all ethnic minority groups. However, the 1981 Rampton Report was an interim report focusing on the education of 'West Indian' children. Just before the Rampton Committee published its interim report its chairman was replaced by Lord Swann, whose name was therefore attached to the final report in 1985. Research for the committee (and both reports) studied school leavers in five inner-city LEA areas where the educational attainment of *every* ethnic group in the study was lower than the national average.

Basing its findings on fieldwork done during 1978/9, the Rampton Report (1981) found considerable underachievement by 'West Indian' children, compared with 'white' and 'Asian' children. Its findings and recommendations included the following:

- Racism was often mentioned in evidence to the committee and it concluded that unintentional racism was widespread and influenced children's performance.
- Discrimination in the labour market led to poor employment prospects for West Indian school leavers and this discouraged some young people.
- Other causes of underachievement included the inadequacy of preschool provision, the prejudice of some teachers against West Indian children's use of English and

inappropriate curricula and teaching materials.
- Some West Indian parents did not do enough to support their children's schools and teachers.
- Careful initial and in-service training of teachers was needed to attune them to the needs of ethnic minority groups and to improve their understanding of a multicultural approach to education.
- Institutions and organizations at all levels were urged to recognize these problems and implement the report's many detailed recommendations.
- The main requirement was for a change in social attitudes towards a greater acceptance of ethnic minorities.

The committee's final Swann Report (1985) was much longer than its predecessor because it investigated underachievement in all ethnic minority groups, including Chinese, Cypriot, Italian, Ukrainian and Vietnamese children, and the particular needs of 'Liverpool blacks' and travellers' children. Its fieldwork was carried out in 1981/2 and its findings and recommendations included the following:

- Differences in IQ were not found to make a significant contribution to underachievement.
- Racism (although largely unintentional) was an important influence on underachievement. This had not undermined the high achievement of Asians, partly because stereotyped views of them were less negative and racism could have different effects on different ethnic groups.
- Although there was still evidence of the underachievement of West Indian children when compared with the other groups, the gap appeared to have diminished in the time between fieldwork for this report and the fieldwork for the Rampton Report.
- A smaller percentage of 'West Indians' (1 per cent) went to university than did people from other ethnic minority groups (4 per cent of 'Indians', 4 per cent of 'Asians' and 4 per cent of 'others' went to university).
- Differences in socio-economic circumstances provided a partial explanation for the

relatively low attainment of Bangladeshi as well as West Indian children and these differences often resulted from racial discrimination, especially in housing and employment.

- Although priority in language teaching should be given to English, linguistic diversity should be considered a positive asset.
- Central government and LEAs should be sensitive to the wishes of some groups to have their daughters educated in single-sex schools.
- It did not favour the creation of separate schools for children from different ethnic groups and believed that the demand for such schools would be reduced if its proposals were adopted.
- More attention should be given to multicultural matters in both initial teacher training and in-service training of teachers, and that effectiveness of racism awareness training be investigated.
- Greater effort should be made to employ and promote teachers from ethnic minority groups, although without positive discrimination or the lowering of standards.
- Problems must be tackled via the education of *all* children, who must learn to understand what was involved in living in a multiracial and multicultural society.

Further evidence of the relationship between the different socio-economic backgrounds of 'West Indian', 'Asian' and 'other' children and their educational achievement was provided from other sources during the 1980s. Craft and Craft (1983) found that, irrespective of social class, 'West Indians' were underrepresented in further and higher education. However, the report also found that a larger percentage of 'Asians' and 'West Indians' took some sort of further education course than was general for the whole population. Eggleston *et al.* (1986) found that in their sample 87 per cent of children from 'Afro-Caribbean' backgrounds had fathers who were manual workers, compared to 73 per cent of 'Asian' children and 69 per cent of 'white' children. In 1985 the first national study of the achievements of young black people in England and Wales was carried out (Drew and Gray, 1989).

It was found that, although social class explained more variation in examination performance than did ethnic group or gender, the combined effects of race, social class and gender still left the larger part of the variation in performance unexplained. Drew and Gray also found that the performance of 'Afro-Caribbeans' seemed to have improved since earlier studies, but still concluded that there had been relatively little change between 1972 and 1985.

The impact of previous research into language codes and Creole interference could be seen in the 1988 Kingman Report (*The Committee of Inquiry into the Teaching of English Language*), which described *variations* in the use of English. It found that, although some dialects and Creole languages differed from standard English, their forms and phrases were not 'bad grammar'. The report recommended that children should learn to write clearly and accurately in standard English but did not favour a return to learning by rote or the 'old-fashioned formal teaching of grammar'. As with the Swann Report, the emphasis was on the priority of the English language; yet there was already an exception in Wales. The 1980 Act provided financial assistance from central government to LEAs, not only for the teaching of Welsh, but also for the use of Welsh as a medium for teaching other subjects.

Throughout the 1980s relatively small-scale studies, taking an interpretive approach, generated further information about racism in the classroom, and how black and Asian pupils responded by forming anti-school subcultures. As part of the research for the Swann Report, Green (1985) analysed interaction in three junior and three middle schools and found that teachers who had highly ethnocentric attitudes differed sharply in their behaviour towards black and white pupils. Boys of European origin were given a lot more individual teaching time and plenty of opportunity to introduce their own ideas into discussions. However, girls and boys of Afro-Caribbean origin received much less individual attention and less encouragement and praise. Wright (1988) conducted classroom observation in a Midlands comprehensive school and found that teachers frequently made racist comments in class. Children who refused to accept these as 'jokes' became known as 'troublemakers', and their disillusionment increased as they moved up the school. By the third, fourth and fifth years they had created an anti-school subculture (structured like a gang), composed entirely of black girls and boys who used West Indian patois to distance themselves from the school and tried to appear threatening. Mac an Ghaill (1988) also described two groups of working-class boys in Kilby School, the Rasta Heads, who were of Afro-Caribbean origin, and the Warriors, who were of Asian (mainly Indian) origin. Both groups saw teachers as authoritarian and had a strong awareness of racism which inspired a celebration of their own cultural origins. They took symbolic possession of certain areas and times within the school and school day and again used language (West Indian patois, Gujerati or Punjabi) as a means of resistance to annoy teachers. Yet the resistance of the Rasta Heads was the most visible, involving open confrontation, whilst the Warriors used more indirect forms of resistance. By adopting such different forms of resistance they seemed to be making their own ironic comments on stereotypes held by teachers about rebellious Afro-Caribbeans and passive Asian schoolboys.

Unlike earlier findings (e.g. Willis, 1977) that white working-class boys resisted both schooling and learning, many of the researchers during the 1980s found that black and Asian pupils often resisted schooling but not necessarily learning. They were generally aware of how disadvantaged they would be in getting jobs when compared to other, white, school leavers. Indeed Eggleston *et al.* (1986) showed that this could be a prime motive behind their decisions to take further education. In theory, black girls would be particularly disadvantaged by both ethnicity and gender, yet Mac an Ghaill (1988) and Fuller (1980, 1983) both found that the black girls they studied tended to use the schools they detested to acquire credentials, because of their realistic appraisal of women's poor chances of becoming independent without such qualifications.

Research during the 1980s generated evidence that the educational experiences of different ethnic groups differed for boys and girls. Driver (1980) studied five multiracial schools and found that 'West Indian' girls did better than 'West Indian' boys but that, among 'whites', boys did better than girls. It was also found that in those schools 'West Indian' children performed better in their 16+ examinations than did 'whites'. This raised the possibility that, although widespread patterns could be discerned, individual school factors might have a significant influence on educational outcomes. Fuller and Mac an Ghaill both found particularly assertive groups of girls of Afro-Caribbean origin. Fuller (1980, 1983) studied girls from Afro-Caribbean backgrounds in a London comprehensive and found them to be critical of many aspects of school and impatient of restrictive routines. They displayed more defiance than many of their white female schoolmates and enough to win the respect of boys in the school. Yet they recognized the importance of credentials and ensured that their behaviour was not so extreme that it could seriously endanger their chance of getting qualifications. Similarly, Mac an Ghaill (1988) found that the Black Sisters, a group of girls of Afro-Caribbean origin, also confused their teachers because of their combination of defiance with efforts to acquire educational credentials.

Bryan, Dadzie and Scarfe (1987) found that black girls described their educational experiences as being primarily defined by their blackness in a negative way. Yet individuals and groups sometimes resisted and not only used education as a source of personal liberation, but also tried to bring about minor or major changes in educational processes. In *Learning to Resist* we see how parents confronted the labelling of their children as 'educationally sub-normal' by, for example, establishing Saturday schools and teaching their children to have pride in their origins. Parents too were resisting the racist knowledge and assumptions they believed that their children were being presented with in schools.

Children were presented with a world view in which blackness represented everything that was ugly, uncivilized and underdeveloped, and our teachers made little effort to present us or our white classmates with an alternative view. Having been raised on the same basic diet of colonial bigotry themselves, they simply helped to make such negative stereotypes and misconceptions about us more credible. According to them, we 'could not speak English' and needed 'special' classes where our 'broken' version of the language could be drilled out of us. We were quiet *and* volatile. Best of all, we were good at sports – physical, non-thinking activities – an ability which was to be encouraged so that our increasing 'aggression' could be channelled into more productive areas.

Bryan, Dadzie and Scarfe, 1987, p 93

Although studies of West Indian children achieved a higher profile during the 1980s, research was also starting to challenge common cultural stereotypes about Asian children, and in particular assumptions that Asian girls who resisted their Asian traditions experienced a strong culture clash. Brah and Minhas (1988) refuted the notion that the education of Asian girls suffered from the tensions between the 'liberal' culture of the school and the 'repressive' culture of home. They pointed out that there was no evidence of greater intergenerational conflict in Asian families than within other communities and that the culture clash argument was based on misleading and ethnocentric comparisons.

Although research into ethnicity and education had a great impact on academia during the 1980s, public debate tended to centre on alleged cases of racism and on the value of anti-racist education. Just as anti-sexist education moved beyond equal opportunities/girl-friendly approaches, so anti-racist education moved beyond multicultural education. Anti-racists argued that it was not enough to simply teach children about different cultures as this did not address racism based on skin colour, which could target people whose families had lived in the UK for many years (perhaps centuries). They also noted (as did the Rampton and Swann Reports) that the multicultural education children experienced in schools often clashed with the racism they were exposed to out of school. What was needed was a change in social attitudes towards a greater acceptance of ethnic minorities. For example, in 1987 many parents refused to send their children to Headfield Primary School in Dewsbury because most of the children there were from Asian families. The children could not mix because their parents did not want them to.

During the 1980s Burnage High School in Manchester had particular problems involving many racist incidents. The school was a single-sex boys' school with a mainly working-class intake. It had already introduced anti-racist policies when,

in September 1986, a 13-year-old pupil of Asian origin (Ahmed Iqbal Ullah) was stabbed to death by a 13-year-old white pupil in the playground. Evidence of a racist motive included the fact that the child who killed Ahmed was later heard by fellow pupils to be shouting, 'I've killed a Paki'. At the time of the third phase of the Greater Manchester Study (and my first interviews), the murder had been receiving a lot of publicity because findings from a lengthy investigation of the circumstances leading up to the murder, and the wider social context in which the murder took place, were gradually emerging. Although the authors of the Macdonald Report (1990) into the murder and the government at Westminster favoured publication, the local authority refused to publish the report because of anticipated legal problems. Parts of the report were released to the press and some newspapers (particularly the right-wing press who associated anti-racial education with left-wing extremism) interpreted the released parts as a criticism of anti-racial education in general.

As the murder at Burnage High School was a topical issue, and the school was not far from Torytown and Labourville, it was included in the interviews in 1988. I tried to assess informants' 'knowledge' about the murder by, first, asking whether the interviewees had heard of 'recent events at Burnage High School in Manchester', second, asking how much interest they had in the subject and, third, what they knew about it. Although many of the interviewees had heard about the 'events', few expressed any interest and very few indeed could provide accurate information. Analysis of the interviews reinforced academic claims that information about the report had been distorted by a biased media before reaching the public, who had then imposed on it their own definitions of reality. Myths had also emerged, based on distorted media reports, hearsay or sometimes half-understood messages. Indeed it was the interviewees with the least knowledge about the murder who tended to make racist comments. Thus, right-wing fears that political education could result in the propagation of left-wing views could be countered by fears that political ignorance could make voters particularly vulnerable to racist or fascist arguments.

Perhaps one of the most probing attempts to understand the circumstances which led to the murder at Burnage High School was provided by Gill *et al.* (1992), who adapted Waddington *et al.*'s (1989) flashpoints model. The original model illustrated various levels of analysis surrounding the individual, who is represented at the central, interactional level. It was originally intended to act as an aid in identifying multicausal influences that could trigger an incident of public disorder. Gill *et al.* adapted these levels to 'provide a lens through which we might specify and interpret the events which led to the murder of Ahmed Iqbal Ullah'.

Gill *et al.* explained the analytical levels as follows:

Structural:	Refers to differential relations of power and structurally-induced conflict between groups perceived as racially different in society.
Political/ Ideological:	Refers to prevailing systems of ideas in play. For instance, racism justified in terms of the prevailing Zeitgeist; anti-racism defended in egalitarian terms.
Cultural:	Refers to the level of lived experience and common-sense understandings within the locality and community, especially as refracted through family and family networks.
Institutional:	Refers to the ideologies, procedural norms and practices which are promoted, sanctioned and transmitted by the school.
Subcultural:	Refers to the children's subcultures.
Biographical:	Refers to factors and characteristics which are specific to the individuals involved.
Contextual:	Refers to the immediate history of a racist incident.
Interactional:	Refers to the actual event or incident, what was done, what was said.

By providing an analysis at various contextual levels this model offers a depth of understanding that would not emerge from analysis at only an individual level. For example, analysis at an institutional level has considered the possible influence of Burnage High School, as a single-sex boys' school, with anti-racist policies. The Runnymede Trust's summary of the Macdonald Report (1989, p 17) asked, 'Did Ahmed Ullah die at the crossroads where the power of masculinity, male dominance, violence and racism intersect?'

The various levels in the model indicate that it would be wrong to suggest that the murder happened simply because Burnage High School was a boys' school. Horrific events such as this are fortunately too rare to simplify in this way. Similarly, when some of the right-wing tabloid press apportioned blame to the school's anti-racist policies, they not only ignored the many other contextual influences, but also distorted the Macdonald Report's criticisms of a certain type of 'doctrinaire anti-racism' that does not integrate the problems caused by other forms of social inequality.

> . . . ostrich-like analysis of the complex social relations which leaves white working class males completely in the cold. They fit nowhere. They become all-time losers. That surely is a recipe for division and polarization, particularly in the area if anti-racist policies.
>
> The Macdonald Committee, quoted in the *Guardian*, 29 June 1988

The Committee wanted to emphasize the importance of effective implementation of anti-racist policies.

> . . . anti-racist policies do not produce racism . . . Badly thought-out and implemented policies may well be counter-productive but certainly no more so than policies that pretend that race does not exist as an issue.
>
> Quoted in the *Guardian*, 29 June 1988

Questions

Does this model absolve individuals of responsibility for their own actions?
How significant was the fact that Burnage High School was a boys' school?
Discuss claims that anti-racist policies produce racism.

> I know about a report that was done on it and about the trouble it's caused with the Asian community. Just general things because in the end I stopped reading it. If it'd been a white boy that had been stabbed, it wouldn't have lasted as long. I thought it got blown out of proportion. It just seemed to go on and on.
>
> Georgina, 1988

Megan commented on media coverage. She had visited the school because of her job and had heard from school staff that the press had got some of their information by asking children questions in the street. The press had also, she said, used cameras with telephoto lenses to peer into the school. She regarded that as unacceptable.

> They get some stories wrong and it makes you distrust the press. The day I went, there was no feeling of racial tension and the children seemed to be mixing well. I did hear a different account to that reported in the press but that was hearsay and I don't know how true it was.
>
> Megan, 1988

Neil worked near the school.

> I'm interested because we see them going to school in the morning and it doesn't surprise me that they have problems because there are some very 'sweet' [being sarcastic] children going to that school and you have to count up to ten! It's not just the whites . . .
>   I don't know why they have to be like that [i.e. racist]. They're growing up together and then all of a sudden they split. Some of the kids I see going to that school are bad news. We were always in trouble but not bashing up people or bus shelters. I don't see why they can't get on together. The other week in our local park [in Torytown] kids were running riot – yobbos. It wasn't racism as they were all white. There were fifty or sixty kids in that park. It was an absolute madhouse. They built a children's playground two weeks ago up the road and the little sods sprayed graffiti all over it.
>
> Neil, 1988

Questions

Discuss Georgina's suggestion that if a white boy had been stabbed, the debate would not have lasted so long.
Discuss the role of the media in reporting racist incidents.

Religion and morality

Throughout the 1980s the Conservative government continued its efforts to reinforce the dominance of its own version of Christianity in schools. Conservatives were not always Christians (or even highly moral in their personal lives) but, under the leadership of Margaret Thatcher, they pursued a belief in the value of schooling as a source of social control, via the perpetuation of 'traditional values'. A distrust of dangerous left-wing influences by trendy educationalists led them (in 1986) to shift the right to decide how sex education was taught in schools from teachers and LEAs to school governors. However, this tended to nullify Clause 28 (of the Local Government Act, 1988), which tried to prevent local authorities (rather than governors) from promoting the 'teaching in any maintained schools on the acceptability of homosexuality as a pretended family relationship'.

Debates leading up to the 1988 Education Reform Act were perhaps more interesting than the Act itself, as the government originally intended a more vigorous approach to the reinforcement of Christianity in schools. Not only did representatives of other religions object, but some Christian priests also objected, partly because it could lead to resentment from non-Christians. Ultimately, the Act required school assemblies to be held, which should be broadly Christian. There would, nevertheless, still be opportunities for the worship of other faiths and individual schools could apply for exemption for all or some of their pupils from requirements that should be broadly Christian. The mixed responses of schools to the requirements of the Act could be seen in complaints from the right-wing pressure group Parental Alliance for Choice in Education (PACE), which claimed that schools in Bradford, Manchester, Ealing and Wakefield had contravened the 'broadly Christian' requirement of the law.

QUESTIONS

Consider arguments for and against the dominance of Christianity in school assemblies.
Discuss reasons why Christian priests might object to attempts to enforce the dominance of Christian religion in schools.

Special needs

It is easy to see progress during the 1980s on special educational needs as consisting of three steps forwards and two steps (or more) back! This is a typical pattern in educational change, as we see that progress often uncovers even more problems than those the changes were originally aiming to address. What follows in this section therefore includes not only lists of changes, but also lists of the further problems that materialized. During the 1980s changes in educational provision for children with special needs were heavily influenced, but not determined, by the Warnock Report of 1978.

The 1981 Education Act, Special Educational Needs, reaffirmed some existing principles but also introduced new measures, including the following:

- It replaced previous categories of 'handicap' with the concept of 'special educational needs' (SEN), defined as existing where a child has 'significantly greater difficulty in learning than the majority of children of his [*sic*] age' or 'a disability which either prevents or hinders him [*sic*] from making use of

educational facilities of a kind generally provided in schools, within the area of the local authority concerned for children of his [*sic*] age'.
- It reaffirmed the principle that children with SEN (and therefore a 'statement') were educated in ordinary schools provided that parental views were taken into account and that such education was compatible with (a) receiving the special educational provision that was required, (b) the provision of efficient education for the children with whom s/he will be educated and (c) the efficient use of resources.
- It noted that some children would be best educated in a special school. At least three groups of children would need such schooling: (a) those with severe or complex disabilities who needed facilities or teaching expertise which would be impossible or very difficult and costly to provide in ordinary schools; (b) those with severe emotional or behavioural disorders who had difficulty in forming any relationships or whose behaviour was so extreme or unpredictable that it caused disruption in an ordinary school or prevented other children from benefiting from education; (c) those whose disabilities may be less severe, but often multiple, and who, despite help, did not flourish in an ordinary school.
- LEAs were given carefully defined responsibilities to identify the needs of children with a learning difficulty and determine the provision required for the child.
- The Act set up a detailed assessment procedure for ascertaining SEN, giving parents the right to be consulted and to appeal against an LEA's decision about appropriate provision.

It has already been noted that, although the 1981 Act was influenced by the Warnock Report, it did not implement all of the report's recommendations. Indeed, Mary Warnock was particularly concerned that, although many of her committee's recommendations were implemented, some of its important features were excluded.

Critics of the Act raised the following points:

- It gave no commitment to the provision of extra resources.
- It did not acknowledge that up to 20 per cent of all children may have special needs. As a result it concentrated on the 2 per cent who were expected to have 'statements' and overlooked the needs of the extra 18 per cent.
- It made school governors responsible for the welfare of children without statements (previously the responsibility of headteachers and LEAs), but governors did not have the resources, expertise or time to help them. No arrangements were made for the training of governors to deal with SEN.
- It stated that one of the reasons for the integration of children with statements of SEN into mainstream schools was the efficient use of resources. Critics said that children should be integrated for educational, not administrative reasons.
- Where children were to be placed had taken precedence over what sort of education they were to receive.
- The necessary in-service training for teachers had not been arranged.
- The Act did not apply to young people aged 16–19 who had been refused places in school or college. A NUT survey in 1982 found that 17 per cent of all LEAs unconditionally guaranteed a place but 10 per cent refused any guarantee.

By the end of the 1980s LEAs and schools were learning to adapt to the requirements of the 1981 Act. However, the 1988 Education Reform Act also had implications for children with special needs. In particular, many people were concerned about how children with SEN would manage to keep pace with other children being assessed at the various stages of the National Curriculum. Ultimately, the effects of the 1988 Education Reform Act included the following:

- Pupils could be temporarily exempted from part of the National Curriculum but continued exemption required a 'statement'.
- Age-related testing on attainment targets meant that many SEN children would be stuck at the low levels.
- The publication of exam results and competition between schools for pupils meant that some schools did not welcome pupils with SEN.
- The extra costs of SEN placed an extra burden on schools which, as a result of the introduction of local management of schools, would now be managing their own budget.
- Special schools were torn between their inclination to include the National Curriculum and their traditionally flexible, developmental curriculum.

As the 1980s ended, new efforts were being made to tackle such issues, including a National Curriculum Council document in 1989 (*A Curriculum for All*) which offered useful advice on school policy (including SEN). Yet problems remained about how to secure excellent, nationwide provision for children with special needs. In addition another 'new' problem was starting to appear on the scene, to be addressed further during the 1990s. Writers such as Jackson (1987) and Morgan-Klein (1985) were raising the profile of the problems experienced by children in the care of their local authority. This was certainly not a new problem, as there have always been orphans and other children without families to care for them. Some educationalists have also been concerned about their welfare in the past. Their particular educational experiences had, nevertheless, been less visible than those of children who were disadvantaged in other ways and it was only late in the twentieth century that research started to highlight their educational needs.

QUESTION

Why has it been so easy for the educational needs of the many children in care to be ignored (e.g. when compared to needs relating to social class, gender and ethnicity)?

Behaviour

During the 1980s public discourse included more and more concern about a supposed lack of discipline in schools. This concern was emerging from a succession of moral panics about rebellious subcultures, teachers with 'subversive' ideas and the unemployability of school leavers. Conservative rhetoric in which an imagined past of order and conformity was compared with current disorder and non-conformity also helped to feed growing anxieties. Many teachers and other educationalists still campaigned for an end to corporal punishment in schools, as they claimed that it contributed to a climate of fear and authoritarianism in schools. As a result, the 1986 Education Act ruled that corporal punishment in maintained schools was to be prohibited from 1987 onwards and that independent schools could not use it on pupils whose fees are paid by the state.

QUESTION

Why do you think corporal punishment was still allowed in independent schools?

Although responses to the abolition of corporal punishment were mixed, many people were asking how teachers could exert discipline in class in a society that seemed to becoming more violent. Before the 1988 Education Act schools were already expected to offer Personal and Social Education but, as more pressure was placed on their timetable by the demands of the National Curriculum, there were fears that the provision of PSE would suffer. The 1988 Act still obliged schools to concern themselves with the moral, spiritual and cultural well-being of their pupils and evidence of this was to be sought by OFSTED inspectors. However, teachers were concerned about how they could provide discipline and moral guidance within a changing framework of control. In the mid 1980s the National Union of Schoolmasters and Union of Women Teachers (NUSUWT) started to monitor the most serious incidents of violence in schools and continued to do so for over ten

TYPES OF DISRUPTIVE BEHAVIOUR

McManus (1989) noted that, although acts of disruption may not be violent, less extreme forms of disruption could cause stress in those sharing the classroom, including teachers and other children. His list of disruptive behaviour has been split into that specifically directed at teachers, that specifically directed at other pupils and that directed (or with little sense of direction) elsewhere.

Aimed specifically at teacher:
   Asking to go to the toilet repeatedly
   Pushing past teacher
   Cheeky/jokey remarks to teacher
   Open abuse of teacher
   Talking when teacher talking
   Refusing to do set work
   Talking when meant to be writing
   Taking teacher's property
   Hitting teachers
   Threatening a teacher
   Rocking on chair defiantly
   Refusing punishment
   Leaving class early

Aimed specifically at other pupils/people:
   Tapping other pupils
   Rude remarks under breath
   Fighting others in class
   Taking pupil's property
   Fighting in yard
   Swearing at pupil in class

Other defiant behaviour:
   Arriving late
   Missing lessons, absconding
   Smoking in toilets
   Playing with matches in class
   Running in corridor or on stairs
   Keeping coat on in class
   Chasing round room
   Setting off fire alarm
   Throwing pencil across the room
   Packing up early, as if to leave
   Unauthorized drawing in book
   Failing to bring homework
   Unruly on way to school
   Graffiti on corridor wall
   Damaging classroom fittings
   Bizarre clothing/make-up
   Attempting smoking in class

THE ELTON REPORT. *REPORT OF THE COMMITTEE OF INQUIRY: DISCIPLINE IN SCHOOLS*

The Elton Report (1989) recommended measures for securing an orderly atmosphere for teaching and learning. It found that the main discipline problem facing teachers was not the rare serious incidents of physical aggression, but the cumulative disruptive effects of relatively trivial but persistent behaviour of the sort described by McManus. Although it offered no simple diagnosis of causes, or simple remedies, it made a wide range of recommendations to teachers, headteachers, governing bodies, LEAs and parents, including the following:

- Ways of helping teachers to become more effective classroom managers through both initial and in-service training.
- Management training for headteachers should help them to encourage a sense of collective responsibility among teachers, and of commitment to school among pupils and parents.
- Schools should try to create a more positive atmosphere based on a sense of community and shared values.
- Parents need to provide their children with firm guidance and positive models of behaviour and schools should do more to prepare pupils for the responsibilities of being parents.
- Pupils should be given more responsibility and their non-academic achievements should be given more recognition.
- School buildings should be kept in a good state of repair and appearance.

Questions

Discuss the positive and negative effects of the abolition of corporal punishment.
Suggest practical ways in which schools can 'try to create a more positive atmosphere based on a sense of community and shared values'.

BALL ON THE EFFECTS OF BANDING AND MIXED ABILITY GROUPING

In 1981 Ball's study of Beachside Comprehensive reinforced earlier findings about the affects of academic grouping on pupils' behaviour. Whilst Ball was carrying out his research the school changed from a system of banding to mixed ability grouping and he was able to monitor the change.

The banding system split pupils into ten classes in each year group: four in Band 1 for the most able, four in Band 2, and two in Band 3 for the least able pupils. This banding system encouraged a polarization between the top and middle bands. Teachers described Bands 1 and 2 in the first year as pliable and a pleasure to teach, but by the end of the second year signs of an oppositional culture were developing in Band 2 (such as absences and the need for detentions, avoidance of extra-curricular activities and the fact that nearly half of them said they disliked school). His findings were similar to those of Lacey in that teachers regarded Band 2 pupils as a discipline problem and Band 1 as ideal type of pupils. Ball saw this anti-school culture as partially a response to failure, with pupils disassociating themselves from a school that devalued their efforts. Pupils also tended to be friends mainly with others in their band and there was some hostility to those in other bands.

When Beachside changed to mixed ability groupings the anti-school subculture that had been concentrated in the middle bands started to disappear. However, the change still did not prevent sharp divisions in friendship according to ability and social class. Teachers still made distinctions between 'bright' and 'average' pupils and regarded some as totally incapable. Moreover, the aspirations of working-class children seemed to have been reduced as they could no longer aim to be top of the class.

years. They, and other pressure groups, argued that something must be done to help teachers to maintain discipline.

Torytown and Labourville

In the mid 1980s both Torytown and Labourville were starting to experience the effects of falling rolls and having to decide how to respond to them. Labourville's large coeducational comprehensive schools experienced problems but had more flexibility than the many single-sex grammar and secondary modern schools in Torytown. By 1985 the Conservative Torytown council was planning to rationalize its system by amalgamating its single-sex schools into coeducational schools. However, they were still faced with the problem of maintaining the viability of some schools as rolls fell even further.

In 1986 the Conservatives lost overall control of Torytown council and it became a hung council with Labour as its largest political group. The Labour and Liberal members together had overall control of the council and agreed to propose a comprehensive system of secondary education. They also started to challenge the practice of paying the fees for some Roman Catholic Torytown children to be privately educated and in this they had some support from the Catholic church. The private Roman Catholic schools to which Torytown sent pupils who had passed the 11+ were split between two diocese outside the Torytown area. One diocese had on various occasions put forward plans to make its school comprehensive in order to match other comprehensive schools in its area. There had, however, been objections from the Torytown council and parents of children currently attending the school. When a Labour/Liberal majority on Torytown council was created in 1986 the council withdrew its objections and submitted plans to the relevant government minister. However, the Conservative minister rejected the plans and did not support comprehensivization. Central government was therefore able to effectively prevent change in Torytown as, by the time the Labour/Liberal majority was lost in a later local election, very little had been done to change a secondary school system that was based on Conservative principles.

Although a system of selection was retained in Torytown, there were some changes to make the process of selection more equitable. In 1989 the complicated system of ranking pupils according to the performance of other pupils (see Chapter 4) was dropped and the Equal Opportunities Commission advised Torytown council that it was discriminating against girls by splitting boys and girls into two groups for selection at 11+.

Unfinished business

The 1980s was a period of such rapid change in education that it hardly seems appropriate to identify unfinished business. Not only were changes introduced and followed up with great speed but it often seemed that as soon as one change was implemented another was launched. Central government was in the hands of one political party throughout the decade and the same party remained in office well into the 1990s. This meant that education did not experience the usual pattern of a new government immediately overturning the plans of its predecessor. Yet this could still happen at a local level as the majority parties controlling LEAs sometimes changed (as in Torytown). The implementation of new policies dictated by central government could also be delayed and some rules could still be adapted at a local level. So, for example, schools sometimes ignored new government guidelines about religious assemblies in order to avoid alienating children who were not from Christian families. Some schools also found it impossible to cope with the demands of the National Curriculum and provided a diluted version until the 1994 Dearing Report reduced the content of the curriculum and simplified assessment arrangements.

Despite the force of change, there were some pieces of unfinished business, and these were often unfinished because they did not fit the Conservative agenda. For example, the recommendations of the 1988 Higginson Report about changes to A level examinations (including more assessment by coursework and a wider range of subjects) were rejected by the Secretary of State as soon as the report was published. A levels had long been regarded as the 'gold standard' of education and any proposed changes were regarded with suspicion.

Discuss the responses of your own schools and/or LEA to central government directives. Can you think of any ways in which they did not follow government directives in the past?

11

The 1990s

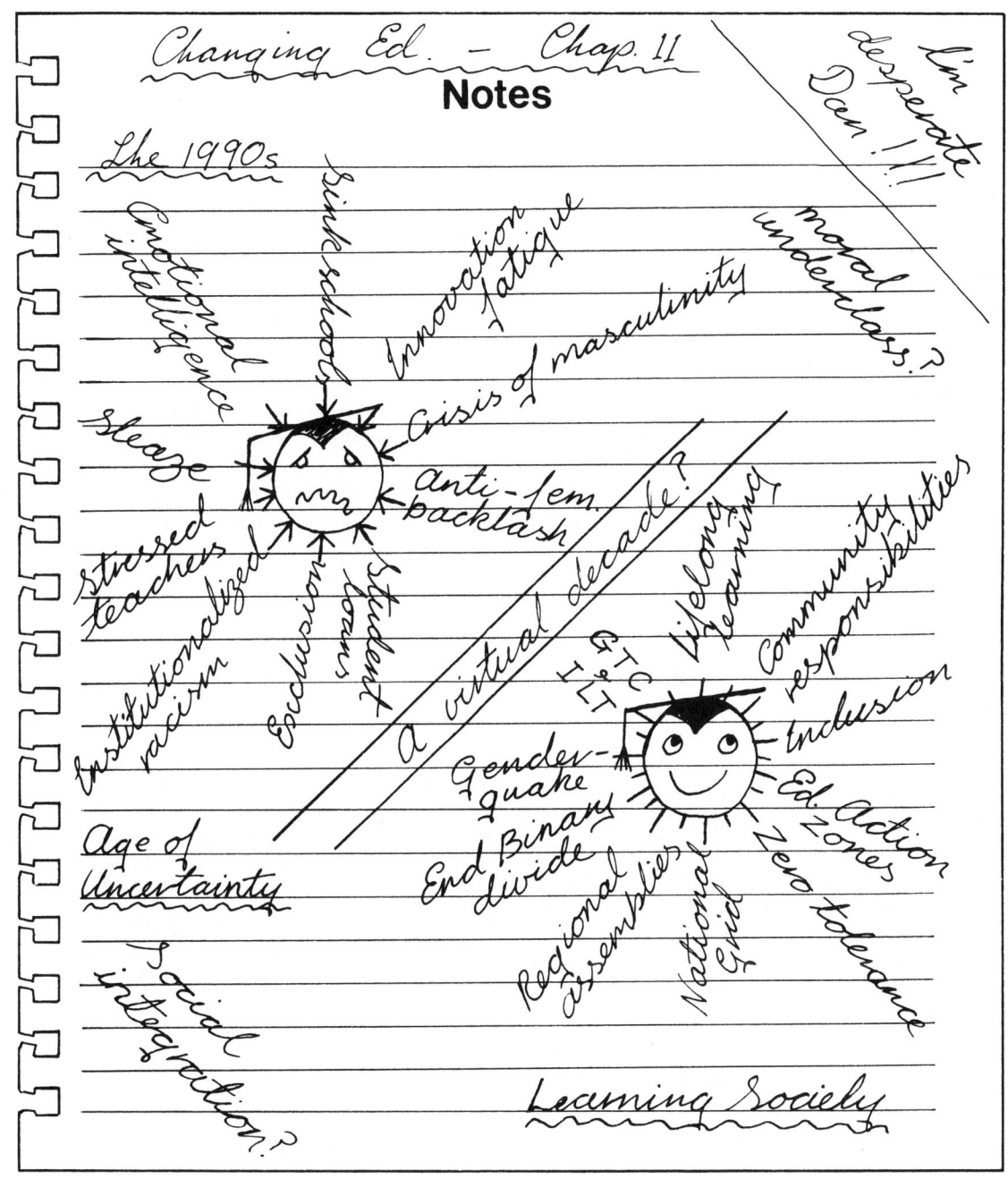

Socio-economic change – Changing perspectives – Changing school systems – Further and higher education – Teachers and lecturers – From class and status to exclusion and inclusion – Gender – Ethnicity – Religion and morality – Special needs – Behaviour – Torytown and Labourville – Unfinished business

. . . the 1990s have often seemed to be a 'virtual' decade, in which history has been abolished, tradition counts for nothing and everything is in a state of flux.

Elliott and Atkinson, 1998, p 250

Socio-economic change

Trying to study present-day society as a historical period demands what may be an impossible leap of consciousness and, as most of this book was written during the late 1990s, hindsight may show that leap to have been unsuccessful. In our everyday lives we are most conscious of our immediate surroundings and what we can physically see, rather than of what is happening to others. This sort of myopia makes it easy to observe events and practicalities but difficult to appreciate trends and changing discourses. Not only does the finding that 'History gets thicker as it approaches recent times' (A.J.P. Taylor, 1970) explain why this book includes more detail about later decades, but it also helps to explain why clarity of vision has gradually become more difficult. Indeed it was more difficult to study this last decade than any other.

It may also be that, as Elliott and Atkinson (1998) suggest, the 1990s were an age of flux and uncertainty, and therefore even more difficult to evaluate. During the 1990s sociologists found it difficult to analyse social structures when they could no longer take for granted structural features such as social class and ethnicity. Definitions of social class became at least problematic and, at most, meaningless, leading studies of social class to become studies of *social exclusion and inclusion*, or of fragmented lifestyles. Similarly, the problems involved in defining ethnicity lead to a greater emphasis on cultural relativism or interculturalism. Sociological studies of work and employment also had to acknowledge that the idea of a job for life, or even for many years, had virtually expired and that it was more meaningful to study fluctuating patterns of work for the majority and long-term unemployment for a minority.

Changing levels of unemployment were difficult to gauge as governments changed the ways the unemployment figures were calculated. However, despite such difficulties, it was clear that levels of unemployment remained high throughout the 1990s and that the social consequences were high. Adult lives had become less predictable as people negotiated many alternative pathways to work or to calamity. One million lost their homes due to mortgage company repossessions between 1990 and 1996; personal bankruptcies in England and Wales peaked at 36,794 in 1992 and even the lower figure of approximately 22,000 a year in 1997 was about three times the 'crisis' level experienced during the postwar recession (Elliott and Atkinson, 1998, pp 151–252). Yet resistance to growing social inequalities seemed muted by comparison with previous decades. The high-profile strikes of the 1970s and 1980s had almost ended by the early 1990s, partly because it was clear that Conservative governments would not give way and partly because the Conservative media seemed to loose interest in reporting them. Even the lengthy industrial action by Liverpool dockers and occasional strike action and demonstrations by teachers, lecturers and students received relatively little attention from the national media. People were still political, and often engaged in direct political action, but the emancipatory politics associated with old social movements, the workplace and the community (as seen in the trade union movement) were being replaced by the sort of identity politics associated with new social movements (such as women's liberation, environmentalism, gay rights, disabled people's rights and animal rights). The loss of long-term community links also meant the loss of a certain type of security.

> Since the Second World War there have been marked trends towards increasing geographical and class mobility. These have brought with them a secular decline in the bonds which historically tied neighbourhood communities, social classes,

religious groups and even families. In one sense this means that societies are less divided. In another, however, and in the absence of new sources of cohesion, it represents a net loss of important sources of collective and group solidarity, and therefore a more individualized society. The indices of this fragmentation – increasing rates of divorce, family break-up and people living alone – are too familiar to require elaboration. As the European Commission report *Accomplishing Europe* notes: 'An individualism not counter-balanced by social obligations is emerging.'

Green, Wolf and Leney, 1999, pp 20–1

Although reductions in the birth rate since the 1960s may have lifted the pressure off the UK's *school* systems in some ways, unemployment and credential inflation actually meant that by the 1990s there was increasing pressure on the *education* system as a whole. The proportion of school leavers in the UK without graded GCSEs, or their equivalent, had been dramatically reduced since the 1970s but there was no certainty that well-qualified school leavers would get good jobs, and there were continuing claims that better results in GCSEs and A levels were not a sign of higher educational standards but of lower assessment standards. Green, Wolf and Leney (1999, pp 34–5) found that between 1990 and 1994 the rate of participation in full-time education per 1,000 people in the UK aged 5–29 rose from 47.1 to 54.7. In every country within the European Union 'pupil and student numbers increased considerably more than would be expected given the universal decline in the 10–19 age group' (Green, Wolf and Leney, 1999, p 35). Thus, more young people were staying in school beyond school-leaving age and more were moving on to further and higher education. The transition of young people from school to the workplace became both more protracted and more complex.

As people learned to expect frequent transitions between different jobs and roles (see Chapter 5 on political and socio-economic change) and the need to acquire new skills, educationalists could see new opportunities but also new challenges. Schools needed to prepare young people to be adaptable, to live with uncertainty and to be imaginative in their career paths. Instead of feeding children with an education, schools had to teach them how to

learn and embrace change. Furthermore, the 'information poor' would lack an adequate preparation for employment by the new and successful 'learning organizations' (Green, Wolf and Leney, 1999, p 9), in which employees would be constantly educated in order to ensure a stock of collective 'organizational intelligence'. Such employers demanded much higher levels of analytical thought than in the past, as well as good communication skills.

Public speculation about the future of education grew throughout the 1990s, promoted by British governments committed to expanding further and higher education in order to generate greater economic prosperity via a 'learning society'. This interest was reflected among social scientists and educationalists. In 1994 the Economic and Social Research Council received 325 applications for its new Learning Society Programme and funded 13 projects (the greatest number of applications in the organization's history). The ESRC programme asked a number of key questions including:

- What are the characteristics of a learning society?
- What are the links between learning and economic success, between training and competitiveness, and between education, innovation and wealth creation?
- What are the theoretical gaps in our understanding of the process of learning and of the complex inter-relationships between employment, training and education?

By the late 1990s there were claims that teachers, lecturers and educational administrators were suffering from innovation fatigue and that consolidation would have been preferred to yet more radical change. Furthermore, there were real concerns about safety in British schools, both in terms of their physical structures and with regard to the people in them. In 1996 16 children and their teacher were shot and killed in a massacre at Dunblane Primary School in Scotland and in 1995 Philip Lawrence, the headteacher of St George's Comprehensive School, Westminster, was stabbed to death at the school gates whilst defending a pupil from a member of a local gang. The Ridings School in Halifax, West Yorkshire, attracted a lot of public interest and was put under special measures for a short time in 1997 because staff could not control many of the pupils (the special measures resulting in dramatic improvements). By 1997 it was clear that the Labour Party could win votes in the general election by promoting its concern about education and it was no surprise that Tony Blair described the three most important issues as 'education, education, education' (*The Times*, 1997).

Interviews in Torytown and Labourville for the fifth phase of the Greater Manchester Study took place just days after the 1997 general election. Some informants therefore reflected at length about the long period of Conservative government between 1979 and 1997. John and Donald took a particularly long-term view, reflecting on how wider social changes impacted on them.

Changing perspectives

As with the 1960s, it is possible to review changing perspectives by splitting the 1990s into separate parts according to which government was in power. During the early part of the decade Conservative education policies still dominated through a Conservative government and towards the end of the decade, after the election of a Labour government in 1997, there were claims that Conservative policies still dominated under a new government! Some people found it difficult to distinguish between the two approaches, although they were emerging from different perspectives (see

---

REFLECTING ON SOCIAL CHANGE: VIEWS FROM TORYTOWN AND LABOURVILLE

I thought it was our last chance to stem a particular attitude of dismantling everything that people of my generation thought was valuable, particularly the National Health Service and the education service. So many things that we took to be the benefits that came out of the Second World War, the 1944 Education Act and all these things, the National Health Service, were set up because these are the promises that are made during a war – the homes fit for heroes and all that stuff. But, nevertheless, a lot of good things came out of that, when you've got a coalition government that were thinking perhaps less selfishly than perhaps governments do at times. This was being dismantled by Thatcherite policies at the time, although they perhaps became watered down a bit eventually (perhaps not so draconian), I felt, and many of the people I work with saw it as our last chance because we could see further education as it stood at the time, just before the election, literally disappearing. I don't think the same threat was there towards higher education, or the school system, but definitely FE was going to be privatized. We're a privatized college now anyway, or a corporation, so we're not fully privatized, but we're a corporation subject to market forces. So that's a *fait accompli*, so we have to live with it and get people in, otherwise you haven't got a job.

John, 1997

Well, I've already said that I think that they [the Conservative governments 1979–97] did a bloody lousy job. Well, I think everything went down, I mean everything. Education, it went a right cropper. Our income, my wife worked damned hard to get a pension, I worked damned hard, never on the dole or anything my full working life, but when I was sixty, well just before I got to sixty, I was made redundant. I was twelve months on the dole, and after that I was told I couldn't get any more dole money, so I asked what I could live on: well you can't have a pension – and I paid all my life, and I had absolutely nothing. When I was made redundant I didn't get a huge pay-out either, I got a minimum payout, but for a couple of years I had to live on my wife's pension, which isn't very nice. It was at the time of my last interview. The only time I got any income, and it was by accident, I got a damned big abscess on the back of neck. So bad I had to go to the hospital with it, and they had to cut it out and all the rest of it. Anyway, while I'm at the hospital they did a blood test on me, and they found out that I'd got diabetes and, through being diabetic and this thing, I had to go on the sick, so I then got an income. I couldn't get another job because of being sick, the diabetes affected my feet, so I just couldn't work, and that's what happened right up until I retired, and that was the only income I got. Now to my mind, if it had been a private insurance company I'd been paying through all my life, I could have sued, but because it was the government, they were just like bloody gangsters taking my money and doing nowt with it. You see, what they do now, they tell everybody to get a private pension scheme going, but when I was younger they told you you didn't need a private pension scheme, we'd be looked after, and this is the way we get looked after.

Donald, 1997

Chapter 3). In general, it seems that weak definitions of equal opportunities and the idealization of parental choice had started to be normalized over a long period of Conservative government and a new government would have expected dramatic change to an alternative perspective to be unpopular. A Labour government was elected not only because it was not the New Right, but also because it was not the 'Old Left'. Just as it took a long time for New Right politicians to promote their opposition to the Keynesian norms of a strong welfare state, so would it take a long time for other politicians to oppose the market-orientated norms that had been entrenched by many years of Conservative government. Efforts by educationalists to promote stronger versions of equal opportunities were suppressed by Conservative and Labour government policies favouring a diverse range of opportunities. What had emerged by the 1990s was an ever-increasing range of different types of schools in the UK and, by the end of the century, little had been done to tackle that diversity.

In 1990 Kenneth Clarke replaced John MacGregor as Secretary of State for Education and Science and in 1992 John Patten replaced Kenneth Clarke, shortly before the election of another Conservative government, led by Prime Minister John Major. During the early 1990s Conservative education policies continued much as they had done during the 1980s, with an emphasis on a competitive market system in which children and parents competed for places in desirable schools, schools competed with each other for pupils, and credential inflation made the competition for jobs even more fierce. Weak definitions of 'equal opportunities' barely entered a political rhetoric that promoted 'choice' and 'parentocracy' and supported moves towards an ever-diversifying schooling system. This could be seen in the titles of government White Papers, such as *Choice and Diversity: A Framework for Schools* (1992) and *Competitiveness – Forging Ahead* (1995). In 1994 Gillian Shepherd replaced John Patten as Secretary of State for Education in the Department for Education (DfE), but in the following year the department merged with the Employment Department to become the Department for Education and Employment (DfEE).

QUESTION

Notice how the name of the government department dealing with education has changed since 1944. Do these changes have any significance?

Although the Conservative government still pursued its New Right policies, its change of leadership, from Margaret Thatcher to John Major, signified a less strident approach to education. Changes continued, but there were fewer radical changes in what seemed to be a period of consolidation as the government was faced with the problems arising from the implementation of the National Curriculum and learning to manage a diversity of school systems. In 1994 Sir Ron Dearing's report on the National Curriculum emphasized the need for some stability within education after a period of radical change. The Labour Party too was changing under the leadership of John Smith, who wanted to 'modernize' the party by moving away from its radical, left-wing traditions and towards a party that emphasized social justice and community spirit rather than the social strife emphasized by traditional socialists.

By the time of the 1997 general election, 'sleaze' had become one of the main talking points in political debate and the cynicism voters had expressed at the time of the 1992 general election was even more extreme when the cohort were interviewed again in 1997. Voters felt sickened by the apparent corruption, low moral standards and hypocrisy of many politicians and many were willing to risk a new government simply because they believed that any change would be an improvement. In the 1997 election campaign the Labour Party tried to associate sleaze with the competitive individualism promoted by the Conservative Party, whilst the Liberal Democrats presented themselves as a party of reason compared with the hot-headed extremists within the other parties. The Liberal Democrats were the only party to suggest an increase in taxation (an extra penny in the pound) in order to support increased spending on education. Conservatives continued to maintain that education could be best supported by effective market forces and Labour claimed that class sizes could be reduced by shifting spending from some areas (such as higher education) into schools. Although not proposing to increase public spending on

EXPLAINING THEIR VOTES IN 1992: VIEWS FROM TORYTOWN AND LABOURVILLE

A few days after the 1992 general election, voters in Torytown and Labourville presented very mixed views about the various parties. In 1988 their spread of allegiances were more strongly Conservative and by 1997 more strongly Labour, but in 1992 they seemed to be at a crossroads, where they were both critical of the current Conservative government and anxious about the prospect of a new Labour government.

[Voted Liberal Democrat.] The education side was not pushed as much as it should have been [in the election campaign]. The Liberal Democrats' ideas were sensible and not too radical. The Tories often changed things dramatically after very little discussion. They have an unwritten agenda. They are by nature divisive and always look after people they think should be in the best jobs.

John, 1992

[Did not vote.] It doesn't matter what party's in, they're all going to do the same thing. They're all in it for one thing – money.

Philip, 1992

[Voted Liberal Democrat.] They were the only one to say what they thought. The others were mud slinging like a lot of big kids.

Donald, 1992

[Voted Labour.] I could just as easily have voted for the other lot because I can't see anything between them. I've never been as disgruntled as I am now about the type of politician we have now. What astonishes me is, given their record, the Conservatives got voted in again. Maggie Thatcher had a lot to do with it because she made a lot of working-class people Conservative and they voted them in.

Bernard, 1992

[Voted Conservative.] If Labour got in – well, the place is in a mess and it'd take years for them to sort things out. If the Conservatives stay then hopefully they'll improve things – and I didn't like the Labour leader.

Eamon, 1992

[Voted Conservative.] I voted Labour in 1945 and they didn't keep any of the promises they made to us service people . . . After that I voted Tory as they have the ability to do a better job, they have the leaders . . . four of my five children have belting mortgages and they will help keep them down. I wouldn't be better off under Labour. I live very comfortably. I pay a lot of income tax and Labour's increase in the pension wouldn't be enough to compensate. And my investments – it's purely selfish [laughs].

Caroline, 1992

education, the Labour Party still managed to promote its image as the party most concerned about education by claiming that 'Education has been the Tories' biggest failure. It is Labour's number one priority' (Labour Party Manifesto, general election 1997, p 7) and describing its three most important policy areas as 'Education, education, education'.

It is interesting to note that in the election campaign an end to grammar schools was no longer seen as a central tenet of Labour policy. Instead it had been replaced by a new version of the previous government's emphasis on parental choice. Whereas the last Conservative government emphasized parental rights and freedoms, New Labour emphasizes parental rights and obligations, with home-school contracts setting out mutual responsibilities and expectations. The aim is to help parents to improve their parenting skills and to link education policies to wider efforts to reduce social inequalities and social exclusion. This seems compatible with the piloting (in 1999) of means-tested maintenance allowances for 16- to 18-year-olds in further education, although critics note that New Labour has broken away from the commitment previous governments had to free education for full-time students in higher education.

Throughout the 1990s sociologists also adapted their perspectives to changing social and political contexts. As the decade progressed their emphasis tended to shift from critiques of the problems associated with current education policies towards identifying new ways of tackling those problems. They were looking for the new 'idea' to replace the New Right agenda in the public imagination. Thus they drew on ideas emerging from the USA, such as communitarianism (Etzioni, 1993) and emotional intelligence (Golman, 1996), before Anthony Giddens's theories about a Third Way started to dominate academic discourse by virtue of their proximity to New Labour policies (see Chapter 3 for the key features of the Third Way and Chapter 5 on social class for theories about social inclusion and exclusion). Giddens explained how a Third Way could mix the principles of individual rights and community responsibilities by offering a system of 'positive welfare'. In such a system the negatives of Beveridge's five evils (see 'Socio-economic change' in Chapter 6) would each be replaced by a positive.

> ... in place of Want, autonomy; not Disease but active health; instead of Ignorance, education, as a continuing part of life; rather than Squalor, well-being; and in place of Idleness, initiative.
>
> Giddens, 1998, p 128

Changing school systems

By the 1990s education in England, Wales and Northern Ireland had become more clearly linked to notions of market forces, with parents as consumers and schools competing with each other for their custom. This meant that individual schools had to demonstrate superiority via their positions in the league tables and image within the local community. Although there had not been a noticeable increase in the number of grammar schools, many other schools which were not deemed as 'selective' (even 'comprehensives') were able to select children by ability and disadvantage many others because of their social origins. Gerwitz, Ball and Bowe (1995) found evidence that schools were using subtle methods of selecting pupils and their parents (including application forms that were difficult to complete, making parents sign contracts for co-operation with the school), ensuring that the more literate, motivated and assertive parents were likely to be the most successful applicants.

There were also growing concerns among sociologists about the increasing number of pupils who were being excluded from school and how this trend reflected schools' efforts to maintain good reputations for discipline.

An emphasis on market forces in education could also be seen, as the proportion of children attending non-maintained schools increased from 5 per cent in 1975/6 to 7 per cent in 1991/2 (*Social Trends*, 1994), but Conservative governments' concern about the availability of private education for some was balanced by a lack of support for social provision at the other extreme. The 1980 Education Act had introduced the Assisted Places Scheme, in order to support some children in private schools, but the same Act withdrew the statutory duty of LEAs to provide school dinners and milk.

During the 1990s annual increases in the numbers of students achieving good passes in their GCSEs, A levels and other school-leaving certificates seemed to suggest that, whatever their problems, schools were still turning out well-educated young people. However, these increases were regularly met with derision (see Chapter 5 for Melanie Phillips's critique, 1996) by those who saw them as an indication of falling standards in the assessments set, rather than improving standards among the candidates. Some critics and educationalists also argued the need to replace A levels with a national baccalaureate (baccalaureates could already be taken at some British schools) in order to broaden the range of subjects. Thus, even apparent successes did not relieve the pressures on teaching staff, who were already suffering from 'innovation fatigue' as a result of a long period of almost constant educational 'reform'. New ideas were constantly being floated by people who did not have to manage change on a daily basis.

The radically changing power relationships that had emerged during the 1980s continued to be a key feature of changing school systems in the early 1990s. Central government continued its policy of shifting powers from LEAs, upward to the Department of Education and Science (DES) and downward to school governors and parents. The Conservative government had been particularly suspicious of the left-wing leanings of the Inner London Education Authority and in 1990 finally transferred its responsibilities to inner-London boroughs.

Responsibilities for education at even the highest level were shifted as the DES lost some of its wider responsibilities. In 1992 responsibility for sport and recreation in England was transferred from the DES to the Department of National Heritage, and responsibility for science in England was transferred to the Cabinet Office. These changes led to the renaming of the DES as the Department for Education (DfE). The 1992 Education (Schools) Act also shifted responsibility for school inspection in England from the DfE to the new Office for Standards in Education (OFSTED, headed by Her Majesty's Chief Inspector of Schools) in England and the Office of Her Majesty's Chief Inspector of Schools in Wales (OHMCI). These were to be non-ministerial departments, independent of the DfE but responsible for training and registering a suitable body of Registered Inspectors and Independent Inspectors, not in the employ of OFSTED or OHMCI. Inspections of schools would be conducted by teams of these Independent Inspectors, headed by a Registered Inspector, and including at least one Lay Inspector, who had not been involved professionally in education. Every maintained school and some independent schools (those catering for children with SEN) were to have four-yearly inspections. These would lead to a report on educational standards, the efficiency of financial management and the 'spiritual, moral, social and cultural development' of the pupils.

Scotland was, however, given more freedom to retain and manage its own school system. In 1992 the Howie Report (*Upper Secondary Education in Scotland*) provided a very critical review of the curriculum and examinations provided in the fifth and sixth years of secondary education in Scotland. The pass rate for Highers was too low and even the ablest pupils compared badly in the breadth of their attainment with those in other European countries. Higher courses give little opportunity for study in depth, as pupils had to learn too much too quickly after the Standard grade (and the pace at Standard grade was too slow). There was too much flexibility, making coherent course planning difficult and many pupils were insufficiently prepared for higher education. Vocational education was too sharply divided from academic education and had low esteem. To meet these criticisms, the report suggested that Standard grade courses should

be started earlier and that in the fourth, fifth and sixth years pupils should follow one of two routes: either a one- or two-year programme leading to a Scottish Certificate (SCOTCERT); or a three-year programme leading to a Scottish Baccalaureate (SCOTBAC). Central government published its response to the report just two years after its publication and, although Howie's recommendations had some influence on the government's plans, most of the recommendations were rejected. Standard grade courses would not start earlier and the proposed twin track of SCOTCERT and SCOTBAC was opposed on the grounds that SCOTBAC inevitably would be held in higher esteem.

The 1993 Education Act further tightened central government's grip on education by ensuring that unsatisfactory schools would be subject to closer supervision. An LEA may appoint new governors and withdraw delegated management from the school but, if the school was still unsatisfactory, central government could put it under the management of an appointed Educational Association (centrally financed) until its performance was deemed acceptable. More schools were encouraged to gain grant maintained status by the creation of the Funding Agency for (Grant Maintained) Schools and the simplification of processes by which LEA schools and independent schools could gain grant maintained status. The Act also replaced two councils, the National Curriculum Council and the School Examination and Assessment Council, with a single council, the School Curriculum and Assessment Authority (SCAA), chaired by Sir Ron Dearing.

Dearing became an increasingly influential figure as the decade progressed because he won the respect of politicians from all of the main parties and, even after 1997, he continued to influence the Labour government's education policies. Indeed, the 1993 Dearing Report (*The National Curriculum and its Assessment*) was unusual in being produced by an individual (Sir Ron Dearing) rather than by a committee named after its chairperson. Dearing was asked to review the National Curriculum in order to make it more manageable, by slimming down the curriculum itself, simplifying its assessment arrangements, considering the future of its 10-level scale of attainment, and improving its central administration. He recommended the following:

- Immediate reviews of Key Stages 1–3 (i.e. ages 5–14) should aim to reduce the statutory curriculum enough to free about 20 per cent of teaching time for use at the discretion of the schools. The essential core for each subject should be identified and the number of attainment targets should be reduced so as to concentrate on that core. Time saved in this way should be used for basic literacy, numeracy and oral work.
- Schools' discretion should be extended for Key Stage 4 (i.e. ages 14–16) by making only English, mathematics, science and physical education compulsory, together with short courses in a modern foreign language and (from 1996) technology. The time saved could be considered for vocational as well as academic education.
- National tests should be simplified.
- The National Curriculum thus described should remain unchanged for at least five years. Dearing recognized the sort of innovation fatigue suffered by many teachers and felt that there should be at least a temporary rest from educational change.

These recommendations were actually accepted by the government, the proposed reviews were conducted and new draft curriculum orders were issued for implementation in 1994.

Dearing's hopes for a period of stability in schools were not entirely sustained, although between 1994 and 1997 most legislation related to subjects other than the curriculum. For example, in 1994 the Education Act established a Teacher Training Agency (TTA) for England and Wales and dealt with students' unions in England, Wales and Scotland. In 1993 two more important reports were published, in which the writers tried to envisage future developments in education (i.e. Institute of Public Policy Research, 1993, *Education: A Different Vision*; National Commission on Education Report, 1993, *Learning to Succeed*) and, in 1994, the Economic and Social Research Council launched its new Learning Society Programme. Meanwhile, the titles of government papers continued to publicize New Right ideals, such as the 1994 White Paper, *Competitiveness – Helping Business to Win*, and the 1995 White Paper *Competitiveness – Forging Ahead*. Education seemed to have become so firmly linked to employment

THE 1997 EDUCATION ACT

This Act was the last piece of Conservative legislation before the general election in May of that year and therefore had some of its provisions overruled by the following Labour government. However, its many provisions concerning discipline were less party-political and had a greater chance of being retained (see later in this chapter about behaviour). It also included the following:

- Schools could be more selective without having to gain central approval to do so.
- The process for allowing schools to opt out of LEA control and gain grant maintained status was simplified and a Funding Agency for Schools was established to finance GM schools in England. A similar agency would be established in Wales if the number of GM schools became sufficient.
- Children would be tested upon entry to primary schools.
- OFSTED was given powers to inspect LEAs.
- The Assisted Places Scheme was extended to independent preparatory schools (40 institutions).
- A new Qualifications and Curriculum Authority (QCA) was set up for England, combining NCVQ and SCAA. The Curriculum and Assessment Authority for Wales was renamed as the Qualifications, Curriculum and Assessment Authority for Wales.

The new Labour government initially left the OFSTED powers in place, believing that the principle of 'zero tolerance of failure' should also apply to them. The QCA came into existence and the testing of children on admission also came into effect, as did the provisions on the exclusions of pupils. Other measures were quickly changed by Labour.

that it made sense when, in 1995, the DfE was renamed yet again, this time as the Department for Education and Employment (DfEE). In 1996 another Dearing Report (*Review of Qualifications for 16–19-year-olds*) recommended that young high achievers should be able to take university courses whilst still at school and that applied and vocational courses should be available to pupils aged 14+ who did not find school of relevance. Reports published in 1997 tended to lend support to plans by both the outgoing Conservative government and the incoming Labour government for a greater emphasis on teaching literacy (*The Report of the Literacy Task Force*, 1997) and tackling failing schools (the OFSTED report about school improvements, *From Failure to Success*, 1997).

A new Labour government was elected in May 1997 under the leadership of Prime Minister Tony Blair and with David Blunkett as Secretary of State for the Department for Education and Employment. Soon after its election, the new government published a White Paper (*Excellence in Schools*) in which it outlined its policy proposals.

WHITE PAPER: *EXCELLENCE IN SCHOOLS*

This paper was based on Labour's six main principles regarding education:

1. *Education is at the heart of the government.*
2. *Education should be for the benefit of the many, not the few.* Independent schools were expected to offer more to their communities (e.g. Saturday classes, sports and language courses and even temporary boarding). Class sizes in maintained schools would be reduced to 30 or less for all 5–7-year-olds (to be paid for by phasing out the Assisted Places Scheme). The practice of partial selection in some schools (where schools pick up to 15 per cent of pupils on academic ability) would be ended. Education would be provided for all four-year-olds whose parents wanted it.
3. *Standards, not structures and institutions need to change.* A Standards Task Force was created, together with a Standards and Efficiency Unit at the DfEE. One hour a day in primary schools would be devoted to teaching literacy and numeracy and new national tests were to be introduced for nine-year-olds. A target was set for the year 2002 of 80 per cent of all eleven-year-olds reaching the required standards of numeracy. All schools and LEAs were required to establish challenging targets for themselves. An Internet system for schools would be created through the 'National Grid for Learning'.
4. *Intervention in what is wrong, not what is working well.* Existing LEA, church and grant maintained schools would be replaced with community, aided and foundation schools. Comprehensive schools would be modernized via a new policy of 'diversity within one campus', the setting of pupils by ability and an end to mixed ability teaching.
5. *Zero tolerance of failure.* Education Action Zones would be set up in 25 deprived areas over a period of three years, as partnerships between local authorities, business and parents. Efforts would be made to reduce exclusions, particularly among some ethnic minority groups. Work-related learning would be provided from the age of fourteen to help retain disaffected pupils.
6. *Commitment to work in partnership with all interested parties.* Efforts to promote the image of parents as partners in learning would include family learning schemes, family literacy projects, primary schools involving all parents in reading, compulsory (but not legally binding) home-school contracts, and compulsory homework with national guidelines on time and content. Efforts to create an effective partnership with teachers would include the creation of a General Teaching Council to represent teachers, a new curriculum for initial teacher training, making a qualification for headteachers mandatory, and policies for valuing teachers by celebrating good practice and excellence. Funding would be provided for better in-service training for those teachers who could act as models of excellence. The White Paper also initiated study support centres (including centres at Premier League football clubs) and specialist schools (particularly in deprived areas, and including some former city technology colleges) with matching sponsorship.

It did not take long for the proposals outlined in *Excellence in Schools* to be activated. In November 1997 another White Paper (*Connecting the Learning Society: National Grid for Learning*) set out further plans for bringing schools and colleges up to date with technology. The new government's first piece of legislation also came soon after its election with the 1997 Education (Schools) Act, which abolished the Assisted Places scheme in England, Wales and Scotland and made transitional arrangements for pupils currently receiving an Assisted Place.

It was in 1998 that the Labour government's first major piece of legislation on education was

SCHOOL STANDARDS AND FRAMEWORK ACT 1998

The main points of this Act were as follows:

- A code of practice was established, defining the role of LEAs.
- Powers to deal with LEAs which fail, sending 'improvement teams' to take over their responsibilities.
- Powers to intervene over failing schools, with some closed down and reopened under a 'fresh start' scheme.
- Powers to set up Education Action Zones, targeting resources at clusters of schools in inner cities and other areas of disadvantage and underachievement to raise standards in the Zone. They would assume some of the LEAs' functions and receive government grants (and contributions from private sponsors, who could second employees to work with the Zones). The government wanted at least one to be run by a business-led consortium. The Zones would have the power to vary the National Curriculum and teachers' pay and working conditions. They were designed to be testbeds for educational innovations and each Zone could operate from three to five years. The aim was to set up at least 25.
- A new framework for schools that would end grant maintained status. Such schools could instead opt for community, foundation, voluntary, community special or foundation special status. Schools previously funded by LEAs, churches or central government (i.e. grant maintained) would be newly designated as, respectively, 'community', 'voluntary' and 'foundation' schools.
- There would be greater representation of parents on schools' governing bodies and parent representatives on LEA education committees.
- Ground rules were set for parental ballots on the future admission arrangements at grammar schools. Unlike past Labour governments, New Labour did not instruct LEAs to replace selective schools with comprehensive schools but, instead, laid down a procedure for parents to vote on future admission arrangements at local grammar schools and allowed some specialist schools to maintain selection for a minority of their intake.
- Home-school contracts would be established with parents, setting out mutual responsibilities and expectations.
- Measures were taken to fulfil the promise to provide nursery places for every four-year-old.
- Measures were taken to fulfil the promise to cut class sizes by restricting parental rights of appeal over admissions.
- Compulsory nutritional standards for school lunches would be established.
- All first-time heads would be required to hold a professional qualification, together with national training arrangements for existing heads.
- A new General Teaching Council would be created to represent the teaching profession.

Questions

Examine the provisions of the 1997 White Paper and the 1998 School Standards and Framework Act, and Teaching and Higher Education Act. How do the Labour government's assumptions and aims differ from those of (a) the previous Conservative government and (b) Labour governments before 1979?

In 1997, majorities of the people living in Wales, Scotland and Northern Ireland voted for the devolution of powers from central government at Westminster to their own regional assemblies (the one in Scotland also having tax-raising powers). Each assembly was given powers to enact some legislation on education, although the Welsh Assembly was given only the power to enact secondary legislation. The assemblies in Scotland and Northern Ireland could amend, repeal and enact legislation. In 1998 three acts were passed to implement those powers:

- The 1998 Government of Wales Act established the National Assembly of Wales (Cynulliad Cenedlaethol Cymru). Responsibilities for education previously held by ministers of the UK Welsh Office were transferred to ministers in the Assembly.
- The 1998 Northern Ireland Act established the Northern Ireland Assembly. Responsibilities for education previously held by ministers in the UK Northern Ireland Office were transferred to ministers responsible to the Assembly.
- The 1998 Scotland Act established the Scottish Parliament. Responsibilities for education previously held by ministers in the UK Scottish Office were transferred to ministers in the Scottish Parliament.

Question

Discuss the advantages and disadvantages of allocating more control over education to the assemblies in Scotland, Northern Ireland and Wales.

Consider this devolution of educational powers to the regions together with the provisions of White Papers and various Acts passed by the Labour government. To what extent can you see a pattern of centralization or decentralization, diversity or uniformity?

passed after many critics expressed concerns that it would centralize power even further, as it gave ministers the right to intervene if teachers, schools or LEAs did not hit performance targets.

Relationships between government, LEAs and teachers improved after 1997, as communications between them seemed to become more effective. Although central government still retained its extensive powers (and even extended some), it was prepared to negotiate and doors closed by the previous government started to open. Labour also favoured the devolution of some powers to regional assemblies and LEAs, encouraged LEAs to apply for extra funding as Education Action Zones and raised teachers' hopes that they would gain more autonomy via the introduction of a General Teaching Council.

Interviewees in Torytown and Labourville who had experience of the education system during the 1990s were often confused and concerned about the many changes that had taken place and explained how they affected them personally. In 1997 cynical attitudes towards Conservative policies were replaced by uncertainties about the future of education under a Labour government.

Further and higher education

The word 'crisis' seems rather extreme and also rather subjective. Yet, whether further and higher education actually experienced a crisis during the 1990s or just thought it did, the word still seems relevant. After years of expansion there were still claims that it had not expanded enough to provide the skilled workers needed for the UK to compete effectively with other countries (especially in the European Union). The UK could compare favourably with most other European countries with regard to the proportion of its population with degrees, but it lagged behind in providing vocational qualifications for its workforce. Unlike other countries (e.g. the Netherlands), training after school-leaving age was not compulsory and vocational training was often regarded as second-

Local Management of Schools

When Local Management of Schools was introduced in the 1988 Education Reform Act it was intended to reduce the power of LEAs and give individual schools more control of their own budgets, but some interviewees pointed out that this could simply mean a shift of the responsibility for managing scarce resources.

Regarding LMS, I agree that schools should have more control but there's no point in having control if the budget is inadequate.

Jeremy, 1992

We now have LMS and it turns out that there's less money in most schools than there was previously. Bringing in the National Curriculum has meant that there is a lot of wasted time for those children who are not being tested. There's been an enormous increase in the workload. The rules keep changing too. My son is going to be a guinea pig and I'm not happy about that.

Natalie, 1992

Nursery vouchers

The nursery voucher scheme was introduced by a Conservative government but scrapped by the new Labour government. Media reports at the time suggested that many parents were anxious that they would not get the vouchers and that their children would loose their nursery places.

I went to a meeting about nursery vouchers. That was the biggest waste of time. I didn't get mine. I went through sleepless nights about that, because they turned around and said to me, 'If you don't get these vouchers back by the end of the week, your child's not coming back after Easter', and I phoned, and phoned, and phoned. Anyway, they eventually came, I got them just in time and, of course, a term later Labour got in and the whole thing got scrapped. It was unbelievable. The point of the whole voucher thing – I couldn't fathom it in the first place. It was just telling you that you had to have them, and who had to have them, because they were at the nursery where some of the children didn't have to, because they weren't going to be four, because they started when they were three.

Sharon, 1997

The curriculum and resources

[Not satisfied with educational opportunities.] I've just been very lucky. Since the Tories got in it was the way the whole system was turned upside down. The changes in the schools themselves in that they were adversely funded, particularly in [Labourville], but maybe in many areas. My eldest girl benefited from the old regime, where she wouldn't have had a degree in music if it had not been for the music service which existed in the 1970s in [Labourville], which disappeared in the 1980s. It's now come back but it's got to be greatly supported by parents, who help fund it over and above the state provision. It's thriving again but it's only because they are now charged. They're a separate unit and they charge the schools and the schools buy-in their services. Whereas a child previously got one-to-one tuition, they now get three or four to one, or five or six, or twelve, depending on the popularity of the particular instrument. In this area we had a music service that was second to none. It's still good compared to some areas, but it's only because a lot of parents in an area like this will pay for private tuition so their children are going to do OK. But what about all the others? In the inner cities they might not get the chance to play on a keyboard. Unless their parents are prepared to pay £6 for half an hour for music tuition, the child won't progress. Yet the child might have the gift to play a musical instrument.

John, 1997

best to academic studies. A Conservative government oriented to ideas of market forces also emphasized the responsibilities of employers and individuals to arrange their own training, with minimum funding from taxation. Yet, as the workforce had become more mobile, employers were reluctant to train employees, who might leave to work elsewhere.

Throughout the 1980s and 1990s governments tried to expand further and higher education at minimum expense, increasing the pressure on lecturers and administrators to educate more students more efficiently (i.e. cheaply), despite redundancies and insecure employment contracts. Expansion was to be partly paid for by the gradual withdrawal of government funding for students in higher education, which meant that students too were facing more pressures. As A level results continued to improve, and competition for places on some particular courses became even more fierce, the 'Robbins principle' (in the Robbins Report, 1962) seemed to be coming under threat. Increasing globalization, and the expansion of the European Union in particular, meant that more students were also arriving from other countries (e.g. on ERASMUS programmes), bringing with them their own expectations and special needs.

Whilst facing such pressures, further and higher education also faced increasing surveillance by a growing number of quasi-government agencies. At the same time, structural changes were taking place, as colleges ceased to be controlled by LEAs and new divides (of status) replaced the binary divide between universities and polytechnics.

Between 1990 and 1997 grants for students in higher education were gradually eroded until students became more dependent on loans and growing debts. The 1990 Education (Student Loans) Act, relating to England, Wales and Scotland, froze student grants at the 1990 level. It also introduced Student Loans and Access Funds as a safety net, with no interest charged on repayments. Students were made ineligible to claim Unemployment Benefit, the majority of students were made ineligible for Income Support and Housing Benefit and, in 1991, the students' Vacation Hardship Allowance was also abolished. Students quickly felt the effects of such changes. Indeed, any assumptions that they could fall back on support from their parents were challenged when a survey in 1991 by the Edinburgh Students' Union found that over 11 per cent of students did not receive the parental financial support that was due to them. In the same year, an education minister, Tim Eggar, criticized the low staying-on rates of young people in many Labour authorities, without acknowledging the traditional link between affluence and voting behaviour (i.e. young people in such areas are less likely to come from affluent families).

By 1992 increasing financial pressures on universities led a committee of university vice-chancellors to consider charging students top-up fees to supplement university incomes. In response, the higher education minister, Alan Howard, observed that such fees were not necessary and that the vice-chancellors had simply put the idea on their agenda to try to get more state aid. In the autumn of 1992 over 320,000 university students were funded by both government grants and state-supported fees but another 70,000 (over 18 per cent of all students) were supported only through tuition fees. Universities were finding it more lucrative to have students supported only by tuition fees, and some admitted a larger proportion of fees-only students than others; for example, nearly half the new students at University College Swansea and Keele University and over a quarter of the new Essex students were fees-only. By comparison, the University of Aston had the lowest proportion of fees-only students and recruited its first in 1992. This trend had been noticed early in the year by students' unions, as in March 1992 sixteen students' unions placed an advertisement in the *Guardian* urging all political parties to accept that access to higher education must be based on academic ability and not personal wealth. In 1993 the government announced that student grants were to be cut progressively by 10 per cent each year from 1994/5 to 1996/7 and loans were to be increased to compensate.

Although it was already clear in the 1980s that the promise of training for 16–17-year-olds could not be fulfilled and that the removal of their entitlement to Income Support was causing hardship, the situation did not improve in the early 1990s. In 1991 attempts were made to increase the provision of vocational qualifications by creating a nationwide network of Training and Enterprise Councils (TECs). However, in 1992 the Social Security Advisory Committee and the Citizens' Advice Bureau (CAB) both published reports calling for a removal of the ban on 16–17-year-olds receiving Income Support. More than half the TECs admitted that they were not able to meet this guarantee and the CAB found that over 1,000 teenagers per week were suffering severe hardship because of failure to get a place on a training scheme.

In 1991 two White Papers about training and further education were published. *Education and Training for the 21st Century* maintained the government's continued plans to extend further and higher education. This involved:

- The extension of degree-awarding powers and the creation of a single funding structure for higher education, as polytechnics could become universities.
- The aim to increase full-time students by 50 per cent and part-time students by 10 per cent by the year 2000.
- Cuts in spending per student of between 10 and 16 per cent.
- An increase in spending on research of about 11 per cent, but this was to be spread over fewer universities.
- The introduction of a vocational qualification equivalent to A levels (which led to the introduction of BTEC Diplomas/GNVQs).
- Non-vocational part-time courses would no longer receive funding, which meant that fees for such courses would increase.

On the last point, critics argued that it was often difficult to distinguish between vocational and non-vocational courses; for example, language classes could be taken for many reasons. Critics also claimed that the change meant that part-time students were being regarded as less important than full-time students. Spending per student in further education had already been reduced by 10 per cent between 1987 and 1990 and this Paper indicated that it was to be cut further.

In 1991 the record number of good results at A level increased pressure for places in higher education and with it the need for more spending. The number of places available expanded rapidly but, again, they were funded in 1992 by substantial cuts in spending per student. Universities expected a cut of 14 per cent for each undergraduate, whilst polytechnics and colleges expected a cut of 16 per cent and they feared that, if this was not enough, there was a possibility that students with good grades might not get places. Nevertheless, in 1994 not all student places were filled on some courses.

When the Universities Funding Council announced its autumn state aid in the autumn of 1992 it indicated that the most money overall would go to universities with rapidly expanding undergraduate programmes, and particularly those with large numbers of fees-only students. Several institutions responded by planning fast-track two-year degree courses (including Kings College, London, and St Martins College, Lancaster). Although the UFC could announce that state aid to higher

1992 FURTHER AND HIGHER EDUCATION ACT

Two pieces of legislation passed in 1992 changed the structure of higher education in England, Wales and Scotland. The Further and Higher Education Act (England and Wales) initiated the following changes, and similar changes were introduced to Scotland by the 1992 Further and Higher Education Act (Scotland):

- Colleges of further education would become corporations, independent of LEAs and funded by central government through separate Further Education Funding Councils (FEFC) for England, Wales and Scotland.
- Sixth-form colleges were removed from LEA control and joined the further education sector as colleges funded through FEFCs.
- The binary divide between universities and polytechnics would end. Polytechnics and other institutions of higher education could become degree-awarding bodies in their own right and take the title of 'university'.
- The funding of higher education would be unified with separate Higher Education Funding Councils (HEFC) for England, Wales and Scotland.

Questions

How significant was the new independent status of colleges of further education to the LEAs and the colleges themselves?

To what extent do institutions of higher education now share the same status?

education had increased by 8.5 per cent (about twice the rate of inflation), this was offset by the increased number of students. Increased money for research was also offset by the fact that it was spread more selectively over a few institutions, reflecting a division into research-dominated, teaching-dominated and 'mixed' universities. Financial adjustments during the early 1990s were therefore quite radical but they still seemed to achieve a lower profile than the structural changes introduced by the 1992 Further and Higher Education Act.

Once the changes initiated by the 1992 Acts were in place, the government also set about controlling the activities of students and staff within the various institutions. In keeping with its policies of limiting trade union power elsewhere, the government expressed concern that students were being forced to join the students' union and aimed to make the union more accountable. The 1994 Education Act regulated the conduct of students' unions in English, Welsh and Scottish colleges and universities, making governing bodies responsible for ensuring that unions operated in a fair and democratic manner and were accountable for their finances. Any student must have the right not to be a member of a union or to be represented by it and other regulations related to appointments to office, allocation of resources and affiliation to other unions. In the same year, the government told universities to freeze student numbers for three years.

During the remainder of the Conservative government it was able to oversee a huge growth industry in quality assessment. Two parallel assessment authorities were created to monitor universities; one initiated by the government, the other by universities which wanted to maintain some control over their own quality assessment. The Higher Education Funding Council for England (HEFCE, and there were separate ones for Scotland and Wales) was initiated by the government. It aimed to carry out detailed three-yearly gradings of the research done in each department and assess teaching quality. Until 1995 it was able to award an 'excellent' grade for teaching but since then has awarded only a pass or fail. The Higher Education Quality Council (HEQC) was, however, initiated by universities for their own self-regulation, assessing the quality of the university itself.

Despite the increasing surveillance of further and higher education, critics were still claiming that an increase in student numbers had brought with it a decline in standards. No matter how hard teachers, lecturers and administrators tried to manage the growing pressures, it seemed that the education they provided would never be good enough.

Higher education is in a state of meltdown. What is happening is nothing less than corruption of the very nature of education itself. It has spread throughout the system and has swept along with

1996 DEARING REPORT, *REVIEW OF QUALIFICATIONS FOR 16–19-YEAR-OLDS*

This report noted the complexity and confusion within the system that made it difficult to understand for students, teachers and employers. Trowler (1998, p 33) noted that 'From a policy sociology point of view this is the almost inevitable result of the micro politics of education policy-making and its implementation. Agencies vie with one another, impose their own agendas and interpretations on policy initiatives and seek to maximize their own gains. The result is a highly complex set of structures and processes.' The Report's recommendations included the following:

- The division between education and training should be replaced by a single national framework of three types of courses: academic and applied courses in schools and colleges and vocational courses in places of work.
- Qualifications for 16–19-year-olds should be simplified into a system of four National Levels (advanced, intermediate, foundation, entry) and all certificates should show which level the award was at.
- The assessment of GNVQs should be simpler but more rigorous and they should be renamed 'Applied A Levels' to indicate comparability with academic A levels. AS levels should be based on the first half of A level syllabuses, allowing students to keep their options open for progressing to A level or National Advanced Diploma courses.
- Quality assurance structures and procedures in the national framework should be simplified and rationalized.

it Britain's brightest and best, the highest achievers and their university teachers. It is not just that university students can no longer spell or punctuate. In some subjects taught at degree level, the gaps in students' knowledge are so fundamental that university dons who can scarcely believe the evidence of their own eyes have had to dilute or extend their degree courses just to cope.

Phillips, 1996, p 6

Critics such as Melanie Phillips often focused their attention on what they saw as a dilution in the quality of the increasing number of A level passes and the other qualifications gained by 16–19-year-olds. Thus it was claimed that the fundamental problem centred on the inadequacies of students on entry to universities. Although it did not accept such criticisms, the 1996 Dearing Report aimed to improve and co-ordinate the structures and processes involved in providing courses for 16–19-year-olds.

Soon after its election in 1997 the new Labour government introduced its Welfare to Work programme, which meant that even more young people would be entering further and higher education. In an effort to reduce the numbers of young people who were dependent on Unemployment Benefit, the government announced that 18–24-year-olds would have just three options: take a job, become a full-time student or do a six-month placement with the Environment Task Force (or an organization in the voluntary sector). Those refusing to take

THE JULY 1997 DEARING REPORT, *HIGHER EDUCATION IN THE LEARNING SOCIETY: THE NATIONAL COMMITTEE OF INQUIRY INTO HIGHER EDUCATION*

This inquiry considered the whole of the UK, looking at the shape, size and cost of higher education, including student numbers and student finance. It noted that during the last twenty years the number of students had more than doubled but that public funding of higher education had only increased by 45 per cent in real terms. Funding per student had therefore effectively fallen by 40 per cent. In the introduction to the Report it noted that:

Over the next 20 years, the United Kingdom must create a society committed to learning throughout life. That commitment will be required from individuals, the State, employers and providers of education and training . . .
We were appointed to advise on the long-term development of higher education. But we express here our concern that the long-term well-being of higher education should not be damaged by the needs of the short term.

The Report's recommendations included the following:

● The lid should be taken off the present freeze in student numbers, and expansion would be mainly through two-year sub-degree courses in further education colleges.
● The present mix of loans and grants for students should continue but with a flat-rate contribution (20 per cent or 25 per cent of average tuition fees) paid by all students. Part-time and full-time students would therefore be on equal terms.
● Students should have a wider choice of courses, including more courses offering breadth across different subjects rather than depth in one.
● Institutions should provide more opportunities for a work experience component in courses.
● There should be various types of institutions. Some universities would be strong in research, others in teaching, and there would be varying subject mixes. Universities should be more prepared to collaborate with each other.
● There should be a new framework for progression through eight levels of qualifications after A levels (Certificate, Diploma, Bachelor's degree, Honours degree, Higher Honours/Postgraduate Conversion Diploma, Masters degree, M.Phil, Doctorate). This would allow for various stopping-off points and credit accumulation and transfer between institutions.
● Several options were suggested for increasing the number of places available in higher education in Northern Ireland. Although Northern Ireland had a high participation rate, there were not enough places available for students wanting to study in Northern Ireland itself.

one of these options would loose entitlement to benefits. Again there was a danger that this policy would lead to a flood of new (perhaps underqualified) students into colleges and universities, which were ill equipped to cope. Since colleges were given their independence from LEA control, funding per student had declined by about a third and they had been facing a financial crisis. An increasing number of colleges were already experiencing well-publicised financial difficulties.

Concerns about the apparent crisis in post-compulsory education had led to a lengthy inquiry into higher education which started long before the end of the Conservative government but reported shortly after the election of the Labour government in 1997. Again the inquiry was headed by Sir Ron Dearing.

The government accepted most of the Dearing Report's recommendations but did not accept the continuation of the system of supporting living expenses via a mix of 50 per cent grants and 50 per cent loans. Instead, in the 1997 Teaching and Higher Education Act, it moved towards a system of enhanced loans only (with a transitional period to support current students). Students would in future pay means-tested contributions to their tuition fees of up to £1,000 per annum and would not begin repaying the increased loans until they were earning an income of a specific level (£10,000 in 1999).

QUESTIONS

Discuss arguments for and against the introduction of the fees described above. This introduction of student fees by a Labour government was greeted with incredulity by many traditional Labour supporters. How could the move be explained by considering a New Labour perspective (see Chapter 3)?

Yet another report into post-compulsory education was also published shortly after the election of a Labour government. This time it focused on further education rather than higher education. Kennedy and others seemed to be arguing that, although all post-compulsory education was facing a crisis, priority for funding should be given to relatively low-level qualifications in further education rather than higher education. Indeed, in the Labour government's early days it seemed that it was also allowing further education to take priority.

THE 1997 GARRICK REPORT, *HIGHER EDUCATION IN THE LEARNING SOCIETY: REPORT OF THE SCOTTISH COMMITTEE*

Another inquiry into higher education in Scotland accepted most of the Dearing Report's recommendations but concentrated on Scottish issues. It noted that higher education in Scotland was distinctive in the following ways:

- 45 per cent of young people participated in higher education (compared with 32 per cent in the UK as a whole) but 40 per cent took sub-degree qualifications (compared with 26 per cent in the UK as a whole).
- Scottish students arrived in higher education having experienced a broader school curriculum (for Highers) than those elsewhere (with A levels).
- Scottish universities offered four-year honours degrees. The report therefore recommended that students' total tuition fees for the course should not be greater than those for three-year courses elsewhere in the UK.
- Scottish universities already offered a great amount of flexibility and opportunities for students to change pathways.
- Levels of qualifications were different in Scotland. A Scottish degree without honours had higher status than a degree without honours elsewhere in the UK and the older universities offered a first degree in the arts as an MA, not a BA. The report recommended that these characteristics should be taken into account when creating a new framework of qualifications for Scotland.
- Universities established since 1993 were more distinctively vocational in character than their counterparts in England.

This was the final report of a committee chaired by Helena Kennedy QC and appointed by the Further Education Funding Council (FEFC) to investigate underparticipation in further education and how participation could be increased. It argued that learning, and further education in particular, was the key to social cohesion and economic prosperity. Its recommendations included the following:

- The government should develop a national strategy for increasing participation in further education, and publicly funded further education should play a major part in this. Market forces alone were not sufficient.
- There should be strategic partnerships at local level. Colleges should be given responsibilities for meeting the needs of local communities.
- The various ways of funding further education should be harmonized.
- Employers should be given financial incentives to help employees with further education.
- The FEFC should alter its funding criteria to favour young people with lower levels of previous attainment and adults from economically deprived areas.
- Those who could afford to pay more towards the costs of their further education should do so, but tax relief should be available for this.
- A national system of information and guidance about further education should be established.

In October 1997 the government announced a target of 500,000 new places in further and higher education by the year 2002, but it soon became apparent that this was particularly aimed at the expansion of further education rather than at moving towards 'mass' higher education. A month later the government announced additional funding of £83 million for further education.

By the end of the 1990s the improved monitoring of further and higher education was starting to provide a further source of evidence about inequalities in access. In 1999 the Higher Education Funding Council for England produced its first annual report on performance indicators, one aim being to highlight differences in performance between institutions with similar intakes of students so that some institutions could learn from the good practice of others. The researchers used various performance indicators to evaluate institutions with regard to widening participation, student progression, learning outcomes, efficiency and research. Indicators were also used to identify certain groups who were underrepresented relative to the population as a whole. For young full-time undergraduates these were as follows:

- Attendance at a school in the state sector.
- Low social class (parents' occupations were unskilled or semi-skilled).
- Home postcode in an area classed as low participation (consisting of about a third of young people in the UK).

For mature full-time undergraduates and part-time undergraduates they were as follows:

- No previous higher education qualification.
- Home postcode in an area classed as low participation.

The first report showed that most universities and colleges had a long way to go in order to broaden access. Young people living in wealthy areas were still ten times more likely to enter higher education than those from the poorest areas and even those institutions with a high proportion of students from state schools tended to select students from higher social classes.

The HEFCE data also revealed that, nationally, 18 per cent of full-time degree students failed to complete their studies. This compares favourably with many other countries; for example, France had a drop-out rate of 45 per cent, the United States 37 per cent and Germany 28 per cent (figures from the Organization for Economic Cooperation and Development, cited in *The Times Higher Educational Supplement*, 3 December 1999). Only Japan had a lower drop-out rate than the UK. However, the drop-out rates for individual institutes varied and could be influenced by the local region served by the institution, students' socio-economic background and age and types of courses.

Interestingly, the indicators revealed a close relation between high income for research and a low benchmark for widening participation among young full-time undergraduates. For example, Oxford and Cambridge had the highest research income from the funding council but benchmarks of only 6.7 and 6.5 per cent (respectively) for the proportion of students from less affluent neighbourhoods. At the other extreme, Liverpool Hope University College and Newman College each received about £10,000 research funding from the council but had benchmarks of 14 per cent of their students coming from less affluent areas.

QUESTIONS

In what ways could drop-out rates be influenced by:

(a) students' socio-economic background;
(b) the local region served by the institution;
(c) the profile of students' ages;
(d) the types of courses provided;
(e) other factors?

Check how the HEFCE evaluated your institution. Do you think this gives an accurate impression?

Teachers and lecturers

During the 1980s and 1990s there was increasing evidence of the strains faced by teachers in their everyday working lives. In their staffrooms teachers were discussing what many of them were experiencing as a form of 'innovation fatigue', as they struggled to cope with the force of educational change. In 1984, and again in 1992, Dunham published his book *Stress in Teaching* and his concerns were reinforced by Hargreaves in 1994. As you read through this section you will see how teachers reacted to their changing experiences throughout the 1990s.

Dunham's research was carried out during the 1980s and early 1990s but findings published at the end of the 1990s also showed extremes of discontent among teachers. After interviewing 7,000 workers every year during the 1990s, Jonathan Gardner and Andrew Oswald, economists at Warwick University, discovered that increasing pressures on the UK's half a million teachers have left them the unhappiest group of workers in the

---

DUNHAM ON *STRESS IN TEACHING*

Dunham (1984, 1992) and his students collected written and oral information from thousands of teachers during the 1980s and early 1990s, aiming to identify the causes of stress and help others to learn from efforts to reduce it. He favoured an interactionist approach and defined stress as 'a process of behavioural, emotional, mental, and physical reactions caused by prolonged, increasing or new pressures which are significantly greater than coping resources' (p 3). Dunham argued that, although teachers had always worked under pressure, pressures during the 1980s and 1990s outweighed their ability to cope with them, resulting in stress-related symptoms (p 101). Environmental pressures included lack of space in school buildings, noise levels, organizational problems within the school, having to manage teaching on a low budget and with inadequate resources, heavy workloads, inadequate time to do work properly, headteachers' leadership styles, and low pay together with poor prospects of promotion.

The usual pressures experienced as a result of children's disruptive or unco-operative behaviour (described by the Elton Report, 1989, as 'persistent low level classroom disruption') were compounded when teachers encountered children with behaviours and attitudes that were beyond their training and expectations and/or when parents refused to support teachers' efforts to deal with such children. Staff could be left feeling confused and uncertain about what actions they should take. Moreover, Dunham explained why stress often remained hidden by citing one informant, who observed that 'Stress is caused because I am unable to ask for extra support because if I did, I would be assessed as a weak teacher by the rest of the staff' (Dunham, 1992, p 1).

Data from the schools A, B and C in Figure 11.1 were collected in the early 1980s for the first edition of Dunham's book and this is compared with responses to the same questions from schools X, Y and Z in 1989 and 1990. Here we can see the proportions of teachers in those schools experiencing common stress reactions.

Stress reactions	A	B	C	X	Y	Z
Large increase in consumption of alcohol	0	10	3	21	29	20
Marital or family conflict	3	5	14	44	27	20
The marked reduction of contacts with people outside school	36	22	35	56	54	30
Displaced aggression – on to children or colleagues or people outside school	20	18	14	33	50	30
Apathy	25	18	14	41	50	50
Wanting to leave teaching	25	15	20	56	62	70
Unwillingness to support colleagues	0	0	3	21	10	10
Strong feelings of being unable to cope	7	16	8	28	25	50
Irritability	18	34	24	48	75	70
Moodiness	7	19	22	30	46	40
Inability to make decisions	0	4	6	16	13	20
Feverish activity with little purpose	7	18	10	35	30	20
Inability to concentrate	14	8	10	28	44	50
Absenteeism	0	0	3	8	6	0
Depression	3	11	8	33	58	20
Tension headaches	14	15	18	46	34	30
Feeling of exhaustion	36	46	41	64	79	80
Frustration because there is little sense of achievement	32	30	16	46	75	80
Withdrawal from staff contact	14	7	14	24	14	10
Anger	7	11	12	44	37	30
Anxiety	3	23	16	41	35	40
Loss of sleep	14	15	14	41	30	70
Loss of weight	0	5	0	2	2	0
Feelings of isolation in school	10	8	11	25	27	20
Feelings of fear	0	8	3	21	15	10
Feelings of guilt	7	10	9	25	33	30
Overeating	14	15	14	16	29	10
Skinrash	3	5	0	14	6	0
Large increase in smoking	0	4	9	8	10	0
Hypersensitivity to criticism	7	11	18	46	23	10
Back pain	7	8	7	16	21	0

% in schools

Source: Dunham, 1992, Table 9.1, p 100

Figure 11.1 Percentage of staff in six English comprehensive schools identifying stress reactions

Dunham went on to observe the following.

The costs of working in the Education Service in the 1990s in terms of stress-related health problems for some of our teaching and non-teaching colleagues can be recognized from these questionnaire findings. But the costs may be even greater as they reach and pass over the exhaustion and burnout threshold. At the exhaustion threshold feelings of tiredness are different from those usually experienced after a day's work. This is a particular type of tiredness which is often described as 'drained' . . . If this level of exhaustion is not relieved by holidays or by absence from school through illness or by taking what our American colleagues call a 'mental health day', there is a real risk that the cost will become much greater through burnout.

Dunham, 1992, pp 102–3

Questions

Comment on changing patterns in the responses over time.
Can we generalize the findings from these schools to others?
Figure 11.1 shows that absenteeism was low but Dunham noted that absenteeism was one of the signs of burnout. How could the various levels of stress affect absenteeism?
How could teachers' stress affect their pupils and students?

public sector. The study (as cited by Elliott, 1999) found that job satisfaction in the classroom has fallen sharply during the 1990s, with the squeeze on pay having a less significant effect than constant assessment and a tougher working environment.

Once again the decade started with an Act superceding another Act, in this case the 1991 School Teachers' Pay and Conditions Act which superceded legislation in 1987. The 1991 Act established a review body, its members being appointed by the government to make recommendations to the Secretary of State about teachers' salaries and conditions of employment. Final decisions were to be made by the Secretary of State after consultation with LEAs, teachers' representatives and other interested parties, and to be set out in a School Teachers' Pay and Conditions Document.

In 1992 changes to teacher training were announced, which were to be phased in over three years. This would start in 1993 with changes to the PGCE (Postgraduate Certificate in Education) course. The amount of time being spent in college or university was reduced so that student teachers could spend 66 per cent of their time in schools. Institutions providing PGCE courses were to identify partner schools and teachers within those schools who would act as mentors to the trainee teachers. New 'articled' teachers would be graduates who would spend 80 per cent of their time in schools over two years, in order to qualify as teachers,

and 'licensed' teachers would follow at least two years of full-time higher education with training in school for a year. In 1994 the Education Act established a Teacher Training Agency (TTA) for England and Wales to fund teacher training courses, involve schools in initial training partnerships with higher education institutions and provide information about teaching as a career. A similar funding agency was introduced for teacher training in Wales (the Higher Education Funding Council for Wales).

The mid 1990s, like the mid 1980s, were marked by disputes, but in this case when teachers refused to teach unruly pupils, some teachers' unions (e.g. the NASUWT) used strike action to force schools and LEAs to exclude pupils who misbehaved. In April 1997 the Secretary of State, Gillian Shepherd, used a speech to the NASUWT conference to note that proposals in the Conservative manifesto would give people a legal avenue to prevent public sector strikes and that parents would be able to use this provision against teachers. In an appeal to professional ethics as a reason not to strike she said that 'Whatever the situation in a school may be, there is never any excuse for a professional person to strike or take industrial action' and 'It is not the way for professional people to behave, and for teachers the interests of the children should always come first' (reported in *The Times Educational Supplement*, 11 April 1997).

QUESTION

Consider Shepherd's comments in the light of claims that teachers have lost their professional status.

The new Labour government elected later in 1997 was committed to a more positive stance towards teachers, aiming to raise their self-esteem by increasing their professional autonomy and tackling their negative public image. In July 1997 the White Paper *Excellence in Schools* included:

- proposals for the creation of a General Teaching Council to raise the status of the profession (although it was instantly criticized for lacking any meaningful powers);
- quicker procedures for disciplining incompetent teachers;
- a new grade of Advanced Skills Teacher;
- a professional qualification for headteachers;
- teacher training for primary staff was to be reformed to focus more on the basics of literacy and numeracy.

Most of these changes were implemented via the 1997 Teaching and Higher Education Act.

The Labour government's apparently more positive attitude towards teachers was, nevertheless, not met with instant delight by teachers themselves, partly because it involved selecting some teachers for extra praise and promoting different pay scales (see Chapter 4). This involved performance-related pay, the creation of a new grade of Advanced Skills Teacher and annual awards for inspirational teachers. Thus, the pressure to shine as a 'superteacher' could just be an additional pressure added to many others.

QUESTION

Discuss arguments for and against the annual national teachers' awards.

Like teachers in schools, lecturers in further and higher education were showing increasing signs of stress during the 1990s. On 29 April 1992 the *Guardian* published a statement signed by more than 900 academics accusing the Conservative governments of the previous thirteen years of undermining the higher education system. There had been a huge expansion of further and higher educa-

TROWLER ON TEACHERS' EXPERIENCES DURING THE 1980s AND 1990s

Paul Trowler was one of many social scientists during the 1990s who were concerned that a move towards more classroom-based training may be emphasizing skills and turning teachers into technicians rather than providing the necessary critical, theoretical and reflexive knowledge. He noted that the new articled teacher and licensed teacher schemes meant that there would very little preparation prior to classroom experience. In particular Trowler observed that the introduction of a National Curriculum had meant the separation of conception from execution (p 95), with planning carried out by curriculum planners, textbook authors and so on, with teachers sometimes just delivering a package.

Trowler's summary of the problems experienced by teachers during the 1980s and 1990s can briefly be described as the following:

- Work degradation; a poor environment, depleted resources.
- Work intensification; more work expected but with fewer resources.
- Deskilling; a decline in the level of skill required to do the job.
- Bureaucratization; an increasing amount of paperwork.
- Work 'flexibility'; more part-time and temporary contracts.
- Loss of control over the work process and hence lack of job satisfaction.
- Reduced control over the use of time as managerialist practices increasingly control what teachers do.

Trowler, 1998, p 96

tion without a comparable increase in the number of lecturers or in government spending. Not only was this causing problems but lecturers also assumed that the problems would worsen with further expansion in the late 1990s. In 1994 the Labour Party was claiming that universities would face an acute staff shortage in the late 1990s as about one-third of the lecturers in the 'old' universities (less so in the former polytechnics) were over 50 and would soon take early retirement. The Labour politician Bryan Davies claimed that 'Fifteen years during which the Government has devalued academic staff have caused significant recruitment and retention problems' (*Guardian*, 28 November 1994).

The mid 1990s also saw a huge growth industry in the quality assessment of universities, primarily by two parallel assessment authorities: one initiated by government, the other by universities who wanted to maintain self-control of their own quality assessment. The Higher Education Funding Council for England (HEFCE, there being separate ones for Scotland and Wales) was initiated by the government to assess teaching quality and carry out detailed three-yearly gradings of research in each university department. Until 1995 these assessments could lead to the award of an 'excellent' grade for teaching, but they have since resulted in only a 'pass' or 'fail'. The Higher Education Quality Council (HEQC) was initiated by universities for their own self-regulation. As a result, lecturers were faced with a formidable amount of extra paperwork as they faced frequent visits by assessors and the need to provide detailed written reports on their work. Just as schoolteachers' complaints about the 'paper mountains' associated with the introduction of a National Curriculum led the government to streamline the National Curriculum, so did lecturers hope that their complaints would lead to some relief from their administrative burdens. In November 1996 a one-day national strike in higher education included all unions (for lecturers and other staff) and was supported by the students' union. John, a Labourville lecturer, explained his grievances.

> I think that they [Conservative governments] used the people in public services as whipping boys for society in general. That was the feeling that many of us perceived. That we were to be punished because we were living off the fat of the land, lazy, idle lecturers, doctors and nurses (perhaps not so much doctors and nurses but certainly in education), that it could be done cheaper by the private sector and better. That sort of attitude was through the broad spectrum of services. Whatever could be privatized had to be privatized and because it was privatized it would be better. I objected to that because I worked in partnership

with people from the private sector in our college and we found that they were not as committed as we were, in any way . . .

> We reached a situation where we were on strike at one point for three colleagues who were going to be made compulsory redundant. That was last Christmas. They were still made redundant, incidentally, but we got them a better deal. In NATFHE.

> John, 1997

Soon after the arrival of the new Labour government in 1997, results were published from an inquiry set up under the Conservative government. The Dearing Report (*Higher Education in the Learning Society: The National Committee of Inquiry into Higher Education*) recommended that teaching in higher education should be more highly valued and teacher training should be provided for academic staff, who should strive to achieve membership of the new professional body for teachers in higher education (the Institute of Learning and Teaching in Higher Education). The report also recommended a review of the conditions of service and pay of staff in higher education.

From class and status to exclusion and inclusion

The concept of 'social class' was problematic for sociologists long before the 1990s (see Chapter 2 for problems involved in operationalizing class) but by the 1990s ideas about an underclass (Wilson, 1987) were starting to be refined into the rhetoric of 'social exclusion' and 'social inclusion'. Even one of the UK's most famous sociologists, Anthony Giddens, was habitually emphasizing 'exclusion' and 'inclusion' in his writings (e.g. 1998) and aligning his theories with New Labour policy. During the 1980s an increasing proportion of the 'working class' who had jobs experienced a higher standard of living; many bought shares in their own companies or in mortgage companies and many voted Conservative. Share ownership meant that they were not only workers but also 'capitalists'. Definitions of social class as relating to the means of production had therefore become problematic and it was much easier to identify the socially excluded as occupying an extreme position of relative deprivation when compared to others who had jobs, increasing levels of prosperity and could see themselves as having a positive stake in society. Thus, it might be easier to identify the underclass or socially excluded than to label others as belonging to particular levels in a social class hierarchy.

The term 'meritocracy' was still commonly used in political debates in which government representatives (whether from a Conservative or Labour government) claimed that their party(ies) had contributed towards the creation of a genuine meritocracy. Yet many sociologists and educationalists were claiming that what had been created was closer to a parentocracy, in which children's educational achievements were likely to be less influenced by their own efforts than by the influence of their parents. In theory parents could 'choose' from a wide range of schools, including private institutions, grant maintained (later called foundation) schools, church schools, city technology colleges (later specialist schools), good schools maintained by their local education authority, or 'sink' schools barely maintained by an impoverished local education authority and/or providing blatantly substandard education. In practice only the children of the least fortunate and/or least assertive parents would have a 'sink' school chosen for them. This was obvious to social scientists such as Dennis Lawton (1992, see Chapter 6) who claimed that parental choice has been oversold as a means of improving education and that, given a choice, most parents would favour a neighbourhood school. Yet, when a neighbourhood school was a 'sink' school it would be the most economically secure parents who had the best opportunities to get their children into distant, but thriving schools (perhaps even moving house into another catchment area). Indeed, many of the interviewees in Torytown and Labourville were acutely aware of a parentocracy rather than a meritocracy; for example, in 1997, Timothy attributed his success in getting a highly paid job in information technology, despite a lack of formal qualifications, to his family rather than to his private school, saying that 'The family's more important than school'.

Timothy was referring to his family's attitudes rather than their wealth, and this could also be seen in poorer homes. Although there was growing evidence of a widening gap between the extremes of wealth and poverty in the UK, it was clear that generalizations could not be made about negative attitudes among poorer parents. In 1997 researchers funded by the Joseph Rowntree Foundation (Middleton, Ashworth and Braithwaite, 1997) described one in ten children as 'poor' on the basis that their families could not afford at least three of the things most families took for granted such as three meals a day, a bed of their own, or shoes bought new and fitted properly. One in thirty children were described as 'severely poor' as they lacked at least five of such things. The authors found that Income Support fell far short of meeting children's needs, with the result that parents were suffering in order to protect them from deprivation. Although the researchers calculated that it cost an average of £50,000 to bring up a child until the age of seventeen, the difference between what was spent by the better-off and the poorer families was surprisingly small. This was because poorer parents (usually lone mothers) often went without various things (such as clothes, shoes, holidays, entertainment or food) in order to protect their children from poverty.

Although some of the least affluent parents deprived themselves for the sake of their children, there would be limits in what they could provide and one crucial limitation could be seen in access to information technology. Lash (Beck, Giddens and Lash, 1994) and others noted that, as information and communication systems became increasingly important in the workplace, those people with a low level of education and lacking in computer skills had started to be socially excluded. Lash has suggested that the production of information and communication goods has become 'the new axial principal of capital accumulation' (Beck, Giddens and Lash, 1994, p 129), replacing the production of heavy industry, and that the new middle class work as experts inside expert systems.

The point is that the accumulation of information (and of capital) in the I & C structures becomes the driving force of reflexive modernity, just as the accumulation of manufacturing capital and its associated social structures had been in an earlier modernity. And reflexive modernity's upgraded (and reduced) working class as well as its expanded middle class find their basis in this informational displacement of the 'motor of industry'.

Lash, in Beck, Giddens and Lash, 1994, pp 129–130

Lash was impressed by Wilson's theories about an underclass (1987), arguing that at the turn of the century we have a 'two-thirds society', consisting of the expanded middle class, who work in the information and communication sectors, the upgraded working class, who have adapted to the shift from manufacturing to information production, and those who have been downgraded from the classical (Marxist) proletariat to become the new underclass. The new working class occupy 'servant' jobs, serving the middle class (for example, as waitresses, taxi-drivers, cleaners and shop assistants). Closure of large factories and movement of smaller industries to out-of-town areas that can only be accessed by car also means that the poor end up trapped in urban ghettos of high levels of unemployment and homelessness. Lash even goes on to say (in Beck, Giddens and Lash, 1994, p 134) that class positions are now more typically determined by ascribed characteristics such as ethnicity and gender. He compares the underclass with the images in Fritz Lang's film *Metropolis*, where the (lumpen-)proletarians could be recognized by ascribed, often physical features.

Although education could provide an escape from such an underclass, access to the funding needed in order to benefit from further or higher education continued to be limited throughout the 1990s. By September 1990 the government had taken almost all 16–17-year-olds out of the benefit system, as they were no longer entitled to either Housing Benefit or Income Support. Income Support had been withdrawn in 1988 on the assumption that youth training places were available for all who needed them but, in 1992, more than half the TECs admitted that they were not able to meet this guarantee and the Citizens' Advice Bureau found that over 1,000 teenagers per week were suffering severe hardship because of their failure to get a place on a training scheme. In 1992 reports by the Social Security Advisory Committee and the Citizens' Advice Bureau called for the removal of the ban on 16–17-year-olds receiving Income Support.

Students over eighteen had also been taken out of the benefits system. In 1991 a survey by Edinburgh University Students' Union found that one in eight Edinburgh students had considered dropping out due to cash problems, students who had paid jobs during term-time worked an average of almost fourteen hours per week, and more than 11 per cent did not receive any of the parental support that was due to them.

By the end of the 1990s further evidence of inequalities in access to, and success in, further and higher education was provided by the HEFCE (see earlier section about further and higher education) when it showed that young people living in wealthy neighbourhoods were still ten times more likely to enter higher education than their counterparts living in poor neighbourhoods. Even those institutions with a high proportion of students from state schools tended to select students from higher social classes. The HEFCE report also indicated that drop-out rates from higher education could be influenced by the students' socio-economic background. Yet some sociologists (e.g. Lawton, 1992) have observed that a student from a privileged public school background and with high scores at A level is probably less academically gifted than a student with the same scores from a school where there were fewer resources (including a less favourable pupil:teacher ratio).

Gender

By the end of the 1990s so much progress had been made towards eliminating the disadvantages of girls in education that new concerns were being expressed about boys being disadvantaged in education. Should boys and men and a supposed crisis of masculinity now be the focus of concerns about gender and education, and had feminists now achieved their goals, thereby making themselves irrelevant? Some feminists perceived a 'backlash' against the women's movement in general and its academic arm of Women's Studies was still struggling to maintain credibility.

Findings about the impact of gender on educational experiences during the 1990s have been confusing and sometimes contradictory. In some ways sexist attitudes were still so entrenched that they were largely invisible to those holding them; for example, in 1992, nearly twenty years after legislation to end sexual discrimination, Birmingham City Council was still appealing against the ruling that it had discriminated against girls by providing fewer grammar school places for them. Yet throughout most of the 1990s (it may have started to balance out by the end of the decade) girls were overtaking boys at various educational hurdles; high-achieving female cohorts were excelling lower down the school, then at GCSE level, then at A level and then in further and higher education. Even the usual pattern of boys achieving better results than girls in certain subjects seemed to have evaporated in 1992 when tests of seven-year-olds showed that girls were achieving better grades than boys in maths, science and technology. There was also some (although often contradictory) evidence that single-sex education was particularly good for girls. For example, from 1992 the annual 'league tables' of schools showed a disproportionate number of single-sex girls' schools among those getting the best academic results. In 1992 seven of the top ten of all schools were girls' schools and seven of the top ten state schools were girls' schools, but this finding was confounded by the fact that single-sex schools were more likely than others to have a selective entry system. Also in 1992 a Department for Education Report (*Preparation of Girls for Adult and Working Life*) found that girls attending single-sex schools were more confident, better prepared for life and had higher expectations than those attending coeducational schools. In March 1997 OFSTED published its report *From Failure to Success*, for which it had studied 260 primary, secondary and special schools in England that were judged to need special measures. Although a small number of single-sex boys' schools had been put on such measures, no girls' schools had been similarly labelled. The report also noted that failing schools tended to have a higher than average concentration of boys, that boys were more likely to be excluded from school than girls and that girls achieved better results in GCSEs.

In 1980 there were fewer females than males taking further education courses, but by 1991 there were more females in both part-time and full-time courses. Between 1980/1 and 1991/2 the number of students taking further education courses increased by a quarter to just over 2 million and female students accounted for 84 per cent of the increase. The gender distribution of higher education students also changed, although not quite so dramatically at the highest levels. Between 1970/1 and 1991/2 the total number of students in higher education more than doubled, and the number of females tripled. In 1992/3 there were, nevertheless, still more male than female full-time undergraduates (approximately 436,000 male and 416,000 female) and many more male full-time postgraduate students (approximately 61,000 male and 44,000 female; *Social Trends* 25). The growing numbers of mature women students also meant that sociologists became more interested in the educational experiences of women as well as girls. Using feminist methods, this research was sometimes used as a source of empowerment for the subjects rather than straightforward academic analysis. For example, one of the themes emerging from *Learning the Hard Way* (The Taking Liberties Collective, 1989) and other publications (e.g. Pascall and Cox, 1993) was that mature women often perceived education as playing a dual role: their experiences in schools encouraged domesticity and low-status jobs, whilst further and higher education provided an escape route from traditional roles and into more rewarding jobs.

To Helen Wilkinson, the dramatic shifts in female attitudes and expectations indicated nothing less than a 'Genderquake' (1994). She was particularly interested in following the advance of the 7 million women aged between 18 and 34 who had come of age since the passing of equal opportunities legislation during the 1970s. Survey data suggested that young women now valued autonomy, education and work more than family or parenting. For example, 79 per cent of women in the sample said that they wanted to develop their careers and find employment, 50 per cent regarded having children as a goal and less than a quarter of women in the youngest age group (16–24) felt that a woman needed a stable relationship in order to be fulfilled. This and other evidence suggested that females (and working-class females in particular) were more likely than their male counterparts to see the long-term value of a good education. Yet we can see in earlier chapters that this is not a new idea.

The result [of the loss of structural institutions of regulation] is not individualization but anomie, and a deficit of regulation. The result is the gang-bonding of young males and racial violence. This of course applies not only to the urban minority ghettos but to the white ghettos of Britain's council estates in Liverpool, Glasgow and Newcastle where working-class fathers breed underclass sons. Where fathers who worked in the mines, on the docks, in the steel mills, in large chemical and machine-building plants have sons who leave school at sixteen without an apprenticeship and invariably find little in the way of steady employment until the age of twenty-five. Of sons who when employed at all are unable to find the industrial labouring jobs they were brought up to do, but wind up behind the counter at Dixons, as a cleaner at the local airport or a porter at the local college . . .

[This is also the case in Eastern Europe.] . . . As in black America, a generation of youth which has been brought up 'learning to labour', a generation of Eastern European working-class kids has grown up only to find this time that there are no working-class jobs. 'Learning to labour', as Paul Willis described it, is also and perhaps mainly the acquisition of a specific sort of *male* habitus. Without an outlet in working-class jobs, the alternative is gang-bonding, the (football) terraces and racial or racist violence. That is, the heteronomous monitoring of simple modernity has not been replaced by reflexive modernity's self-monitoring.

Lash, in Beck, Giddens and Lash, 1994, p 131

Questions

Compare the first paragraph with the extract from Dennis *et al.* (1956) in Chapter 7, 'Learning to be miners'. What had changed?

The second paragraph refers to Eastern European countries. Does it also apply to British society?

Discuss the claim made in Lash's last sentence.

See the extracts from Willis in Chapter 9, 'Learning to be lads', and compare the laddishness of the 1990s with the experience of learning to be lads in the 1970s.

Compare Wilkinson's findings about female attitudes (1994) with those of Sue Sharpe in 1976.

During the 1990s it was possible to appreciate the impact of the sort of 'enforced' subject choice for boys and girls that was introduced with the National Curriculum. More girls had started to take the traditionally 'male' science subjects and more boys were starting to take the traditionally 'female' arts subjects. Yet the influence of schooling alone has its limitations and mainstream sociologists were also starting to acknowledge wider gender differences in access to technology. Returning to Lash we can see that, in an era in which the global focus was on information technology and communication systems, many females were still disadvantaged as a result of the unwillingness of males to surrender their control of technology, both inside and outside the home.

. . . the line separating the 'life zones' from the 'dead zones', which sets the middle-class neighbourhoods from the ghettos also runs right through the centre of the private sphere of the household. Here men typically have access to equipment highest in the information content, such as the camcorder, the remote-control switch of the television and operation of the time-shift on the video recorder, while women – with less access to the 'brown goods' – tend to concentrate their usage in the 'white goods' of refrigerator, cooker and vacuum cleaner, washer and dryer in which there is a higher ratio of mechanical components to electrical components. This holds even for the young boys, and not girls, who have privileged access to the Sega and Nintendo consoles, the home computers and electric guitars.

Lash, in Beck, Giddens and Lash, 1994, pp 133–4

Male domination in information and communication structures also applied to the top jobs in education for much of the 1990s. The decade started with continuing worries about the feminization of the primary school workforce: in 1990, 81 per cent of all primary school teachers were female (an increase from 78 per cent in 1985), and the relative lack of female primary school headteachers (in 1990, only 65 per cent of deputy heads and 49 per cent of heads were women). There was also a relative lack of prospects for promotion at secondary school level, as in 1990 48 per cent of all secondary school teachers were female (in 1985 it was 46 per cent), but only 34 per cent of deputy heads and 20 per cent of heads were women (Statham *et al.*, 1996, Fig. 7.3). In 1992 approximately 30 per cent of lecturers in the 'new' universities were women, and this fell to 10 per cent or less at grades above senior lecturer level (Universities' Statistical Record, 1993). In the 'old' universities approximately 6 per cent of senior lecturers were women and only 3 per cent of professors (Hart and Wilson, 1992).

Yet by the end of the decade there were some signs that more women were breaking through the 'glass ceiling' to take up top jobs in primary and secondary schools. By 1999, 57 per cent of all primary school headteachers in England and Wales were female and 27 per cent of all secondary school headteachers in England and Wales were female (DfEE statistics cited in TES, 15 October 1999). However, as is typical of educational analysts, the breaking down of barriers in the educational job market is also seen as symptomatic of a worrying trend towards the feminization of schooling, as not only do many boys see educational achievement as unmanly, but few male graduates are drawn to work in schools where they know that their wage and status will be lower than that of their counterparts in other jobs. There is growing concern that a lack of male role models for boys in primary schools will reinforce the impression that men are not associated with education.

By the end of the 1990s educationalists were introducing various schemes designed to subvert male assumptions that educational achievements were 'uncool'. This involved exploring the construction of masculinity (e.g. Roper and Tosh, 1991) and opened up new avenues for the sociology of education (see Chapter 5).

QUESTION

Evaluate the influence your gender has had on your educational opportunities.

Ethnicity

In 1991 the British Census asked a question about ethnicity for the first time and this provided more accurate information than had been possible in previous estimates. Yet, the UK had had a multicultural society for so long that it was still difficult to evaluate ethnicity. Common perceptions of a multicultural society seemed to be challenged by findings that in 1991 only approximately 5.9 per cent of the population of England and Wales and 6.2 per cent of the population of England were drawn from ethnic minorities (Owen, 1992, pp 1–2). Such a low figure may relate to the problems involved in operationalizing the concept of 'ethnicity' (see Chapter 2) and to the geographical dispersion of various ethnic minority groups or individuals.

As most people accepted that a multicultural society had become entrenched in the UK (and in most of the Western world), those who still felt that ethnic minorities were in Britain but not British were less likely to focus on negative stereotypes than the supposed problems of managing a 'multicultural society'. Thus, anti-racist policies were still regarded with suspicion. Campaigns to establish separate Muslim schools, and to ban Salman Rushdie's novel *The Satanic Verses*, were sometimes portrayed as yet more evidence of the incompatibility of 'non-British' cultures. In the opposite corner, anti-racists who were appalled by the response of the police to the murder of Stephen Lawrence argued that the Macpherson Report's challenge to eliminate institutionalized racism must be rigorously applied in education.

Such was the growing awareness of the many different ethnic groups that a new wave of analysts challenged the right of black feminists to speak on behalf of all women from the diverse range and social locations of ethnic minorities. According to Tariq Modood (1992), many analysts are guilty of 'racial dualism', or essentialism in which racism is seen as the only factor shaping the life-chances of black Britons and largely ignoring the significance of ethnic differences. Modood highlighted the different attitudes and experiences of various Asian groups, noting, for example, the major divide between the many Hindus and Sikhs from India (who were gaining educational success, entering the professions and building businesses) and the Sunni Muslims from Pakistan and Bangladesh (who were suffering from acute disadvantage). Even apparently positive patterns of employment could have been influenced by discrimination, as, for example, the professions may be attractive to ethnic minorities because they hope that educational credentials provide some protection from racism in recruitment. Indeed, unemployment figures suggested that such beliefs had some grounding in fact. In 1993 figures from the national Labour Force Survey for the period 1989–91 indicated that black unemployment rates were approximately double those for whites (Jones, 1993). Moreover, the experience of schooling continued to be problematic for some, as indicated by an OFSTED report in 1993, which found that the number of Afro-Caribbean pupils excluded from schools was disproportionately high and that a disproportionate number attended referral units.

Throughout the 1990s such negative images of the educational problems associated with ethnicity continued to be countered by growing evidence of the different educational achievements of pupils and students from various ethnic groups. In 1992 Reid reported on his study of socio-spatial indices and 16+ examination results in Bradford schools. From a very complex picture he found that the average score at GCSE of 'Asian' girls was higher than for 'white' boys. Using some indices, 'Asian' girls' achievements were also higher than those of 'Asian' boys and 'white' girls and boys. This structural approach obviously raises various questions that can only be investigated by interpretive research and it also raises questions about the impact of gender differences on educational achievements. Mirza (1992) carried out a more interpretive study of young Afro-Caribbean women. She argued that a common focus on the education of boys had led to a distorted picture of race and educational performance, and a spurious analysis of educational 'underachievement'. The young black women Mirza interviewed had aspirations and experiences which were distinctive from those of both young black men and young white women and their prospects were limited by factors which had little to do with their background. The girls suffered from inadequate schooling and low teacher expectations and

later had to cope with a racially and sexually segregated labour market.

It is clear now that not only do experiences differ according to gender, but also according to socio-economic circumstances. Rattansi (1988, p 354) argued that, if differences in economic circumstance were properly allowed for, the gaps in attainment between whites and blacks cited by studies such as the Swann Report would be much less marked. The ethnic minorities who performed least well (such as Turkish and Bangladeshi children) were those where the adult population was most heavily concentrated in manual work.

Perhaps the most interesting data to emerge from research during the 1990s related to the 'academic drift' (see Chapter 4) of many people from ethnic minorities into further and higher education. Although the economic context meant that many more young people were drifting into further and higher education in order to improve their prospects in a highly competitive job market, some ethnic minority groups were overrepresented in further and higher education. Indeed, findings during the 1990s often contradicted earlier negative images of the achievements of 'West Indians' or 'Afro-Caribbeans'. For example, the 1988–90 Labour Force Surveys found that not only had the numbers of young people taking some sort of further education increased, but that 'Afro-Caribbeans' and 'South Asians' have maintained a tendency to be overrepresented compared to 'whites'.

In 1991 PCAS and UCCA reported for the first time on the ethnic background of applicants to higher education. They found that nearly 7 per cent of new students at universities in the autumn of 1990 came from non-white families and nearly 16 per cent of all admissions to polytechnics in the autumn of 1990 were black or Asian (i.e. about three times their estimated percentage in the British population as a whole). In 1994 the Policy Studies Institute published its findings about the different rates of entry of ethnic minorities into higher education in 1992. It too considered the percentages of successful applicants from various groups and found radical differences in access to universities and polytechnics. When looking only at success in access to universities it was found that:

- 'Chinese' and 'black African' applicants were overrepresented compared to their presence in the population as a whole.
- 'Black Caribbeans' and 'Bangladeshis' were underrepresented compared to their presence in the population as a whole.

When looking only at success in access to polytechnics it was found that:

- 'Black Caribbeans' were overrepresented compared to their presence in the population as a whole.

However, the Policy Studies Institute indicated that a simplistic cause/effect interpretation based on racial categorization should be avoided. For example, they found that a larger proportion of 'black Caribbeans' applied for access to highly competitive courses (such as medicine and law) and to courses in a relatively small number of universities near to their homes. This meant that competition for places was not evenly spread. It was also noted that the socio-economic inequalities highlighted in the study fell disproportionately on certain ethnic minority groups.

Religion and morality

During the 1990s both Conservative and Labour governments emphasized the value of schooling as a way of implementing their strong moral agendas. Whilst Conservatives tended to focus on religious beliefs (and Christianity in particular) and family values as the source of morality, New Labour tended to focus on the community and family responsibilities. Although politicians differed in their personal religious beliefs, Conservatives focused (as with most of their policies) on individual rights, whereas New Labour focused on shared rights and responsibilities. At the start of the 1990s the Conservative government was promoting a discourse that was critical of a supposed moral underclass, but by the end of the 1990s the Labour government was promoting a social integrationist discourse, with an emphasis on communitarian ideals (see Chapter 3 and Levitas, 1998). Indeed the different approaches of the two political parties can be seen in how they balanced their educational legislation with religious interest groups. In 1993 the Education Act, passed by a Conservative government, included a provision to extend religious education even further. However, in 1997, Church of England bishops in the House of Lords expressed their concerns about the proposal in the Labour government's School Standards and Framework Bill to dilute Church of England representation on schools' governing bodies and amend admission procedures that secured the religious character of church schools. The Bill was redrafted to placate them.

In 1993 Sir Ron Dearing's report on the National Curriculum promoted philosophical thinking skills among secondary school children via ethics-orientated short courses in religious education (which could include the nature of knowledge and morality). This was to be made possible by reducing the workload imposed by the ten National Curriculum subjects. Religious education and sex education would be compulsory at Key Stage 4 (i.e. ages 14–16) but outside the National Curriculum. In his report, Dearing not only reflected the ideas of many educationalists, who favoured a stronger moral agenda in schools, but also helped to legitimize their efforts. This could be seen in 1995 when the National Foundation for Educational Research, The University of London Institute of Education and various other educationalists established a Values Education Council to provide a forum for groups involved in religious, moral, personal and social teaching.

Many educationalists favoured the inclusion of a secular moral agenda, accommodating children from families with a wide range of religious, or non-religious, beliefs. This was intended to generate social unity at a time when religious fundamentalism was apparently increasing together with a growth of many forms of non-denominational spirituality. British education systems had traditionally accepted church schools of various types and now included Jewish and Muslim schools as well as the usual Christian church schools. This is in contrast to some other European countries where schools are more obviously designed to promote cultural unity and therefore less tolerant of religious differences. For example, in 1994 the French education minister issued a directive banning 'ostentatious' religious symbols in schools (crucifixes and Stars of David were seen as discreet). During 1994

Governors of a primary school have come under attack for barring a 10-year-old Sikh girl from classes for carrying a small ornamental dagger under her uniform. The girl was banned from lessons at Glodthorn Park primary school in Wolverhampton for the winter term. She was only allowed to return this year provided she was excluded from activities such as PE, breaktimes and school visits.

The governors ruled that the short-bladed kirpan, worn as a religious symbol, posed a threat to the safety of staff and pupils. The decision was taken shortly after the machete attack at the nearby St Luke's primary school in which pupils and staff were injured. Local councillor Bob Jones suggested the governors had overreacted to the attack, coupled with a wider public concern over knife-related crime after the fatal stabbing of London headteacher Philip Lawrence. Mr Jones, who is also chairman of the West Midlands police authority, said: 'They have legitimate concerns, especially in the aftermath of St Luke's, but if they had done more research then their concerns would have been allayed.' Many other schools in the country permitted Sikhs to wear the kirpan and had experienced no problems, Mr Jones said.

Matthew Beard, *The Times Educational Supplement*, 21 February 1997

Questions

Who has the power to make decisions about the exclusion of children from schools?

On what basis are such decisions made?

How much freedom do you think children should have to express their religious beliefs whilst in school? Are some forms of expression acceptable and some not?

As sociologists refer to cultural relativism and personal values are regarded as relative, is it possible to teach 'good' values in schools?

several French schools sent Muslim girls home for wearing the Islamic headscarf or hijab. The wearing of the headscarf was seen as a challenge to the French tradition of secular education established in the nineteenth century. Yet in the UK a history of church schools and the teaching of religion in schools made intolerance more difficult to justify, although there were still some difficult cases.

Special needs

Throughout the 1990s continuing efforts were made to improve educational provision for children with special educational needs, including the recognition of needs that had not been previously identified. Some of the loopholes found in the 1981 Education Act were addressed when it was almost entirely repealed by the 1993 Education Act.

The general aim of the 1993 Education Act was to clarify, speed up and generally improve relevant practice in schools.

- It aimed to help both the 2 per cent of children with statements and the 20 per cent of others with special needs who were not statemented.
- The Secretary of State was empowered to issue regulations and a code of practice concerning the education of children with special educational needs.
- All schools were required to follow the code of practice to be introduced in 1994.
- All schools were required to appoint a member of staff as SEN co-ordinator.
- Children with disabilities were given an equal right to school sex education.
- The category of indefinite exclusion from school was abolished and pupils could now be excluded either permanently or for a fixed term not exceeding fifteen school days in any one term. Local education authorities were obliged to provide education for excluded pupils in Pupil Referral Units, which must offer a broad and balanced curriculum, but need not offer the full National Curriculum.

The 1993 Dearing Report stated that the National Curriculum should still be available for children with SEN and that the levels defined in the curriculum should be broadened to take account of this. It also noted that the teachers and parents of pupils with SEN should be consulted and involved in the development of an appropriate curriculum for their children.

The code of practice introduced in 1994 stated that:

- school governors had a duty to publish a policy on special educational needs and report on its management in their annual reports to parents;
- schools should now adopt a 'whole school policy' regarding SEN, which meant that the whole school was involved in developing policy;
- local education authorities were required to complete assessment and statement procedures within a fixed timetable;
- parental rights would be strengthened; and
- any maintained school named in a child's statement would be required to admit that pupil.

QUESTION

Look in Chapter 5 at Jeremy's comments on how his school catered for children with SEN. To what extent do descriptions of good practice mirror actual experience?

By the late 1990s the special needs of new groups of children were starting to be identified. There was, for example, a growing appreciation of the social exclusion and educational problems of children in the care of local authorities (whether fostered or living in children's homes; see Armstrong, Clarke and Murphy, 1995). Children in care may be fostered or living in children's homes, but in both cases the state has effectively taken the role of parent. Although it is estimated that at any one time there are approximately 50,000 of them in the UK (and it often costs more to support a child in care than to send a child to Eton), it was easy to ignore them in a society promoting ideas of a parentocracy. Communitarianism also emphasizes the need to improve standards of parenting but it is becoming clear that the state may have been the worst parent of all!

In 1997 Sir William Utting produced a disturbing study of children in local authority care which led to the setting up of a ministerial task force, and in 1998 the Downing Street Social Exclusion Unit (SEU) considered children in community care as part of its wider remit. It found that three-quarters of children in care left with no qualifications of any kind and were ten times more likely than other children to be excluded from school. Many experienced several moves between homes and half of care leavers were unemployed. The SEU set a target for local authorities to ensure that half of all children in care achieved some qualifications by the year 2000; a very modest target, set at a time when very few children in the population as a whole were leaving school with no qualifications.

At the end of the 1990s other special educational needs were also being acknowledged. For example, in 1999 Dobson published her interim report (*Pupil Mobility in Schools*) on the needs of the increasing numbers of pupils who were constantly changing schools, including the children of members of the armed forces, refugees, travellers, victims of family breakdowns and children whose parents regularly moved to new jobs. She found that in some schools in inner-city areas classes changed from week to week, sometimes with a yearly mobility rate of 88 per cent. In a class of 30 children, as many as 27 could have moved in or out during the year. Most worryingly she found that many of these children were extremely vulnerable, more likely than the general population to be eligible for free school meals and more likely to have English as a second language. In general, the academic attainment of many mobile pupils was significantly lower than that of other children and large numbers of such children in one school could affect the school's position in league tables.

At the turn of the century we can now appreciate that, although educationalists are constantly trying to improve the help they provide for children with SEN, the identification of SEN will continue to change as more problems are uncovered.

Behaviour

In 1992 Nicholas in Torytown said that education should be given first priority for increased government spending 'because we might not need a police force then'. He was not seriously suggesting that a police force would some day be unnecessary but, like some other interviewees, was indicating a link between a good education, good behaviour and public safety. The high moral agenda of the 1990s (associated also with opposition to political 'sleaze') could be seen in continuing public concern about 'sink' schools and the social consequences of behavioural problems in schools. Indeed, Daniel Goleman's book *Emotional Intelligence* (1996) became a best-seller as more people looked for ways of managing the pressures of schooling and everyday life. Goleman claimed that children had lost the ability to handle their emotions and did not know how to interpret the emotions of others. He offered practical solutions, including classroom activities. Yet, if we consider the case of the Ridings School, we will see that what happens in the classroom cannot be separated from external influences.

PROBLEMS AT THE RIDINGS SCHOOL

The Ridings School is in Halifax, West Yorkshire, and under the control of Calderdale Local Education Authority. By 1995 it was clear that the school had severe problems. It had an above average proportion of children with special educational needs (139 pupils, or about 23 per cent of the school roll) and there were additional pressures associated with the behavioural problems of some children. In 1995 the school introduced a behaviour management scheme with a five-step system of sanctions but this proved to be ineffective as, after insufficient training, some teachers moved to the final sanction too quickly and removed pupils from the classroom into an isolation unit staffed by just two members of staff. In 1995 Calderdale LEA made an unsuccessful bid for £5.5 million from central government to tackle the school's problems. The bid included requests for:

- resources to improve core curriculum work in English, maths, science and technology (all later criticized in the OFSTED report);
- extra training for teachers at the school;
- help with truancy and discipline problems.

By 1997 problems in the school had escalated and, when OFSTED inspectors moved into the school at the end of October, they had to abandon their observer status and intervene to break up fights. In November the school was closed for five working days after a male teacher was bombarded with books and a young woman supply teacher was assaulted. A new headmaster, Peter Clark, was seconded from a local grant maintained school. Teachers threatened to strike if troublemakers were not removed and Clarke excluded twelve disruptive pupils and suspended twenty-three others (for between five and thirteen days).

When OFSTED published its report in November 1997 it noted the following:

- The quality of teaching was unsatisfactory in more than two-fifths of lessons.
- Leadership and management were weak.
- There were sufficient resources but '. . . the school does not evaluate the consequences of its spending decisions and as a result offers poor value for money'.
- Some senior staff had lost the will to bring about improvement.
- Standards were adversely affected by staff illness and turnover. For example, there was no subject leader for French and inexperienced teachers were given inadequate support.
- There were stark variations in the quality of teaching; for example, a lesson on the weather was taken up by asking eleven-year-olds to draw and colour a snowman.
- Relationships between teachers and pupils ranged from very good to confrontational.

- There was poor attendance and punctuality. At least twenty fifteen-year-olds had not appeared at school at all in the autumn term.
- Levels of 'internal truancy' were high as children skipped lessons without teachers knowing where they were.
- In 1995/6 about 150 children were excluded from the school, but there was no exclusion register and staff could not explain this 'unacceptably high' number.
- Four in ten pupils left school with no GCSEs.
- There was an atmosphere of underlying distrust and uncertainty.

Inspectors found that spending per pupil was £2,800 (above the national average) and class sizes were low compared with other secondary schools. Although this might be explained by the high proportion of children with special educational needs, it might also explain why central government refused the LEA request for extra funding. The new headteacher Peter Clarke was given three weeks (until 29 November) to devise a solution to the problems of indiscipline and underachievement and the LEA was given until 12 December to provide a support plan. On 6 November 1997 a phased return to school of senior pupils started and 250 of the school's 600 pupils returned.

The Secretary of State for Education and Employment, Gillian Shepherd, blamed Calderdale LEA for most of the school's problems because of its 'scandalous' neglect. The LEA blamed central government for its failure to provide the necessary financial aid. The national media suggested that the school's teachers were lacking the necessary disciplinary skills.

Question

How would you set about trying to discover the causes of the problems at the Ridings School or any other school in difficulties?

Since 1997 the Labour government has introduced various measures aiming to improve discipline in schools and reduce truancy. These started with the 1997 Education Act which had many provisions concerning discipline:

- Schools may make the admission of children conditional on their parents signing a home–school agreement and accepting certain responsibilities.
- Detention outside school hours may be imposed on pupils without their parents' consent.
- The exclusion of pupils for up to 45 days per year (previously 15) was permitted and arrangements were made for appeal against exclusion.
- The powers of teachers to restrain pupils physically were defined.

By the end of the 1990s the government was also introducing fines for the parents of children who regularly truanted from school.

QUESTIONS

Do you think that fines will work?
Identify and discuss various ways of tackling (a) poor discipline in schools, and (b) truancy.

Torytown and Labourville

Between the interviews in 1992 and those of 1997 political changes and their impact on education in Torytown and Labourville were very noticeable. In 1992 many of the interviewees were focusing their political discontent on the Conservative government, whilst having relatively few complaints about their Conservative council. Distrust of the Labour Party seemed to be the deciding factor for many when they noted that, despite their complaints, they still voted Conservative in the 1992 general election. Thus, Torytown in 1992 was still primarily Conservative territory, despite the

On 29 April 1997 the *Manchester Evening News* published a double-page spread with the headline 'Questions for the party leaders'. In an introduction to a series of questions it noted that:

> Tony Blair tells north-west voters today that if they trust him he will cut class sizes and keep [Torytown] grammar schools. John Major insists the electorate can 'only be sure' with him that there will be more grammar schools and no hiding place for slacking schools. And Paddy Ashdown promises only he will 'make the difference' by raising extra cash for schools with a penny on income tax.
>
> Labour, Tory and Liberal Democrat leaders all put education at the top of their election agenda when they answered ten questions from the *Manchester Evening News*.

Reporters asked politicians 'What changes will we see in education in the north-west if you win the election? What will happen to grammar schools?'

Conservative

After ten years of step-by-step reform, the next stage of our education reforms will be to offer parents a guarantee of standards. There will be no hiding place for poor-performing Labour councils who have failed the last four places in exam league tables for the north-west over the last two years. Where schools or local authorities fail we will intervene. We are pledged to keep existing grammar schools and to help more schools to become grammars where parents want that. Contrast this clear commitment with Labour's confusion. Their spokesmen contradict themselves almost daily and their own councillors in [Torytown] have voted against giving parents the power to decide their own grammar schools' future.

Labour

Education will be the No. 1 priority. Under the Tories, a third of five, six and seven-year-olds in the north-west – more than 80,000 children – are taught in overcrowded classes of more than 30. We will reduce class sizes to 30 or less for every five, six and seven-year-old by phasing out the government's £140m subsidy to a few private schools.

We will raise standards by setting strict literacy and numeracy targets; linking every school to the information superhighway; tackling underachievement; increasing the power and responsibilities of parents and improving teacher training.

On grammar schools, it will be up to the parents to decide their future. Labour will not close any good school. Our priority is to raise standards in the 4,000 state secondary schools where most children are educated.

Liberal Democrats

Our first priority is education. Every party says they care about our children's future, but only we will guarantee the extra investment that schools need. An extra penny on income tax would ensure nursery education for every three and four-year-old, and make sure that no child between five and eleven is in a class of more than 30. We will also double the amount which schools spend on books and equipment next year – an extra £16,000 for a primary school of 250 pupils and an extra £110,000 for a secondary school of 1,000 pupils.

The Liberal Democrats oppose Conservative plans for the wholesale expansion of grammar schools. But we would leave it to each local community to decide on the issue locally.

Question

See Chapter 5 about the instrumental nature of voters' interest in education and identify any reasons why the double-page spread in the *Manchester Evening News* might, or might not, influence individual votes.

electorate's reservations and the regular experience of hung councils, which meant that Conservative councillors had to win the support of Liberal Democrats or Independents on the council in order to pursue their policies.

When interviews took place in the summer of 1997 it was clear that many of the voters in this small sample strongly associated Conservative politicians with sleaze and that, for some, this had finally allowed them to change their vote, or vote in 1997 when they had not voted in 1992. As Donald noted, 'At the end they were falling apart'. Indeed, the association between Conservatives and sleaze was strengthened by a negative report in the *Manchester Evening News* about the Conservative candidate in Labourville, who was refused permission (by the school's headteacher) to visit a Labourville primary school. Despite the refusal he posed for a photograph beside the school sign and the picture was published in a Conservative campaign leaflet next to a statement of his support for testing in Labourville schools. Claiming that testing would show parents which schools were performing well, he observed that, thanks to selection, schools in a neighbouring authority continually out-performed those in Labourville. Yet the Labourville school he chose to be photographed outside was recognized as a school of excellence in an OFSTED report and one of the top 60 in the country.

The influence of such a critical report in a local newspaper during the general election campaign is difficult to estimate. However, after five interview phases from 1980 to 1997, it had become clear that the *Manchester Evening News* was a popular paper among the cohort. Some had it delivered instead of a national newspaper, some read it as well as a national newspaper and some just read other people's copies.

Since 1997 Torytown could more appropriately be called New Labourtown, a label that still distinguishes it from the old Labour traditions of Labourville. In the 1997 general election a swing of nearly 10 per cent to the Labour Party resulted in a Labour MP being elected for the Torytown constituency. Yet distrust of Conservative politicians did not necessarily indicate trust in Labour politicians, just a willingness to give Labour a chance. Labour's chance in 'New Labourtown' has,

as in similar areas, allowed local parents to vote on whether the local grammar schools should become comprehensives.

Unfinished business

At the end of Chapter 10 it was noted that a lengthy period of Conservative government meant that education did not experience the usual pattern of a new government immediately overturning the plans of its predecessor. In 1999 the Labour government was still only two and a half years into its administration and publicly trying to fulfil its election commitment to 'education, education, education' by introducing a rapid succession of new programmes. It was the newness of the administration that left the public wondering what unfinished business there was and what the long-term impact of such changes would be.

Some particular uncertainties are perhaps worth noting. First, the future of grammar schools and selection for other schools looked uncertain because Labour policies neither supported selection nor forcibly opposed it, and this may be a reflection of the fragmented views within the party. In June 1998 David Blunkett announced that from September 2000 it would be unlawful for schools to introduce any additional selection on the grounds of general academic ability. Yet some schools could retain the right to select up to 15 per cent of their pupils unless challenged by their education authority or local parents. Although the government rules that parents should not be interviewed as part of the admissions process, Catholic schools could still carry out interviews to assess religious or denominational commitment. Second, the government's policies on private education sometimes seem ambiguous and this may again be because of divisions of opinion between Old Labour and New Labour. Non-maintained schools still had a remarkable amount of freedom (e.g. from OFSTED inspections) and many of them seemed to be thriving under a government party that was traditionally opposed to private education. Third, the implications of the government's policy of 'lifelong learning' are still uncertain. From 2000 onwards the only age group to be expanding will be that of retired people and the already increasing demands for new forms of education for this group are likely to grow. It is uncertain how continuing demands for more further and higher education can be met by the system, even with the introduction of fees for higher education. Finally, the government's ambitious plans for the expansion of education are dependent on continued economic growth. By the end of the 1990s there were heartening signs of general economic improvement and even claims that the British economy was starting to boom. Yet many schools, colleges and universities were still struggling to provide a good service on a very tight budget and it is possible that for them economic expansion may continue to mean increasing demands not matched by increasing funds. The next chapter will consider more long-term scenarios for the future.

12
Changing education in the future

Changing Ed. - Chap. 12

Notes

Notes in for Wed.

The Future   Dystopian   Utopian

Giroux -

Discourses of
possibility   Nostalgia   Open future

Some scenarios -

A/ Continuing   B/ Regulating the
   pressures   economy

Kirsten — The whole   Keynes — Capitalism
   point is to enjoy   is not a self-
   it & he doesn't   correcting system

C/ Ecological   D/ Reflexive
   development /   knowledge
   modernization

                          Einstein —   An
Using Giddens et al   intellect   with
                             personality ?

Avoid pollution

McKenzie — let's discuss
   when we're going   *ring ticket office*

Social expectations – Modern schools in a post- or late modern world – Fears and anxieties – The relationship between education and the economy – Discourses of possibility – Scenario 1: Maintaining the 'eduction myth' – Scenario 2: Regulating the economy – Scenario 3: Ecological development – Scenario 4: Reflexive knowledge – Which scenario?

Unhappiness is best defined as the difference between our talents and our expectations.

Edward de Bono, 1977

Social expectations

Unhappiness in late twentieth century education seemed to emerge from an early tendency to expect too little of the majority of the population and a gradual propensity to expect too much. In the mid twentieth century it was assumed that most people would achieve very few educational qualifications. Assessment at the age of eleven defined the majority as incapable of academic work, incapable of studying certain subjects, such as foreign languages, and incapable of passing examinations at school-leaving age. These assumptions were based on what seemed to be common sense, on an acceptance that abilities could be measured and an understanding that no more than basic skills were needed anyway in order to succeed in manual-labour. Although some individuals might challenge such assumptions, this was part of public knowledge and public discourse. We *knew* that destinies could be determined at the age of eleven, and in most cases they were. Compare this with what is *known* at the start of a new millennium. It is now assumed that most people will achieve educational qualifications across a wide range of subjects, not only demonstrating abilities in one subject, but also showing the versatility needed in order to thrive in a constantly changing workplace. A basic grasp of a (generally European) foreign language is expected of even those who struggled to achieve good grades in lessons taught in English. All are expected not only to have good literacy and numeracy skills but also be computer literate and open to future technical developments. Although some individuals are clearly not able to match superhuman expectations, notions of infallibility have become part of public knowledge and public discourse. We *know* that the job market dictates a competitive ethos, insecurity and fear of failure.

Sociology challenges common assumptions, and the associated public knowledge and discourse, and this book has shown how understandings have changed over time. We have seen how the optimism of postwar society gave way to pessimism as it was realized that, despite the expansion of mass education, hopes for a genuine meritocracy were dashed by continuing inequalities of educational opportunities. That pessimism includes assumptions that British education systems are failing to deliver the skills needed to support a thriving national economy able to compete in an increasingly demanding global market. Yet what German sociologists call a *Zeitdiagnostische Soziologie* can study the interaction between education and social change and not only challenge such assumptions but also question the continuation of such trends. Writing at the turn of the century it is possible to see how we can learn from the past, understand the present and anticipate various alternative futures.

Modern schools in a post- or late modern world

Let us start by considering what sort of education systems we have at the turn of the century. Of course we have a very wide range of school types, incorporating a variety of educational cultures, standards and so on, but the existence of so many types may simply camouflage more significant features. Some writers (e.g. Hargreaves, 1994) have observed that schools have not changed enough and that most are still basically modern institutions, looking out of place in an increasingly postmodern or late modern world. This can be seen if we compare schools with other large places of work occupied by adults. Whilst other forms of mass production have gradually declined to be replaced by smaller units offering more personalized services, schools remain as large, often impersonal establishments geared to a treadmill of expectations. It therefore seems reasonable to compare them with other workplaces occupied by hundreds or even thousands of workers. In most labour-intensive workplaces, barn-like halls with row upon row of anonymous workers have gradually been replaced by smaller work units and a variety of work experiences. Yet schoolwork often takes place in crowded classrooms, pupils may shuffle into crowded assembly halls, resources may be scarce and the playground may be a threatening place occupied by bullies. Children's names may or may not be known to teachers, who must manage large numbers of pupils together with increasing amounts of paperwork. Even in the 1990s some schools did not have inside toilets, adhere to health and safety regulations or have the attractive environments expected of most large workplaces. Indeed, it seems that the sort of working environment that was acceptable fifty years ago, when most children experienced similar working conditions to those of their parents, is looking less acceptable when shared with only a minority of adult workers. Schoolwork in smaller units/classes and pleasant surroundings is usually experienced only by those children attending particularly affluent schools or remaining in education after school-leaving age.

Fears and anxieties

Although parents, teachers and administrators may try hard to compensate for the experience of mass education it is also clear that education has been, and continues to be, a fearful experience in many other ways. Although children have, throughout history, dreaded the public ridicule they faced in class or at home when they did something wrong, the threshold of failure has moved and become more challenging as unreasonable expectations have been placed on all children, instead of the few. As one among many children, all becoming increasingly aware of a future of economic uncer-

tainties in a competitive world, a schoolchild today faces different fears to those encountered by the children of fifty years ago. It is even possible that children may fear both failure and success.

Writers such as Elliott and Atkinson (1998) argue that by the late 1990s two decades of globalization and economic liberalization had produced even greater anxieties. Green, Wolf and Leney (1999) observed that, although globalization is in some ways a continuation of past trends, the current 'internationalization' is qualitatively distinct from the globalization of the past. In particular they note that its expansion is likely to be accelerated because of the scale and impact of multinational enterprises, the quickening pace of scientific and technical innovation, and the communication revolution which now encompasses not only goods but also services such as knowledge and ideas. Those individuals and/or states who cannot keep pace with change of this sort will be marginalized and the social consequences may be dire.

> Some of the most fundamental social changes now occurring in European states are those which serve to fragment and atomize society. Maintaining social cohesion and mutual solidarity in a world of centrifugal forces may yet be the greatest challenge facing the societies and education systems of the next century.
>
> Green, Wolf and Leney, 1999, p 20

The relationship between education and the economy

The big question is whether education can best support social cohesion by giving its highest priority to preparation for work or by aiming to develop wider intellectual and creative capacities. In the light of continuing dissatisfaction with the vocational emphasis in British (particularly English and Welsh) education, some writers challenge even the assumption that raising education standards will have a clear and positive effect on economic performance. Elliott and Atkinson see it as a deeply entrenched 'myth'.

HOW CHILDREN FAIL

Nobody starts off stupid. You have only to watch babies and infants, and think seriously about what all of them learn and do, to see that, except for the most grossly retarded, they show a style of life, and a desire and ability to learn, that in an older person we might well call genius. Hardly an adult in a thousand, or ten thousand, could in any three years of his life learn as much, grow as much in his understanding of the world around him, as every infant learns and grows in his first three years. But what happens, as we get older, to this extraordinary capacity for learning and intellectual growth?

What happens is that it is destroyed, and more than any other one thing, by the process that we misname education – a process that goes on in most homes and schools. We adults destroy most of the intellectual and creative capacity of children by the things we do to them or make them do. We destroy this capacity above all by making them afraid, afraid of not doing what other people want, of not pleasing, of making mistakes, of failing, or being wrong. Thus we make them afraid to gamble, afraid to experiment, afraid to try the difficult and the unknown. Even when we do not create children's fears, when they come to us with fears ready-made and built-in, we use these fears as handles to manipulate them and get them to do what we want. Instead of trying to whittle down their fears, we build them up, often to monstrous size. For we like children who are afraid of us, docile, deferential children, though not, of course, if they are so obviously afraid that they threaten our image of ourselves as kind, lovable people whom there is no reason to fear. We find ideal the kind of 'good' children who are just enough afraid of us to do everything we want, without making us feel that fear of us is what is making them do it.

Holt, 1964, 1990, pp 273–4

OUR DEEPEST FEAR

Our deepest fear is not that we are inadequate. Our deepest fear is that we are powerful beyond measure. It is our light, not our darkness, that most frightens us. We ask ourselves, 'Who am I to be brilliant, gorgeous, talented, fabulous?' Actually, who are you not to be? You are a child of God. Your playing small doesn't serve the world. There is nothing enlightened about shrinking so that other people won't feel insecure around you. We are all meant to shine, as children do. We were born to make manifest the glory of God that is within us. It is not just in some of us, it's in everyone. And as we let our light shine, we unconsciously give other people permission to do the same. As we're liberated from our own fear, our presence automatically liberates others.

Nelson Mandela

Questions

Discuss Holt's claim that adults destroy the intellectual and creative capacities of children.
Discuss Mandela's claim that people fear success more than they fear failure.
Can anything be done to tackle these problems?

Discourses of possibility

So far we have considered problems rather than solutions, but writers often baulk at the prospect of anticipating or promoting one particular future. Indeed, the lessons learned from the rest of this book should be enough to suggest that predictions are impossible and that it is not wise to make them. Educationalists and politicians have regularly introduced changes in education that have not born the fruit expected. Yet not every writer is prudent and the findings emerging in this book seem to flow naturally from past, to present, to future. Perhaps such a flow may be regarded as more prudent if we consider discourses of possibility as utopian, rather than dystopian.

> What is central to develop in response to this position [a cynical rejection of all utopian images] is a discriminating notion of possibility, one that makes a distinction between a language that is 'dystopian' and one that is utopian. In the former, the appeal to the future is grounded in a form of nostalgic romanticism that calls for a return to a past, which more often than not serves to legitimate relations of domination and

. . . it is not easy to see what the policy of 'education, education and education' is actually going to achieve. It may be that education is desirable in its own right – indeed it certainly is, provided that what is delivered is education rather than merely a training checklist demanded by business. It may be that education and training have a part to play within a package designed to improve economic performance. But on its own, raising educational standards will not be the magic ingredient that will ensure higher levels of growth.

Why should that be? First, supply does not necessarily bring forth its own demand. If it did, the establishment of a training school designed to churn out astronauts and rocket scientists would ensure that Britain had its own space programme. What actually happens, in a period of low growth, is that there are not enough good jobs for those with qualifications, and they start to take the jobs for which they are over-qualified, thereby displacing people further down the ladder. There is evidence that those at the bottom of the ladder are disadvantaged because of poor levels of attainment in literacy and numeracy. However, the government's education is not aimed at them specifically, but is rather concentrated on raising the average performance.

Second, as with stability and low inflation, it is hard to find proof which links educational attainment with growth levels. A recent study by Peter Robinson, of the LSE's Centre for Economic Performance (1997), says that once the vast majority of the adult population is functionally literate – the case in most developed countries for many years – any link between the attainment of literacy and numeracy and economic performance is very hard to demonstrate. He says that much has been made of a recent cross-country comparison showing that British fourteen-year-olds lagged well behind pupils from Singapore, Hong Kong, South Korea and Japan in a recent mathematical study. But what does this actually prove? America, which has the highest GDP per capita in the world, came out of the study as badly as Britain, and what possible influence could the performance of students at least two years away from leaving school have on economic performance? A more meaningful study carried out in 1982–83 showed that children in Hong Kong and Singapore did not have significantly higher scores in maths than those in England. 'Any notion that the impressive economic growth of these countries in the last decade or so is a product of past superior attainment in mathematics is not borne out by the evidence. Indeed, the relative improvement in mathematics attainment of Hong Kong students has followed economic growth and not precipitated it' (Robinson, 1997).

Elliott and Atkinson, 1998, pp 240–1

Elliott and Atkinson argue that what most people want can be described as 'security' (including a good job and reasonable pay), but this is one thing that will not be provided as it is perceived as standing in the way of competitiveness, and that this is a frightening proposition for those who cannot 'compete in the cut-throat game' (p 247). They argue that, although comparisons over time using the Gross Domestic Product suggest that most people have never been richer, this is a crude way of evaluating society's well-being. Instead they cite comparisons over time using an Index of Sustainable Economic Welfare (recently developed by radical economists as an attempt to monitor crime rates, unemployment, environmental degradation, stress-related illnesses and other social concepts). These comparisons suggest that during the 1950s both the GDP and ISEW rose together but that from the mid 1970s onwards the two measures moved apart. The GDP per head continued to rise, whilst the ISEW started to decline and by the 1990s was almost back to the levels of the early 1950s.

Questions

How do Elliott and Atkinson distinguish between 'education' and 'training'?

Discuss the claim that a link between literacy and numeracy and economic performance is hard to prove.

oppression. . . . In contrast to the language of dystopia, a discourse of possibility rejects apocalyptic emptiness and nostalgic imperialism and sees history as open and society worth struggling for in the image of an alternative future.

Adapted from Giroux,
in Halsey *et al.*, 1997, p 126

Within sociology there is a growing discourse which focuses on uncertainties about the future. Indeed, the fascination with the future has become even more mesmerizing when combined with claims by some sociologists (such as Elliott and Atkinson, 1998) that today our futures are more uncertain than they were in the past. They see a different type of uncertainty because they believe that we have a different capacity to shape our futures. More sociologists are working together and using their imagination to identify alternative 'scenarios' for the future, based on an understanding of current trends, issues and priorities (e.g. Ling, 1998). They do not claim that such scenarios will happen, but simply claim that they could. The scenarios are created by building on a wide range of existing data about various trends, searching for key issues and finding the 'drivers' for change (main theories about how the world is changing). In this way scenarios can be used to aid lateral thinking (including awareness of possibilities and uncertainties), improve current practice (by identifying those practices which could succeed and those which would be undermined in each scenario) and form the basis for various workshops (involving people from relevant organizations).

Scenario 1: Maintaining the 'education myth'

Our first scenario is one in which current trends continue unabated. This is not real continuity because education is constantly changing, even if that change simply means adaptation, or gradual incremental change. Yet just suppose that there is no radical departure from current pathways, or from continued assumptions that higher educational standards will stimulate the economy (Elliott and Atkinson's 'education myth'), no change of government and no radical change of government policies. This means that pressure on educational systems and on pupils, students and teachers to constantly achieve more will continue.

Green, Wolf and Leney (1999) claim that, in order to remain competitive and prosper, European states will need to move even further into knowledge-intensive, information-rich production and services with an emphasis on innovation and rapid change (p 6). They cite the European Commission's White Paper *Teaching and Learning: Towards the learning society*, which says that 'The European Union's greatest asset for boosting its industrial competitiveness is its capacity to generate

and use knowledge, with the aid of the great potential of its labour force and the social consensus laying the foundations for harnessing it' (European Commission, Brussels, 1995, p 29). Furthermore, they see the success of many organizations as centred on their ability to promote their 'collective intelligence', with a focus on multi-disciplinary problem-solving skills, teamwork and communication (p 12). Whilst becoming even more competitive, organizations will have to study the activities of adjacent organizations and even create more interlinking of those organizations with mutual interests. Thus, the search for good practice may not necessarily mean separation or lack of co-operation.

The search for good practice will, however, mean that individuals continue to strive for an unattainable perfection, always conscious that if they cannot achieve it, someone else may make a good impression of having done so. What Giddens calls the 'manufactured risk' resulting from human intervention in the conditions of life and nature could be extended to the workplace and the education workplace. When unreasonable expectations are imposed on human beings, the consequences of failure become more acute. Such expectations will look even more unreasonable if modern school systems are not adapted to keep pace with postmodern or late modern societies. This means that the input of computer systems into schools will not be enough, as they need to be supported by new learning environments in keeping with the knowledge-intensive, information-rich workplaces for which future workers are being prepared.

A continued emphasis on vocationalism as the prime purpose of education will mean a continued emphasis on the transferable skills needed to cope with changes in technology and a constantly changing job market. Thus specialization at school age will still be frowned on and the generalist will be prized more highly than the individual whose talents primarily lie in one area. There is also the risk that some of the joy will be taken out of learning, as children are given little choice about what they want to study. Some of the Labourville and Torytown cohort expressed concerns about this.

As pressures continue, even those who are the most successful in education may suffer as they discover that the rewards do not fit their efforts.

Children are expected to be able to do more than we did. It's a different sort of work now and they like parents to take an active part. Me and my husband have arguments about that. I don't agree with him bringing reading books home. I feel as though it's taken something from me. I'm used to reading our own books with him and he doesn't like the school books. The whole point is to enjoy it and sometimes he doesn't. It puts too much pressure on him.

Kirsten, 1992

[Disagrees with the ruling that applicants for teacher training must have the equivalent of a pass in O level' mathematics.] They will not accept that, for example, somebody from the arts side may be brilliantly gifted at art, or the arts, at English, but hopeless at maths and vice versa. And now they're going back to this idea that if you're not good at a broad spectrum then it's not good enough. I personally disagree.

[Cited members of his family who were not good at maths but excelled in the arts.] And now we see in this business where there was a great emphasis on dyslexia and now it's beginning to bubble-up that people have problems with numbers, but that they can be gifted in other areas. It's a worry to me that we're now going back to this standardizing and that, unless you're good at a broad spectrum of subjects, there's something wrong with you.

[What would you like to see?] I would like to see a child have a chance to progress to their maximum ability and not be held back because they are not good at one particular subject, and whatever subjects that they are good at, that they're given the maximum chance to show brilliance in those subjects.

John, 1997

In 1999 Gardner and Oswald (economists at Warwick University) reported on their yearly interviews with 7,000 workers, which they had conducted during the 1990s. They discovered that those people with degrees tended to be less happy than those with A levels or GCSEs, who in turn scored less well than those with no qualifications. Gardner and Oswald's conclusions tended to match the quote at the start of this chapter, as they suggested that education raised people's targets and satisfaction depended upon the gap between outcomes and aspirations. As students face the debts incurred whilst gaining their further or higher education, it is likely that monetary rewards will become even more important, a *genuine* meritocracy will be regarded as even more essential and resentments will escalate as we see further evidence that the UK is not a meritocracy. Problems for the highly qualified lie not only in the possible lack of monetary reward but also in their heavy workloads, as many learn to work without lunchbreaks, take their work home with them and constantly strive to justify their privileged positions in a competitive job market. Yet an information-rich society can only thrive if it is remembered that it is populated by people rather than computers. Perhaps the comedian Alexei Sayle was being particularly perceptive when he observed that, although scientists have talked about intelligent computers, computers would only be intelligent if they did not work all the time! A continuation of the present scenario involves a loss of balance, a failure to distinguish between the human and the technical and real dangers for both the high achievers and those who cannot, or do not want to, face the pressures of an inhumane model of education.

> It may come as a surprise to those who favour home-school contracts and would willingly send a homework police force round to check that seven-year-olds are learning their tables rather than watching videos, but most people endure rather than enjoy education. They do enough to get by, but no more. Given the choice between a night in the pub and an interesting paper from the Internet on aboriginal culture from the University of New South Wales, we would hazard a guess that they would choose the former, even if Mr. Blair gave them all a free PC.
>
> Elliot and Atkinson, 1988, p 271

Scenario 2: Regulating the economy

Our second scenario involves a radical change from free-market economics to the sort of government intervention in the economy favoured in the 1940s to 1960s. Elliott and Atkinson offered recent evidence to support Keynes's claim that capitalism is not a self-correcting system and should not be left to its own devices. For example, they cited the events of 'Black Wednesday' in the UK (16 September 1992), when the pound sterling was ejected from the Exchange Rate Mechanism. Although, in principal, committed to New Right monetarist policies, John Major responded with Keynesian-style intervention (which he called a 'growth strategy') to regulate the economy, and it worked. Perhaps the key is to reclaim power ceded to the 'institutions of money'.

> Instead of looking at the world through the one-way mirror of big business, we should look at the sort of world we would like to see. We are not asking for much. We would like to see full employment, we would like a high-wage rather than a low-wage economy, we would like job security, we would like a fairer distribution of income between and within countries, we would like to have some certainty that the planet will outlast us. Now ask whether the culture of big business helps in that process?
>
> Elliott and Atkinson, 1998, p 269

There is, indeed, some evidence of a change of direction since 1997 by a Labour government committed to monitoring the free market and challenging some of the wilder excesses of big business. However, even if they accept that capitalism is not a self-correcting system, politicians and economists are still wary about the risk of returning to the high inflation associated in the past with Keynesian economics. They are, moreover, concerned about the consequences (to the economy and on voting behaviour) of raising taxes in order to finance increased spending on education. Survey data (including findings from the Greater Manchester Study) have regularly indicated that voters are willing to pay extra in taxation in order to provide more generous support for education, but analysts are concerned that there may be a difference between what voters say and what they actually do. Informants may claim that they are willing to pay higher taxes, because this suggests a social conscience, but actually vote against them because their instrumental values outweigh their social conscience at the ballot box. At any one time only a

minority of the population have been involved in the education systems themselves (or linked through their children) and it seems safe to say that many others will attach greater importance to other issues when deciding how to vote (see Chapter 5). Yet government efforts to introduce market principles, and their associated risks, into education and other social services have only been partially successful (e.g. in encouraging careful budgeting and greater enterprise) and led to many voters labelling politicians as mean-spirited and ignorant of the reality of social inequalities.

Scenario 3: Ecological development

Our third scenario involves applying ecological rhetoric to the education system. Many scientists and social scientists are concerned about the long-term prospects for a form of economic development that will not damage the environment. As Dryzek notes

> Ecological modernization implies a partnership in which governments, businesses, moderate environmentalists, and scientists cooperate in the restructuring of the capitalist political economy along more environmentally defensible lines.
>
> Dryzek, 1997, p 145

According to this scenario, the ecological modernization of education involves a partnership in which policy-makers, administrators, educationalists, social scientists and businesses co-operate in the restructuring of British education systems along more humane and environmentally defensible lines. There are parallels with the aim of environmentalists to replace 'end of pipe' technologies with modes of production designed to avoid or limit pollution. In the case of education the aim would be to generate sustainable educational development by maximizing positive educational products whilst avoiding the 'pollution' (side effects) of its negative impact, such as stress, mental illness, credential inflation and so on. If we are conscious of the damaging effects of large-scale industrial workplaces in the past, we can surely be conscious of the detrimental effects of a dehumanizing type of mass education. Should not education, like industry, be excused from the pressures of time and motion, overcrowding and otherwise unsafe working conditions?

Yet little or no public debate has taken place about the 'pollution' caused by education. As a result, some state schools have been allowed to become 'sink' schools; overcrowded, a scarcity of basic resources, still using outside toilets, and with less concern about health and safety than factories and offices. Long before their problems have been officially recognized, such schools have already failed many of their children and possibly caused irreparable damage to their long-term prospects. At the other extreme, some of the more successful schools could become sweatboxes, squeezing the maximum output from anxious, but 'successful', pupils. Many adult workers have refused to tolerate unsafe working conditions, overcrowding or the pressures of the conveyor belt and time and motion studies. Yet some schools still look less like late modern workplaces than the impersonal, alienating industries of the nineteenth century.

Can the theories of ecological modernization be successfully applied to education? First, it would currently be difficult to modernize education along ecological lines when few policy-makers are likely to recognize that educational 'pollution' exists. Indeed, such pollution often takes the form of very individual, personalized responses to educational experiences, and these can be overlooked. Second, it is unlikely that action will be taken whilst the needs of the economy are seen to take priority over the needs of the individual. Only a perceived link between educational pollution and major social problems is likely to persuade policy-makers of the need to change their priorities and the necessary evidence to support that link has not yet been acknowledged. Third, most politicians tend to address relatively minor educational issues whilst failing to see the wider picture. As a result, they not only believe in their existing education policies but also believe that their policies will tackle effectively any current problems. Finally, it would be easy to dismiss the demands associated with the development of education along ecological grounds as too excessive, unreasonable or utopian without making any effort to identify what would actually have to be done.

Scenario 4: Reflexive knowledge

Our fourth scenario involves looking at what we mean by 'knowledge' afresh. It is simply not possible, or humane, to insist that all students internalize the mass of information available today. The consequences of trying to learn more and more are too dire, not only in terms of the 'failures' who fall by the wayside, but also in terms of those 'successes' who must face a never-ending struggle to maintain an image of perfection. Even one of the twentieth century's most formidable minds, Albert Einstein, suggested that although the intellect has powerful muscles, it has no personality and therefore should not be elevated to a godlike status. Yet to suggest that students should learn less, rather than more, appears blasphemous and has a history of failure.

This scenario involves progress towards what Einstein might have called an 'intellect with personality', and this process could be aided by adding an extra R of 'Reflexivity' to the original three Rs of reading, writing and arithmetic. It means encouraging an opening of minds through education so that individuals can appreciate the ephemeral nature of knowledge and engage in genuine creativity instead of the artificial creativity dictated by the problem-solving exercises espoused by technicists.

> The really able thinkers in our class turn out to be, without exception, children who don't feel so strongly the need to please grownups. Some of them are good students, some not so good; but good or not, they don't work to please us, but to please themselves.
>
> Holt, 1964, p 29

> We ought also to learn, beginning early, that we don't always succeed. A good batting average in baseball is .300; a good batting average in life is a great deal lower than that. Life holds many more defeats than victories for all of us. Shouldn't we get used to this early? We should learn, too, to aim higher than we think we can hit. 'A man's reach should exceed his grasp, or what's Heaven for?'
>
> Holt, 1964, pp 67–8

Genuine creativity is, of course, a dangerous thing because it can challenge accepted norms and even appear subversive (see Chapter 4 about the curriculum) and, for this reason, fear can lead some children to fail. If we look at the list of educational principles drawn up by Giroux, we may find that the freedoms they suggest only seem attractive if they generate a form of education that does not challenge our own beliefs and way of life.

HENRY GIROUX ON 'PRINCIPLES OF CRITICAL PEDAGOGY'

1. Schools should be constructed as democratic public spheres, which means that the knowledge, habits, and skills of critical citizenship, not simply good citizenship, are taught and practiced.

2. Ethics must be seen as a central concern of critical pedagogy, involving a social discourse that refuses to accept needless human suffering and exploitation, is grounded in historical struggles and attentive to the construction of social relations free of injustice.

3. Critical pedagogy needs to focus on the issue of difference in a challenging and politically transformative way. This involves an attempt to understand how student identities and subjectivities are constructed in multiple and contradictory ways and how differences between groups develop and are sustained around both enabling and disabling sets of relations. Teachers can offer students the opportunity to read the world differently, resist the abuse of power and privilege, and construct alternative democratic communities.

4. Curriculum knowledge should not be treated as a sacred text but developed as part of an ongoing engagement with a variety of narratives and traditions that can be reread and reformulated in politically different terms. Knowledge has to be constantly re-examined in terms of its limits and rejected as a body of information that only has to be passed down to students.

5. Critical pedagogy needs to create new forms of knowledge through its emphasis on breaking down disciplinary boundaries and creating new spheres in which knowledge can be produced. It reclaims the historical and the popular as part of an ongoing effort to critically appropriate the voices of those who have been silenced. At stake here is a pedagogy that provides the knowledge, skills, and habits for students and others to read history in ways that enable them to reclaim their identities in the interests of constructing more democratic and just forms of life.

6. The Enlightenment notion of reason needs to be reformulated within a critical pedagogy. First, educators need to be skeptical regarding any notion of reason that purports to reveal the truth by denying its own historical construction and ideological principles. Second, the limits of reason must be extended to recognizing other ways in which people learn or take up particular subject positions.

7. Critical pedagogy needs to regain a sense of alternatives; as postmodern feminism has done both in its critique of patriarchy and its search to construct new forms of identity and social relations. Educators need to construct a language of critique that combines the issue of limits with the discourse of freedom and social responsibility. They need to explore a language of possibility that is capable of thinking risky thoughts, that engages a project of hope, and points to the horizon of the 'not yet'. It does not have to dissolve into a reified form of utopianism but can be developed as a precondition for nourishing convictions that summon up the courage to imagine a different and more just world and to struggle for it.

8. Critical pedagogy needs to develop a theory of educators and cultural workers as transformative intellectuals who occupy specific political and social locations. Rather than defining teacher work through the narrow language of professionalism, a critical pedagogy needs to ascertain more carefully what the role of teachers might be as cultural workers engaged in the production of ideologies and social practices.

9. Central to the notion of critical pedagogy is a politics of voice that combines a postmodern notion of difference with a feminist emphasis on the primacy of the political. This suggests taking up the relationship between the personal and the political so as to engage rather than withdraw from addressing those institutional forms and structures that contribute to forms of racism, sexism, and class exploitation. First,

the self must be seen as a primary site of politicization. That is, the issue of how the self is constructed in multiple and complex ways must be analyzed . . . Second, a politics of voice must offer pedagogical and political strategies that affirm the primacy of the social, intersubjective, and collective. This begins with what bell hooks [sic] calls a critical attention to theorizing experience as part of a broader politics of engagement. In referring specifically to feminist pedagogy, she argues that the discourse of confession and memory can be used to 'shift the focus away from mere naming of one's experience . . . to talk about identity in relation to culture, history and politics' (hooks, b., 1989, Talking Back, Boston: Southend Press, p 110)

Adapted from Giroux, in Halsey *et al.*, 1997, pp 123–128; in the original Giroux, 1992, pp 39–88.

Questions

Discuss arguments for and against Giroux' claim that educators should 'explore a language of possibility that is capable of thinking risky thoughts' (item 7).
Can you identify practical teaching strategies that could be used to promote this sort of critical thought?

'EDUCATION IS OUR FUTURE': VIEWS FROM TORYTOWN AND LABOURVILLE

Education is the future of the country.

Eric, 1992

Education is the future of the country.

Kirsten, 1992

Education is important for the future.

Polly, 1992

Education is for the future.

Paul, 1992

Education is the future and you've got to spend for the future. You've got to give kids a chance.

Bernard, 1992

Education's the most important [government spending priority] because it's the future. If children are not educated, there's no hope for us.

Michelle, 1992

I think it [education] is a long-term investment, for the next twenty years. Therefore, you need to start it tomorrow rather than in a year's time. The payback is in twenty years. Its value is crucial to the competitiveness of the country and to social stability.

Richard, 1992

Education is the future. We can't spend enough on that.

Henry, 1997

I think education, it's the future. I mean, the children of today are going to be the government of tomorrow really, and the voters.

Kirsten, 1997

Education is important, obviously, because it benefits certain people while they're going through the process, and afterwards, but in the long run everybody benefits from a good education service.

Jeremy, 1997

Which scenario?

The problem as we reach the end of this book is that it is not possible to suggest that any one scenario, or combination of scenarios, is most likely to dominate the early part of the twenty-first century. It is, however, possible to formulate a personal conclusion that there is an urgent need for a national debate about where British education seems to be going at the turn of the century. Without such a debate it will continue to career along its existing tracks at breakneck speed, with passengers unable or unwilling to check its progress. It will move forward but we will have little control over its safe destination or whom it may harm in its path.

It was the destination of education that most concerned members of the Torytown and Labourville cohort. Of the many concepts used by interviewees it was the 'future' that they most clearly associated with education, even if they were unsure about what they meant. Not only did they use the word 'future', but some even used identical phrases when talking about the future. To them education had a long-term impact and was an experience that could influence opportunities for themselves, their families, friends and country. Their commentaries in this book show that, even if they did not understand or express a strong interest in educational issues, they appreciated that changes in education would have more wide-ranging repercussions than any of us could anticipate.

Appendix 1 Family biographies

Informants interviewed in the last three phases of the Torytown and Labourville research are listed below in order of age, from the oldest to the youngest. Where an individual has not provided a date of birth, a rough estimate is provided (i.e. that the person was born before a given year at the latest). Efforts to maintain some sort of anonymity include giving interviewees different names and making some of the information intentionally vague (e.g. describing someone as a 'skilled manual worker' rather than stating the actual occupation). Other information was accurate at the time of the last interviews. Jobs and votes were consistent in all of the interviews with an individual informant, unless indicated as otherwise. Experience suggests that there will have been significant changes in the cohort's circumstances by the time this book is published, three years after the last interview.

Where the dates of interviews are noted as 1980 or 1984 they actually refer, respectively, to the first two phases of fieldwork for the Greater Manchester Study in 1980/1 and 1983/4. The first two phases of the Greater Manchester Study provided quantitative data and no quotes. Therefore most of the information provided here relates to circumstances affecting the views quoted in 1988, 1992 and 1997.

Fieldwork dates: 8 June–11 July 1988; April 1992; July 1997.

A similar, short biography of the author of this book is also provided at the end of this appendix.

Albert   Torytown, born 1910
Interviewed in 1980, 1984, 1988 and 1992. Not willing in 1997.

Parents: Father attended elementary school, school-leaving age unknown, but left with no qualifications and had no further formal education. Did not know what sort of school his mother attended or her school-leaving age. She left with no qualifications and had no further formal education. Both parents were manual workers. Did not know how they voted.
Education: Passed scholarship to attend a single-sex grammar school but left at 13 with no qualifications. Since then attended evening classes, not leading to any qualifications.
Work: Trained on the job as a (private sector) skilled manual worker. Retired in 1975.
Partner, children etc.: Wife was a sales assistant but by 1988 was retired. They had no children living at home and none in further education.
Vote: In 1983 voted Liberal. Did not vote in the 1987 general election or local election. In 1992 too ill to vote but would have voted Liberal Democrat.

Annie   Labourville, born 1916
Interviewed in 1980, 1984, 1988 and 1992. Not willing in 1997.
Parents: Both parents attended elementary school, left at 14 with no qualifications and had no further formal education. Father was a semi-skilled manual worker, employed in the public and the private sector and voted Labour. Mother gave up work when she had children and voted Liberal.
Education: Attended a technical central school and left at 15 with RSA qualification(s). Trained as a nurse.
Work: Worked as a nurse in the public sector but gave up when she had children. Now retired.

Partner, children etc.: Married. Husband was a skilled manual worker, self-employed (with his own shop). No children living with them.
Vote: Consistently voted Conservative.

Anthony Torytown, born 1917
Interviewed in 1980, 1984 and 1988.
Parents: Knew nothing about his father's education. He was a non-manual worker in a routine but supervisory position, working in the private sector and voted Conservative. His mother attended elementary school, left at 12 with no qualifications and had no further formal education. She worked as a sales assistant and voted Conservative.
Education: Passed a scholarship, attended a 'high' school and left at 15 with no qualifications. He attended evening classes, not leading to qualifications.
Work: Retired. Was previously employed in the private sector in a supervisory position.
Partner, children etc.: Widowed. No children.
Vote: Consistently voted Conservative.

Audrey Torytown, born 1918
Interviewed in 1980, 1984, 1988, 1992 and 1997.
Parents: Both parents attended elementary school, left at 14 with no qualifications, had no further formal education and did unskilled manual work in the private sector. Mother voted Conservative and did not know how her father voted.
Education: Attended coeducational state/church elementary school, left at 14 with no qualifications and had no further education.
Work: In the past did clerical work, worked in a hospital laundry and on a market stall. In 1997 retired with only a state pension.
Partner, children etc.: No partner and no children.
Vote: Did not vote in 1987 general election or in last local election before 1988. In 1992 voted Conservative in general election and local election. In 1997 did not vote in general election and voted Labour in local election.

Bernard Labourville, born 1920
Interviewed in 1980, 1984, 1988 and 1992. Died before 1997.
Parents: Knew nothing about his father's education. He was a skilled manual worker in the private sector. His mother attended an elementary school, left at 14 with no qualifications and had no

further formal education. She gave up work when she had children. Both parents voted Labour.
Education: Did not know what type of school he attended, took no selective examination, left at 16 with no qualifications. Gained some qualifications at evening classes. Well read about educational philosophy.
Work: Low-level management/supervisor in the public sector. Was retired in 1988.
Partner, children etc.: Widowed. In 1988 his daughter (not living with him) was taking a degree.
Vote: Voted Conservative in the 1987 general election and did not vote in the last local election before 1988. Voted Labour in the general election and local election in 1992.

Brenda Labourville, born 1920
Interviewed in 1980, 1984, 1988 and 1992.
Parents: Father attended elementary school, left at 13, with no qualifications and had no further formal education. He was a skilled manual worker in the private sector and voted Conservative. Mother attended elementary school, left at 14 with no qualifications and had no further formal education. She worked in family business and voted Conservative.
Education: Passed an examination to attend a technical central school, left at 15 with no qualifications and had taken evening classes, not leading to a qualification.
Work: Routine non-manual work. Was retired in 1988.
Partner, children etc.: Married. Husband in a supervisory non-manual job in the public sector. No children living at home.
Vote: Consistently voted Conservative.

Brian Labourville, born 1922
Interviewed in 1980, 1984 and 1988. Could not contact in 1992.
Parents: Father attended an elementary school, left at 12 with no qualifications and had no further formal education. He had a supervisory non-manual position in the public sector and voted Conservative. Mother attended elementary school, left at 13 with no qualifications and had no further formal education. She gave up work when she had children and voted Liberal.
Education: Attended an elementary school, left at 14 with no qualifications and later took evening classes, not leading to a qualification.

Work: Worked as a low-level manager in the private sector. Retired in 1983.
Partner, children etc.: Married. In 1988 wife did routine non-manual work in the public sector. No children living at home or in education.
Vote: Consistently voted Conservative.

Caroline   Torytown, born 1922
Interviewed in 1980, 1984, 1988, 1992 and 1997.
Parents: Both parents attended a private/direct grant school, left at 13 with no qualifications and had no further formal education. Father was a semi-skilled manual worker in both private and public sectors and voted Labour. Mother gave up work when she had children and voted Labour.
Education: Passed examination to attend grammar school, left at 15 with no qualifications and had since taken courses, not leading to qualifications.
Work: Gave up work when she had children. In 1980 was disabled. In 1997 living in sheltered accommodation. Supported by husband's company pension and income from investments.
Partner, children etc.: Widowed. In 1992 lived with her son, who had his own shop. Had five children. In 1997 four surviving children aged 35–45. First (daughter) attended a private, single-sex grammar school, took a degree and became a teacher. Second (son) attended a single-sex comprehensive school, left at 16 with two O levels and became an engineer. Third (son) attended single-sex grammar school, left with seven O levels and became a manager of his own business. Fourth (son) attended single-sex grammar school, left with seven O levels, studied catering, had various jobs, was made redundant earlier in 1997 and currently unemployed. Fifth (daughter) attended single-sex secondary modern school, left with seven O levels, trained and worked as a secretary.
Vote: Only voted Labour in 1945. Since then has consistently voted Conservative.

Cecil   Labourville, born 1923
Interviewed in 1980, 1984 and 1988, ill in 1992.
Parents: Both parents attended elementary schools, left at 12 with no qualifications and had no further formal education. Father was a semi-skilled manual worker (supervisor) in the public sector and voted Conservative. Mother gave up work when she had children.

Education: Attended a special school, left at 14 with no qualifications and attended evening classes without a qualification.
Work: In 1983 unemployed. In 1988 was retired.
Partner, children etc.: Married. Wife had given up paid work by 1983. No children living at home.
Vote: Consistently voted Labour.

Clifford   Labourville, born 1925
Interviewed in 1980, 1984, 1988, 1992 and 1997.
Parents: Father attended elementary school, left at 14 with no qualifications and took evening classes without qualifications. Employed at intermediate and supervisory level in the private sector. Mother attended elementary school, left at 14 with unspecified qualifications and took evening classes with no qualification. She had a routine non-manual job in both the public and private sectors. Both parents voted Labour.
Education: Attended a 'council school' in London. Passed a scholarship examination at 11 for a free place at a [probably direct grant] single-sex secondary/technical school. Not sure at what age he left school [14–16] but left with a distinction in his diploma. Took job as a draughtsman, joined the airforce in 1943 and trained as a pilot. After the war moved to Labourville, where he attended college and acquired an OND and HND. Took O level mathematics in his 60s.
Work: In 1992 and 1997 retired.
Partner, children etc.: Married. Wife a part-time waitress. Has four children. First (daughter) passed 11+, later went to teacher training college and became a teacher. Second and third (both sons) passed 11+ and went to grammar school. One left with two O levels. The other was expelled and became an affluent businessman. Fourth (daughter) attended comprehensive school, left with no qualifications and in 1997 was working as a shop assistant.
Vote: Consistently voted Labour, except in 1992 when he described himself as a floating voter.

Constance   Labourville, born 1925
Interviewed in 1980, 1984 and 1988, refused in 1992 (done enough).
Parents: Father attended private/direct grant school, left at 14 with no qualifications and took a day-release course. He worked as a foreman in the private sector. Mother attended elementary school,

left at 14 with no qualifications and took evening classes without qualification. She did not have paid employment. Father voted Labour and did not know how mother voted.

Education: Passed examination to attend single-sex grammar school, left at 16 with matriculation and had various further education since then.

Work: In 1983 was retired.

Partner, children etc.: Married. Husband was a professional in the public sector. No children living at home or in education.

Vote: In 1983 voted Conservative. Voted Conservative in 1987 general election and Labour in the last local election before 1988.

David   Torytown, born 1926

Interviewed in 1980, 1984 and 1988. Died before 1992.

Parents: Knew nothing about his parents' education. Father had a supervisory non-manual job. Mother worked in personal service and gave up when the children were born. Did not know how they voted.

Education: Did not know what sort of school he attended (but no selective examination), left at 16 with the equivalent of O levels and had no further education.

Work: In 1983 disabled and unemployed. Previously did various jobs.

Partner, children etc.: Married. In 1988 wife was in personal service in the public sector and one adult child was a student.

Vote: Consistently voted Labour.

Derek   Torytown, born 1928

Interviewed in 1980, 1984 and 1988. Died before 1992.

Parents: Both parents attended elementary school, left at 14 with no qualifications and had no further formal education. Father did unskilled manual work in the public sector and voted Labour. Mother worked in personal service before giving up to have children. She voted Conservative.

Education: Took no examination for selection and attended single-sex secondary modern school, left at 14 with no qualifications and had no further formal education.

Work: In 1983 self-employed as a credit traveller (intermediate level).

Partner, children etc.: In 1988 no children currently being educated.

Vote: Consistently voted Conservative.

Donald   Torytown, born 1929

Interviewed in 1980, 1984, 1988, 1992 and 1997.

Parents: Did not know what type of school his parents attended but his father left at 12 and mother left at 11, both had no qualifications and had no further formal education. Father had various jobs in both the public and private sectors. Mother did unskilled manual work in the private sector. Both parents voted Labour.

Education: Took no selective examination and attended a single-sex secondary modern school, left at 14 with no qualifications and had no further formal education.

Work: Was a semi-skilled manual worker with a supervisory role in the private sector. In 1992 he was interviewed on the day that he was made redundant. In 1997 he was retired.

Partner, children etc.: Wife also retired. Had six children (none still in education in 1988). One passed the 11+ and attended a single-sex grammar school. The rest failed and attended single-sex secondary modern schools. The four eldest all went to college after school and 'did well'. The youngest (Donald is Ryan's father) left school in 1979 or 1980 and was nearly 24 when he got his first permanent job.

Vote: In the 1987 general election voted Liberal Alliance and did not vote in last local election before 1988. In 1997 voted Labour in the general election and local election.

Eamon   Torytown, born 1930

Interviewed in 1980, 1984, 1988, 1992 and 1997.

Parents: Knew that his parents both attended elementary school, did not know at what age they left or if they had any qualifications or further education. Father was self-employed, running his own farm and supervising others. Mother was not employed outside the farm. Both parents voted Liberal.

Education: Attended a single-sex elementary (National School) school in Ireland and left at 14 with no qualifications. Has had no further formal education since then.

Work: In 1988 did unskilled manual work in the private sector. In 1992 was a part-time unskilled manual worker in the private sector. In 1997 was retired on a state pension.

Partner, children etc.: Married. In 1992 wife was full-time nurse and in 1997 a part-time nurse in the NHS. Five children. In 1988 the two youngest were still in (grammar) school. In 1992 they were taking degrees and a son was taking an evening class.

Vote: In the 1987 general election voted Conservative. Did not vote in last local election before 1988. In 1997 voted Conservative in general and local elections but said he was glad they lost the general election.

Edward   Torytown, born 1931

Interviewed in 1980, 1984, 1988 and 1992.

Parents: Did not know what type of school his parents attended, but they left at 12 with no qualifications and had no further formal education. Father was a foreman in both the private and public sectors. Mother had various jobs in the private and public sectors. Father voted Labour, mother voted Conservative.

Education: Failed the 11+ and attended a single-sex secondary modern school, left at 14 with no qualifications and had no further formal education.

Work: Semi-skilled manual work in the private and public sectors. In 1992 had taken voluntary redundancy two weeks earlier, but it was amended to early retirement.

Partner, children etc.: Married. In 1988 and 1992 wife in routine non-manual work in the private sector. In 1988 one child taking a degree.

Vote: Voted Labour in the 1987 general election but did not vote in the most recent local election. Voted Labour both times in 1992.

Elizabeth   Torytown, born 1931

Interviewed in 1980, 1984, 1988 and 1992.

Parents: Knew nothing about her parents' education. Father a skilled manual worker in the private sector. Mother not in paid employment. Both parents voted Conservative.

Education: Passed an examination to attend private/direct grant school, left at 15 with no qualifications and had no further formal education.

Work: Consistently employed in domestic work in the public and private sectors.

Partner, children etc.: In 1988 divorced and no children currently in education. In 1992 still single.

Son still lived with her but he was permanently unemployed due to mental disability.

Vote: Consistently voted SDP or Liberal Democrat.

Emma   Labourville, born 1932

Interviewed in 1980, 1984, 1988 and 1992.

Parents: Father attended elementary school, left at 12 with no qualifications and had no further formal education. He had various jobs, including a supervisory role, in the private and public sectors. Mother attended a grammar school, left at 16, matriculated but had no further formal education. She had a supervisory non-manual job in the private sector. Both parents voted Labour.

Education: Attended an elementary school, left at 14 with no qualifications and had no further formal education.

Work: Semi-skilled manual work in the public sector. In 1992 worked on a school crossing patrol.

Partner, children etc.: Married. Husband a semi-skilled manual worker in the private sector and in 1992 he was retired. In 1988 two children were living with her, one attending a primary school and one attending a comprehensive school.

Vote: Voted Conservative in 1987 general election and in the most recent local election. Did not vote in 1992 general election.

Eric   Labourville, born 1933

Interviewed in 1980, 1984 and 1988.

Parents: Both parents attended elementary school, left with no qualifications (father at 11, mother at 13) and had no further formal education. Both were unskilled manual workers in the public sector (father had a supervisory role). Both voted Conservative.

Education: Attended elementary school, left at 14 with no qualifications but gained some qualifications at evening class.

Work: In 1988 a building foreman in the public sector.

Partner, children etc.: Married. Wife an unskilled manual worker in the public sector. In 1988 he had no children currently in education.

Vote: Voted Conservative in the 1987 general election and did not vote in the most recent local election.

Frank   Torytown, born 1935

Interviewed in 1980, 1984 and 1988. Died before 1992.

Parents: Knew nothing about his parents' education or how they voted. Father was self-employed in the family business. Mother was in service but gave up employment when she had children.

Education: Attended a coeducational secondary modern school. Left-handed and forced to write with his right hand. Left school at 15 with no qualifications and had no further formal education. Still illiterate in 1988.

Work: Various unskilled manual jobs. In 1983 unemployed living on invalidity benefit. In 1988 receiving benefits for disability.

Partner, children etc.: Widowed. In 1988 two children living with him who were students.

Vote: Did not vote.

Freda   Torytown, born 1936
Interviewed in 1980, 1984, 1988 and 1992.

Parents: Knew nothing about her parents' education. Father was a skilled manual worker in a supervisory post in the private sector. Mother was a routine non-manual worker in the private sector. Both voted Conservative.

Education: Took no examination for selection and attended a single-sex secondary modern school, left at 15 with no qualifications but gained qualifications in further education.

Work: Routine non-manual work in the public sector.

Partner, children etc.: In 1988 separated, no children in school. In 1992 married, husband a sales executive and one daughter a teacher.

Vote: Conservative.

Frederick   Torytown, born 1939
Interviewed in 1980, 1984 and 1988, refused in 1992 (done enough).

Parents: Did not know what type of schools his parents attended, mother left at 13, they left with no qualifications and had no further formal education. Father was a foreman in the public and private sectors. Mother was in service but left when she had children. Both voted Labour.

Education: Attended elementary school, left at 14 with no qualifications and had no further formal education.

Work: Between 1983 and 1988 a semi-skilled manual worker in a power station.

Partner, children etc.: Married. Wife a sales assistant. In 1983 and 1988 no children currently in education.

Vote: Consistently voted Liberal/Alliance.

Georgina   Torytown, born 1939
Interviewed in 1980, 1984, 1988, 1992 and 1997.

Parents: Father attended elementary school, left at 13 with no qualifications and had no further education. Mother attended a comprehensive/high school, left at 14, did not know whether she had any qualifications but she had no further formal education. Father was a self-employed skilled manual worker. Mother was a routine non-manual worker in the private sector. Father voted Conservative, mother's vote varied.

Education: Failed 11+ examination and attended single-sex secondary modern school. Left at 15 with no qualifications and took a one-year evening class course in shorthand typing.

Work: In 1988 was a manual worker for the local social services department. In 1992 and 1997 a clerical officer working for social services.

Partner, children etc.: Married. In 1988, 1992 and 1997 husband a self-employed skilled manual worker. In 1992 no children in education. Eldest child (aged 28 in 1997) failed the 11+ examination, attended a single-sex secondary modern school, left at 16 and took a secretarial course at a college of further education. In 1997 she was working as a secretary. Other daughter (aged 25 in 1997) passed the 11+ examination, attended a single-sex grammar school (still there in 1988), left at 16 with low-grade O levels and took a two-year catering course. In 1997 she was working as a chef. Also a son, who lived with his father.

Vote: Floating voter. Voted Alliance in 1987 general election and Labour in most recent local election before 1988. In 1992 voted Labour. In 1997 voted Labour in general election and Conservative in local election (because the Conservatives 'run [Torytown] very well').

Graham   Torytown, born before 1940
Interviewed in 1980, 1984, 1988. Had died by 1992.

Parents: Did not know what type of school his parents attended but they both left at 14 with no qualifications. His mother had further formal education (unknown type) but his father had none.

Father was a skilled manual worker in the private sector. Mother was a self-employed professional. Both voted Labour.
Education: Attended technical school, left at 16 with unspecified qualifications and later took an HNC.
Work: Police officer.
Partner, children etc.: Married. Wife a routine non-manual worker in the public sector. In 1988 one adult child still in further education.
Vote: Liberal/Alliance

Helen   Torytown, born 1940
Interviewed in 1980, 1984, 1988 and 1992.
Parents: Both parents attended elementary school, left with no qualifications and had no further formal education. Father left at 14 but did not know when mother left. Father was a semi-skilled manual worker in the private sector. Mother did various jobs in the private sector. Both voted Labour.
Education: Failed 11+ and attended single-sex secondary modern school, left at 15 with no qualifications and had no further formal education.
Work: Previously worked as a sales assistant. In 1983 a housewife, in 1988 unemployed and in 1992 a cleaner in the private sector.
Partner, children etc.: In 1988 was divorced and had one child just about to leave a single-sex secondary modern school. In 1992 her daughter and baby granddaughter were living with her.
Vote: Floating voter. Liberal Alliance in the 1987 general election and Conservative in the most recent local election. In 1992 voted labour.

Henry   Torytown, born 1941
Interviewed in 1980, 1984, 1992 and 1997.
Parents: Father attended a single-sex high school, left at 15 or 16 with no qualifications and had no further formal education. Mother attended a single-sex secondary modern school, left at 15 or 16 and was not aware of her having any qualifications. Father was a skilled manual worker. Mother was a routine non-manual worker in the public sector. Both voted Labour.
Education: Passed 11+ and was due to attend grammar school but was hospitalized and had to go to a technical school. Left at 16 with O levels.
Work: Worked in several supervisory non-manual jobs in the public sector. From 1984 to 1992 regularly took on-the-job training courses.

Partner, children etc.: Married. In 1992 and 1997 wife a legal secretary. One daughter (Henry is Sharon's father).
Vote: In 1992 voted Conservative in general and local elections. In 1997 voted Labour in general and local elections.

Hugh   Labourville, born 1942
Interviewed in 1980, 1984, 1988 and 1992.
Parents: Knew little about his parents' education but said that they left school at 14 with no qualifications and had no further formal education. Father worked in his family business in a supervisory role. Mother had no paid employment after having children. Father voted Conservative, mother voted Labour.
Education: Failed the 11+, attended a single-sex secondary modern school, left at 15 with no qualifications and gained some qualifications at evening classes. Had no further education between 1988 and 1992.
Work: In 1983 a skilled manual worker in the public sector. Since 1988 in an administrative post with a regional health authority.
Partner, children etc.: Married. In 1988 and 1992 wife was a sales assistant. In 1988 no children in education. In 1992 son (living with parents) working in the building trade but currently unemployed, grandchildren in nursery and school.
Vote: Labour.

Ian   Labourville, born 1942
Interviewed in 1980, 1984, 1988, 1992 and 1997.
Parents: Both parents attended elementary school, left at 14 with no qualifications and had no further formal education. Father had various jobs in the private sector. Mother did semi-skilled manual work in the private sector.
Education: Had a lot of time off school due to illness. Failed 11+, stayed at coeducational elementary school until left at 15 with no qualifications. Took various evening classes (not leading to qualifications). Between 1992 and 1997 passed an O level.
Work: A skilled manual worker in the private sector until 1993. Since then unemployed due to illness and receiving invalidity benefit.
Partner, children etc.: Married. In 1988 wife was in routine non-manual work. In 1992 she was a housewife and in 1997 she was unemployed,

caring for her elderly mother and not claiming any benefits. In 1988 one daughter was on a YTS scheme and taking day release at college. In 1997 both daughters were over 15. Eldest daughter was dyslexic and he did not know what type of (mainstream) secondary school she attended. She left at 16 with three or four O levels, had various jobs and in 1997 was doing semi-skilled non-manual work in a university. Youngest daughter attended coeducational secondary school (he was not sure whether it was a comprehensive), left at 16 with O levels and trained on the job for skilled non-manual work.

Vote: Voted Liberal/Alliance in the 1987 general election and the last local election before 1988. Voted Labour in 1992 and 1997 general elections. Did not vote in 1997 local election.

Iris   Torytown, born 1943

Interviewed in 1980, 1984, 1988, 1992 and 1997.

Parents: Father attended a grammar school, matriculated at 16 and gained a degree. Mother attended a single-sex grammar school, matriculated at 16 and had no further formal education. Father was a professional in a supervisory role employed in the private and public sectors. Mother did no paid work after having children. Both parents voted Labour.

Education: Attended council and single-sex direct grant schools, left at 18 with O levels and A levels. Qualified as a State Registered Nurse and health visitor. Gained more work-related qualifications. Between 1992 and 1997 took an Open University course to gain a professional certificate in management.

Work: In 1988 a nurse and in 1992 and 1997 a care centre manager.

Partner, children etc.: Married. In 1988–97 husband a shop-manager. In 1988 one adult child still in education. In 1997 adult son and daughter, neither living with parents. Both attended a single-sex grammar school. Son left school at 16 with three GCSEs, took an ONC, but was made redundant, had various other jobs and in 1997 was working as a credit controller. Daughter left school at 18 with O levels and A levels, took a diploma in business studies and in 1997 worked in insurance.

Vote: Labour.

Jane   Torytown, born 1944

Interviewed in 1980, 1984, 1988, 1992, 1997.

Parents: Knew nothing about parents' education. Father an unskilled manual worker in the private sector. Mother had various jobs in the private sector. Both voted Conservative.

Education: Failed the 11+, attended a coeducational secondary modern school, left at 15 with no qualifications. Between 1988 and 1992 took evening classes in word processing.

Work: First job after leaving school was as an office junior. In 1988 was working as a buyer. In 1992 unemployed (for the last two weeks). In 1997 an administrative assistant for a private company.

Partner, children etc.: Married. Between 1988 and 1997 husband was a sales assistant. In 1988 no children in education. Son failed the 11+, attended single-sex secondary modern school, left at 16 with no qualifications and in 1997 worked as an upholsterer.

Vote: Did not vote in 1987 general election or last local election before 1988. In 1992 voted Conservative in general and local elections. In 1997 did not vote in general or local elections.

Jean   Torytown, born 1944

Interviewed in 1980, 1984, 1988 and 1992.

Parents: Know nothing about her father's education. He was a skilled manual worker in the private sector. Mother attended private single-sex boarding school but left when her father died. Did not know where she went, when she left or any school leaving qualifications. She later acquired a qualification in shorthand typing and was a routine non-manual worker in the private sector. Both voted Conservative.

Education: Failed the 11+, attended a single-sex secondary modern school, left at 15 with CSEs and later took day-release training and evening classes leading to a City & Guilds qualification.

Work: In 1988 was a tracer in an office in the private sector. In 1992 working in computer aided design in the private sector.

Partner, children etc.: Married. Husband an intermediate (junior management level) post in the private sector. In 1992 he was a CAD draughtsman in the private sector. In 1992 one child was a student in higher education.

Vote: Labour

Jennifer Labourville, born 1945
Interviewed in 1980, 1984 and 1988. Moved house and could not trace in 1992.
Parents: Father attended a secondary modern school and left at 14. Did not know of any qualifications but had no further formal education. Mother attended elementary school, left at 14 with no qualifications and had no further education. Father was a skilled manual worker in the private sector. Mother not in paid work after having children. Both parents voted Labour.
Education: Failed the 11+, attended secondary modern school, left at 15 with ULCI qualifications and had no further formal education.
Work: In 1983 a housewife. In 1988 in routine non-manual work in the private sector.
Partner, children etc.: Married. Husband a self-employed skilled manual worker. In 1988 one child was soon to start a course of further education.
Vote: In 1983 and 1988 did not vote.

Jeremy Labourville, born 1945
Interviewed in 1980, 1984, 1988, 1992 and 1997.
Parents: Both parents attended elementary school and left at 14 with no qualifications. Father later took a course by day release and mother had no further formal education. Father was a skilled manual worker with a supervisory role in private and public sectors. Mother was an unskilled manual worker in the private sector. Both voted Labour.
Education: Attended private preparatory school from 8–11. Passed 11+, attended direct grant grammar school, left at 18 with A levels. Took a teaching certificate at teacher training college and then a part-time B.Ed degree. Later took a part-time M.Ed degree and another course about special educational needs.
Work: Headteacher of a primary school (voluntary aided, outside Labourville).
Partner, children etc.: Married. Wife a primary school teacher. In 1988 Jeremy was taking a course himself and had two children attending comprehensive school. In 1992 one child taking a degree and the other in sixth-form college. In 1997 daughter had a degree and was teaching in an infants school (i.e. Jeremy is Susan's father), son was working with disabled people whilst waiting to start a degree course soon. One grandchild was currently living with Jeremy (attending a LEA/church playgroup).

Vote: Floating between Labour and the Liberal Democrats. Voted Liberal/Alliance in the 1987 general election and did not vote in the last local election before 1988. 1992 voted Liberal Democrat. 1997 voted Labour in general election and did not vote in local election.

John Labourville, born 1946
Interviewed in 1980, 1984, 1992 and 1997.
Parents: Unknown.
Education: Failed the 11+ and attended a comprehensive school. Left school at 15 with no qualifications. Later gained a City & Guilds qualification, Member of the Institute of Clerk and Works and a certificate in education (for teaching).
Work: Apprentice in the building trade. Became a lecturer in a college of art and technology, teaching courses in building skills.
Partner, children etc.: Married. Wife a skilled technician in the NHS and a (comprehensive) school governor. All three children attended comprehensive schools. In 1992 the eldest was just about to leave a sixth-form college. (She later went to university, i.e. John is Teresa's father). In 1992 the middle (daughter) was just about to start at a sixth-form college. The youngest (son) later went to sixth-form college to resit exams and to a preservice course, before joining the army.
Vote: Floating between Labour and Social Democrats. 1992 Liberal Democrat. 1997 Labour.

Justin Torytown, born 1946
Interviewed in 1980, 1984, 1988 and 1992.
Parents: Father attended single-sex secondary modern and mother attended grammar school. Both left at 14 with no qualifications and had no further formal education. Father was a semi-skilled manual worker in the private sector. Mother was manager of a small business. Both voted Labour.
Education: Did not take the 11+. Attended private boarding school from 10 to 13, when he moved to a secondary modern school, left at 16 with no qualifications and had no further formal education.
Work: Privately employed taxi driver.
Partner, children etc.: Married. Wife also a taxi driver. In 1988 had two children in primary school. In 1992 they were both attending a single-sex secondary modern school.

Vote: In 1987 general election voted Conservative. Did not vote in last local election before 1988. In 1992 general election voted Labour.

Karl Labourville, born 1946
Interviewed in 1980, 1984 (not in 1988), 1992 and 1997.
Parents: Left school at 14. Both were manual/factory workers and both voted Labour.
Education: Failed his 11+ examination and went to a secondary modern school. Left school at 15 with no qualifications.
Work: Had various low-paid manual jobs. In 1992 temporary job working on a factory conveyor belt, unemployed for five months since 1988. In 1997 a cleaner in the private sector. Was unemployed for one month in 1997.
Partner, children etc.: Single. Niece at university training to be a teacher. Grown-up children.
Vote: Floating between Labour and Liberal Democrats. He had sometimes voted differently in local and general elections. In 1992 voted Liberal Democrat in general election. In 1997 voted Labour in general election and Liberal Democrat in local election.

Katherine Torytown, born 1946
Interviewed in 1980, 1984, 1988, 1992, 1997.
Parents: Did not know the type of school her parents attended or what qualifications they left with. Both left at 14, father took evening classes, not leading to qualifications, and mother had no further formal education. Father had an intermediate/supervisory job in the private sector. Mother worked in personal service and gave up when she had children. She did not know how they voted.
Education: Failed 11+, attended secondary modern school and left at 15 with no qualifications. Took a City & Guilds course. Later qualified as a State Registered Nurse. Between 1988 and 1992 took other part-time work-related courses at polytechnic. In 1994–6 took part-time university diploma in sexual health.
Work: Nurse in the NHS.
Partner, children etc.: Married. Husband was an accountant, in 1988 he was employed, in 1992 he was unemployed (made redundant) and in 1997 was self-employed. No children.
Vote: Voted Conservative in the 1987 general election and did not vote in the last local election before 1988. In 1992 voted Conservative in general and local elections. In 1997 voted Liberal Democrat in general and local elections.

Kathleen Torytown, born 1947
Interviewed in 1980, 1984, 1988.
Parents: Did not know what type of school they attended. They left at 14 with no qualifications and had no further formal education. Father was a semi-skilled manual worker in the private sector. Mother did not have paid work after having children. Father voted Conservative and mother voted Labour.
Education: Failed the 11+, attended a single-sex secondary modern school and left at 16 with ULCI qualifications. Took evening classes, not leading to a qualification.
Work: Clerk-typist in the public sector.
Partner, children etc.: Single, living alone. No children.
Vote: Conservative.

Kirsten Labourville, born 1948
Interviewed in 1980, 1984, 1988, 1992, 1997.
Parents: Both attended elementary school and left at 14. Did not know if father had any qualifications but he had no further formal education. Mother took evening classes, not leading to a qualification. Both parents were routine non-manual workers in the private sector. Both voted Labour.
Education: Failed 11+, attended a secondary modern school, left at 15 with no qualifications and gained some qualifications at evening classes. Between each of the interviews in 1988, 1992 and 1997 she gained more qualifications (O level standard) at evening classes.
Work: Full-time housewife from 1984 to 1996 (i.e. since birth of son). In 1997 working as a clerk-typist for a children's charity.
Partner, children etc.: Married. Husband manager (not supervisory) in a private company. In 1988 no children in education. In 1992 son in primary school. In 1997 son attending a coeducational comprehensive school in Labourville.
Vote: Voted Liberal/Alliance in the 1987 general election and did not vote in the last local election before 1988. Voted Labour in 1992. Did not vote in 1997 general election. Otherwise tended to vote Labour in local and general elections.

Laura Labourville, born 1949

Interviewed in 1980, 1984, 1988 and 1992. Too ill in 1997.

Parents: Originally lived in the West Indies ('white' appearance with a slight West Indian accent) and moved to UK. Knew little about her parents' education but knew that father attended a grammar school and mother left school at 14. Father was manager of a large business. Mother was in personal service. Did not know how father voted but mother voted Labour.

Education: Passed 11+, attended single-sex grammar school, left at 16 and later gained A levels and a teaching certificate.

Work: Primary school teacher.

Partner, children etc.: Single and no children. Shared her home with her retired mother.

Vote: Labour.

Lawrence Torytown, born 1949

Interviewed in 1992 and 1997.

Parents: Father attended a 'kind of grammar school', left at 15 and he did not know what qualifications he had. Knew nothing about his mother's education. Father was a structural engineer and he knew nothing about his mother's work (she died young). Both voted Conservative.

Education: Passed the 11+, attended single-sex grammar school, left at 16 with five O levels. Apprenticed in an engineering drawing office. Gained an ONC and HNC in mechanical engineering and a City & Guilds qualification in computing.

Work: In 1997 a technical clerk in the private sector.

Partner, children etc.: Married. Wife had many jobs. In 1992 she was a skilled manual worker in the NHS. In 1997 she had two part-time jobs. She had recently completed a part-time City & Guilds course in computing. In 1992 had one child in a primary school and one child attending a grammar school. In 1997 had children aged 15 and 17. Both took the 11+ examination. The eldest child attended a coeducational grammar school, passed GCSEs and in 1997 was taking A levels. The youngest was attending a single-sex secondary modern school.

Vote: In 1992 voted Conservative. In 1997 voted Labour in general election but did not vote in local election. Described himself as a floating voter.

Leonard Labourville, born before 1950

Interviewed in 1980, 1984 and 1992. In 1992 was considering emigrating and could not be contacted in 1997.

Parents: Both educated at Roman Catholic schools and left at 14 with no qualifications. Father worked for the post office and mother worked as a cleaner. Assumed they both voted Labour.

Education: Attended church (Roman Catholic) schools. Could not read when he moved to a cathedral school at the age of 9. Left school at 15 with no qualifications. Qualified with the Industrial Training Board by working on the job.

Work: In 1992 a skilled builder. Experienced occasional periods of unemployment.

Partner, children etc.: Married. Wife a credit controller. Daughter attended comprehensive school and in 1992 waiting for results of O levels. Son aged 22 an electrician.

Vote: In 1992 voted for a minor party (unknown) in protest against Conservatives (mainly) and Labour.

Luke Labourville, born before 1950

Interviewed in 1980, 1984 and 1992.

Parents: Both parents left school at 14 without any qualifications. Father was an electrician and mother worked in a shop. Both voted Labour.

Education: Attended secondary modern school, left at 15 with no qualifications. Later took a day-release course in electronics. In 1992 was taking work-related training (quality assurance).

Work: In 1992 a technical clerk of works in the public sector.

Partner, children etc.: Married. In 1992 wife a cleaner at a school and taking an evening class in typing. In 1992 eldest son taking an Open University course and younger (11-year-old) son attending primary school.

Vote: In 1992 voted Conservative.

Margaret Labourville, born 1950

Interviewed in 1980, 1984, 1988, 1992 and 1997.

Parents: Did not know what type of school her father attended. Mother attended a secondary modern school. Both left at 14 with no qualifications and had no further education. Father was a semi-skilled manual worker in the private sector. Mother had no paid work after having children. Father voted Labour and did not know how mother voted.

Education: Failed the 11+, attended a single-sex secondary modern school and left at 15 with no qualifications. Later took day release (City & Guilds) and evening classes. Qualified as State Registered Nurse and had since taken a (work-related) diploma by distance learning.

Work: Worked in an office and a shop until nurse training. In 1988–97 a nurse in the NHS.

Partner, children etc.: Married. Husband a manager in the private sector (privatized since 1980). In 1992 one child attending junior school, two at a coeducational comprehensive school and husband completing an Open University degree. In 1997 one son still attending coeducational comprehensive school. One other child in final year of a four-year degree course (in England) and another due to start a degree in two months' time (i.e. Margaret is Zoe's mother).

Vote: Did not vote in 1983. Voted Labour in 1987 and 1997 general elections. Did not vote in 1988 and 1997 local elections.

Marie Torytown, born 1950

Interviewed in 1980, 1984, 1988 and 1992. In 1997 had left Torytown.

Parents: Father attended grammar school, left at 14 with no qualifications but had some further education. Mother attended elementary school, left at 14 with no qualifications and had no further formal education. Father did routine non-manual work in the public sector. Mother did unskilled manual work in the public sector. Both voted Labour.

Education: Failed 11+, attended secondary modern school, left at 15 with no qualifications and had no further formal education.

Work: In 1983 a school meals assistant (supervisor in 1988). In 1992 school meals assistant cook.

Partner, children etc.: Married. Husband assistant manager of a business. In 1988 two children; one attending a grammar school, one attending a secondary modern school.

Vote: Labour.

Mark Torytown, born 1951

Interviewed in 1980, 1984, 1988 and 1992.

Parents: Did not know what type of school father attended. Mother attended elementary school. Both left at 14 with no qualifications and had no further formal education. Father was a skilled manual

worker with a supervisory role in the private sector. Mother was a semi-skilled manual worker in the public sector. Father voted Labour. Did not know how mother voted.

Education: Passed 11+, attended single-sex grammar school, left at 18 with A level and gained a degree. Since then had taken work-related courses (teaching).

Work: Teacher in a state secondary school. In 1992 also had senior management role in the school.

Partner, children etc.: Married. In 1992 wife was a manager in the NHS. In 1988 and 1990 wife was studying part-time. No children.

Vote: Labour.

Megan Torytown, born 1951

Interviewed in 1980, 1984, 1988 and 1992. In 1997 in the process of emigrating.

Parents: Both parents attended elementary schools, left at 14 without any qualifications and had no further formal education. Father was a skilled manual worker in a supervisory role in the private sector. Mother was in personal services in the public sector.

Education: Failed 11+, attended secondary modern school and left at 15 with ULCI qualifications and trained as a State Registered Nurse.

Work: In 1983 a housewife. In 1988 a nurse. In 1992 a school nursing sister.

Partner, children etc.: Married. In 1988–92 husband a consultant (computers). In 1988 both children at primary school. Son later passed 11+ and in 1992 was attending coeducational grammar school. Daughter failed 11+ and in 1992 was attending a single-sex 'high' school.

Vote: In 1983 voted Conservative. In the 1987 general election voted Labour and did not vote in the latest local election. In 1992 voted Labour.

Michelle Labourville, born 1951

Interviewed in 1980, 1984, 1988, 1992 and 1997.

Parents: Father attended elementary school, left at 14 with no qualifications and had no further formal education. Mother attended a technical school, left at 16 with unknown qualifications and had no further formal education. Father worked in the family business in a supervisory role. Mother did various jobs in the private sector. Both voted Liberal.

Education: Failed the 11+, attended a comprehensive/high school, left at 16 with CSEs and later had some further education.

Work: In 1983 a housewife. In 1988 was doing routine non-manual work in the private sector. In 1992 and 1997 a clerical officer for the local social services department.

Partner, children etc.: In first three interviews was married. Husband a self-employed skilled manual worker with a supervisory role. In 1988 had two children attending primary school. In 1992 they were attending a coeducational comprehensive school. By 1992 her marriage had broken up. In 1997 both children were still living with their mother and were students taking vocational courses at a college of further education (i.e. Michelle is Valerie's mother).

Vote: Labour.

Monica   Labourville, born 1951
Interviewed in 1988 and 1992.
Parents: Knew nothing about her parents' education. Father was a skilled manual worker in the public sector. Did not know what job her mother did. Both parents voted Labour.

Education: No 11+, attended single-sex grammar school, left at 16 with O levels and had further education, not leading to a qualification.

Work: Routine non-manual work in the private sector.

Partner, children etc.: Married. Husband a skilled manual worker in the private sector. In 1992 had two children in primary school.

Vote: Voted Labour in the 1987 general election but did not vote in the last local election.

Naomi   Labourville, born 1951
Interviewed in 1980, 1984, 1988 and 1992.
Parents: Only knew that her parents attended elementary school and had no further formal education. Father was an unskilled manual worker in the public sector. Mother was an unskilled manual worker with a supervisory role in the public and private sectors. Both voted Labour.

Education: Failed the 11+, attended a comprehensive/high school, left at 15 with no qualifications and had no further formal education.

Work: Sales assistant.

Partner, children etc.: Married. Husband a supervisor in a small business. In 1988 one child in a primary school and one (adult child) taking a day-release course. In 1992 one child still attending a comprehensive school.

Vote: Labour.

Natalie   Labourville, born 1951
Interviewed in 1980, 1984, 1988 and 1992.
Parents: Both attended elementary school, left at 14 and she did not know whether they had any qualifications. They had no further formal education. Father had an intermediate job in the public sector. Mother did unskilled manual work in the private sector. Father's vote varied and mother voted Conservative.

Education: Passed 11+, attended a single-sex grammar school and left at 17 with O levels. Later got a teacher training certificate and gained more qualifications.

Work: In 1988 teacher in a state primary school.

Partner, children etc.: In 1988 separated and one child attending primary school. In 1992 child attending a comprehensive school.

Vote: Labour.

Neil   Torytown, born 1951
Interviewed in 1980, 1984, 1988 and 1992.
Parents: Knew nothing about his parents' education. Both were unskilled manual workers, father in the private sector, mother in the public sector. Both voted Labour.

Education: Passed the 11+ but attended a secondary modern school, left at 15 with no qualifications and took a day-release training course.

Work: Unskilled manual worker in the public sector.

Partner, children etc.: Married. Wife a sales assistant. In 1988 one child attending a single-sex secondary modern school. In 1992 one child taking a day-release course at college.

Vote: Labour.

Nicholas   Torytown, born 1952
Interviewed in 1980, 1984, 1988, 1992 and 1997.
Parents: Knew nothing about his parents' education. Parents split up and he lived with his mother. Father self-employed skilled manual worker. Mother had an intermediate job in the private sector. Did not know how father voted. Mother voted Liberal.

Education: Passed the 11+, attended grammar school, left at 15 before he was due to take examinations and had no further formal education.

Work: Playing in a pop group. Then trained as a builder, initially in his father's business, and by 1980 had his own business. Some periods of unemployment due to irregularity of his work. In 1992 his business was failing but in 1997 it was thriving again.

Partner, children etc.: Married. Wife worked in his business. In 1988 two children in school. Eldest son (i.e. Nicholas is Timothy's father) had an assisted place at a single-sex private school, youngest in a state primary school. In 1992 one child attending a state grammar school and the other still had an assisted place. In 1997 the eldest had passed A levels, started a university degree but left and started work. Youngest left at 16 with GCSEs, was unemployed (but not claiming benefit) for one year before started equivalent of A level/NVQ, which he completed in 1997.

Vote: Voted for the first time in 1979. In 1988 voted Conservative both times. In 1992 did not vote. In 1997 voted Conservative in general and local elections.

Olivia Labourville, born 1954
Interviewed in 1980, 1984, 1988, 1992 and 1997.
Parents: Did not know what school father attended, he left at 14 with no qualifications but later got qualifications via evening classes. Mother attended elementary school (passed scholarship for grammar school but could not go), left at 14 with no qualifications and had no further formal education. Did not know how they voted.
Education: Passed 11+, attended coeducational secondary modern school, left at 15 with O level and CSEs and passed more GCSEs via evening classes.
Work: Various jobs with short periods of unemployment. In 1988 a semi-skilled manual worker with a supervisory role in the public sector. In 1992 a shop assistant. Between 1992 and 1996 had short period of unemployment. Since 1996 worked as a home carer for the local social services.
Partner, children etc.: In 1988 unmarried and cohabiting. Partner a self-employed skilled manual worker. In 1988 no children in education. In 1992 was single with three children attending primary school. In 1997 still a single parent with twins attending primary school, and moving shortly to the comprehensive school currently attended by her eldest child.

Vote: Voted Liberal/Alliance in 1987 general election and last local election. Voted Liberal Democrat in 1992. Voted Liberal Democrat in 1997 general election and did not vote in 1997 local election.

Owen Labourville, born before 1955
Interviewed in 1980, 1984 and 1992.
Parents: Father attended secondary modern school and left at 14. He later took various engineering courses at evening classes and worked as a post office engineer. Did not know what sort of education his mother had. She worked as a machinist. Thought both parents voted Labour.
Education: Attended secondary modern school, left at 15 with no qualifications. Day-release City & Guilds course in electrical fitting.
Work: In 1992 an electrical fitter for a private company.
Partner, children etc.: Separated from wife and living alone.
Vote: Conservative.

Paul Torytown, born before 1955
Interviewed in 1980, 1984 and 1992.
Parents: Father attended elementary or secondary modern school (not sure), left at 14 and unsure about any qualifications. He later studied accountancy at evening classes. Mother attended coeducational secondary modern school and left at 14 with no qualifications. Father worked as an accountant. Mother worked in the Air Force during the war and then became a housewife. Both parents voted Labour.
Education: Attended single-sex secondary modern school, left at 15 with no qualifications. Took apprenticeship in mechanical engineering, including day release and City & Guilds qualification. Later took technical drawing CSE at evening class.
Work: In 1992 a firefighter.
Partner, children etc.: In 1992 a single parent with two sons. One son soon being made redundant. Other son on an access course. Both sons had recently (in 1992) been attending college one day per week.
Vote: In 1992 voted Labour.

Philip Labourville, born before 1955
Interviewed in 1980, 1984 and 1992.
Parents: Both attended elementary schools. Father had various manual jobs. Mother sewed clothes. Father voted Labour. Did not know mother's vote.

Education: Failed 11+, attended a single-sex secondary modern school, left school at 15 with no qualifications. No further education since then.
Work: A process worker in a factory.
Partner, children etc.: Wife working as a (supervisor) cleaner. Adult daughter living with them.
Vote: In 1992 voted Liberal Democrat in local election. Did not vote in general election.

Polly Torytown, born 1956
Interviewed in 1988 and 1992. In 1997 had left Torytown.
Parents: Did not know what type of school they attended. Father left at 18 with A levels and had no further formal education. Mother left at 18 with A levels and had (unknown) further education. Father was a foreman in the private sector. Mother was an unskilled manual worker in the public sector. Did not know how they voted.
Education: Failed the 11+, attended a single-sex private school, left at 16 with CSEs and had further education.
Work: Computer consultant.
Partner, children etc.: Was separated in 1988 and married in 1992. Husband a construction manager for a private company. No children currently in education.
Vote: Voted Conservative in 1987 general election and did not vote in last local election. Voted Conservative in 1992.

Richard Torytown, born 1961
Interviewed in 1992 and 1997.
Parents: Father attended a 'ragged school', left at 14 and had no further formal education. He was a skilled manual worker. Mother attended an 'ordinary state' school, left at 15 with no qualifications and had no further formal education. She started her own dressmaking business and ultimately had her own factory. Both parents voted Conservative.
Education: Failed the 11+, attended a secondary modern school and left at 16 with O levels. In 1992 was part-way through a part-time (engineering) degree. Later took a part-time MBA (awarded in 1993). Both were sponsored by his employers.
Work: 1997 an engineering manager for a privatized company. Also has investments.
Partner, children etc.: No partner and no children.

Vote: In 1992 voted Liberal Democrat in general and local elections. In 1997 voted Labour in general and local elections.

Robert Torytown, born before 1962
Interviewed in 1980, 1984 and 1992.
Parents: Did not know what sort of education his parents had but they left school with no qualifications. Father worked as a chief engineer. Mother did administrative work for an insurance firm. Both parents voted Conservative.
Education: Attended single-sex secondary modern school, left at 16 with three O levels. No further education.
Work: In 1992 had been unemployed for one and a half years.
Partner, children etc.: In 1992 living with retired parents. No children.
Vote: Consistently voted Labour.

Rodney Labourville, born before 1962
Interviewed in 1980, 1984 and 1992.
Parents: Both attended elementary school until the age of 14 and left with no qualifications. Father was a machine minder and mother a home help. Both voted Labour.
Education: Passed 11+, attended grammar school for a while before moving to a secondary modern school, left school at 16 with three O levels. In 1987–8 took a one-year employment training course (internal credits).
Work: Made redundant and was unemployed off and on for four years between 1984 and 1988. In 1992 teaching computer-based skills in the public and private sectors.
Partner, children etc.: Married. In 1992 wife working as a welfare assistant (during the lunch break) at the children's school. Two children, both attending primary school.
Vote: Strong Labour supporter.

Roger Labourville, born 1962
Interviewed in 1980, 1984 and 1992.
Parents: Lived with parents. Did not know what education parents had. Father self-employed. Mother a home help. Both parents voted Conservative.
Education: Attended grammar school, initially single-sex but changed to coeducational while there. Left at 16 with nine O levels. Took two A levels and building

qualifications at a college of technology. Between 1984 and 1992 took a course in the management of a small business at a college of further education. *Work:* In 1992 self-employed as a building consultant. Had experienced occasional periods of unemployment. Business partner had left him with his debts. *Partner, children etc.:* No partner. In 1992 he was living with parents but he sometimes lived with his girlfriend (a primary school teacher). *Vote:* Did not vote.

Ronald   Labourville, born 1963
Interviewed in 1988.
Parents: Only knew that father attended a grammar school. Father was a semi-skilled manual worker in the private sector. Mother was in personal service in the public sector. Both voted Labour.
Education: No 11+, attended secondary modern school, left at 15 with O levels and took evening classes without qualifications.
Work: Unskilled manual worker in the private sector.
Partner, children etc.: Married. Wife a routine non-manual worker in the private sector. No children currently in education.
Vote: Voted Conservative in 1987 general election and Liberal/Alliance in most recent local election.

Ryan   Torytown, born 1964
Interviewed in 1997.
Parents: **Son of Donald.** See his details.
Education: Failed 11+ examination, attended single-sex secondary modern school and left at 16 with one O level and five CSEs. BTEC unit in computer literacy. NVQ in gas services. In 1997 studying for an ONC in building services at a college of further education.
Work: Various periods of unemployment between 1992 and 1997. In 1997 warehouse assistant (manual and clerical).
Partner, children etc.: Wife a machine operative in a factory. In 1997 had two children attending primary school and one attending a comprehensive school (outside Torytown).
Vote: Labour.

Samantha   Labourville, born 1968
Interviewed in 1988 and 1992.
Parents: Only knew that father attended a comprehensive/high school and mother attended a single-sex secondary modern school. Neither had any further education. Father was a semi-skilled manual worker in the public sector. Mother was an unskilled manual worker in the public sector. Both voted Labour.
Education: Attended a comprehensive school, left at 16 with CSEs and had since had day and evening classes.
Work: In 1988 she was a self-employed childminder. In 1992 she described herself as a housewife with no paid work in four years.
Partner, child etc.: In 1992 she was living with her parents but soon moving to live with her boyfriend. Had one pre-school child attending a church playgroup. One brother attending comprehensive school.
Vote: Labour.

Scott   Labourville, born 1969
Interviewed in 1988.
Parents: Father attended a comprehensive school, leaving age unknown, left with GCEs and took a day-release course. Mother attended a comprehensive school, left at 15 with no qualifications and had no further formal education. Father was a non-manual worker with a supervisory role in the public sector. Mother was a routine non-manual worker with a supervisory role in the public sector. Father voted Labour and mother voted Conservative.
Education: Attended comprehensive school, left at 16 with O levels and had since taken a day-release course.
Work: A skilled manual worker in the public sector.
Partner, children etc.: Single, living with parents. One sibling attending comprehensive school.
Vote: Voted Labour in 1987 general election and did not vote in last local election.

Sharon   Torytown, born 1972
Interviewed in 1997.
Parents: **Daughter of Henry.** See his details.
Education: Passed 11+ examination and attended single-sex grammar school. Met husband when the girls' and boys' grammar schools merged. Left grammar school at 16 with GCSEs, took a BTEC course at a college of further education. Started a degree course but left after two terms because she disliked the subject. In 1997 considering taking a part-time degree in another subject.
Work: Not in paid employment.
Partner, children etc.: Husband a mechanical

engineer. One baby daughter and another had attended LEA nursery school part-time and was due to start local authority infants school soon.
Vote: Did not vote.

Susan   Labourville, born 1973
Interviewed in 1997.
Parents: **Daughter of Jeremy.** See his details. Both parents teachers.
Education: Voluntary aided Roman Catholic coeducational comprehensive school, sixth-form college and university.
Work: Primary school teacher.
Partner, children etc.: Married. Husband a sales administrator. They were currently living with her parents until able to move into a house they had just bought. One child had been attending a church playgroup and was soon starting a LEA nursery school.
Vote: Did not vote.

Teresa   Labourville, born 1973
Interviewed in 1997.
Parents: **Daughter of John.** See his details.
Education: Attended mixed comprehensive school in Labourville, followed by sixth-form college and university.
Work: Peripatetic music teacher for all age groups.
Partner, children etc.: Lived with parents. No children.
Vote: Did not vote in general election 1997, voted Labour in local election.

Timothy   Torytown, born 1974
Interviewed in 1997.
Parents: **Son of Nicholas.** See his details.
Education: Had an assisted place at a single-sex private school (girls in the sixth form), left in 1993 with GCSEs and A levels, started a university degree but left after one month (did not like long hours, lack of freedom and distance from home).
Work: Computer artist, drawing computer graphics for educational software.
Partner, children etc.: Lived with his parents and younger brother, aged 19.
Vote: Did not vote.

Valerie   Labourville, born 1977
Interviewed in 1997.
Parents: **Daughter of Michelle.** See her details.
Education: Attended coeducational comprehensive school. Left with six high-grade GCSEs (i.e. grade C+) and two others. Diploma in nursery nursing/NNEB.
Work: Nursery nurse, working in a nursery class attached to a school.
Partner, children etc.: Lived with parents. Brother currently taking vocational NVQ course at college of further education.
Vote: Voted Labour in local and general elections in 1997.

Zoe   Labourville, born 1979
Interviewed in 1997.
Parents: **Daughter of Margaret.** See her details.
Education: Attended coeducational comprehensive school. Took A levels at a sixth-form college. Starting degree course soon after the interview.
Work: Waitress and barmaid.
Partner, children etc.: Lived with parents. No children. Brother starting final year of a degree course.
Vote: Did not vote in 1997 (but was old enough).

The writer – Janet McKenzie, born 1950 in Horwich, Lancashire (now in Bolton, Greater Manchester).
Parents: Father failed a scholarship, attended a secondary modern school (one existed in Horwich during the 1930s) and left at 14 with no qualifications. Mother passed a scholarship for grammar school, left at 16 with no qualifications. Both parents attended evening classes, not leading to qualifications. Father was a skilled manual worker for British Rail. Mother did several jobs involving unskilled manual and non-manual work in the private sector. Both parents voted Labour.
Education: Failed 11+, attended coeducational secondary modern school (starting in a low stream), left at 16 with GCEs and CSEs, took A levels at grammar school, left with one A level pass, failed resits, failed correspondence course in hospital administration, took BA degree as a mature student, then PGCE, M.Sc and Ph.D.
Work: Various jobs involving unskilled manual and non-manual work (in the private sector and public sectors). Currently senior university lecturer.
Partner, children etc.: Married. Husband was an unskilled manual worker before qualifying as a State Registered Mental Nurse in 1998. Two adult daughters, both with degrees.
Vote: Usually Labour, but has also voted SDP/Liberal Democrat.

Appendix 2 Glossary of terms

ABILITY GROUPS The division of pupils according to assessment of their ability; for example, banding, setting, streaming. Can be mixed ability groups.

ACADEMIC DRIFT The tendency of the public to perceive academic qualifications as superior to non-academic or vocational courses and therefore follow academic routes.

ACHIEVED STATUS Status gained by one's own efforts.

ACTION RESEARCH Research that studies changes before, during and after they happen and actually involves the researcher as a participant in the process of change. This means that implementation is not an afterthought, but built into the actual research, and that the research involves a partnership between the researcher and other participants.

AIDE MÉMOIRE An informal and often loosely structured memory aid to remind the interviewer what topics should be covered in an interview.

AIDED SCHOOLS Until 1998 these were a type of voluntary aided (i.e. church) school. There were over 4,000, about half Church of England, half Roman Catholic, some Jewish – providing their own premises and meeting some of the maintenance costs in exchange for a degree of self-control. Since 1998 the name aided school has been given to any type of church school that is partly funded by a church and partly funded by the state.

ANTI-RACIST EDUCATION Aimed at eliminating the practice of labelling people according to the colour of their skin or racial identity.

ANTI-SCHOOL CULTURE Group(s) of pupils who refuse to conform to the school's expectations/culture.

ANTI-SEXIST EDUCATION Aimed at challenging male domination of the education system and society in general. Ultimately aiming for a less competitive, less authoritarian system.

ASCRIBED STATUS Status awarded by others, with no personal effort; for example, inherited.

ASSISTED PLACES SCHEME Scheme introduced in the 1980 Education Act whereby pupils can be transferred from maintained (state) schools to selected non-maintained (private) schools, with the government paying all, or part of, the tuition fees. Gradually phased out by the Labour government elected in 1997.

BACCALAUREATE A school qualification indicating success across the whole breadth of a group of subjects. Common in France and becoming more popular in British schools. The European Baccalaureate is recognized in all member states of the European Union.

BANDING Pupils are subdivided into broad ability groups such as above average, average and below average (a type of streaming). Within these groups parallel classes are established which contain pupils of similar ability (i.e. no streaming in these parallel classes).

BIOLOGICAL DETERMINISM Theory that educational achievement is primarily based on innate abilities.

BIPARTITE SYSTEM Pupils sent to grammar schools and secondary modern schools according to their performance in an examination (11+ or scholarship). See Tripartite.

BLACK PAPERS Series of papers published (in the *Salisbury Review*) during the late 1960s to mid 1970s. They were strongly critical of trends towards progressive education, the introduction of comprehensive schools and Labour Party education policies in general. Contributors included Brian Cox, Rhodes Boyson, Caroline (later Baroness) Cox and Richard Lynn.

(THE) BRITISH DISEASE (Weiner) Theory that British culture is biased against manufacturing industry.

BUREAUCRACY Weber's model involves an administrative hierarchy with a structure of command, specialized training and a clear career structure, and division of labour among experts. Specific rules and procedures according to which the bureaucracy completes tasks. Formalized and impartial methods of dealing with clients.

CASE Each of the individuals or other subjects of the research; for example, each school or each class.

CITY TECHNOLOGY COLLEGES Schools introduced during the 1980s for pupils aged 11 to 16 or 18. Although the National Curriculum was to be taught, each city technology college would offer a particular specialism, such as science and technology. Conservative governments expected these new schools to be financed by private sources but had to step in to provide most of the funding when private finance was not forthcoming.

COHORT STUDIES A type of longitudinal research in which the same people (called a 'cohort' or 'panel') are studied at different points in time.

COMMUNITY COLLEGES Schools serving the needs of, and providing facilities for, the whole community. These have been particularly popular in rural areas (e.g. Cambridgeshire) where it makes sense to pool local facilities. They are likely to provide a centre for evening classes and may allow local adults to use the school library, sports facilities and rooms for group meetings.

COMMUNITY SCHOOLS Schools under the control of local education authorities. This name was introduced in 1997 by the new Labour government.

COMPENSATORY EDUCATION Attempts to compensate for the social or cultural disadvantages experienced by some children; for example, see Educational Priority Areas.

COMPREHENSIVE SCHOOLS It was originally hoped that comprehensive schools would be attended by children with the widest possible range of abilities and socio-economic backgrounds. The aims were (and still are) to generate more social mixing and more opportunities for children to pursue a diverse range of educational paths. However, it was found that some children were 'creamed-off' by their parents who sent them to more prestigious schools.

CONCEPTS Provide meaningful summaries and images of certain aspects of the world.

CONSUMER SOVEREIGNTY Theory/recommendation that consumers ultimately determine what is produced; for example, parents would determine the sort of schools to be provided.

CONTEST MOBILITY (Turner) Status awarded as a prize in an open contest. Similar to meritocracy.

CONTROLLED SCHOOL A type of aided or church school. They are virtually all Church of England and provide their own premises but the LEA meets all the school's costs. Before the 1988 Act the governing bodies had control only over religious instruction.

CORRESPONDENCE PRINCIPLE (Bowles and Gintis) Similarities between social relationships in the school and the division of labour at work.

CREDENTIAL INFLATION The qualifications required for jobs are raised as more people get more qualifications.

CREOLE INTERFERENCE (Edwards) Creole is a West Indian language/dialect sharing a large part of the vocabulary of English, but different in grammar and sound system. Children using Creole are often at a disadvantage when educated through the medium of standard English.

CRITERION REFERENCED ASSESSMENT Used when there is some sort of list of criteria available to provide guidance concerning the standard that has been reached. An individual is assessed according to how the criteria have been satisfied, and the assessment can be made by a tutor or by the student (e.g. self-assessment using a tutorial on computer).

CRITICAL RESEARCH Assumes that social inequalities are maintained by false consciousness and that research should aim to enlighten people about the nature of their oppression. Once enlightened, the oppressed can be empowered in order to overthrow their oppressors, be emancipated and transform society.

CULTURAL CAPITAL (Bourdieu) Linguistic and social competencies, and such qualities of style, manners, know-how, aspirations and perception of chances of success. See Habitus.

CULTURAL DEPRIVATION In terms of experiences and the values shared by their cultures (background), some (e.g. working class and ethnic minority) children have been considered to be culturally deprived.

CULTURAL DETERMINISM Theory that educational achievement is primarily the outcome of individual experiences, social conditions and so on. Compare with biological determinism.

CULTURAL RELATIVISM Acknowledges the social and cultural forces affecting the conditions under which knowledge is produced. It notes that it is impossible to distinguish between 'real' knowledge and culturally produced knowledge and denies that any one way of living is superior to others.

CULTURAL REPRODUCTION (Several writers, e.g. Bourdieu, Young) The ways in which schools, in conjunction with other social institutions, help to perpetuate social and economic inequalities across the generations.

CULTURAL RESTORATIONISTS (Ball) Emphasize tradition, heritage, strong state control, formal relationships between teachers and pupils/students, rejection of 'non-subjects' and 'politicized' curriculum.

CURRICULUM Courses (and their contents) offered by educational institutions.

DEDUCTION (Sometimes called the hypothetico-deductive method) A process involving moving from a theory or theories (i.e. the general) to the creation of a hypothesis, the operationalization of concepts and then to observation (i.e. the particular) in order to test the hypothesis.

DEPARTMENT FOR EDUCATION AND EMPLOYMENT (DfEE) Central government department responsible for overseeing the British education system, although various responsibilities are devolved to other departments for Wales, Scotland and Northern Ireland.

DE-SCHOOLING (Illich) Claims that the system of compulsory education has many faults and schools in their present form should be abolished and replaced by the provision of resources for everyone who wants to learn – at any time in their lives. This would lead to the diffusion of knowledge and more personal choice over what is studied.

DIAGNOSTIC ASSESSMENT Is likely to include a summative assessment, but will go further by providing an indication of what the next stage of the learning process should be (e.g. by identifying special educational needs). Positive action can be taken.

DISCOURSE Speech conversation including a mixture of beliefs, ideas, concepts and rhetoric which become established as knowledge or as an accepted world-view and create a powerful framework for understandings and actions in social life.

DISCOURSE OF DERISION (Ball) Long-term criticisms of the education system since the 1970s including claims that education has failed to serve the needs of the economy.

EDUCATIONAL PRIORITY AREAS (EPAs) Advocated by the Plowden Report, 1967. Areas, regarded as particularly deprived, in which positive discrimination was intended to compensate for social disadvantages. Included extra spending on facilities, remedial teachers and so on.

EDUCATIONAL RADICALISM Strength of support for left-wing education policies. However, the term 'radical' is also used to refer to 'extreme' left- or right-wing policy changes; for example, Mrs Thatcher had 'radical' policies.

ELABORATED CODE (Bernstein) Complex language, analytical and abstract. Explicit meanings, that is, not dependent on shared understandings. Difficult to anticipate. See Restricted Code.

ELEMENTARY SCHOOLS Single, free schools attended by the majority of British children (until the age of 14) before 1944.

EMPIRICAL TESTING Involves testing by observation.

EPISTEMOLOGY Philosophical theories about knowledge and how we know what we know.

EQUAL OPPORTUNITIES Can be weakly defined as equal access to scholarships (or similar) for entry to high-quality institutions, with lower-quality education for those who 'fail'. The strongest definition suggests that the proportion of people from different social categories at all levels of education should be roughly the same as the proportion of those people in the population as a whole.

EQUAL OPPORTUNITIES (APPROACH TO GENDER) Changes in the curriculum, books and so on aimed at reducing the differences in course (and ultimately occupational) choices made by boys and girls. See Anti-sexist for a stronger approach.

ETHNICITY Relates to a sense of identity, of belonging to a community with common cultural traditions.

ETHNOGRAPHY A term originally used to describe the study of the institutions and customs in small, well-defined communities in relatively simple societies. It is now also used to refer to the detailed study of small groups of people within a complex society. The emphasis is usually on forms of social interaction and the meanings which lie behind these, and it may involve a wide range of methods of data collection.

FEMINIST RESEARCH Although feminists may use any of the methods used by other researchers, their feminist ontologies and epistemologies make them particularly aware of how research can relate to inequalities of power. They are critical of research for having provided knowledge which supports the continuation of male domination, and are particularly critical of positivist approaches for having treated (and exploited) the people studied as objects rather than real people. Feminists challenge any claims to objectivity and see the research process as a shared experience that should empower rather than exploit the person being studied.

FOUNDATION SCHOOL Schools supported by a central government grant instead of funding from a local education authority. Label given by the Labour government of 1997. See Grant Maintained Schools.

FRAME (Bernstein) The power relationships of interaction in education, the control students and teachers have over the selection, organization and timing of the knowledge delivered, and communications between subjects and other aspects of the curriculum.

GENDER Social divisions associated with notions of masculinity and femininity which vary according to changing contexts.

GENERALIZABILITY The extent to which research findings apply to people or settings other than the ones which the researcher used.

GOVERNANCE The term *governance* can be widely defined beyond the image of a 'government', in a traditional sense, to include various processes of co-ordination and collective decision-making from micro (e.g. family) through to macro (e.g. government agency) levels. It includes an interest in how institutions are changing the way in which they are 'governed', in ways that might be perceived to be legitimate or illegitimate.

GRADING Allocation of pupils to a class according to attainment and irrespective of age group. Not used in the UK but used in the USA, Australia and elsewhere. The term is now associated in the UK with 'years'; that is, since the introduction of the National Curriculum, pupils aged 14–15 are now labelled as year (or grade) 10.

GRAMMAR SCHOOLS Secondary schools attended by pupils who, following examination or other assessment at 11+, were labelled as being particularly academic.

GRANT MAINTAINED SCHOOLS These schools were supported by a central government grant instead of funding from a local education authority. Conservative governments encouraged schools currently maintained by LEAs to apply for grant maintained status (i.e. opt out of LEA control). In theory a grant maintained secondary school could still have the characteristics of a comprehensive, grammar or secondary modern school. The Labour government elected in 1997 discouraged schools from opting out and renamed most of these schools Foundation Schools.

(THE) GREAT DEBATE Public debate said to commence with the speech by James Callaghan in 1976 at Ruskin College, Oxford. Concerning the idea that education was/is failing the nation and that increased government control is needed to make education more work-related.

HABITUS (Bourdieu) Habits of thought, perceptions, dispositions and manners. Provide the basis for the child's 'durable disposition'. Some habituses constitute Cultural Capital.

HEURISTIC VALUE Is useful as an analytical tool.

HIDDEN CURRICULUM Traits of behaviour or attitudes learned at school but not included within the formal curriculum. 'Unstated' agenda involved in schooling; for example, gender differences. See Paracurriculum.

HIGH SCHOOLS This label can be given to almost any type of school providing a secondary education (i.e. for children over 11).

HILLGATE GROUP Pressure group publishing pamphlets (mid 1980s onwards) to promote right-wing, neo-liberal education policies. Included Baroness Cox. See Black Papers.

HORIZONTAL (OR LATERAL) MOBILITY Change from employment in one place to employment in another, with little or no change in the status of the job.

HUMAN CAPITAL THEORY (Schultz) Economic theory which sees education as an investment. Individuals in whom education has been invested would yield 'profits' in the form of higher earnings. Schultz claimed that this helped to account for the productive superiority of technically advanced countries.

HUMANIST (According to Ball, 1990, p 4, 'old humanists') '... argued that "man's spiritual health depended on a kind of education that was more than training for some specialised work".'

IDEAL MATCHING (Hargreaves) A model of typification. Teachers have an image of the ideal pupil and good pupils are those who come nearest.

ILEA Inner London Education Authority. Abolished by the 1988 Education Reform Act. From April 1990 its responsibilities were transferred to inner-London boroughs.

INDEPENDENT SCHOOLS See non-maintained schools.

INDICATORS When of a concept these are observable and measurable entities which define the concept in a practical way.

INDUCTION (Sometimes called *ex post facto* theory or grounded theory) A process which involves moving from observation or findings (i.e. the particular) through analysis towards the development of a theory (the general). This theory may lead to the development of a hypothesis which is tested by further observation, analysed and so on.

INDUSTRIAL TRAINERS (Ball) Emphasize the needs of industry and the economy, consumer sovereignty in education, profiling, social skills and so on. Schools are too academic and anti-industry. See British Disease.

INFANT SCHOOL For children aged 5 to 7. See Primary School.

INTERCULTURALISM Promotes a recognition and acceptance of the uniqueness of the individual and the superficiality of labelling anyone simply by their skin colour, 'culture', social class, gender, disability and so on.

INTERGENERATIONAL MOBILITY How much difference there is between a parent and child's occupation.

INTERPRETIVE SOCIOLOGY An interest in discovering the meanings behind actions and investigating what is often taken for granted. These sociologists include phenomenologists, symbolic interactionists and ethnomethodologists.

INTERVIEW SCHEDULES May look similar to questionnaires but require an interviewer to note the answers on behalf of the interviewee.

INTRAGENERATIONAL MOBILITY How far a person has moved up or down the social scale during his or her lifetime.

JUNIOR SCHOOL For children aged 7 to 11. See Primary School.

KEYNESIAN ECONOMICS Involve government intervention to regulate the market. Emphasis on the need to increase public spending and minimize unemployment in order to stimulate the market by increasing public spending power, demand for products, investment and profits.

LAISSEZ FAIRE The state should not intervene.

LOCAL EDUCATION AUTHORITIES (LEAs) Educational administration operating through locally elected authorities (i.e. councils).

LOCAL MANAGEMENT OF SCHOOLS (LMS) Introduced in the 1988 Education Reform Act. Required LEAs to delegate certain responsibilities for financial management to the governing boards of schools.

LONGITUDINAL RESEARCH Data is gathered over a long period of time and research can last for several years. This can involve cross-sectional longitudinal studies or retrospective longitudinal studies.

MAINTAINED SCHOOLS All types of 'state' schools financed (i.e. maintained) by public taxation. This may be taxation paid to central government, which funds foundation (previously grant maintained) schools or taxation paid to local councils, which funds community schools (previously local education authority schools). Although some maintained schools may be partly funded by private sources, parents are not officially required to pay fees for their children to attend.

MERITOCRACY A society in which social rewards are allocated not according to ascribed characteristics but according to talent and effort (achieved).

MESSAGE SYSTEMS (Bernstein) The three systems through which educational knowledge is realized are: the curriculum (what counts as valid knowledge), pedagogy (transmission of education), evaluation (realization of knowledge).

METHODOLOGY Philosophical and theoretical debates about how research should be carried out.

METHODS Practical aspects of social research, such as surveys, interviews and observation.

MIDDLE SCHOOL In some areas children leave primary school early (e.g. aged 8) and move to secondary school late (e.g. aged 13). The intervening years are spent at a middle school.

MIXED ABILITY GROUPS Pupils distributed randomly into classes, or classes designed to contain an assortment of abilities.

MULTICULTURAL EDUCATION Aimed at teaching pupils/students about a wide range of cultures.

NATIONAL CURRICULUM Introduced by the 1988 Education Reform Act. Standardization of curriculum and testing in state schools for all pupils. Includes core subjects and foundation subjects. Attainment targets set out what pupils are supposed to know. Programmes of study set out for each subject. Testing (standard assessment tests) at 7, 11 and 14. Four key stages for different age groups; that is, 5–7, 7–11, 11–14, 14–16.

NEW PROGRESSIVES (Ball, 1990, p 6) '. . . those advocates, especially as represented in the mathematics and science subject communities, of pedagogical and assessment innovations like the use of investigations and 'practical mathematics', and, crucially, process and graded assessments'.

NEW SOCIOLOGY OF EDUCATION Origins early 1970s. Emerged from criticisms of previous emphasis on functionalism. 'New' emphasis on activities within the school and in the classroom and on the content of the curriculum. More interpretive approaches, meanings, interaction and so on.

NON-MAINTAINED (independent or private) **SCHOOLS** These are not maintained by state funds. Although they may receive some state funds they are at least partly financed by fees charged to families who 'buy' their children's education. During the 1980s and 1990s some 'academically able' children from less affluent backgrounds were granted an 'Assisted Place,' which meant that central government at least partly financed their education at a suitable independent school.

NON-PARTICIPANT OBSERVATION The researcher does not participate in the setting and may observe via a two-way mirror, video cameras and other secret ways of viewing a scene.

NON-RANDOM (NON-PROBABILITY OR PURPOSIVE) **SAMPLING** Does not allow the researcher to claim that all the members of the relevant population had a known probability of being selected at the outset. As a result, the findings cannot be generalized to the wider population. The sampling techniques falling into this category allow the researcher to choose certain types of people within the whole population. This is commonly done via quota sampling, or snowball sampling.

NORM-REFERENCED ASSESSMENT This is used when the performance of one individual is ranked in comparison with that of others. Usually the aim of this approach is to ration the number of 'passes' or qualifications.

ONTOLOGY Perception of the nature of reality.

OPEN SYSTEMS APPROACH (Parsons) Looks at the way that parts of the system (school) interrelate internally and externally (with society and the educational system). Sees schools taking the raw product (pupils) and processing them with the result that an 'educational product' emerges when the child leaves school.

OPERATIONALIZATION of concepts The process of finding observable indicators of concepts; for example, deciding to use someone's occupation as an indicator of social class.

PARACURRICULUM (Hargreaves) Term promoted as an alternative to 'hidden curriculum'. All that is taught alongside the formal curriculum.

PARADIGM A consensus or model of 'normal' research, the rules to be followed and what constitutes acceptable knowledge.

PARENTOCRACY A free market education system in which access to a good education is largely determined by parental choice and parental pressure and only those high-quality schools that attract parents will survive. As schools and families become more self-sufficient, the pressures of education on the state should decrease and consumer-led education should lead to optimum consumer satisfaction. See Consumer Sovereignty.

PARITY OF ESTEEM The original intention of the 1944 Education Act that children should be regarded as 'equal' irrespective of whether they were allocated to a grammar, secondary modern or technical school.

PARTICIPANT OBSERVATION This may be covert or overt (i.e. the subjects know that they are being watched) and involves the researcher joining a group of people in their natural setting, participating to a greater or lesser extent in what they are doing, observing patterns of social interaction, and talking informally with them.

PEDAGOGY Related to teaching and the transmission of knowledge.

PLURALISM A plurality of influences (and participants) on policy. A relatively impartial government adjudicates.

POLITICAL PARTISANSHIP Strength of support for a political party.

POSITIVISM The belief that social scientists can objectively identify laws governing human nature and generalize them. This means that detached observers should monitor and measure behaviour and often involves numeric comparisons between clearly operationalized variables in order to identify laws of cause and effect.

PREPARATORY SCHOOLS Non-maintained schools for pupils in the primary or middle school age range. They prepare such children for entry into non-maintained secondary schools.

PRIMARY SCHOOLS Attended by children aged 5 to 10 or 11. Primary provision could consist of one school covering the whole age range, or children may be split into two schools: an infant school for children aged 5 to 7, and a junior school for children aged 7 to 11. In some areas children leave primary school early (e.g. aged 8) and move to secondary school late (e.g. aged 13). The intervening years are spent at a middle school.

PRIVATE SCHOOLS This is a general label that may be attached to any school not financed by either LEA funds or a central government grant (although they may receive some government subsidies, such as tax concessions). Also called independent, fee-paying or (more correctly) non-maintained. Some are 'public' schools. The quality of these schools can vary, as they are often not subject to the sort of inspection that maintained schools now expect. Private preparatory schools are for pupils with the primary or middle school age range.

PROFILING The creation of a profile or file, describing a pupil or student's achievements, experiences and abilities. Now used to supplement GCSE and A level GCE results.

PROGRESSIVE EDUCATION Although its origins were earlier, the term usually refers to 1960s and early 1970s movements towards child-centred learning, mixed ability groups, open-plan schools, informal teaching methods, less authoritarian and more democratic organization, and comprehensive schools.

PROGRESSIVE FOCUSING A process of gradually narrowing the focus on to a relatively small area of research, a central theme, a central question or a research hypothesis.

PUBLIC EDUCATORS According to Ball (1990, p 4) they '. . . put the view "that man had a natural right to be educated, and that any good society depended on governments accepting this principle as their duty".'

PUBLIC SCHOOLS (a) In England, Wales and Northern Ireland these are an elite number of high-status, non-maintained secondary schools (e.g. Eton, Harrow, Winchester). Some can be identified by their headteacher's membership of the prestigious Headmasters' Conference. Unlike other private schools, public schools are not profit-making. (b) Public schools in Scotland are what are called maintained or state schools in other parts of the UK.

PUPIL TEACHER RATIO (PTR) The proportion of pupils to each teacher (e.g. number of pupils divided by number of teachers).

QUESTIONNAIRES Structured lists of questions on which respondents write their own answers. These are sometimes delivered by post.

RACE This term emphasizes biological differences often based on skin colour but there are debates about whether it has any meaning at all.

RANDOM (OR PROBABILITY) SAMPLING All members of the chosen population have a known and equal chance of selection. Potential bias should be eliminated from the selection procedure as the researcher cannot just choose people who seem to be particularly approachable, easy to contact, helpful, attractive and so on.

RECORD OF ACHIEVEMENT Used in schools. See Profiling.

REGULATION In political science this is concerned with particular aspects of public policy-making (such as public choice theory) and includes specific areas such as environmental regulation, the regulatory state, deregulationism and so on.

RELIABILITY The extent to which a test or observation would give consistent results if applied more than once to the same people under standard conditions.

RESTRICTED CODE (Bernstein) Simple language, limited range, descriptive and narrative. Implicit meanings; that is, it relies on shared understandings. Speech can often be predicted by the observer. See Elaborated Code.

SECONDARY MODERN SCHOOLS Secondary schools attended by pupils who, following examination or other assessment at 11+, were labelled as non-academic.

SECONDARY SCHOOL Any type of school attended after the age of 11. (Note that a secondary modern school is, like other schools, a type of secondary school.)

SELF-FULFILLING PROPHESY Pupils strive to achieve their own self-images which may be positive or negative.

SEMI-STRUCTURED INTERVIEWS Planned by the researcher in advance in order to ensure that various topics are covered and, whether this involves the preparation of a detailed interview schedule (a list of questions) or a more flexible aide mémoire (noting the topics to be covered), they still allow the interviewee considerable freedom of response.

SETTING Allocation of a pupil to a particular group according to ability in that subject; for example, may be in top set for English and bottom set for maths.

SOCIAL CLASS Individual or group position within the economy, relationship to the means of production. This is influenced by the sort of paid work done by an individual, or by that individual's family members.

SPECIAL AGREEMENT SCHOOL A type of aided or church school. Mostly Roman Catholic, they were established as a result of a government offer in 1936 to pay 50–75 per cent of the cost of building new secondary schools.

SPECIAL EDUCATIONAL NEEDS (SEN) Personal conditions affecting an ability to learn or thrive in an education environment. These may include temporary or permanent physical or mental conditions.

SPECIAL SCHOOLS Schools attended by children with special educational needs. The 1981 Education Act had a commitment to integrating most children with SEN into mainstream schools ('mainstreaming'). However, thousands of children still attend special schools.

SPONSORED MOBILITY (Turner) Elite recruits are chosen by the established elite or their agents.

STATUS The respect or esteem attributed to an individual or group by others. It may be achieved through one's own effort or ascribed by others with no effort on your part.

STRATIFIED CURRICULUM (Young) Hierarchy of subjects (school knowledge) and access to them related to the stratification of society.

STREAMING Results when assessment in several subjects are averaged to provide one grade representing the overall ability of each pupil. The whole year group of pupils is divided into different classes according to overall ability. This results is a 'top' class and 'bottom' class.

SUMMATIVE ASSESSMENT Aims to describe an individual's current intelligence, knowledge or ability. This may lead to a grading, or some other type of summary or label.

SURVEY The systematic collection of data from more than one person which is then studied by identifying variables for each person. This data is then analysed via a variable-by-case matrix, which allows the researcher to compare responses.

SYMBOLIC VIOLENCE (Bourdieu) The oppression of the working class by cultural domination rather than physical coercion.

TECHNICAL-FUNCTIONAL THEORY Skill requirements for jobs increase with technical change, and education provides specific job skills or capacity for various jobs.

TECHNICAL SCHOOL Secondary schools attended by pupils who were labelled as having technical/practical abilities as a result of assessment at 11+.

TEACHER PROLETARIANIZATION Claim that teachers now have more in common with other 'workers' than with other 'professionals'. This results from low pay, erosion of teacher autonomy and an increase in management controls.

THEORETICAL SAMPLING Decisions about sampling that will help the researcher to focus on testing an existing theory, or theories.

TRIANGLE OF TENSION Up to the mid 1970s the Department of Education and Science, local education authorities and teachers' unions negotiated policy decisions. This resulted in a fragile consensus and incremental change. LEAs and teachers have since then become less influential.

TRIANGULATION (of methods, of theory or of data) The use of more than one method or theory, or collection of more than one type of datum, in order to improve the validity and depth of the findings.

TRIPARTITE SYSTEM Introduced by the 1944 Education Act. Pupils were allocated to grammar, technical or secondary modern schools according to their performance in an examination or other assessment at 11+. A bipartite system became more common.

TVEI Technical and Vocational Education Initiative. Created in 1983 by the Manpower Services Commission and the government for young people aged 14+. Introduced in some schools and colleges.

TYPIFICATION Accounts of typification show how people understand things by labelling and categorizing them. For example, Hargreaves identified three models: ideal matching, characteristics (comparing an identikit of different characteristics), dynamic interactionist.

UNDERACHIEVMENT Failure to reach potential.

UNIT COSTS Used in the presentation of official statistics. Average total spending on each pupil.

UNSTRUCTURED INTERVIEWS These are generally unplanned and allow the interviewee to identify topics of interest to themselves.

UTILITARIAN Useful. Utilitarianism is a belief that the morality of actions is to be tested by their usefulness.

VALIDITY The extent to which the findings can be trusted, and accurately represent reality. Researchers often evaluate internal validity, external validity, population validity and ecological validity.

VARIABLES Characteristics that vary and consist of two or more values; for example, gender, age and social class.

VERTICAL MOBILITY Movement up or down the social scale. Upwardly mobile or downwardly mobile.

VOCATIONALISM Education with the emphasis on job-related training.

VOLUNTARY AIDED OR AIDED (church) SCHOOLS Schools partly financed by the state and partly by a church. Since the 1944 Education Act three types of schools established by a church body became voluntary aided schools, differing mainly in the extent to which the LEA financed and controlled them: aided, controlled and special agreement. In 1997 the new Labour government effectively renamed voluntary aided schools as aided schools.

Appendix 3 Useful websites

Government information

www.open.gov.uk = The main website for the British Government Information Service.

www.dfee.gov.uk = Department For Employment and Education.

www.standards.dfeegov.uk = Help for school teachers in England, with an emphasis on raising standards in education.

www.ofsted.gov.uk = Office of Standards in Education.

www.scotland.gov.uk = The Scottish Office.

www.wales.gov.uk = The Welsh Office.

www.nics.gov.uk/deni = Department for Education in Northern Ireland.

Newspapers and journals

www.educationunlimited.co.uk = The Guardian Education Supplement, includes general information and situations vacant.

www.tes.co.uk = The Times Educational Supplement

www.learnfree.co.uk = The Times Educational Supplement site providing advice for teachers, parents and learners.

www.thes.co.uk = The Times Higher Educational Supplement.

www.carfax.co.uk = Provides access to British Carfax journals about education.

Research

www.socresonline.org.uk = Sociological Research Online publishes applied sociology and engages in current debates.

www.bera.ac.uk = The British Educational Research Association provides information about research, education journals and links to other sites.

www.scre.ac.uk = The Scottish Council for Research in Education (SCRE) provides access not only to research about education in Scotland, but also to the contents (and in some cases full texts) of many British and international education journals and newsletters.

Other sites

www.rmplc.co.uk = EduWeb provides information for schools and a range of teacher support resources.

www.feda.ac.uk = The national Further Education Development Agency.

www.mandolin.demon.co.uk/case.html = The Campaign for State Education provides general information about education and links to other education websites.

www.education-quest.com = Helps teachers and parents to find resources and services quickly.

www.lycos.com/L/d40 = Information about a wide range of education topics and access to other sites.

www.geocities.com/Athens/Troy/4579 = EduLinks UK, a 'one-stop service station for the UK Education Super Highway'.

www.pscw.uva.nl/sociosite = An information system based at the University of Amsterdam. It provides information about a wide range of sociological topics worldwide.

www.vts.rdn.ac.uk = The Resource Delivery Network provides web-based tutorials on what the Internet offers in various subjects. Includes tutorials for 'sociologists' and 'politicians'. From May 2001 additions include 'educators'.

Bibliography

Ackland, H. (1980) 'Research as stage management: the case of the Plowden Committee', in Blumer, M.I.A. (1980) *Social Research and the Royal Commissions*, London: Allen and Unwin.

Adler, M.E., Petch, A.J. and Tweedie, J.W. (1989) *Parental Choice in Education Policy*, Edinburgh University Press.

Aggleton, P. (1987) *Rebels without a Cause? Middle class youth and transition from school to work*, London: Falmer Press.

Althusser, L. (1971) 'Ideology and ideological state apparatuses', in *Lenin, Philosophy and Other Essays*, London: New Left Books.

Ambler, J. (1994) 'Who benefits from educational choice? Some evidence from Europe', *Journal of Policy Analysis and Management*, vol. 13, no. 3, pp 454–76.

Amos, V. and Parmar, P. (1984) 'Challenging imperial feminism', *Feminist Review*, vol. 17.

Armstrong, F., Clarke, M. and Murphy, D. (1995) ' "... some kind of bampot." Young people in care and their experiences of the education system', in Potts, P., Armstrong, F. and Masterton, M. (1995) *Equality and Diversity in Education 1: Learning, teaching and managing schools*, Open University / Routledge.

Arnot, M., Bullock, A. and Thomas, H. (1992) 'Consequences of local management: an assessment by head teachers', in Whitty, G. 'Creating quasi-markets in education: a review of recent research on parental choice and school autonomy in three countries', *Review of Research in Education*, 22.

Arnot, M. (1986) *Race, Gender and Educational Policy Making*, Module 4, E333, Milton Keynes: Open University Press.

Arnot, M. and Weiner, G. (eds), (1987) *Gender and the Politics of Schooling*, London: Hutchinson.

Askew, S. and Ross, C. (1988) *Boys don't cry: boys and sexism in education*, Milton Keynes: Open University Press.

Ball, S. (1981) *Beachside Comprehensive: A case study of secondary schooling*, Cambridge University Press.

Ball, S.J. (1990) *Politics and Policy Making in Education*, London: Routledge.

Banks, O. (1955) *Parity and Prestige in English Secondary Education*, London: Routledge and Kegan Paul.

Banks, O. (1968) *The Sociology of Education*, London: Batsford, p 283.

Barker, M. (1981) *The New Racism*, London: Junction Books.

Barker-Lunn, J. (1970) *Streaming in the Primary School*, Windsor: NFER.

Baudrillard, J. (1983) 'The ecstacy of communication', in Foster, H. (ed.) *The Anti-Aesthetic: Essays on postmodern culture*, Port Townsend, Washington: Bay Press.

Bauman, Z. (1992) *Intimations of Postmodernity*, London: Routledge.

Beck, U. (1992 original, 1998 reprint) *Risk Society: Towards a new modernity*, London: Sage Publications.

Beck, U. 'The reinvention of politics', in Beck, Giddens and Lash, 1994.

Beck, U., Giddens, A. and Lash, S. (1994) *Reflexive Modernization*, Cambridge: Polity Press.

Bell, D. and Kristol, I. (1969) *Confrontation: The student rebellion and universities*, New York: Basic Books.

Bell, D. (1973) *The Coming of Post-Industrial Society*, New York: Basic Books.

Bernstein, B. (1970) 'Elaborated and restricted codes: their social origins and some consequences', in Danziger, K. (ed.) *Readings in Child Socialization*, Oxford: Pergamon, pp 165–86.

Bernstein, B. (1971) 'On the classification and framing of educational knowledge', in Young, M.F.D. (ed.) *Knowledge and Control: New directions in the sociology of education*, London: Collier-Macmillan.

Bernstein, B. (1975) 'Class and pedagogies: visible and invisible', an extract from *Class, Codes and Control*, vol. 3, London: Routledge and Kegan Paul, pp 116–56; in Halsey *et al.* (1997), pp 76–8.

Best, J.W. (1970) *Research in Education*, Englewood Cliffs, New Jersey Prentice-Hall. Cited by Cohen and Manion (1994), pp 53–4.

Beveridge, W. (1942) *Social Insurance and Allied Services*, London: HMSO.

Blackstone, T. [and others] (1969) *Students in Conflict: LSE in 1967*, London: London School of Economics and Political Science, Weidenfeld and Nicolson.

Blair, T. 'Why schools must do better', in *The Times*, 7 July 1997.

Blaxter, L., Hughes, C. and Tight, M. (1996) *How to Research*, Buckingham: Open University Press.

Blundell, J. and Gosschalk, B. (1997) *Beyond Left and Right*, London: Institute of Economic Affairs.

Bosely, S. (1986) 'Crisis warning on school books', in the *Guardian*, 31 March 1986.

Bourdieu, P. 'The forms of capital' (original 1983) in Halsey, A.H., Lauder, H., Brown, P. and Wells, A.S. (1997) *Education: Culture, Economy, Society*, Oxford University Press.

Bourdieu, P. and Passeron, J.C. (1977) *Reproduction in Education, Society and Culture*, London: Sage.

Bowe, R. and Ball, S. with Gold, A. (1992) *Reforming Education and Changing Schools: Case studies in policy sociology*, London: Routledge.

Bowles, S. and Gintis, H. (1976) *Schooling in Capitalist America*, London: Routledge and Kegan Paul.

Brah, A. and Minhas, R. (1988) 'Structural racism or cultural difference: schooling for Asian girls', in Woodhead, M. and McGrath, A. (eds) (1988) *Family, School and Society*, London: Hodder and Stoughton.

Bransma, J., Kessle, F. and Munch, J. (1995) *Continuing vocational training in Europe: state of the art and perspectives*, Utrecht: Force, Lemma, p 24.

British Medical Association (1987) *Deprivation and Ill Health*, BMA.

Broadfoot, P. (1985) 'Changing patterns of educational accountability in England and France', *Comparative Education*, vol. 21, no. 3.

Broadfoot, P. (1988) 'Educational Research: two cultures and three estates', in *British Educational Research Journal*, vol. 14, no. 1, adapted from pp 4–7.

Brown, P. (1990) 'The "third wave": education and the ideology of parentocracy', *British Journal of Sociology of Education*, vol. 11, pp 65–85.

Brown, P. (1989) 'Schooling for inequality?' in Cosin, B., Flude, M. and Hales, M. (eds) *School, Work and Equality*, London: Hodder and Stoughton with the Open University.

Brown, R. and Howell, D.A. (1983) *Educational Policy Making: An analysis*, London: Heinemann.

Bryan, B., Dadzie, S. and Scafe, S. (eds) (1987) 'Learning to resist: black women and education', in Weiner, G. and Arnot, M., *Gender under Scrutiny*, London: Hutchinson in association with the Open University.

Buck, N. and Scott, J. (1994) 'Household and family change', in Buck, N., Gershuny, J., Rose, D. and Scott, J. (eds) *Changing Households: The British Household Panel Study 1990–1992*, Colchester: Economic and Social Research Council Research Centre.

Burt, C. (1961) 'The gifted child', in *British Journal of Statistical Psychology*, vol. 14, no. 2, pp 123–39.

Burt, C. (1975) *The Gifted Child*, London: Hodder and Stoughton.

Bush, T., Coleman, M. and Glover, D. (1993) *Managing Autonomous Schools*, London: Chapman.

Butler, D. and Stokes, D. (1974, 2nd edn) *Political Change in Britain: The evolution of electoral choice*, Macmillan Press.

Butler, R.A. in newsreel *From Butler to Baker*, BBC2 1993.

CACE, Central Advisory Council for Education, Wales (1949) the Evans/Aaron Report, *The Future of Secondary Education in Wales*, London: HMSO.

CACE, Central Advisory Council for Education, England (1954) the Gurney-Dixon Report, *Early Leaving*, London: HMSO.

CACE, Central Advisory Council for Education, England (1959) the Crowther Report, *Fifteen to Eighteen*, London: HMSO.

CACE, Central Advisory Council for Education, England (1963) the Newsom Report, *Half our Future*, London: HMSO.

CACE, Central Advisory Council for Education, England (1967) the Plowden Report, *Children and their Primary Schools*, London: HMSO.

CACE, Central Advisory Council for Education, Wales (1967) the Gittins Report, *Primary Education in Wales*, London: HMSO.

Carby, H. (1982) The Empire Strikes Back: Race and racism in 1970s Britain, London: Hutchinson in association with the Centre for Contemporary Cultural Studies.

Castles, S. and Kosak, G. (1985) *Immigrant Workers and the Class Structure in Western Europe*, Oxford University Press.

Centre for Contemporary Cultural Studies (CCCS) (1981) *Unpopular Education: Schooling and social democracy in England since 1944*, London: Hutchinson.

CERI (1996) *Education at a Glance, Analysis*, Paris: OECD, p 56.

Chubb, J. and Moe, T. (1990) *Politics, markets and America's schools*, Washington DC: Brookings Institute.

CIPFA (1988) Financial Information Services, vol. 20, Education, London: Chartered Institute of Public Finance and Accountability.

Education Statistics 1985–86 Actuals, CIPFA, Statistical Information Service, SIS Ref. 52.87.

Citizens' Advice Bureaus (CAB)(1992) report calling for a removal of the ban on 16–17 year olds receiving income support.

Cohen, D. (1990) *Being a Man*, London: Routledge.

Cohen, L. and Manion, L. (1994, 4th edn) *Research Methods in Education*, London: Routledge.

Cohen, S. (1973) *Folk Devils and Moral Panics*, London: Paladin.

Cohn, T. (1988) 'Sambo – a study in name calling', in Kelly, E. and Cohn, T. *Racism in Schools – New Research Evidence*, Stoke-on-Trent Trentham Books.

Cole, M. (1989) *The Social Contexts of Schooling*, Lewes: Falmer Press.

Comte, A. (1853) *The Positive Philosophy of Auguste Comte*, translated and condensed by Martineau, H., vol. 1, London: John Chapman.

Conran, S. (1975) *Superwoman*, Sidgewick and Jackson; in 1977, Harmondsworth: Penguin Books.

Conservative Research Department (1985) *Education, Politics Today*, no. 14.

Cox, B. and Dyson, A.E. (1969) *Fight for Education: A Black Paper*, The Critical Survey, 1968–70, The Critical Quarterly Society.

Cox, B. and Dyson, A.E. (1970) *Black Paper Two: The Crisis in Education*, The Critical Survey, 1968–70, The Critical Quarterly Society.

Cox, B. and Dyson, A.E. (1971) *Black Paper Three: Goodbye Mr. Short*, The Critical Survey, 1968–70, The Critical Quarterly Society.

Cox, B. and Boyson, R. (1975) *Black Paper 1975: The Right for Education*, J.M. Dent and Sons Ltd.

Cox, B. and Boyson, R. (1977) *The Black Paper 1977*, London: Temple Smith.

Craft, M. and Craft, A. (1983) 'The participation of ethnic minority pupils in further and higher education', *Educational Review*, vol. 25, no. 1, pp 10–19.

Crewe, I. (1987) 'Tories prosper from a paradox', *Guardian* 16 June 1987.

Crisp, Q. (1985; original in 1968) *The Naked Civil Servant*, 1985 London: Flamingo.

Crosland, A. (1956) *The Future of Socialism*, London. Revised edns 1963 London: Cape; 1994 London: William Pickering.

Dahlerup, D. (1986) *The New Women's Movement: Feminism and political power in Europe and the USA*, London: Sage.

Dale, R. (1989) *The State and Education Policy*, Buckingham: Open University Press.

Dale, R. 'The state and the governance of education: an analysis of the restructuring of the state-education relationship', in Halsey, A.H. *et al.* (1997) *Education, Culture, Economy, Society*, Oxford University Press.

Davis, A. (1981) *Women, Race and Class*, New York: Random House.

Dawkins, R. (1989; original in 1976) *The Selfish Gene*, Oxford University Press.

Dearing, R. (1993) *The National Curriculum and its Assessment: An interim report*, York: National Curriculum Council.

Dearing, R. (1997) *Higher Education in the Learning Society: The National Committee of Inquiry into Higher Education*, London: HMSO.

de Beauvoir, S. (1953; original publication 1949 in France, *Le Deuxieme Sexe*) *The Second Sex*, translated and edited by H.M. Parshley, London: Jonathan Cape.

Deem, R. (ed.) (1980) *Schooling for Women's Work*, London: Routledge and Kegan Paul.

Degroot, G. (1998) *Student Protest: The sixties and after*, Longmans.

Dempster, J.J.B. (1954) *Selection for Secondary Education*, London: Methuen & Co.

Dennis, N., Henriques, F. and Slaughter, C. (1956) *Coal Is Our Life*, London: Tavistock Publications, as cited in (1986) *E333 Policy-making in Education*, Module 1, Part 1, pp 29–30, Milton Keynes: Open University Press.

Dennison, W.F. (1985) 'Education and the economy: changing circumstances', in McNay, I. and Ozga, J. (eds) (1985) *Policy-making in Education: The breakdown of consensus*, Pergamon Press and the Open University.

Denver, D. and Hands, G. (1989) *Elections and Voting Behaviour in Britain*, Philip Allen.

Denver, D. and Hands, G. (1992) *Issues and Controversies in British Electoral Behaviour*, Harvester.

Denzin, N. (1970) *The Research Act*, Chicago: Aldine.

DES (1970) *Education and Science in 1969*, London: HMSO.

Disraeli, B., Earl of Beaconsfield (1835) *Vindication of the English Constitution in a letter to a noble and learned Lord*, London: Saunders and Otleg.

Dixon, B.R., Bouma, G.D. and Atkinson, G.B.J. (1987) *A Handbook of Social Science Research*, Oxford University Press.

Donald, J. and Rattansi, A. (1992) *'Race', Culture and Difference*, London: Sage.

Douglas, J.W.B. (1964) *The Home and the School*, London: McGibbon and Kee.

Douglas, J.W.B., Ross, J.M. and Simpson, H.R. (1968) *All Our Future*, London: Panther.

Douglas, J.W.B. (1976) 'The use and abuse of national cohorts', in M.D. Shipman, *The Organization and Impact of Social Research*, London: Routledge and Kegan Paul.

Drew, D. and Gray, J. (1989) 'The fifth-year examination achievements of black young people in England and Wales', University of Sheffield Educational Research Centre, reported in Gillborn, D. (1990) *Race, Ethnicity and Education*, London: Unwin Hyman. Paper also in *Educational Research*, vol. 32, no. 3.

Driver, G. (1980) *Beyond Underachievement: Case Studies of English, West Indian and Asian School Leavers at 16 Plus*, London: Commission for Racial Equality.

Dryzek, J. (1997) *The Politics of the Earth*, Oxford University Press: Oxford.

Dunham, J. (1992; 1st edn 1984) *Stress in Teaching*, London: Routledge.

Dunleavy, P. and Husbands, C. (1985) *British Democracy at the Crossroads: Voting and party competition in the 1980s*, London: Allen and Unwin.

Durkheim, E. (1956) *Education and Sociology*, New York: Free Press.

Durkheim, E. (1973) *Moral Education: A study of the theory and application of the sociology of education*, edited by E.K. Wilson, translation by E.K. Wilson and H. Schnurer, London: Collier Macmillan.

Durkheim, E. and Pickering, W.S.F. (1979; original 1916) *Durkheim, Essays on Morals and Education*, edited by W.S.F. Pickering, translation by H.L. Sutcliffe, London: Routledge and Kegan Paul.

Durkheim, E. (1970; original 1897) *Suicide: A study in sociology*, London: Routledge.

Easton, D. (ed.) (1966) *Varieties of Political Theory*, Eaglewood Cliffs: Prentice-Hall.

Edgell, S. and Duke, V. (1991) *A Measure of Thatcherism*, London: HarperCollins.

Edgell, S., Walklate, S. and Williams, G. (1995, eds.) *Debating the Future of the Public Sphere*, Avebury.

Edwards, V. (1976) *West Indian Language: Attitudes and the school*, London: National Association for Multiracial Education.

Edwards, V. (1979) *The West Indian Language Issue in British Schools*, London: Routledge and Kegan Paul.

Edwards, R. (1993) *Mature Women Students: Separating or Connecting Family and Education*, London: Taylor & Francis.

Eggleston, J., Dunn, M., Anjali, M. and Wright, C. (1986) *Education for Some*, Stoke-on-Trent: Trentham Books.

Elliot, L. (1999) 'Too much education leads to discontent in the workplace', *Guardian Weekly*, 21 March, p 9.

Elliott, L. and Atkinson, D. (1998) *The Age of Insecurity*, London and New York: Verso.

Etzioni, A. (1993) *The Spirit of Community: The reinvention of American society*, New York: Simon and Schuster.

European Commission (1995a) *Teaching and Learning: Towards the learning society*, Brussels: European Commission.

European Commission (1995b) *Key/Core Competencies – Synthesis of Related Work Undertaken within the Eurotecnet Programme*, Brussels: European Commission.

European Commission (1996) *Key Data on Education in the EU*, Brussels: European Commission.

EUROSTAT (1997) Education Across the European Union, *Statistics and Indicators, 1996*, Luxembourg: Office des Publications Officielles des Communautes, European Commission 1996f.

Exley, H. (ed.) (1993) *The Best Women's Quotations*, New York: Exley Giftbooks.

Eysenck, H. (1971) *Race, Intelligence and Education*, London, Temple-Smith.

Eysenck, H. (1973) *The Inequality of Man*, London: Temple Smith.

Finn, D. (1984) 'Leaving school and growing up', in Bates, I. *et al.*, *Schooling for the Dole?* London: Macmillan.

Firestone, S. (1970) *Dialectic of Sex*, New York: Paladin.

Fitz, J., Halpin, D. and Power, S. (1993) *Grant Maintained Schools: Education in the market place*, London: Kogan Page.

Floud, J. and Halsey, A.H. (1957) 'Social Class, Intelligence Tests and Selection for Secondary Schools', *British Journal of Sociology*, VIII.

Floud, J.E., Halsey, A.H. and Martin, F.M. (1956) *Social Class and Educational Opportunity*, London: Heinemann.

Foucault, M. (1977; original 1975) *Discipline and Punish: The birth of the prison*, London: Allen Lane.

Foucault, M. in Rabinow, P. (ed.) (1984) *The Foucault Reader*, London: Penguin.

Fraser, S. (1995) *The Bell Curve Wars: Race, intelligence and the future of America*, Basic Books.

Freire, P. (1970) 'A few notions about the word "Conscientization",' in Schooling and Society Course Team (1976), *Schooling and Capitalism: A sociological reader*, Open University.

Freire, P. (1972; original 1970) *Pedagogy of the Oppressed*, Harmondsworth: Penguin.

Friedan, B. (1963) *The Feminine Mistique*, Harmondsworth: Penguin.

Friedman, M. (1962) *Capitalism and Freedom*, Harmondsworth: Penguin.

Fukuyama, F. (1989) 'The end of history?' in *The National Interest*, vol. 16, pp 3–18.

Fullan, M. (1991, 2ⁿᵈ edn.) *The New Meaning of Educational Change*, Cassell.

Fuller, M. (1980) 'Black girls in a London comprehensive school', in Deem (1980) pp 52–65, and in Hammersley and Woods (1984) pp 166–190.

Fuller, M. (1983) 'Qualified criticism, critical qualifications', in Barton, L. and Walker, S. (eds) *Race, Class and Education*, London: Croom Helm.

Further Education Development Agency (FEDA), Institute of Education, The Nuffield Foundation (1997), *GNVQs 1993–1997, Final Report of a Joint Project: The evolution of GNVQs: Enrolment and delivery patterns and their policy implications*, London: FEDA.

Gannaway, H. (1976) 'Making sense of school', in Stubbs, M. and Delamont, S. (eds) *Explorations in Classroom Observation*, Chichester: Wiley, pp 45–82.

Gewitz, S., Ball, S.J. and Bowe, R. (1995) *Markets, Choice and Equity*, Buckingham: Open University Press.

Giddens, A. (1991) *Modernity and Self-identity*, Cambridge: Polity Press.

Giddens, A. (1994) *Beyond Left and Right: The future of radical politics*, Cambridge: Polity Press.

Giddens, A. (1998) *The Third Way*, Cambridge: Polity Press.

Gill, D., Mayor, B. and Blair, M. (1992) *Racism and Education: Structures and strategies*, London: Sage.

Giroux, H. (1992) *Border Crossings: Cultural workers and the politics of education*, London: Routledge; pp 39–88 in Halsey *et al.* (1997).

Glaser, B. and Strauss, A.L. (1968) *The Discovery of Grounded Theory*, London: Weidenfeld and Nicolson.

Glass, D.V. (ed.) (1954; reprinted in 1963) *Social Mobility in Britain*, London: Routledge and Kegan Paul.

Goldthorpe, J.H. and Llewellyn, C. (1977a) 'Class mobility in Britain: three theses examined', *Sociology*, vol. 11, no. 2, pp 257–87.

Goldthorpe, J.H. and Llewellyn, C. (1977b) 'Class mobility, integrational and worklife patterns', *British Journal of Sociology*, vol. 28, no. 3, pp 269–302.

Goldthorpe, J.H., Llewellyn, C. and Payne, C. (1980) *Social Mobility and Class Structure in Modern Britain*, Oxford: Clarendon Press.

Goleman, D. (1996) *Emotional Intelligence*, London: Bloomsbury.

Government Statistical Service (1989) *Educational Statistics for the United Kingdom 1989*, London: HMSO.

Gramsci, A. (1971) *Selections from the Prison Notebooks*, London: Lawrence and Wishart.

Grant, D. (1989) *Learning Relations*, London: Routledge.

Green, A., Wolf, A. and Leney, T. (1999) *Convergence and Divergence in European Education and Training Systems*, Bedford Way Series, London: Institute of Education.

Green, P. (1985) 'Multi-ethnic teaching and the pupils' self-concepts', *Annex B* in the Swann Report, 1985.

Greer, G. (1971) *The Female Eunuch*, London: Paladin.

Griffin, C. (1985) *Typical Girls? The Transition from School to Un/employment for Young Working Class Women*, London: Routledge and Kegan Paul.

Griffin, C. (1986) 'It's different for girls', *The Social Studies Review*, November 1986.

Griggs, C. (1989) 'The rise, fall and rise again of selective secondary schooling', in Cole, M. (ed.) *The Social Contexts of Schooling*, Lewes: Falmer Press.

Habermas, J. (1975) *Legitimation Crisis*, Boston: Beacon Press.

Habermas, J. (1987a) *The Theory of Communicative Action, Vol. II, Lifeworld and System: A critique of functionalist reason*, trans. T. McCarthy, Boston: Beacon.

Habermas, J. (1987b) *Toward a Rational Society: Student Protest, Science and Politics*, Cambridge: Polity Press.

Hall, S., Critcher, C., Jefferson, T., Clarke, J. and Roberts, B. (1978) *Policing the Crisis: Mugging, the state and law and order*, Basingstoke: Macmillan Press.

Halsey, A.H., Floud, J. and Anderson, C.A. (1961) *Education, Economy and Society*, Glencoe: Free Press.

Halsey, A.H. (1972) *Educational Priority. EPA Problems and Policies*, vol. 1, London: HMSO.

Halsey, A.H., Heath, A. and Ridge, J.M. (1980) *Origins and Destinations: Family, class and education in modern Britain*, Oxford, Clarendon Press.

Halsey, A.H., Lauder, H., Brown, P. and Wells, A.S. (1997) *Education, Culture, Economy, Society*, Oxford University Press.

Hammersley, M. and Woods, P. (1984) *Life in School: The sociology of pupil culture*, Buckingham: Open University Press.

Hargreaves, A. (1994) *Changing Teachers, Changing Times*, London: Cassell.

Hargreaves, D.H. (1967) *Social Relations in a Secondary School*, London: Routledge and Kegan Paul.

Hargreaves, D. and Hopkins, D. (1991) *The Empowered School*, London: Cassell.

Hayek, F.A. (1976) *The Road to Serfdom*, London: Routledge and Kegan Paul.

Hayek, F.A. (1976) *The Constitution of Liberty*, London: Routledge and Kegan Paul.

Hayek F.A. (1979) *Law, Legislation and Liberty: a new statement of the liberal principles of justice and political economy*, London: Routledge and Kegan Paul.

Hearnshaw, L.S. (1979) *Cyril Burt, psychologist*, London: Hodder and Stoughton.

Heath, A.F. (1981) *Social Mobility*, London: Fontana.

Heath, A.F. (1989) 'Class in the classroom', in Cosin, B., Flude, M. and Hales, M. (eds) (1989) *School, Work and Equality*, London: Hodder and Stoughton with the Open University.

Herrnstein, R.J. and Murray, C. (1994) *The Bell Curve: Intelligence and class structure in American life*, New York: Free Press.

Hillgate Group (1986) *Whose Schools?* London: Hillgate Group.

Hochschild, A. (1983) *The Managed Heart: Commercialisation of human feeling*, Berkeley: University of California Press.

Holdsworth, A. (1988) *Out of the Dolls House: The story of women in the twentieth century*, BBC Books.

Holt, J. (1990) *How Children Fail*, revised edition (first published in the USA by Pitman Publishing 1964), London: Penguin Books.

Hopper, E. (1971) *Readings in the Theory of Educational System*, London: Hutchinson.

Hughes, D., Lauder, H., Watson, S., Hamlin, J. and Simiyu, I. (1996) *Markets in Education: testing the polarisation thesis*, Wellington, NZ: Ministry of Education.

Humphries, S. and Gordon, P. (eds) (1992) *Out of Sight: The experience of disability 1900–1950*, Plymouth: Northcote House Publishers.

Hutton, W. (1995) *The State We're In*, London: Cape.

Huxley, A. (1941) *Grey Eminence: a study in religion and politics*, London: Chatto and Windus.

Illich, I. (1971) *Deschooling Society*, London: Penguin.

Inglehart, R. (1977) *The Silent Revolution: Changing values and political styles*, Princeton University Press.

Institute of Public Policy Research (1993) 'Education: a different vision.'

Jackson, B. and Marsden, D. (1963) *Education and the Working Class*, London: Routledge and Kegan Paul.

Jackson, S. (1987) *The Education of Children in Care*, the Bristol Papers in Applied Social Studies, no. 1, University of Bristol School of Applied Social Studies.

Jensen, A. (1969) 'How much can we boost IQ and scholastic achievement?' *Harvard Educational Review*, vol. 39, no. 1, pp 1–123.

Jensen, A. (1973) *Educability and Group Differences*, London: Methuen.

Jephcott, A.P. (1942) *Girls Growing Up*, London: Faber and Faber.

Johnson, R. (1983) 'Educational politics: the old and the new', in Wolpe, A.M. and Donald, J. (eds) *Is there Anyone here from Education?* London: Pluto Press.

Jones, C. and Mahony, P. (1989) *Learning our Lines, sexuality and social control in education*, London: Women's Press.

Jones, K. (1983) 'Teachers and their organizations', in Wolpe, A.M. and Donald, J. (eds) *Is there Anyone here from education?* London: Pluto Press.

Jones, K. (1985) 'The National Union of Teachers', in McNay, I. and Ozga, J. (eds) (1985) *Policy-making in Education: The breakdown of consensus*, Pergamon Press and the Open University.

Jones, T. (1993) *Britain's Ethnic Minorities*, London: PSI.

Jowell *et al.* (1984) British Social Attitudes: the Report, Aldershot: Gower.

Jowell, R. and Witherspoon, S. (eds) (1985) *British Social Attitudes: the 1985 Report*, SCPR, Gower.

Jowell, R., Brook, L. and Witherspoon, S. (eds) (1986) *British Social Attitudes: the 1986 Report*, SCPR, Gower.

Jowell, R., Witherspoon, S. and Brook, L., (1990) *British Social Attitudes: the 1990 Report*, SCPR, Gower.

Joynson, R.B. (1989) *The Burt Affair*, London: Routledge.

Kamin, L. (1977) *The Science and Politics of IQ*, Harmondsworth: Penguin.

Kellecher, M. and Scott, P. (1996) 'Convergence and fragmentation? Vocational training within the European Union', *European Journal of Education*, cited by Green, Wolf and Leney (1999) pp 31–2.

Kennedy, H. (1997) *Learning Works: Widening participation in further education*, Further Education Funding Council.

Kenway, J. (1997) 'Having a postmodern turn or postmodern angst: a disorder experienced by an author who is not yet dead or even close to it', in Halsey *et al.* (1997) p 131. Original in Smith, R. and Wexler, P. (eds) *After Postmodernism: Education, politics and identity*, Lewes: Falmer Press, p 36.

Kelly, A. (ed.) (1981) *The Missing Half: Girls and science education*, Manchester University Press.

Keynes, J.M. (1985; original 1936) *A General Theory of Employment, Interest and Money*, vol. VII of his *Collected Works*, London: Macmillan.

Kuhn, T. (1962) *The Structure of Scientific Revolutions*, University of Chicago Press.

Kluckhohn, F.R. and Strodbeck, F.L. (1961) *Variations in Value Orientations*, Illinois: Row Peterson.

Labour pamphlet *A policy for Secondary Education* (1951) cited in Morrish, I. (1972) *The Sociology of Education: An introduction*, London: George Allen and Unwin Ltd.

Labov, W. (1969) 'The logic of non-standard English', Georgetown Monographs on Language and Linguistics, no. 22 in Giglioli, P.P. (ed.) (1972) *Language and Social Context*, Harmondsworth: Penguin.

Laclau, E. (1988) 'Politics and the Limits of Modernity', in Ross, A. (ed.) *Universal Abandon? The Politics of Postmodernism*, Minneapolis: University of Minnesota Press, p 80.

Lacey, C. (1966) 'Some sociological concomitants of academic streaming in a grammar school', *British Journal of Sociology*, vol. 17, no. 3.

Lacey, C. (1970) *Hightown Grammar: The school as a social system*, Manchester University Press.

Laing, R.D. (1960) *The Divided Self*, London: Tavistock.

Lambart, A. (1976) 'The Sisterhood', in Hammersley, M. and Woods, P. (eds) *The Process of Schooling*, London: Routledge and Kegan Paul.

Lawton, D. (1992) *Education and Politics in the 1990s: Conflict or consensus?* Lewes: Falmer Press.

Lee, D. and Newby, H. (1983) *The Problem of Sociology: An introduction to the discipline*, London: Hutchinson.

Lees, S. (1986) *Losing Out: Sexuality and adolescent girls*, London: Hutchinson.

Levacic, R. (1995) *Local Management of Schools: Analysis and practice*, Buckingham: Open University Press.

Levitas, R. (1998) *The Inclusive Society? Social Exclusion and New Labour*, Basingstoke: Macmillan Press.

Ling, T. (1998) *The Madingley Scenarios*, London: NHS Confederation.

Lipset, S.M. (1969) *Revolution and counterrevolution: change and persistence in social structure*, London: Heinemann Educational.

Little, A. (1975) 'Performance of children from ethnic minority backgrounds in primary schools', *Oxford Review of Education*, vol. 1, no. 2, pp 117–35.

Little, A. (1978) *Five Views of Multiracial Britain*, London: Commission for Racial Equality.

Little, A. and Mabey, C. (1972) 'An index for designation of Educational Priority Areas', in Shonfield, S. and Shaw, S. (eds) *Social Indicators and Social Policy*, London: Heinemann, pp 67–93.

Locke, J. (1966; original 1690) *The Second Treatise of Government . . . and a letter concerning toleration*, ed. J. Gough, Oxford: Blackwell.

Lovenduski, J. and Randall, V. (1993) *Contemporary Feminist Politics*, Oxford University Press.

Lynn, R. (1970) in Cox, C.B. and Dyson, A.E. (eds) (1970) 'Black Paper Two: The Crisis in Education', *The Critical Survey 1968–70*, The Critical Quarterly Society.

Lyotard, J.F. (1984) *The Postmodern Condition: A report on knowledge*, trans. G. Bennington and B. Massumi, Manchester University Press.

Mabey, C. (1981) 'Black British literacy', *Educational Research*, vol. 23, no. 2, pp 83–95.

Mac an Ghaill, M. (1988) *Young, Gifted and Black*, Milton Keynes: Open University Press.

Mac an Ghaill, M. (1996) 'Sociology of education, state schooling and social class: beyond critiques of the New Right hegemony', *British Journal of Sociology of Education*, vol. 17, no. 2, June 1996, pp 163–76.

Macdonald, I. *et al.* (1989) *Murder in the Playground*, The Burnage Report, London: Longsight.

Mackinnon, D. and Statham, J. (1999) *Education in the UK: Facts and figures*, Open University and Hodder and Stoughton.

Mackintosh, N.J. (ed.) (1995) *Cyril Burt: Fraud or framed?* Oxford: Oxford University Press.

Maclure, S. (1988) *Education Re-formed*, London: Hodder and Stoughton.

Maclure, S. (1989, 2nd ed.) *Education Re-formed*, London: Hodder and Stoughton.

Maclure, S. (1992, 3rd edn) *Education Re-formed*, Hodder and Stoughton.

Macnair, M.R.T. (1989) 'Homosexuality in schools – Section 28, Local Government Act 1988', *Education and the Law*, vol. 1, no. 1, pp 35–9.

Maguire, M.J. and Ashton, D.N. (1981) 'Employers' perceptions and use of educational qualifications', *Educational Analysis*, vol. 3, no. 2, pp 25–36.

Mannheim, K. (1943) *Diagnosis of Our Time: wartime essays of a sociologist*, London: Routledge and Kegan Paul.

Marcuse, H. (1964) *One Dimensional Man: Studies in the ideology of advanced industrial society*, London: Routledge and Kegan Paul.

Marshall, T.H. (1947) 'Citizenship and social class', in Marshall, T.H. and Bottomore, T., *Citizenship and Social Class*, London: Pluto.

Marx, K. 'Critique of the Gotha Programme', in Feuer, L.S. (ed.) (1969) *Marx and Engels: Basic Writings on Politics and Philosophy*, London: Collins, pp 170–1.

Marx, K. and Engels, F. 'Manifesto of the Communist Party, Preface to the English edition of 1888', in Feuer, L.S. (ed.) (1969) *Marx and Engels: Basic Writings on Politics and Philosophy*, London: Collins, pp 66–7.

Maychell, K. (1994) *Counting the Cost: The impact of LMS on schools' patterns of spending*, Slough: National Foundation for Educational Research.

McFadden, M.G. (1996) 'Resistance to schooling and educational outcomes: questions of structure and agency', in *British Journal of Sociology of Education*, vol. 16, no. 3, Sept 1996, pp 293–308.

McKenzie, J. (1993) *Education as a Political Issue*, Avebury.

McKenzie, J. (1995) 'The process of excluding "education" from the "public sphere"?' in Edgell, S. *et al.* (1995) *Debating the Future of the Public Sphere*, Avebury.

McManus, M. (1989) *Troublesome behaviour in the classroom: a teachers' survival guide*, London: Routledge.

McNay, I. and Ozga, J. (eds) (1985) *Policy-making in Education: The breakdown of consensus*, Pergamon Press and the Open University.

McPherson, A. and Willms, J.D. (1987) 'Equalization and improvement: some effects of comprehensive reorganization in Scotland', Chapter 45 in Halsey *et al.*, 1997.

Measor, L. and Woods, P. (1988) 'Initial fronts', in Woodhead, M. and McGrath, A. (eds) (1988) *Family, School and Society*, London: Hodder and Stoughton.

Merton, R.K. (1957) *Social Theory and Social Structure*, Glencoe: Free Press.

Middleton, S., Ashworth, K. and Braithwaite, I. (1997) *Small Fortunes*, Joseph Rowntree Foundation and York Publishing Services.

Mies, M. (1993) 'Towards a methodology for feminist research', in Hammersley, M. (1993) *Social Research: Philosophy, politics and practice*, London: Sage in association with the Open University.

Miles, R. (1993) *Racism After 'Race Relations'*, London: Routledge.

Mirza, H.S. (1992) *Young, Female and Black*, London: Routledge.

Morgan-Klein, B. (1985) *Where am I going to stay? A report on young people leaving care in Scotland*, Edinburgh: The Scottish Council for Single Homeless.

MORI and TES polls, reported in *The Times Educational Supplement*, 5 June 1987.

The Munn Report (1977) *The Structure of the Curriculum*, HMSO.

Nash, R. (1971) 'Camouflage in the classroom', *New Society*, no. 447, 22 April, pp 667–9.

Nash, R. (1973) *Classrooms Observed*, London: Routledge and Kegan Paul.

National Commission on Education Report (1993) *Learning to Succeed*.

National Union of Teachers prepared by the Trade Union Research Unit, Ruskin College, Oxford (1985) *Education: Investment or impoverishment?* London: NUT.

Neill, A.S. (1962) *Summerhill*, first published by Victor Gollancz and in 1968 published by Pelican Books.

Nightingale, F. (1863) *Notes on Hospitals*, Preface, London: Longmans Green and Co.

National Curriculum Council (NCC) (1989) *A Curriculum for All*, York: NCC.

Oliver, M. (1990) *The Politics of Disablement*, London: Macmillan.

Ollerenshaw, K. (1961) *Education for Girls*, London: Faber and Faber.

Ottoway, A.K.C. (1953) *Education and Society*, London: Routledge and Kegan Paul.

Parry, G., Moyser, G. and Day, N. (1992) *Political Participation and Democracy In Britain*, Cambridge University Press.

Parsons, T. (1937) *The Structure of Social Action*, New York: McGraw Hill.

Parsons, T. (1949) *Essays in Sociological Theory*, New York: Free Press.

Parsons, T. (1959) 'The school class as a social system: some of its functions in American society', *Harvard Educational Review*, vol. 29.

Parsons, T. (1951) *The Social System*, New York: Free Press.

Parsons, T. (1968) 'Social systems', in Sills, D.L. (ed.) *International Encyclopaedia of the Social Sciences*, vol. 15, New York: Macmillan and Free Press.

Pascal, G. and Cox, R. (1993) 'Education and domesticity', *Gender and Education*, vol. 5, no. 1.

Peterson, R.E. (1968) 'The student left in American higher education', *Daedalus*, vol. XCVII, pp 311–12.

Phillips, Angela, 'By the people, against the people', *Guardian*, 12 June 1993.

Phillips, M. (1996) *All Must Have Prizes*, London: Little, Brown and Company.

Philpott, H.B. (1904) *London at School: the story of the School Board*, London: T. Fisher Unwin.

Polanyi, M. (1975) *Meaning*, University of Chicago Press.

Popper, K. (1961) *The Poverty of Historicism*, London: Routledge.

Postman, N. and Weingartner, C. (1971; first published in the USA by Delacort Press), *Teaching as a Subversive Activity*, Penguin Books Ltd.

The Rampton Report (1981) *West Indian Children in our Schools*, HMSO.

Rattansi, A. (1988) 'Race, education and British Society' in Dale, R., Ferguson, R. and Robinson, A. (eds) (1988) *Frameworks for Teaching*, Milton Keynes: Open University Press.

Reid, I. (1978) *Sociological Perspectives on School and Education*, Open Books.

Reid, I. (1986) *The Sociology of School and Education*, London: Fontana.

Reid, I. (1992) 'Socio-spatial indices and 16+ examination results 1991 for Bradford schools', Bradford Directorate of Education, Strategic Development Unit. An unpublished report.

Rex, J. and Tomlinson, S. (1979) *Colonial Immigrants in a British City – A Class Analysis*, London: Routledge and Kegan Paul.

Richardson, E. (1973) *The Teacher, the School and the Task of Management*, London: Heinemann.

Richardson, E. (1975) *Authority and Organization in the Secondary School*, London: Macmillan.

Ritzer, G. (1996, 4th edn) *Sociological Theory*, London: McGraw-Hill.

The Robbins Report (1963) *Higher Education*, HMSO.

Robinson, P. (September 1997) 'Literacy and numeracy and economic performance', paper for the London School of Economic's Centre for Economic Performance.

Roosevelt, E. (1884–1962) cited in Exley, H. (ed.) *The Best Women's Quotations*, New York: Exley Giftbooks.

Roper, M. and Tosh, J. (1991) *Manful Assertions: Masculinities in Britain since 1800*, London: Routledge.

Rosenthal, R. and Jacobson, L. (1968) *Pygmalion in the Classroom*, New York: Holt, Rinehart and Winston.

Rousseau, J.J. (1973; original 1762) *The Social Contract and Discourses*, translation and introduction by G.D.H. Cole, revised and augmented by J.H. Brumfitt and J.C. Hall, London: Dent.

Rousseau, J.J. (1974; original 1762) *Emile*, translated by B. Foxley, London: Dent.

Runnymede Trust (1989) *Racism, Anti-racism and Schools: A summary of the Burnage Report*, London: the Runnymede Trust.

Sanderson, M. (1987) *Educational Opportunity And Social Change in England*, London: Faber and Faber, pp 86–7.[1] Dennis Potter (1960) *The Glittering Coffin*, London: Victor Gollancz, pp 13 and 89.

Sanger, J. (1997) *Young Children, Videos and Computer Games*, London: Falmer Press.

Santos, B. (1991) *State Wage Relations and Social Welfare in the Semi-Periphery: The case of Portugal*, Universidade de Coimbra: Centro de Estudos Sociaias.

Schagen, I. (1997) 'Value added taxes the statisticians', *The Times Educational Supplement*, 7 March 1997.

Schultz (1961) Human Capital – Chap 8, Chap 9.

Schultz, T.W. (1991, ed.) *Investment in Human Capital*, Chicago: University of Chicago Press.

Scott, J. 'Changing attitudes to sexual morality: a cross-national comparison', in *Sociology*, vol. 32, no. 4, November 1998, pp 815–45.

Sexton, S. (1987) *Our Schools: A radical policy*, London: Institute of Economic Affairs.

Sharpe, S. (1976) *Just Like a Girl: How girls learn to be women*, a Pelican Original, Penguin Books.

Shaw, G.B. (1946) 'Maxims for revolutionists', in *Man and Superman: A comedy and philosphy*, Harmondsworth: Penguin.

Shaw, G.B. (1972) *The Bodley Head Collected Plays With Their Prefaces*, vol. V, London: Bodley Head.

Siltanen, J. and Stansworth, M. (eds) (1984) *Women in the Public Sphere: A critique of sociology and race*, London: Hutchinson.

Simon, B. (1953) *Intelligence Testing and the Comprehensive School*, London: Lawrence and Wishart.

Sivanandan, A. (1982) *A Different Hunger: Writings in Black resistance*, London: Pluto Press.

Skellington, R. with Morris, P. (1992) *'Race' in Britain Today*, Open University Press and Sage.

Smith, A. (1970; original 1776) *The Wealth of Nations*, Harmondsworth: Penguin.

Social and Community Planning Research, British Social Attitudes survey dataset, 1994, Economic and Social Research Council (ESRC) Data Archive, Essex University.

Social Security Advisory Committee (1992) *The Social Fund: A new structure*, London: HMSO.

Social Trends 24 (1994 edn), Central Statistical Office and Government Statistical Service, London.

Spelman, E. (1990) *Inessential Woman*, London: Women's Press.

Spender, D. (1985) *For the Record: The meaning and making of feminist knowledge*, London: Women's Press.

Spender, D. (1982) *Women of Ideas and What Men Have Done to Them: From Aphra Benn to Adrienne Rich*, London: Routledge and Kegan Paul.

Spender, D. and Sarah, E. (1980) *Learning to Lose: Sexism and education*, London: Women's Press.

The Speus Report (1938) *Secondary Education*, HMSO.

Stanley, L. and Wise, S. (1983) *Breaking Out: Feminist consciousness and feminist research*, London: Routledge and Kegan Paul.

Stanley, L. (1990) *Feminist Praxis, Research, Theory and Epistemology in Feminist Research*, London: Routledge.

Stanworth, M. (1981) *Gender and Schooling: A study of sexual division in the classroom*, London: Women's Research and Resources Centre; reprinted by Hutchinson in 1983.

Statham, J. (1986) *Daughters and Sons: Experiences of non-sexist childraising*, Oxford: Blackwell.

Statham, J. Mackinnon, D. and Cathcart, H. (1989) *The Education Fact File*, London: Hodder and Stoughton.

Statham, J. and Mackinnon, D. with Cathcart, H. and Hales, M. (1991, 2nd edn) *The Education Fact File*, Hodder and Stoughton.

Stubbs, M. and Delamout, S. (eds.) (1976) *Explorations in Classroom Observation*, Chichester, Wiley.

Study Group on Education and Training (1997) *Accomplishing Europe Through Education and Training*, Brussels: European Commission.

Sugarman, B.M. (1966) 'Social class and values as related to achievement and conduct in school', *Sociological Review*, vol. 14, no. 3.

Swann Report (1985) *Education for All*, London: HMSO.

Swift, D.F. (1967) 'Social class, mobility ideology and 11+ success', *British Journal of Sociology*, vol. 17, no. 2.

The Taking Liberties Collective (1989) *Learning the Hard Way: Women's oppression in men's education*, Basingstoke: Macmillan Education.

Tawney, R.A. (1922) *Secondary Education For All*, London: Allen and Unwin.

Tawney, R.A. (1931, fourth edition in 1964) *Equality*, London: Unwin Books.

Taylor, A.J.P. (1970) *English History, 1914–1945*, Harmondsworth: Penguin.

Tong, R. (1989) *Feminist Thought: A comprehensive introduction*, Sydney: Unwin and Hyman.

Tomlinson, S. (1980) 'The educational performance of ethnic minority children', *New Community*, vol. 8, no. 3.

Travers, R.M.W. (1969) *An Introduction to Educational Research*, London: Collier-Macmillan.

Trenchard, L. and Warren, H. (1984) *Something to Tell You – The experiences and needs of young lesbians and gay men in London*, London: London Gay Teenage Group.

Trowler, P. (1998) *Education Policy*, Eastbourne: the Gildredge Press Ltd, in the Gildredge Social Policy Series; series editor Pete Alcock.

Turner, R.H. (1961) 'Modes of social ascent through education: sponsored and contest mobility', in Halsey, A.H., Floud, J. and Anderson, C.A. (eds) (1961) *Education, Economy and Society*, Oxford: Free Press, pp 221–39.

Underwood Report (1955) *Report of the Committee on Maladjusted Children*, chairman J.E.A. Underwood, London: Board of Education.

Universities' Statistical Records (1993) *University Statistics 1992–3*: Vol. 1: Students and Staff, Cheltenham: Universities Statistical Record.

Ussher, J. (1989) *The Psychology of the Female Body*, London: Routledge.

Vaizey, J. (1958) *The Costs of Education*, London: Allen and Unwin.

Van Sertima, I. (ed.) (1987) *Great African Thinkers*, vol. 1., Transaction Books.

Vincent, C., Evans, J. Lunt, I. and Young, P. (1995) 'Policy and practice: the changing nature of special education provision in schools', *British Journal of Special Education*, vol. 22, no. 1, pp 4–11.

Waddington, D. (1989) *Flashpoints: Contemporary Issues in Public Disorder*, London and New York: Routledge.

Walford, G. and Pickering, W.S.F. (1998) *Durkheim and Modern Education*, London: Routledge.

Walker, A. and Walker, C.A. (1987) *The Growing Divide: A social audit 1979–1987*, London: Child Poverty Action Group.

Waller, W.W. (1965; original 1932) *A Sociology of Teaching*, New York: Wiley.

Warnock, M. (1977) *Schools of Thought*, London: Faber.

Warnock, M. (1992) 'Special case in need of reform', in the *Observer*, 18 October.

Weber, M. (1949) *The Methodology of the Social Sciences*, trans. E. Shils and A. Henderson, Illinois: Free Press, p 72; cited in Lee and Newby, p 173.

Weber, M. (1968; original 1922) *Economy and Society – an Outline of Interpretive Sociology*, trans. G. Rothe and G. Wittich, Towater: Bedminster Press.

Wedge, P. and Prosser, H. (1973) *Born to Fail?* London: Arrow.

Weeks, J. (1995) *Invented Moralities: Sexual values in an age of uncertainty*, Cambridge: Polity Press.

Wellings, K. and Wadsworth, J. (1990) 'AIDS and the moral climate', in Jowell, R., Witherspoon, S. and Brook, L. (eds) *British Social Attitudes: The 7th Report*, Aldershot: Gower.

West, Rebecca (1892–1983) cited in Exley, H. (ed.) *The Best Women's Quotations*, New York: Exley Giftbooks.

Wiener, M. (1981) *English Culture and the Decline of Industrial Spirit*, Cambridge University Press.

Weiner, G. (ed.) (1985) *Just a Bunch of Girls*, Milton Keynes: Open University Press.

Weiss, L. (1990) *Working Class Without Work: High School Students in a De-industrializing Economy*, New York: Routledge.

Wilkinson, H. (1994) *No Turning Back: Generations and the genderquake*, London: Demos.

Williams, R. (1961) *The Long Revolution*, Harmondsworth, Penguin; since published in 1992, London: Hogarth Press.

Willis, P. (1977) *Learning to Labour: How working class kids get working class jobs*, Aldershot: Gower.

Wilson, W.J. (1987) *The Truly Disadvantaged*, University of Chicago Press.

Wiseman, S. (1964) *Education and Environment*, Manchester: Manchester University Press.

Wolcott, H. (1991) *Writing up Qualitative Research*, London: Sage.

Wolf, A. (1997) 'Growth stocks and lemons', *Assessment in Education*, vol. 4, no. 1.

Wollstonecraft, M. (1792) *Vindication of the Rights of Women*, London: Penguin.

Wolpe, A.M. (1974) 'The official ideology of education for girls', in Flude, M. and Ahier, J. (eds) *Educability, Schools and Ideology*, London: Croom Helm, pp 138–59.

Woodhead, M. and McGrath, A. (1988) *Family, School and Society*, London: Hodder and Stoughton and the Open University Press.

Woods, P. (1976) 'Having a laugh: an antidote to schooling', in Hammersley, M. and Woods, P. (eds) *The Process of Schooling*, London: Routledge and Kegan Paul.

Woods, P. (1979) *The Divided School*, London: Routledge and Kegan Paul.

Wright, C. (1988) 'School processes: an ethnographic study', in Woodhead, M. and McGrath, A. (eds) (1988) *Family, School and Society*, London: Hodder and Stoughton.

Wright Mills, C. (1970; original 1959) *The Sociological Imagination*, Harmondsworth: Penguin Books.

Yates, A. and Pidgeon, D. (1957) *Admission to Grammar School*, London: Newnes.

Young, M.F.D. (ed.) (1971) *Knowledge and Control: New directions for the sociology of education*, London: Collier-Macmillan.

Index

moral underclass discourse 6
morality 163–164
  1980s 262–263
  1990s 299–300
Moray House tests 45
Mulley, F. 218
multicultural schooling 256
multiculturalism 159, 297
Munn Report *The Structure of the Curriculum* 219–220
murder in playground *see* Burnage High School
muslim schools 299

National Curriculum 77, 97, 101, 113, 244, 255, 267
  Dearing Report 276–277, 299, 301
  influence on contents 113
  views of Labourville and Torytown 113–114
national identities 79
nature-nurture controversy 44
neo-Marxist critiques 27
new public management 75
Newsom Report *Half our Future* 201, 203, 206–209, 211, 213
non-maintained *see* private/public schools
non-oppressive methods of research 28–29
non-probability sampling 19
non-random sampling 19
norm-referencing 77
North/South Ministerial Council 96
Northern Ireland 95–96, 211
  1940s 177
  1970s 220
  bipartite system (1970s) 219
  Chilver Reports
    The Future of Higher Education 247
    The Future Structure of Teacher Education 248
  devolution 280
  Education and Library Boards 95
  Education Reform Order (1989) 245
  integrated schools 95, 96
  organization of schools on sectarian lines 95
  religious education 177
  sectarianism 182
  selection at 11+ 95
  single-sex schools 95
  types of schools 95–96
Northern Ireland Assembly 96
Northern Ireland Council for Integrated Education 95
NUD*IST 33
numeracy 278
  views of Labourville and Torytown 136, 138
nursery provision 176, 207, 213, 236, 279
  Labourville 98
  Torytown 98

nursery voucher scheme, views from Torytown and Labourville 281

OFSTED 97, 101, 276
one-parent families 229, 236, 238
ontological insecurity 59
ontologies 15, 43
open enrolment 81, 85
Open University 205, 218, 241
open-plan buildings 213
operationalization of concepts 12–14
  ethnicity 12–13
  social class 13
opinion polls 18
opting out of LEA control 123–124
  views of Labourville and Torytown 124
organizational intelligence 140
Oxford Mobility Study 225, 250
Oxford University 181, 252

panel study 11
paradigm 16
Parental Alliance for Choice in Education 263
parental choice 65, 241, 273, 274, 293
  Scotland 85–86
  Torytown and Labourville 86
parental responsibility 65
parental rights and obligations 274
parental values, influence on educational opportunities 226
parenting skills 274
parentocracy 144, 293
parents
  attitudes towards education 207
  as partners in learning 278
parents' charter 241
parity of esteem 142, 174, 175, 176, 177, 189
part-time employment, female workers 253
participant observation 23
participation rate in full-time education 271
partnerships 76
party policies April 1997 304
patriarchal knowledge 53
Patten, J. 273
Personal and Social Education (PSE) 265
PGCE 290
Plowden Report *Children and Their Primary Schools* 27, 144, 201, 203, 205, 206, 207, 210, 211, 213
pluralist system 62, 142
political attitudes towards educational research 37–40
political bias 38
political changes 138–141
political partisanship and educational radicalism 166–167
polytechnics, university status 90
Polytechnics and Colleges Funding Council 247

positivism 17, 27, 46–47, 51
  compared with anti-positivist approach 17–18
post-graduate students 222
postmodernism 57–58, 67
postmodernity
  dimensions (Hargreaves) 56
  shift from modernity 55–56
poststructuralism 58
Powell, E. 210
power relationships 1990s 275–276
predetermined life chances 186–187
pregnant schoolgirls 229
Prentice, R. 218
pressure of experience 110
primary research 14
primary school teachers, gender imbalance 151, 296
primary schools 80
priority of basic needs 110
private businesses, contribution towards state system 252
private/public schools 119
  1940s 181, 184
  1950s 191
  1960s 201–202, 203
  1970s 220
  1980s 252
  1990s 275, 305
  assisted places 119
  charitable status 65
  community benefit 278
  registration 191, 201–202
  views of Conservative Party (1940s–1960s) 143
  views of Labour Party (1940s–1960s) 142–143
  views of Labourville and Torytown 119–121, 147–148
privatizers 144
probability sampling 19
problem solving 140
progressive education 198
progressive focusing 14–15
proletarianization 102
PSE 265
public awareness of educational issues 106–109
pull of tradition 110
pupil:teacher ratios 99
pupil mobility 301
Pupil Referral Units 300
pupils' evaluation schema for teachers 223, 224
purposive sampling 19
Putnam, Lord David 102

quasi-markets, further and higher education 91
questionnaires 22
quota sampling 19

race 157–161, 182
  compared with ethnicity 157
  and educational outcome 161–162